√ FE 5 '82

B&T

W9-BKQ-011

# China and the West

# China and the West

Society and Culture 1815–1937

*Jerome Ch'en*

**Indiana University Press**
Bloomington and London

Wingate College Library

Copyright © 1979 by Jerome Ch'en

All rights reserved

No part of this book may be reproduced or utilized in
any form or by any means, electronic or mechanical,
including photocopying and recording, or by any
information storage and retrieval system, without
permission in writing from the publisher. The Association
of American University Presses' Resolution on Permissions
constitutes the only exception to this prohibition.

Manufactured in Great Britain

*Library of Congress Cataloging in Publication Data*

Ch'en Jerome, 1919 –
    China and the West.
    Includes bibliographical references and index.
    1.   China – Civilization – Occidental influence.   I.   Title.
    DS72.C47545   301.2950181

Library of Congress catalog card number: 79-2704

ISBN 0-253-12032-2

084659

*For Mary*

# Contents

*List of maps and plates*                                                11
*Preface*                                                                13
*Chronology*                                                             15

Introduction: China through war and peace                               23

## Part 1 Agents

1 **Images and image-makers**                                           39
  The West's view of China                                              39
  China's image of the West                                            59

2 **Missionaries and converts**                                        92
  The Catholic Church                                                  92
  The Protestant Church                                                94
  Conversion and converts                                             103
  Chinese Christian theology and the growth
    of autonomy                                                        112
  Secular influences                                                   116
  Missionary education                                                 122
  Medicine                                                             129
  Social work                                                          134
  The anti-Christian movement and anti-imperialism                     138
  Conclusion                                                           147

3 **Students and scholars**                                            151
  Overseas study programmes                                            151
  Cultural ambivalence in 'returned' students                          158
  The Chinese student abroad                                           159

The Work-Study Scheme                                          166
The 'returned' students in China                               168
The spread of Western scientific thought                       173
The impact of Western philosophy                               179
Translation, literature and the arts                           194
Conclusion                                                     202

4   **Residents and immigrants**                               206
Shanghai                                                       206
San Francisco                                                  234

Part 2   **Changes**

5   **Process of change**                                      265
The crisis of 1895                                             270
The reform of 1898                                             271
Towards revolution                                             273

6   **Politics and the law**                                   285
Attempts at constitutional government                          285
The provincial issue                                           296
The National Assembly                                          300
The growth of political parties                                304
The establishment of consular jurisdiction                     317
The mixed courts of Shanghai                                   318
The decline of consular and extraterritorial jurisdiction      320
Law reform                                                     324
Modern law courts and judicial independence                    328

7   **Economy**                                                332
The growth of international trade and tariffs                   332
Exports                                                        336
Imports                                                        338
Balance of payments and the maritime customs                   340
Industrial development: the growth of government-
  financed industries                                          348
Foreign concessions: the railways                              359
Private enterprise                                             361
The failure of industrialization                               362
The benefits of imperial economic penetration                  377

8   **Society**                                                380
Emancipation of women                                          380

Morality and love                     387
The family revolution                 396
—Chinese youth                        399
The labour movement                   413

9   **Culture**                       426

*Select bibliography*                 453
*Index*                               466

# Maps and plates

## Maps

Three views of the East *page* 36
The provinces of China in the 1920s *page* 286

## Plates *(between pages 224 and 225)*

*Misconceptions*
Brooklyn Bridge, New York, 1880s
The Sphinx and the Pyramids, 1880s
An American theatre, 1880s
St Paul's Cathedral, London, 1880s

*The Chinese in Western eyes*
Reception of the Chinese family by Her Majesty Queen Victoria,
    late 1840s
Collection formed by Nathan Dunn
San Francisco Chinatown just before the earthquake of 1906 (photo
    by Arnold Genthe)
An American smile, under an American hat, and above a Chinese
jacket. Chinatown, New York City, 1915
'They don't trouble him any more', 1888

*Changing city life*
The Confucian village, Ch'ufu, Shantung, 1931 (photo by White
    Bros.)
Street scene in Peking (photo by White Bros.)
Rickshaws in Peking, 1931

American warehouse at Hankow (Bain Collection)
Well-to-do Peking home, 1931

*Westerners in Shanghai*
Shanghai Race-course, 1880s
Cricket, Shanghai, 1880s
French opium addicts, Shanghai, 1880s
Explanation of Western diving techniques, 1880s

*Changing fashions and clothes*
Wealthy Manchu family, 1931 (photo by White Bros.)
Ladies' fashions, Shanghai, 1921
A Chinese couple, 1931 (photo by White Bros.)
Dr Wellington Koo – Western hair-style and Western clothes
Chinese Christian pastor and family, Canton, 1900

(Plates in the first and fourth sections by permission of the British Library; plates in the second, third and fifth sections by permission of the Library of Congress)

—

# *Preface*

This is a general book with a difference, for it is not entirely based on secondary works by those who wrote before me in this and related fields. It is not a political or diplomatic history of modern China either, as its title clearly indicates. Considerable original research has gone into the making of this volume in the hope that the result would please both the general reader and the specialist. A broad survey, it should serve to reveal to the reader, and to me, where the gaps of our knowledge and the weaknesses of our research lie; the revelation may stimulate others to follow up in the pursuit of a deep and fuller understanding. From a functional point of view like this, I would like to entertain the belief that even a general book, a broad survey, should not merely present 'the state of the game'; it should also explore new areas and seek new interpretations.

In such pursuit I have been ably assisted by Ms Irene Jones who made meticulous use of the archives of the China Inland Mission and the British Baptists. To guard against my Chinesisms I was glad to have the watchful eye of Ms Judith Lucas. I am grateful to them both.

I cannot express how grateful I am to Ms Sue Hogg for her painstaking and critical editing of my manuscript, without which this book would have more inconsistencies and repetitions, woolly passages and careless mistakes than it does. However, the remaining mistakes are, needless to say, my responsibility.

In addition to the libraries of the China Inland Mission and the British Baptists, I myself have used the library of the School of Oriental and African Studies in London, the Toyo Bunko in Tokyo, the Library of Congress in Washington, the State Library of Cali-

Wingate College Library

fornia in Sacramento, the Municipal Library in San Francisco, the Chinese collection of the Hoover Institution in Stanford, the Church Research Libraries in New York, and the Hankow Club Collection and the Feng P'ing-shan Library at the University in Hong Kong. I owe them and the courtesy of their staff my thanks.

In the period of research for this book I received a sizable grant from the Canada Council and in the period of writing the Joint Centre on Modern East Asia of the University of Toronto and York University provided me with a teaching assistant so as to allow me more time for the undertaking. My own university, York University in Toronto, financed my reading at the Church Research Library in New York and later offered me its typing service for the manuscript. I am deeply thankful for their generosity.

My close colleagues, Professors Stephen Endicott, Margo Gewurtz, Diana Lary and Peter Mitchell, have read parts of the manuscript and shared their insights and criticisms with me. Here I acknowledge my gratitude to all of them. Professor Mary Sheridan's stimulating discussions throughout the preparatory stages of this book up to the final draft, her patience and care, and her love have been an important source of inspiration and strength for me, without which the book may never have been completed. To her, this volume is affectionately dedicated.

As it is, the book is already too long, longer than any other volume in this series; its cost of manufacture is therefore already very high. Understandably both my editor, Professor J. H. Plumb, and my publishers insist that all the notes should be eliminated, leaving only the footnotes. If the elimination disappoints or inconveniences my specialist readers, I hereby offer my apologies. However, they, more than anyone else, should be able to see that much of the information contained in the pages below has come from a wide range of primary sources, including Church archives and missionary correspondence, Chinese and other newspapers and periodicals, travelogues and personal memoirs, official papers and government statistics.

# Chronology

1814    Ts'ai Kao, probably the first Protestant Chinese convert, is baptized.

1816    Lord Amherst mission to China fails over the ceremonial question of *kowtow*.

1820    John Marshman and Joannes Lassar complete their translation of the *New Testament* into Chinese.

The Livingstone and Morrison Clinic is established in Macao.

1823    Robert Morrison and W. Milne publish their translation of the *New Testament*.

1830    British and American missionaries organize the Christian Union in Canton.

1831    The *Chinese Repository* is founded in Macao (its publication ceased in 1852).

1832    Elijah Bridgman's School for Chinese boys begins teaching.

1834    J. Matheson, D. W. C. Olymphant, R. E. C. Bridgman and C. Gutzlaff organize the Society for the Diffusion of Useful Knowledge.

1838    The Medical Missionary Society in China comes into being.

1839    Commissioner Lin arrives at Canton to take charge of the prohibition of the opium traffic.

The Opium War begins.

1842    The Opium War ends with the signing of the Nanking Treaty between China and Britain. This is followed by the Sino–French and Sino–American Treaties in 1843.

Steam shipping to the Far East begins.

1843    By the Sino–French (Whampoa) Treaty, the Catholic Church obtains rights to construct churches in China.

1844    Wei Yuan's *Illustrated Gazetteer of the Maritime Nations* is published.

1847      The Royal Asiatic Society sets up its China branch.
1848      S. Wells Williams completes his *Middle Kingdom*.
1849      The first Chinese immigrants arrive at San Francisco.
1850   The Taiping Rebellion breaks out.
          The *North China Herald* begins publication in Shanghai.
          W. P. A. Martin arrives at Canton, to begin his career as a
          missionary and educationist in China.
1853   The Small Swords Society occupy Shanghai and foreign consuls
       in Shanghai organize the Provisional System of Tariff Collection.
          Chinese inhabitants in Shanghai move into the foreign settle-
          ments for safety.
1854      The Chinese newspaper, *Golden Hill News*, begins publication.
1856   Auguste Chapdelaine, a French priest, is murdered in Kwangsi and
       the lorcha *Arrow* is searched by Chinese police.
       The Anglo–French Expedition (or the second Opium War) begins.
1857   Lord Elgin and Baron Gros are sent to command the Expedition
       in China.
1858   The Sino–American, Sino–Russian, Sino–British and Sino–French
       Treaties are signed in Tientsin.
1860   The Anglo–French Expeditionary troops occupy Peking and
       destroy the Summer Palace, Yuan-ming-yuan.
       The Sino–British, Sino–Russian and Sino–French Peace Treaties
       are signed in Peking.
       F. T. Ward organizes an army which is to be renamed the Ever
       Victorious Army in 1862 and disbanded in 1864.
          Young J. Allen comes to China.
1861   H. N. Lay is appointed the Inspector-General of the Chinese
       Imperial Maritime Customs.
          The Peking Language Institute is founded.
1862   The controversy over the control and command of a flotilla of
       warships, known as the Osborn Flotilla, which the Chinese have
       bought from Britain, breaks out.
1863   R. Hart replaces Lay as the Inspector-General of China's Maritime
       Customs.
          The International Settlement in Shanghai is formed.
1865      The Kiangnan Arsenal in Shanghai is founded.
          Hudson Taylor sets up the China Inland Mission.
1866   The Foochow Shipyard and the Tientsin Arsenal are established.
          R. Hart goes home on leave, with a number of Chinese
          officials.
          The Peking Language Institute begins its courses on astro-
          nomy and mathematics given by foreign instructors.
1867   The American Minister, Anson Burlingame, resigns and is

appointed the Chinese envoy at large, assisted by John Mcleavy Brown of Britain and E. de Champs of France and a number of Chinese officials on a visit to the USA and European countries.

1868         John Fryer edits the *Chinese Scientific Magazine* sponsored by the Kiangnan Arsenal.

1869   The Suez Canal opens.

1870   The Tientsin Massacre takes place and twenty-four foreigners, including seventeen French citizens, are killed.

Tseng Kuo-fan resigns the viceroyalty of Chihli and is replaced by Li Hung-chang.

Ch'ung-hou is sent to France on a mission of apology.

California unleashes its anti-Chinese movement.

Timothy Richard arrives in China.

1871         Shanghai begins its telegraph communication with Europe.

The Mandarin *Bible* is published.

1872         The first group of Chinese students sail for the USA.

The *Shen Pao* of Shanghai begins publication.

The Zikawei Observatory in Shanghai is established by the Catholic Church.

1873         The Merchants' Steamship Navigation Company is founded by Li Hung-chang.

1875   A. R. Margary, a British legation translator, is murdered in Yunnan.

A group of boys are led by Prosper Giquel of the Foochow Shipyard to study in France.

Young J. Allen edits the *Globe Magazine* (its publication is discontinued in 1883 and resumed under the name of the *Review of the Times* from 1889 to 1907).

Jardine and Matheson Co. plan to build the Woosung Railway (which is purchased by the Chinese authorities in 1876 and dismantled).

1876   The Chefoo Convention is signed between Britain and China as the settlement of the Margary case, and Kuo Sung-t'ao is appointed the Chinese Minister to Britain.

1877         The Kaiping Coal Mines are opened.

The Shanghai Steam Navigation Company of Russell and Co. is merged into the Merchants' Steamship Navigation Company. The Society for the Diffusion of Christian and General Knowledge is founded in Shanghai by Alexander Williamson (it changes its name to the Christian Literature Society in 1906).

Shanghai has its first epidiascope theatre.

The Conference of the Protestant Missions in Shanghai is held.

1881    The Chinese Telephone Company of Shanghai begins operation.

1882    Li Hung-chang establishes the Shanghai Textile Factory.

1884    The Sino–French War takes place and ends in the Sino–French Tientsin Treaty which establishes France's domination of Indo-China.

1889    The construction of the Peking–Hankow Railway begins.

1890    Chang Chih-tung plans for the foundation of the Hanyang Foundry.

1891    Emperor Kuang-hsu learns English.

1892    The American Oriental Society (forerunner of the Association for Asian Studies) is organized.

1894    The Sino–Japanese War breaks out.

1895    The Shimonoseki Treaty brings the Sino–Japanese War to an end and the scholars assembling in Peking petition the throne against the signing of the Treaty.
YMCA is established in China.
Yen Fu's translation of Thomas Huxley's *Essay on Evolution and Ethics* is published.

1896    Li Hung-chang goes on a mission to Russia and Europe.
Modern postal service is organized by R. Hart.
Liang Ch'i-ch'ao edits the *Shih-wu Pao* in Shanghai and compiles the *Catalogue of Books on the West*.
Shanghai sees its first motion picture show.

1897    The first modern bank is established; so are the Commercial Press and a number of modern schools.

1898    The Hundred Days Reform begins and the Open Door Principle is proposed by Britain and the USA.
Dowager Empress gives a party in honour of the diplomatic wives in Peking.
Peking (National) University is founded.
Chang Chih-tung's *On Learning* is published; so are the Chinese translation of Robert Mackenzie's *Nineteenth Century – A History* and the *Ch'ing-i Pao* (The China Discussion) in Yokohama.

1900    The Boxer War leads to the exile of the Ch'ing Court.
Chang Chien establishes the Nant'ung Textile Company.
A women's conference is organized by a number of missionary women in Shanghai.

1901    Modern schools come into existence in the provinces.
Adam Smith's *Wealth of Nations* appears in Chinese.

1902    Emperor Kuang-hsu receives diplomatic representatives and the Mackay Treaty of Commerce is signed between Britain and China.

An edict prohibiting foot-binding is issued.

The Peking Language Institute is incorporated into the Peking University.

1903     The *T'oung Pao*, the authoritative sinological journal of Europe, begins publication.

The Bank of the Board of Revenue is established.

1904     Soccer is introduced to China.

The *Tung-fang tsa-chih* (Eastern Miscellany) begins publication.

The USA excludes Chinese immigration.

1904–5   The Russo–Japanese War begins; the traditional Chinese examination system is abolished; the Alliance Society is founded in Tokyo (and to change its name to the Kuomintang in 1912);and because of the American Exclusion Act, the boycott of American goods is organized at the Chinese treaty ports.

The City Council of the Chinese city of Shanghai comes into being (to be abolished in 1914).

The official organ of the Alliance Society, *Min Pao*, begins publication.

1906     The Church Self-Government Society holds its first national congress in Shanghai.

An abridged version of the *Communist Manifesto* appears in Chinese.

1907     The Ministry of Education forbids students' participation in political activities.

The Chinese government sends girl students to study abroad.

Yale-in-China establishes a medical college in Ch'angsha.

The Shanghai Electricity Corporation is established.

1908     The Dowager Empress and the Emperor die.

1909     The Political Advisory Council is convened.

Peking has its first national library.

The first group of Boxer Indemnity scholars are sent to study in the USA.

1910     The Ginling Women's College is established in Nanking.

China organizes her first National Games.

1911     The Revolution takes place.

China adopts the Gregorian calendar.

Tsinghua College is organized (to change its name to Tsinghua University).

The English paper, *China Weekly Review*, begins publication in Shanghai.

1912     The Emperor abdicates; the Provisional Government in Nanking adopts the Provisional Constitution; Yuan Shih-k'ai is elected the

President of the Republic of China; general elections are held for the election of the National Assembly.

The work study scheme for Chinese students to study in France begins.

1913  The Chinese Geological Institute is founded.

1914  The Constitution Compact replaces the Provisional Constitution.

The Christian West China Union University in Chengtu founds its medical and dental schools.

1915  Japan presents the Twenty-One Demands to China.

The magazine *New Youth* begins publication.

The Peking Union Medical College comes into being.

1916  Yuan Shih-k'ai calls off his monarchical attempt and dies.

1917  China sees her abortive monarchical restoration fail, declares war against the Central Powers, and organizes her second parliamentary election under the leadership of the Anfu Club.

1918  The Chicherin Declaration renounces Russia's privileges in China.

1919  China participates in the Paris Peace Conference.

Peking students demonstrate against the Paris decision on the German possessions in Shantung on May 4th.

John Dewey arrives in China.

1920  The war between the Chihli and Anhwei cliques of warlords breaks out and the movement of provincial autonomy begins.

Bertrand Russell visits China.

The Christian Yenching University is founded.

1921  The first national congress of the Chinese Communist Party takes place in Shanghai and the Washington Conference is held.

The Creation Society and the Association for Literary Studies are established.

Lu Hsün publishes his short story, 'The True Story of Ah Q'.

1922  Chinese students lead an anti-Christian education movement.

The Star Co., a Chinese motion-picture company, begins production.

Margaret Sanger visits China to lecture on birth control.

1923  The Peking Government adopts a new constitution and the workers of the Peking–Hankow Railway stage a strike which is defeated by violent suppression.

1924  Against the background of a large-scale civil war, the Kuomintang is recognized with Russian assistance, the Kuomintang and the Chinese Communist Party form their first united front, and Chiang Kai-shek is appointed the commandant of the Whampao Military Academy.

Sun Yat-sen gives a series of lectures on his Three Principles of the People.

The Crescent Moon Society comes into existence.

1925 A nation-wide strike against Britain and Japan begins on May 30th and the Tariff Conference to discuss the restructure of the Chinese maritime customs is held in Peking.

Sun Yat-sen dies.

The Institute of Pacific Relations and the Catholic (Fu-jen) University of Peking are founded.

1926 The Northern Expedition commanded by Chiang Kai-shek is launched against the warlords of the North and twelve treaty powers hold the meetings of the Commission on Extraterritoriality in Peking.

Chinese representatives are elected on the Shanghai Municipal Councils of the International and French Settlements.

The demonstration against imperialism organized by Peking girl students is ruthlessly suppressed by the military police of the Provisional Government.

The first six Chinese Catholic bishops are consecrated.

James Yen begins his Mass Education Movement in Tinghsien.

1927 The British Settlements in Hankow and Kiukiang are overrun by Chinese demonstrators and are to be renditioned to China; the Nanking Incident in which foreign residents are killed and molested takes place; the first united front between the Kuomintang and the Chinese Communist Party splits.

Chiang Kai-shek becomes a Methodist.

1928 The Northern Expedition is completed and Nanking is made the capital of China.

The new penal code comes into force.

The Academia Sinica is founded.

1930 China regains her tariff autonomy.

The Left-wing Writers' League is established.

1931 Japan occupies Manchuria.

The new civil code is proclaimed.

1932 Japan invades Shanghai.

The magazine *Lun-yü* (The Analects) begins publication.

1933 President Roosevelt raises the price of silver.

1934 President Roosevelt introduces his Silver Purchase Act; the Long March of the Chinese communists begins.

1935 The Nanking Government reforms China's currency system and Chiang Kai-shek launches his New Life Movement.

The Kuomintang sponsors the Indigenous Cultural Movement.

Hitler's *Mein Kampf* appears in Chinese.

Peking students hold a demonstration against Japanese aggression on December 9th.

1936    The May 5th Constitution is proclaimed and Chiang Kai-shek is
        kidnapped by the mutineers in Sian.
            Edgar Snow visits the Chinese Communists in Paoan in
        preparation for his *Red Star Over China*.
1937    The Sino–Japanese War breaks out.

# Introduction:
# China through war and peace

Peace was restored to Europe after the second defeat of Napoleon. As if in vengeance, it was a Europe imbued with the conservatism of the 'Holy Alliance', which even Metternich called 'a high-sounding nothing'. But the dream of a European *t'ien-hsia* – a great empire built on an institutionalized cultural tradition – vanished at long last.

It was also a Europe still to some extent influenced by the new French modes of thought, liberal, to some degree egalitarian, and nationalistic. Politically, this meant the sovereignty of the people, which implied the protection of civil liberties or natural rights of man by broadening the basis of the national government; economically, it meant the promotion of greater material well-being and freer trade, with the increasingly optimistic belief in progress based on the advancement of science and technology; socially, it meant a more humanitarian approach to alleviate the sufferings of those who had been 'divorced from nature' by urbanization and industrialization but were still 'unreclaimed by art'. Though the hereditary aristocracy still held much of their old power, new leaders were clearly emerging from the ranks of an intelligent, hard-working and profit-seeking middle class.

None of the ideals of individual freedom, democracy, a higher standard of living, progress and benevolence towards the under-privileged clashed absolutely with the basic tenets of the Church. No one challenged the truth of Genesis; few were agnostic. If anything, with the romanticization of Christianity by Rousseau and Wesley, the Church became more tolerant and more anxious to bring the Gospel to uneducated Europeans as well as to the heathen overseas. Morality, Bible study, prayer and preaching appealed more strongly to the liberated individual than ritual splendour; and thus religious life played a more vital and more meaningful part among the new pursuits of Western man.

The Napoleonic Wars inevitably forced the countries of continental Europe temporarily back upon themselves, partly because of the loss of their possessions abroad and partly because of the immediate concerns of their own reconstruction. Britain, on the other hand, emerged as unchallenged mistress of the seas with her peerless navy and merchant fleet, which had by now established itself as far away as Singapore and even Nagasaki. In spite of her military supremacy and rapid industrial development, Britain was preoccupied mainly with internal reforms in the two decades after the Congress of Vienna. Her overseas interests scarcely extended beyond the suppression of the slave trade and the administration of her white colonies. This was the background to Lord Amherst's ill-starred mission to China in 1816 which foundered on the question of *kowtow*.

There is hardly any doubt that the majority of the British merchants engaged in overseas trade came from the urban middle class; the China trade was no exception. The sons of minor civil servants, naval and army officers, small businessmen and small manufacturers, these men had seen poverty but aimed at riches. They aspired to a position of importance in society, a country house if possible, and even political influence. At any rate they wished to be free from the drudgery of working for their living. They were intensely family-centred men, saving for security but spending unsparingly on the education of their children, demanding obedience from their wives, and living in comfortable but over-decorated homes. Mostly devout Nonconformists, they attended Sunday worship together with their families, neighbours, and friends; they also read the Bible, edifying stories, and later magazines and newspapers with their families. By thrift, hard work, and robust common sense they had improved their own lives materially and socially and therefore they adopted a utilitarian attitude in their search for knowledge and happiness and were antagonistic towards antiquated customs and laws. Their faith in science and progress was as strong as their disdain for Kantian moral law or for intricate theological argument. Their taste in music was limited to playing popular tunes on the family piano; in literature it was no more advanced than that of the *Westminster Review* or the

*Economist*; in art it extended no further than appreciation of conventional portraits and landscapes. There exists no better picture of these hard-headed and dynamic people than Samuel Smiles's *Self Help*.

It was such confident and self-righteous Britons as these who virtually monopolized the foreign trade at Canton. Two years before the French Revolution, out of a total of seventy-three Western ships anchored off Canton, fifty-two were British. The Napoleonic Wars put an end to all hopes of a challenge to British domination from continental Europe, while American competition could safely be ignored. Apart from the restriction imposed by the Chinese that all foreign trade must be handled by the chartered merchants, the Co-hong of Canton, and the restriction of imports of Chinese silk and cotton textiles into Britain there was no official policy on either side governing the trade till the ending of the British East India Company's monopoly and the appointment by the British government of Lord Napier as superintendent of trade in 1833. By this time the new commodity from India – opium – had finally tipped the balance of trade in favour of the British merchants and China's determination to stamp out this traffic had crystallized. Napier's appointment was significant, not because of any clearly defined instructions from Palmerston (he did not even carry letters of credence), but because he came as his King's representative, empowered to negotiate as an equal with the Chinese viceroy at Canton. Thus he came armed with the assumptions of modern diplomacy to China, only to find that that ancient empire was not a nation-state and did not share those assumptions. Trade was not regulated by any treaty until 1842.

At this time the Ch'ing empire had neither any clearly defined boundaries based on international agreements (except for those laid down by the two agreements already signed with Russia) nor a law of nationality based on either *jus sanguinis* or *jus soli*. Therefore 'China' (the 'Great Ch'ing') and 'the Chinese' ('Hsia' or 'Hua-hsia') could be defined only in cultural terms. 'China' was the land where the Chinese lived; 'the Chinese' were that people who adhered to a certain distinct set of values and norms suited to their way of life. Naturalization was possible only in the sense that a foreigner could adopt (or a Chinese reject) this set of values and norms and take up a new mode of life. The process of naturalization in either direction was purely cultural, needing no legal sanction, though the Chinese traditionally treated any of their number who became 'barbarians' with universal condemnation. History consequently records in detail the mass sinocization of foreigners (barbarians) from the Torba Wei in the fifth century down to the Manchus in the seventeenth, but remains tactfully silent about the 'barbarianization' of Chinese emigrants in Central Asia and overseas.

Since the 'barbarians' were ignorant of Chinese values and norms, they were seen as having no values or norms at all. Logically, then, they could only be motivated by crude instinctive desires for food and sex, like animals. They would stop at nothing until their desires were satisfied. This was why the Chinese saw them as quarrelsome, stubborn, greedy, and licentious, with little awareness of those finer human qualities, such as flexibility, moderation, kindness and consideration, which were so essential for the smooth functioning of human relationships. China should show these people benevolence and understanding, in the hope that her moral example would lead them to repay her with obedience and respect.

The whole system of thought and action was based on Confucianism; it was Confucianism alone that distinguished the Chinese from the barbarians. Within Chinese society, the theory ran, the higher one's social level, the more one was permeated with Confucian ideals, and this hierarchy extended outwards to include the barbarians – but their position in it was below even the lowest class of Chinese. At the apex of the hierarchy was the emperor of China himself, whose main interest in the management of 'barbarian' affairs was to maintain peaceable relations between his own subjects and the outsiders. In the days when overseas trade mattered little to the Chinese government, and when the exchange of ideas with the outside world meant practically nothing to the Chinese, this policy was reasonable and understandable.

The barbarians' goodwill in responding to China's benevolence was shown symbolically by their tribute mission. Foreign delegations seeking trade concessions were invariably treated by the Chinese as if they were tribute missions, even though they did not always go through the elaborate rituals which were expected of such missions. Both Pieter van Hoorn in 1667, who was granted an audience by the Ch'ing monarch in 1667, and Lord McCartney, who was treated likewise in 1794, were described in the Chinese records as tribute-bearers, and the countries they represented were classed with Korea, Annam, and Liu-ch'iu. In return, their merchants were allowed to reside and trade in China, enabling them to share the benefits of the empire's superior culture.

Culturally and economically, China regarded herself as far above the 'barbarian' countries; there was no question of equality. But there were reasons for her arrogance. Her staple exports – principally tea and silk – were highly marketable and yielded high profits, for the Europeans had considerable difficulty in finding commodities that the Chinese wanted in exchange before the introduction of opium. China had enjoyed a continuously favourable balance of trade for as much as two centuries at a time when mercantilism dominated economic thought. Moreover, as an assistant magistrate at Hong Kong, Mitchell, pointed out in 1852:

It seems a strange result after ten years of open trade with this great country, and after the abolition of all monopolies on both sides, that China with her swarming millions should not consume one half so much of our manufactures as Holland or as our own thinly populated North American or Australian colonies.

But this seemingly strange result is a perfectly natural one to those who are sufficiently acquainted with this peculiar people and have marked their thrifty habits and untiring industry . . .

or as Sir Robert Hart pointed out, some fifty years later:

The Chinese have the best food in the world, rice; the best drink, tea; and the best clothing, cotton, silk and fur. Possessing these staples and their innumerable native adjuncts, they do not need to buy a penny's-worth elsewhere.

One might add 'except of opium' in which China was not self-sufficient until the twentieth century.

The trade, confined to Canton as we have said, was actually handled on the Chinese side by officials and their assistants and by the chartered merchants (the Co-hong), with the officials firmly in control. The system they operated was cumbersome, restrictive and corrupt. The officials, educated in the Confucian classics, believed that China was the most civilized community on earth just as un-shakably as Macaulay believed that England held that distinction. They were no less self-confident and self-righteous than the late eighteenth- and early nineteenth-century English, and they were also stubborn.

It was the opium question that brought these uncompromising

attitudes into head-on conflict. China's defeat in the war of 1839–42 was no surprise to the British, but did teach the Chinese a lesson that their military preparations had not been sufficient. None the less, they were defeated again by the Anglo–French Expedition of 1856–60, in the Sino–French War of 1884–5, in the Sino–Japanese War of 1894–5, and in the Boxer War of 1900. China's foreign policy was born in military humiliation.

In the long run no foreign policy could succeed unless backed by efficient military power. This belief has been shared by all schools of Chinese diplomatic thought from 1860 to the present day. In the second half of the nineteenth century this line of thought gave rise to what came to be known as the Self-Strengthening Movement. In the short run, however, the pragmatists, especially those who were in control of Chinese foreign policy and consequently knew better than most what the real situation was, hoped to keep the foreigners on a 'loose rein', either by setting up a system of checks and balances ('using one barbarian to check another') or by observing carefully the letter of treaties and agreements. Both these short-term policies required a fresh interpretation of the nature of the 'barbarian'. If he was driven by greed and self-interest alone, how could he be trusted, however briefly, either as an ally or as a foe? It is interesting that this re-interpretation became a problem in the 1860s. By then the Chinese policy-makers' knowledge of the foreigner had changed considerably. Chinese diplomats now knew something of Western diplomatic practice, international law and Christianity. However arrogant they might be, the Europeans were not to be dismissed as 'dogs and goats'; they had their culture too, inferior to that of China as it might be.

Not all the high officials at court accepted the new interpretation, nor were all of them possessed of the new information about the foreigners. Indeed, high-minded gentlemen like the Grand Secretary Yen Ching-ming considered that to dirty one's fingers by handling foreign affairs was utterly despicable. Many such men thought that China's weakness lay in the government's reluctance to make good use of 'the spirit of the people' (*min-ch'i*) which had shown its power on the question of British entry into the city of Canton in the 1840s and 1850s. The defeat in the war of 1856–60 did not put an end to this school of thought, for the activities of foreigners often touched on the interests and provoked the resentment of the ordinary people, compelling the government to take cognizance of their feelings.

Sometimes popular feeling was expressed indirectly, but more articulately, through the mouths of certain officials who took it upon themselves to uphold Confucian orthodoxy (*ch'ing-i*); sometimes it was expressed directly by mass action, as in the anti-missionary riots. Caught between foreign and popular pressure, the Chinese authorities found themselves in an exceedingly difficult position during the period from 1840 to 1937. Sometimes they acted according to the popular will, as in the Boxer War of 1900, sometimes they gave in to the demands of a foreign power, as in the *de facto* cession of Manchuria to the Japanese in 1931.

The rise to power of a new generation of diplomats, mostly Western-trained, after 1900, brought a deeper understanding of the West to China's foreign service, against the background of an upsurge of nationalism that came to dominate Chinese political thinking in the twentieth century. But these officials were, like their predecessors, elitist pragmatists, sceptical of the reliability and staying power of 'the spirit of the people'. They regarded earlier attempts to make use of this spirit as foolhardy, absurd, yet did not themselves take the trouble to find out how the masses could be mobilized, organized, disciplined, and led in effective action. Their personal attachment both to China and to the West – more particularly to the country where each individual had been trained – led them into an ambivalence. China must be strong in order to recover her lost sovereign rights; each of the new-style officials thought she could become strong only by learning from whichever country he had studied in. Social Darwinism gave coherence to their theories; China's general weakness was due to her specific weaknesses; her salvation depended on her own efforts to make herself fit to survive. Since the previous attempt at self-strengthening had failed, China must adopt a new approach, beginning with a merciless self criticism to expose her weaknesses and then designing ways and means of curing them. The whole process was fraught with almost insoluble problems – what the methods were to be, how they were to be financed, who was to give the lead, and finally, the suitability or otherwise of the Western model. In the long term, if China could emulate the West well enough to fulfil her nationalistic aspirations, she would eventually become another Britain or another Germany – i.e. another imperialist power. Imperialism was seen as the final stage of nationalism; Japan provided a recent example of this process of development, which was seen as constructive and admirable – there was no anti-imperialist sentiment yet. In fact the expression 'anti-imperialism' (*ta-tao ti-kuo chu-i*) had not yet entered the Chinese language.

The short-term goal was 'recovery of rights' (*shou-hui chu-ch'uan*), but while China lacked military power and the ruling class distrusted the strength of the people this could be attempted only in a piecemeal fashion, as opportunity offered. In essence, China's foreign policy now became one of introspective nationalism, using appeasement and compromise to buy time in which to work towards that distant vision of a strong country. The new generation of diplomats were not in tune either with radicalism or with the spirit of the people. Over such issues as the Twenty-One Demands (presented by Japan to the Chinese government in 1915), the Shantung resolution (which came out of the Paris Peace Conference of 1919), the Nanking Incident of 1927, and the December 9th Movement of 1935, they took up a stance opposed to the radicals and the masses.

The 'spirit of the people' itself underwent a process of rationalization during this period. After the May 4th Movement of 1919 it was no longer the crude xenophobia shown by the Boxers in 1900 but the anti-imperialism of the age of Lenin that lay at the heart of Chinese nationalism. Popular methods of resisting imperialism also changed. In place of the chanting of magical incantations and the indiscriminate killing of foreigners, we now find organized boycotts, strikes and demonstrations. These new methods gained their first important success in the recovery of the British settlements in Hankow and Kiukiang in 1927; their second was in persuading the country to go to war against Japan in 1937.

Before the inauguration of the treaty system in the years after 1842 the Western nations had no coherent China policies at all, except a vague expectation that, once 'opened', China would provide an unlimited market for Western manufactured goods. It was this expectation, the importance of the China trade to British India, and China's intransigence that, taken together, caused Palmerston to decide on war in 1839. Between 1840 and 1860 ideas of mutual accommodation were debated by both sides and were embodied in a series of treaties. Although Whitehall did not realize that the stories of China being another El Dorado were sheer fantasy until the time of Lord Elgin's expedition in 1857-8, Britain had never entertained the notion of turning China into another India. Her aims were limited to the maintenance and gradual expansion of her mercantile

interests and their protection by a negotiated tariff, consular jurisdiction and gunboats. Contact between British subjects and the
Chinese native should be kept to a minimum to avoid trouble; it was
hoped that commerce could then be conducted in a less stormy
atmosphere. The other powers shared the fruit of the war with
Britain under the 'most favoured nation' formula. In more concrete
terms, the new treaty system, which in part preserved and in part
broke down traditional Chinese diplomatic practice, consisted of the
stationing of resident envoys at Peking and of consuls at the treaty
ports, the establishment of foreign settlements, the organization of
a modern maritime customs service under joint control, and the
creation of mixed courts presided over by Chinese and foreign
officers. In addition, as France was interested in protecting and
furthering the efforts of missionaries, China was forced to open her
doors to the Gospel, Western missionaries, like Western traders,
coming in under the protection of extraterritoriality.

These agreements were made in 1860 when the Ch'ing empire was
threatened not only by the Anglo–French Expedition but also by
internal rebellions. Its survival was in the balance; the rebels, of
whom the Taiping (1850–64) were the most important, might reduce
the gains won by this and the earlier war and by many arduous
sessions of negotiation to nothing. The Western nations therefore
switched from attacking to defending the Ch'ing regime. To call
this policy 'co-operative' evades the question of the purpose of the
co-operation. Was it to protect China's national interests or the
vested interests of the West in that country? These two sets of interests were incompatible. However, the system worked out at this time
was to remain effective up to 1917, when the Czarist government was
overthrown and China declared war on the Central Powers.

Throughout the second half of the nineteenth century Britain was
supreme in east Asia. The French War in the 1880s did not really
alter Britain's position or the structure of the treaty system. But
thereafter the international situation changed rapidly because of
Russia's eastward expansion, mounting competition from Germany
and the United States of America, and the emergence of Japan as an
imperialist power. In the years immediately after the Sino–Japanese
War of 1894–5 these powers threatened to carve up China into
separate spheres of influence, within which each one would have
exclusive rights and privileges. To arrest this anarchic, and, to China,
potentially lethal process, Britain and the United States put forward

the formula of the 'Open Door and Equal Economic Opportunities'. A dismembered China without an effective central government would naturally mean the collapse of the treaty system. Russia was, in effect, to reject the Open Door principle, and because of this neither France nor Germany showed any enthusiasm for it. Japan, on the other hand, equivocated, paying lip-service to the formula while consolidating her gains after the defeat of Russia in 1905.

During the First World War Japan's continental expansion gathered momentum to the detriment of the treaty system which was further weakened by Russia's voluntary renunciation of some of her rights in the Chicherin declaration of 1918 and the loss of the treaty rights of the Central Powers at the end of the war. Meanwhile the fast-growing anti-imperialist nationalist movement in China itself was calling for a recognition and sympathy which only Soviet Russia would give. The delegates to the Peace Conference at Versailles ignored it in a manner which showed contempt for its impotence; the Western powers decided to hand the former German possessions in Shantung to Japan.

It was Wilson who realized the explosive nature of the problems created by the Peace Conference; it was Harding who convened the Washington Conference in an effort to hinder its consequences. But the achievement at Washington in 1921–2 was meagre. Re-affirming the principles of the Open Door and Equal Opportunity, the nine powers at Washington sought to uphold China's territorial and administrative integrity – in other words, to bolster up the warlords' government in Peking; they wanted the door of China to be open to foreign trade and investment but did not appoint a 'door-keeper' to keep it open. Unlike the Anglo–Japanese alliance, the Washington formula was not provided with any mechanism to enforce its general acceptance. Its workability rested on three hypotheses: (a) that the British and American Pacific fleets would retain their preponderance; (b) that Russia would not become strong enough to upset the balance of power in east Asia; (c) that Chinese nationalism would continue to be ineffectual. If any one of these hypotheses turned out to be incorrect, the formula would become a dead letter; and even if that eventuality happened, neither the United Kingdom nor the United States would resort to force to guard their interests in China.

While these hypotheses held true, peace among nations did prevail in the East. Then came the Depression and the arms race between Japan and the Anglo–American powers, which swiftly changed the situation. Japan's seizure of Manchuria in 1931 shocked the Western powers into a panic-stricken disunity. The League of Nations could do nothing beyond sending a fact-finding mission, while the major powers behind the League, faced with Japan's military might, confined themselves to refusing to recognize the puppet state set up on the soil of Manchuria. After that the spectacle of Europe's retreat from east Asia was, to use a Chinese metaphor, like that of watching mercury poured upon the ground and seeing its scattered beads rolling into holes and crevices.

Apart from pursuing their individual imperialist aims, the Western powers had never, in the past hundred years, had a concerted policy towards China. From the Western point of view, the treaty system of the 1860s was probably the best thing they had done. Once erected, the system became the status quo and its architects conservative and passive. The West's lack of initiative and dynamism in the 1920s was in acute contrast with the communism of Russia, the expansionism of Japan, and the nationalism of China, all of which sought to destroy the status quo. That the status quo was undesirable weakened the West's case, and it finally became untenable after 1937. When the West first came to east Asia, it represented a new, progressive force; when it withdrew, it was already out of date.

In the hundred years from 1842 to 1942, China had been treated by the West with distrust, ridicule, and disdain, mingled from time to time with pity and charity, only occasionally with sympathy and friendliness. No Western head of state while in office lowered his dignity by paying a visit to China; no Chinese head of state was ever invited to visit a Western country. The first time China took part in a major international assembly was at Versailles, but her second appearance at the Washington Conference was greeted by Briand's embarrassing question: 'What is China?' Chiang Kai-shek's trip to Cairo in 1943 and Chou En-lai's to Geneva in 1954 were therefore landmarks in her progress as a member of the family of nations.

This brief summary of China's international relations will, I hope, provide adequate background for the rest of the book which, after all, is not a diplomatic history. The book is mainly concerned with China's cultural and social contacts with the West in a dynamic process of change; the process is called 'Westernization' or 'modernization', which involves institutions of all sizes from the state and political parties down to voluntary organizations, and also, of

C.A.T.W.—B

course, many individuals, on whom this study will focus. The book will be concerned throughout with society below the level of government.

To make the book manageable in scope and size, I propose to treat China as she was from the beginning of the nineteenth century down to the outbreak of the Japanese War in 1937, and to define the West to include Europe west of Vienna, the United States of America, and the white dominions of the British Empire. The period and geographic area are so chosen as to exclude Japan and to minimize the impact of communism, though I am fully aware of the profound influence Russia and Japan had on China. Japan can hardly be regarded as a Western nation; Chinese communism, like Chinese diplomatic history, has been discussed in detail in several existing works. Nevertheless these topics will be referred to from time to time, for narrative clarity.

My analysis will open with a chapter on how China and the West saw each other. Attitudes and policies are formed, approaches and procedures are chosen, on the basis of things as they are perceived, not as they really are. Therefore the role of image-makers and the images they created will be analysed. The image-makers are also agents of changes; they include missionaries and converts, scholars and students, traders and emigrants. Diplomats, too, perform this role, but, with few exceptions, only those who addressed their views to the general public in an unofficial capacity are discussed in this study. Among the groups of people mentioned above, a comprehensive coverage of the traders and emigrants is extremely difficult owing to a dearth of recorded material. Therefore I shall limit myself to treating the Western community in Shanghai and the Chinese one in San Francisco as two case studies.

The remainder of the book will then deal with the process of change induced by the ideas brought to China or the West by these agents. After outlining the basic attitudes, I shall go on to describe political, social, economic, and cultural developments. It is hoped that, on the one hand, the book will help to settle some controversial problems, such as the nature of the T'ung-chih Restoration – China's first attempt at modernization in the 1860s–1890s – and that of the reform movement after 1900, and, on the other, to fill in some of the gaps in our knowledge. By means of a review such as this, some of the strains and stresses of China's modernization may be better understood.

For the purposes of this book, the basic elements of China's modernization must be sought in stimulus and response. When looking at these in political and economic affairs alone, one receives an impression of China's lethargy and passivity, almost like that of 'a patient etherised upon a table'. But China becomes alive, dynamic, buzzing with activity, if one looks below this level, at the *feng-ch'i* (climate of opinion) and the *min-ch'i* (spirit of the people) with their biases towards either tradition or radicalism. By exploring these depths one may come to realize what an obstacle the government of China was to the modernization of the country.

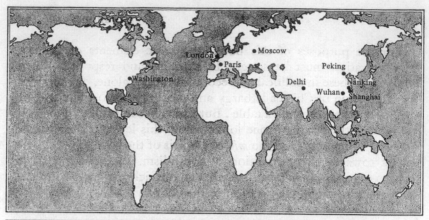

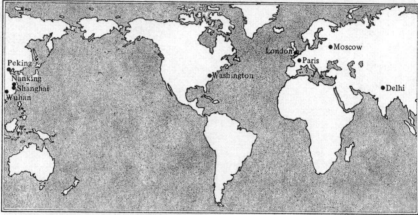

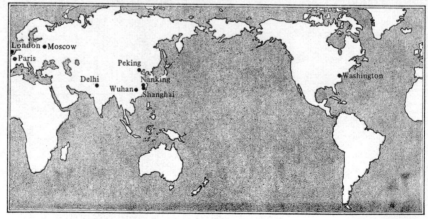

*Three views of the East*

# Part 1
# *Agents*

# Chapter 1

# *Images and image-makers*

## The West's view of China

The idealized, sinophile picture of the great empire in the East as depicted by the Philosophes and the Physiocrats, Voltaire, Jean-Baptiste Du Halde, Rousseau, Quesnay and Turgot, which influenced even David Hume and Oliver Goldsmith, was only one side of the story, a whip in the hands of the reformers with which to beat the *ancien régime*. Father Louis Lecomte's *Mémoires sur La Chine* of 1696 was ordered to be burnt, Christian Wolff's eulogy of China was stigmatized as atheistic; Montesquieu's denunciation of Chinese despotism gave rise to sinophobia. Even so, Quesnay could still argue that this despotism, being based on 'wise and irrevocable' laws, was legal, not arbitrary. The American and French revolutions and the political reforms in Britain, demonstrating the rationality of a new political philosophy and the superiority of new forms of political practice, drastically changed the Western view of China. Although the Chinese government was still thought of as 'excellent', it was none the less oppressive.

As European and North American commercial involvement in the East expanded, more detailed and accurate knowledge of China became available. In peacetime most of the visitors were hard-headed merchants and their assistants, missionaries, and officials; in times of war, most were sailors or soldiers. What they saw was an empire in rapid decay, as portrayed by Charles Gutzlaff in his *Journal* of three illegal voyages along the coast of China in 1831, 1832 and 1833. But the Far East remained too remote, interesting only to those who were concerned with the profits to be gained from trade or the souls to be saved through the propagation of the Gospel – both these aims being considered as beneficial to Christians and heathen alike. Even the exhibition of a Chinese lady with a pair of small bound feet at the Grand Salon, 94 Pall Mall, London, in July 1827 (admission one shilling), and of a large collection of exotic Chinese things, including, inevitably, the shoes of bound feet and an opium-smoking set, sponsored by an enterprising American by the name of Nathan Dunn at Hyde Park Corner from April 1843 to May 1851, aroused only ephemeral curiosity among the inhabitants of London. Books on China were not published in any considerable number for wide circulation until after the Anglo–French Expedition in the late 1850s. Thereafter China was to attract European attention again only during and immediately after the Sino–Japanese War of 1894–5 when Britain was breaking out of her 'splendid isolation' and seeking a possible alliance with Japan.

In China itself, what followed was a series of violent convulsions, causing more books on the state and society of China to be published. The Boxer War of 1900 engaged more Western pens and consumed more Western ink than any other event before the communist revolution of 1949. The revolution of 1911, the Washington Conference of 1921, Chiang Kai-shek's seizure of power in 1928, the Japanese occupation of Manchuria of 1931, and the outbreak of the second Sino–Japanese War of 1937 were stormy intervals between seasons of calm. Hardly a 'power' in the true sense of the word, China aroused Western interest only by her irrelevance or when some other uncontrollable force threatened to disrupt the status quo. She existed either to amuse the Westerner or to prick his conscience and make him uneasy.

The swift progress of the West in the nineteenth century threw China and most other Oriental and African countries into sharp contrast. China had a predilection for stability; her great fear was of progress. In stagnation, de Quincey remarked, the empire 'was rotten in one part and she is hollow in another. On this quarter you detect cancer; on that quarter you find nothing on which cancer could prey.' The unchanging nature of China was also observed by, for instance, Victor de Laprade. Hegel, like many of his contemporaries, shared this view of 'a static, unchanging society'. Even the thoughtful Max Weber was struck by the enduring stability of China at the turn of the twentieth century.

The *rigor mortis* by which China was gripped, diagnosed as such by the consensus of European and North American commentators, was of course the result of Oriental despotism, a theme that had run through European writing on China even before the French Revolution. Despotism allowed freedom and power only to the ruler while depriving the governed masses of both freedom and the chance to express their opinions, with the result, as a dismayed John Stuart Mill remarks, that there was 'one man of superhuman mental activity managing the entire affairs of a mentally passive people'.

The enduring political and social structures and the long-established moral values of China were noticed at the same time as the revolutionary tradition of her peasants. But Western observers failed to see any systemic or ideological changes brought about by the peasant uprisings. After all, 'what sort of human beings can be found under such a [despotic] regime?' as Mill said, summarily dismissing the multitude of the Chinese masses. To be sure, the attention of nineteenth-century Europe, when it looked at China, was focussed on the elite, the mandarinate; one elite was trying to understand another.

Naturally, these leading European intellectuals obtained the information on which they based their analysis of China from the 'old China hands' on the spot, who professed to refrain from judging China 'by our own civilized standard' but could nevertheless not avoid comparing China with Europe, particularly with England after the Age of Reform. To begin with, let us see what they thought of the Chinese ruling classes. The Confucian mandarin was described by the authoritative *Chinese Repository*, a monthly founded by an American medical missionary-cum-diplomat, Dr Peter Parker, as 'intellectually a proud, self-sufficient fatalist'. Such a man could not conceivably be an agent of change, as the influential American missionary, S. Wells Williams, noted in his well-known *Middle Kingdom* in 1848 and the learned English missionary, W. H. Medhurst, pointed out in a more emphatic tone:

. . . it is not in the *nature* of the Chinese to imitate reform or carry it honestly and steadily out. Neither the ruler nor the ruled appreciate its necessity; and could they be enlightened sufficiently to perceive it, they do not possess the strength of character or fixity of purpose to follow implicitly the course pointed out.

Their lack of intellectual curiosity and their habit of throwing temper tantrums made them appear to John Fryer, a Briton who had worked with the mandarins for many years, as 'more like children than men'. Another Briton, Sir Thomas Wade, who had also had long experience of mandarins, described them as 'mostly corrupt'. Corruption was deemed by Paul S. Reinsch, the American Minister to China from 1913 to 1919, to be the root cause that reduced China to utter insignificance: 'At every turn we seem to get into a blind alley leading up to a place where some spider of corruption sits, the whole tribe manipulated by a powerful head spider.' Conducive to none of the Confucian public virtues, e.g. benevolence, righteousness and a sense of shame, which were essential to good Confucian administration, corruption was a hindrance to the growth of patriotism in the age of growing Chinese nationalism in the twentieth century. The most important specialist in Eastern affairs at the Foreign Office in the 1920s, Sir Victor Wellesley, pitied China 'stewing in her own juice', that is to say of corruption. There was no hope for the country under the Nationalists and things would be the same under the communists, for both leaders and masses were thoroughly corrupt. The change from empire to republic and the replacement of the warlords by Chiang Kai-shek made little impression on the civil service discipline; they only turned the people into a flock of sheep without a shepherd and the country into an object for others to act upon. In Metternich's term, China was 'a mere geographic expression'.

There were two other, modified ways of looking at the Chinese body politic. After the beginning of this century a considerable body of opinion, especially in the United States of America, saw the limits of China's despotism. Beyond the reach of the tentacles of authoritarian rule lay vast stretches of the country controlled by the self-governing clans and guilds to which most Chinese belonged. This self-governed China 'was a sound basis for a new kind of democracy'. From this observation, one could proceed to elaborate, if one chose, on the democratic spirit of the Chinese. They were after all 'represented by a government for the people'; they had a sincere belief in peace and a love for freedom. Above all, they were willing to co-operate with true believers in democracy in the Republican period between 1912 and 1949. The fact that China never had had a democratic tradition and would by all indications be unlikely to initiate one did not trouble this body of opinion. The democracy observed by those who belonged to it could at best be described as democracy by default or 'beggars' democracy'. There was also the sophistry of the writer Lin Yutang, which presented yet another way of looking at the despotic corruption of China. In his widely read book, *My Country and My People* (1939), Lin compared this despotic corruption to a banyan tree that spread wide and fast. 'We Chinese do not fight the banyan tree, we try to come under its shade. We do not impeach officials, like the Americans, or bring down the houses of [the] rich, like the Bolsheviks. We try to become the doorkeepers and enjoy their official umbrage [*sic*].' Because, on the one hand, the Chinese were conservative, having no desire to change; on the other, they were as divided as grains of sand. Both their conservatism and their disunity were praiseworthy attributes in the sense that they helped to preserve the race and its cultural tradition.

In the eyes of an Oxford country parson, James Woodforde, the Chinese were 'uncommonly ugly' like 'the runabout gipsies'. Not having had any previous contact with them, Woodforde might have been shocked by the strangeness of the physical appearance of a Chinese he saw on 13 June 1775. Later, a learned American mission-ary, J. Edkins, found 'many a pretty face . . . among the women, but in general the men of China are more interesting-looking than the females'. Edkins' impression was not widely shared, for in the Western cartoons and caricatures (Hop Lee with his goggles, flirta-tious fan, and swishing pigtail, for example) the Chinese was often represented as a comic figure with slanting eyes and high cheekbones, toothy and clumsy, with either an unsightly pigtail at the back of the head (if a man) or a pair of bound feet below the skirt (if a woman). He or she was sometimes disgusting, sometimes pitiable, depending on the mood of the time or the theme of the drawing. He or she was seldom good looking. After the First World War there was a spate of motion pictures about China made in Hollywood and Germany all of which contrasted the beauty of the Caucasian with the beast-like appearance of the Mongolian. Mr Wu, as presented by Harry Maurice Vernon and Harold Owen, and Dr Fu Manchu, imperson-ated by Sax Rohmer, could hardly be described as handsome; even the podgy Charlie Chan was not in any sense physically attractive.

To date, I think the most comprehensive survey of Chinese characteristics is still A. H. Smith's study under that title published in 1894. In social behaviour, Smith noted, the Chinese had an 'ante-diluvian concept of time', never punctual and never sensible enough to take his leave when his company was not wanted. He was indiffer-ent to crowding and noise and completely incapable of appreciating the value of privacy. But he was hypersensitive to a loss of 'face' when he was accused or made aware of a fault of whatever description, either personal or collective. Once lost, the 'face' must be 'saved' regardless of evidence or logic. When the effort to 'save it' failed, or when, for instance, a command from him was not readily accepted, he might lose his temper also, usually by letting fly a tirade of invective which Smith called 'a ball of filth'. Even women would behave like this, in the very street. The conditions in which the Chinese lived were characterized by a total lack of sanitation and a stoic disregard for comfort and convenience. In addition to his ugliness, unpunctuality, 'indirection' and filth, the Chinese was cruel to animals, an attitude that shocked the Westerner just as the Westerner's fondness for pets amused and puzzled the Chinese.

With his puny physique, thin whiskers, and effeminate manners, the Chinese male perplexed the Westerner. The famed scholar, Wang T'ao, who assisted James Legge in translating the Confucian classics, was mistaken for a woman in Scotland in 1868. President Hsü Shih-ch'ang (1918–22) was known as 'Susie' among the foreigners in Peking. 'In China, most of the positive qualities (courage, honesty, generosity, industry, and restraint) which we [Westerners], at heart, admire in a man are positive nuisances.'

But the Chinese fault that Westerners remarked upon most often and denounced most vehemently was dishonesty. The Chinese 'love of specious falsehood' was noticed by the early missionaries, diplomats, and traders alike. W. A. P. Martin, an American missionary and educationist, held that ' . . . truth is not a point of honor with the Chinese, and adroit lying is with them admitted to be one of the prime qualifications of a mandarin'. A. H. Smith really went to town on this subject, devoting a whole chapter of his book to the Chinese skill in cheating and deviousness in the use of polite words, circumlocution, and hinting of all sorts, and he came to the conclusion that 'one never has any assurance that a Chinese ultimatum is ultimate'. Reports on the Chinese disregard of truth continued into the twentieth century. It was Rodney Gilbert, a sinophobe with a sardonic turn of phrase, who wrote *this* diatribe: 'Polite lying is everywhere an accomplishment; in China [it]is an art, and the Chinese when busy adhering to their rule of propriety, are past masters in insincerity.'

There was the Chinese disregard for human life, an example of which Hudson Taylor, founder of the China Inland Mission, and a fellow missionary, J. Jones, witnessed in 1856 when a Chinese was

drowning and no one would rescue the poor man unless the foreigners on the spot were willing to put up some money for the operation.
Early missionaries sent back hair-raising reports on the practice of
infanticide. The same reports appeared much later in American school
textbooks on geography and in Pearl Buck's books in the 1920s. One
can go on endlessly listing Chinese moral deficiencies – the absence
of public spirit, indulgence in gambling, the use of obscenity,
prostitution, etc.

The general picture was, then, of a depraved race governed by a
despotic and corrupt ruling class. In the words of Thomas de
Quincey, these people were natural connoisseurs of cowardice but
had no vital stamina nor mercy. The moral standards of the past
had collapsed, but no new ideas had emerged to replace them. This
was a China surviving in immorality. There were only three rational
reactions possible – to wipe the race from the face of the earth; to
treat it with the utmost contempt; or to reform it. These attitudes
corresponded roughly to the consensus of opinion among three
different groups of foreigners in China – the Shanghai merchants,
the diplomats, and the missionaries. Among the last group, A. H.
Smith advocated a moral reconstruction by instilling a new value
system, that of Western Christian morality, into the minds of the
Chinese masses. By this means alone could there be a gleam of hope
for China:

There is wealth enough in China to develop the resources of the Empire,
if there were but the confidence, without which timid capital will not
emerge from its hiding-place. There is learning enough in China for all
its needs. There is no lack of talent of every description. But without
mutual confidence, based upon real sincerity of purpose, all these are
insufficient for the regeneration of the Empire.

But the question was, were the Chinese intelligent enough to see
their country's compelling needs? Were they intelligent enough
either to pull themselves up by their own bootstraps or to be brought
up to the generally accepted standard of civilization with foreign
help? To put it more bluntly, were the Chinese an intelligent race
and willing to learn? In the intellectual atmosphere prevailing after
the publication of Darwin's theory of evolution most Western observers held the view that China had sunk to her present state of
abject misery because of the inferiority of the Chinese race. In 1847
Captain S. Shaw of the USA gave his opinion on these questions

thus: the Chinese 'can imitate most of the fine arts, [but] do not possess any large portion of original genius'.

On top of this, the Chinese were so conceited that they believed themselves to be superior to everyone else. Therefore they felt no need to understand other people, asked no questions about them, and learnt no foreign languages. They were, in the estimation of de Quincey, 'imbecile' and 'obstinate' because of a 'feeble brain'; C. Currie Martin, a missionary, called them 'this vilest and silliest among nations'. Even education, de Quincey believed, would not help the Chinese, for 'no native Chinese, educated at a native school, ever advanced . . . to the Fourth Book of "Euclid".' T. G. Selby wrote in his *Chinaman at Home* of 1900:

In fact, when nature made the Chinaman, wishing to forestall the inventions of the future, she made an auto-laundry with the chemistry of digestion for a motor, and then covered the contrivance with a skin of cheap vellum.

The Chinese mind, as described by those who appear to have known it well, was characterized by its slowness. Samuel Drake remarked in the 1880s: 'Hurry it, then it is thrown into confusion, and an act of folly is the result.' In greater detail, A. H. Smith pointed out three obvious traits: disregard of accuracy; a talent for misunderstanding, and a propensity to be opaque. 'A hundred cash [*wen*] is not a hundred, a pound is not a pound, a pint not a pint.' The disregard for accuracy might be blamed, Smith suspected, on the way the Chinese language was constructed. After all, it was without the conditional clauses or phrases which help to make statements clear. Nor did it have any means of showing the tense of a verb or the number of a noun; nor, in speech, was there any way of telling the gender of a pronoun. To make things worse, the users of this language took advantage of its ambiguities purposely to create misunderstanding. Frank Goodnow, the American expert on constitutional law who advised President Yuan Shih-k'ai to restore the monarchy in 1915, believed that the cumbersomeness of the language actually retarded the Chinese mind. It burdened the memory of the learner and slowed him down in the study of any subject; lacking an alphabet, it permitted only a fumbling method of classification so that Chinese reference works were veritable nuisances; its spoken and written forms diverged so sharply that it practically fostered illiteracy. Instead of clarity, this language produced only muddleheadedness, an inability, for instance, to distinguish between facts and reasons. If a Chinese was asked why he did not keep the ice in winter for his use in summer, he would reply that he did not keep it for use in summer. As to logical contradictions, A. H. Smith insisted, they were absolutely beyond the grasp of the Chinese mind:

He knows nothing about logical contradictions, and cares even less. He has learned by instinct the art of reconciling propositions which are inherently irreconcilable by violently affirming each of them, paying no heed whatever to their mutual relations.

If the Chinese were as depraved and dense as these Western writers had made out, how then could one explain the glorious achievements of their past history, a fact that anyone with a nodding knowledge of the country could not possibly overlook? How could one explain the durability of the Chinese civilization? These may well have been the questions in Goodnow's mind when he gave his opinion that the Chinese, Asiatic though they were, were none the less intelligent. Some half a century before him, Maclay had described the Chinese mind as having 'an intuitive logic of rare vigour and certainty'. Maclay praised its quickness, shrewdness, and pragmatism, an observation in which Medhurst concurred. It was this practical bent of the Chinese intellect that gave both the race and its civilization their durability.

Throughout the whole period under consideration, all Western writers, with Rodney Gilbert as perhaps the only exception, acclaimed Chinese industriousness. This was the image of the Chinese peasant Wang Lung, in the most popular book on China ever written by a Westerner, Pearl Buck's *Good Earth* (1931). Unconcerned with politics and Christianity, the simple and gracious, dignified and practical, industrious and frugal peasant was China's only hope for survival and revival, according to Buck, in spite of his lust, quarrelsomeness and ignorance. Drawing from her own experience as a child and later as the wife of an agronomist, John Lossing Buck, Pearl Buck's novel persuaded the West to accept a more favourable image of the Chinese. For those the novel had failed to reach, there were the Broadway stage production based on it in 1933 and the film version in 1937. Tens of millions of Western people came under its influence.

Their industriousness, patience and fortitude in the face of dire misfortunes made the Chinese content, cheerful, a lovable people.

From the 1920s to the 1940s more and more favourable pictures were drawn and the subjects of these were depicted more and more like faithful, innocent, and happy children. The Western businessmen liked them because they respected the white people. Diplomats liked them, too, because the house servants, club boys, and the Westernized Chinese with whom the diplomats were in frequent contact were friendly. Some went even as far as to find no fault with the Chinese at all, like the little known, starry-eyed James Marsh, not to mention many Western collectors of Chinese antiques, who were completely captivated by the beauty of the Orient, a beauty 'beyond description'. From that position, one could easily become a staunch defender of the old China 'with all its oriental glamor'.

## The challenge of radicalism

The charm and lovability of old China! The virtues of industriousness, perseverance, fortitude, and contentment belonged to an oppressed people desperately attempting to raise a smile under the crushing burden of inhuman misery. Were there some Chinese who actively defied this destiny, stridently calling for change, destruction of the old order, and progress?

Indeed there were, and these were the radical youth. To Stalin's envoy in China, Mikhail Borodin, they were 'all good when they are young'. The Chinese indeed had their revolutionary tradition in the peasant uprisings which had overthrown past dynasties, as noted by Pearl Buck. It is perplexing that the Westerners so often applaud the meekness of the Chinese and yet ignore the frequent riots against missionaries, boycotts, demonstrations against foreign aggression, civil wars, and rebellions against all forms of oppression.

But it was after the First World War that the radicalization of China presented a challenge to a West whose self-confidence was shaken by the war itself and was to be shaken further by the Great Depression. Although the old colonial system with some modifications was reaffirmed at Versailles, the Western concept of the world was changing, hence the Western re-evaluation of China. In that process, the hardest element for the West to accept was Chinese radicalism with its fervour for independence, justice and modernization. Before the West could approve and support Chinese radicalism it must condemn traditional China, and, what is more, the activities of the Westerners in China up to that date would have to be judged anew and perhaps condemned also, for China after decades of efforts at modernization still remained hopelessly backward.

Clinging tenaciously to Victorian values and the Darwinian world order, conservative Westerners put all the blame for this on the Chinese themselves, as did Rodney Gilbert in his *What's Wrong with China?* (1923):

There are inferior races in the world, just as there are inferior men in every community. There are nations that cannot govern themselves, but must have a master, just as there are men in every community that need a guardian and are a menace to the community if granted the unqualified 'right to life, liberty, and the pursuit of happiness'. Races, like men, have their limitations. Education and environment, law and the exercise of it, may make the inferior man a more useful and less dangerous member of the community, but he is born with certain distinct limitations beyond which no amount of education or training can carry him.

On the other hand, radical Westerners, losing their faith in the old Western values and sensing a new hope for China and the world as a whole, went to China through the traditional channels, as missionaries or journalists, not to teach or to aid the unfortunate, but to observe, report, or join in working for a worthy cause. These were the Edgar Snows, Agnes Smedleys and Norman Bethunes.

Gilbert spoke of China as if she was a homogeneous entity which could be judged by judging her officials, scholars and other city dwellers. Their faults were the faults of the whole race; to attack their futility was to attack the futility of the whole race. The unfairness of this approach was obvious and was partly responsible for Lin Yutang's reply, *My Country and My People*. Lin had the advantage that he knew China and her cultural tradition far better than Gilbert and was thus able to distinguish the corrupt and unscrupulous bureaucrats from the scholar gentry – the refined and propertied people who had both the taste and the means to develop an ethos, an attitude and a life-style of their own. Even if they were called upon to serve the empire or the republic, their hearts remained most of the time in their studios hidden away behind the wooded hills, encircled by murmuring streams, lit by the bright moon and gently brushed by autumn breezes.

Such people were mellow, rich in passive, calm strength rather than in youthful vigour and romantic ideals. They sought peace under any circumstances, rather than progress and conquest. Such people were indifferent to organized action for the protection of civil rights and the like, and to the effect on living conditions of overpopulation, economic pressure and even war. They were old in cunning with a dove-like gentleness and serpent-like wisdom. Their essentially mellow culture inculcated in the people a spirit of contentment and a tolerance which were the highest human values. Neither political revolution nor social reform, however thorough it might be, was likely to alter these characteristics of Chinese culture.

The twentieth-century successors of these recluses were the intellectuals in the political wilderness pursuing their various callings – university professors, newspaper editors, freelance writers, lawyers, and rural reformers such as Hu Shih, Wang Yun-sheng, Lo Wen-kan, Pa Chin, James Yen, and Lin himself. Lin's picture of a homogeneous China was no less distorted than Gilbert's, but both were concerned with an unchanging China. The China Lin wanted to preserve was almost totally unknown to Gilbert; the China Gilbert wanted to destroy was not defended by Lin. The battle between them was never really joined.

Gilbert saw China as 'the world's greatest contemporary burlesque'. How could it be fit for self-government or representative government in the Western fashion? Having failed in Western democracy and republicanism, it turned to the 'extremism' of the 1920s – Russian Bolshevism. Infantile and lawless as ever, the Chinese extremist 'is a medieval product, crazy drunk with modernism, like a Mongol shepherd out of the wireless wilderness with a magnum of champagne under his belt'.

Was the Chinese form of extremism a legacy from the Middle Ages as Gilbert asserted? Since the opening of China to foreign contacts, the less educated masses such as the fringe elements in the cities and market towns and the peasants on both sides of the law had consistently shown a tendency to violence against the foreigner. The resistance at Sanyuanli near Canton in 1841, the innumerable anti-Christian riots, and the Boxer Uprising of 1900 were enough evidence to the West of a violent opposition among the masses. In the majority of cases, the secret societies played a role. While officials and soldiers treated the foreigner with respect out of fear of reprisal, the bandits treated white men and women with scanty deference. These acts of violence were described as the result of Chinese 'xenophobia' stirred up by the lawless elements in society. Even after the dawn of nationalism in China, boycotts such as those of 1905 and 1915 and demonstrations and workers' strikes such as those of 1919 and 1925, in which the participation of either merchants or students or both was obvious, tended to be interpreted by the foreigner in terms of 'medieval' xenophobia. The British consul in Ch'angsha regarded the nationalist revolutionaries in 1905 as 'notorious rowdies'. These 'rowdies' were to become what J. O. P. Bland labelled as 'a small and semi-alien class', whose nationalism crystallized into anti-foreignism.

Bland – a journalist of considerable experience in China – expressed these views after the momentous strikes and demonstrations touched off by the shooting of Chinese workers in Shanghai towards the end of May 1925 which gave rise to what was called the May 30th Movement. During the strikes and demonstrations the *China Weekly Review*, an influential American paper in Shanghai, used such epithets as 'over-excitement' and 'anarchy' to imply the traditional failings of xenophobia and disorganization. Since the Chinese were incapable of organized action, the dimensions of the 1925 strikes and the staying power of the strikers must have been due to foreign help, as *The Times* declared:

The novel fact in this summer's outbreak against certain classes of foreigners in China is that the discontent is being organized, taught, guided and directed by a type of foreigner who is in perpetual revolt against all the institutions of Europe. . . .

The young China is at once ardently and defiantly national and extraordinarily susceptible to inflammable foreign influence. Its young men and women have broken with the old Chinese tradition. They are adrift in the modern world, and the Bolsheviks have caught them in a receptive mood.

The 'type of foreigners' in perpetual revolt against Europe were mostly, but not all, Bolsheviks who stirred up and made use of Chinese radicalism. Whatever interpretation was put upon these events in the West, radicalism attracted the attention of Western commentators who made it a point of debate. *The Times* and the *Manchester Guardian* persisted with their theory of a Moscow conspiracy whose tools were the youth of China. But this theory was contested by Bertrand Russell in the *New Leader* of 19 June 1926 and the *Guardian* of 14 March 1927, and by the more radical British papers like the *New Statesman* (29 August 1925) and the *Daily Herald* (8 June 1925). Even the *Christian Century*, a leading American religious journal, wrote on 18 June 1925, repudiating the conspiracy theory:

It is absurd to see in such an outburst as this only another evidence of the machinations of Moscow. . . . But all the Russian agents in the Far East could have done nothing had not the other foreign nations given them plenty of grievances on which to play.

Perhaps the whole May 30th Movement of 1925 was explained best by a foreigner, not widely respected but none the less widely experienced, Lennox Simpson (Putnam Weale):

. . . the parallel movements of foreign communism and Chinese nationalism were suddenly joined, and, like the guilty lovers in Dante's *Inferno*, were condemned to journey to the end together.

How could an alien ideology like communism take root in China as it was perceived by the West? J. D. Whelpley's views as expressed in the *Fortnightly Review* (1 March 1927) were typical of Western thinking then:

The nationalistic movement would have come into being if the Soviet Government had never materialized, and China will never go 'Bolshevic'. [*sic*] The psychology and tradition of the Chinese render them less susceptible to Marxian doctrines than any people in the world. They are a nation of individualists, the entire social and economic system being founded upon the dignity and value to the community of the individual trader.

The year 1925 and the appearance of a virulent new form of nationalism and radicalism in China marked the beginning of re-thinking in the West. The age-old image of the Chinese as easily excitable and hopelessly disorganized made it difficult to distinguish between modern Chinese radicalism and traditional forms of rebellion. In the same way the conservative Chinese mind was apt to see the radicals as dangerous rebels against the established society and political system. Once the radicals took up arms either in their own defence or for the furtherance of their cause, they became, in conservative eyes, mere 'bandits'. After 1925, and especially after the split of the Kuomintang–communist coalition in 1927, the conservative Chinese and the conservative Westerner, influencing each other mutually, were to reach a curious unanimity. Another age-old view, that the Chinese were incapable of organized action, which was the basis of the Moscow conspiracy theory, led both Chinese and Western observers to doubt the patriotism of the radicals. Neither group was sure whether the radicals were not Moscow agents working against the interests of their own country. As Chinese radicalism between

1925 and 1927 was confined to the city, both Western opponents and Western advocates of the Chinese radicals focussed their attention on the urban intelligentsia; peasant radicalism was not yet there to be observed.

The split in the first united front between the Kuomintang and the Chinese Communist Party in 1927 was followed by a continuous armed struggle amid various forms of civil strife. Occupying the key economic areas of China, Chiang's government in Nanking was the strongest among the contenders, recognized by the powers, and in control of the major sources of information which enabled it to create an image of the communists as mere rabble-rousers. Foreign observers in China, official and unofficial, being in no position to differentiate between the power struggle between Chiang and territorial leaders on the one hand and the social revolution being conducted by the communists against Chiang on the other, were easy victims of Chiang's propaganda. For instance, the *China Weekly Review* reported Chiang's victory over the communist 'bandits' from an official Nanking source without any editorial comment on 1 August 1931 and the *Chinese Recorder*, a leading missionary magazine in China, continually reported the atrocities supposed to have been committed by the communists from 1932 to 1936. Even the famous evangelist and YMCA leader, Sherwood Eddy, subscribed to the 'bandit' theory, saying that:

Had the communists been wise they would have relieved the poor so that the peasants would have turned to them for deliverance from oppression by soldiers and officials, but their savage cruelty piled great heaps of dead at the entrances to the villages they held. They not only killed the rich, the 'reactionaries', and all suspected of being their enemies, but they killed the aged as well when food grew scarce or when they retreated. Their cruelty struck terror into the hearts of the people of Szechwan.

It was true that the communists expelled missionaries from the areas under their control, confiscated their property, and abolished mission schools. But later, when the second united front was in the offing, the communists ceased to regard missionaries as 'imperialist spies' and suspended their anti-Christian campaign altogether in 1936. Generally speaking, the Protestant, especially the Congregationalist, missionaries did not swallow the Nanking 'bandit' theory hook, line and sinker. As early as 1927, Henry Hodgkin, the secretary of the National Christian Council, recognized the communists as a party dedicated to a cause which they regarded as the only solution to China's multitudinous problems. Even in 1931 an article in the *Chinese Recorder* stated that the communists had the 'support of millions of peasants and workers'. The same observation prompted the social gospel missionaries to consider the communists seriously as a challenge to the Christian mission in China. This being so it is easy to see why the missionaries occupied themselves with the rural reconstruction of China after 1930, for though the communists were godless and against religion, their approach to China's problems – changing the social milieu before trying to change man – struck the missionaries as more efficient than the Christian approach of changing man in order to change society.

Foreign journalists first began to doubt the truth of the 'bandit' theory when it became clear that Chiang was having considerable difficulty in quelling the 'bandits'. If the strength of the communists came from popular support, why did the people support 'bandits'? The *China Weekly Review* began to ask these questions from 1932 on. But the first opportunity for foreign journalists to visit the areas formerly under the communists did not come until the central China Soviets had been abandoned and the Long March begun in 1934–5. Hallett Abend of the *New York Times* and Anthony Billingham went to Fukien and found that the peasants there preferred the communists to the Chiang government, because redistributed land had now been restored to the landlords. Another American reporter, Haldore Hanson, journeyed to Kiangsi where he discovered the peasants complaining about high taxes, rents and rates of interest, and talking about the period of Red rule with nostalgia.

But for the time being Chiang's victory in central China seemed to have sealed the fate of Chinese communism. This was the view held by the *China Weekly Review*. Before long, there came the news of the communist proposal of an anti-Japanese united front with the Kuomintang, as reported by the *China Weekly Review* on 21 September 1935 and 21 March 1936. Could the communists, inspired by an alien philosophy, sincerely work for the interests of the Chinese nation? Some newspapermen were prepared to give them the benefit of the doubt; the majority, however, dismissed the proposal as sheer opportunism. But soon yet another American journalist, Earl Leaf, reported from Shansi, saying that the peasants of that province were willing to follow the communists in their effort to repel Japanese aggression.

At this time Edgar and Helen Snow (writing under the name Nym Wales) were teaching at Yenching University in Peking while writing for various newspapers in the United States and England. Like everyone else, Edgar Snow had been influenced by Chiang's propaganda and reported the atrocities of the Reds. But as time went on, his liberal and inquiring mind began to search for an explanation of the 'powerful something holding them [the communists] up' – so powerful, they had successfully withstood Chiang's relentless efforts to suppress them and the tough test of the Long March. His personal contacts with radical students in Peking in 1935–6, his friendship with Madame Sun Yat-sen, and his conversations with Colonel Joseph Stilwell, at that time American military attaché, deepened his interest in gaining a fuller understanding of the communists. Snow made his epic journey to Red China in the summer of 1936. He carried with him a letter of introduction from Liu Shao-ch'i, then in charge of the North China Bureau of the Chinese Communist Party (CCP). The outcome was a report on his conversation with Mao Tse-tung published in the *China Weekly Review* on 14 and 21 November 1936 and his first pictures of Red China appeared in *Life* on 25 January and 1 February 1937. Having already aroused considerable interest by these publications, Edgar Snow was to change the world's view of the CCP with his *Red Star Over China* in 1937. The seven editions which came out in quick succession in the United States ran to over 23 500 copies. In Britain, thanks to the Left Book Club, over 100 000 copies of *Red Star Over China* were sold within a few weeks. Soon it appeared in six other languages. Unlike Buck's and Lin's books, *Red Star Over China* has stood the test of time superbly. Even today, forty years after its first publication, it continues to inspire young radicals and to shape the image of Chinese communism.

It is superfluous to reproduce in detail the new image Snow's *Red Star* conveyed to the world. In short, it was the image of a number of Chinese dedicated to national integrity and social justice, embodying some of the traditional virtues and at the same time developing what was to be realized as the consciousness of socialist man. The exciting news Snow brought out of Paoan (then the Red capital) induced others to follow his example. Before the outbreak of the war against Japan in 1937, Agnes Smedley, Helen Snow, Anna Louise Strong, James Bertram, George Hatem, Philip Jaffe, Owen Lattimore, and several others made the journey and came out with their equally good impressions of the communists, which were to be reinforced by the 1944 group of reporters and to be sustained throughout the war period.

Western official views on the Chinese Communist Movement as represented by diplomatic dispatches were inclined to be more cautious. Among the American officials in China there were a few independent-minded souls whose inquiring minds led them to look deeper into the Red mystery. A military officer under the pseudonym of 'P' wrote in 1931, recognizing the CCP as 'a social force'. 'Because of the clarity of the objectives,' he said, 'and the capacity of its leaders, its extirpation – nothing less will serve to subdue it – can be achieved only with the greatest difficulty.' Its 'masterly adoption of Bolshevik methods to Chinese conditions' had laid 'the ground work of an out-and-out Soviet state . . . in the heart of China', without Russian help but with strong ties with the Communist International. The American vice-consul in Hankow, O. Edmund Clubb, carried out perhaps the most thorough study of the communist movement yet, and concluded that the movement was home-grown, ably led by a group of educated revolutionaries, and supported by the peasants because of its land policy. This revolution, according to Clubb, could not be defeated by arms alone; it could be halted only by economic and social reforms. As if he had had a premonition of the future, Clubb remarked:

It has very often been true in the history of nations that efforts at suppression, whether from within or outside the State, have proved in the end to be of considerable assistance to revolutionary movements, the pressure integrating the separate elements into a strong unity and giving it shape.

Few, however, shared Clubb's expectation that Chiang's military operations against the 'Red Bandits' would eventually fail. Nelson Johnson, the American ambassador, who knew China well, spoke the language, and was an open-minded man, believed that Chiang's efforts to exterminate the communists could succeed. So Chiang's victory in 1935 heartened not a few Western diplomats. Even in 1937 the British ambassador, Sir Hughe Knatchbull-Hugessen, saw no danger of the communists 'being able to regain a footing in the Government or seriously to affect national policy'. Yet the communists had survived the rigours of the Long March during which the American vice-consul in Kunming reported on their strong morale and 'almost fanatical unity of purpose', which report rekindled both curiosity and anxiety. Joseph Stilwell, for example, burst out to Edgar Snow one day:

Those Reds may be bandits, as Chiang says they are, but bandits or not, they're masters of guerilla warfare. I don't know what they're preaching but to me it looks like they've got the kind of leaders who win. I mean officers who *don't* say, 'Go on, boys!' but *'Come on*, boys!' If that's the case and they had enough of them, they could keep the Japs busy here till kingdom come.

Another American officer in naval intelligence Evans Fordyce Carlson, who made contacts with the communists in 1937–8, confirmed Stilwell's impression of the martial prowess of the communist army and went as far as to suggest learning from them, much to the disgust of his fellow military observers at the idea that Carlson 'thought *we* had anything to learn from any Chinese'.

By the time the Japanese War broke out in 1937, the issues of whether the communists were bandits or revolutionaries, and whether they were agents of Moscow under the control of the Communist International or masters of their own fate and capable of defending the honour of China, were largely settled. Western observers – missionaries, journalists, and officials alike – were sure that the communists were fighting for the welfare of the under-privileged, but communist practice in China appeared bafflingly different from that in Russia. Few observers had access to communist documents or other writings; few could have read them if they had; even fewer had any knowledge of the institutional arrangements or the ideological discussions which were held in the Soviet areas and in the party. Hardly any of them had the slightest understanding of Marxism–Leninism. Therefore they could not hope to grasp issues of theory, policy, and the establishment of new systems.

## The threat of China

In the confusion of admiration and disdain, eulogy and criticism, the basic facts of China's territorial size, vast population, and durable civilization did not escape the notice of any observer. These basic facts led such an experienced man as A. H. Smith to ask whether the 'nervous' European or the 'tireless, all pervading, and phlegmatic Chinese' would eventually win the struggle for survival. The old Napoleonic image of a 'sleeping giant' was to be revived, ironically, at a time when European and American imperialism was at its zenith. The danger of a strong China without the restraint of Christian discipline was perceived by A. T. Mahan; the fear that Chinese capital, cheap labour, and mercenary troops would one day turn the tables upon the West was in the mind of J. A. Hobson; anxiety lest the over-ripeness and corruption of European civilization should cause the West to lose the battle of cultures was expressed by Emile Zola:

Would it be possible to have a revolution from within our old race corrupted by monarchism? Would we not need a new race? It would be a race of barbarians . . . perhaps the Chinese if we waited long enough and if they threw themselves upon us.

Even in the minds of those who professed to understand China and the Chinese well, the thought of the 'yellow peril' was present. Lying behind his wholesale condemnation of the Chinese was Rodney Gilbert's feeling that

He [the Occidental] would rather be an Occidental and *control* the East, than submit to Oriental standards, sooner or later, and be dominated by the East.

The policy of Europe and America in China must finally be determined by this choice.

Conscious of the wrong the West had done to China, Pearl Buck

. . . has feared them [the Asians, particularly the Chinese], for she has long known that some day they would take revenge for the cruelties of white people in their country. Yes, she has seen unbelievable cruelty committed by white people in Asia and she has told me often that her greatest dread is the day when the dark races rise up and rebel against the minority of the world's population that is white.

The image of an inferior civilization destroying a superior one (for that was what the 'yellow peril' thesis was about) was clearly evoked by the historical experiences of Europeans – the destruction of the Roman Empire by the barbarians and the invasions of the Mongol hordes. Also it was a result of the guilt feelings of Europeans and of their consciousness that their civilization was in decline. This fear surged up whenever the West felt a loss of confidence in itself, which was usually a time when it became more aggressive. A parallel phenomenon can be observed in China's recent past. Whenever she was conscious of her own weakness she appeared to become more xenophobic and more aggressive. If this conclusion can be justifiably extrapolated to predict China's future course, a strong and therefore self-confident China may be the least dangerous to the world at large.

## China's image of the West

When Matteo Ricci was finally permitted to proceed to Peking in 1601 and presented a map of the world to Emperor Wan-li of the Ming dynasty, at least the Emperor himself and some of his ministers learned of the existence of five continents on which peoples of different races and cultures lived. But this information had largely been forgotten by the time of the war of 1839. The inhabitants of Canton, where trade with maritime nations was conducted, and the officials who dealt with foreigners knew that the Hollanders were 'the red-haired barbarians' 'with their sunken eyes, long nose, red hair, red eyebrows, red beard, and their feet when bare measuring some 14 inches long. They are unusually big.' There were also the Franks (*fo-lang-chi*) or Portuguese who possessed the best weapons and had even once bombarded Canton. The last piece of information referred, of course, to the coming of Fernao Peres Andrade in October 1517, whose action in firing off his guns as a salute was mistaken for a show of force. Subsequently his search for boys to work as servants was misconstrued as kidnapping tender flesh for food. In the north, where contacts were made with Russians, another oral tradition was established, consisting of stories of the *Lo-sha* (Russian) devils with their eyes like green lanterns and heads as large as bushels, who also survived on human flesh and blood. The white 'barbarians' were fearsome with their devilish, fierce, ugly physical appearance, which suggested all kinds of ominous possibilities. Foreigners were given the odious title of 'devil' or the equally derogatory name of *fan kow* (foreign dogs). The elite of China, unfortunately, had the same image of the foreigner as the common people, and it was to be one of the basic assumptions behind their handling of 'barbarian' affairs. It was hardly surprising that this myth persisted, in view of the fact that the *lingua franca* used in contacts between Chinese and foreigners was pidgin English, which at its best was inadequate even for communication on trade and everyday matters. The old books on the West had not been read for generations; no new ones were compiled. In the Chinese view, these physically hideous and socially repulsive foreigners who had come across vast seas were driven by their greed (or in modern terms, bourgeois acquisitiveness) and sustained by their obstinacy. Rapacious and stubborn, they were compared to goats and dogs that never willingly gave anything up.

Defeat at the hands of a mere 10 000 British soldiers in 1839–42 caused the Chinese to re-examine their hypotheses about the foreigner. The war completely destroyed the old beliefs that foreign guns could not shoot upwards at an angle, that foreign ships could not be sailed in the shallow waters near the coast, and that foreign soldiers could bend neither their backs nor their knees. Ch'i-shan, the Grand Secretary, Viceroy of the Metropolitan Province, and China's negotiator for peace with Britain, observed in 1841 that the power of the 'barbarians'' guns was a total surprise, that their ships could be manoeuvred nimbly even in shallow waters, and that their soldiers could fight on land more skilfully than the Chinese. Ch'i-ying, the chief negotiator of the Nanking Treaty, was absolutely convinced of the invincibility of the British war machine. To make things worse, the Chinese discovered during the negotiations that the 'barbarians' were also cunning, intelligent, and unpredictable.

Now that the martial prowess of the barbarians was admitted, China must obviously keep peace with them. Their weakness was their avarice, and so the way to pacify them was to lure them with some trumpery material bait such as the cession of Hong Kong and frequent banquets and exchange of gifts. The basic principle was to 'weigh our gains and losses, not their rights or wrongs', a method of proceeding that the reigning emperor thought to be 'fair and honest'. The watchword, as put forward by the Viceroy at Nanking, Ho Kuei-ch'ing, was 'to tame the barbarians by refraining from rubbing them up the wrong way'. To be tactful was the secret of diplomacy.

This, in essence, was the policy of *chi-mi*, using compassion and personal friendship to keep the 'barbarians' on a loose rein so as to outmanoeuvre and control them. But this policy had a built-in flaw. When the stubborn, avaricious, and fickle 'barbarians' had pushed China to the sticking point, it would become impossible to sustain. This was precisely the situation on the eve of the second Opium War (or the Anglo–French Expedition) in 1856. After the second war, the frequent resort to gunboat diplomacy on the Westerners' part, the frequent occurrence of anti-missionary riots which led once again to the use of gunboats to protect the carriers of the Good

Message into the hinterland of China, and the frequent changes in international alignment among the European powers rendered the *chi-mi* theory of diplomacy utterly useless.

In the meantime, the Chinese Court and high officials were changing their image of the foreigner. Far-sighted men like Commissioner Lin Tse-hsü, having studied the maritime nations while handling the opium question in Canton before the 1839 war, criticized his colleagues for their ignorance of Europe, and even for regarding the Europeans as 'barbarians'. His learned assistant, Wei Yuan, author of the famous *Illustrated Gazetteer of Maritime Countries (Hai-kuo t'u-chih)* of 1844, went even further:

Do we honestly know that among the visitors from afar there are people who understand propriety and practise righteousness, who possess knowledge of astronomy and geography, who are well versed in things material and events of past and present? They are extraordinarily talented and should be considered as our good friends. How can they be called 'barbarians'?

Immediately after the second war, Feng Kuei-fen, a wealthy scholar-official, felt deeply ashamed that China knew so much less of the West than the West knew of China. Even the less learned and less sensitive gradually ceased using such descriptions as 'with a nature like dogs and goats' and 'aware only of profit and gains' on official papers. The foreigners' 'obstinacy' and 'persistence' became 'tenacity' and 'perseverance'. The co-regents, two empresses of little education, realized that the foreigner was pragmatic and truthful. The chief cause of this changed image of the Westerner was his assistance in suppressing the Taiping Rebellion, especially in the campaigns in east China in 1862–3, as is shown by another edict issued by the co-regents in the name of the emperor:

Since the exchange of the instruments [of the Peking Treaties], we [Chinese and foreigners] have treated each other with trust and goodwill. Their help in quelling the bandits near Shanghai was unquestionably a demonstration of their peaceable intentions and friendship.

Prince Kung, who headed the newly created Tsungli Yamen, which dealt with all foreign affairs, and wielded great power at the Imperial Court, even dared to quote, unprecedentedly, a mere secretary in the British legation, Thomas Wade, to prove the need to train Chinese officers so that they could take over the command of the contingents organized by Frederick Ward and Charles Gordon. The foreign troops' conduct in military operations impressed the Chinese authorities with their courage and discipline, superior deployment and organization. At the entreaties of Robert Hart, Horatio Nelson Lay, and Anson Burlingame, W. A. P. Martin undertook to translate into Chinese the most lucid and authoritative treatise on international law of the time, Henry Wheaton's *Elements of International Law*, in 1863 and Prince Kung had it published the next year, since the Prince thought that although it was 'not entirely in conformity with Chinese institutions, there are points in it which may be adopted'. This beginning was followed by the translations of de Marten's *Guide Diplomatique*, Bluntschli's *Völkerrecht*, Fawcett's *Political Economy*, Tytler's *Universal History*, and other works. Thus it became known that the Western countries had their own laws and institutions and Chinese concepts of the West and diplomacy rapidly changed.\*

In the coastal provinces a new attitude towards the foreigners appeared. Tseng Kuo-fan, Viceroy at Nanking and perhaps the most respected minister of the realm after the pacification of the Taiping Rebellion, expounded the value of sincerity and good faith, refusing to promise what could not be done but carrying out to the last letter what had been promised. At court, Prince Kung instructed all local officials to handle affairs concerning foreigners with justice and fairness. Of the slightly younger generation, Li Hung-chang, whose weight in diplomatic affairs was increasingly to be felt, memorialized the throne on 4 May 1863:

I beg to suggest that in dealing with foreigners, we must first fathom their goals and intentions in order to ascertain their sincerity or insincerity [maximum and minimum demands]. Only then we can form a proper assessment of the situation and arrive at a just solution.

And the first Chinese Minister to the Court of St James, Kuo Sung-t'ao, stressed equally the three elements of reason, circumstances, and human understanding in search of a just solution. The old tactic of *chi-mi* with its attention to ritual and decorum, though not abandoned, gave up its central position in favour of larger considerations to do with the interests of the country. In the midst of changing attitudes and changing policies, an old assumption remained; right

---

\* The best case to illustrate this is the seizure of three Danish ships by a Prussian man-of-war just outside Taku within Chinese territorial waters in 1864. China, applying her newly gained knowledge of international law, forced Prussia to relinquish the Danish prizes and pay the sum of $1500 in compensation (I. C. Y. Hsü, *China's Entrance into the Family of Nations*, Cambridge, Mass., 1960, p. 133).

had to be shielded by might and diplomacy in whatever sense had only a limited use. In the view of Li Hung-chang, there could be only two types of international relations – those between the suzerain and its protectorate which were never on an equal footing, and those between two mutually belligerent states, which were on an equal footing. There could not be equal states co-existing in amity. Throughout the second half of the nineteenth and the first half of this century the firm belief held by the Chinese was that the relationship could be made equal only by a test of force. Another noteworthy point in Chinese diplomacy after the relegation of *chi-mi* to a secondary position was the revival of an age-old rule: 'No minister of the realm could enter into private contact with foreign envoys' (*jen-ch'en wu wai-chiao*). The revival of this dictum made what Kuo Sung-t'ao called 'human understanding' (*ch'ing*) between Chinese officials and foreigners utterly impossible in China itself and created a difference between the image held by the Chinese officials dealing with foreign affairs at home and that held by Chinese diplomats abroad. The officials at home discussed issues and disputes in stiff and often argumentative interviews with foreigners while the diplomats, in addition to discussing issues and disputes on an official level, met foreigners on social occasions in a more relaxed and amicable atmosphere.

Consequently Robert Hart suggested that a number of Chinese in the T'ung-wen Kuan (the Language Institute founded in 1861) should be selected to accompany him when he went back to England on furlough in 1866, passing through several European countries on the way. A year later when Anson Burlingame retired from his post as American Minister, he was, surprisingly, persuaded to become the Chinese ambassador at large, taking a number of Chinese with him on a world tour. The motive, as Tung Hsün of the Tsungli Yamen pointed out, was to learn 'their situation' and 'our deficiencies'. After the 'Tientsin massacre' of 1870 in which thirteen French people including the Consul, H. V. Fontainier, were killed, the first Chinese high official ever to be sent abroad, Ch'ung-hou, went to France on a mission of apology. Later more high officials, even members of the imperial clan, made trips overseas to broaden their views. At home, the Dowager Empress herself reverted to the old *chi-mi* tactic by inviting all the diplomatic wives to an audience, more precisely a dinner party, plus a command performance of Peking opera, plus tea, plus valuable gifts, on 13 December 1898.

Following the Empress's lead, Li Hung-chang invited some diplomatic ladies to his residence in Peking on 3 June 1899. This modest beginning was to become a fashion after the dust of the Boxer War had settled.

While Ch'ung-hou was on his way to a Paris under German occupation, Tseng Kuo-fan's proposal that thirty boys should be sent to study in the United States of America received imperial approval. This, too, was to become a fashion, especially after 1895. What Tseng and other proponents of this project intended to achieve was to unravel the mysteries of Western learning for the enrichment and strengthening of their own country, a task that the students at the Language Institutes in Peking and other places could not fulfil.

Long before officialdom awoke to the need to send members of the government service and candidates for the examinations abroad, many Chinese of lesser social standing, peasants, workers, and even some defeated rebels of the 1850s and 1860s had already made their appearance in Europe and America in far greater numbers. The earliest to arrive at San Francisco did so in 1849, either lured there by the news of the discovery of gold or driven there by the hardships at home. The migration of Chinese to maritime Siberia probably co-incided with the founding of the city of Vladivostok in the 1860s. The construction of the Southern Pacific, Union Pacific, Canadian Pacific, the Trans-Siberia, and even the railways in British Malaya depended on Chinese labour; so did the opening of the gold mines in Victoria and the Transvaal. Many of these wayfarers were indeed merely sojourners, eager to acquire a pot of gold and when it had been acquired, eager to go home. Through them and the scholar-official and student emissaries the image of the West underwent yet another change.

The Chinese now saw the military might of the West as an object of fear and its material wealth as something to be envied. Foreigners in China purposely tried to make the Chinese afraid of them. Throughout his career in that country, Sir Harry Parkes believed that it would be 'disastrous to show the slightest weakness to the Chinese'. With China's military weakness further exposed by the French War of 1884–5, the Japanese War of 1894–5, and the Boxer War of 1900, both the fear the Chinese felt and their readiness to soothe the foreigners' ill-temper by flattery grew. The Taiping Rebellion drove many Chinese to the foreign settlement in Shanghai for protection in 1860. At the same time, the presence of a single foreigner in a convoy of Chinese junks sailing on inland waters from government-controlled into rebel-controlled areas was sufficient to insure the convoy against harassment by both the official and the rebel side. The Legation Quarter in Peking became a sanctuary for Chinese political leaders and a strongbox for their property whenever there was a crisis. President Li Yuan-hung, General Chang Hsün, Prime Minister Tuan Ch'i-jui, and ex-Emperor P'u-yi, to name only a few, took refuge there at different times. Elsewhere in the country a foreign concession, a church, or even a foreigner's home served the same purpose for the less important Chinese. Sometimes a Chinese business could even escape looting or destruction in a civil war just by hanging out a foreign flag.

Taking cognizance of the unpleasant results of offending foreigners, the Ch'ing imperial government and later the warlords' governments in Peking repeatedly proclaimed that one of its policy goals was to see that foreign interests in China were meticulously protected in spite of internal disturbances. On the eve of the outbreak of civil war in the neighbourhood of Peking, the Prime Minister, Tuan Ch'i-jui, pronounced:

The capital is the most important city of our country where legations are as many as trees in a forest. Merchants and residents of various nationalities live here. The slightest disturbance may offend countries friendly to us with the dire result that the very foundation of our country may be affected.

## Western studies in China

The questions foremost in the Chinese mind were how had the West become as strong as it was and how could China emulate it? China's first intellectual response to the war of 1839–42, Wei Yuan's *Illustrated Gazetteer* of 1844, was written precisely to answer those questions. Conceding no cultural superiority to the West, Wei admitted that the Europeans were quite different from the barbarians known in Chinese history, for Europe had literature and education. The only way he could find of explaining the existence of another civilization was to assert, without producing a shred of evidence, that Jesus had the Confucian classics translated into Latin, which helped him found the Christian religion,* a religion of God in

---

\* This was the beginning of a school of thought which believed in Chinese civilization being the origin of all other civilizations.

C.A.T.W.—C

Heaven, i.e. Catholicism, which was in time embraced by all Europeans. This taught them to love God and their fellow men, hence their philanthropy towards the old, the young, and the less privileged. Their language being simple, they were people of few words, but they had a well-developed judicial system which needed neither torture nor threat to arrive at a fair judgement. Their rules and regulations were so comprehensive that no room was left for unscrupulous 'law clerks' to manoeuvre. Theirs were mercantile countries, unlike physiocratic China, and thus had such institutions as banks and insurance companies to facilitate commerce. Their mercantile system was so complex that only people of complex minds could have evolved it. To connect the mercantilism and martial skill of the Europeans, Wei advanced the view that for the protection of their overseas trade, they perfected ship-building and maritime warfare.

In the strict sense the title of Wei's widely influential work was misleading, as it went far beyond the scope of a mere gazetteer. Four years later Hsü Chi-yü published his *Ying-huan chih-lüeh* (A Brief Account of the Oceans around Us, preface dated 1848) after the style of some American geographic works which had come to his knowledge. It was straightforward geography. Hsü corrected an earlier piece of misinformation, that the Dutch were all red-haired. As a matter of fact, most Europeans had brown hair. He went on to give, none the less, his own contribution to the fund of misinformation – 'When he has lived in China for some time, a European's hair is likely to turn black.' Like Wei Yuan, Hsü described the European nations as being founded on commerce; their government finance depended on tariffs rather than on land taxes as was the case in China. Unlike Wei, Hsü knew of the Reformation and the work of Martin Luther, the religious wars, and the schism between the Catholics and the Protestants. Perhaps because of his personal contacts with Americans, he observed that the Westerners were exceedingly clean, since they bathed every day.

These two pioneer scholars in what might be called the field of Western studies in China set the pattern for the books to be published in the next few decades. Most of these books were written by Chinese envoys, who were required to keep a diary while abroad. They contained a mixture of analysis of Western institutions, whose purpose was to learn the secret of Western strength, and of observation of Western life-styles and social customs, intended to help Chinese to live and work in peace with Westerners.

Writing to Li Hung-chang from London in 1877, Kuo Sung-t'ao remarked:

The [Western] governments and people co-operate in their common effort to protect and enhance their common interests. The wealth created by the people is used to support the country and there lie the roots of their countries' wealth and power.

Needless to say, Kuo's eulogy of the co-operation between Western people and their governments implied a criticism of the lack of it between the Chinese and their bureaucracy. His thesis of co-operation was echoed in the best travelogue so far written by a Chinese diplomat, Hung Hsün's *Yu-li wen-chien tsung-lüeh* (Summing up my Travels, 1884). Hung maintained that in all the European countries the interests of government and people were complementary. Births, deaths, and marriages, emigration, and naturalization were all registered so that the government knew the condition of the people. The complementary nature of their interests explained, in Hung's view, why taxes were gladly paid and bonds gladly bought by the people so long as the government managed its finances according to an approved budget. Like his forerunners, Hung observed that commerce was the foundation of these countries' economies, for there was a shortage of raw materials needed by their manufacturing industries. Mercantilism with profit as its driving force could lead to a situation of too much idle capital, declining rates of profit and trade depression. These defects apart, the European system allowed no room for cornering of goods, thanks largely to the matchless ease of transport. If the European economic system did not impress Hung to the same extent as it had Kuo Sung-t'ao and Marquis Tseng before him, he was full of admiration for European education, especially the compulsory education of every boy of school age, for the wide spectrum of employment opportunities for the educated in addition to the civil service, and the courses for refinement and practical use offered to students. The scope of knowledge was wide; the logic was rigorous; the judgement was well considered.

As to the legal systems of Europe, Hung saw them as intended to instil a sense of shame into the minds of people rather than to protect the rights and liberties of the citizens. However, he was aware of the tradition of Roman law and the importance of human life enshrined in it. Therefore the legal officials must have a thorough grasp of the law itself. A conviction was a public humiliation, and this shame was a heavy enough penalty in itself which rendered more brutal punishment unnecessary, although fines, imprisonment and the death sentence were the three usual forms of penalty meted out. The prisons, clean and well organized, sometimes compared favourably with a poor man's home.

What law and administration could not do for the people was left to religion. Here Hung had an inkling of the contribution of Christianity to the freedom enjoyed by the Europeans. A little amazed, he found men and women worshipped together in the same church. He had scarcely any more to say on either the doctrines or the work of the Church. But regarding more tangible achievements, he spoke enviously of the roads, hospitals, libraries, theatres, waterways, and harbours, but he thought that in agriculture Europe had nothing to teach China. After all, it was an activity that the Europeans themselves avoided if they could.

Writing as the Chinese Minister in London in 1890–2, Hsüeh Fu-ch'eng had even less understanding of Christianity than Hung Hsün.* He made fun of its absurd supersitions, regarding the entire corpus of its doctrine as more contemptible than some lowbrow Chinese novels. He foresaw its inevitable decline when Confucianism should become known in the West through ever increasing intercourse with the East. Disagreeing with Wei Yuan, Hsüeh thought Jesus derived his doctrine from the philosophy of Mo-tzu (*c.* 478–392 BC), a view put forward, also quite seriously, by a mid-nineteenth century chronicler, Wang K'ai-yün, who could not resist the temptation of identifying Mo-tzu with Moses on the grounds of the phonetic similarity of the two names. Since Mo-tzu's philosophy contained some elements of proto-science, Jesus, having acted as a catalyst, had given European science a good start. The strength of the West therefore lay in its ability to develop ancient Chinese scholarship whereas the weakness of China originated from neglecting her own traditions. The contrast between East and West was thus explained by Hsüeh in terms of the lack of educational facilities in the former and their ready availability in the latter.

By the end of the nineteenth century China had acquired some knowledge of Western science and industry, less of Western law and

---

* Because of his position and successful career, Hsüeh enjoyed during his lifetime and after his death an exaggeratedly high reputation as a modernizer. But his understanding of the West, compared with that shown by Hung Hsün in his account published several years earlier, was, to say the least, shallow and confused.

institutions, and almost none of Western philosophy, art and literature. Summing up the state of Western studies in China, Liang Ch'i-ch'ao compiled and published his *Catalogue of Books on the West* (*Hsi-hsüeh shu-mu piao*) in 1896, a year after China's defeat by Japan and a year after the first publication in a limited edition of Yen Fu's translation of Thomas Huxley's *Essays on Evolution and Ethics*. The defeat made the Chinese mind more receptive to new ideas and theories and Yen's exquisite style made social Darwinism more appealing. The impact of both the defeat and of the theory of evolution was shattering. China suddenly found that she was only one of many states in the world, and to make things even worse, she was not even 'fit to survive' in the Darwinian sense. The most perplexing task now facing the Chinese mind was to interpret the new situation in Confucian terms; if this could not be done, the Darwinian wind would blow Confucius clean out of the window. The Confucian concept of *jen* (humanism-cum-humanitarianism) could now be extended to the whole of humanity – 'within the four seas, all men are brothers'. This was obviously a rearguard action on the part of Confucianism.

Yen's translation of Huxley was most influential, and created a belief in Anglo-Saxon superiority in the minds of such intellectual leaders as Liang Ch'i-ch'ao, Sun Yat-sen, and of course Yen himself. To illustrate what Huxley said, a far inferior work, though no less influential than that of Huxley in China, Robert Mackenzie's *Nineteenth Century – A History*, was translated by a Welsh Baptist, Timothy Richard, and his Chinese assistants and published in 1898. With official help it was sold out in a fortnight and several editions of it had to be issued, reaching the incredible number of nearly one million copies. In the years of rapid political change these were great eye openers. Thereafter Chinese officials, for instance the Minister at St Petersburg, Yang Ju, could comment on the secret of the West's strength in 1901 more penetratingly than, for example, Hsüeh Fu-ch'eng had done ten years before:

Let us observe their [the foreigners'] domestic rule and study their history. Then we know that their methods of governance, selection of officials, and employment of the people are derived from their comparative studies of the systems of scores of countries. These methods are the results of the accumulated experience of thousands of years and have been tested in generations of crises and changes. It is only by concentrating their spirit and wisdom that the foreigners can enjoy their achievements today.

The adulation of the West reached its zenith and became more sophisticated in the decade before the outbreak of the First World War. Now the courage and determination of the Westerner in the pursuit of his ideals and in invention of all kinds, from *Utopia* and *New Atlantis* to aeroplanes and submarines was acclaimed by a young man studying under John Dewey at Columbia in 1915. Two years later Hu Shih was to return to a China of social disorder, moral decay, and civil wars, but also of bubbling intellectual ferment – the classic situation on the eve of a revolution. As professor of philosophy at the famous National Peking University, Hu Shih was to write in 1918:

We are not yet qualified to criticize other people's [the Westerners'] shortcomings. We should do well to notice only their strength. . . . When I spoke on Chinese civilization when I was in the United States, I discussed only its good points; when I speak on American civilization now, likewise I stress only its good points.

This uncritical attitude was not widely shared by his contemporaries, particularly after the Paris Peace Conference had decided to hand the former German possessions in Shantung to Japan instead of returning them to China. Overnight, Wilson's Fourteen Points, the principle of self-determination, and other high-sounding ideals of the West became as worthless as a returned cheque in the eyes of a number of Chinese intellectuals, whose interest gradually shifted to Moscow and communism. The image of the West therefore underwent another radical change.

The life-style and social customs of the West at once fascinated and disgusted Chinese observers. Pin-ch'un, who accompanied Robert Hart to Europe, was dazzled by the luxury of the French liner he travelled on – the beautiful crockery and cutlery and the delicious food, the lavish use of lighting, and the presence of mirrors everywhere 'made my head spin'. That was in 1866. Exceedingly clean, the Westerner spat only into a spittoon and flushed the water closet each time he used it. At dinner, ladies took their seats before men; no one overate; and everyone talked right through the meal.* Soup was never sucked in audibly; nor was food chewed noisily. Everyone treasured his privacy to such an extent that his door was always closed and no one could enter without knocking on it and obtaining his permission first.

* Confucius said in his *Analects* that one should not speak while eating.

What puzzled the Chinese most were Western human relations. A throne could be inherited by a woman; parents lived apart from their married children; they left wills to their children concerning the disposal of their property after their deaths; and among the five cardinal relations (sovereign subjects, father–sons, husband–wives, elder and younger brothers, and friends), the husband–wife relation, instead of that between father and sons, took precedence over all the others. By 1877 the Chinese began to realize that inequality between the sexes in the West was of a different sort from what they had understood before. It was the man who held important positions and dealt with important matters. Even a manservant earned more money than a maid. But at home and on social occasions, Western women played a more dominant role. To a Chinese, this was a topsy-turvy situation in which most men appeared to be henpecked and most women domineering. Women often abused the freedom they had by indulging in extravagance so as to make themselves physically more attractive to men. Their over-sized busts and under-sized waists, their azure eyes and auburn hair did not seem to the Chinese observer in the nineteenth century to be adequate compensation for their over-abundance of hair, such as moustaches, and their vixenish body odour. Stranger still to the Chinese eye was the frequent use of the naked female body as the subject of painting. But a good thing to come out of this practice was the excellence of Western erotic art, which tended to confirm the Chinese impression that Western sex life was 'murky'. The small countries of Europe had a kaleidoscopic variety of styles of life and social customs at wide variance from the Confucian values and norms. 'How can they be made uniform?' asked one Chinese traveller in 1877. 'The only way is for China to unify the whole world.'

Among the Western countries the British Empire of course stood head and shoulders above the rest. A Chinese anglophile, Hsü Chih-mo, wrote in 1924:

Too stupid and rigid are the Germans; too incontinent are the French who know no inhibitions in whatever they do and never fail to go to extremes; too chaotic are the Southern Europeans whose heads are never sober as long as the grapes grow abundantly on each side of the Rhine; too parochial are the Americans whose majority rule based on majority ignorance at best leads only to a sentimental democracy. The rest are not worth considering. Only the British are passable. As is generally known, the British are the only modern political race; their body politic is like a termitary gnawed to its very centre [by the political animals within]. Politics is more than just interwoven as closely as possible with their daily life; their daily life *is* their politics. Like [fish] forgetting each other in rivers and lakes,* the British forget each other in politics. They are free but never radical; they are conservative but never obscurantist.

Such sentiments require a degree of understanding of the British.

Perhaps the first Chinese anglophile was Wu T'ing-fang who was educated in Hong Kong and at Lincoln's Inn, called to the bar, and served as a distinguished Chinese diplomat. He was 'a perfect English scholar', in the words of the American Minister to China, Charles Denby. Wu's praise of the British Empire was embarrassingly fulsome.

Under the influence of a spate of English books translated into Chinese, including those by Adam Smith, John Stuart Mill, Thomas Huxley and Herbert Spencer, the image of the empire upon which the sun never set certainly evoked envy. Even as late as the early years of this century, hardly a Chinese knew that the industrial preponderance of Britain was threatened by Germany and the USA which were also overtaking her in scientific invention. Therefore in 1902 Prince Tsai-chen, who was in Europe chiefly to apologize to the Kaiser for the murder of Baron von Kettler at the beginning of the Boxer War, was still able to pose the question: how is it that British trade dominates the whole world? In his view the answer lay in British perseverance and the policy of *laissez-faire*. This perseverance was interpreted as the fruit of a calm, disciplined, and orderly approach to problems. In 1903 a Chinese magazine published an (illustrated) article on the funeral (five years before) of Gladstone, the serene solemnity of which was in sharp contrast to the pandemonium of the Chinese mourning rituals. In sport as well as in more serious matters, like parliamentary debates, the British did things by rules and regulations. But, as Liang Ch'i-ch'ao reflected in Britain in 1919:

We Chinese have our rules and regulations, too, when we play *mahjong*. However, the loser often kicks over the table. Our republican politics has for years been a game that usually ends in the losers kicking over the table.

In contrast to this, the procedure of the House of Commons struck Liang with a feeling akin to awe:

* An allusion from *Chuang-tzu*.

I listened to a debate for more than two hours and my admiration for [Parliament] is beyond description. The two sides discussed matters of the state as frankly and forthrightly as [our Chinese] ladies talk about their everyday affairs round a table. They yielded not an iota of their views and yet sincerely respected the opinions of the opposition. Without this attitude, any republicanism, any constitutional rule would be like building a road to the north but driving the carriage to the south.

Both cause and effect of the rule of law, British orderliness depended also on a gradual approach to problems, on people's refraining from rash action. This was the essence of British conservatism; this fact first dawned upon Liang when he was in Westminster Abbey, an architectural wonder which he saw consisted of many parts added on to it at different times.

In politics and law, in religion and morality, in customs and etiquette, [one sees] the same additions bit by bit [that, all together, amount to a total] change. . . . This [British] conservatism we share, but we don't share their tolerance and conciliatory spirit.

In fact, the British and Chinese forms of conservatism were different – the British preserved the old bottle while changing the wine; the Chinese changed the bottle while preserving the old wine.

The casual visitor usually noticed the visible achievements of Britain – the magnificence of her great cathedrals and her high standard of living. But it was those who had the opportunity to live in the country for some time and the sensitivity and education to appreciate the refinement and culture of the British who probed deeper into the psychology and spirit of the people. The green lawns, the weeping willows and the ancient colleges along the Backs at Cambridge gave Hsü Chih-mo, a young man who knew Katherine Mansfield and Middleton Murry, a feeling of absolute solitude. To him, that was the highest pleasure he had ever experienced.

It was Cambridge which opened my eyes, gave me my craving for knowledge, and awakened the consciousness of my own existence. . . . It was Cambridge which preoccupied me with strolling, punting, cycling, smoking, idle chatting, taking tea with buttered scones at five, and reading for fun.

For Lin Yutang, Oxonians were educated men who excelled in scholarship and moral sentiments as well as in stimulating conversation. 'The British are more attached to their tradition than we to ours. Probably that is why they are great and Oxford is great.

Oxford is in no sense a fashionable place. Its refusal to be fashionable has preserved its personality for five centuries. Irrational to the extreme, it remains the highest seat of learning and the hub of English thought and ideas.'

For Lin and Hsü, all this was what was meant by 'the ethos of the English gentleman', which was less well known to the urban Chinese than its outward manifestations – the quiet voice, the even temper, and the stiff upper lip, with all the paraphernalia of bowler hat, pinstripe trousers and umbrella. These gentlemanly appurtenances were familiar sights to Ch'en Yuan at the London School of Economics in the late 1920s. Ch'en's anglophile sentiments were aroused by de Quincey's art as a translator, the literary judgement of Arnold and the narrative skill of George Moore. For him, there could be no higher achievement in literature.

Humour, British humour, was a household word to any Chinese who had a nodding acquaintance with the country. To Lin Yutang, its most important champion in China, humour was 'a state of mind', 'a way of looking at life'. 'A humorist is often a defeatist and delights in recounting his own failures and embarrassments and the Chinese are often sane, cool-minded defeatists', and therefore capable of being humorous. Instead of condemning them, a humorist takes 'a tolerant view of vice and evil' and laughs at them, for life itself 'is a huge farce'. Unfortunately for Lin, the China of the 1930s was a far cry from Balliol or Magdalen. In such a China, neither the British concept of 'fair play' nor British humour could take root and both were vehemently attacked by the leading left-wing writer Lu Hsün, who, in his last will and testament, told his son 'not to go anywhere near anyone who preaches tolerance'. Moreover, even the right-wing writers repudiated Lin's doctrine, because 'our society needs people who work seriously and hard' while humour, like the opiate of the people, 'is a hindrance to progress'.

What is meaningful for our China in our time is not joking, not the so-called 'humour', but truly brave men who use iron and blood to fight for freedom and truth.

Politically, China realized quite early on that Britain was interested mainly in trade rather than territorial expansion. Not all Chinese visitors to Britain were uncritical of the British administration and economy, although none of them had the temerity to tell the British how to run their own business. It baffled Wang Chih in 1876 that machines were invented by the British to save people from toil, but also to render them idle and unemployed:

[I] can understand that heaven and earth create things of all description for man to use and man produces goods to serve other men. I have never heard of the principle of inventing things to make men redundant. If men can be made redundant; so can their country.

To be sure, neither Wang Chih nor Lin Shu, the translator of *Oliver Twist* and many other European novels in the 1900s and 1910s, had any inkling of socialism. Lin was shocked by the sordid civil administration of Britain as described by Dickens. Between the two world wars, a scholarly traveller, Sheng Ch'eng, paid two visits to England, to find the once great empire living in a dream and leading a shadowy existence with most of its erstwhile colonies already independent. The island country had, he thought, almost no agriculture one could speak of, hence the need to import food and raw materials; its largest market, India, was in turmoil, craving independence and freedom; unemployment and its relief had created a race of loafers. These were also the observations of a Christian educationist, Chang Po-ling. In the gloom of the Depression, Tsou T'ao-fen saw the same problems and analysed them in Marxist terms. But contrary to Marx's prophecy, Tsou did not believe Parliament could be the vehicle for Britain's transformation into a socialist country. He supported his view by pointing out that even the piecemeal social reforms attempted by the Labour Party had encountered so many obstacles and so many difficulties.

The United States of America was believed to be the only country which was strong enough to resist Britain, as it had won its war of independence. It differed from Western Europe in many ways – a vast country which liked to think it was without imperialist ambitions, conceived in and dedicated to liberty, and therefore free from class and racial discrimination.

Probably because of the Americans' lack of rigid class distinctions and their easy approachability, the doors of their homes were more often opened to the Chinese visitor than in Europe. The harmony between husband and wife in an average American home contrasted noticeably with the constant bickering in an extended Chinese family. In town and country a middle-class family enjoyed ample space and all the amenities American wealth and industry could provide. In the words of Lin Yutang, the New World was a world for women and children who were happier there than anywhere else in the world.

At the Philadelphia Exposition of 1875 a Chinese visitor was not at all sure whether the corseted waist of an American woman was more comfortable than a pair of Chinese bound feet. This criticism was soon dissipated; the Chinese Minister in Washington was pleased by and reported on the politeness and good looks of the sales girls behind shop counters. After the First World War, as China's own image of the ideal woman changed through more contact with the West, the American woman appeared to the Chinese as:

the most modern, the most lovely and admirable. They are intelligent and vivacious, often using their charm to subjugate their husbands, with wonderful results. Every one of them knows how to dance and understands music. The happiness enjoyed between husband and wife when they are in each other's company can be imagined. Our Chinese women cannot in any sense be compared with them.

Generally, American girls began to work from the age of sixteen and married at twenty-two. They had ample opportunities for employment and for taking part in politics. Even if they did not seek gainful employment, they worked hard at home. This, however, was not to say that the sexes in the United States were equal. Women's wages were between a quarter and a half lower than those of men in similar jobs. For a Marxist like Tsou T'ao-fen this was a capitalist device to exploit cheap female labour while keeping down the wages of men. In 1931 some women earned only $3–$7 a week, but the basic cost of living for a single woman was at least $17.20. Among the unemployed, more than one-fifth were women, some of whom had to turn to streetwalking for a living.

Quite unlike Chinese babies who were constantly carried by their parents or nannies, American babies were often left to play by themselves and slept alone in their own cots. When they grew older they were trained to be independent by doing such work as delivering newspapers. Their socialization was always democratic, never through parental coercion. As a result, an understanding developed between the generations, forming the basis of their mutual affection. The school developed their intellect, moral sense, and especially their physical health by such activities as cycling, baseball, swimming, etc. The Chinese Minister in Washington, Chang Yin-huan, questioned a thirteen-year-old boy about China and was amazed by the boy's knowledge, which made the diplomat apprehensive of the coming generations of Americans. Traditionally minded as he was, Chang did not approve of the 'simple' way American children were brought up. He wondered how the bond of love between the generations could be strengthened when a child was fed on cows' milk, slept apart from its parents, and learnt to walk under the tender age of one.*

In spite of the large number of Chinese students in the United States, not one wrote about the intellectual and character development on campus in such a readable and attractive way as Hsü Chih-mo portrayed Cambridge and Lin Yutang Oxford. The snippets they did write read like gossip columns or a guide book. The widely uneven qualities of American universities and something of the students' activities were naturally known to the Chinese, especially those who aspired to study there. It was again left to Tsou T'ao-fen to give a Marxist, therefore extremely critical view of American education. According to him (he was obviously drawing on information given by his American left-wing friends), in 1933, 1253 schools in nine states were closed down, sixteen universities and 1500 colleges suspended their work, 119 000 children had no school to go to, and nearly 250 000 teachers were unemployed. A working-class child rarely went beyond the sixth grade; thus the public schools were left for the benefit of middle-class children. As far as Tsou could see, American education was in a blind alley.

In the 1840s, Chinese scholars knew scarcely more than the great landmarks of American history – the discovery of the new continent by Columbus, the Boston Tea Party and the War of Independence. What won Wei Yuan's special admiration was the fact that presidential elections took place every four years. In his understanding, this was a system which made sure of having the most virtuous man at the helm of power without going through the agony of a violent struggle. Influenced by Elijah Bridgman, Hsü Chi-yü saw Washington in 1843 as the personification of the long-cherished Chinese political ideal of 'voluntary abdication'. This early, rudimentary impression was to be confirmed by Wu T'ing-fang – the country, the

---

* It may be of some interest to note that Chinese visitors to America learned something of American home life by first-hand observation, while it was left to an American missionary, Young, J. Allen to introduce English home life to Chinese readers in his *Nu-su t'ung-k'ao* (A General Description of the Life of [an English] Woman, Shanghai, 1903).

states, the cities, towns, and villages were orderly and unostentatiously governed, the people being trained in the practice of democracy. To contrast this image with China, another Chinese diplomat wrote in this preface to Liang Ch'i-ch'ao's *Travels on the New Continent*:

We have failed to govern our country . . . our villages . . . even our own homes. What we walk on is not a road; what we live in is not a house; what we sleep on is not a bed. It is not that we [scholars refuse to follow the ancient warning against being] ashamed of simple clothes and simple food; it is that our standard of civilization falls a long way below theirs [the Americans']. When I compare our nation with theirs, I can only sigh and weep.

Under a good government and blessed with a good social order, the Americans lived in happiness and pursued their enterprises with success. Therefore they could concern themselves with the welfare of the whole society in a humanitarian and philanthropic manner. Even their prisons, already a hundred times better than Chinese prisons, were constantly being improved, as Hu Shih remarked in his student diary. Having established himself as a distinguished scholar and served as China's wartime ambassador to America, Hu looked back at the United States he had known well for half a century. Since the introduction of income tax in 1913, the United States had eliminated class distinction and become a classless society:

In fifty years, social sanction and political sanction, strengthened by social legislation, have created in America a system of liberty and democracy. With its large-scale industrial production, its free and egalitarian economic system has raised the American people's standard of living. There exists no disparity between rich and poor; there is only a uniform level of enjoyment. America has reaped the result of revolution without even having to go through a revolution.

The American achievements were so many and so wonderful that they overwhelmed and over-awed most Chinese visitors and residents and made them 'americophiles'. The educationist Chang Po-ling attributed the wealth and scientific progress of the United States to its leaders' tireless service to the masses. They were more concerned with work than money; they were old and experienced but also able and healthy. This was something China could never successfully copy. Lin Yutang's understatement was more subtle. He did not regard the United States 'as a den of vice, nor a paradise of mechanized civilization. It is merely a livable place and the future of its civilization may promise a greater measure of welfare to its people.' The conference of the refugee intellectuals from Nazi Germany held in New York City early in the summer of 1937 was itself proof enough to Lin that liberty was far from dead in the United States of America.

America was, and still is, a multi-racial nation and therefore the existence of racial discrimination there after the Civil War was a matter of interest to the Chinese visitor. As the Chinese themselves were at the receiving end of American racial prejudice, only a very few of them such as the starry-eyed 'americophile' Tzu-wei and the extraordinarily diplomatic Wu T'ing-fang could bring themselves to deny or ignore this problem. In a predominantly white nation, the Chinese' own feeling of present inferiority and their pride in China's past glory made them reluctant to identify with the black minority.

Chang Yin-huan, for example, noticed that blacks generally took on menial jobs, but he unreservedly placed the blame for their lowly social status on the laziness of the blacks themselves. The one-time Chinese Minister for Foreign Affairs, Ch'en Yu-jen (Eugene Chen), decided against bringing his wife, a Trinidadian lady, to China because he knew that even among his revolutionary colleagues there existed a racial prejudice. Old Chinese residents in America were known to be die-hard anti-blacks. They were known to turn blacks away from their restaurants, and in the deep south the greatest shame for a Chinese was to marry a black woman, because their children could only enter schools reserved for black children. The Chinese–black animosity persisted throughout the Second World War till very recent times. For instance, Madame Chiang refused to be interviewed by a black journalist when she visited the United States in 1942. In spite of their own poor command of English, some Chinese criticized the Negroes for their loquacity, strange accent and weak grammar. Even highly educated Chinese were not free from contempt for black Americans. The brilliant Liang Ch'i-ch'ao, under the influence of Darwinism, was outraged by the Americans' excluding Chinese while allowing blacks to stay. He made the following revealing remark in 1903: 'True, the type of Chinese [excluded from the United States] are lowly and undisciplined. Are they not better than the blacks?' He had heard stories of the lynching of Negroes in the south and was puzzled that such things could happen in a civilized society. But he went on:

The black people's behaviour is despicable. They die without regret only if they have a chance to touch a white woman. Therefore they wait in the darkness of the woods to pounce on white women who are invariably murdered afterwards so that the women will not talk. Nine out of ten cases of lynching are caused by this crime.

Liang's remarks, based on hearsay, were reproduced verbatim in Hsü Cheng-k'eng's *Liu Mei ts'ai-feng-lu* (American Observations, 1926). A critic of America, Hsü ascribed the squalid practice of lynching to the pseudo-emancipation of the blacks and the existence of strong racial discrimination. Tsou T'ao-fen, however, did travel to the south to see for himself the racial segregation in Birmingham and Selma, Alabama. He had enough sense and background knowledge to compare the political rights enjoyed by the whites with those of the blacks; he set the use and abuse of black women by the whites against the image of the 'black rapist'; he also referred to the Grandfather Act, the Jim Crow laws, and the poor education given to black children. He believed that racial prejudice was worse in the United States than in Britain.

Convinced of Anglo-Saxon superiority, Liang Ch'i-ch'ao was apprehensive of the admission of 'inferior' Europeans into the United States. Since 'the *yuan-ch'i* (the real strength) of America comes from Teutonic people, the immigration of large numbers of southern Europeans, mostly ignorant peasants and lawless riff-raff, would eventually mean that the Teutonic Americans would be outnumbered. I am worried over the future of that country.' Indignant at the exclusion of the Chinese, disdainful of the blacks and apprehensive of the southern Europeans, Liang – the patriotic Chinese – conceded superiority only to the Anglo-Saxons. But there were also the Jews in America. According to Liang, they were the most united, hence the most powerful in banking and other business enterprises. They were avaricious and uncultured, and as dirty as the Chinese. In spite of the loss of their ancestral land, making them 'stateless' to Liang's mind, Jewish financial genius commanded his respect.

Chinese critics of the United States also pointed out that all sorts of vices plagued American urban life and that all sorts of corruption permeated American political parties and the administration. Political and administrative corruption in the United States was reported in the Shanghai *Shen-pao* as early as 30 March 1875, with the comment that the much-admired America was just as bad as China in this respect. The failure of Prohibition proved the corruptibility of both the legislature and the judiciary in that country. Its roots penetrated deeply into American democracy; as Liang Ch'i-ch'ao put it in a speech in 1906:

In [American] elections those who are eloquent can flatter the public and be returned to office while those who are learned and righteous often receive no attention. Hence many stupid and ignorant men sit in the Assemblies. [American electoral] history is indeed a farce.

Because the United States government was in the hands of the capitalists, the renowned wealth of the country did not prevent 1 200 000 people from being unemployed at the lowest point of the Depression. Since the ordinary people were indifferent to politics, democracy was a mere empty word. So observed Li Kung-p'u, a student then and a prominent left-wing intellectual leader in the 1940s. The equally renowned mechanized civilization of America was not for the welfare of the people but for the profit of the capitalist. That was why in the midst of all the wealth of New York City the slums were a veritable hell on earth, where unemployed blacks lived in dilapidated houses, without bathrooms, but at higher than normal rents. The dirt and stench and the frequent brawls among the inhabitants shocked Tsou T'ao-fen, who was perplexed by the fact that Harlem was listed as a point of interest in the *Complete Guide to New York*. The New Deal had solved neither industrial nor agricultural problems; the labour movement, controlled by such 'proletarian aristocrats' as Sam Gompers and Bill Green, was a lap dog of the bourgeoisie. Even more absurd was the destruction of thousands of gallons of milk and tons of Californian fruit while children and migrant workers went hungry. To soothe the discontent of the underprivileged there emerged the strange phenomenon of the popular radio priest, Charles E. Coughlin. In such circumstances what difference was there between the apparently sublime and the ridiculous? What difference could there be between Al Capone and William Randolph Hearst? In Tsou T'ao-fen's eyes the United States was already a country in decline. It was not a country for colonies and semi-colonies to emulate.

However, from the point of view of China's international relations, the image of the United States had always been consistently better than that of the major powers of Europe, including Russia. 'A country of good faith', Emperor Hsien-feng called it in his edict to the Grand Council on 16 June 1853; it was 'never troublesome or petulant', according to the Viceroy at Nanking, I-liang, in a memorial of 20 July 1853; it was 'quiet and peaceable', according to Prince Kung in his report to the throne on 21 November 1867. Wu Ting-fang summed up some sixty years of Sino–American relations as peaceful, friendly and generous, and interpreted John Hay's principles – the Open Door and Equal Economic Opportunity – as almost altruistic. The greatness of the United States sprang not only from its system of freedom and equality, but, according to Wu, from the characteristics of its people – their earnestness and perseverance, dauntless courage, remarkable genius for organization and punctuality.

To illustrate the characteristics of the Americans, Lu Yüeh-chang cited Roy Sloane's successful gaol break in 1930:

I bow to his perseverance in seeking a way to freedom. He persisted with his plan after several failed attempts till he finally achieved success. This is the characteristic of Western man of which we must beware. It is this characteristic that carries him in whatever he does to his final goal of which he never stops short.

Travelling from China to Europe by French liner, one's first European port of call was Marseilles, which city impressed Pin-ch'un, accompanying Robert Hart in 1866, Wang T'ao, on his way to Scotland to assist James Legge in his great enterprise of translating the Confucian classics in 1867, and Marquis Tseng who was the Chinese Minister in both Paris and London in 1877. The multistorey buildings, gas street lamps, the streets humming with omnibuses and cabs, and machines of all descriptions, for instance, elevators, dazzled the inexperienced eyes of both the diplomats and the scholar. Then Paris! The Palais Bourbon, the Louvre, and the Opéra, with all their magnificence and splendour, were beyond imagination. Pin-ch'un was taken to see an opera. What the opera was he did not bother to remember, but the brilliance of the costumes, the beauty of the actresses (some of them half-naked!), and the grandeur of the sets tested his command of the Chinese classical language to the limit. Wang T'ao thought the Bibliothèque Nationale was the best library in the whole world. They both enjoyed the circus and perhaps were themselves a source of amusement to performers and audience. Wang was full of praise for Parisian cuisine, but none of those early visitors in the periods of the Second Empire and Third Republic noticed the existence of the ancient cathedrals and churches.

At one extreme, the self-righteous modern defender of the Confucian faith, K'ang Yu-wei, disliked everything in Paris in 1904 – 'The palaces lack splendour; the streets are not particularly beautiful; the river is polluted. It may be less damp and gloomy than London . . . , but it is inferior to the clean and spacious city of Berlin. It has nothing like the majesty of New York.' At the other extreme, Hsü Chih-mo was completely captivated by the Paris of 1925 – 'having been to Paris, one loses one's wish to go to heaven; having tasted [the life of] Paris, one is sure to lose one's appetite for hell. It is superfluous to applaud Paris just as it is to applaud heaven; it is superfluous to condemn Paris just as it is to condemn hell.' K'ang's sincere disgust and Hsü's needless condemnation referred to the same thing – the easy availability of women. K'ang was horrified to learn that there were 150 000 licensed whores and many more un-licensed ones in the city, some of whom were even from good families. The Westernized Hsü merely asked his envious Chinese readers: 'Sir, have you ever seen a blindingly beautiful naked body?' He obviously had, in the bohemian-style studio of a Chinese friend of his on the Left Bank.

Moral and amoral views on sex in Paris continued to be expressed into the years of the Depression. Tsou T'ao-fen disapproved of it from his Marxist stance. All the passionate kissing in public, extra-marital affairs and the general deluge of sensuality were due to in-equality between the sexes. Since French women were either under-paid in whatever jobs they did or without an independent income at all, they depended on their men friends to take them out for enter-tainment and fun. In such a situation, no ideas of propriety could be maintained and so they behaved like trollops. Tsou took a friend of his to a 'glass house' (brothel), where they found themselves sur-rounded by a circle of naked harlots who 'had only francs on their minds'. He and his friend stayed for five minutes and left without even having a drink. Hsü Yü, the novelist, took a 'sophisticated' view – 'Sex in the West is as common as seeing a movie.' Then why should one try to make a mystery of sexual love at *the* place for pleasure? It would, however, be unfair to say that Chinese visitors to France lost sight of the majority of French women who worked hard at home, in an office, or in the fields. Rather conservative in their outlook, French women did not have the vote and did not fight for it, although they enjoyed the other rights of citizens. All of them had some education which was so disciplinarian in tone as to be incongruous against the background of general moral laxity.

French education and culture had been admired by the Chinese since the 1840s. As time went on, her art, literature, and philosophy were to win great esteem among Chinese scholars. Of her seats of learning, the Sorbonne naturally commanded high respect among Chinese students.

The best-known event in French history was of course the Revolution of 1789. But when Wei Yuan came to describe it in his *Gazetteer* of 1844 there was no word for 'revolution' in the Chinese language.* Wei attributed the Revolution to the pugnacity of the French people, particularly that of Louis XVI whose costly intervention in the American War of Independence had depleted the financial resources of the government. The King's attempt to levy more taxes alienated all the three estates which abandoned the monarch, committed regicide and created chaos. Hsü Chi-yü in his book of 1848 added the King's lust and Marie Antoinette's influence on the administration to the other aspects of the misgovernment which brought about the downfall of the Bourbon dynasty. This perfectly Chinese interpretation established itself as a tradition, which was accepted even by such an enlightened scholar as Wang T'ao when he wrote his *Fa-kuo Chih-lüeh* (General History of France) in the 1880s. The book, published in 1890, showed the whole process as nothing but a dynastic change which resulted from the appalling abuse of monarchical power and equally appalling mob violence. None the less, Wang lauded the elected National Assembly as a political system close to the Confucian ideal of saintly rule. The Revolution continued to be censured by Chinese constitutional monarchists like Liang Ch'i-ch'ao, who visited France in 1903 and lamented Robespierre's dream of a 'republic of virtue' that turned out to be a reign of terror. Liang's mentor K'ang Yu-wei castigated the Revolution in these words:

Before it, France had already begun to destroy the Church and slaughter the priests. People had neither a doctrine nor a code of propriety to tame their hearts. Without discipline, they turned into beasts, committing violence in the name of liberty. There was left neither a king nor a teacher, neither religion nor education, neither rite nor righteousness.

In the anarchy after the Revolution, unscrupulous and homicidal men like Robespierre and Marat rose to seize power. It was, according to

* '*Ke-ming*', an old Chinese term, had to be taken back from Japanese.

K'ang, heaven's mercy alone that saved France from disappearing from the face of the earth.

The Chinese republican revolutionaries drew inspiration from both the American and French Revolutions. Their early adulation of Washington and Napoleon and acceptance of revolution as the only feasible way to social and political change in China developed into a more penetrating understanding, embodied in Ch'en Tu-hsiu's 'On literary revolution' in 1917:

How did Europe achieve its magnificence and splendour? Through its revolutions. In Europe, 'revolution' means the elimination of the old and the introduction of the new. It bears no similarity to our dynastic changes. Since the Renaissance, Europe has witnessed political, religious, moral, literary, and artistic revolutions which have brought revival and progress to the continent. Its modern history is a history of revolutions.

The vicissitudes of France after the Revolution were seen by Wang T'ao as a result of weak leadership, far inferior to the acumen of Bismarck and Moltke, which eventually led to the defeat of Napoleon III in 1870. China, to be sure, knew of France's defeat, as Ch'ung-hou's mission found Paris under German occupation; she also knew that France paid the indemnity of 1870 six months before the time limit. But K'ang Yu-wei, following up his disapproval of the Revolution, reproached the French for their indulgence in metaphysical discourse with little pragmatic foundation, hedonistic pursuits and parochial self-satisfaction. K'ang's biased views did not explain away the fact that France was a great European power and colonial empire, a country of modern industries and modern defence forces. The revolutionary tradition of liberty, equality and fraternity had become ingrained in the nature of the French people who were a race with a rich emotional life and refined aesthetic sense. Ts'ai Yuan-p'ei, the Chancellor of National Peking University, in 1915 expressed his belief, based on these observations, that the French had the calm of mind to deal with any exigency and overcome any adversity. After the war, Liang Ch'i-ch'ao paid his second visit to France, and concluded that the foundation of French national strength lay not in the central government but in the chief towns of the départements. French patriotism was an extension of the citizens' concern with their own local affairs. Another Chinese observer traced the roots of French strength to her countryside and agriculture which he regarded as the foundation of her body politic.

After the First World War and the Depression unreserved admiration gave way to sympathy for a declining civilization, as Sheng Ch'eng commented in 1936:

Her life is about to end, though not yet ended. Her mission is almost, though not yet completely, finished. The basic ideas [of the nation] have been destroyed; so have the proper relations among men. The shrugging-off of humiliation becomes a daily routine and this is a far worse crisis than the economic crisis.

Germany was a Johnny-come-lately on the Chinese scene, where her first act of political significance was to join Russia and France in the Tripartite Intervention, forcing Japan to disgorge the Liao-tung Peninsula in 1895. Before Germany defeated France in 1870 no Chinese envoy had set foot on German soil. Then Li Hung-chang called on Bismarck in 1896, when the Iron Chancellor advised China to strengthen her defences. Later, after the First World War, when the German people were demoralized and the mark was suffering a rapid inflation, Germany attracted many Chinese students to her universities, for it was cheaper to study there than anywhere else in Europe or America. But the rapidity of Germany's recovery, itself an impressive performance, was ascribed by the Chinese to her people's martial courage, industry and patriotism.

The rigorous discipline of the Germans, wherein, according to Chinese observers, lay the secret of the rise of the Reich and its post-war revival, contrasted with the *nil admirari* and dishonesty of the Italians. The hordes of poor people, thieves and street urchins following visitors spoilt the architectural elegance of Rome and Venice, which in any case the Chinese did not quite understand nor appreciate.

Italy and Germany made their deepest impact on China in the early 1930s when a group of admiring Chinese formed themselves into an organization called the Blue-shirts with Chiang Kai-shek's approval and active support. The situation in China after years of civil wars and in the face of the communist challenge was apparently similar to that of Mussolini's Italy and Hitler's Germany. For the sake of building up national wealth and power as a necessary step towards the restoration of her past glory, a new nation had to be created by the state which would necessarily subjugate individual and group interests, including those of the various social classes, to the interests of the state. The fascist doctrine of class harmony, which implied a denial of any need for class struggle, seemed to fall in with Sun Yat-sen's analysis of China as a nation of two kinds of people only – the poor and the yet poorer. Communism was therefore judged to be totally alien, and totally unsuitable for Chinese conditions. On the other hand, Spengler's spartan recovery programme based on strength of will, national vengeance and a charismatic leader, which was taken over by the Nazi movement, and the concept of the state as basically embracing the whole of life, fitted in well with the ascetic tradition of Confucianism and the Kuomintang watchword of vitalism. Chinese intellectuals, who had been looking for a way that might lead to national glory since 1919, had succeeded only in creating a talking-shop. Unlike the intellectuals, the Blue-shirts appealed to instinct in a manner reminiscent of Joseph Goebbels' dictum: 'When I hear the word "culture", I reach for my gun.'

The Chinese 'führer' was of course Chiang Kai-shek, a man like Hitler and Mussolini in the sense that he had no distinct class, past or family, but was a 'nobody-hero'. Chiang had a strong will, was bent on personal success, and was supported by the military as he proceeded to tackle the problems of a society and nation near collapse. He felt that he had to cut the Gordian knot by making himself the giver of laws, founder of institutions, educator and promoter of spiritual life. These political and social functions used to belong to the emperor and were therefore not entirely strange to Chinese political culture. A spate of books on Nazism and fascism, on Hitler and Mussolini, including *Mein Kampf* (translated and published in 1935), appeared in China. In addition, the Blue-shirts also helped promote the New Life Movement in 1935, founded the Youth Corps of The Three Principles of the People in 1938, and fought a war of counter-espionage against the communists.

But what Tsou T'ao-fen saw in Germany in 1934 was a frightening picture of the ruthless persecution of Jews and liberals by the SS. The illogicality of *Mein Kampf* appalled him. Although he admitted that in a country without a liberal democratic tradition like China, there was a need for a strong leader, 'the leader we need must be one who is willing to sacrifice his own interests for the masses'. By implication, Chiang was not such a leader. When the war against Japan broke out in 1937 and the enemy was drawing closer to Germany and Italy, the Blue-shirt movement came to its official, but not its actual, end.

The rest of Europe, Switzerland, the Low Countries and Scandinavia, attracted the Chinese by their scenic beauty, well-regulated social order, and material wealth. The Dutch, for example, fought against the sea in order to create tiny tracts of land, while China had handed over the whole of Manchuria to Japan. 'What futile people we are!' commented Tsou T'ao-fen. Spain and Portugal, in spite of their early contacts with China, disappointed the Chinese by their laziness and poverty. 'What sort of bravery is it to fight a bull?' Chang Yin-huan wondered in 1889. Ireland fascinated China because of her own struggle for independence, and won her gratitude by de Valera's support for China when the League of Nations discussed the Japanese invasion of Manchuria. The Sinn Fein leader even received Tsou T'ao-fen on 4 December 1933. At the interview Tsou expressed his admiration for the Irish independence movement, while de Valera offered him his opinion that China, big and populous as she was, needed tight organization and a social revolution.

In the century of East–West intercourse before 1937 there had been two choruses – a Western chorus denigrating China and a Chinese chorus lauding the West. The few discordant voices in each seem to have come from singers who were following a different score. In the 1920s and 1930s, only the left-wing liberals of the West, who had enough suppleness of mind to see the serious defects in their own civilization and the merits in the Chinese radical movement, and the Marxists (including Russian communists), were prepared to accept the proposition that there was hope and a future for China. Consequently they could both by instinct and by intellectual conviction treat the Chinese masses as their equals. Only the Chinese radicals, few of whom had a chance of visiting the West, had the analytical tools to uncover the deficiencies of the West and dared to criticize it. These radicals, too, belonged to the post-war era.

On the whole, the century had been a century in which a strong and wealthy West despised China and urged her to imitate Western ways, of a poor and weak China admiring the West which she wanted to imitate, but was unable to do so. At least the knowledge, if not the aims, of the elite on both sides were no longer parochial, so that cultural comparison with an empirical and later even a theoretical frame of reference was more possible. The ground for a deeper mutual understanding was thus laid after the first shocks had been absorbed.

Psychologically, this century produced in the minds of the Chinese a deep inferiority feeling, which had its roots in the undeniable robustness of Western civilization, in Western aggressiveness in both war and peace, and in the ineffectual efforts of the Chinese themselves to meet the challenge. Dr Hu Shih admitted this inferiority at the end of the 1920s:

*We must acknowledge our own mistakes.* We must acknowledge that in a hundred ways we are inferior to others, and that it is not only in the material way and with respect to mechanization that we are not equal to others, but that we are not equal to others politically, socially, or morally either.... We have never once repented our past misdeeds, or thoroughly reproached ourselves, or fully acknowledged our errors. [We must] *give up all hope, and go to study others.* Speaking frankly, we must not be afraid of imitating.

Even towards the end of the Sino–Japanese War (1937–45), Professor Wen I-to developed the same theme, speaking in a much sharper tone:

Compare Chinese and Western styles? What do you have to compare Western styles with? Are you good enough for any comparison? In spite of your mealy mouth and silver tongue, you cannot conceal your smallness, vulgarity, cowardice, and hypocrisy; nor can you hide your greed, stealth, selfishness, and other ugly characteristics. Your filial piety, brotherly love, loyalty, and reliability; your rites and righteousness; your incorruptibility and sense of shame. All the so-called philosophy of your ancient sages makes me sick! I have seen through all of it. You have no soul. You have no knowledge of the Kingdom of Heaven. You are a sheet of sand without any concept of nationhood. You are a horde of impotent people who have no idea what love means (and therefore no idea what hate is). You have neither compassion nor a concept of truth. However, you have a little cunning and tremendous powers of procreation. Because you are cunning, you know how to steal like a rat, how to embezzle money, and how to hoard goods; because you can multiply at a fantastic rate, you and your kind in your great multitudes can all wrap yourselves up in tattered uniforms, get yourselves a number each, and then bleed, starve, sicken and die. That is your style, your morality, your ethics. What else do you have to compare with the West?

Again and again in this chapter I have referred to the European War as the turning point in the history of the East's and West's perception of each other. While the war was still being fought, most Chinese commentators interpreted it as a contest between might and right, with China anxious to join the side of right in the hope that in the post-war peace settlement China could have a voice in matters concerning her own interests. This hope was strengthened by the enunciation of President Wilson's principle of national self-determination. The war shattered Europe's confidence in her own values and skills that had once promised unlimited progress. Now its landscape was littered with the scars of war, while cynicism grew in the place of her old belief systems. The war had been the most disastrous experience for Europe since the Enlightenment that had given Europe this confidence. But now Spengler and Toynbee wrote of the senility of their declining civilizations; Eliot grieved over the Waste Land; Proust chronicled the degeneration of France. Communists and fascists alike condemned, from their own points of view, the general decadence of the West. Of these critics, Spengler became immediately known in China through Liang Ch'i-ch'ao who was in Europe in 1919; while there Liang listened to the uncertain judgements of such learned men as Bergson and Eucken.

The intellectual crisis taking place in Europe fraught with the danger of a social revolution affected the mind of China too, and compounded its confusion. Liberals like Hu Shih, the educationist Chiang Monlin, and even Liang Ch'i-ch'ao, did not entirely lose their faith in democracy and the development of the potentials of the individual. Yen Fu, however, summed up his disappointment in the West: '. . . three hundred years of European progress had only achieved a situation of "profit for oneself and kill others, diminish incorruptibility and banish shame".' The translator of Huxley, Mill, and Smith now turned to Confucius and Mencius, for the difference in the level of civilization between East and West was like that between Heaven and Earth.

The radicalized Sun Yat-sen, though not always consistent, did write:

. . . this war was a conflict of imperialism between states, not a struggle between savagery and civilization or between Might and Right. So the effect of the war was merely the overthrow of one imperialism by another imperialism. What survived was still imperialism.

Both Ch'en Tu-hsiu and Li Ta-chao, the founders of the Chinese Communist Party, castigated the Peace Conference as worthless, as a conference of robbers sharing out their spoils. But Lu Hsün saw the futility of blaming the Europeans for their insensitivity to humanity. 'Humanity is for everyone to fight for, to protect, and to cultivate. It is not something that can be taken for granted.'

In 1923, the twenty-fifth anniversary of the founding of the Peking National University, the faculty and students organized an opinion poll with the aim, among other things, of finding out which foreign personalities were the most admired. Two hundred and twenty-seven people voted for Lenin, only fifty-one for Wilson and six for Lloyd George. China was already engaged in the process of intellectual and political reorientation.

## Chapter 2

# *Missionaries and converts*

### The Catholic Church

Immediately after the French Revolution Christian evangelical work in China entered a dark age. The Catholic revival in France early in the nineteenth century slowly revived the various orders in China. The 1843 Whampoa Treaty with France restored to the Catholics* the right to construct churches and they gained further rights to practise their religion and had their confiscated church property renditioned to them by two imperial edicts, in 1844 and 1846. The work of proselytization was largely revitalized all over China, where it had once flourished early in the eighteenth century. Not satisfied by the limited rights to buy or lease land for constructing churches in the treaty ports, Fr Delamarre abused his position as the official translator of the French delegation at the Tientsin negotiations in 1858 by inserting a few words of his own in the Chinese version of the Treaty which granted the Catholics the right to buy or lease land in the interior of China as well. In 1870 the Church had nearly 400 000 converts in the pastoral care of 250 priests. But the end of the second empire did not end French support for the Catholic missions. The great famine in North China in 1877 saw the Catholics insisting on conversion as a precondition for giving aid to the famine refugees. This quite improper insistence swelled the number of Catholic converts to 558 980 in 1885. On the eve of the First World War the Church claimed no less than 1.5 million baptized Chinese and in 1924 over two million. Throughout the century under discussion the

* By applying the most-favoured-nation clause in the American treaty of the same year, the Protestants, too, acquired the same rights. Strictly speaking, this should not have been so, as the clause referred chiefly to economic interests.

Catholic missions always had four or five times the numerical strength of the Protestant missions in China.

The financial resources of the Roman Catholics, derived mainly from investment in land, could never match the wealth of the Protestants, derived mostly from the voluntary contributions of the wealthiest nations of the world. As a result, priests and nuns enjoyed no furloughs and very few worldly comforts. To be sent to China was virtually banishment for life. As time went on they became depressed, overtaken by their nostalgia for Europe, while their calling still compelled them to discharge their duties with vigour. By an imperial decree issued in March 1899, the Catholic priests acquired yet another extraordinary privilege – official status, which enabled them to communicate and deal with Chinese officials of comparable rank as equals. Even before gaining this advantage, Catholic priests, the worse offenders by far in this respect than their Protestant colleagues, had already begun to interfere with Chinese local administration and jurisdiction. The French Bishop of Kweichow, for example, gave his personal guarantee to the Muslim rebels there that they would be leniently treated if they surrendered to the government. Fortunately the decree of 1899 was rescinded in 1908 and thereafter the priests behaved with greater circumspection.

The slender financial resources provided by the Catholic countries, mainly France, prevented the Church from sending more priests to look after the Chinese flock and to develop their mission work. In Shantung, for instance, the ratio of the missionaries to converts in 1894 was 28 to 25 000 in the north of the province; 14 to 11 000 in the east; and 42 to 42 000 in the south. But in 1890 there were 1296 Protestant missionaries in China ministering to only 37 000 communicants. When foreign priests were recalled to serve as chaplains in the First World War Chinese Catholic clergy grew in strength from 35 per cent of the total priesthood in China in 1918 to 41 per cent in 1926. It was under these circumstances that the Lazarist memorandum on the 'nationalization' (self-government) of the Roman Catholic Church in China in 1919 was approved by Pius XI in his *Rerum Ecclesiae*. These moves eroded the earlier distrust of the abilities of Chinese priests and the fear of their vulnerability *vis-à-vis* the Chinese government because of their lack of extraterritorial privileges. On 28 October 1926 the first six Chinese bishops were consecrated.

In 1872 the Jesuits and Lazarists, with several distinguished scholars among them, founded the Zikawei (Hsuchiahui) Observatory to make meteorological reports and publish a monograph series under the general title of *Variétés Sinologiques*. The diversion of funds from propagation of the doctrines to that of science suggests a shift of emphasis towards demonstrating the power of the white man's science to the Chinese. It was also a reflection of a change in the intellectual climate of Europe itself. The Observatory proved to be one of the lasting memorials of Catholic work in China. Another was the Fu-jen University, founded in Peking in 1925. This small group of learned priests, including Fr Leon Wieger, Teilhard de Chardin, and others, had a great impact on sinology and the study of Chinese meteorology, geology and archaeology. None the less, the chief purpose of the missions remained the salvation of the heathen souls, hence their focus on conversion and on closely related work such as orphanages, hospitals and famine relief rather than on education, social reform and secular cultural activities. Unlike their predecessors in the seventeenth and eighteenth centuries, the nineteenth-century Catholics in China chose to address their message to the less educated classes, hence their general neglect of the intellectual ferment in a rapidly changing China at the end of the nineteenth and the beginning of the twentieth century. The reform and revolution in that period left the Catholics, both foreign and indigenous, out of the main stream of the political and cultural life of the nation.

## The Protestant Church

The early co-operation between Catholics and Protestants, first in Portuguese Macao and then in Canton, ironically broke down after the door of China was forced wide open by the Peking Treaties of 1860. After that each side regarded the other as 'heretical'. However, with their strong political and financial backing, the 130 Protestant denominations, representing thirteen countries with the British and American churches as the major forces in the field, showed a much greater vigour than the Catholics, in every area of their evangelical activities, except in the number of converts.

Why did the missionaries of the Protestant churches choose to go to China? Robert Morrison, a Presbyterian sent by the London Missionary Society in 1807, defined his goal: 'the light of science and revelation will . . . peacefully and gradually shed their lustre on the Eastern limit of Asia and the islands of the rising sun'. Dr Peter

*Strength of Protestant churches in China*

|  | Chinese communicants | Missionaries |
|---|---|---|
| before 1840 | less than 100 | |
| 1853 | 350 | |
| 1858 | | 81 |
| 1864 | | 189 |
| 1874 | | 436 |
| 1876 | 13035 | 473 |
| 1881 | | 618 |
| 1886 | 28506 | |
| 1887 | 32260 | |
| 1888 | 34555 | |
| 1889 | 37287 | 1296 |
| 1890 | 37000 | |
| 1893 | 55093 | |
| 1900 | 95943 | |
| 1905 | | 3445 |
| 1910 | 207747 | 5144 |
| 1914 | | 5462 |
| 1921 | 366524 | 6204 |
| 1922 | | 7663 |
| 1925 | | 8300 |
| 1928 | | 5375 |
| 1929 | | 4744 |
| 1933 | | 5775 |
| 1936 | | 6020 |
| 1937 | 960000 | 5891 |

(From various sources, mainly K. S. Latourette, *A History of Christian Missions in China*, NY, 1929, 1967 edn, pp. 405–6 and 606.)

Parker, another pioneer in the China field and also a Presbyterian, was motivated by the idea of spreading the benefits of science and Christianity to the whole globe.

The Chinese Empire, which had the largest idolatrous population on earth, was obviously the greatest challenge to Christians. Charles Gutzlaff, a Prussian sent to China by the Netherland Missionary Society, was shocked by the use of obscenity by half-naked Chinese sailors in 1831: 'A person who has lived among these men would be best qualified to give a description of Sodom and Gomorrah as well as to appreciate the blessings of Christianity.' The utter blindness of the missionaries to Chinese values and norms, which caused them to regard the Chinese as barbarians and children, and their firm belief in the superiority of Christian morality were balanced by the Chinese bigotry in the Chinese attitude towards the Christians. The difference was that the Chinese did not aggressively dispatch 'missionaries' of their own to Confucianize the West;* Confucianism was there for the barbarians to come and appreciate and learn about, not for its followers to propagate on foreign soil. In comparing China to Sodom and Gomorrah, Gutzlaff did not, mercifully, lower China to the same level as the even 'less civilized' races of the world. His aim was to instil a different, and, in his view, superior set of values into the Chinese mind. Up to 1928 this 'fundamental' approach, as laid down in 1905 by Hudson Taylor, the founder of the China Inland Mission, remained unaltered. The emphasis was still on saving and regenerating lost souls. Like the Catholics, those who followed Hudson Taylor's line allowed the reform and revolution to pass them by, leaving them behind to become antiquated and insignificant.

The focus on conversion and saving souls did not mean that the early missionaries paid no attention whatever to the need for secular reform in the fields of medicine, education and public morality. Rather, they placed their faith in the power of the true religion to change individual Chinese, to draw them away from idolatry and immorality, in order to lay the foundations for China's progress. It would be unfair to accuse the early missionaries of ignoring 'the modes of thought' of the Chinese, but learning the Chinese language, practising the medical arts and teaching secular subjects to the Chinese were secondary and subservient.

But at the 1877 Conference of the Protestant Missions in Shanghai a change of attitude occurred. This change reflected the cultural and social changes in the nations from which the missionaries came. When the first missionaries were sent to China, or any other un-christianized parts of the world, for that matter, they had the support of a climate of unbounded faith in progress guided by the universal creed. Their approach to theology was intuitive and emotional. Admittedly, progress depended on science, but science limited men's knowledge to what was phenomenal, not noumenal, in the Kantian

* W. A. P. Martin related an amusing conversation between him and his colleague in the Peking Language Institute, the mathematician Li Sheng-lan. Li asked him why China did not send any missionaries to the West. Martin did not answer, but later he wrote that his answer would have been: 'Because water does not flow uphill' (W. A. P. Martin, *A Cycle of Cathay*, N Y, 1896, p. 370).

terminology; therefore it had nothing to do with the reality of God. Essentially, this was a romantic approach to Christianity in general and to missionary work in particular. The Oxford Movement from 1833 onward did not depart from it to any significant degree. As to the doctrine of Divine Creation, no one raised the slightest doubt.

But socially Europe entered a period of optimism after the revolutions of 1848 because of its industrial and commercial expansion. The grip of patriarchal and masculine authority on the middle-class Europeans was loosened; so were bourgeois sexual inhibitions. The naturalist literature and theatre of the period reflected a keener and franker interest in sexual matters, especially premarital and extra-marital love. The middle class itself became more hedonistic and consequently its concern with religion declined. In education, the growth of *lycées* and state schools intensified what was called 'the war of the schools' in Belgium and hastened the secularization of education in the West, culminating in the discontinuation of religious tests at Oxford and Cambridge in 1871. This trend of social development had its parallel in the USA after the Civil War. The war itself and the pleasure-seeking mood that followed it lowered the standard of public morality while the issue of slavery weakened the spiritual leadership of the Church.

Amid all this, the growth of philosophical radicalism in England, the confluence of liberalism and positivism, the publication of Darwin's *Origin of Species*, and the emergence of the Young Hegelians and Materialists aligned the most advanced natural and social sciences against the basic doctrines that had held since before the French Revolution. Belief in the natural goodness of man, his natural rights and duties, and the universality of reason was discarded. Belief, according to Bentham, must be solidly placed on rational grounds and nothing else.

Morality was not belittled, but was freed from the fear of an external authority. It thus became autonomous, dependent entirely on the attitude and motive of the person concerned who sought a good life as a member of society. It should have nothing to do with the hope for heaven or fear of hell. The *Origin of Species* shocked Darwin's contemporaries, because for the first time in history it placed man in the biological natural order. The denial of the Divine Creation necessarily implied the repudiation of the Fall, the Flood and Divine Revelation. The great tide of rational science engulfed even

C.A.T.W.—D

the irrational Nietzsche, who labelled Christian morality as slavish and ignoble and pronounced all religions to be untrue.

If God had not created man, man had created God as the symbol for his ideals and goals, as the Young Hegelians would have it, or as a reflection of the misery of this world as Marx would interpret it. The concept of 'man' and his progress to what he was were now open questions that led to an intellectual crisis. The answers lay possibly in science – in an open-minded, dispassionate, sceptical search for them. Instead of depending on Divine guidance, man's progress in history came as a result of his struggle for survival in a process of selection or through the class struggle. Thus evolved historicism and the laws of social development. To stem the tide of this intellectual revolution, the Catholics put forward scarcely more than the *Syllabus of Errors* of 1864 and the convocation of the Ecumenical Council to solemnize the doctrine of Papal Infallibility of 1870. Both were incongruous phenomena in the cultural world of the West in the second half of the nineteenth century.

Against this background Calvin Mateer drew the attention of the 1877 Conference in Shanghai to science as the only effective means of bringing religion to the elite of China, for science appealed to their reason rather than to emotion. Science by then had come to be appreciated by the Chinese elite who were prepared to concede a certain amount of intellectual ground to it. On their side the missionaries, too, were prepared to concede the same amount of ground. After some sixty years of Protestant missionary work, Kipling's 'twain' finally found their meeting point.

But although they might meet on science, at the back of their minds the old tension continued to loom large. The Confucians, defeated and humiliated in war, were not yet willing to yield their superiority in moral judgement and governance of the state whereas the Christians insisted upon the necessity of Western tutelage – 'the white man's burden' – to lead China to progress. It required three more wars, the Sino–French of 1884–5, the Sino–Japanese of 1894–5, and the Boxer War of 1900, to break down the Confucian adamancy which had so far dammed up the flood of the intellectual change, while the missionaries themselves had their supply lines thrown into chaos, as it were, by developments in theology in the West. In 1862 George Smith drew the attention of theologians to a Babylonian record of the story of the Flood which brought the accuracy of the Old Testament as a historical chronicle under scrutiny. This beginning led on to the discovery of evidence that the chronological order of the Four Gospels was quite wrong and that the life of Jesus Christ as recorded by the Evangelists was not, historically, entirely correct. Secular approaches to human religious experience, on the one hand, made religion into a branch of humanity studies and, on the other, denied unique supremacy to Christianity. In 1870 J. F. Clarke produced his book on the ten religions of the world to further research on comparative religion. At one extreme of this trend was Ernest Renan's *Life of Jesus* which appeared in 1863. Renan rejected Christianity on positivist grounds and suggested the replacement of religion by aesthetics. Bertrand Russell's *Free Man's Worship* of 1910 even expressed doubts about the historicity of Christ. The other extreme was represented by the publication, also in 1910, of the *Fundamentals* in twelve volumes, financed by Californian conservatives, which reached the astronomical circulation of 2 500 000 copies!

Between these two extremes were William James's Gifford Lectures on 'The Varieties of Religious Experience' with the emphasis on belief. If faith in the Christian God or any other gods bestowed joy and happiness on men, so be it. But a benevolent God, not being supernatural, was not unique to Christianity; other gods of other religions could be just as benevolent. There was also the growth of progressivism in the USA which stimulated the eclectic social gospel movement. It exhorted the various denominations to put aside their theological differences in a co-operative effort to do social work in the congested cities of America and in backward countries like the Philippines and China.

Both the fundamentalist reaction to this new intellectualism and the social gospel movement gave rise to a religious revival in Europe and America. Even university graduates, like the Cambridge Seven, were attracted to missionary activities overseas. Money flowed from the prospering businesses of the 1880s and 1890s into the treasuries of the churches while political leaders, especially those of the newly awakened American expansionism, encouraged the missions to work on a world wide scale. The Student Volunteer Movement thus began. Canada, too, joined in this wave of evangelical enthusiasm by sending young university-trained people to China.

The conflict in importance between saving souls and that of social work and the introduction of science raised a difficult question which had never occurred to churchmen before: which should come first, Christianity or secular civilization?

In the China field Young J. Allen (who arrived in China in 1860), Timothy Richard (who arrived in China in 1870), and Gilbert Reid (who arrived in China in 1883), to name only a few, instigated a reorientation of the Protestant work. In essence, Christianity was interpreted as predominantly 'remedial', – first, remedying moral impurity which was traditional and, second, remedying social injustice which was modern. From this, Richard, a Baptist with considerable technological training, went on to define a new goal for the whole missionary enterprise, which was to save the Chinese nation through the collective efforts of regenerated souls, so that China now in decay could one day become 'perhaps the foremost empire of the world' which, after all, was her ambition. As long as the entire process of her renaissance was guided by her spiritual reformation based on the Gospel, then there would be no need to share Mark Twain's fear of the person sitting in darkness who suddenly saw light and sprang into action. This would entail not so much a change in China's antiquated institutions as the injection of Christian spirit into them. This would certainly entail the missionaries' addressing their message to the educated elite, including the students, of China. This also meant that the West must bring its best, particularly its science, to China in order to enhance the welfare of the Chinese people.

The Indian summer of the Christian missions in China began with the defeat of the anti-foreign Boxers and ended with the chilly wind of the First World War. The war shattered many dreams and invalidated many assumptions. Different cultures could no longer be ranked in higher and lower orders. Religions, including Christianity, were thought of as a neurotic manifestation derived from the Oedipus complex. In such an intellectual context, what could the civilizing function of the missionaries possibly be? To eradicate indigenous values was deemed undesirable; to graft Christianity on to them plainly absurd. The spread of anthropological and psychological knowledge thus dampened the zeal of young people either to save souls or to improve social conditions overseas. Having produced such a holocaust as the First World War, which was in contradiction to all Christian ideals, Western civilization now bred disillusionment and cynicism. On the wider horizon the triumph of the Bolsheviks loomed large as a dangerous challenge to both capitalism and Christianity. With the passage of time the challenge grew in size, as the West plunged into the Depression.

In the 'backward' countries the missionaries were no longer the only source of knowledge of things Western. A much more powerful agent, the motion pictures of Hollywood, came upon the scene, revealing various facets of the intimate life of Western men and women. The Fairbankses, Clara Bows, Charlie Chaplins, Gloria Swansons presented an image of the West vastly different from that imparted by the missionaries. Through the importation of films, gramophone records, popular literature and consumer goods, the Gay Twenties made its impact on a few treaty ports of China. In the country at large the anarchy of the warlords' era reigned, with the result that agriculture suffered grievous disruption from the incessant civil wars and a militant, anti-imperialist nationalism spread like a prairie fire. Against such a background the irrelevance of the missionary and his work found expression in Maxwell Chaplin's letters:

1919: I am ashamed to confess that I have caught myself falling into that superior, apologetic attitude about being a missionary. It is so utterly disloyal and contemptible – to be ashamed of the fact that we are ambassadors of Jesus Christ and messengers of the love of God to the world.

1924: How far away and how futile all this theological discussion seemed the other day as I sat with that little company of Christians in the chill, dirty, little village schoolroom, with its dirty floor and paper windows, and listened to the pastor as he broke the bread and poured out the wine for the communion service!

Criticism of this irrelevance came from all directions, including the missionaries themselves. Nathaniel Peffer attacked the naivety and misjudgement of the old missionaries in their way of tackling Chinese problems. D. W. Lyon censured the Church for neglecting the development of Chinese initiative and responsibility in the Christian movement itself. F. S. Brockman advised his colleagues to 'get into the stream of national life'. These critics and their missionary friends were in a quandary as to whether they still wanted to Christianize China. If they did, how could they do it? None had anything positive to suggest. Even the crucial report of the Laymen's Foreign Missions Inquiry, drawn up by W. D. Hocking in 1930, only managed to arrive at a series of negative prescriptions – no preaching on Future Punishment, no conflict between free science and free religion, no claim to be the sole possessor of truth, no claim to superiority over other religions, and no need to expand mission work unless by a change of method. Yet what was to follow was nothing more remarkable than an emphasis on education which the 1877 Conference had already stressed. The crisis was real and deepening; the 'poverty of philosophy' was painfully obvious. It was then, in response to the Chinese communist challenge, and mainly on Chinese initiative, that the rural reconstruction programme was conceived. When this programme came to an abrupt end with the outbreak of the Japanese War and on account of its own failure, the 'Christian century' of China quietly faded into history.

Apart from the desire to spread the Gospel, there were also other, more personal reasons for going to China which spurred on a minority of the missionaries. Some were inspired by the glamour of the 'Livingstone' image as described by the young Lord Lugard in 1876:

Proud as England is of her warriors and statesmen, her inventors and her martyrs, of none is she so justly proud as of the humble missionary. . . . Justly we may regard him as a pattern of British courage and we shall not disparage England's other heroes by selecting him as the greatest among them.

At the other extreme there were the discontented and the misfits, unsettled by the frustrations of the English city or the insecurity of the English countryside, who sought to emigrate or to go overseas as missionaries. Some of them found it pleasanter to work among the Chinese than the English. There were also 'rice missionaries' like John Fryer who hoped to gain wealth and honour in China, and a Miss Wilson whose only aim in working in China was to earn enough money to pay off the mortgage on her father's house. Mr Ballou's letter to Dr Brown from Peking (or Peiping as it was called then) on 5 April 1932 put it frankly: 'I am sure [that] many of us would have been home many years ago if we had not had things somewhat comfortable'.

The long history of mission work in China produced its second and third generations, e.g. Dr W. W. Pettus, Dr James Endicott, and the renowned Pearl Buck, who became emotionally and culturally involved with China and the Chinese. They followed in the footsteps of their parents, continuing with missionary work, teaching, or working for the diplomatic service in that country. In some individual cases, a desire to found a girls' school or to emancipate Chinese prostitutes may have served as strong enough motive for taking the long voyage to China.

The first step for the missionaries was to have the Bible translated into Chinese, a work undertaken by Dr John Marshman and Joannes Lassar in 1811 and completed in 1820. But the 500 copies of their translation of the New Testament printed in 1822 were not allowed to be distributed in the Chinese Empire. Dr R. Morrison and Dr W. Milnes began their translation in 1813; this proved to be a more satisfactory rendering and was completed in 1823. Two thousand copies of the New Testament, together with 10 000 copies of a tract and 5000 copies of the Catechism, came out of the mission press at Malacca which Morrison also founded. Three years later the Bible made its first appearance in the empire. It went through several revisions, all of which were in classical Chinese, compounding the incomprehensibility of such outlandish names as Jacob and Isaiah, such strange allusions as those to the shepherd and his sheep, and such alien customs as holy kisses. The 'mandarin' vernacular version of 1871 reduced the general obscurity of Christian literature slightly; it was issued by the American Bible Society.* Between 1833 and 1914, the Bible, the Old and New Testaments, and portions of them together reached the incredible circulation of 20 088 736 copies. But neither the old versions nor the new bore a single explanatory note on Biblical symbolism, terminology, customs, or historical background, for the Bible Society which issued the literature was interdenominational and any note might run the risk of offending against the interpretation of the doctrine held by one or other of its financial backers.

## Conversion and converts

Conversion was, of course, the central task of the missions and a Chinese convert usually went through three stages of development – the arousal of his interest in the doctrine (the hearer or inquirer), the possibility of being received into the Church (the probationer), and the baptism (the communicant).

Of the three stages of conversion the second was the most crucial, the one during which the probationer was put under close observation, usually for as long as a whole year. During that time the probationer studied the tracts and the Testaments, if he was able to read, demonstrated his faith by deeds (e.g. giving up idolatry, gambling, opium-smoking, or concubinage, depending on what his chief

* The work of improving the translation of the Bible continued into the 1930s.

sins had been, and taking part in church activities including the attendance at services and helping with proselytization). The stage usually ended with a visit by a missionary to the probationer's home, to pray with him and to verify that the probationer was actually living like an honest Christian. At the baptismal ceremony the probationer was subjected to questioning, as recorded in Alexander Stronach's letter to Arthur Tidman on 10 March 1848:

Saturday, March 4th. This forenoon the two accepted applicants attended the meeting usually held once a month with the Chinese members of the church, preparatory to their partaking of the Lord, supper on the following day. All were highly pleased with the evidant [*sic*] truthfulness, and with the warmth of Christian love manifested by our two new brethren.

Lord's day, March 5th. This morning the two Chinese converts were baptized at our chapel.... Before baptizing them I asked, 'Why do you wish to receive baptism and to become professed Christians?' They both answered in harmony, – first the father and then the son, – 'We wish to obey the Lord's commands, believing that Christianity is the only true religion.' 'What do you believe regarding the natural state of your hearts?' 'We are by nature only, and altogether, evil.' 'Then you believe you could not do anything to save yourselves from hell; – on what do you trust now for salvation?' 'Our trust is entirely on the Lord Jesus Christ, who came into the world to save sinners, and who died on the cross to redeem us unto himself.' 'How has it taken place that you are become sensible of your need of a Saviour, and that you now love to think of the Lord Jesus as your almighty Redeemer?' 'We believe that it is by the power of the Holy Spirit that our hearts are become changed, and that we have been enabled to see the divine glory of Christ while hearing his gospel preached.' 'You have rejected the idols that you formerly worshipped, and you knew that your countrymen around you still worship many things which they call gods; – how many gods do you now believe there are?' 'We believe that there is only one, – the living and true God, – the Father, the Son, and the Holy Ghost, – three persons but one God; and in this faith we wish to be baptized.' 'Are you willing to cast off for ever all idolatrous practices, including the worship of ancestors, going to inquire about lucky days, and every thing that God has forbidden?' 'Yes, we cast them all off; and henceforth desire only to obey and follow the Lord's revealed will.' 'Do you suppose that by your future obedience to the will of God you may be able to merit the happiness of heaven?' 'No, not at all. We will pray for strength from above to enable us to live as disciples of Christ; still our best acts are defiled with sin, and we can never have any merit in ourselves; our only trust is in the merits of the Redeemer.' 'In desiring to become members of the Christian church, do you hope by being admitted into it to gain any worldly advantage?' 'No, we desire and hope for only heavenly blessings.' 'You know that when the Lord Jesus lived on earth the world hated him, and persecuted him even unto death. The evil heart of man has still the same enmity against God; and our Lord tells us that all who will devotedly follow him must expect to be persecuted for his name's sake?' 'We know this, and have maturely weighed the matter in our minds; but we are not at all afraid; men can only kill the body, and Jesus will graciously receive our Souls into his heavenly kingdom.' After stating to all present that what was now to be done was in obedience to the expressed command of Christ, I baptized the two men 'in the name of the Father, and of the Son, and of the Holy Ghost'. Prayer having been again offered up, and another hymn sung, the congregation was dismissed. The whole service was, of course, conducted in the Chinese language.

The whole ceremony, including the questions and answers, had been rehearsed beforehand and therefore its validity as a test of the convert's understanding of the doctrine could be open to doubt. In 1850 some missionaries asked unprepared, trick questions such as 'Which came first, chronologically, Father, Son, or Holy Ghost?' But this practice was soon discontinued. As the Chinese were trained to commit written texts to memory, the questions and answers at baptism were not hard work for them.

For the missionary, the main difficulties lay in making sure that the probationer truly understood what he was supposed to believe and in overcoming the language barrier. To resolve the latter, the missionary usually relied on the help of an assistant whose integrity the missionary had to trust. In any case, he had no other recourse than his own judgement and the observable behaviour of the probationer and the assistant. As the Confucian tradition had always linked knowledge with action, both the assistant and the probationer believed that as long as they behaved in the Christian way, they also understood the doctrine. They were apt to equate the concept of sin with observable sinful acts. Neither probationer nor assistant was normally of a reflective cast of mind; neither thought faith alone was essential and sufficient.

With a conversion scheme so designed, it was little wonder that most of the early inquirers had had a blatantly sinful personal history; some even had criminal records. The churches themselves purposely addressed their message to the less fortunate and less educated before the reorientation of the 1880s and 1890s. Many converts were of modest origins and had material gains in view, which gave rise to talk of 'rice Christians'. To attract followers the early evangelists dished out 'free breakfasts', set up 'soup kitchens', and gave medical treatment. In order to create a suitable environment in the convert's home, the churches made use of the Chinese family ties. After a man became converted, the rest of his family soon followed, as happened for instance with the conversion of Go T'o (Wu T'u), a corporal in the Chinese army stationed in Amoy in 1848. The corporal was totally illiterate and his family's conversion was a simple act of illumination. In Tz'uchow, Chihli (now Hopei), early in this century, when J. Goforth met a Mr Shen at dinner, another case of simple illumination occurred, in spite of the fact that Mr Shen had read J. S. Mill and Darwin. The missionary asked Shen about the solar system and whence it came. He then went on to discuss Ezekiel and the fulfilment of prophecies. Silenced, Shen 'looked up with tears in his eyes and said: "I believe there is a God." Bringing his hand down with a bang on the table, Shen continued: "No other book in the world is going to *save China* but this book." ' In a year, all those who had been present at this dinner were admitted into the Church. Conversion by sudden illumination came under severe criticism and conversion by growth in a country without a Christian tradition was hardly feasible unless in a limited way. Consequently even a shift of focus to the educated class of Chinese did not bring more people into the Church. Very few, 'no more than 10 per cent', as one missionary admitted, could be counted as true Christians and among the students at Christian schools and colleges perhaps 15 per cent were favourably inclined to the Church, an equal proportion violently against it, while the rest were utterly indifferent.

Examples of successful conversion illustrate the personal and social impact Christianity had on the Chinese. Liang Fa (Leangafa), a wood-block engraver working for Dr Robert Morrison, was baptized in 1816. In Canton early in the 1830s, Liang served as an ordained minister while continuing to print Christian literature for distribution. Elijah Bridgman, Thomas Fisher, Dr W. Milne, and other missionaries, who knew him, spoke of his progress in glowing terms. One of the tracts he distributed fell into the hands of one Hung Hsiu-ch'uan, later the Heavenly King of the Taiping Rebellion (1850–64), which came within an ace of overthrowing the Ch'ing Dynasty. Ch'en Tai (also known as Tan Tai), a common soldier of twenty-five years of age stationed in Amoy, was a remarkable convert in two ways. First, he demonstrated the spirit of a Christian martyr after his conversion in 1848 by showing his steadfastness when he was made a subject of persecution and reproach in front of the whole of his regiment. His superior officer reviled him and his comrades mocked and shunned him. Second, having sustained these trials with fortitude, his gallantry in an action against pirates earned him, though after some hesitation and delay, a promotion in 1851.

The Hu family were the first Methodist Episcopal converts in Foochow. Old Hu Ngieng Sen, a *yamen* clerk, took his wife and two sons to be baptized on 9 May 1858. The eldest son, Yong Mi, was to become the pastor of East Street Church in 1864; all his six sons and a daughter were brought up as Methodists. Three of the sons were ordained ministers and the daughter went to study at the Ohio Wesleyan University and the Women's Medical College in Philadelphia. The old man's second son, Bo Mi, began his career as a non-commissioned officer in the imperial army and some time after his conversion was appointed the steward of the Methodist Episcopal Church of Foochow. The old man's youngest son, Sing Mi, followed Dr E. Wentworth to New York to study and was an ordained deacon in 1864. The Hu family set an example as a sincere Christian family who, through the channels of the Church, developed their ecclesiastical careers to the envy of their friends and neighbours.

There was Pastor Hsi Liao-chu in Pingyang, Shansi, an educated opium addict, who received religious instruction from J. J. Turner and won a prize for religious essays from Timothy Richard and David Hill. Hill then invited Hsi to teach him to read the Chinese classics and to live with him. In November 1880 Hsi was baptized. Hsi's great contributions to the church work included the founding of an opium refuge through which 700 men were converted and he travelled to other parts of his province to spread the good message and convert hundreds more to the Christian religion. But in private life, Hsi was against his wife, also a Christian, spending too much time on church work and unbinding her feet. Only after his death was his widow able to free herself from the agony of foot-binding. She started a women's opium refuge.

Nearly all the examples of successful conversion were drawn from the lower classes. After the reorientation of mission work in the 1880s more educated people were attracted; this was also partly due to a change in the government's attitude from contempt and antagonism to tolerance and flattery and partly due to the emergence of a

Christian career-pattern like that of the Hu family in Foochow. Although the government had not yet begun to appoint foreign-trained students to posts of substantive power, the scheme to send students abroad which started in 1871 initiated a fashion which increasingly commanded the attention and admiration of the educated classes. The Church had been known as a channel through which Christian youth could go abroad to further their training. Starting from Charles Gutzlaff's charitable act in sending a blind girl to England in 1856, there followed a generation of talented Christian 'literati' such as Jen Pao-lo (Paul Jen), who became Young J. Allen's assistant in the translation and publication of religious and other works after a period of study in the USA; Chang Wen-k'ai, the well-paid editor with security of tenure of a church magazine for twenty-five years; Liang Hsiao-ch'u, a poor boy who was to distinguish himself as an important leader of the YMCA; and Wang Chih-ping, for twenty-five years a leading pastor in north China, holder of American MA, PhD, and DD degrees, and later in 1930, a bishop of the Methodist Episcopal Church.

With the changing attitude of the government towards the Church after 1870 and the deepening crises in the empire, social intercourse between political leaders and the clergy became possible. Marquis Tseng saw W. A. P. Martin in Peking as frequently as three or four times a week and his uncle, Tseng Chi-tse, invited Timothy Richard to be the tutor of his own children. In the 1890s Richard had extensive contacts with Chinese leaders in both the central and local governments such as Chang Chih-tung, Weng T'ung-ho, Li Hung-chang, Ts'en Ch'un-hsuan of Shansi and Chou Fu of Kiangsu. He and his colleagues influenced the Hundred Days' Reform of 1898. Two years before that Emperor Kuang-hsü had even contemplated the establishment of Christianity as the state religion of China. As yet none of these government leaders had ever considered embracing the faith. The leaders of the early Republic, Yuan Shih-k'ai, Li Yuan-hung, even old Marshal Chang Tso-lin, continued to show friendliness to missionaries. Sherwood Eddy, for example, was asked to preach to President Li Yuan-hung's family. Important government posts, especially in the Ministry of Foreign Affairs, were given to Christians. Lu Cheng-hsiang, a Catholic, who retired to and died in a monastery in Bruges, was several times China's Minister of Foreign Affairs; Wang Cheng-t'ing (C. T. Wang), son of a pastor and a leader of the YMCA, was also several times her Minister of Foreign

Affairs; Yen Hui-ch'ing (W. W. Yen), another pastor's son, was a veteran diplomat.

The leader of the 1911 revolution, Dr Sun Yat-sen, was baptized by J. Lewis Shuck of the Southern Baptist Church in Macao, and his widow, Soong Ch'ing-ling, was the daughter of Charles C. J. Soong, a Methodist Episcopal pastor from North Carolina. But because of her left-wing political views, she became estranged from her church friends, being regarded as 'an adventuress'. Her more moderate sister, Mei-ling (Mayling), married Chiang Kai-shek in 1927. When dealing with a complex personality like Chiang's, it is difficult to tell when he was in honest communion with God and when he was simply polishing up his public image or playing to the international political gallery. Before his conversion in 1931 he had shown his goodwill towards the churches by his promise to protect clergymen, pastors, and mission property in 1926, a none-too-easy step for him to take when the country at large witnessed a rising tide against Christianity. He continued to maintain a pro-Christian stance after taking power in 1928. In his New Life Movement, essentially a Confucian revival with some Christian content, in 1935, he even employed several YMCA functionaries as leaders and ordered the Movement to co-operate with the YMCA. From his address at the graduation ceremony of the Ginling College, a Christian women's college in Nanking, in 1934 to his broadcast speech in 1938 under the title 'Why I believe in Jesus', Chiang held the view that Jesus was a national, social, and religious revolutionary leader, almost a model for himself to emulate. He was audacious enough to advance the proposition that the Three Principles of the People, the guiding philosophy of the Kuomintang, were derived from the teachings of Christ. These eclectic principles suited the eclectic cast of Chiang's mind; to be sure, he was neither a pure Christian nor a pure Confucian. Many and contradictory political theories dwelt together in his mind in a stolid harmony. By means of this harmony, he hoped to gain support from the conservative landowning gentry whose values were principally Confucian, from the more enlightened capital-owning gentry whose values were an incoherent blend of Confucianism and Christianity, and from the urban lower classes whose guilt culture based on traditional Chinese religions might be replaced by the guilt culture of Christianity. With the former two social groups controlling the latter, Confucianism would eventually dominate and sinocize Christianity. Chiang's scheme was, then, one which served both tradition and nationalism – rather as folk Buddhism and Taoism had been syncretized by the neo-Confucianists in the twelfth century, with a Chinese moral revival as the final goal.

Another eminent convert, Major (as he was then) Fen Yü-hsiang, was received by the Methodist Episcopal Church in 1911. While still a common soldier, Feng had been ordered to protect missionaries and their property in Paoting during the Boxer disorders, and had been deeply impressed by the courage of a Miss Morrell and the Presbyterians. After his conversion, many of his officers and men were sometimes persuaded and sometimes commanded to take part in Holy Communion and the mass conversions of his soldiers, hundreds at a time. Hymn singing, Bible reading and services became a part of his army training. This famed Christian general was concerned to create 'a spiritual revival' in China, for he believed that Christianity could instil a sense of shame (not the concept of sin) into his fellow-countrymen's hearts.

Concern over China's moral degeneration and anxiety for a moral rearmament were shared by Chiang, Feng, and many others who had a regard for the destiny of China and her people. When the missionaries resumed their proselytization after the Second Opium War, the neo-Confucians, led by Tseng Kuo-fan, were engaged in reviving the Ch'ing Dynasty with propriety as the central criterion and the sense of shame as the yardstick for any deviation from it. To be sure, the shame culture of the Chinese elite was then in a state of ambiguity, resulting in moral confusion in both public and private conduct. The missionaries, whose understanding of the Confucian philosophy and literature was inadequate, but who had ample opportunities to travel and observe the depravity of the upper and lower classes in cities and towns, came to the easy conclusion that the shame culture was capable of evoking only a shallow moral sense in men, if it was not actually amoral. As one missionary put it:

There [in Confucianism] is no consciousness of the deep guilt of sin, no groaning in the struggle with a heart that is desperately wicked.

Other missionaries, too, tended to overdraw the contrast between the guilt culture of Christianity and the shame culture of Confucianism, scarcely aware that articulated Confucianism was mainly urban. The vast expanse of rural China was only marginally touched by it as peasants with their folk religions – Buddhism and Taoism – also had a sense of guilt which they might incur *vis-à-vis* the supernatural

beings to regulate their lives while they seldom had any temptation
or opportunity for corrupt conduct. Addressing their message
chiefly to city- and town-dwellers, the missionaries succeeded first
only in converting the 'marginal men' who were open to intellectual
compromise, even gullible, showing a tendency towards eclecticism
like that of Chiang Kai-shek and Fen Yü-hsiang. For instance, a
Hupei government student who later became prefect of Kuangchow
wrote in the *Chiao-hui hsin-pao* (Chinese Christian Review) edited by
Young J. Allen:

The holy and powerful God, born according to the wish of Heaven to be
the unique God is the trinity of Father, Son, and Holy Ghost of the
Western religion. His desire to become established and widely known by
experiencing [other people's] starvation and [other human] predicaments
as His own is for the purpose of redeeming the guilt of man. To comfort
the old and care for the young is the significance of prayer. To examine
one's conscience thrice a day and to preach on the auspicious days of each
month is the meaning of the services. Only Crucifixion, Resurrection, and
other strange events recorded in the Old and New Testaments arouse
people's suspicion that it [the religion] is absurd. However, the [Bible]
reader should not interpret the texts too literally at the expense of the
intended meaning behind the words. . . . The differences between China
and the West amount to nothing more than differences in diction and
phraseology, habits and customs. The anxiety to correct what is wrong is
common to both.

In spite of the reorientation of the Church in 1877 towards converting the Chinese elite and the sending of promising converts to
Europe and America for theological training, no Chinese Christian
had emerged who could command the respect of Western theologians or Chinese intellectuals. True, there were eminent Christian
educationists like Wu Yi-fang, the President of Ginling College from
1928 to 1952; Mei Yi-ch'i, President of the famous Tsinghua
University in Peking; Ma Liang, the founder of Fu-tan College in
Shanghai; Chang Po-ling, the founder of Nankai School and
University; James Yen, the renowned mass educationist. True, too,
there were many distinguished Chinese clergymen who attained the
rank of bishop or even archbishop or were outstanding social workers in the YMCA. But the question remained: why should China
become a nation of Bible readers?

## Chinese Christian theology and the growth of autonomy

The May 4th Movement of 1919, anti-imperialist as it was, awakened searching minds not only among the laity but also among the Chinese Christians. Thereafter the embryo of a Chinese Christian theology began to grow. This growth was also closely related to the movement for the autonomy of the Chinese churches in the early 1920s, as if demonstrating their intellectual maturity.

Hsieh Fu-ya, an educationist and YMCA worker, was inspired by Alfred Whitehead's *Religion in the Making* while he was studying at Harvard in 1926. Hsieh took it upon himself to interpret the Christian doctrine in terms of Chinese philosophy, as Whitehead's ideas turned him away from social work towards the individualization of religion with emphasis on the cultivation of a complete personality through family socialization and school and social education. For him, the complete personality consisted of the ultimate good (represented by China-Confucianism), the ultimate beauty (represented by India-Buddhism), and the ultimate truth (represented by West-Christianity). Confucianism cultivated a personality which could be the motive force of revolutionary action; Buddhism led to *nirvana* which through its mystical experiences could lend support to mass participation in such action; and Christianity sought after reason which could guide action. Whatever logic there was in Hsieh's schema, his interest lay in the *way* (*tao*) of action, not in contemplation and union with the supernatural being. Rather than a coherent theological system, Hsieh's theory is an illustration of the ponderousness, hesitancy and indecision in the thinking of most Chinese Christians of the 1920s, who were troubled by problems such as individualization versus popularization and intellectual conviction versus practical action.

Towards the end of the 1920s and in the early years of the 1930s, the problems resolved themselves, partly due to the mounting crisis in China and the search for a solution on the part of the more radical Christians. Wu Lei-ch'uan, who embraced the faith in 1915, was greatly influenced by the social-gospel and modernist movements; he used science and empirical knowledge as the basis of his theological understanding. To his mind, Christ was a social reformer and Christian love had no meaning other than social justice which could be fulfilled only through a bloody revolution. As he put it:

'Christianity is a revolutionary religion which opposes oppression and unjust economic systems.'

As a Christian he was not satisfied by material reform alone. He regarded it as the first step in a continuous revolution working towards a society based on human values and mass welfare. This Methodist Episcopal theologian had considerable influence on Wu Yao-tsung, who went much further, denying that Christianity was spiritual and individual at all. Instead, it was socially and politically reformist. On the one hand, there was no hope of reviving Chinese tradition; on the other, there might be a hope of reforming the Church so as to develop its reformist ethos. Christian love could unite individuals and Christian truth must unite man to his God. Such a religion could help reconstruct Chinese culture and foster a new generation of Chinese leaders. The two Wus thus paved the way to the formation of an activist church in China which defied foreign domination and sought to be autonomous, as if in preparation for the total severance of its ties with the Western churches after 1949.

The British Protestant missionaries in the China field were sent by the British societies such as the Baptist Missionary Society, the London Missionary Society, the Church Missionary Society, the British and Foreign Bible Society, and the Methodist Missionary Society. These early organizations were followed by the China Inland Mission, founded by James Hudson Taylor in 1865. At first the Americans went to China through the sponsorship of the American Board of Commissioners for Foreign Missions which became the agent of the Congregationalists while the Methodists and Presbyterians had their own mission societies. After the civil war the Presbyterians (North), Methodist Episcopal (North), the American Baptist Missionary Union, and the American Board were the predominant groups up to the end of the nineteenth century. During the religious revival in Europe and America (including Canada) in the 1880s the missionary work in China, Japan and Korea expanded considerably. This was the time when the American Student Volunteer Movement was formally inaugurated under the auspices of the YMCA, aiming ambitiously at spreading the Gospel throughout the world in one generation. Between the last decade of the nineteenth and the first decade of this century, the Student Volunteer Movement took on China and India as the two major fields of its work. Then came the secularization of American education, decreasing financial support, a demand for social work to be done in the USA, and the split between the fundamentalists and modernists which contributed to the decline of the Movement when its goal was still far from being attained.

Before the schism between the fundamentalists and modernists, the various Protestant denominations co-operated well. As early as 1830 the idea of an Anglo–American Christian Union was broached. There followed two attempts at co-operation: at the Hong Kong Conference of 1843 and the Edinburgh Conference of 1909. But the schism mentioned above gravely affected the Protestant work in China. The Chinese clergy and laity at the 1922 Conference in Shanghai tried to patch up the differences by calling for unity among missionaries and pointing out the irrelevance of the whole issue to the Chinese. The Conference also demanded autonomy for the Chinese Church without cutting its ties with the West.

When Hudson Taylor founded his China Inland Mission, the idea of an autonomous Chinese Church was already on his mind. But in tune with the general condescending attitude towards the Chinese mixed with a genuine fear of heretical and sinocizing tendencies, Bishop James Bashford in 1907 still doubted 'the wisdom of an independent Chinese church at any time which would lead to heresies and difficulties'. The Church, like China herself, must grow under the tutelage of the Westerners. This explains why no Chinese bishop was consecrated before the First World War. The years after the war were the years of growing militant nationalism which encouraged the Chinese clergy to push ahead with their movement towards autonomy. The Church Self-Government Society (Tzu-li-hui) which began in Shanghai in 1906 convened its first national congress attended by the representatives of eighty branches. By 1924, it had 330 branches all over the country. The 1922 Shanghai Conference of the Protestant Missions, at which half of the attendance was Chinese, voiced (a) its lack of interest in denominational and doctrinal feuds which were of Western historical and cultural origin; (b) a desire for the sinocization of the churches to suit Chinese historical tradition and national characteristics; (c) a wish for autonomy in the sense of financial control, government and proselytization by the Chinese themselves. The fact was that with the expansion of the mission enterprise into a gigantic structure, most of the missionaries had been promoted to office work or were preoccupied with secular activities like education and medicine, leaving the actual pastoral work to the Chinese. This development on the one hand accentuated the importance of the Chinese clergy and on the other demonstrated that there was racial discrimination in the church hierarchies. The conference referred tactfully to the racial problem. After this, steps were slowly taken towards the goal of autonomy – Chinese was made an official language at church conferences held in China, more Chinese became ordained ministers and even consecrated as bishops, and church property came under a form of joint control. None the less the Chinese churches could not carry out all their work without foreign financial aid; nor could the Chinese clergy marshal enough authority, as could foreign missionaries under the protection of extraterritoriality when they encountered the Chinese bureaucracy. The nationalist aspirations of the Chinese clergy were thus frustrated by the imperialist reality both within and without the churches themselves. They remained unfulfilled till the Liberation of China in 1949.

More fundamental and insoluble were the problems concerning the sinocization of the Christian doctrine. What could Chinese Christian theology mean? How could Christianity be adapted to suit Chinese patterns of thinking, cultural traditions, and social conditions? To fit Christianity into the Confucian mould would eventually mean the elimination of all that was supernatural and transcendental; to fit it into the Buddhist mould would negate all its earthly concerns. Confucians certainly frowned upon any form of evangelism, except formal education and the *hsiang-yüeh* system which explained the holy edicts of the saintly emperors to the illiterate; Buddhists had their own methods of proselytization which were passive compared with those of the Christians, showing less concern with welfare work such as education, medical care, and famine relief. There was also the question of how to sinocize Christian rituals. When all these questions had been asked but not answered or not satisfactorily answered, church autonomy amounted to no more than Chinese control over the administration of the missions. It was a movement of shallow nationalism without much religious or social significance. Its success in 1949 did not increase the appeal of Christianity to the Chinese. Throughout the whole movement, no theological schism comparable to that between the Eastern and Western Churches or the Reformation had ever occurred. The churches remained unnaturalized on Chinese soil. With their social and moral functions taken over by the powerful Chinese Communist Party guided by a truly sinocized ideology, Maoism, and with a vastly more efficient conversion scheme, the churches lost their role in society. They could only wither away.

## Secular influences

If the work of conversion was largely a failure, the Protestants contributed more to the Chinese understanding of the West and Western sciences than their Catholic colleagues. In 1834, three years after the foundation of the *Chinese Repository* in Macao, J. Matheson, D. W. C. Olymphant, Elijah Bridgman, and Charles Gutzlaff organized the Society for the Diffusion of Useful Knowledge whose prime object was to enlighten the Chinese minds by means of the arts and science of the West. The columns of the magazine devoted to *belles lettres* were pedestrian and certain subjects, e.g. philosophy, politics and economics, were deemed useless; the Society concentrated on Western history, geography, natural history, medicine, mechanics and of course theology. These articles influenced Commissioner Lin Tse-hsu in his management of the opium question in Canton and also scholars like Wei Yuan and Hsü Chi-yü. By 1842, *Pilgrim's Progress* and works on English history, European astronomy and arithmetic had been translated into Chinese. This line of work was continued by W. A. P. Martin, especially in the field of international law and diplomatic usage, when he worked at the Language Institute in Peking and also by John Fryer, in the field of natural science and technology, when he was the chief translator at the Kiangnan Arsenal from 1868 to 1896 and edited the *Ke-chih hui-pien* (the Chinese Scientific Magazine).

The 'modernists' at the 1877 Conference, Young J. Allen and Timothy Richard, and later Gilbert Reid, stood out as intellectual giants among the ranks of lesser missionaries. Allen, perhaps earlier than anyone else, relied on writing and publication as the most effective means of promoting the religious and secular influence of the Church. In 1868 this young churchman began his first literary venture – the *Globe Magazine* (1875–83) which was revived under the title of *Review of the Times* (1889–1907). It attacked Chinese immorality and inhuman social praxis while introducing Bible stories, theological discourses and Western practical knowledge in the tradition of the Society for the Diffusion of Useful Knowledge of the 1830s. In seven years this long-surviving magazine leapt from a circulation of 200 to 96 000 copies. The *Review of the Times* was finally taken over by the Society for the Diffusion of Christian and General Knowledge (Kuang Hsüeh Hui) which was the full fruition of Alexander Williamson's original idea of 1877. Williamson laboured for years to see his dream translated into reality in 1887. After his death in 1890, the work of the Society was taken over in 1892 by Timothy Richard under whose directorship it blossomed into the most influential publishing house in China, which position it held from the Japanese War in 1895 until the First World War. These were years of reformist and revolutionary experiments in China and consequently years of anxiety and crises, during which Richard himself wrote copiously – *Lieh-kuo pien-t'ung hsing-sheng chi* (An Account of the Reforms and Revivals of Various Countries) in 1895, *Hsin cheng-ts'e* (New Policies) in 1896, *Hsi-to* (The Warning Bell from the West) and *Chung-hsi ssu ta-cheng* (Four Chinese and Western Major Policies) in 1899. In 1898 he also had Robert MacKenzie's *Nineteenth Century* rendered into Chinese. The immediate, if not more lasting impact of these publications was tremendous. At the same time, John Fryer wrote his *Tso-chih ch'u-yen* (Some Advice on How to Rule) and Young J. Allen published his *Chung-tung chan-chi pen-mo* (A Complete Account of the China–Eastern War). After the abolition of the traditional examination system in 1905 the Minister of Education, Chang Chih-tung, invited the Society (which changed its name to the Christian Literature Society in 1906) to edit textbooks to meet the demands of China's new schools and universities. But soon the 1911 Revolution rendered many of the policy proposals out of date and threw the people they had supported out of authority. With the sharpening competition from China's own publishing enterprises like the Commercial Press and the outbreak of the First World War which greatly reduced the personnel and financial support of the Society for the Diffusion of Christian and General Knowledge, its public shrank until it consisted only of church circles while its wider influence gradually faded away. Even the YMCA's efforts in later years failed to reach the same height and extent as the churches' authority in the years of reform and revolution. China's own intellectual reorientation and progress after the May 4th Movement in 1919 left the Christian publishing houses looking hopelessly ineffectual and old-fashioned.

Nevertheless, in introducing natural science, knowledge of the Western countries, and the use of the vernacular language for the translation of the Bible, the Church played a pioneer role and made a lasting impact on the cultural life of China.

In social praxis and life-style, the missionaries and Chinese affected each other. For reasons of economy and also of social acceptance the missionaries donned Chinese clothes, even the queue, for Hudson Taylor was particularly insistent on this 'mass line' approach to the Chinese. In his view it was not the religion, which was superior and universal, but the foreignness of the missionaries – their appearance, the architectural styles of their churches, and the interior arrangements of their homes – to which the Chinese took exception. When Taylor went to meet a newcomer, a Mr Judd, in November 1873, he not only rode in a Chinese wheelbarrow, but was dressed in a padded gown and jacket, with, over his head, a windhood with side pieces which fitted close to the face, leaving nothing but a medallion-shaped opening for nose, eyes and mouth. In his hand he grasped a huge Chinese umbrella, which he carried in true native style, handle foremost. In his padded clothes he looked almost as broad as he was tall 'and to our foreign eyes was the oddest figure we had ever seen'. Dr David Hill, too, assumed Chinese clothes and the queue when he was doing famine relief work in 1878. This custom does not seem to have ended until the 1880s when the Chinese showed their appreciation of Western aesthetics and in 1908 the Pope decreed that all Catholic priests in China must wear the costume appropriate to their order.

On the other hand the converts were required to give up all forms of idolatry, including ancestor-worship. This practice gave rise to a belief that the foreign missionary was so powerful that his presence in a non-Christian home could scare all gods and spirits away. After his departure the timid gods and spirits had to be invited back home by performing a special ritual. A consequence of abandoning idolatry was that the converts would refuse to contribute any money or take any part in worshipping the Dragon King to bring rain or the local gods to give protection against epidemics, thus creating an impression among the local people that the converts were arrogant and unco-operative. By and by, disbelief in idols spread, so that in the 1900s it became possible for temples to be taken over by local authorities to be used as premises for new schools. Discontinuation of idol-worship was bound to change the pattern of funerals and weddings; and from the change a new concept of marriage emerged. A marriage arranged by parents was likely to be opposed by their Christian children, as in the case of Chao Shih-kuang, whose mother eventually relented and allowed him to choose his own wife. Parents' consent was, however, always sought, as in the cases of Liang Hsiao-ch'u and Wang Ming-tao. Even in 1943 when Wang visualized an ideal Christian marriage, he still insisted on the primacy of parental consent, because parents or other senior members of a family had more experience and wiser judgement in matters of this importance.

The Christian opposition to sexual immorality (including prostitution and the performance of obscene plays) and polygyny eventually reshaped the Chinese attitude towards women. At first, men and women worshipped in the same chapel but were separated by a curtain or a wooden partition. Later, the partitioning was taken away so that families could sit together for worship. Women converts were the first to unbind their feet voluntarily. In 1875 a missionary sponsored an anti-foot-binding society, thus anticipating other organized efforts to wipe out this cruel custom by nearly twenty years. The converts may not have been the first to cut off their queues, but they were encouraged to do so after the 1911 Revolution. On a more refined plane, hymn-singing gave the Chinese a new style of music besides their operas and folksongs as well as modern musical instruments; likewise preaching and sermons taught them the art of public speech. Church music was the beginning of the growth of modern Chinese music whereas public speaking added a new element to Chinese social and political life. Speech-making had never been a part of the public life of a prominent Chinese who had grown up before the 1890s. Such a man would be often overcome by shyness and stammer and stutter on a rostrum. Prince Tsai-chen, for example, made the lame excuse of having a cold to spare himself the agony of addressing a group of students – but, anticipating the cold, he had the speech printed and distributed to the students.

Because of the nature of their work, the missionaries were the first foreigners to learn the Chinese language, including its many dialects, and thus were the pioneers of Western sinology. Inheriting the tradition set by the Jesuits with such works as *Notitia Linguae Sinicae*, *Confucius Sinarum Philosophus* and the *Lettres Edifiantes*, the French were in a more advantageous position than other European countries, with perhaps the sole exception of Russia. Organized French research in sinology began in 1815 when a chair was created at the

Collège de France. The illustrious names such as Julien, Wieger, Cordier, Maspero, Chavannes and Pelliot belonged to men with either missionary or civil service experience in China. At the turn of the twentieth century the *Bulletin de l'école française d'Extrême-Orient* was founded in Hanoi and three years later Cordier of Paris and Schlegel of Leyden launched the authoritative *T'oung Pao*. These pioneer scholars concentrated on language teaching, philological research, religious studies, and description of Chinese geography and social customs, laying the foundation for Henri Cordier's *Bibliotheca Sinica* (1878–95) as well as Edouard Chavannes' and Paul Pelliot's works on history, philosophy and archaeology. At Leyden, G. Schlegel's chair was inherited by J. M. de Groot, who specialized in folk religion and secret societies; in Berlin, Hamburg and Leipzig there were Forke, Franke and von der Gabelentz in the 1870s, not forgetting Ernst Faber's studies of Confucianism in China and Ferdinand von Richthofen's geological reports and travels.

The Royal Asiatic Society came into being in 1832 and its China branch in 1847. To these organizations as well as by the translation of the Chinese penal code, Sir George Staunton made a seminal contribution. Leaving aside civil servants, e.g. John Francis Davis, Thomas Wade and Frederick Mayer, whose studies in Chinese literature, political institutions and linguistics were precursors of better and more solid works to come, James Legge's gigantic undertaking of getting the basic Confucian classics rendered into English and Herbert Giles's compilation of a Chinese dictionary and a biographical dictionary remained unsurpassed. Legge was professor of Chinese at Oxford and Giles held the equivalent post first at Aberdeen and then at Cambridge. Other chairs of Chinese were established at University and King's Colleges, London, and Owen's in Manchester before the foundation of the School of Oriental and African Studies.

The *Chinese Repository* introduced, though in an unsystematic way, some popular Confucian classics, some short stories, and some Yuan dynasty dramas before 1839. Then there followed the redoubtable S. Wells Williams's *Easy Lessons in Chinese* of 1842, *An English and Chinese Vocabulary in the Court* of 1844, and the *Middle Kingdom* of 1848, the last of which remained an indispensable general treatise on China for many decades. Works by American missionaries included A. H. Smith's studies on Chinese villages and characteristics; F. H. Chalfant's research on oracle bones; J. C. Ferguson's works on Chinese art history for the wealthy collectors of Chinese antiquities in Europe and America. During the high tide of the Student Volunteer Movement J. L. Buck laid the foundation of Chinese agricultural economics, G. B. Cressey published on Chinese geography, H. H. Dubs translated Chinese chronicles, A. W. Hummel compiled Ch'ing biographies, H. F. MacNair wrote on contemporary problems, Ida C. Pruitt recorded Chinese family life, and F. W. Price made his authoritative translation of the Three Principles of the People.

In terms of human and financial resources for sinology the USA surpassed all the European countries. From the modest beginnings of Caleb Cushing's and William Rockhill's collections of a few thousand volumes, the Library of Congress rapidly caught up with the British Museum and the Bibliothèque Nationale in its Chinese holdings. Under the influence of Ernest Fenollosa, Freer Gallery and Boston Museum of Fine Arts started acquiring Chinese works of art. Organized efforts were represented by the American Oriental Society, started in 1892, the forerunner of the Association for Asian Studies; the East Asiatic Committee, founded in 1904; and the China Foundation, established in 1924. At Berkeley, Cornell, Columbia and Harvard Chinese studies, including magnificent bibliographical collections, were to thrive and the first professorial appointments went mostly to missionaries. Unfortunately for Australia, the library of the renowned correspondent of *The Times*, Dr George Morrison, was bought by the Toyo Bunko of Tokyo, but fortunately for Canada, the Gest Collection of Chinese books came from New York to Montreal and the fabulous collection of tomb figures and other works of art and oracle bones made by Bishop W. White was and still is housed at the Royal Ontario Museum in Toronto.

Apart from a few landmarks in research and the work of the missionaries and the civil servants, early sinology was still concentrated principally on philological and pre-modern studies, an accumulation of knowledge rather than a developing discipline. It was not until after the Second World War that this tradition gradually came to an end. On the one hand, sinology helped to further the general understanding of China, but, on the other, it created a mutual contempt between Chinese and Western scholars in Chinese studies. The very need for Western sinology implied, among other things, a dissatisfaction with the way the Chinese scholars went about interpreting their own civilization. At the other end, Chinese scholars were often dismayed by and hypercritical of their Western colleagues.

## Missionary education

None of the early treaties conceded to the foreigner the right to educate Chinese children, although the Sino–French Whampoa Treaty and the Sino–American Burlingame Treaty mentioned the possibility of French and American missionaries establishing schools for the education of foreign children in China. Not until the Ministry of Education decision on 3 October 1906 was the existence of many missionary schools recognized legally; they were exempted from registration with the government.

The missionaries set up schools in China to aid the propagation of Christianity and they were pioneers in modern education from primary school to university, for both girls and boys, and in vocational training and the education of the physically and socially handicapped. Elijah Bridgman 'has a small school of Chinese lads' in 1832; Mrs H. V. Rankin in Ningpo and Mrs W. Young in Amoy founded schools for girls in the 1840s; Robert Morrison even started a programme for training the deaf and dumb by using a system 'invented in Spain and practised in France and England'.

The schools had neither a uniform curriculum nor a standard organization, except for the commonly agreed purpose of religious propaganda. There was no competition either, except from the traditional Confucian education which served an entirely different goal. The schools were normally free, collecting no tuition fees and supplying books, lunches and sometimes even clothes to the children. Local dialects usually being the medium of instruction, foreign teachers and native children may have had considerable difficulty in communicating with one another. Compared with the learning by rote and authoritarian style of the instructors in Chinese schools, missionary pedagogical methods were lively, ensuring better results. The boys and girls learnt to play Chinese and foreign games, listened to stories from the Bible and history, and, much to the disgust of old-fashioned scholars, also sang hymns and other songs. At Christmas time they contributed money to buy decorations for the festival. Designed in this way, the mission schools were obviously for poor children who would otherwise have had no education at all. In this sense they and the traditional system of education were complementary rather than competitive. Even so, there were two obstacles – the general unfavourable attitude towards the mission and the fact that poor boys and girls had to start work at an early age in order to supplement the income of the family.

The story of a Fukien boy, Lim Jin-gi, provides an illustration of the typical career pattern of a mission school student. The son of a poor widow, Lim was introduced to the Church by an old convert and was admitted into a mission primary school where he had spent three 'happy years' while his mother worked in a different county. After finishing the primary course, Lim went to the Livingstone Easter School in Tungan – a move that showed the Church's recognition of his promise. His mother, now too old and too weak to work, was hired as a chapel keeper. When his education was completed in 1925, Lim became a preacher, first in Shantung and then in Fukien. He ended his career as the minister of the largest church in Amoy. Generally speaking, graduates of mission schools took up evangelism, teaching, employment in foreign firms, or posts in the Customs Service or Postal Service as their careers. These jobs offered them greater security than any other in China at that time.

By educating girls, the missionaries wanted to form 'intelligent Christian wives and mothers anewing the Christians of the next generation'. Even with a purpose as limited as this, the churches had to combat the prejudice against educating girls which fostered an indifference to their own education in the girls themselves, fight the debilitating custom of foot-binding, and resolve the conflict between being a good Christian and being a good daughter-in-law. Before 1900 most of the girls at mission schools were destitute – like the beggar girls at Mrs Eliza Bridgman's school in Peking, founded in 1864. A change of name to Bridgman Academy at the time of the addition of a secondary section in 1895 meant that the school was no longer for poor girls but for girls from good families. Its college section, founded in 1910, was to be incorporated into the famous and decidedly bourgeois Yenching University in 1920.

After the churches' reorientation in 1877 two extraneous factors hastened changes in Christian education. The wars of 1895 and 1900 made Western knowledge and the Western life-style fashionable and the Chinese government introduced its own educational modernization programme in the opening years of this century. Mission schools had to meet new demands from gentry and bourgeois parents who wanted their children to have a Western-style education and the schools also had to keep ahead of the growing competition from Chinese state and private schools. They expanded and multiplied;

they also modified their curricula for the wealthy students. At that juncture the Church happened to have enough human and financial resources to do all these things, for those were the years of the rising Student Volunteer Movement and increasing donations to overseas mission enterprise. With inadequate funds, the Chinese local authorities could not run government schools unless on a fee-paying basis, thus linking educational opportunities more closely with wealth; the mission schools followed this example, but offered scholarships to talented but poor Christian children.

*Courses offered at Chinese and mission schools*

| Chinese School *1903* (high primary) | | Tientsin Intermediate School (missionary – for the 7–20 age group) *1907* | Chengtu Mission School *1910* |
|---|---|---|---|
| Morals | 2 hrs | Chinese etiquette | |
| Chinese classics | 12 | Chinese classics | Chinese classics |
| Literature | 8 | | Chinese grammar |
| Mathematics | 3 | Mental and written | Arithmetic |
| Science | | arithmetic | Science |
| Chinese history | 2 | Chinese and foreign history | History |
| Geography | 2 | Geography | Geography |
| Drawing | 2 | | Maps and drawing |
| Physical drill | 3 | | Drill |
| | | Physiology | |
| | | Bible catechism | Bible |
| | | | English |
| | | Sunday-school lessons | |

Sources: *Social and Political Journal*, vol. IX, no. 1, March 1925, p. 16, Mrs B. L. St John's letter, Tienstin, 15 January 1907; J. F. Goucher gapers, Methodist Correspondence. For comparison with other schools, see J. F. Goucher papers, China I, and A. M. Cable, *The Fulfilment of a Dream of Pastor Hsi*, the story of the work in Hwochow, London, 1918, pp. 265–8. When I went to my junior high and senior high, Goucher and the West China Union Middle School, in the 1930s, there was hardly any Bible study at all.

Inevitably this trend led to the secularization of mission schools, which the wealthy students regarded as their 'preparatory' schools for studying abroad. The general impression was that at a mission school a student could receive better instruction in English, especially conversational English. Ironically, some mission schools were reluctant to impart that precious knowledge to the Chinese for the same reason as lay behind the German Minister of Education's question to Timothy Richard during a conversation in 1885: 'And when you have educated the Chinese nation what will become of us?' From the 1880s to the 1900s, the question of teaching English, which does not seem to have been debated up to then, drew the attention of mission schoolteachers. Against the background of the reorientation of church work, the raising of objections to introducing English as a subject of study was only a conservative rearguard action. The subject was introduced to take its place along with Chinese and mathematics as one of the three major courses at secondary schools and universities.

Secularization brought with it its own problems, not entirely different from those facing the Chinese schools of the same period. Conservatives like H. T. Hodgkins of the Friends' Mission in Chengtu remarked that the Chinese, being pragmatic, were interested only in 'money-making and armament' rather than 'character forming' and should be given more spiritual training, while Professor E. D. Burton of the Burton Commission, after his survey of Christian schools in China, came to the conclusion that their better moral tone was 'a dangerous excuse for low standards'. The trend then was for the newly arrived, university-educated missionaries to replace the old-fashioned missionaries as teachers. Secularization brought another problem – the secular subjects taught by Chinese teachers in Chinese unavoidably increased the number of Chinese on the faculty. That a Chinese teacher was paid less, sometimes one-third of what his missionary colleague received and sometimes even less, was accepted as the established rule. Other inequalities – Chinese teachers always ranked lower than foreigners and had no voice in school administration – were to provoke complaints and protests in the 1920s. A revealing case was the appointment of Y. L. Hwang to Fowler Biblical School. Hwang, an American-trained student of divinity, accepted this appointment in preference to a government post which carried a much higher salary and a place at Columbia University as a graduate student. Upon his acceptance Dr Stuart warned Bishop Bashford:

Note that *we do not ask* that he be appointed a *member of the mission*. We are not yet ready to have natives so connected with the mission that they will be in a position to deal with matters affecting the Society and our relationships thereto. We think that this should remain in the hands of the foreign missionary, so long as the church in America furnishes nearly all the money.

The questions arising from the secularization of education were closely related to *Chinese* goals of education and the *Chinese* way of administering a mission school. They were part and parcel of Chinese nationalism and could not be solved by the Chinese teachers and students alone. Their solution had to wait for the upsurge of nationalism over wider issues – issues such as the imperialist nature of the mission enterprise.

The Christian universities, like any other university, were for the elite or were designed to train the successors to that class. In north China they admitted mostly students from wealthy landowning families and in east China mostly those from bourgeois families.* They shared many of the attributes of mission schools – they were the first universities in the country, anticipating the first truly Chinese university by some twenty years; they were the first to introduce modern subjects in the liberal arts and sciences including medicine; they were the first to initiate co-education; they were qualitatively and quantitatively to be overtaken by Chinese universities. By 1922 Christian universities accounted for only 11.2 per cent of the total student population and in spite of their efforts to increase enrolment between 1926 and 1936, they still accounted for no more than 12 per cent. Enrolment at a Christian university tended to be lower than at a Chinese university; the teacher–student ratio was therefore better for pedagogical purposes. Apart from the cost of capital construction which was estimated at $19 million† the current expenditure of the eighteen Christian universities in the 1920s came to $3·25 million, i.e. about $500 per student, per annum! With the average rural family income hovering between $50 and $200, university education was beyond the wildest aspirations of the peasants.

The libraries and laboratories of Christian universities, though inferior to those of the best government universities, were infinitely better than those of Chinese private universities. S. M. Gunn of the Rockefeller Foundation commented in 1934 that the Chinese Chris-

* Such as the University of Shansi which began by admitting a number of *hsiu-ts'ai* and *chü-jen* – traditional degree holders – to study at a level slightly higher than that of the London matriculation (W. E. Soothill, *Timothy Richard of China*, London, 1924, pp. 261–2).

† Predominantly financed and administered by Americans and modelled on American campuses, these universities were remarkably beautiful in an environment of squalor and stench, like so many medieval castles or cathedrals.

tian universities were academically mediocre by American standards. This seems too harsh. Perhaps Alice H. Gregg's assessment in her *China: An Educational Anatomy* was more balanced. It conceded the impossibility of Christian universities' competing with government universities due to a lack of financial resources and scholarship and therefore most of their graduates went into teaching, social work, businesses, journalism, medicine, etc. Not research oriented, these graduates won few government scholarships to study abroad; distrusted by the government because of their manners, life-style and religious influence, they gained few positions in the civil service; dissatisfied with the intellectual barrenness of the theological studies available to them, they did not choose to enter the ministry.

The secularization of Christian education, the European War, and the cultural revolution known as the May 4th Movement in 1919 left the mission schools in China with reduced foreign faculties and reduced financial support, but, even more lamentably, without a set of clearly defined goals or well-formulated policies. To be fair, Chinese education as a whole was in the same state of confusion. The fact that Chinese schools and universities were Chinese-run, Chinese-financed and Chinese-taught spared them many of the searching questions levelled at mission education. Both the Burton Commission of 1921 and the Laymen's Inquiry into Missionary Education of 1931 were highly critical. 'Why prepare students for Harvard and heaven rather than for China?' What these inquiries did not ask was what were the needs of China and how could they be met? It may have been true that the general standard of instruction on Chinese subjects at Christian schools and universities left much to be desired and after the May 4th Movement their contents appeared to be old-fashioned.* This may have been due to a deficiency in intellectual leadership on the part of Christian educators. But a pertinent question remained unanswered: what was the generally accepted standard of instruction?

Like the issue of church autonomy, the issue of educational autonomy in the 1920s, an offshoot of the surging nationalism in China, had little theoretical significance. Rather it was an outburst of pent-up grievances against foreigners' control of Chinese schools and universities, the compulsory religious courses, and, perhaps most

---

* I remember submitting a school essay in 1938 in which the term 'May 4th [Movement]' was used. My Christian Chinese teacher commented in the margin: 'There is no such term!'

important of all, the socialization of Chinese youth in a life-style, manners and values which were neither purely Chinese nor purely Western. The result of all this was to create a political apathy and indifference that alienated the students at Christian universities from nationalist movements.

Still, to say that the students at Christian universities were unpatriotic is to oversimplify their feelings. A few examples should suffice to testify to this point. Students of the Canton Christian College joined their compatriots in boycotting American goods in 1905 in a protest against the American exclusion policy. During the anti-Christian education movement of the 1920s, students at the mission schools in Canton and Ch'angsha agitated against their own teachers. In the 1930s, Yenching University students played an active role in the anti-Japanese demonstrations such as that on 9 December 1935.

The great wave lashed against Christian education was stirred up by the convocation of the World Student Christian Federation in Peking, April 1922. Chinese educationists and anti-Christian organizations thought it was an affront to hold such a conference in China and protested indignantly. This first emotional reaction was to harden into the concrete proposals for educational autonomy put forward at the Conference of the National Association for the Advancement of Education held in Nanking, 1924. These included the total separation of education from religious propagation, the denial of the right to teach anyone who was not a Chinese citizen, and government registration and supervision of all schools and colleges, the underlying assumptions being that education should foster a sense of citizenship, strengthen national consciousness and develop Chinese cultural tradition. These proposals did not differ much from the memorandum presented by Chinese Christian students at the World Student Christian Federation meeting in 1922. In response to this, the Chinese Christian educationists issued a declaration explaining that Christian education, with its aim of character formation, was not contradictory to the nurturing of national consciousness or a concept of citizenship. The religious courses at mission schools were entirely voluntary.* However, if private individuals, be they foreign missionaries or Chinese Christians, were deprived of the right to educate the young, it would be a grievous infringement of personal freedom with detrimental consequences to educational

* The fact this change had to be made in 1929 belied the statement in the 1925 declaration that religious instruction was voluntary.

advancement. The declaration argued that all private schools, Christian as well as secular, should be registered and supervised by the government so that they could become a recognized part of the national educational system.

But there was the ticklish problem of which government was to register and supervise the schools. Riding on the crest of nationalism, both the warlords' government in Peking and the Kuomintang government in Canton claimed these rights. By 1929, when the political situation became more settled and there was a semblance of central authority in Nanking, Christian schools decided to register, and when they did so, religious subjects were made elective except for students of divinity and the Chinese staff gradually took over the administration of the schools.

Under attack, Christian education suffered a temporary decline – several colleges were closed and the number of mission schools fell from 11000 to only a half of the number during the period from 1922 to 1927. But in the 1930s when factional dissension dominated the politics of Nanking and the Chinese Communist Party was under relentless persecution, Christian education came into its own, while the churches directed their attention to China's rural reconstruction. But now the Christian student population had decreased from being the majority at any Christian university or college to somewhere between 20 and 30 per cent. Religious courses were poorly subscribed and sparsely attended – so were those on the Three Principles of the People.

## Medicine

Unlike education, medical work had always been looked upon as an integral part of the missionary enterprises, as Hudson Taylor put it: 'The foreign doctor was always *persona grata*, and if he must tell more or less about his religion – well, his medicines were so good that the preaching could be tolerated.' Ever since the founding of a clinic by Dr Livingstone and Dr Morrison in Macao in 1820 and of the Ophthalmic Infirmary by Dr P. Parker in Canton in 1835, missionary medical work had been in a limited sense a success. Parker, Colledge, Bridgman and Jardine helped organize the Medical Missionary Society in Canton inaugurated on 21 February 1938 and a few Chinese, such as Kwan Ato and Wong Fun, were given Western medical training. The pattern of the work – treatment and training –

was thus set from the very beginning, but there remained the problems of how to break down the resistance to Western medicine and how to expand the service for humanitarian and evangelical purposes.

The first generation of medical missionaries were little more knowledgeable than modern medical auxiliaries. European doctors had only just progressed beyond the stage of diagnosis by merely looking at the patient; the stethoscope was not invented until 1819. The initial use of the new instrument was no more advanced than the Chinese art based on feeling the pulse at the wrist. Morrison, Parker and Hudson Taylor were equipped with unsterilized surgical instruments, but had no ophthalmoscope (invented in 1852), hypodermic syringe (invented in 1845), or clinical thermometer (invented in the 1860s). Even in the surgical operations about which they boasted so much they were unaware of the existence of 'germs' (a term which then meant 'life' itself) for Pasteur and Koch did not develop their theories till the 1860s and 1870s; hence there was no conception of antisepsis and no efficient way of dealing with the formation of pus in the hot climate of south China. Their pre-Listerian operations were also excruciatingly painful as nitrous oxide, ether and chloroform did not come into use until the end of the 1840s.

Surgery, restricted by Confucian filial piety which forbade one to submit one's body voluntarily to be hurt, was the least developed branch of the Chinese medical art. There, the Western physicians found little competition. Even Commissioner Lin, in charge of the stamping out of the opium trade in Canton, was prepared to ask for Dr Parker to treat him for a hernia. After the Anglo–French Expedition, which opened up the interior of China to the missionaries, the use of anaesthesia, though it greatly eased the suffering of the patient, gave rise to rumours that Christian doctors had magic powers of bewitching people, thus reviving dreadful memories of practices once attributed to foreigners and contributing to the causes of anti-foreign riots.

In the 1870s and 1880s the medical profession in China was not a gentleman's pursuit. As Chinese physicians seldom wrote, their observation of Western medical practice is not known to historians. What are known are the views of the gentlemen who did write about their experiences as patients. Ch'ien Teh-p'ei, the diplomatic traveller, was puzzled by the fact that a Western doctor only timed his pulse:

Apart from timing the pulse, he knows nothing else of it. His prescription deals only with one ailment, taking cognizance of nothing else. Even when treating a fever, he does not inquire whether the illness comes from external or internal causes, from 'substantive' or 'insubstantive' (*shih* or *hsü*) causes. His is indeed a piecemeal sort of medicine.

Although a 'minor art', the spread of Western medical facilities caused 'major concern', as the *Shen-pao* editorial of 1 November 1881 pronounced, going on to say:

Our view is that the Chinese and Western medical arts are different. Chinese physicians use plants and herbs whereas Western physicians use minerals and metals. The latter are strong drugs which the Westerners, who eat strong meat like beef and mutton to strengthen their bodies, can take without harmful effects. The Chinese, however, may not be able to withstand such potent substance because of their weak physique, nourished on a daily diet of cereals which enfeeble their stomach and intestines. It is therefore inadvisable to apply Western medicine to the Chinese.

Since it was impossible for the Chinese to fathom the mystery of Western medicine, the editorial argued, it might not be foolish for a Chinese to see a foreign doctor, but he would certainly be unwise to consult a Western-style Chinese physician. It might not be foolish for him to see a foreign doctor for skin and external diseases; he would be stupid to do so for internal sickness.

Such a climate of opinion could be changed only by convincing the leaders of the empire of the efficacy of Western medicine. The editorial quoted above was a sign of change. The same newspaper reported on 30 August 1879 that Li Hung-chang's wife had been cured by a Western physician after seventeen Chinese doctors had thrown up their hands in despair. In spite of the *Shen-pao*'s expressed concern, Li Hung-chang made a donation, as did Dr J. F. Goucher, to assist Dr Leonora Howard in founding the Isabella Fisher Hospital for Women in Tientsin. To be sure, Marquis Tseng frequently consulted Western doctors. Hsüeh Fu-ch'eng, a successor to the Marquis at the Court of St James in the early 1890s, wrote in his diary that the strength of Western medical science lay in its positivist approach (*shih-shih ch'iu shih*), the result of which was that seven or eight cases of external illness out of every ten were successfully treated. But with regard to internal ailments, it was, according to Hsüeh, more successful in 'substantive' than 'insubstantive' cases, for its medication had only a 'warming' (*wen*) effect and lacked the subtle power of 'cooling', 'concentrating', 'diffusing', 'elevating', 'lowering', 'repairing', and 'loosening' (*han, liang, lien, san, sheng, chiang, pu,* and *hsieh*). What was material was his lamentation over the loss of much of the implied subtlety of Chinese medicine through an imperfect system for disseminating medical knowledge. About the same time the Chinese Minister to Washington, Chang Yin-huan, was indelibly impressed by an army hospital he had visited and American dentistry he had experienced. His dignity as an educated Chinese did not allow him to record these impressions without a note of comment. He criticized American dentists for being less subtle in killing tooth-ache than the Chinese and for being oblivious of the protective function of dirt on the tooth!

This mildly critical attitude could no longer be maintained after two major wars in the East. Chinese doctors, weak in surgical work, were virtually useless in treating the wounded soldiers who arrived at Chefoo in the 1895 war against Japan; they were treated by the missionary doctors there. And taking advantage of the Russo–Japanese War, American physicians and nurses organized the first Red Cross in Canton and sent 600 Chinese to Manchuria to help the Japanese. By January 1906, even the Dowager Empress was resorting to Western medicine when she was ill. The superiority of Western medicine, after its rapid progress in the second half of the nineteenth century, was by now firmly established. The death of President Yuan Shih-k'ai in 1916 was blamed on the use of Chinese medication; so was the death of General Hsiao Yao-nan in 1926. The debate between Chinese and Western medicine in July and August 1934 marked the nadir of the reputation of the former. But in humiliation and under suspicion Chinese medicine survived the challenge.

It could not disappear entirely because of the simple fact that China had an immense sick population which it was beyond a handful of Western-style doctors to treat. Even when its reputation was highest, the Western-style medical service consisted of only 392 hospitals together with perhaps one or two hundred more dispensaries. There were no more than 5 000 Western-style doctors for 450 million people. Had he been the only physician available, each Western-style doctor would have had to look after some 100 000 people. To make the situation worse, most of these doctors lived in the cities, leaving the vast countryside almost entirely to Chinese physicians. In 1933 it was estimated that there were still 1 200 000 practising Chinese doctors, who were to survive the Japanese War and the civil war into the communist era when their value was properly re-assessed, a marriage of the two bodies of medical knowledge was arranged, and this mixed marriage for the first time gave rural China the benefit of modern medicine.

The success of the missions' pioneer role in introducing modern medicine to China can be shown by the fact that in 1934 there were two missionary hospitals to each Chinese hospital. The situation was the same in medical education. In that same year, China had only twenty-six medical colleges, including two army ones, of which fourteen were missionary-run. The famous seats of medical learning – the Peking Union Medical College whose establishment was financed by the Rockefeller Foundation in 1915–16, the Medical and Dental Schools of the West China Union University in Chengtu, founded with Canadian missionary funds in 1914, the Yale-in-China Medical College set up in Ch'angsha in 1907, etc. – were all administered by foreigners and all had foreign teaching staff. But the salient fact to be mentioned here is that only 315 doctors graduated from the Peking Union Medical College in the period from 1924 to 1950.

W. H. Dobson thought the medical missionary was an 'icebreaker' from the point of view of the Church, as the doctor could preach to his patients while treating them. But working 297 to 303 days a year, the medical missionaries had neither time nor energy to spend in proselytization, even if they were interested in it. The treatment of a patient did not often lead to conversion, though in China medicine and the Bible frequently went hand in hand. The missions' medical enterprise must then be assessed in secular terms and measured against China's health needs. In that sense, S. M. Gunn of the Rockefeller Foundation was justifiably sceptical while Pearl Buck was more outspoken:

I used to fight it [professionalism] in China against the American doctors and the Western-trained Chinese doctors. While millions of people died of preventable disease and millions more went blind from trachoma, the doctors went on with their high professional standards. That is, anyone who practiced medicine must be a graduate physician. But there were few who could be graduates, it was too expensive and there were too few medical schools.

## Social work

Christian social work in China was not systematically done until the arrival of D. Willard Lyon and Fletcher Brockman in 1895, half a century after the YMCA's foundation in London. This doctrinally liberal organization was to develop rapidly into the group doing the most comprehensive social work, transforming Christianity into a truly social religion, as John Dewey observed. Take the YMCA in Shanghai for instance. Its regular work embraced famine relief, mass education, organized sports, opium prohibition, and youth and labour welfare, in addition to providing a venue where Chinese and foreign businessmen could meet. Geographically, the YMCA was urban-based; socially, it was much more successful among the elite than among the workers. Therefore its sponsors and supporters included many famous names, prominent educators and leading diplomats. In fact, its first Chinese general-secretary, C. T. Wang, was to become Chinese Minister for Foreign Affairs more than once. With the Christian convert Chiang Kai-shek at the helm of power, the KMT and the YMCA forged strong ties.

The YMCA's student work and its leading role in promoting organized sports (again for the students) were particularly pronounced successes. The first soccer match in Tientsin, 1904, was between the YMCA and Western soldiers. By the 1920s, soccer had become a popular sport among the Chinese. Without the assistance of the YMCA, especially that of Dr Exner, it was doubtful whether the first Chinese National Games of 1910 could ever have been staged. Thereafter the physical appearance of Chinese campuses changed with the addition of sports grounds, signifying a changed attitude.

Through their social work the YMCA spread to thirty-six cities, having a total membership of 54000. In its educational work the YMCA stressed moral, physical and intellectual discipline and a sense of community; in social work, its principle of service to mankind had a lasting influence. In the final analysis the YMCA was a gradualist, formalist organization based on voluntary co-operation rather than revolutionary coercion. Consequently its welfare work among the workers produced few results. In this respect, as in others, it worked through and with authority as if it did not know that it was authority itself that was the stumbling block for the YMCA's demands for labour legislation.

Up to 1922, nearly a whole century after the first Protestant missionary had set his foot on Chinese soil, 66 per cent of the missionaries and 34 per cent of Chinese Christian workers chose to live and work in the cities where only 6 per cent of the Chinese lived. These mission workers usually had a contemptuous and critical attitude towards their brethren in rural China. Two factors* shifted the attention of the churches to China's agrarian problems. First at the invitation of the Institute of Pacific Relations Professor R. H. Tawney, the well-known economic historian and social critic, undertook a trip to China in 1930, the outcome of which was his book, *Land and Labour in China*, published in 1932. The second, much more powerful, factor was the communist challenge in Kiangsi and Fukien. Social Gospellers like Kenyon Butterfield, George Shepherd and Hugh Hubbard began to evolve their plans for saving China from the Red atheists.† They turned their eyes to James Yen's work in Tinghsien, Hopei, where Yen's mass education movement had been going forward since 1926.

Armed with a simple, 1000-character scheme for teaching the illiterate to read, and with great personal charm,‡ Yen volunteered through the YMCA to educate the Chinese trench-diggers and porters on the Western front in the First World War. A proven success, he then transferred his work to Hengshan in Hunan after the war, only to have his mass education work stopped by the civil war of 1922. Then, at the invitation of the leading citizens of Tinghsien, he took his Mass Education Association thither in 1926, at a time when the churches were disoriented by militant nationalism and an internal intellectual crisis. To the clergy, Yen's endeavours in Tinghsien seemed a godsend, 'a gleam of hope', 'a true Christian communion'. In a conversation with Fletcher Brockman Yen defined his aim as the creation of a truly democratic China and Brockman remarked: 'If China is to be made a Christian nation, there must be

---

* I am not sure how much Pearl Buck's *Good Earth* also changed the missions' attention to China's peasants. Her picture of an unchanging or satisfied peasant went against the rural programmes being conceived by the churches. Also her criticism of the missionaries must have been known to the churches. Both would militate the clergy against her.

† Revivalists too reacted to the Red challenge with emotional orgies, trances, faith healing and attacks on education in preparation for the Second Coming and the Last Judgement (Paul Varg, *Missionaries, Chinese and Diplomats*, New Jersey, 1958, pp. 229–30).

‡ I met Yen a few times in the 1930s when he and a couple of his colleagues, including my brother, were invited to Szechuan by the provincial government.

a great deal of work similar to what Yen and his colleagues are doing at Ting Hsien.' The travelling evangelist Sherwood Eddy acclaimed Yen as 'an outstanding Chinese leader'. In the space of less than five years at least twenty similar rural reconstruction projects sprang up all over China among which the better known were Hugh Hubbard's at Fanchuang near Paoting, Hopei, the Nanking University's at Shunhuachen on the outskirts of Nanking, and Liang Shu-ming's at Tsoup'ing, Shantung.*

The mushrooming of such projects aroused the interest of the Rockefeller Foundation and at S. M. Gunn's recommendation the Foundation decided to regard rural reconstruction as its central task in China from 1934 to 1942. Gunn's recommendation itself was disappointing. It criticized the Western-trained students on the one hand but advocated sending them to lead the rural project on the other, while leaving the Japanese threat to north China and the question of land ownership out of consideration. The Foundation none the less allocated $1·9 million for this task. With money, personnel and the encouragement of Chiang Kai-shek's government,† the projects were under way.

The Shunhuachen project is a good example. The churches appointed Dr Frank Price, assisted by a Chinese pastor, Chu Ching-yi, to direct its religious programme while the government appointed Professor Mei Ssu-p'ing of the Central College of Political Science as magistrate of Chiangning county. Apart from technological improvement in agricultural production, the churches, the university, banks, government and foreigners worked together for the spiritual elevation, moral uplifting, social welfare and public hygiene of the town. The values and norms these enthusiasts wanted to impose on the peasants were decidedly urban and to a large extent Western. They organized harvest festivals, sports, public lectures, and religious services. They taught the peasants to bathe regularly, use separate basins for washing themselves, open windows, whitewash walls, and eat high-protein food. Under their guidance more wells were sunk. They lost a great deal of 'face', perhaps to the amusement of many old peasants who knew the country, for there was no water. Then the professors, doctors, and other experts invited even greater experts

* A famed philosopher, Liang had nothing to do with the Church. He was in fact fighting on two fronts, against alien ideologies of Christianity and communism.

† Chiang even appointed a Christian rural worker, Chang Fu-liang, as the director of the Government Rehabilitation Programme in Kiangsi after the Red Army had gone on the Long March.

to come and give wiser advice to the Marxian 'sacks of potatoes'. The new advice was to use the mountain spring water – a project which would cost about $10000, a sum which the peasants did not possess. Even the chronicler of the Shunhuachen project, Pastor Chu, had to admit that by 1937, when the project came to an end with the outbreak of the Japanese War, little had been achieved.

The failure of the Church's rural reconstruction movement can be ascribed to two major factors. Working under the existing social order, the Church and their co-workers saw no need for a drastic change in the tenure system, thus ignoring the basic agrarian problem of China. This, however, is not to say that some of them were not aware of it. The Anglican Bishop Ronald O. Hall called the system 'un-Christian', because it was plainly exploitative and even George Shepherd, who co-operated with Chiang Kai-shek, suggested that the absentee landlords should be bought out by farmers' co-operatives. But a powerful government leader like Dr H. H. Kung, a Christian himself, insisted during his conversation with the American ambassador, Nelson Johnson, that the gentry was 'the pillar of moral stability' in China. The rural reconstruction movement in China in the 1930s was basically the same as the Green Revolution in the Third World in the 1960s. It was a technological change without accompanying social and political reform or revolution. The other factor was that it was reform on behalf of the peasants, not with them. Any such reform programme was bound to find that the urban input of money and expertise fell far short of the need and was truly a drop in the ocean. The well-trained urban experts in rural reconstruction work often adopted a similar attitude to that of a girl student from the London School of Economics working in the co-operative movement in north-west China. She showed Graham Peck, an American writer, her beautifully printed plans in Chinese and English, but had achieved nothing in reality. When she was questioned as to why she had failed, she shrugged her shoulders and blamed everything on the ignorance and passivity of the peasants. The thought of arousing the peasants to help themselves and to develop their own ingenuity and intelligence never occurred to her and her kind.

## The anti-Christian movement and anti-imperialism

Although they were politically cautious, the missionaries' ways of dealing with Chinese officials and their own affairs helped expose the corruption and ineptitude of the Chinese civil service. By implication they awakened a desire for reform and revolution. In the 1890s Timothy Richard and Young J. Allen actively promoted political reform, like Robert Hart and Thomas Wade before, and Bishop James Bashford after, them. But from the missionary perspective, in order to change herself either by reform or by revolution, China needed Christian guidance, as George L. Davis stated in a letter to H. C. Stuntz on 14 December 1911 when China was still in the throes of the revolution:

The truth is that nothing will save China, but a radical change of the heart. The revolutionary leaders are just as corrupt as the leaders of the old school, and unless China is Christianized it will mean a new set of theories, instead of the experienced [existing?] ones.

Politically Christianity could serve China's cherished goals of national power and wealth; it could also keep her as a peaceful member of the international order designed by the West. With the China Inland Mission as the only dissenters, the majority of the missionaries sympathized with her nationalist aspirations even when they took on a violent form and manifested themselves in such ways as in 1925–6. That this sympathy was seldom understood and that most missionaries were regarded as imperialist spies was due to China's having accepted them under duress from foreign gunboats and also to a lack of communication between them and the Chinese.

In opening China to God and trade (initially to opium), the churches and Western imperialism shared a common goal. That was why John Robert Morrison, James's son, and his Christian colleagues in China urged England to fight; that was why Charles Gutzlaff's 'heart throbs with mighty joy' when China was opened by British guns; why Peter Parker wanted the USA to join forces with Britain and France in the Arrow War of 1856; why S. Wells Williams insisted on the inclusion of the article on religious toleration in the Sino–American Tientsin Treaty of 1858; why the missionaries welcomed the Chefoo Convention of 1876 which gave a greater measure of safety in the interior of China; why some missionaries thought the Sino–Japanese

War of 1894 was an Act of Providence and why Gilbert Reid felt able to justify the 'ethics of loot' after the Boxer War of 1900. Each imperialist blow was interpreted as a blow to the empire of Satan, of the dark forces, whose destruction would hasten the arrival of the Christian era.

Imperialism needed moral justification and the missionaries provided it. Imperialism also needed well-informed people who could help in wars of aggression and in the conduct of trade. In both, the missionaries gave their services and this service was acknowledged, in the words of Theodore Roosevelt, '. . . because their work helped to avert revolutionary disturbances in China and to lead her into a position for peace and righteousness' and by an American Minister to China, Charles Denby:

For nearly a century the missionary men and women have labored to carry our prestige, our language, and our commerce into China. . . . If we turn them adrift, our national fame will be dimmed. It cannot be doubted that by their disappearance our commerce would greatly suffer, and our diplomacy would lose its chief support.

The list of the members of the Laymen's Missionary Movement of the USA in 1906 reads like that of the China Association of London. Little wonder then that it was said: 'Every missionary is a salesman for the manufactures of Christendom.' Though protected by the gunboats and extraterritoriality of their countries and financed by big businessmen, the missionaries had none the less to grapple with moral, psychological and social problems and to win the respect of their Chinese colleagues and students. By their daily contacts with Chinese Christians and students, they were the first to feel the strength of Chinese nationalism and its demands for church autonomy and the abrogation of the unequal treaties, just as they were the first to realize the challenge of Chinese communism. From 1920 onward they voluntarily asked their own governments, especially the American government, to withdraw the privileges they had so long enjoyed.

In judging whether the missionaries were the willing tools of imperialism a distinction must be made between those who worked in China before 1914 and those who came to work there afterwards. The European War had destroyed the status quo and swung Chinese nationalism away from its mood of Darwinian introspection into one of Leninist anti-imperialism. No longer blaming all her weaknesses on herself, China now wanted to drive out the weakening agents of imperialism. Unwilling to be kicked out and yet uncomfortable about clinging to their superior position, the missionaries adapted themselves to the new mood and new circumstances in order to keep their foothold in China and carry on their work. To go back to imperialist domination again was impossible; to go forward to communism was undesirable. Through emancipation reached by way of Christianity, she was destined to take her place among the great nations of the world. It was thus imperative, in the view of the missionaries of the 1920s, that she be treated as an equal immediately.

The propagation of the Gospel had provoked many anti-Christian riots in many of which, it was true, xenophobia and anti-Christianity were inseparably mixed. Still, it may be safe to say that before 1860 there had been instances only of xenophobic outbursts. Had there already been anti-Christian feeling among the masses there would have never been the Taiping Rebellion which, after all, was inspired by a nativized form of Christianity. After the Peking Treaties of 1860 when the interior of China was opened to missionary work, local inhabitants, sometimes acting in a spontaneous fashion and sometimes in an organized way, began to attack missionaries and damage their property. The era of 'religious incidents' (*chiao-an*) was therefore at hand. These incidents were to culminate in the Boxer Movement in the last years of the nineteenth century. Between then and the time of the First World War, they gradually subsided, to be replaced by the rationalized anti-Christian movement of the educated elite.

Different classes naturally reacted differently to the presence of the missionaries. The common people in small market towns (not in the villages, for neither the government nor the churches had enough manpower to penetrate so far) projected their various religious beliefs and practices, largely superstitious, on to the followers of the new religion of whom and their dogmas they had but scanty knowledge. The Catholic anxiety to give Absolution to dying children aroused the suspicion that priests and nuns took young virgins into their churches, and had their genitals and eyes hacked out for the manufacture of aphrodisiacs and elixirs for longevity. When men and women gathered in the same church hall behind closed doors and began to sing merrily, there arose the rumour that they bathed (baptized) naked and indulged in orgies. The strong physique of the priests served only to confirm these suspicions. The presence of missionaries could offend local gods with dire consequences such as drought, flood, or epidemic. The building of the missionary's church might have disturbed the geomantic equilibrium of a place, bringing misfortune on all the inhabitants. Folk superstition of this kind persisted into the twentieth century, causing, for instance, an anti-Christian riot in Chaot'ung, Yunnan, in 1910.

More serious in the scale of its effects was the direct confrontation of the churches with folk religions themselves. Idolatry was attacked head on by the missionaries; the rituals of folk religions and their claims to magic powers were ridiculed. In retaliation, the organized religious sects and secret societies, led by articulate men of organizational ability and experience, agitated against the local church and its converts, who, after conversion, adopted an unco-operative and sometimes haughty attitude towards their fellow townsmen. Many 'religious incidents' were caused by such organized agitation, of which the Boxer Uprising is the best known.

Soldiers did not like the missionaries either, for many of them during the suppression of the Taiping Rebellion joined secret societies in order to secure their livelihood after demobilization. They, too, were agitators against the churches, especially along the Yangtze Valley. In 1861-3 militia units were organized in Kweichow for the pacification of the Miao tribal uprisings. These militia groups were utilized by the anti-Christian commander of the armed forces in that province to attack Catholic missionaries. Even as late as 1929, H. Gabb, an American missionary in Changteh, Honan, was stripped, tied up, dragged through the mud, and stabbed by soldiers.

The gentry, who dominated rural China, feared the churches' challenge to their social, economic and cultural supremacy. Christian charity work and Christian education threatened the gentry's traditional roles; Christian justice clashed headlong with the gentry's manipulation of the law. Institutionally, they had clan associations, country schools and militia units under their control and all of these could be militated against the Church. The worship of gods and spirits was defended for it was the only strong bulwark against immorality. The gentry also gave expression to the grievances of the religious sects by issuing a great many broadsheets and pamphlets attacking the evil, immoral and heretical practices of the missionaries. Under parental influence, the children of the gentry staged demonstrations and riots against Christianity when they gathered for prefectural or provincial examinations.

At a higher intellectual level, the gentry could also challenge the Church on ideological and theological grounds. Christian equality was repudiated, because it might reduce the Confucian familial and societal hierarchies to anarchy or at best disorder. Thus, they questioned the myth of the Virgin Birth which by implication would undermine patriarchal authority. Upon close examination, the Bible contained not a single piece of evidence to prove that Jesus was filial to his parents. This was interpreted as a threat to the Confucian family system. Other dogmas were also questionable. Since Christ did not know of the presence of a traitor among his disciples, how could he be relied upon as a man of wise judgement? Since he failed to protect even himself, how could he be expected to protect anyone else? Truth needed no proselytization and it could not possibly give rise to so many different interpretations and so many schismatic divisions. Worse still, the Christian factions even instigated wars among themselves. If kings could be humbled by the Pope, what was the meaning of loyalty to one's monarch? If faith alone was enough to secure a place in heaven, what safeguard was there to prevent the treacherous from devoting all his life to vice and yet being redeemed before breathing his last by confessing the faith?

The 'religious incident' caught the Chinese central and local governments on the horns of the most agonizing dilemma. They did not dare to alienate the people whose support they needed, however despotic they might be; nor did they dare to offend the Western powers, armed with treaty rights and gunboats to protect their missionaries. The normal *modus vivendi* was the payment of indemnities for the damages done; the punishment of culprits; apologies to the offended countries; and demotion of the officials responsible. This was called 'the co-operative policy' by some historians and 'the sycophantic policy' by others. When humiliation of this kind became intolerable and the anger of the people uncontainable, the government was capable of swinging to the side of the people to fight for the honour and integrity of the country. Such a war was the Boxer War of 1900, the sobering effect of which ensured that it was the only war of the kind China ever fought. She had to pay even heavier indemnity than previously, punish even more distinguished officials, and apologize to even more countries.*

* For the Boxer Movement and the war, see Victor Purcell, *The Boxer Uprising, a Background Study* (Cambridge University Press, 1961) and Chester Tan, *The Boxer Catastrophe* (Columbia University Press, 1955). The details of that episode, like those of the Taiping Rebellion, are well known and are therefore omitted here.

Like the quarter of a century after the Anglo–French Expedition, the twenty years after the Boxer War saw Sino–Western relations flow smoothly till the sudden eruption of anti-imperialism in 1919. In the wake of this came the Anti-Religious League formed in 1920, the Students' Anti-Christian Movement in 1922, and the Anti-Christian League in 1924, which heralded the nation-wide strikes against Britain and Japan, the May 30th Movement in 1925. Whereas the anti-Christian and xenophobic riots began among the common people, the anti-Christian and anti-imperialist movement of the 1920s was led by the intellectuals and later spread to the merchants and urban proletariat. Its vibrations were to be felt during the Northern Expedition of 1926–8 on such occasions as the suspension of the teaching and medical work at Yale-in-China in Ch'angsha, the rendition of the British concessions in Hankow and Kiukiang, and the killing of an eminent missionary and attack on other foreigners and their property in Nanking early in 1927. That, however, was already the Indian summer of urban anti-imperialism.

The Young China Study Society, whose leading members were mostly under the influence of the agnostics of post-war France, championed the Anti-Christian Movement. In their view, the conservatism and blind faith of all religions hindered intellectual growth; their superstition slowed down scientific advancement; their prayers and reliance on supernatural forces impaired the free development of youthful potentials; their sectarianism disrupted co-operation and harmony among men; their stoicism and disregard of the physical body perverted the growth of personality. If this reasoning lacked originality, its social arguments were a reflection of the *élan* among the Chinese intellectual community at the time. The society objected to the Church's dependence on the unjust capitalist social order and its role as the forerunners of imperialist aggression. Missionaries and converts also cajoled Chinese officials into working for their interests. Through mission work and education they fostered a sycophantic attitude towards the foreigner. As most members of the Society were educators, they naturally criticized the way mission schools were run, which was described as old-fashioned, despotic and unpatriotic. These views were, to a large extent, also those expressed in the manifesto of the anti-Christian students meeting in Shanghai, on 9 March 1922, on the eve of the conference of the World Student Christian Federation. The leftists of the Kuomintang and the handful of Marxists, too, sympathized with them. From the ranks of the KMT came Chu

Chih-hsin who, in his article, 'What was Jesus?', called Christ an illegitimate son, dishonest, narrow-minded, self-important and short-tempered. Another KMT leftist, Tan Leang-li, forthrightly pointed out that, arriving with opium, the missionaries caused China to lose her independence and the West to misunderstand her civilization.

Among the early Marxists, Ch'en Tu-hsiu had at one time admired Jesus (as a social reformer) and Christianity (as a religion of love) while cherishing a fierce hatred of the manners, behaviour, and style of life of the missionaries. But he criticized the churches' support for the First World War and for the policy of colonization. The Church's motto, according to him, was: 'I give you the Bible; you concede your rights.' His conversion to Marxism led him to accept the thesis that all religions were the opiate of the people, while in a semi-colonial country like China Christianity was used as a tool of imperialist aggression. Ch'en's younger comrade, Ts'ai Ho-sen, went further in his *Chin-tai ti Chi-tu-chiao* (Modern Christianity), in 1925, maintaining that, without Christianity, it would not be possible to justify the fact that the bourgeoisie – a class of people who used neither their hands nor their brains – could enjoy such comfort and fortune, nor would it be possible to explain why there should be regular economic crises. The Christian religion was essentially irrational in spite of its followers' efforts at rationalization.

Whereas the consensus of the radicals was to regard Christianity as a hindrance to China's modernization, Liang Ch'i-ch'ao, ageing but still highly respected, took religion to mean only faith which was a personal and emotional thing, quite unnecessary to be put under rational scrutiny. Thus ignoring the social and political aspects of religion, Liang held strong reservations about the anti-religious movement but did not explain his own views in a coherent and clear-cut manner. Liang Shu-ming, philosopher and rural reconstruction-ist, gave a series of lectures on the anti-religious movement, stressing the transcendental and emotional needs of man which could be satis-fied only by a religion. Social movements could never obliterate such needs. The pragmatist Hu Shih saw little use of the theory of the immortality of the soul. It would be much better if it was replaced by the Chinese theory of three immortalities – immortal words, immortal deeds and immortal ethical standards. Hu invented the term 'social immortality' which meant that 'The individuals die, but their community never dies.' Moral sanction could be based on the individual's responsibility to his community, thus rendering all religious sanctions superfluous. Wang Hsing-kung and Ts'ai Yuan-p'ei, both agnostic positivists, conceded two useful functions to religion – promoting progress and alleviating human misery. But the former could now be performed by education and the latter by aesthetics. All these and the other liberal moderates too accepted the common hypothesis that religious freedom had to be defended in order to preserve whatever freedom there was in China and to remould her into a democracy. They regarded Christianity as helpful in a limited sense or replaceable by other systems of thought, but did not see any possible justification for its suppression either by a despotic government or by mob violence. In their view religion was made by man for man's needs; it should not be treated differently from other intellectual activities such as art, literature and philosophy. The tendency of their arguments to relegate the churches to a secondary position in China's nation-building and cultural development merely reflected a *fait accompli*.

The Christians were naturally not prepared to accept these views. The social-gospellers counter-attacked by pointing out the radicals' utter ignorance of Christianity and by underlining the immense contribution the Church had made to social welfare, medicine and education. What the social-gospellers urged was that Christians should go to the grass roots and aid the underprivileged so as to create a just and virtuous society. The Christian theologians, on the other hand, stressed that neither science nor philosophy based on empirical knowledge and rational analysis had any hope of superseding revelational religions like Christianity. The suggestion of substituting aesthetics for religion was so elitist as to mean nothing to the masses. In their view, personal faith in God and Christ, far from being superstitious, would in no way contradict science and its advancement. At the Shanghai conference of the Protestant missions in 1922, Timothy Lew denied that the churches had any connection with imperialism. Acts of aggression had been committed by the so-called Christian governments over which the churches had no control and of course the churches could not be called upon to shoulder responsibility for them. The missions, on the contrary, had always preached love and peace among men. They were a force for international friendship rather than international hostility.

In a welter of criticism and refutation, the churches examined their conscience. The leading American religious journal, *Christian Century*, laid down the guideline in its issue on 18 June 1925:

Certainly if there is any hesitation to make the break clean between the commercial and political aims of the West and the aims of our religious enterprise, there is no chance to win back the confidence of the already suspicious Chinese.

Within the missions themselves, the 'break away' meant a process of development towards Church autonomy so as to refurbish the tarnished image of the Chinese churches as lorded over by foreigners. In this process, theologians engaged themselves in sinocizing both doctrine and ceremonies to suit the Chinese milieu; moderate Christians gave their support to the KMT government and its political principles; and radicals criticized racial prejudice in the churches and labelled such missionaries as John R. Mott and Sherwood Eddy 'agents of imperialism'. In all three respects, social work, sinocization of the doctrine and the creation of a new image, little was achieved. The churches wanted all the credit for the splendour of Western civilization and yet declined responsibility for all the unjustifiable things the West had done to China and other countries. The churches' claim to be associated with the former while denying any part in the latter was not a tenable one, especially now that China was in a militant nationalist mood.

The anti-Christian and anti-imperialist movement during the Northern Expedition reached its height in the early months of 1927 when communist-led mobs overran the British Concessions in Hankow and Kiukiang. Then Britain, the USA and Japan struck back in retaliation for the Nanking Incident in which a prominent missionary had been killed, other foreigners in the city molested, and foreign property damaged by the expeditionary armies. Chiang Kai-shek reacted in the same pattern set in the 1860s – indemnity, making apologies and punishing the officers and men responsible. In conjunction with Chiang's persecution of the communists, the mood of the nation suddenly changed. The anti-Christian movement fizzled out and the missionary enterprise in China was thus reprieved for the next twenty years.

On the eve of the communist victory the number of Christians in China was slightly larger than the total membership of the CCP – 2.7 millions; yet their relative power positions were vastly different, in spite of the fact that the churches wielded greater influence than the communists in social, medical and educational work. After only twenty-nine years of existence the CCP had successfully challenged the churches and all the political and social forces supporting them and the missionaries had to leave the country which they and their predecessors had worked for almost one and a half centuries to Christianize. Some native Christians survived the revolutionary change, only to find their spiritual and social influence steadily diminishing, like that of the followers of other religions in China, to a point of utter insignificance. The great enterprise, which had cost so many lives and so much money, and had lasted so long, ended in nothing.

## Conclusion

If one seeks to appraise the missions' work in terms of conversion it was undeniably a failure. Quantitatively speaking, the Catholic Church had done better than the Protestants, but then what was the quality of Catholic conversion? The Protestants sought true spiritual revelation and moral reform. In the words of Hudson Taylor, 'There must be heart-contact with the Chinese and personal contact too, if our lives are to be invested to the utmost profit.' This individualist approach meant that it took the Methodists and the Anglicans ten years to receive their first convert. Although later the rate increased, Bishop Bashford estimated in 1907 that assuming, as did the Student Volunteer Movement, that China was to be Christianized in one generation and assuming that one missionary could guide a flock of 25000 Chinese into the fold, the Church in China would need 16000 foreign evangelists. But then there were only 4000, each of which had to cover an area of two or three counties, sometimes as large as five and a half counties. This made his position even less enviable than that of a county magistrate who was expected to govern, on the average, 250000 people. This perennial problem of insufficient human resources was never solved and it was a great obstacle facing the missions.

Language, too, was a real barrier. Donald MacGillivray of the United Church of Canada was said to have learnt the whole Gospel according to St John – 12000 Chinese characters – in a month. Even if one could believe that any man was able to learn 400 new words a day, this achievement would truly have been a miracle. Nearly all missionaries complained about the difficulties of learning the Chinese language. Some managed it, like Frank Price and James Endicott; most of them never did. The story of a missionary in Nanch'ang in 1911, who set out to buy a donkey, but found he had bought a pig instead, was recorded by J. R. Trindle. From this, one can imagine how much more difficult it was to make the Chinese understand such theories as that of Jesus sacrificing himself for the redemption of men. Disease also took its toll; many missionaries had their careers cut short by death.

When the churches redirected their work to the educated elite of China in the 1880s they confronted other, sophisticated ideologies. All educated Chinese in the nineteenth century were well versed in the Confucian classics and practised ancestor worship, which was a facet of Confucian filial piety. A host of problems arose here and nearly all of them were beyond the intellectual powers of the missionaries to overcome. Some advocated a form of compromise but were not able to formulate a theory on which the compromise could be based. Theologians like Wu Lei-ch'uan went no further than semantic comparison between Christianity and Confucianism in their efforts to draw these two great systems of thought closer. Nothing like the synthesis of Christian doctrine and Greek philosophy was achieved. The less patient wished for the removal of 'the incubus of Confucianism', to make room for Christianity, but did not know how this could be done. The conversion of the educated elite proved as difficult, in Fletcher Brockman's metaphor, as 'drilling a hole in a great monolith with a pin'. Where the theologians had failed, the Christian soldier Chiang Kai-shek hoped to succeed. His simultaneous Christianization and Confucianization of Christianity was, to follow Brockman's metaphor, like dropping a pin in the intellectual bedlam of the 1930s. Leading scholars and thinkers, including Ts'ai Yuan-p'ei, Hu Shih, Hsü Chih-mo, and Ch'en Tu-hsiu, were either searching for secular ways to meet men's religious needs or denying such needs altogether. Having failed to convert the best brains of China, as Bertrand Russell pointed out, and having failed to produce a powerful theologian from among the ranks of the clergy, Christianity had never managed to put even a toe in the mainstream of China's cultural life, except as a pioneer in secular education and in introducing Western secular knowledge.

Individual conversion being a lost cause, evangelists like A. L. Warnshuis and Sherwood Eddy resorted to collective conversion in the Billy Graham style. Eddy's tours in China in 1907 and 1913 harvested thousands of new converts. Normally such conversions lacked firmness. In the 1920s and 1930s voices of despair were heard. Frank Gamewell admitted: 'We cannot evangelize China, we cannot cure China's multiplying diseases, we cannot educate her multiplying millions or feed them.' A woman missionary, having spent her life in China, confessed the futility of her work and advised young Americans not to do what she had done. Others, like J. V. A. Mac-Murray, the US Minister to China, forecast the decline of missionary work in a nation whose intellectuals were hypercritical of the Christian religion. And Joseph F. Rock, a naturalist, asked Edgar Snow: 'What's the use of wasting money by sending soul savers here if they only add one kind of ignorance to another?'

Advised by the British and American, sometimes even by the French governments to refrain from close contact with the Chinese in order to avoid unnecessary disturbances and riots, the missionaries lived in their secluded compounds.* Few of them made true friends among the Chinese; fewer still treated the Chinese as their equals. In spite of advice against it, racial prejudice undeniably existed among the ambassadors of God. D. W. Lyon said at the Meeting of Commission on 9 February 1932: 'I don't know that I ever heard of a missionary who invited one of his Chinese co-workers to come to eat with him on a par.' Pearl Buck recalled: '. . . the small white clean Presbyterian American world of my parents and the big loving merry not-too-clean Chinese world, and there was no communication between them.' In the small clean world, life was comfortable and superior as if to sustain the image of a superior race. Even in church work, the missionaries tended to neglect spiritual leadership for office work, as the edifice of the missions grew in complexity. Through the decades, there were a few mixed marriages between missionaries and Chinese Christians – all ended in the ostracization of these married couples by both the 'small clean' and the 'large not-too-clean' worlds. There was no such friendship as that forged between, for example, Edgar Snow and Mme Sun Yat-sen and between Norman Bethune and his Chinese co-workers. The social chasm between the missionary and his Chinese colleagues was almost unbridgeable, as is shown by the case of a boy brought up in a family of three generations of Catholic converts who still called the local priest 'the foreign devil'.

Handicapped by their foreignness, their small numbers, the language barrier, their intellectual mediocrity, their racial prejudice, their sectarianism, and their growing bureaucratism, what little the

* The Catholic priests, being without family ties, moved more freely among their followers.

missionaries had succeeded in achieving collapsed like a house of cards in 1949. Perhaps the worst obstacle they faced was the assumption that they must carry out their task of Christian conversion within the existing social framework, which they could try to change only by changing the people living in it. Their observation of China's tragic and fearsome moral decay was correct; their assumption that the people could be changed without changing the social framework was wrong. Even in their secular work – famine relief, medicine and education to which they had made remarkable contributions' – they were constantly hampered and inhibited by that very social framework. Famine relief was troubled by the 'squeeze pidgin' (official embezzlement of funds). Their hospitals and medical education were damaged or disrupted by the armies of warlords and Chiang Kaishek. They were aware that all would be in vain unless China could be regenerated and a new China came forth, but in their occluded view they could only pray God to cleanse China by the blood of the blessed Saviour.

When the cleansing and regeneration did come, would the missionaries interpret it as being done by the blood of the Saviour? Why do the followers of the Saviour find no place in that regenerated country? The answer must be either that they were not truly the ambassadors of Christ or that the new China was not brought forth by the will of God.

# Chapter 3

# *Students and scholars*

## Overseas study programmes

It is obvious that the Language Institute in Peking could never train graduates of the calibre of Yung Wing* who was educated by Mrs Charles Gutzlaff and the Reverend S. R. Brown when he was a boy and then at Yale as one of the earliest Chinese students there. The need to send Chinese students to the fountainhead was seen by Viceroys Tseng Kuo-fan and Li Hung-chang in 1870 and at Yung's urging a programme for sending Chinese boys to school in the USA was formulated. In view of China's defence needs at that time, the selected boys were to study subjects closely related to the army and navy for a period of fifteen years from the age of twelve. Each year the government was to send a group of thirty boys under the supervision of two appointed officials, of whom Yung was one. Four such groups were planned.

The programme ran into its initial difficulty in 1872 when Yung Wing could not recruit the specified thirty students until he went south to Canton and Hong Kong, because the employment and career prospects for boys so trained and their living conditions in such a distant country were uncertain. Parents, especially those of substantial and educated families, were reluctant to let their boys go. This reluctance remained unbroken in the hinterland of China till the 1910s. As they were so young, the students needed to study the Chinese language and receive a classical education to foster a sense of

* About the same time as Yung there were other Chinese students being trained in the USA and Europe, e.g. Yen Hui-ch'ing's father, uncle, and others, whose studies abroad were sponsored by the Church. See Yen Hui-Ch'ing, *Tzu-Chuan* (Autobiography, Taipei, 1973 edn, p. 1).

propriety and deference to their own cultural tradition so that they would retain their identity while acquiring the useful skills American schools could offer them. But it was too much to expect boys at an impressionable age to understand this dichotomous scheme – Chinese scholarship as the essence with Western scholarship only for application – as they quickly took up American sports, manners and even dating habits, which, incidentally, gave the Americans in Hartford, Connecticut, a pleasant impression of the boys. Alarmed by the supervisors' reports of the Americanization of the boys, Li Hung-chang bought a house in Hartford in 1874 so as to have all the students and their supervisors under one roof and hired two teachers of Chinese classics to provide them with additional training. The boys disliked this new arrangement so much that they referred to the Hartford house as 'the hell house', and it did not put a stop to their Americanization. One Sunday, the supervisor, Wu Tzu-teng, saw a student returning from a church service accompanied by an American woman. In an indignant report to Li Hung-chang, Wu proposed the discontinuation of the whole programme. In response, a fact-finding envoy was sent and he discovered that some of the boys had even cut off their queues and donned American clothes. Their Americanization caused the *Shen-pao* of Shanghai to comment on 22 September 1881:

None of the first group of Chinese boys to study abroad has come from a respectable or wealthy family. . . . They are a motley collection of people with whom one can hardly talk about Western learning or army and naval affairs.

Opinion seemed to be against the continuation of the programme, which was thought to be a failure. Coincidentally, the USA announced its first Exclusion Act at this time and so the abandonment of the programme also appeared to be an act of protest against this. Of the 120 boys only five or six distinguished themselves in their later careers.* Only Chan T'ien-yu (Tien Yow Jeme) followed his training, becoming a well-known engineer.

Of the students sponsored by this programme, the first group in 1872 consisted of twenty-four from Kwangtung, one from Shantung, and the rest from the Yangtze delta; the second group in 1873, twenty-four from Kwangtung and the rest from the Yangtze delta;

* Among these few were Liang Teng-yen, Liang Ju-hao, T'ang Shao-yi, Ts'ai Shao-chi and Ts'ai T'ing-kan – all diplomats and statesmen.

the third group in 1874, seventeen from Kwangtung, one from Fukien, and the rest from the Yangtze delta; and the last group in 1875, nineteen from Kwangtung and the rest from the Yangtze delta. The end of the programme, the end of an era in itself, broke the Kwangtung domination in sending students to study abroad, although other students continued to sail to the USA, Japan, and Europe. Meanwhile the system of supervision went on into the 1920s and 1930s.

The dispatch of a group of boys by the Foochow Shipyard led by Prosper Giquel and Li Feng-pao in 1875 and that of army officers to Germany and naval cadets to England began the sponsorship of studying abroad by regional authorities. These regional programmes were carried into the 1880s. Between the French War of 1885 and the Japanese War of 1895 a general mood of relaxation and a distrust of the semi-Chinese and semi-foreign 'returned' students contributed to a loss of direction in sending students abroad on the part of central and regional authorities. But the war of 1895 and the reform of 1898 brought all the vital issues of the times, including studies abroad, into sharp focus. The Viceroy of Hupei and Hunan, Chang Chih-tung, in his widely known essay, *On Learning*, proposed the first clear-cut policy after a long period of confusion:

One year at a foreign school is better than five years' reading of Western books at home. . . . Three years at a foreign school is better than three years at a Chinese school. . . . As to receiving the benefit of studies abroad, a mature scholar is better than a boy, a man of noble birth is better than a commoner.

Chang's argument was reproduced almost verbatim in a memorial of the Tsungli Yamen in August 1899 which was enacted as law by an imperial edict soon afterwards. The goals of the new decision shifted from strengthening defence to enriching the country by emphasizing practically useful subjects like agriculture, industry, commerce and mining. Imperial clansmen were encouraged to travel abroad and 'returned' students were to be awarded the Chinese degrees of *chin-shih* or *chü-jen*, thus making them eligible for government appointments. This new policy was not implemented until after the Boxer War of 1900 when further urgings came from Chinese ministers abroad, exhorting members of the imperial clan to travel and study in foreign countries. This suggestion no doubt sprang from the horrifying display of ignorance and bigotry by the clansmen during the Boxer episode. Therefore, in the 1900s, Prince Ch'un was sent to Germany, P'u-lun to the St Louis Exhibition, Tsai-chen to England, Tsai-tse on a world tour, and so on. But the result of these visits was disappointing, as hardly any of them had any European language or knew much about the countries of the West. The fashion for learning English at the Imperial Court led by the Dowager Empress herself in 1906 also came to nothing.

In 1902 an imperial edict instructed the provincial authorities to draw up plans for sending students abroad and to finance them. Chang Chih-tung, then in Kiangsu, and Tuan-fang in Hupei were the first to respond to the edicts. Soon other provinces – Hunan, Szechuan, Anhwei and Kwangtung followed. That the central government had not sponsored its own programme since 1885 was obviously due to financial stringency which was not relieved until 1908 when the USA returned its share of the Boxer Indemnity. The policy of encouraging provincial sponsorship without adequately trained personnel at the disposal of provincial authorities to select qualified students led to chaos and absurdity. Szechuan, for instance, sent a totally illiterate student to the USA. The more advanced provinces of Kwangtung set up a preparatory school for students going abroad, to be rewarded only by student unrest and endless troubles. The original purpose of the policy, to allow backward provinces a chance to draw level with the more advanced ones, proved to be illusory, for the more competent students from backward provinces chose upon their return to work at more advanced places where the intellectual atmosphere was more congenial, salaries better, and opportunities for further personal advancement more readily available. The provinces drastically reduced the number of students they sent to study abroad after the US Exclusion Act of 1924.

Hitherto the government had not concerned itself with the academic standards of the 'returned' students. On the suggestion of Chang Chih-tung in May 1903, a series of examinations were designed to test their ability before sailing abroad and their fitness for government appointments after their return. First, a palace examination was instituted in 1905 to scrutinize Japanese-trained students who, if passed with first-grade honours, were given the *chin-shih* degree, and if passed with second-grade honours, were given the *chü-jen* degree. But the same year saw the traditional examination system abolished altogether, so that continuing to award traditional degrees to foreign-trained candidates became anomalous. Chang Po-hsi, Superintendent of Educational Affairs, advised the throne to discontinue such awards, but to continue holding the palace examinations. In the examination of that year all the examiners – T'ang Shao-yi, Yen Fu and Chan T'ien-yu – were Western trained and the questions and answers were in English. Not unexpectedly all the first grade awards went to American-trained candidates while a few Japanese-trained ones won a poor second. Complaints from the Japanese camp were heard, grumbling against the bias of the Western-trained examiners. The palace examination system was scheduled to be abolished in 1912. After the revolution of 1911–12 the President, Yuan Shih-k'ai, revived it (in 1915). With the downfall of Yuan in 1916 the system finally came to an end.

The examination of government students before they went abroad was introduced in 1908 to discourage ill-qualified young people from wasting time and money in such a venture. The 1908 Act stipulated that those who entered for political and law studies should not be younger than twenty-five, but should already be well versed in Chinese literature and classics and also experienced in education or administration. Those who were planning to go to school in the USA should pass a qualifying examination before being admitted into the preparatory school, Tsinghua College, founded in 1911, for a period of study of eight years. The College was placed surprisingly under the jurisdiction, not of the Ministry of Education, but of the Ministry of Foreign Affairs. It was financed by the American Boxer Indemnity and the quotas of students from each province were determined according to the size of each province's contribution to the Indemnity. The poorer and more backward provinces therefore had smaller quotas but had difficulty in finding enough interested and qualified students to fill even those. The first such examination was held on 4 September 1909 and out of a field of 2500 candidates, 100 were selected for preparatory studies.

The policy of sending young students abroad was changed by the Act of 1916 which made only graduates eligible to take government examinations to qualify for study abroad. At the same time Tsinghua College became Tsinghua University. The rationale for the change was that graduates, having already specialized in a subject, needed less time abroad to attain a professional standard to fit them for service at home. This new arrangement might, on the one hand, save time and money for the students and their country, but, on the other, older students making a shorter stay in a foreign country could hardly achieve the same standard of linguistic proficiency as their younger predecessors. The policy outlined by the Act of 1916 was to be elaborated and generally followed by the Kuomintang government in the 1928–37 period, except that the importance of Chinese literature and classics was now matched by political indoctrination in the basic philosophy of the Kuomintang party. How thorough this ideological control was is not easy to define. However, ideological control rendered the study of social and political sciences unnecessary in the government's view, hence the discouragement of students from taking up such areas to study abroad. Fewer scholarships were allocated to social and political scientists during the Nanking period, reversing the intellectual trend established earlier on in the twentieth century.

Before sailing the student had to see to it that his passport and visa were in order, go to Shanghai or Hong Kong to have his Western clothes made, and cut off his queue when the queue was in fashion. Those who were bound for the USA were advised to travel first class in order to save unnecessary troubles at the port of entry in the years when the Exclusion Act was in force. Expenses for a student studying in America or Europe amounted to at least 20 000 *yuan* per annum at the beginning of this century, rising to about twice as much in the 1930s. Because of this high cost, government scholarships and missionary sponsorship were the only hope for talented but poor youths who aspired to rise in the social scale. The competition for scholarships was therefore extremely keen and the successful candidates were, generally speaking, of a higher academic calibre than the self-supporting students who were largely beyond the control of government policies. As the majority of Chinese students abroad were supported by their well-to-do families, the social status conferred by foreign degrees became more closely linked with personal wealth than ever. The internal political disorder from 1919 onwards put the poorer government students in an even less enviable position, for the remittance of government funds for their support was frequently interrupted, inflicting even greater hardships on them. Another predicament of the government students was the supervisory system which turned into a system of political surveillance. It did not come to an end in the USA till 1924 and elsewhere not till the 1930s. To make things worse, most of the supervisors were old-fashioned and insensitive to student problems. For example, a supervisor in the

USA in 1914 even forbade Chinese students to take summer courses, for no explicit reason. Some others were simply corrupt officials enjoying a sinecure which allowed them to live abroad.

Statistics concerning Chinese students abroad are as inconsistent and unreliable as other statistics relating to China in the first three decades of this century. However, it is probably safe to say that because it was academically less rigorous and financially less expensive more Chinese students went to study in Japan than in any other country, and that because the USA was the first nation to formulate a policy of educating Chinese students and institutionalized it through the rendition of the Boxer Indemnity, more Chinese students studied there than in any other Western nation. Of the European countries, France accommodated thousands of Chinese students during the war years and up to 1925, due to the Work-Study Scheme; Germany received about a thousand Chinese students in the period of her hyperinflation which drastically reduced the cost of living and studying in that country. Over the years the number of students, both government and self-supporting, increased. This trend was both the cause and the effect of a changing attitude towards studying abroad. Earlier reluctance gave way to an eagerness comparable to the eagerness for success in the traditional examinations. A scholarship enabling one to study in the USA or Britain was no less enthusiastically celebrated than a *chin-shih* degree. In this atmosphere, a zealous young man in Kwangtung decided to take up a career as a beggar in order to gather enough money to study in a foreign country. In the same spirit, the father of Liang Shu-ming, the famous philosopher remarked:

Even if I have no chance to study abroad, I must save enough to send my son to a foreign country. Anything else can be forgotten, but not this one!

This changed attitude had its roots in the improved employment opportunities and career patterns of the 'returned' students and in the establishment of a tradition of sending brothers and sisters, sons and grandsons on the same road to success. To mention only a few in illustration of this point, there were Sun Yat-sen's family and Wu T'ing-fang's family in Kwangtung, Marquis Tseng's family in Hunan and Ku Yü-hsiu's family in Kiangsu.

Chaff and wheat inevitably became mixed in this breathless rush for distinction. Some were serious scholars with laudable intentions, fulfilling their set goals and then rendering valuable contributions to their country; some were fakes and time-servers who merely sought to acquire the prestige of having studied abroad so that they could shine like fool's gold on their return. A student of engineering in the USA spent much of his time in fortune telling; a teacher who went to Chicago spoke not a word of English; a student in France was caught smuggling Chinese antiques. It was so important to have studied abroad that even men of distinction struggled to go through the process in order to obtain the special status it conferred. A professor, vice dean of the faculty of arts at a university and editor of a popular magazine, was sponsored by the Associated Boards for Christian Colleges in China to study Western literature and journalism at Columbia University and this fact, he thought, deserved an advertisement in the magazine he edited. Other professors disguised their study trips as '*chiang-hsüeh*' – a vague term which could mean a 'lecture tour' or 'lecturing and learning'. In fact it was more often learning than lecturing, as in the case of Shen Yu-ch'ien's '*chiang-hsüeh*' at Harvard in 1939.

## Cultural ambivalence in 'returned' students

Out of 400 000 or so 'returned' students from the West many outstanding scholars emerged to promote the cultural changes of modern China. Their contribution will be discussed presently. For the time being, it may be of some help to outline a few of the salient characteristics of their cultural attitudes resulting from their contacts with a totally alien, immensely useful and profoundly complex intellectual tradition. Their exposure to this tradition set off a chain reaction in the students themselves. Some were superficially affected by the contact and returned later to display only their superficiality. The generation of 'returned' students of the 1870s broke away from Confucian restraints by learning to sing and engage in sports; the 1910 and 1920 generations affected long hair and adopted a bohemian life-style. Even at such inconsequential levels, the clash between Eastern and Western values was evident and the clash induced change. Those who changed faster disdained those who lagged behind, on the grounds that the latter caused their nation and race to lose face and honour. A moot point here was whether, in order to preserve the face and honour of the race-nation, the students should become Westernized as fast as possible or should retain their Chineseness as much as they could. A satisfactory answer to their question was by no means easy to find. Therefore as soon as contact between the East and West was made, the question of appropriate manners and etiquette cropped up and a cultural ambivalence began to evolve.

The intellectual ambivalence of the 'returned' students naturally percolated deeper than the levels of life-style and languages. Their love of China and Chinese values was just as intense as their hate. They were quite incapable of resolving the conflict between Eastern and Western values and yet they were emotionally committed to both China and the country in which they had studied. Most Western-trained students in humanities and the social sciences unbashfully displayed their two sets of mutually contradictory loyalties; they defended Chinese values against Western criticism and defended Western values against Chinese criticism. In so doing they were culture mongers rather than original thinkers trying to arrive at a coherent synthesis of these two great traditions. Throughout the whole period when students were sent abroad this cultural ambivalence remained; so did the contradictions between the two sets of values.

Such ambivalence generated personal identity crises. Consciously and semi-consciously the students alienated themselves from and at the same time integrated themselves into the Chinese tradition. Few were convinced of the wisdom of total alienation (*ch'uan-p'an hsi-hua*); few were prepared to reject any change at all (*pao-ts'un kuo-ts'ui*). Compromise solutions – '*chung-hsüeh wei t'i; hsi-hsüeh wei yung*' (Chinese scholarship as the essence while Western scholarship only for application), '*hsüeh-shu tu-li*' (cultural independence), and '*pen-wei wen-hua*' (indigenous culture) – lacked cogency and depth. For the majority of 'returned' students the issue was buried and alienation, both facetious and substantial, was cheerfully turned into a status symbol. A minority, like Hu Shih, endeavoured to rise above nationalism in the hope that when one had elevated oneself to the cosmopolitan level only the humanity of Goldwin Smith's vision could remain. Yet the reality of the hierarchy of nations and races belied such a vision.

## The Chinese student abroad

The social life of Chinese students abroad was governed by a few voluntarily or involuntarily accepted rules. Racial discrimination against them was the basic one, especially in English-speaking countries and Hitler's Germany. They encountered considerable difficulty in obtaining accommodation and sometimes Chinese were refused service in barbers' shops. To this and to even worse types of racial prejudice, even the radical Tsou T'ao-fen became resigned, asking – 'How can we protest when we are powerless?' Another radical, Wen Yi-to wrote to his parents:

The US is not a place for me to stay in long. For a young Chinese of principle, the flavour of life here cannot be described. When I come home at the end of the year after next, I shall tell you all about it beside our fireside and I shall weep bitterly to get rid of the accumulated indignation and frustration in my heart.

On the other hand, the Chinese students themselves disliked Korean students to the extent of refusing to dine at the same table with them because they were 'stateless slaves'; they laughed at Indian coolies and bejewelled Indian ladies for their 'ugliness'; they regarded East Africa as the 'lair' of 'the most inferior races' on earth. They even warned themselves to refrain from looking down upon the Jews. In other words, they were prepared to concede superiority to the Anglo-Saxons, perhaps also to the Germans and French, but not to the Jews or the coloured races.

The second rule was that imposed by the fact that they were not only individuals but also ambassadors of their country; hence nothing they did or said must be detrimental to the face and honour of the race-nation. This rule required them to conform to both Chinese and Western norms of conduct. They greeted the achievements of such scholars as Dr Wu Lien-te and Dr Wang Ch'ung-hui as a great honour to the entire yellow race. The Nobel Prize shared by Drs Li Cheng-tao and Yang Chen-ning had the effect of 'restoring the self-confidence and self-respect of the Chinese nation'. On a lower plane there was Miss Yang Man-hua who

showed her natural-size feet to Belgian ladies, to prove to them that Chinese women do not bind their feet any more. This gesture made them apologize to her. Miss Yang also denied that China was reduced to a hell on earth by her soldiers and bandits. She has certainly won a great deal of face for our country.

One could resort to all sorts of devices to 'win' face for China; staging traditional plays in order to let foreigners know of her glorious cultural tradition, protesting against the publication of Pearl Buck's translation of a classical Chinese novel, *All Men Are*

*Brothers,* because it depicted a renegade priest eating human flesh, or pointing out that corruption, illiteracy, and even flies also existed in England so that 'in an instant of time, my respect for Britain waned while my confidence in my own nation waxed'. The irony of all these injunctions and inhibitions was that the Chinese students during their sojourn in the West failed to put up an impressive performance. They were far from being paragons of the virtues they admired.

Thirdly, the Chinese students abroad worked excessivly hard, at the expense of their social life and relaxation. They travelled little, except for those in Europe in the 1920s, and they rarely took part in organized sports and other extracurricular activities on campus. When they travelled, they were silent wanderers, as their travelogues demonstrate. Hsü Chih-mo visited more graves of the famous dead than he did ordinary living people during his European tour. Hu Shih, by no means an inactive student at Cornell, did not make his first appearance at a university ball until he had spent more than a year on the campus and did not dance until four years after that.

A few brilliant students had genuine foreign friends. V. K. Ting's association with Teilhard de Chardin and Davidson Black, Hu Shih's with L. E. Patterson, and Ku Yü-hsiu's with B. A. Behrend were based on mutual respect and admiration; they could not be described otherwise. Later, a new type of friendship based on ideological ties grew up among radical Chinese and radical Westerners, especially radical Americans, e.g. Tsou T'ao-fen's communist comrades. The majority of the Chinese students, however, spent their time in isolation from the white community and from the Chinese in Chinatown. The famous writer Lao She (Shu She-yü) attributed this isolation to the social restrictions of status and tabooed subjects of conversation which made friendship with the Englishman difficult. Chinese scholars in the USA found the same arduousness. To be sure, there were other inhibiting reasons. A feeling of inferiority discouraged them from approaching fellow students; their faulty English or French hardly helped embolden them. Some particularly insightful observations were recorded by Wei Su-yuan describing his visit to a Russian poet living in Peking in 1925. On his way, Wei felt lonely and timid, a psychological reaction which he called melancholia. When the poet asked him about conditions in China, Wei depicted them as 'sad' and 'as lifeless as a desert'. On his way out, Wei again felt sad, cold and melancholy. He was so weighed down by his disappointment that he could scarcely breathe.

Conversation between most Chinese and most Westerners had never flowed easily, perhaps due to the feeling of inequality between them. Before the awakening of nationalism, Chinese cultural superiority dictated a pattern of conversation which would reflect that superiority. It invariably ended in the foreigner being thoroughly convinced and silenced. Any other pattern was inconceivable, at least in official reports. With the establishment of the authority of social Darwinism, the tables were turned and Chinese were too easily convinced of the wisdom of a foreigner's argument and reduced to taciturnity.* Yet after the split of the nationalist–communist alliance in 1927, anti-communist politicians were reportedly capable of browbeating Stalin and his representative in China, Mikhail Borodin. It is an irony that only as stubborn culturalists or vehement anti-communists could Chinese politicians talk down on Westerners; as nationalists of the Darwinian persuasion, they lost their tongue.

Since their concerns were less political, scholars should have been able to converse more fluently with their foreign counterparts. Unfortunately, their conversations followed the same patterns; the Chinese silenced the foreigner or the foreigner the Chinese. Chang Hsing-lang's meeting with Bremen and Liang Chi'i-ch'ao's with Boutroux ended in their being silenced by the foreigners, whereas Liang Shu-ming when he met Tagore silenced Tagore.

Some scholars and statesmen made a habit of interviewing foreign celebrities. Liang Ch'i-ch'ao called on John Hay, J. P. Morgan and Theodore Roosevelt in 1903, Hsü Chih-mo on Thomas Hardy in 1927 (?), Ts'ai T'ing-k'ai on Mussolini in 1935, and Ku Yü-hsiu on Bertrand Russell and Bernard Shaw in 1945–6. None of them seem to have prepared himself for the interviews and consequently in each case the conversation dried up quickly. The lack of preparedness for these momentous interviews can probably be ascribed to a lack of intellectual curiosity about the fields of study or activities of the foreign interviewees. To illustrate this point one should browse through Chang Yin-huan's *Diary*, written when he was the Chinese Minister to the USA and Spain. Never in all the conversations recorded throughout his term of office did Chang ask a single question

* *The Chinese Mail*, 5 August 1905, when the Japanese Minister to China, Naida, reduced Prince Ch'ing to saying nothing but 'Yes, yes'; Chang Chi-chih, *Chüan-chi* (Complete Works), Shanghai, 1935, p. 232, relates an incident in 1912 when Chang Chien found no answer to Timothy Richard's forceful reasoning; and Feng Yu-hsiang, *Wo-ti cheng-huo* (My Life), vol. III, Chungking, 1944, pp. 638–9, where the Christian General remained in agonized silence after a long speech about the misery of Chinese women by a Belgium or Italian lady.

that might have touched off a dialogue between him and his foreign colleague. This conspicuous absence of inquisitiveness may have been shaped by the conversational style of the Confucian *Analects* in which the master did all the talking. Even there, the disciples at least asked questions occasionally. Perhaps in addition to being held back by a feeling of deference, the Chinese student used his silence to cover up his ignorance. A naive question could betray the shallowness and inadequacy of a diffident inquirer.

Even if a Chinese had a fair command of the language of his foreign interlocutor, he might not be able to interpret the foreigner's manners or detect innuendos, flippancy, or arrogance. The following exchange took place at the London School of Economics in 1936:

'I have heard that you Chinese can have concubines. Is that true?' a German student demanded.

I felt embarrassed and did not know how to answer. At length I replied: 'Yes, but our law forbids concubinage.'

'What a pity!' He seemed disappointed and added: 'How could you give up such a wonderful custom?'

'How can you think it's a wonderful custom?' I was taken aback.

Sometimes the common ground on which a conversation could be built simply was not there as, for instance, when a descendant of Confucius talked about the Shantung Question with Sir John Jordan, the British Minister to Peking, who naturally referred to the Fourteen Points of President Wilson. Innocently the Confucian duke asked: 'Who is President Wilson?' At the very worst level of conversation comes General Wei Li-huang who gave a sumptuous banquet for his foreign friends. It was consumed in complete silence. No wonder the *Chinese Repository* regretted: 'We are no great talkers with the natives.' In conversation at least it seems to have been a wasted century.

Intellectually bewildered and socially isolated, the highly motivated Chinese students abroad preserved their equanimity by the comforting comparisons between their lot and that of their less fortunate compatriots at home and with thoughts of the glorious future that awaited them upon return. But they were sexually frustrated. Marriage between a government student and a white woman was repeatedly prohibited by law in 1910, 1913, 1918, and as late as 1936, on the grounds that a foreign girl was extravagant, that it would be far beyond the studen'ts power to maintain her, that marriage would distract the student's attention from his studies, and that the married student might decide to settle in his wife's country. The government based its decision on the experience obtained with the students of the 1870s. But this prohibition could hardly be enforced even with the threat of withdrawing financial support to back it up. Han Suyin tells how her father married in Belgium in 1907 and many prominent figures of the Nanking government married their American, British, French and German wives in about the same period.

The law did not mention other, perhaps more pertinent social reasons against miscegenation. It was hard to work out how a white wife could play her proper role in an extended Chinese family as wife (or concubine), daughter-in-law, cousin and the mistress of servants. Her role as the wife of a friend or colleague would be even more difficult to define. Uncertainty about how she was expected to behave could easily be a cause of family discord and an insurmountable handicap for her husband's career. In addition there was racial discrimination both in China and abroad. In China a white woman walking in the street, accompanied by a Chinese male, was likely to be stared at and followed by a group of children, shouting 'Foreign devil, foreign devil!' just as in the West at that time the Chinese would be greeted with 'Chin-chin Chinaman!' To cite Han Suyin again, her parents could not be admitted into the same restaurant, the same hotel, or the same park in Shanghai. When they travelled from Shanghai to Hankow on an English steamer, the mother and her son were sent to a first-class cabin while the father stayed below. Arguments on eugenic grounds in favour of mixed marriage were put forward by Wu T'ing-fang and Wu Chih-hui, the second of whom did not forget his patriotism in his reasoning – 'It is because of the relaxation of sexual inhibitions that European men are manly and women attractive, enabling them to dominate the world.' But Chang Ching-sheng, the sex revolutionary of the 1920s, cautioned Chinese students abroad against 'marrying a negress or a red Indian'.

Mostly virgins and completely ignorant of women, the Chinese boys sometimes found the experience of suddenly being in close proximity to pretty females in the same classroom or common room could be a traumatic one, as one of them recorded his reaction to a girl sitting beside him while powdering her nose:

My heart pounds wildly. All my moral upbringing, all my Confucian ethics, go straight out of the window when I am so close to physical temptation.

So Chinese students learnt to dance and overdid the ritual of dating by taking white girls out to dinner and the cinema and showering them with expensive gifts, in most cases only to be rebuffed when they sought the expected rewards. Misconceptions of the relationship between the sexes in the West ran wild among Chinese students. Some thought Western girls were downright loose whereas others idealized the relationship between the sexes. Because of the freedom of social contact,

Western men and women regard each other as schoolmates, friends, simply *human beings*. The barrier disappears; the sense of physical difference is forgotten. As the sense of difference fades, men and women have found the only way of controlling themselves in their social intercourse.

In a Christian country, a Chinese lady with a likable personality had far fewer social handicaps than a Chinese man. Dr Mary Stone (Shih Mei-yü) in America and Miss Cheng Yü-hsiu in France were examples of this. The sending of Chinese girls to study abroad was one of the great initiatives taken by the Church and at first they were all mission-sponsored. The Chinese government did not enter into this field until 1907 when Kiangsu sent three girls to study at Wesleyan College. Finally the Ministry of Education adopted the policy of granting scholarships to women on the principle of equality with men, and from 1914 onward Tsinghua College followed suit. By 1925 there were 640 Chinese girls studying in the USA out of a total of 1600 Chinese students. The Work-Study Scheme in France, too, had its women's programme which at the beginning of the 1920s had more than twenty girls from Hunan and seventeen from other provinces out of a total of 1700 students. On the whole, too few girls were lucky enough to go abroad; fewer still made any impact on Chinese culture. Judging it in terms of scholastic achievement alone, the policy was a failure, even taking into consideration Ch'en Heng-che's professorship in European history, Hsieh Wan-ying's delightful essays, Tai Ai-lien's influence on choreography, and Wu Yi-fang's presidency of the women's college in Nanking.* But in terms of their impact on Chinese politics and society, the 'returned' women students were a notable force, far outweighing their small numbers, in the 1920s and 1930s. The three Soong sisters are a good example. On the side of the revolution, women's influence had been

* All these and other Chinese names mentioned in this chapter can be found in H. L. Boorman and R. C. Howard, *Biographical Dictionary of Republican China* (NY, 1967).

felt from the very foundation of the Chinese Communist Party in 1921 onward. Several Moscow-trained women attained positions on the Political Bureau and several others who had studied in France were outstanding leaders or martyrs. 'Returned' girl students left a deep impression on medical and social-welfare work and also on the movement for women's emancipation.

Their marriages with Western men seem to have worked out more happily once the initial parental objections were overcome. Their social acceptability and their being frequently invited to balls and dinners 'provoked an acid feeling' among some Chinese males who sneered at and taunted them, even wrote threatening letters to them, in an endeavour to keep them 'pure'.

## The Work-Study Scheme

Of all the programmes for studying abroad, the most remarkable was the Work-Study Scheme founded by Li Shih-tseng, Wu Chih-hui and Wang Ching-wei in 1912 on the basic assumption that studying abroad was the *only* way to reform the Chinese and their society. Three preparatory schools for those intending to study in France were established in Szechuan, Peking and Shanghai. Only eighty students left for France in the first year of the scheme. The founders broached the idea of part-time study and part-time work in 1914, but the scheme was interrupted by the war. Two years later they revived the scheme in response to France's need for manpower, to attract large numbers of young people from the inland provinces who had hitherto had only scant opportunities for studying in the West. The leaders of these provinces eagerly assisted, setting up branches of the Sino–French Education Society and contributing money. The fare for a fourth-class passenger then amounted to only 100 *yuan*. In addition each Work-Study student needed 300 *yuan* for other expenses. For students in Szechuan, Hunan, Kiangsi, Fukien and Kwangtung, after years of continuous civil war and the impoverishment of the lower middle class, this low-cost scheme was a godsend. Hitherto they had been unable to compete scholastically with their contemporaries in the more advanced provinces. It was therefore from these provinces that the majority of the Work-Study students were to come. Starting from a few score in 1917, their number was to swell to a staggering 2000 in 1921 when the scheme reached the peak of its popularity. Li Shih-tseng founded the Université Franco–Chinoise

at Lyons in 1920 with the specific object of accommodating, finding
jobs for, and registering the new arrivals at various colleges in the
city. The financing of the whole scheme depended heavily on the
students' own initial contribution towards their own passage and
subsistence for the first few months in France, on the subsidy from
the Sino–French Education Society which, in turn, relied on provincial and warlord support, and on allocations from the Chinese and
French Ministries of Education and a few Chinese universities. In
the context of the internal disorders in China, none of the Chinese
financial sources was certain, while many students could not find
jobs. When they were employed, the average wage of three or four
*yuan* a day was insufficient to pay their living and tuition. In January
1921 the Sino–French Education Society withdrew from its financial
commitment to the scheme with the result that a sense of crisis
seized the students in Lyons. They went on strike against the
Chinese government while hundreds of them died of hunger and
cold during the winter. The Chinese Minister in Paris responded by
repatriating those who could not support themselves and 104 were
literally deported. The news of a French loan of F 500 million to
the Chinese government added to the general dismay. But with the
activists removed from the scene, calm was finally restored by the
end of the year and the scheme survived by the skin of its teeth.

Most of the Work-Study students in Lyons specialized in science
and engineering subjects and at the same time worked in factories.
Fourteen of them were awarded doctorates, thirty master's degrees,
twenty-four certificates in engineering, and no less than twenty-eight
first-class prizes in architecture in the year 1930 alone. It would be a
false impression to regard them as so many loafers and hot-headed
agitators. They made a notable contribution to the advancement of
science and technology in modern China. In the field of fine arts, the
scheme produced sculptors like Li Chin-fa and painters like Lin
Feng-mien and Hsü Pei-hung – prints of Hsü's drawings of horses
are widely obtainable in the West.

Politically the Work-Study students were active and influential.
Coming from impoverished middle-class backgrounds, they were
particularly susceptible to radical ideas. In post-war France they
were drawn to French Marxists and converted to their doctrine, at
approximately the same time as the founding of the Chinese Communist Party. From their ranks emerged such eminent leaders of the
Chinese communist movement as Chou En-lai, the party theoretician

Ts'ai Ho-sen, the economic planner Li Fu-ch'un, the party organizers
Li Li-san and Teng Hsiao-p'ing, brilliant soldiers like Ch'en Yi and
Nieh Jung-chen, and women leaders like Hsiang Ching-yü and Ts'ai
Ch'ang. Through some of them the movement itself was to receive
intellectual nourishment which affected Mao Tse-tung himself.

### The 'returned' students in China

What did the 'returned' students do? How did the government of
China make use of their special training? The early ones, if they were
not connected with the Church, were treated with suspicion and were
frequently unable to find a suitable job. Yung Wing's career before
1870 was a case in point. Upon his return from Yale, Yung worked
as Dr Peter Parker's secretary and then in the supreme court of
Hong Kong. His interest in law gave him the idea of studying for the
bar, but the British solicitors there would not have a Chinese intrude
into their territory. Yung therefore left for Shanghai where he acted
as an interpreter at the customs office. Filled with disgust at the corruption of the customs officers, he resigned and drifted from job to
job until he met Tseng Kuo-fan. The Yung Wing boys who were
trained in the USA in the 1870s fared no better. Summoned home
in 1882, they were carried in small carts to a college in Shanghai to
be given filthy lodgings and awful food and kept there under police
surveillance for two weeks before being allowed to leave under the
guarantee of their relatives and friends.

Not all of the boys returned. Liang Ch'i-ch'ao met about ten of
them in the USA in 1903; most of them were working either as
interpreters in the Chinese diplomatic service or as clerks in American banks. All of them had married American wives and settled in
the USA. Their departed colleagues were employed in China as
follows:

|  | 1872 Group | 1873 Group | 1874 Group | 1875 Group |
|---|---|---|---|---|
| Industry and commerce | 10 | 9 | 3 | - |
| Law clerks and interpreters | 8 | 3 | 1 | - |
| Teaching | 1 | 11 | 21 | 21 |
| Total | 19 | 23 | 25 | 21 |

Source: Based on Hsü Jun, *Hsü Tzu-bsü Yü-chai nien-p'u*, in *Yang-wu Yung-tung*,
Shanghai, 1961, vol. VIII, pp. 104–16.

It is not clear when Hsü Jun recorded these statistics, but a safe guess is that he did so before 1907. Before 1907 even the Ministry of Foreign Affairs did not make a point of hiring Western-trained students except for work in the legations and consulates abroad. The Yung Wing boys were simply not trusted. It was to Yuan Shih-k'ai's credit that an order was issued in 1907 in the name of Liang Tun-yen, one of the 1872 group and Yuan's henchmen in the Ministry, disqualifying anyone who had no foreign language for the post of commissioner for foreign affairs in the provinces. Yuan himself introduced several American-trained students, T'ang Shao-yi, Liang Tun-yen, Ts'ai Shao-chi and Ts'ai T'ing-kan, into the administration. The order of 1907 was followed by an edict of the Regent in 1909 prohibiting anyone who knew no foreign language to any diplomatic post abroad, and another stipulating that the tax collectors at the Ch'ungwenmen office in Peking had to have a good command of a foreign language. In the same year the Ministry of Civil Affairs inaugurated a scheme of grading its staff: first class – graduates from foreign universities; second class – undergraduates from foreign universities; third class – graduates from Chinese schools; and fourth class – the rest. The door of the bureaucracy was thus flung open to the 'returned' students; a foreign degree or any other foreign qualifications superseded the traditional degrees as the ladder to social distinction. For instance, the Ministry of Finance in 1912 was headed by a Japanese-trained man and all its departments were under either Japanese- or American-trained students (at a ratio of 5:2); the only exception was the deputy minister. A similar situation existed in the Ministry of Foreign Affairs, the Ministry of Communications and Transport, and the Maritime Customs Office. In 1919 the Who's Who section of the *Year Book* specified the educational background of some eminent Chinese thus: 145 foreign-trained, forty-three Chinese-schooled, and only thirty-seven traditional degree holders.

The majority of the 'returned' students, however, took up teaching, practically monopolizing all the important posts in higher education. This state of affairs in 1937 portended three causes of conflict – first, the chasm between the central government manned by a Westernized staff and local governments manned by Chinese-educated administrators was widening as more 'returned' students joined the central government; second, a similar chasm also existed between the higher education system, which was in the hands of professors and lecturers using Western teaching material and methods, and the secondary education system which was in the hands of Chinese-educated teachers; third, the majority of the Western-trained students were not using their specialized training in industry or engineering, but in administration and teaching, a situation for which the backwardness of Chinese industry was surely responsible. At all Chinese universities the total lack of research facilities except in mathematics and subjects related to China made sure that the 'returned' students, even the brilliant ones, would in time fall behind their Western contemporaries. The slogans of 'Catching up with the West', and 'Intellectual Independence', were so many empty words.

Government sponsorship of programmes for study abroad was based on the hypothesis that a cultural disparity existed in some or all areas of scholarship between the East and West. As long as the hypothesis held good, the programmes remained. That was why Liang Ch'i-ch'ao wrote in a fulsome manner in their support in the *Hsin-min ts'ung-pao* (New Citizens' Review) he edited on 26 September 1902:

The 'returned' students, . . . having been civilized and influenced by the commendable tradition of a foreign country, possessing both patriotism and youthful capabilities, are the masters and rulers of the future of China. They alone can be trusted with the country's affairs in the years to come.

Others were much less sanguine. The ultra-conservatives and, ironically, the British diplomats in China, had formed a highly critical attitude towards the 'returned' students precisely because of their cultural alienation which pleased Liang Ch'i-ch'ao. Sir Walter Medhurst, for example, thought they were 'most insufferable' and Sir Meyrick Hewlett preferred their conclusions on all matters when they 'could suppress the imported part of themselves and argue with a Chinese mind'. However, neither the Chinese conservatives nor the British diplomats had taken the trouble to define their criteria of judgement; they simply felt a vague aversion to any degree of cultural alienation. Their unexpressed opinion seems to have been that the 'returned' students should learn only what was useful to China but reject all that was culturally disagreeable to her. This line of criticism, so ambiguous as to be difficult to rebut and so trivial as sometimes to be absurd, was carried on by Lin Yutang, himself a 'returned' student, under the label of 'the slavery of foreign culture' (*yang-nu*) in contradistinction to the political term, *yang-nu* (treason), employed by the nationalists. Lin wrote, in his usual flippant manner, in the *Lun-yü* (Analects), No. 39, of 16 April 1934:

With a mouthful of English and ungrammatical Chinese, such men [the 'returned' students] must don Western clothes. Having acquired a foreign doctorate by hook and by crook, read a couple of books on literary criticism to give themselves an excuse for barging in here and there talking about literature, and developed a yearning for women; such men must don Western clothes. But when they grow older, more mature, more understanding, and calmer, they invariably shed their Western clothes and go back to their Chinese dress. After all, when they have attained some social status and succeeded in their careers, there would be no need for Western clothes to conceal their poor English and infantility. They must then abandon their Western clothes.

Surely, the cultural alienation of the 'returned' students went far beyond Lin Yutang's 'English language' and 'Western attire'. A more serious complaint against them was directed at their confused values. Hu Hsien-hsü expressed this in his essay on the educational crisis of China in the *Hsüeh-heng* (the Critical Review), No. IV, in April 1922:

As for their personality development, they lack a firm commitment to any ethical standard, and so easily lose heart and become confused. When frustrated they tend to blame society and other people; even under favourable conditions, material desires tend to disorient them.

These confused values manifested themselves in two forms. First, these students tended to over-praise the wisdom and superiority of the country to which they had become acculturated in an attempt to press home a point they were making or simply to increase the importance of the country they represented in China. Sir Eric Teichman, for example, observed that American-trained students looked to the USA as their spiritual home for security and to provide final authority for their judgements. For this reason, their excessive praise often stemmed from articles of faith and personal vested interests which compounded intellectual chaos if they worked in education or aggravated administrative disarray if they were in the government service. At a less significant level, it made the 'returned' students appear boastful as the essay, 'Oxford – Carrel for Taming Rebels', betrays. To begin with, its author refers casually to the Italian and Chinese scholarships he has acquired which have enabled him to live in comfort for three years; then he plans to give lectures in Italian at an Italian academy during which he would swear by Santa Maria and Karl Marx at the same time; he wanders in Rome and Florence; when his money is gone, he steals grapes from vineyards and sleeps under a bridge; he mentions Timbuctoo to illustrate a point and gives a footnote in case his readers do not know where the place is. All this glib, smart talk is designed to impress his readers with his learning and carefree, enviable life-style. Ignoring both racial discrimination and intellectual honesty, the author seems to see his ability to live as he did in a white man's country as proof enough of his superiority to all those who care to read him.

Secondly, 'returned' students appeared to be unnecessarily reverent of foreigners, especially those from the country where they had studied, and irreverent towards their own country and their own people. This made them easy meat for satirists like Li Po-yuan and Lu Hsün, who depicted them as 'foreign bootlickers', 'high-class Chinese', and 'cultural compradores'. In the view of nationalists, they were 'traitors'; in the view of revolutionaries, they were 'reactionaries'. Their refraining from participation in anti-imperialist movements and the communist revolution lent force to both the nationalist and the communist charges.

The 'returned' students' own incompetence and false pretences laid them open to adverse criticism. Quite early on, in an editorial of 14 November 1879, the *Shen-pao* of Shanghai noted their shallow scholarship, which went little further than a command of English or French. Even their language proficiency was publicly challenged by a 'returned' professor of English literature, Dr George Yeh, in the prestigious *Independent Review* (No. 166, 1 September 1935). A student in Germany of three years' standing could hardly make himself understood by a cab driver; the author of a book on English literature rendered 'The Ballad of the Reading Gaol' as 'a ballad by someone reading in a gaol' and 'At the Mermaid' as 'with a mermaid', or another who turned the Milky Way in Wordsworth's 'Daffodils' into 'the milk way'.

Lu Hsün saw through most of the 'returned' students' pretences, suspecting that they had whiled away their time abroad 'stewing beef in their digs'. He also exposed their culture mongering and mutual compliments; their theses written on Li Po, Yang Chu or any Chinese 'Tom, Dick, or Harry' which apparently entitled them to offer courses at Chinese universities on Bernard Shaw and H. G. Wells. They published memoirs of twenty minutes with Katherine Mansfield, forty minutes with Thomas Hardy, or an hour with André Gide, in which they described such moments as 'unforgettable', 'divine inspiration', and 'being in the presence of a heavenly god', without even hinting at the intellectual content of the conversation. On the strength of such dubious claims, the 'returned' students found their way to university chairs, high government posts, and editorships in publishing houses. Lu Hsün advised them:

Stop acting, strip yourselves of your nauseating airs, forget your professorial titles, abdicate from your positions as mentors of the youth, . . . stand out nakedly and say something honest.

Another serious charge against the 'returned' students was their imperfect understanding of Chinese conditions and Chinese life-styles and thought-patterns. There is a grain of truth in this, although their critics did not quite know what the said conditions, life-styles and thought-patterns were, let alone whether these Chinese traditions should be preserved. Early criticism tended to dismiss all the 'returned' students in crude terms as 'useless, since they know neither Chinese nor Chinese social usages', or 'utterly foreign, quite unable to handle Chinese affairs'. Condemnation of this kind implied a difficulty on the part of the students in readjusting themselves upon their return, and a lack of understanding of Western scholarship and customs on the part of their critics. Later, people who were qualified judges of Western learning attacked the shoddy scholarship of many 'returned' students, which was more to the point – Hu Shih thought they lacked the critical faculty and the Scottish-trained Ku Hung-ming regarded then as 'half-educated'. Geologists and engineers were good at making maps and graphs, but entirely at sea with practical work; social scientists knew nothing about Chinese crops, law courts, or prisons; educationists freely transplanted foreign theories and methods to China without inquiring whether conditions there were congenial to them. As professors, they used their teachers' lecture notes as their own and sometimes even published them without a qualm of conscience.*

## The spread of Western scientific thought

However well founded, these criticisms do not blot out the fact that the 'returned' students and the Western knowledge they introduced were the most powerful agents of social and cultural change in

* J. R. Levenson, in his article in A. F. Wright (ed.), *Studies in Chinese Thought*, Chicago University Press, 1953, stresses the point of the alienation of the 'returned' students. They had other, equally serious problems, e.g. lack of intellectual honesty and competence.

modern China. Science and technology were the first territories Confucian traditionalists conceded to the West, and one can hardly imagine such a concession being made without the help of 'returned' students and visiting Western scholars. China, as J. Needham has shown in his monumental work, did have both a tradition of scientific inquiry and a remarkably advanced technology. Before the Galilean and Newtonian revolution, the Chinese were particularly strong in mathematics and empirical disciplines, e.g. medicine, geology, hydraulics, astronomy and biology, but weak in theoretical natural history. Their empirical strength and epistemological weakness pointed to a lack of a scientific way of thinking and a scientific approach to natural phenomena. When the first groups of Chinese students were sent to the USA this weakness had not yet been understood, as the students were still instructed to study empirical sciences and engineering.

The difficulty in the way of introducing science to China was that few highly qualified Western scientists chose to waste their time in what Chiang T'ing-fu once called 'intellectual exile' in that country, and those who actually went were, with few exceptions, 'science' missionaries, intellectually quite incapable of formulating a systematic programme for science education. The science that John Fryer and others could bring to the Chinese was of a practical not a theoretical nature; thus they contributed unwittingly to the view of 'Chinese scholarship as the essence and Western scholarship only for application'.

With the return of V. K. Ting from Britain and the establishment of the Chinese Geological Institute in 1913 the old piecemeal, unsystematic approach began to change. In Ting, China had her first accomplished scientist. Through his enterprise and inspiration, Chinese and foreign geologists, paleontologists, and archaeologists, e.g. Weng Wen-hao from Belgium, Li Ssu-kuang from Britain, A. W. Grabau from Columbia University, Teilhard de Chardin from France, Davidson Black from Canada, Ferdinand von Richthofen from Germany, Sven Hedin and J. G. Andersson from Sweden, co-operated as friends and colleagues for the first time in modern Chinese history, conducting geological and geographic surveys and carrying out amazing archaeological and paleontological excavations including the discovery of Peking Man and the oracle bones of Anyang. It was this small group of scientists who revolutionized the study of Chinese history and pre-history.

As yet there was no comprehensive understanding of science *per se*. K'ang Yu-wei's *wu-chih-hsüeh* (studies of matters) of 1905, whose object was to 'save the country' by strengthening and enriching it, consisted of a motley collection of subjects like ship-building, industry, the manufacture of clocks and watches, astronomy, mathematics, the textile industry, strategy, fine arts, and ceramics. Among these, industry, steam and electricity, guns and warships, and the army were deemed to be the most urgently needed. This incongruous juxtaposition can hardly suggest an understanding of science; the basic disciplines – chemistry, physics, and biology – find no place in it. Yen Fu, however, seemed to be closer to the quintessence of science when he singled out truth and sincerity as the heart of the Western learning in his essay on 'The Speed of World Changes' (*Lun shih-pien chih chi*) in 1895. But a firm grasp of the significance of science did not appear until the years immediately after the May 4th Movement, in the early 1920s.

For John Dewey, who spent the period from May 1919 to July 1921 in China, the essence of science did not lie in technology; instead it manifested itself in the development of a new spirit and the cultivation of a new attitude which, like the Confucian tradition, encompassed life itself. This spirit and attitude permeated all spheres of man's activities and their adoption meant nothing less than an intellectual revolution such as had occurred in early modern Europe. The absence of such a revolution in China, in Dewey's words, provided evidence that 'the new [scientific] thought does not have much influence on their [the Chinese] lives. And when this is the case, the development of new thought is slowed down and narrowed.' For Dewey's disciple in China, Hu Shih, the scientific spirit, attitude, and mode of thinking could be equated with the whole realm of observational and experimental methods, scepticism, and critical analysis. This understanding was further confirmed by Bertrand Russell, who came to China in the autumn of 1920 to impart his empirical thinking to a Chinese audience. Russell's adherence to objective truth and intellectual honesty, impressed a whole generation of inquiring Chinese. For Russell, the scientific method was also sceptical and analytical – a characteristic which made the separation of philosophy from empirical science meaningless and the destruction of mysticism imperative. Equally meaningless was the dichotomy usually seen between Chinese and Western learning with the former lying beyond the realm of analytical and empirical understanding.

The introduction of science in this new sense stimulated the Chinese to raise at least two major questions. Why had China had no science, in contradistinction to Europe? Was science able to answer all the questions life itself posed? Answers to these questions would help to throw light on another: under what conditions could science thrive? A chemist and educationist, Jen Hung-chun, attempted to answer the first question, by paraphrasing the Comtean three stages of civilization – superstition, experience and science – and came to the conclusion that Chinese civilization had not yet reached the third stage. A philosopher, Liang Shu-ming, ascribed the absence of science to the Confucian urge to conquer oneself, so different from the Promethean urge to conquer nature. The youthful Feng Yu-lan, the future historian and philosopher, put forward the forthright explanation that it was:

because according to her own standard of values she has not needed any.... The Chinese philosopher had no need of scientific certainty because it was themselves that they wished to know; so in the same way they had no need of the power of science, because it was themselves that they wished to conquer. To them, the content of wisdom was not intellectual knowledge and its function was not to increase external goods.

Explanations of this kind seem to suppose that the Chinese mind had been immune from external stimuli, however random, to have become an isolated organism, working entirely for itself, and that external stimuli had somehow totally failed to goad it into action. Such theories are not only illogical, but also patently untrue. What can be said of the Chinese mind was that it was syncretic, interested in synthesis rather than analysis, in similarities rather than dissimilarities. It was happier when arranging things and ideas, past and present, in patterns than when developing theories to explain the patterns.

China's repeated defeats in war proved to be strong stimuli to which even the 'immune' Chinese mind responded. In 1919, the Chancellor of Peking University, Ts'ai Yuan-p'ei succinctly described the stages of this response:

It has been sixty years since our country began its Westernization. From ship-building, [we] went on to train our army, reform our institutions, and emphasize education. In education, [we] started from technology, then moved on to establish regular schools, and finally recognized the need for science.

Still unaccustomed to differentiating between what was empirically possible and what was emotionally desirable, China's need for science was seen not so much in terms of solving the problems of human existence as in terms of increasing her wealth and power. But a scientific view of life and the application of science to tackle the problems of life was what V. K. Ting advocated; the achievement of the Great Harmony as envisioned by ancient sages, the creation of a utopia by machines, was what Wu Chih-hui longed for. Science was identified with modernity. In a tangential sense, this seemed to their hosts to be the message brought to China by John Dewey and Bertrand Russell.

Neither Ts'ai Yuan-p'ei nor Ch'en Tu-hsiu, respectively a great educationist and a great publicist, was prepared to yield the entire realm of knowledge to science. Ts'ai clearly saw the role of the arts side by side with that of science, while Ch'en, using science as a weapon against traditional metaphysics, wanted democracy also. Stressing the grand role of science in European progress, they both still failed to see science as an all-embracing ideology which would replace Confucianism. The European War brought a shattering despair to the Chinese admirers of the West. For Yen Fu, three hundred years of European progress had ended in self-seeking and homicide, corruption and shame. For Liang Ch'i-ch'ao, 'the dream of the omnipotence of science was rudely shattered'.

In 1922–3 Liang's message that science in the West was bankrupt, though in no sense banishing science altogether, revived interest and confidence in the traditional values of China, which were now categorically labelled 'spiritual'. This revival can be also interpreted as a reaction against the scientism of the May 4th Movement a few years earlier. But it was different from the traditionalist stance of a few decades earlier still, in the sense that it now had the blessing of Western sages like Russell, Bergson, Eucken, Boutroux, and Hans Driesch who had taught in China. It was Carsun Chang (Chang Chun-mai) who sparked off in the early 1920s the great controversy on scientism versus metaphysicalism with his discussion of Science and the Philosophy of Life. Influenced by Bergson and Eucken, Chang drew the attention of the intellectual world to the psychological and spiritual dimensions of life, stressing its subjective and intuitive aspects in contrast to its rational analytical facets. The freedom of the will and the uniqueness of personality belied Jeremy Bentham's assumption of the uniformity of human nature. Science alone must be then inadequate and useless in man's endeavours to understand himself. Scientists like V. K. Ting responded to Chang's challenge without producing a more cogent argument than that Carsun Chang had confused 'what was' with 'what was to be'. Science was perhaps not yet in a position to provide all the answers to life's problems, but given faith in future progress in psychology and sociology, it would be able to do so one day. Fan Shou-k'ang, another scientist, divided the sciences into the descriptive and the normative, for instance, psychology and ethics. However immutable or changeable were the laws governing these two kinds of science, the approach to them was the same. The general feeling among the scientists was that if China's trust in science was to be shaken, the future would be unimaginably bleak.

The polemic raged on. Its subject matter, the priority of mind over matter or vice versa, mingled with practical considerations of the role of Western science in China's modernization and China's role in the modern world, was obviously one which could not be dealt with in a year or two. One of the outcomes of the debate was a clearer definition of science. Any branch of knowledge in which the judgement of truth was respected and to which the empirical and analytical method could be applied was a branch of science, thus opening the way to the establishment of the social sciences as legitimate and respectable subjects for teaching and research in China. Another, equally important outcome was the unresolved issues raised during the controversy. The value of the Chinese tradition had neither been endorsed nor denied, but this was to be left for a future debate on the choice between total Westernization or the restoration of the indigenous culture.

A new orientation in the selection of subjects for study by Chinese students abroad seems to have set in after the controversy. In the USA, the number of Chinese students of engineering temporarily declined between 1924 and 1927; the subject did not recover its popularity until 1942. At the same time, the number of students in pure science and social sciences rose. In Great Britain the same trends were observable. In pure science China was to produce men of high international reputation, e.g. Ch'en Hsing-shen, Chung K'ai-lai, Hua Lo-keng and Wang Hao in mathematics; Tseng Chao-lun, Yuan Han-ch'ing, Sa Pen-t'ieh in chemistry; Wu Yu-hsun, Wu Ta-yu and Yen Chi-tz'u in physics.

Following in the footsteps of C. H. Robertson of Purdue University, who came to China to give a lecture tour on engineering and science in the 1900s, American mathematicians like G. Birkhoff, W. F. Osgood, N. Wiener and others visited China. Marconi, too, made his trip in 1933. Co-operation between Chinese and foreign natural scientists, especially in the fields in which Chinese scholars distinguished themselves, ignored national and racial boundaries. There, close personal ties also influenced Chinese scientists' attitude towards politics and their life-style. Fame and security afforded the Chinese scientists a measure of independence from the sordid business of politics in the 1920s and 1930s, while the Western style of life converted them to the pursuit of monetary gain. The satisfaction of their intellectual curiosity and the attainment of international recognition* overshadowed the former desire to strengthen and enrich their country. They became a class of Westernized individualists striving for academic freedom and better research facilities instead of the amelioration of the predicament of their compatriots.

Other visiting scholars beside Dewey and Russell were invited by the Society for Lectures on the New Learning. The American educationist Paul Monroe came in 1921, Hans Driesch in 1922, and Rabindranath Tagore in 1924. The Society's invitations to Bergson and Eucken, however, did not materialize. In the 1930s, the visits of E. Smith, Radcliffe-Brown and W. Schmidt helped develop anthropological studies. In comparison, Eugene O'Neill's visit in 1928 and that of Bernard Shaw in 1933, like those of W. H. Auden and Christopher Isherwood in 1938 and Ernest Hemingway in 1941, left behind hardly a ripple.

## The impact of Western philosophy

When a humble pastor, Yen Yung-ching, translated Herbert Spencer's *Education: Intellectual, Moral, Physical* of 1862, *Principles of Psychology* of 1857–73, and *Genesis of Science* of 1855 into Chinese in the 1880s, neither the political nor the intellectual atmosphere of China was ready for them. Not until the crisis of the 1895 war against Japan did China bury her self-strengthening policy based on the formula of Chinese scholarship as the essence and Western scholarship only for application and open her mind to new philosophies which might

* For instance, the science papers published by the Academia Sinica in 1948 were mostly written in English – 1707 out of a total of 1815 to be precise.

provide the basis for a new policy. Coincidentally, a 'returned' student from the Greenwich Naval College, Yen Fu, was engaged in the translation of Thomas Huxley's *Essays on Evolution and Ethics*, a work which he completed in the very year of China's defeat. The conjunction of these two events was a situation liable to produce revolution; an intellectual revolution indeed occurred. Between the war of 1895 and the Russo–Japanese War of 1905, Yen had rendered into Chinese other works of epoch-making importance; his labours included the translation of Adam Smith's *Wealth of Nations* in 1901, J. S. Mill's *On Liberty* and Herbert Spencer's *Study of Sociology* in 1903, and Mill's *System of Logic* in 1905. These annotated renderings in exquisite style brought a generation of Chinese scholars under the sway of what may conveniently be called social Darwinism. It threatened to replace Confucianism in the minds of the elders like K'ang Yu-wei and Liang Ch'i-ch'ao, of the younger intellectuals like Hu Shih and Kuo Mo-jo, even of students in remote provinces like Mao Tse-tung and Han Suyin's father. 'Natural selection' and 'the survival of the fittest' were the starting points of almost all the discourses on Chinese politics and society in the 1900s.

Social Darwinism showed the Chinese scholars an evolutionary process of human society and gave them faith in progress. It caused the Chinese to stop looking backward to history for a model of benevolent administration and turn to look forward into the future with optimism. Evolutionary change was nothing to be feared, for the death of the old was prompt and 'the vigorous, the healthy, and the happy' would always survive and multiply. The equivalent process in politics was reform and all reformists stressed the need to enlighten the people through education.

Change, reform, and education were all forces for progress in Yen Fu's view:

Wealth and power entails no more than the interests of the people. A policy designed to meet the interests of the people must begin from the people working for their own interests. No people can do so without having obtained freedom in the first place. And the precondition for acquiring freedom is the self-government of each individual, lest freedom should lead to chaos. All the other peoples who are free and self-governing are superior [to us] in physical, intellectual, and moral education. At the moment, there are only three urgent policies [for us to adopt]: the enhancement of the physical strength, development of the intellect, and renewal of the morality of the people.

Here the influence of Spencer's theory of education on Yen was evident. When the Chinese were so educated and so emancipated from the shackles of tradition, their 'energy of faculty' would be released to achieve the long-term goals of modernization. Like Spencer and Huxley, Yen believed that the process of evolutionary change in China would take decades, if not a century, before she became strong and self-reliant. He also believed that change depended on the one hand upon the respect for people's freedom and on the other upon the capacities of the present-day sages (the elite) as leaders of the people. Influenced by Yen's translations and by those of Timothy Richard, Liang Ch'i-ch'ao sought a moral revival to release the energy of the new citizens of China. To both Liang and Yen, the aim was not so much individual freedom and individual happiness, as Huxley and Spencer insisted, but the power and wealth which could bring freedom and independence to the Chinese nation. Liang even turned to Johan Kaspar Bluntschli to solidify his argument that a strong Chinese state had to be his central consideration. Identifying the Confucian examination of things as a means of achieving knowledge with the Darwinian pragmatic interpretation of science, Yen Fu went on to focus his attention on the utility of knowledge in rectifying the mind so that it would become totally sincere. In sincerity knowledge found its value, which could make its possessors equal to the tasks of rectifying themselves and ordering the state. In this way, Spencer's sociology became Yen's science of social order and of national power and wealth.

Yen, however, was sufficiently faithful to social Darwinism to believe in the unchangeability of the laws of total evolution and by implication also in the unchangeability of the sages (the elite) themselves. What should be changed was all the rest, including institutions and policies. Liang Ch'i-ch'ao, on the other hand, rejected the concept of total evolution. In the final analysis, Liang was prepared to accept revolution as a method of change. By means of voluntarism and the identification of knowledge with values, the first generation of Chinese social Darwinists Confucianized this powerful European doctrine. Similarly, in equating 'the greatest happiness of the greatest number' with the Confucian concept of *jen* (humaneness) and free trade with the 'wealth of a nation' (not nations), they also sinocized Bentham and Smith. These signs of their lingering love of the Chinese tradition and fervent nationalism reflected an underlying dissatisfaction with social Darwinism which would in time lead them back to the spiritual civilization of China when, sixty years after the publication of *On the Origin of Species*, the Great War shook Europe's self-confidence and their confidence in Europe.

The hegemony of social Darwinism ended with the shock of the European war and changes in European thought before and after the war. In China the theory came to be regarded as a new superstition which 'humbled ethical standards without bringing forth an understanding of life', and 'transformed morality and co-operation into a camouflage of the struggle for survival'. The result of this was aggression, the replacement of right by might, and even the belief that civilization was created by war. In the wake of the collapse of the authority of social Darwinism, John Dewey arrived in China with his pragmatism.

For Dewey and other pragmatists,* experience is truth. Truth or falsity is determined by results, not causes. This simple device had the merit of cutting a multitude of Gordian knots and thereby suited the needs and aptitudes of many Chinese scholars, especially educationists with only a peripheral interest in philosophy. In a world of struggle, man needs experience as a weapon for defence and offence; knowledge is therefore no more than an instrument for enriching man's material and emotional life; it is not achieved for the sake of solving problems. Experience or knowledge is, and must be, useful for oneself and for society. This pragmatic approach to knowledge with action consequence and focus on social benefit conforms to the neo-Confucian dialectic of the unity of knowledge and action. Indeed, in some cases, the term 'pragmatism', was translated as 'the dialectic of knowledge and action'. By the time the Deweyan epistemology became known in China, traditional Chinese studies were being increasingly attacked by the modern minded as 'useless', while Deweyan experience, controlled by scientific methods, could yield new knowledge powerful enough to change China. Because of this hope, Dewey's theory was welcomed with open arms just as it had recently been in the USA.

* Before Dewey's arrival none of his works had been made available in Chinese for the benefit of his audience in China, though a series of lectures on C. S. Peirce and Dewey had been given by Hu Shih in the spring of 1919 (*Wen-ts'un* (Collected Essays), Shanghai, 1921 and 1924, vol. II, pp. 409–79). Dewey's *Reconstruction in Philosophy* and W. James's *Varieties of Religious Experience* and parts of his *Principles of Psychology* appeared in translation after 1923 (D. W. Y. Kwok, *Scientism in Chinese Thought*, New Haven, 1965, p. 113). Dewey's *Democracy and Education* was used in China either as a textbook or as a reference work for several years. As to his other works translated into Chinese, see his *Lectures in China, 1919-1920*, Honolulu, 1973, p. 38, n. 49.

Dewey accepted the Kantian concept of autonomous morality without stressing its religious implications. His avoidance of any discussion of religion made his views even more acceptable. The aims of morality were for individual growth and the common good of society. Morality must be flexible enough to change with society; consequently it must be conceptualized as general guidance and not as a set of concrete precepts regulating specific human relations and conducts. By defining the functions and principles of morality in this way, Dewey was in effect criticizing the rigid Confucian ethics which impeded individual growth.

For the same reasons Dewey also criticized authoritarianism and championed democracy. Authoritarianism suppressed the growth of individual talents and reoriented them towards servitude and dishonesty, while the class of people who wielded authority became cruel, extravagant and decadent. Psychologically it bred frustration, disenchantment and abnormality. For Dewey, neither social and political institutions nor customs and political culture must ever become dead weights; they must leave room for individuals to choose, criticize and judge. To that end, the political system must protect people's rights and freedoms with such apparatus as a constitution and a parliament while the socio-economic system must provide equal opportunities for all. Such a state of affairs could not be arrived at through either conservatism or radicalism, but through what Dewey called the third political philosophy:

We need the ability (and the disposition) to look for particular kinds of solutions by particular methods for particular problems which arise on particular occasions. In other words, we must deal with concrete problems by concrete methods when and as these problems present themselves in our experience.

Rome was not built in a single day; nor was the new society the Chinese wanted. Clearly Dewey was not in search of a cosmic inspiration or messianic message, which would be contradictory to his scientific and empirical approach. He was interested only in specific solutions to specific problems and the key to them all was education.

To link education directly to life itself for the development of the individual personality and democratic spirit was to deny it any other extraneous purposes, e.g. nurturing the martial spirit of citizens, preserving the cultural heritage of a nation, or validating an authority.

Dewey's lectures in 1919 and 1920 and his books, which were translated afterwards, expounded this philosophy. His Columbia students, together with other supporters of Dewey's theory, formed the China Society for the Promotion of New Education, with *New Education* as its official organ. The persuasiveness of Dewey's theory and the important positions his students held in Chinese higher and adult education ensured that his influence would be great for several years to come. Thanks to him the Chinese educational system was Americanized by the Educational Act of 1922.

Outside the field of education Dewey had a short-lived methodological and political influence on the Chinese intelligentsia, especially the Americanized section of it. Hu Shih, for example, following his mentor's gradualism, repudiated any all-embracing ideology which might effect a sudden and total change in China, as shown in his controversy with the early Marxists in China over the choice between studying specific problems and embracing a totalist ideology in order to solve all interrelated problems, the controversy known as 'Problems versus "Isms" '.

Dewey's exposition of political democracy and his influence on Chinese liberalism were, however, more complicated, since Western theories on democracy and liberalism had been introduced to China long before his visit. Rousseau, Bentham, Mill and Smith were all introduced in the early years of this century and Hu Shih himself accepted the doctrine of democracy through the study of the Declaration of Independence while he was at Cornell. But in Hu's later discourses on liberty and human rights traces of Deweyan influence are to be found. Dewey's aversion to party politics and his fear of revolution as a means of political change were shared by Hu. Later still, Hu's comments on current affairs published before 1937, particularly his sharp criticism of the decree protecting citizens' rights issued by the Kuomintang government on 20 April 1929,* followed the Deweyan tenets.

However, Ch'en Tu-hsiu, who in 1919 was already in the process of conversion to Marxism did not accept the Deweyan concept of

---

* The decree stipulated that 'any individual or public body under the jurisdiction of the Republic of China shall not illegally interfere with the persons, freedom, and property of other people'. Hu questioned the definitions, or the lack of them, of the citizens' three rights. Why were government organizations not specifically mentioned among the public bodies which might interfere with personal freedom and individual rights? Where were the laws by which the guilty would be punished? See the *Hsin-yüeh*, vol. II, p. 2, and Hu and Lin Yutang, *China's Own Critics*, Shanghai, 1931, pp. 22–3.

democracy 'whole-heartedly'. In his important statement on 'The Basis for the Realization of Democracy' of December 1919, Ch'en wrote:

Dr Dewey's explanation of socio-economic democracy (i.e. livelihood [of the people]) can be regarded as a belief shared by all schools of socialism. I think it is acceptable to all those who are just and unbiased.

Earlier in the same year his image of the future of China had ceased to be modelled on Anglo-Saxon democracy because of his increasing antagonism to capitalism and to the imperialist exploitation of China. He may still have had a lingering concern for the idea of democracy, only in a different sense, with much broader mass participation than with the Anglo-Saxon model. He called for something akin to a people's dictatorship, to be achieved by means of a social revolution of the workers and peasants overthrowing the rule of the elite. Just before the publication of the statement quoted above he launched a fierce attack on the moral decay of the system based on private ownership:

In the West, men are lazy and profit-seeking while women are extravagant and licentious. Wars, strikes, and all sorts of lamentable unrests – which of these is not caused by the moral decay of the system of private property?

He could then go along with Dewey on the equality of economic opportunity and a more equitable distribution of wealth and income, but what he had written implies that he would certainly disagree with Dewey on the need for democratic procedure and on the in-applicability of the class analysis to China.

Even in the field of education, Dewey's influence began to decline from 1927 on, in spite of the visit to China of Helen Parkhurst. In the first place the new ruling party, the Kuomintang, reintroduced political aims into education in order to foster nationalism and 'Chineseness' among students. In the second place the slavish emula-tion of the American educational system provoked a reaction from an eminent student of Dewey. T'ao Hsing-chih declared that he was against 'pulling a rickshaw with a foreigner sitting in it'. The foreign-er he referred to was the Deweyan educational philosophy, which he thought should be replaced by Chinese educational theories and methods. Instead of following Dewey's dictum that 'education is life' and 'a school is society', T'ao expounded his anti-elitist approach – 'life is education' and 'society is a school'.

In so far as empirical thinking, a commonsensical approach to reality, and individual freedom were concerned, Russell and Dewey differed little. However, the abstruseness of Russell's philosophy in the eyes of his Chinese admirers may have restricted the impact of his more academic lectures on mathematical logic, matter and mind, notwithstanding the enthusiasm his visit evoked. But his more popular lectures on freedom of thought and his criticism of Western civilization in the wake of a disastrous war had widespread and long-lasting influence. His antagonism to any attempt at the unification of thought appealed strongly to Chinese liberals, as did his praise of Chinese spiritual civilization –

. . . those who value wisdom or beauty, or even the simple enjoyment of life, will find more of these things in China than in the distracted and turbulent West and will be happy to live where such things are valued.

– sounding most agreeable to the ears of Chinese conservatives. In a sense, remarks like this made by Russell abetted the conservative revival that was to take place soon after his departure from China.

Upon his return from his European trip of 1919 to 1920, Liang Ch'i-ch'ao, like many of his younger contemporaries, evinced doubt of the wisdom of the West. His conversations with Bergson and Eucken had given him the impression that Western philosophers in the post-war years wanted, but did not know how, to unite ideals with reality and harmonize social concerns with freedom from such concerns.

Through Liang's and also Dewey's references to Bergson, the French vitalist came to hold the centre of attention of both Chinese philosophers and Chinese politicians for nearly a quarter of a century; his influence far outstripped that of Dewey and Russell and was more comparable to that of Darwin and Marx.

The Bergsonian approach to knowledge was a reaction against the rational, analytical scientism of late nineteenth-century Europe (and for that matter, early twentieth-century China). For Bergson the only sure knowledge man possessed was of his own existence through inner experience. By the same token, whatever true knowledge of the external world he could possibly have must come in the same way. Man changed incessantly and change was a continuous stream, never a static state however he dissected it, for neither time (the essence) nor space (the illusion) could be so treated. Man's existence was therefore a process of indivisible change and must be understood as such. To project this understanding on to external things, the things were seen to be bound together in a manner of existence analogous to man's own. Thus they became truly understandable.

In terms of time and space, reality was a continuum which could neither be divided up nor be held fast in an immobilized state for analysis; it could not be conceptualized by man's intellect. Science could do no more than make reality useful to man; it could never make it theoretically meaningful to him. For a meaningful understanding, reality must be grasped by intuition, as only intuition could keep pace with the ceaseless change of life and external things. Intuition was intellectual sympathy and immediate experience which alone could take man close to the *élan vital* – a force in man that broke the resistance of matter and enabled man make matter serve his needs.

Without the *élan vital*, evolution became at once purposeless and inexplicable. The new and unpredictable forms life evolved, and reality itself, were creative, and created by a purposive force, an impulse to action. The ethical value of man's action, according to Bergson, should be assessed in terms of fulfilment, creativeness and satisfaction of the undefined wants of man rather than in terms of the results of his actions. By emphasizing fulfilment and satisfaction, Bergson laid the foundation of a new morality. He also opposed the kind of education which gave exclusive attention to the development of man's intellect. Good education must be designed to enrich man's *élan vital* also, enabling him to participate creatively in the making of the unending flux which was his universe.

The new philosophy struck a Francophile, Li Shih-ts'en, as the work of the greatest genius since Kant, and the historian, Chang Yin-lin, as a totalist theory of 'flesh and blood' instead of an unexciting, cold formalist analysis. The periodical, *Min-to* (the People's Bell), issued a special supplement on Bergson's philosophy on 1 December 1921 and another periodical, *Hsüeh-heng* (the Critical Review) began to introduce it from 1925 onward. As expected, Chinese scholars of the Anglo-Saxon tradition took exception to it, for its anti-intellectualism throve 'on the errors and confusions of the intellect', while Chinese Francophiles and native metaphysicians welcomed it as a new stimulus for the revival of the Chinese tradition. Carsun Chang and Chang Tung-sun were particularly active in translating and popularizing Bergson's works,* as if purposely to break the dominance of Anglo-Saxon analytical philosophy.

Liang Shu-ming was notable among Bergson's admirers and critics, and his attempt to link Bergson with Oriental philosophy opened the way to the growth of the Chinese vitalism of the Kuomintang. In the hands of Ch'en Li-fu and his comrades the integration of Bergson and Confucius laid the foundation for a new monism – the 'life only' theory (*wei-sheng lun* or vitalism) – in contrast to the 'idea only' (*wei-hsin lun*, idealism) and 'matter only' (*wei-wu lun*, materialism). Being the official philosophy of the ruling party of China, KMT vitalism was to play havoc in Chinese politics, if not in Chinese philosophy.†

There is no doubt that the Russian October Revolution powerfully influenced Chinese radical intellectuals in the direction of sympathy with, or even conversion to Marxism and Leninism. The Chinese radicals saw the revolution as having destroyed the world's strongest autocracy; its leaders had voluntarily renounced Czarist Russia's privileges in China; the new Bolshevik regime in Moscow represented a triumph of the popular masses, lighting the way for the future of mankind. It would be, however, a gross simplification to say that the Russian Revolution was solely responsible for the radicals' conversion to communism. A mood of disappointment with Western civilization, stemming from the European War and the rendition of the former German possessions in Shantung to Japan instead of their return to China as justice demanded, had already become prevalent among the politically aware Chinese. Their disappointment was compounded by the failure of China's own experiments in parliamentary democracy since 1912 and the misery

* Nearly all Carsun Chang's writings of the 1920s were based on Bergson's theories, while Chang Tung-sun, a Japanese-trained philosopher, rendered Bergson's *Creative Evolution, Matter and Memory* and *Time and Free Will* into Chinese.

† Chinese literature on Rudolf Eucken in the 1910s and 1920s was considerably less extensive than that on Bergson. Liang Shu-ming also made an attempt to identify Eucken's theory of harmony between man and nature with Confucianism (*Tung-hsi wen-hua chi ch'i che hsueh*, Shanghai, 1923, pp. 179–80) and came to the conclusion that Western civilization must sooner or later develop in the same way as Chinese civilization. Liang's view had been anticipated to some extent by Chang Shih-chao in his article in the *Eastern Miscellany* (vol. XIV, no. 12, December 1917, pp. 6–7). Both were criticized by Carsun Chang who pointed out that Eucken's religious view of life contrasted with the Confucian secular view of life (*Eastern Miscellany*, vol. XIX, no. 3, February 1922, pp. 171–18). Eucken's religious revival could not legitimately be identified with a Confucian revival in China. As to Ch'en's vitalism, see below.

endured by the oppressed classes in factories, mines and villages. Many of the radicals had, like Ch'en Tu-hsiu, experienced a turning point in their intellectual development. Before it, they had addressed their messages for the reconstruction of China to the intelligentsia; afterwards they shifted their attention to the labouring people. The turning point was the May 4th Movement of 1919.

As Ch'en Tu-hsiu put it, 'since the revolutionary situation of the world and the domestic conditions of China indicated [the way] so clearly, my change of view was inevitable'. As Ch'en turned away from Anglo-Saxon democracy because of his increasing antagonism to capitalism and imperialist exploitation, Li Ta-chao, another pioneer Marxist in China, voiced his objection to capitalist exploitation while regarding democracy as having already been defeated in the USA. In the spring of 1919 the radical paper *Weekly Review* (*Mei-chou p'ing-iun*) carried an editorial under the title of 'The crimes of the Chinese elite class', calling for a social revolution of the workers and peasants to overthrow the rule of the elite. Thence, the radical view progressed to an attack on private property and on the exploitation of surplus value by the capitalists.

Except for some radical students who went to France under the Work-Study Scheme and who became Marxists, none of the early communist sympathizers was a 'returned' student from the West and very few of them could be regarded as leading intellectuals from a well-to-do background. As time passed, the chasm between them and the high intellectuals holding professorial chairs and newspaper editorships increased; so did their lack of mutual understanding. But in 1919 and 1920, the shift of the radicals' focus from the oppressed youth and oppressed women – subjects which had been under discussion since the 1900s – to the oppressed labouring masses amounted to a new identification for them. Their scope of view being thus widened, their sympathies now encompassed all the underprivileged. Externally they ceased to be chauvinistic: instead of identifying China with the great powers of the world, they now identified her with the oppressed nations like Korea, Ireland and the Philippines. Internally a spate of articles on social survey, covering a wide range of topics concerned with the working and living conditions of workers in Shanghai, Hankow, and T'angshan and the misery of the peasants in Shantung, Kiangsu and Fukien, appeared in their periodicals, the *New Youth*, the *Weekly Review* and the *Morning Post*. Before the founding of the Chinese Communist Party in 1921 there were even special magazines for or about working people which provided information on workers and peasants, fostered a new attitude towards labour and drew attention to some of the most urgent social problems.

As radicals they were moved to ask: could China's national aspirations be fulfilled and social justice be done without recourse to a violent revolution? Would the ruling class allow these purposes to be achieved by a process of peaceful transformation? By the time of the May 4th Movement the enemies of the nation – the imperialists, militarists and corrupt bureaucrats – had been identified, but could not be driven from positions of power merely 'by a few citizens' meeting' as Li Ta-chao said. Here the failures of the reforms of 1898 and the 1900s and the experiences of the 1911 and 1917 (Russian) revolutions furnished indubitable evidence. To the mind of Ch'en Tu-hsiu, the glory of Europe resulted chiefly from her revolutions; to the mind of Li Ta-chao, the greatest success could only follow the greatest sacrifice and suffering. As a famous editorial 'The new era' in the *Weekly Review*, January 1919 explained, evolution was based on co-operation rather than competition. Since the greed of the few that drove man to exploit man created a competitive instead of a co-operative situation, social injustice was the outcome. This injustice could not be eliminated by means other than violence. By violence, the old would be destroyed and the new would be brought forth. The solutions to all social problems had to come after the victory of the revolution. In the words of Ch'en Tu-hsiu, 'Problems concerning women, youth, and workers can be solved by a class war only.' It was then logical to accept the materialist interpretation of history and the dictatorship of the proletariat.

As radicals they must also ask: why Marxism? What did they know about it before taking the plunge into organized political action? Prior to the founding of the CCP, several translations of the *Manifesto of the Communist Party* were available; there were also essays introducing historical materialism in the *New Youth* and the supplement of the *Morning Post*. Kautsky's *Karl Marx's Ökonomische Lehren* was translated twice, but *Das Kapital* itself was available in Chinese only in drastically abridged forms. Also obtainable in Chinese were *Wage Labour and Capital, Critique of the Gotha Programme, Civil War in France, On the Jewish Question, The Holy Family, The Poverty of Philosophy, A Contribution to the Critique of Political Economy*, and *Socialism: Utopian and Scientific*. Apart from these, the October Revolution naturally drew the attention of the radicals to Russia under the Bolshevik leaders. Lenin's *State and Revolution, Imperialism: the Last Stage of Capitalism*, and *Left-wing Communism: an Infantile Disorder*, and Trotsky's *Communism and Terrorism* and *Bolshevism and World Peace* were translated into Chinese. The Chinese version of Lenin's report on the Constitution of the Communist Party of the Soviet Union at the party's Eighth Congress found a space in the *New Youth* in two instalments – 'National Self-determination' and 'The Economy in the Period of Transition'. The work of introducing Marxism–Leninism gained momentum with the founding of the monthly, *Communist* (Kung-ch'an tang-jen), in Shanghai in November 1920, while various aspects of the party, state and society of Russia, together with Russia's new arts and literature, were reported on in several radical periodicals.

With these publications, the main analytical tools of Marxism–Leninism – dialectical materialism, the class struggle, surplus value, proletarian dictatorship, etc. – were within the grasp of the early converts. The faults of their country and the suffering of the working people were seen as the outcome of imperialist, capitalist and landlord exploitation and their monopoly of state power. In this perspective, Chinese society was viewed as being made up of oppressor and oppressed classes and its nature as semi-colonial and semi-feudal, an image quite different from that of the proud empire of a couple of decades before. Admittedly a revolution was needed to transform it, but why a revolution guided by Marxism–Leninism and led by a communist party when China had neither a developed bourgeoisie nor a massive proletariat? Li Ta-chao's answer to this question, in an editorial of the *Weekly Review* on 4 May 1919, was a simple one – since the Chinese bourgeoisie was under-developed, the Chinese revolution might be more easily accomplished than those in Russia, Germany, Austria, and Hungary. On the eve of the founding of the CCP, he argued that in a world of rising labour movements, it would be theoretically as well as practically unthinkable for China to develop capitalism. The vision of Chinese capitalism struggling against endless labour unrest and striving to catch up with the West was almost intolerable for Li. China must therefore leap over the capitalist stage of social development. Ch'en Tu-hsiu, while subscribing to the leap-over theory, thought the embryonic capitalism of China in 1920 was no less developed than that of Germany in 1848 or that of Russia in 1917. Since Russia had successfully made the jump, why not China? Dialectical or otherwise, the dreary prospect of a lengthy 'capitalist stage' was too repulsive for all the radicals to contemplate.

At the time of the founding of the party, methods of party organization, the strategies to be followed in the Chinese anti-imperialist and anti-feudal revolution, and patterns of party life were introduced to the members of the burgeoning CCP. As the revolution they led progressed, some Chinese Marxists developed theories of art and literature in the areas under the control of the KMT, whereas their comrades evolved theories of government organization, military strategy and mass work in the revolutionary base areas. The significance of the entire enterprise of introducing and developing Marxism–Leninism lay in waging a two-front struggle against enemies outside the party as well as among its rank and file, in order to bring the revolution to victory. They were faithful to the Marxist tradition;

truth, i.e., the reality and power of thought, must be demonstrated in practice. The contest as to the reality or non-reality of a thought which is isolated from practice is a purely scholastic question. . . . Philosophers have only interpreted the world in various ways, but the real task is to alter it.

Another important political doctrine imported into China with the aim of altering the Chinese reality was fascism. But, unlike liberalism and communism, fascism anywhere, anti-intellectual and irrational as it was, had hardly anything which could be described as a coherent body of theories. The common characteristics of fascist movements were, on the negative side, anti-capitalism in the sense of a curtailment of individual acquisitiveness which might be detrimental to the state; anti-communism, because of the fascist belief in class co-operation for the interest of the state; and opposition to democracy, because of the cumbersomeness and inefficiency of the democratic procedure. As to the positive views of these movements, they were for the restoration of the glory of a nation as symbolized by its past conquests and cultural achievements; they also sought for ideological unity under a strong dictator who, in the name of national glory, could justifiably use coercion, violence and even terror to ensure the unity and efficiency of each of the movements. The paramountcy of unity and the interests of the state made it mandatory that the state be ruled by only one party organized along Leninist lines, and by the same token the youth of the country must be trained to become physically fit and ideologically united to give service to the state.

The introduction of fascism through the German officers working as Chiang Kai-shek's advisers, e.g. Colonel Max Bauer and Lieutenant Colonel Herman Kriebel, both ardent supporters of Hitler, and through Chiang's special envoys, Ho Chung-han, P'an Yu-ch'iang and Feng T'i, to Germany, Italy and the Soviet Union suggests that the Chinese fascists perceived a similarity between Europe in the 1920s and China early in the 1930s. Democracy for a time did not seem to be working well in Europe whereas it had never been a success in China. Although China had not suffered a calamitous defeat and a runaway inflation like Germany, her economy had been in chaos since Chiang's assumption of power in 1928. The disgruntled ex-servicemen in Italy and Germany and the defiant soldiers in China joined forces with disillusioned middle-class and landowning people in their respective countries to express their wish for a strong leadership and their fear of a left-wing challenge; the sentiment of 'better Hitler than the communists' or 'better Chiang than the Reds' was essentially the same in both East and West. Under these circumstances, even convinced liberals like V. K. Ting and Ch'ien Tuan-sheng, Chiang T'ing-fu and Lo Chia-lun began to break away from their erstwhile belief in democracy in the hope that China might yet be saved from her almost inescapable fate of destruction by Japan. The elitist V. K. Ting had no faith in the people's ability to practise democracy; as he put it: 'two smelly cobblers can make only two smelly cobblers'. When the Japanese were advancing into north China from their newly gained base in Manchuria, dictatorship in China became urgent and necessary. The Harvard-trained political scientist, Ch'ien Tuan-sheng, wrote in a provocative article published in the *Eastern Miscellany* in January 1934:

I think what China needs is also a competent and imaginative dictatorship [like the Soviet Union, Germany, and Italy] which can in a short spell of time turn her into a country of considerable military strength. . . . If [we] desire to industrialize the coastal provinces, our country must possess the powers of a dictatorial state.

These liberals were evidently disappointed by the bungling of the democracies during the Great Depression and impressed by the economic progress of the Soviet Union and Germany. And that was why the American- and British-trained Lo Chia-lun felt able to recommend *Mein Kampf* as a standard book for the Sunday edition of *Shen-pao* on 1 January 1936.

It was precisely with a call for unity in order to defend and save the nation that the Chinese fascists addressed the nation. They insisted that their movement was for action and had a scientific basis, although the scientific basis was never explained. Instead, they wrote:

[Fascism] has no definite contents; it takes social contents [*sic*] as its own. When society needs statism, fascism is the most lively statism. When society needs socialism, fascism is the most progressive socialism. In sum, fascism is the crystallization of will power and [the spirit] of sacrifice. With its fearless *élan*, it aspires to save society and mankind.

By stating its political principles in this flexible manner, Chinese fascism opened the way to its operating within the framework of the KMT under the personal leadership of Chiang Kai-shek. Under Chiang's tutelage the KMT paid lip service to the principles of democracy and the livelihood of the people, thus dressing Chiang's personal dictatorship up as the party's tutelary rule according to Sun Yat-sen's *Three Principles*. Also unnoticed was the fascist insistence on the state creating the nation, which fundamentally differed from the KMT's belief that the nation created the state. Otherwise, fascism and the Three Principles of the People agreed in that their basic philosophy was the vitalism which would give China a vision, develop into a faith, and lead her people to strength and wealth. They also agreed on the state supervision and planned control of all activities of the nation, especially its economic activities. Both the fascists and the KMT wanted to restore the traditional glory of China; both were longing for a supreme leader. In their heyday, the Chinese fascists made Chiang such a revered *führer* that, whenever his name was mentioned in a public speech, the entire audience was required to stand to attention.

## Translation, literature and the arts

Very few Western-trained students who had an interest or specialized in literature took up translation as a career. The most diligent translator, Lin Shu, had never set foot in the West whereas Wu Kuang-chien, Li Ch'ing-yai and Li Chi-jen were exceptional rather than typical. This observation certainly applies to Lin Yutang, Lao She and Ch'ien Chung-shu, and to a lesser degree to Hsü Chih-mo, Chao Yuan-jen and P'an Chai-hsün. The result of this tendency was that although there were large numbers of English-speaking 'returned' students, fewer literary works in English than in Japanese, French, and Russian were rendered into Chinese and much of the translation from English was left to professional translators trained in Japan. A prominent example of this was T'ien Han's tackling of *Hamlet* and *Romeo and Juliet*. Professional translators as a rule had neither the time nor the facilities for research. In their hands, translation was apt to become a hack job of doubtful quality. Marketability, the common concern of both publisher and translator, rather than any intellectual consideration, was the weather-vane of the entire enterprise of translation, which affected the level of understanding and taste of the reading public. In the 1920s and 1930s two strands of development in this field emerged. On the one hand, highly sophisticated academics in literature, confining themselves to their small circles of friends and students and oblivious of the fact that their self-imposed isolation was directly responsible for the low standard of appreciation of Western literature, tended to be esoteric and stale in their attempts at introducing Western literary works; on the other, professional translators, working without much knowledge or methodology, looked only for popularity and monetary gain. The chasm between them failed to generate a dynamic process of mutual influence and stimulation; instead there was mutual contempt and acrimony. That was why in the 1930s Chinese readers had to be satisfied with Shakespeare and Wilde, Washington Irving and Walt Whitman, Shelley and Hardy, Conan Doyle and Jules Verne, with little thought of sampling Hemingway and Steinbeck, Eliot and Pound. Less lucky in securing academic appointments, the 'returned' students from France, Japan, and Russia had little choice but to take up professional translation to obtain fame or just a living. In the majority of cases they *were* the professional translators, introducing the newest French and Russian, and to a lesser extent Japanese and German, works of literature into China.

The English-speaking 'returned' students, with academic security behind them, influenced the development of Chinese literature through their own writings which were in turn influenced by English or American mentors, e.g. Hsü Chih-mo under the influence of Keats and Byron, Wen Yi-to under Tennyson, Browning and Housman, Lao She under Dickens and Hardy, and Wu Mi under

Irving Babbitt and P. E. Moore. Their works, coupled with translations of such works as Goethe's *Werther* and *Faust* and Ibsen's *Doll's House* stimulated Chinese writers to evolve their own theory of literature. Regardless of their philosophical or political persuasions, they generally rebelled against the Confucian canon of literature as being a vehicle for the exposition of moral principles; they came to accept that the primary aim of literature was the expression of human emotions. Self-expression in an age of social transformation and intellectual rebellion easily led to individual or social romanticism and to writing poems and novels for art's sake or for life's sake. Chinese literature suddenly blossomed into variegated forms and lively vernacular language, a new movement that was both a cause and an effect of the social change of the period.

Representing the students from English-speaking countries, the romantics of the Crescent Moon Society formed in 1924 (named after an anthology of Tagore) defined its attitude towards literature in a series of 'don'ts', in the inaugural issue of the society's organ, *Hsin-yüeh* (the Crescent Moon). It dared not endorse the idea of art for art's sake or any tendency towards decadence, for life itself was too magnificent to be wasted on mere beauty; it dared not support sentimentality or fanaticism, for it believed that emotions unrestrained by reason were muddy and extravagant; it dared not subscribe to any extremism, for love was always stronger than hate and mutual co-operation stronger than mutual harm; it did not adopt utilitarianism, for price was no substitute for value and material gain no substitute for spiritual satisfaction. Living in the rarefied air of academies, members of the Crescent Moon unashamedly displayed their elitist distrust of the lesser breeds. For them the portrayal of reality, of the immutable universal human nature, was the only reliable criterion for evaluating a literary work. A valuable piece of writing could be created only by a genius. Democracy in literature was a mirage; literature for the majority was only a slogan. Since its attitude was defined only negatively, the literary output of the members of the Crescent Moon displayed a concern with form rather than content. As long as the author did not commit the four listed sins, any subject matter could make good literature. Moreover, the Society's elitism was no bar to lack of perspicuity. Take Liang Shih-ch'iu's essay on 'Literary discipline' in the first issue of the *Crescent Moon* for instance. In it, the author referred to more or less the entire corpus of European literary criticism from Aristotle to Robortelli, from Goethe to Arnold. Out of necessity, the references were so brief as to become incomprehensible and the essay read like a directory of European writers and critics, as if purposely written to bore its readers to tears.

Two years before the foundation of the Crescent Moon Society the Creation Society had come into being. Romantic and elitist like the Crescent Moon, the Creation, dominated by Japanese-trained students, showed a more positive and less individualistic approach to literature. It sought to give comfort to those who had been defeated in life's battles on account of their righteousness and to promote reform of the irrational structure of society. Both the Creation and the Crescent Moon followed the doctrine that literature and art were a vehicle for self-expression of the writers and artists. This was particularly true of the poems by Kuo Mo-jo, Hsü Chih-mo and the 'Modernists' (*Hsien-tai p'ai*) led by French-educated writers like Tai Wang-shu, Ho Ch'i-fang and others. But the left-wing writers, romantics with a strong social consciousness, doubted the so-called 'universal human nature' and therefore also the function of art and literature as self-expression. In Lu Hsün's words,

True, joy and anger, sorrow and happiness are human nature. But a poor man can never be troubled by his losses at a stock market; nor can Mr Rockefeller share the misery of an old woman in Peking who scraped a living by rummaging rubbish heaps for pieces of unburnt coal. Famine refugees will probably not follow the wealthy in nursing a few shoots of orchids. . . . If the best literature must express the most universal human nature, the literature that shows the even more universal animal instincts – eating, breathing, moving, and procreating – . . . must be even better. If we agree that since we are people [our literature] can express only human nature, then the proletarians have every justification for writing proletarian literature.

The left-wing writers' denial of the universal human nature logically led to their insistence that literature must serve the interests of the labouring masses instead of mere self-expression. What would be the significance of a few falling flowers and the autumn moon, which so sentimentally concerned the aristocrats, to a man working in a dark and dingy factory, Fen Nai-ch'ao asked. Left-wing writers also opposed the elitist view of civilization as being the creation of a few geniuses. In their view it was the creation of collective labour. Founded in 1930, the Left-wing Writers' League declared that in a period of social transformation, art and literature unavoidably served either conservatism and reaction or progress and revolution. Progressive and revolutionary art and literature must therefore reflect the feelings and sentiments of the proletariat and other working people in a gloomy, 'medieval' society and their longing for a better world.

Either directly from the originals or indirectly through Japanese renderings, Chinese translations of Western works of literature had a tremendous impact on the Chinese language. Foreign idioms and proverbs, allusions and sentence structures, even punctuation and other morphological features, invaded Chinese, much to the chagrin of the purists. First, the learning of a foreign language made the Chinese conscious of the grammatical structure of their own language, resulting in the French-trained Ma Chien-chung's *Ma-shih went'ung* (1903 edition) – a Chinese grammar based on the framework of Latin – and Hu Shih's similar attempt in 1921. Later revisions and improvements did not seem to break away from the methodology adopted by these two pioneers. Second, in order to render foreign ideas and the names of material objects, translators inevitably had to coin their own words and phrases or borrow from the Japanese. An extremist in this endeavour was Wang Chih who favoured transliteration instead of translation, e.g. *'p'u-lo-le-t'a-li-ya'* rather than *'wu-ch'an chieh-chi'* (property-less-class) for the 'proletariat'. In fact, except for a few cases like 'gallon', 'dozen', and 'the Pound', translators imitated either Yen Fu in inventing new phrases or Liang Ch'i-ch'ao in borrowing from Japanese. The regrettable feature here was that despite the authority of a government institute of translation – the National Bureau of Translation – both the new coinages and the loan words from Japanese were by no means uniform. Third, whatever method was adopted by the translator, many erstwhile monosyllabic words were replaced by polysyllabic compounds and phrases to gain precision and to create a new fashion. Take the old expression, *'kung'* (work, industry and worker) for instance. Its place was taken by *kung-tso* (work), *kung-yeh* (industry) and *kung-jen* (worker) and sometimes even *kung-jen-men* (workers). Fourth, sentences tended to become longer by the addition of conditional phrases, adverbs, and adjectives; they also became more varied and complicated in structure, for instance by the more frequent use of the passive voice and subjunctive mood.

The last bastions of Chinese linguistic conservatism – correspondence, official documents and newspaper editorials – stood firm against the rising tide of vernacularism, perhaps on the ground of appropriateness to the occasion of writing and the social status of the writer and of the expressiveness of the well-developed language. Chinese writers of the 1920s and 1930s still felt that the vernacular style tended to bring the reader down to the same level of social standing as the writer. The suggestion of equality appeared to be embarrassingly informal and impolite, and therefore inappropriate for personal and official letters or for the government to use in addressing its messages to the people. Furthermore, when finer sentiments, grandeur, ambiguity and other subtleties were called for, the vernacular was deemed inadequate, and so writers continued to use the classical styles. These were the reasons why the Ministry of Education prohibited the use of the vernacular styles in its order of 15 September 1927, and as late as 1933, almost fifteen years after the launching of the vernacular campaign at the time of the May 4th Movement, the Ministry still insisted that at least 50 per cent of the Chinese lessons at the secondary school must be in the classical style; in the same year the central government adopted modern punctuation in its official pronouncements for the first time. To show the sharp contrast between two different attitudes to the adequacy of the vernacular, the Kuomintang's official news agency translated the Japanese Emperor's order of surrender of 15 August 1945 into classical Chinese, while all the communist papers published it in a vernacular translation. The KMT government's effort at preserving classical Chinese was tantamount to keeping the less educated from any fuller knowledge of affairs of state.

The earliest Chinese student of Western painting was probably Wu Mo-ching who pioneered the application of Western techniques to Chinese art in the 1680s. In the 1830s and 1840s, Cantonese artists who worked with foreigners, as did Langua with George Chinnery, used oil on canvas and some of Langua's works are still to be seen in the Medical Library of Yale and at Guy's Hospital in London. They were regarded by traditional critics as lacking in intellectuality. Widespread appreciation of Western art had to wait for Miss Carl's Portrait of the Empress Dowager in 1903 and the 1911 Revolution. At the popular and commercial level, Cheng Man-t'o hired sing-song girls as models when designing advertising posters and calendars; and at the academic level, a French-trained student, Liu

Hai-su, founded the Shanghai College of Arts to teach the development of European painting from the Renaissance down to the Impressionists. In the meantime, illustrated periodicals carried reprints of European masterpieces, from those of ancient Greece down to the nineteenth century. Then the return of Hsü Pei-hung and Lin Feng-mien from their Work-Study sojourn in Paris marked a decisive step towards the development of oil painting in the Western idiom and the reform of Chinese traditional art by adopting Western techniques.

Amateurs flourishing in an amateurist tradition, Chinese statesmen did not hide their impressions of Western art. The redoubtable Commissioner Lin preferred the realism and attention to detail of the Western tradition, but he disliked the dismal background of the Western portrait. That was in the 1830s. A Chinese visitor to the Philadelphia Exhibition of 1876, Li Kuei, learned to admire the Western skill in the use of light and perspective and to appreciate the difficulty of depicting the nude, but he roundly condemned the Western inattention to brushwork. Chinese beholders still felt uneasy in the presence of paintings of the female nude and K'ang Yu-wei ascribed the European predilection for them to hedonism. K'ang nevertheless, was overwhelmed by the works of Raphael which he compared to Wang Hsi-chih's calligraphy and Li Po's poems – the highest praise a Chinese could offer.

To be sure, K'ang and other Chinese critics before the May 4th Movement had hardly any inkling of Western aesthetics. Through the writings of Ts'ai Yuan-p'ei, its importance came to be known to a new generation of Chinese intellectuals. So Li Shih-ts'en, arguing from his study of Nietzsche and Bergson, urged the importance of self-expression which, to him, made all the difference between the sterility of Chinese art and its vigorous Western counterpart. Liu Hai-su went further, commenting on the strength and weaknesses of classicism as represented by David and Ingres and romanticism as represented by Delacroix. A Chinese literary man, Wang T'ung-chao, could linger in front of a Rembrandt or a Vermeer in Amsterdam, transfixed by the artists' magical power, sincerity, and serenity; a Chinese woman, Chiang Pi-wei, could be overpowered by the wisdom and creativeness of Michelangelo; and a Chinese communist leader, Ch'ü Ch'iu-pai, could be moved by the anxiety and hope expressed by the Futurists in Moscow. The originality, methods of composition and freedom from moral concerns of Western art were all new, exciting and evocative to the few fortunate Chinese who saw the original paintings and sculpture in European and American galleries and museums.

In an atmosphere like this, whither should Chinese traditional art go? Liu Hai-su, true to his reputation as a rebel, demonstrated his defiance of convention by placing a nude model in his classroom for his students to study and by showing his own painting of a nude woman at an exhibition in 1919. The outcry he succeeded in provoking can be imagined by the demand of the warlord, General Sun Ch'uan-fang, that he should be shot. However, ten years later, Liu, like Hsü Pei-hung and Lin Feng-mien after him, went back to the Chinese tradition. He ceased to paint in the Western style altogether after 1926. When Yi-to, the American-trained artist and poet, after a period of admiration of Velasquez and van Gogh, concluded that in the final analysis Western art was inferior to Chinese, for Chinese paintings reached beyond mere forms and sensations to the soul and heart of man – a height that was undreamt of in the West. Apart from a shallowness of understanding, these artists and art critics were caught in a dilemma between cosmopolitan taste and national pride. Perhaps they were also influenced by the climate of opinion in China and left behind by the rapid change in artistic thinking in the West.

Western architecture drew little attention from Chinese travellers, not to speak of the Chinese in China. Liang Ssu-ch'eng's attempt at a compromise by putting a Chinese roof on an otherwise Edwardian building was unoriginal and incongruous. Only Wang T'ung-chao, on his tour of Europe in 1939, was struck by the disturbing gloom and sombreness of a medieval city which transported him to the distant past and made him feel small and insignificant.

Slightly more attention was given to European music; after all, modern Chinese music, in spite of all its Chineseness, was essentially Western in form and technique. The revolutionary movements since 1920 had bestowed on the Chinese many revolutionary songs which were all Western in form and spirit, accompanied by Western instruments. From 1900 onward systematic efforts had been made to introduce Western music by publishing music magazines, organizing brass bands and teaching music in schools and colleges. There was a realization of the simplicity, crudeness and even vulgarity of the Chinese musical tradition and an urge to emulate the West, although the Peking and provincial operas continued to play to full houses.

It was one thing for a Chinese soldier to be able to sing the *Marseillaise*; it was another for the Chinese to appreciate Western classical and popular melodies. The philosopher Liang Shu-ming's comments on a Beethoven recital were, to say the least, superficial and irrelevant. Even the well-known aesthete, Chu Kuang-ch'ien, could only vaguely describe Beethoven's Symphony No. 5 in C Minor as 'exciting' (*k'ang-kai lin-li*). Perhaps he had heard the story of the singer Malibran's bout of convulsion upon hearing the symphony. The legend around the so-called *Moonlight Sonata* completely misled him into fantasizing dreamy, intoxicating and serenely elegant qualities in the piece. Another art critic, Li Chien-wu, quite inappropriately compared a short piece of prose by Ho Ch'i-fang to a symphony that ended suddenly in a coda of disorder like broken pieces [of glass?]! The superficiality here is even more disconcerting.

## Conclusion

For nearly a hundred years, Chinese students either relied on their own financial resources or were sponsored by the government or voluntary organizations when they went to study abroad, while a small number of foreign scholars came to teach in China. These interchanges of visits perhaps contributed more than anything else to the importation of Western learning, with the intention of enriching the cultural life and of modernizing the political, social, and economic structures of China. Christian and non-Christian Chinese students studying in the West shared the same national concerns, although they would follow different approaches to a better life for the Chinese and a higher status for their country among the family of nations. Their failure to fulfil these large goals cannot obviously be blamed entirely on them, for the 'returned' students, small in number and without a solid power base, were not the ultimate decision makers. If they decided to join the government, they had to serve their more powerful masters in the Imperial Court or later in the republican governments. This was the position of T'ang Shao-yi and Liang Tun-yen under Yuan Shih-k'ai, of C. T. Wang and V. K. Ting under the warlords, and of T. V. Soong and H. H. Kung under Chiang Kai-shek.

It was this position of subordination to forces which most 'returned' students regarded as archaic and irrational that alienated them from government service. Remaining in the political wilderness and teaching at colleges and schools, the majority led the life of a teacher, a journalist, a doctor, or a lawyer. At the teaching institutions research facilities were meagre, unless one was prepared to pursue a topic or field related to China – Chinese geology, Chinese archaeology, Chinese zoology or Chinese demography. For those who had been trained in pure science, medicine, engineering and the Western humanities, it was hard to keep abreast of progress in the West, let alone extend the frontiers of knowledge.

Academically the practice of sending students abroad resulted in an admiration of foreign authorities, while at the same time it was not possible to jettison the age-old tradition to which the 'returned' students still felt a close attachment. This cultural ambivalence, exacerbated by a grievous lack of research facilities, could lead only to intellectual confusion; the 'returned' students' writings were, and still are, full of quotations from foreign authorities while the authors themselves had almost nothing new, nothing original to say on academic subjects The less gifted among them simply indulged in plagiarism.

Had the 'returned' students devoted their hours of leisure to translation they would have made a much greater contribution to China's cultural enrichment. As it was, translation was left to people less qualified than the well-known professors at prestigious universities; for instance, *Das Kapital* was handled by two incompetent economists who produced an utterly incomprehensible Chinese version, while *Mein Kampf* had to be translated from its English edition.

The 'returned' students were often criticized for their unsystematic way of introducing foreign works on the social sciences and the humanities into China, while none of their critics, except the Marxist ones, laid down a set of acceptable principles or guidelines to make the whole enterprise systematic. No one was sure for what specific purposes foreign knowledge should be introduced into China. To learn from the 'barbarians' in order to deal with the 'barbarians'? For the power and wealth of the nation? These old-fashioned goals seemed to be totally inadequate after 1900. For enrichment of Chinese cultural life? A pertinent question here was: the cultural life of what type of Chinese? The confusion in China was further compounded by the confusion in the West after the Russian Revolution, the First World War, and the Great Depression. What would and could be the significance of Dadaism and sexual emancipation to the Chinese intellectual life or their national struggles, or the significance of *Alice in Wonderland* to Chinese children? Should the Chinese foster a spirit of fair play and an Anglo–Saxon sense of humour as Dr Lin Yutang advocated?

Deficient in both Chinese and Western learning, the ambivalent and confused 'returned' students, except for the scientists and engineers, made a pitifully small contribution to knowledge and introduced too few Western works into China. Their admiration of the West and Westernized ways of thinking turned them into naive critics of Chinese society and culture. They also carried with them the habits and life-styles which they had acquired while studying in Europe or America and which served to set them apart from the rest of their compatriots in a separate class of high-caste Chinese. This attitude was typified by the following incident. In 1925 a couple of American soldiers in Peking who had beaten up their rickshaw boys were chased by a policeman and a large crowd of Chinese onlookers to the Legation Quarter. They turned to the crowd and challenged them: 'Come on and fight!' The crowd simply dispersed. Incensed by the cowardice of his compatriots who could do no more than shout threats and slogans, an anglophile commented: 'Hit them! Hit them! War! War! This kind of Chinese, phew!' Twenty years before this incident, in 1905, there was a Chinese medical student studying at Sendai, Japan, where a teacher screened for him and his classmates a newsreel of the Russo–Japanese War. The newsreel showed a group of Chinese standing silently watching a number of Chinese spies for the Russian army who had been captured and were being beheaded by the Japanese. The Chinese medical student decided after seeing the newsreel that however physically robust his medical training might help the Chinese to become, they would be fit for no better roles than those criminals or spectators of a public execution. Thereupon he gave up his medical studies for popular writing in order to cure the mental deficiencies of his people. When the former student heard about the anglophile's comment on the incident in Peking in 1925, he questioned whether the crowd should have beaten up the American soldiers or not. If they had done, they would have been called lawless Boxers; as they had not, they had been subjected to the scorn of the anglophile. In any case, the crowd could do no right in the anglophile's eyes. It was this sort of Westernized, high-caste Chinese that the erstwhile medical student thought should be 'phewed' and 'phewed' again.

# Chapter 4

# *Residents and immigrants*

The two cities of Shanghai and San Francisco lie at 42° and 48° north respectively, with the widest ocean of the world between them. They are the subjects of the case studies of this chapter, chosen for the obvious reasons: in Shanghai there resided the largest concentration in China of Caucasian traders, civil servants, and intellectuals including missionaries; in San Francisco there lived a large concentration of Chinese immigrants. Both communities were surrounded by a vast population racially and culturally different from themselves; both could be the agents of municipal and cultural changes; both underwent a process of limited acculturation themselves.

## Shanghai

The presence of some fifty Caucasians among a population of approximately 500000 in the county of Shanghai, like the arrival of thirty-four Chinese men and two Chinese women in San Francisco in 1849, caused quite a stir. The cultural shock for both inhabitants and new arrivals being so great, it was considered better for the sake of harmony that the two races should live separately. Foreigners were forbidden to buy land in China, but they circumvented this law by leasing or renting land in perpetuity. The idea of a concession (controlled by a consul who was responsible for paying taxes to the Chinese government) or a settlement (controlled in the same way, although the leaseholders paid their taxes directly to the Chinese government) emerged. The Land Regulations of the British Concession in Shanghai were agreed upon in 1845. Three years later, because Americans did not like living under the British authorities,

Bishop W. Boone initiated negotiations with the Chinese for the Americans to lease land from Chinese owners. His work was

*The growth of the foreign community in Shanghai**

| 1844 | 50 | 1900 | 6774‡ |
|---|---|---|---|
| 1846 | 134 | 1905 | 11497 |
| 1848 | 159 | 1910 | 13536 |
| 1849 | 175 | 1915 | 18519 |
| 1850 | 210 | 1920 | 28000§ |
| 1851 | 265 | 1927 | 44000 |
| 1854 | 250 | 1929 | 40000 |
| 1860 | 569 | 1930 | 59188 |
| 1865 | 5129 | 1931 | 65182 |
| 1870 | 2773† | 1932 | 69797 |
| 1876 | 1673 | 1933 | 73504 |
| 1880 | 4000 | 1934 | 68308 |
| 1885 | 3673 | 1935 | 69429 |
| 1890 | 3820 | 1936 | 73040 |
| 1895 | 4184 | 1937 | 37273§§ |

Sources: The *Chinese Repository*, vol. V, no. 9, January 1837, p. 432; the *Shen-pao, Shanghai Nien-chien* (Shanghai Year Book), 1936, quoting from the census taken by the Municipal Council; H. Lang, *Shanghai Considered Socially*, 2nd edn., 1875, p. 24; Manley O. Hudson, 'International Problems of Shanghai', *Foreign Affairs*, 1927; Shanghai T'ung-chih-kuan, *Ch'i-k'an* (Journal), vol. I, pp. 64–5; *Shanghai Chih-nan* (A Guide to Shanghai,) 1930, vol. I, p. 4.

accomplished by Consul J. A. Griswold and later Consul E. Cunningham, and the American Settlement came into existence. The French, too, had their settlement which, together with the British and American ones, was put under a single governing body during the emergency of the Small Sword Rebellion within the city and the threat of the Taiping Rebellion from without in 1853. The history of these settlements was full of legal ambiguities and sometimes blatant illegality from the beginning, persisting until their occupation by the Japanese at the outbreak of the Pacific War in 1941.

* The total population in Shanghai grew from 544415 in 1852, to 1 million in 1900, over 1.5 million in 1920, close to 3 million in 1929, and close to 4 million in 1937.

† This decrease in foreign population was due to the evacuation of foreign troops after the Taiping Rebellion.

‡ Japanese immigration began in large numbers and in 1915 the number of Japanese in Shanghai overtook that of the British.

§ White Russians came to Shanghai.

§§ The Sino–Japanese War began.

The settlements were designed to segregate the Caucasians and their Indian and African servants from the Chinese. But driven by the two rebellions, Chinese flocked into the settlements for protection, thus nullifying the intention of segregation. The Chinese population in the settlements leapt from 500 in 1850 to over 50000 in 1854 and to 70000 in 1872. The decision to admit Chinese to live in the settlements was not entirely humanitarian; the additional tax revenue brought in by the wealthy Chinese refugees opened up new possibilities for the settlement authorities – the organization of a municipal council, a volunteer corps for defence, and excuses for territorial expansion. The International Settlement (Anglo–American), after several enlargements, was to reach a final size of nearly nine square miles, and the French Settlement about half that size.

The Municipal Council administered all three settlements in the years of crisis. When the crisis was over, in 1863, the British and Americans decided to continue with the merger while the French, for religious reasons and because of national pride, split away to form their own council. Both settlements went on to thrive through all the tribulations of the imperial and republican periods – the Boxer Uprising, the 1911 Revolution, the 1925 anti-British and anti-Japanese strikes, the Northern Expedition of 1927 when Shanghai saw the bloodiest purge of the communists by Chiang Kai-shek, and the Japanese invasion of 1932 which destroyed much of the Chinese city.

Though the settlements were never in danger despite all these grave occurrences, their character unavoidably changed. The entry of Chinese to form 96 per cent of the population replaced the old tranquillity with new overcrowding and pollution. It also enabled foreigners to expand their commercial and industrial activities. The great influx of Japanese after 1895 did not seem to change the character of the settlement noticeably in the way that that of the White Russians did after 1917. The latter preferred the French Settlement, where the control over the opium traffic and prostitution was less strict than in the International Settlement. Their presence accelerated the demoralization of the Western Europeans who, from the 1880s, began a trend of rebellion against Victorian morality, due not so much to intellectual defiance as to money proving easy to make and to comfort being cheaply obtainable. With the Caucasians leading the way, the whole of Shanghai became what John Gunther called 'a political ulcer on the face of China' or what Edgar Snow called 'Sodom and Gomorrah'. Eddy Miller entitled his book on the city, *Shanghai, the Paradise of Adventurers.*

But the first generation of the Victorians was of tougher moral fibre. Their main concern during the years of the crisis was the maintenance of law and order; their first contribution to modern municipal government in China was the formation of a police force. The police were trained to respect personal rights, as no policeman could make an arrest without a warrant signed by the consul. They were, however, authorized to drive away beggars and street-walkers, and put a stop to opium and gambling dens. They could also stop anyone urinating in the street, selling rotten meat or fish, carrying a fowl upside down, making a loud noise to disturb neighbours, and other misdemeanours. These measures helped tremendously to improve public order and living conditions in the settlements.

Missionary hospitals came into existence in Shanghai as early as in the 1840s, and news from home and about the rebellions was circulated in the *North China Herald*, a weekly founded in 1850. The Municipal Council surprised the inhabitants and the Chinese elsewhere by introducing kerosene street lamps, allowing an enterprising Englishman to build a wooden bridge across the Wusung and laying out a race-course – all in the 1850s at the height of the military crisis. These public works provided a good reason for the Chinese to call the Council, the *Kung-pu Chü* (Works Bureau). When the crisis ended in 1863, the settlements introduced gas and gaslights in the streets, a regular steamer service, a modern postal service and the Huangpu Park. The peace of the 1870s brought greater prosperity and further development to the city. Shanghai saw its first bicycle and its first rickshaw (*jinrikisha*), which necessitated the macadamization of roads. The telegraphic service began in 1872 and vaccination against smallpox the year after. There was even a building as tall as three storeys – the Shanghai and Hong Kong Banking Corporation. By then the foreign sector of the city, in contrast to its Chinese surroundings, was truly a modern metropolis.

Outside the settlements, the Chinese city squatted in filth and mud, in the darkness of night. To drive home the security and comfort of modern municipal living, the fire-brigade of the settlement staged a public display of its engines ('water dragons' as the Chinese called them). It was a wonderful spectacle, as reported by the *Shen-pao* on 2 December 1872; ten years later the paper drew the conclusion –

*The modernization of Shanghai and other cities*

|  | Shanghai | Peking | Tientsin | Canton |
|---|---|---|---|---|
| Piped water supply | 1883 | 1908 |  |  |
| Street lamps – |  |  |  |  |
| kerosene | 1850s |  |  |  |
| gas | 1866 |  |  |  |
| electric | 1888 | 1904 |  |  |
| Rickshaw | 1874 |  | 1897 | 1903 |
| Telephone | 1878 | 1904 |  |  |
| Tramcar | 1908 | 1924 |  | 1919 |
| Trolley bus | 1914 |  |  |  |
| Postal service | 1863 | 1878 | 1878 | 1878 |
| Police | 1854 | 1900 | 1881 |  |
| Automobile | 1901 | 1913 |  |  |
| Macadamization | 1860s |  |  | 1919 |
| Telegraphic service | 1872 |  | 1878 |  |
| Radio | 1908 |  |  |  |
| Airline | 1921 |  |  |  |
| Public library | 1849 |  |  |  |

Sources: *Shen-pao*; Shanghai T'ung-chih-kuan, *Ch'i-k'an*; *Shanghai nien-chien*, 1936; Hsü K'o, *Ch'ing-mi lei-ch'ao* (Classified Jottings on the Little Known Facts of the Ch'ing Period, Shanghai, 1928); the *Hua-tzu jih-pao* (China Mail, Hong Kong).

'In starting great projects, we Chinese lack the resolve of the Westerners.'

The Western challenge in Shanghai was thus noticed and at length accepted. In 1905 the gentry and bourgeoisie (*shen, shang*) got together to form their own city council. The new council copied the settlements in public works, social control, hygiene and education. The Chinese telephone company, essential for business competition with the foreigners, was founded in 1881, the electricity corporation in 1907, the tramcar service in 1912, and civil aviation in 1924. Like other modern Chinese enterprises in this period, the Shanghai public utilities suffered from conflicts between its interests and the concerns of the gentry and the bourgeoisie. Take the demolition of the city wall to make way for road building as an example. The businessmen were naturally in favour of the project whereas the gentry, through the official apparatus which was still under their control in 1906, objected strenuously in the name of the people living in the shadow of the wall. As a result, the project was delayed for six years.

In the reformist mood of the 1900s, the imperial government recognized the city council of Shanghai, which later was split into two during the 1911 Revolution and then abolished by Yuan Shih-k'ai in 1914. The abolition of the first and only modern city council in China signified the re-emergence of the conflict between the gentry and the bourgeoisie, the conservatives in Peking and the radicals in Shanghai and elsewhere where local self-government was attempted. After Yuan's demise in 1916, a new element – the military – intruded into the power struggle over the immense tax revenue and economic resources of Shanghai, thus further delaying the city's progress towards self-government. The strength of the Shanghai bourgeoisie, however, increased considerably during the First World War and after the last warlords' war which affected the welfare of Shanghai, fought in 1924–5, General Sun Ch'uan-fang from central China made great concessions to the bourgeois interests of the city. Though the city was still under military domination, Sun appointed V. K. Ting as Director-General of the Port of Greater Shanghai in 1926. In the long history of the city, Ting was to be the only 'mayor' who was a thoroughly modern and highly educated man, though even he had to serve the warlord. The year 1926 also saw the reconstitution of the city council under a different name. Then came Chiang Kai-shek and his expeditionary armies in the spring of 1927, and the threat of the city being taken over by the communists. Chiang's triumph over the communist challengers led to Shanghai being made a special metropolis under the direct control of Chiang's central government and the Kuomintang. The city council under Chiang consisted of the mayor, two advisers, nine heads of bureaux (all appointees) and only three to five elected members. The citizens of Shanghai, businessmen and workers, paid all the rates and taxes and yet the city had still not achieved self-government.

In the foreign settlements, the structure of power was similar, the only difference being that the foreigners instead of the government were at the helm of power. The governing bodies of both the International and French Settlements were elected by their respective ratepayers' meetings at which the Chinese ratepayers had no voice. In 1919 the Chinese bourgeoisie, conscious of its strength and influenced by the nationalist movement that was sweeping across the whole nation, adopted the principle of 'No representation, no taxes' at a meeting of the recently formed Chinese Ratepayers' Association.

A Chinese advisory body was set up with the intention of advising the governing councils of the settlements. It had no legal basis; the foreigners refused to recognize it on the grounds that the Chinese lacked the experience and ability for municipal self-government, and that their participation in settlement administration would therefore be a retrogressive rather than a progressive step. Besides, to take such a step would endanger the political neutrality, and hence the security, of the settlements at a time when China was being rent by frequent civil wars. That the Chinese Ratepayers' Association had only 3000 members out of one million Chinese living in the International Settlement alone did not make the Association's voice any stronger.

The decisive moment came in May 1925 when a Chinese worker in a Japanese textile factory was shot dead, and a couple of days later when demonstrating students and workers were fired on by the British police. This incident touched off a nation-wide strike against Britain, the chief target of the Chinese anti-imperialist movement in the 1920s. In the settlements themselves, the main grievances were the increase in wharf dues, which added to the financial burden of the Chinese business community, and the new publication law, which restricted the freedom of speech of the radicals. After a protracted investigation of the May 30th Incident and negotiations in Peking and Shanghai, the burgeoning strength of the militant nationalism was recognized by London, Washington and Paris. Compromise was the order of the day. The French Settlement added two Chinese representatives to its governing council in 1926 and three more in 1927; there were thus five Chinese out of a total membership of seventeen. Following the French lead, the Municipal Council of the International Settlement added three Chinese deputies in 1928 and two more in 1930; there were five Chinese out of a total membership of fourteen. Needless to say, all the Chinese were leading businessmen or leading professional men who, acceptable to their foreign equals, tended to transform, on pragmatic grounds, wider political issues of sovereignty and nationalism, labour legislation, and social justice, into economic and social welfare issues. Take, for instance, the committees of the Council in 1935–6. Only on the Library Committee and the Board of Film Censors did the Chinese have a measure of power and influence, while the foreigners controlled all the other, more important committees, e.g. Finance, Public Utilities, Rate Assessment, etc.

The 'third estate' of Shanghai, obstructed and 'squeezed' by its government on the one side and the foreigners on the other, in spite of efforts at obtaining self-government, still paid rates and taxes for the maintenance of the city over which it had only nominal control. Even in the 1930s, its political life was no more democratic than that of France before 1789.

## Life in the International Settlement

In a letter dated 24 April 1833, one Thomas Fisher wrote to a friend:

To the best of my recollection you expressed yourself very favourable to the unrestricted expatriation of *well disposed* Englishmen, possessed of commercial skill and capital, who might be induced to colinize [*sic*] in any part of the world, and thereby to benefit their species by carrying with them, together with European science, the light of the Gospel. I certainly acquiesce in these views. . . . [But] those were just the kind of people to stay in England, while the 'trash' element would be more likely to go abroad to trade.

From the very beginning the foreign community in Shanghai, and for that matter, elsewhere in China, consisted of a motley collection of people, whom the British government decided after 1860 were not worth another war. Still, there were Alexander Wylie and Walter Medhurst, Rutherford Alcock and Robert Hart, Young J. Allen and Timothy Richard, as the leading lights of a growing community. By the end of the century the prominent figures of the Shanghai foreign community were no longer ardently religious and morally upright, but were people like Sir Victor Sassoon (known locally as 'Sassoon the lame'), famous for his land speculation, a lavish building named after him and his high living. There was also a British Jew of perhaps Syrian origin, Silas Hardoon, who arrived in China in 1874, worked his way up in the Sassoon empire to become its deputy director and a member of the Municipal Council in 1897. He, too, made his fortune (estimated at £4 million in 1931 when he died) and was known as a great patron of the ancient divine rituals and classical learning at a time when Chinese intellectuals were attacking 'Confucius and Co.' (*K'ung-chia tien*). The purchasing power of his money was so enormous that it bought Chang T'ai-yen, a great classicist and revolutionary, to write his obituary.

The moral degeneration of the Shanghai foreign community and the city at large is clearly reflected in the following two quotations, representing two different views. The first is from Alexander Michie, referring to the nineteenth century:

Truth, honour, courage, generosity, nobility were qualities common to the whole body. . . . Black sheep there were, no doubt, but being never whitewashed, they did not infect the flock, as happens in more advanced communities.

Such a body of people were expectedly self-righteous, taking upon themselves the task of civilizing the lesser breeds and changing the environs in which they lived. When the civilizing mission produced undesirable results and the Chinese national interests demanded recognition, the confidence of this body of people evaporated. Its ethos was described by Sir Eric Teichman in these terms, referring to the 1920s: 'An anti-Chinese, treaty port complex had regarded all manifestations of the new nationalist China with soured and jaundiced eye.'

Indeed, the old generation dealt in opium, but it was done in a manner described by William Jardine as 'a gentleman's pastime'. That generation was predominantly male and young, indulging in excessive drinking and overeating in their leisure hours. Later, their womenfolk came to set up house at a cost considerably lower than in England, France, or the USA. Wang T'ao seems to have been invited into one of these Tudor or Victorian-style houses and described the garden, the paved path, the carpeted floor, the shining glass windows, and, above all, the cleanliness with admiration.

The heavy doors are shut to insulate the house from noise. The green wall-papers and silver hooks [of curtains] serenely decorate [the rooms]. When the attendance of a servant is needed, [the master] pulls the bell; when a visitor comes, he announces his arrival by the knocker on the front door. Even if one knows that there is someone in a room, one still knocks on the door before making one's entry.

The home-loving foreigners attended to their gardens and played with their pets. Some even had Pekinese from the West, or 'fire-chickens' (turkeys) which led to wild misconstructions like this: 'Fire-chickens' from Holland eat fire. They peck at burning pieces of coal like grains of rice.

For the outdoor types there were organized sports – cricket, soccer, boat racing and horse-racing. For the more studious, there were a Short Story Club, the Shanghai Branch of the Royal Asiatic Society (started in 1847), and libraries. In the 1860s new indoor recreations such as billiards, fencing, bowling, gymnastics and clubs (for instance, the German Concordia) became available. The cricket matches and boat races attracted much Chinese attention. Wang T'ao remarked on Westerners' fondness for boating: 'Even wealthy merchants and scholars take part in it', implying that these Westerners, unlike their Chinese equivalents, actually took physical exercise. They were so skilled that 'Chinese boatmen look on with envy'.

Life was further diversified by regular balls, the flower shows organized by the British Consul from 1875 on, public lectures, and so on. There was a dramatic group, the Rangers and Footpads, whose performances, put on in warehouses, had been known to the Chinese since the 1840s, although no Chinese were admitted to them.

Those who lead a jejune life yearn for thrills and excitement; only an exciting life calls for recreation. Life in Shanghai after the founders' generation had passed on was jejune indeed. Newcomers had the tourist's curiosity about Shanghai – the ancient temples and Chinese restaurants – and were pleased to meet new friends at dinner or cocktail parties. The curiosity was quickly worn down by constantly seeing the same faces and hearing the same gossips; the intellectual few were driven to scholarly pursuits and the majority to diversions, e.g. pelota or basque tennis (known in Shanghai as *hai-a-lai*), and greyhound racing, tolerated in the French Settlement in 1928. People gambled on both and the Chinese nicknamed the greyhound course, Canidrome, '*K'an-ni-ch'iung*' (See you go broke). While the Chinese easily took up these new games from the West, Westerners learnt to play *mahjong*.

The trend towards the degeneration of the foreign community in Shanghai began in the 1880s. It did not escape Chinese eyes: 'Rites and propriety, literature and scholarship are difficult to learn, but extravagance and excitability are not.' This was written by a correspondent of the *Shen-pao* on 25 November 1883, who also remarked on the good manners the Westerner had displayed in public in the past. But now, he regretted that Westerners quarrelled and fought the Chinese as boisterously as the Chinese themselves. This trend was exacerbated by the arrival of White Russians and Western mercenaries fleeing from the Depression. Hence a quack evangelist preached in the pelota court like a Pharisee, while the greyhound managers pretended charity by organizing a race in aid of the refugees from the great Yangtze flood of 1931.

The number of white prostitutes in Shanghai also increased from an occasional report of their activities in 1872 and 1881, to the concentration of 'American houses' near Kiangsi and Soochow roads, claiming to have 'American girls' for the entertainment of sailors in the 1920s. Prostitutes in the settlements numbered no less than 48 000 in 1929, excluding amateurs and part-timers. The need for the presence of women in Shanghai to counteract the demoralizing influence of association with an 'inferior race' did not on the whole achieve its intended purpose. The Westerner was not humanized by the presence of the whore.

The moral degeneration of the Shanghai Caucasian community can be observed in the crimes committed by foreigners. Walter Medhurst referred to the existence of white vagrants, mostly deserters from ships in the 1860s. They were apt to commit such misdemeanours as breach of the peace and petty larceny. They also terrorized the Chinese, provoking them into taking retaliatory action. Many cases of fighting between Chinese and foreigners were reported in the middle years of the 1870s. Of the crimes committed by members of the middle class, there were only two cases of embezzlement of public funds, reported in the *Shen-pao* on 5 July and 21 November 1872, but the number of murder cases increased from the autumn of 1881. There were also cases of fraud and vagrancy. On the whole the community was well able to deal with its criminal elements and sent them home. The situation changed rapidly after the First World War. Fugitives from the law now came to Shanghai for sanctuary and a good life. Like other citizens of the treaty powers, these undesirable aliens were protected by extraterritoriality and the Chinese government seldom deported them. Peter Grimes was a case in point. Having spent a year in San Quentin for forgery, he came to Shanghai in 1919 to continue his fraudulent life. On his way back to San Quentin under escort, he escaped in Nagasaki, was arrested in Yokohama, and came back to Shanghai again. C. C. Julian, an oil promoter in California, was indicted in Oklahoma, skipped bail, fled to Canada, arrived in Shanghai where he took to wine, opium, and Russian women, and finally committed suicide. These people, together with quack evangelists, opium traffickers, gamblers, and prostitutes, made up the 'paradise of adventurers'. 'Without their help, China might not have become what she is now.'

Betting at race meetings was a sport that the Chinese took up quickly from their foreign neighbours. For business reasons, Chinese spectators were admitted to the race-course when it was completed in

1854 and wagers were formally allowed. As one would expect, no Chinese was admitted into a foreign club; however, the Chinese soon organized their own. Western bars and restaurants existed in the French Settlement in the 1870s. Great epicures, the Chinese curiosity was tickled by what they called '*ta-ts'ai*' (big dishes). *Yi-p'ing-hsiang* was one of the earliest Chinese restaurants in Shanghai to specialize in English and French cuisine, as advertised in the *Shen-pao* on 3 September 1879. From that beginning, the Chinese went on to drink beer, sherry, whisky, brandy and champagne. Drinking tonic water (known as 'the Dutch water') was believed to protect one from the effects of the harmful effluvia of summer, but it was unsuitable for anyone of a weak constitution. Pool rooms and bowling alleys for Chinese clients first opened in 1881. Social dancing, however, had to wait until the Chinese changed their style of dress during the First World War. In the Gay Twenties the Chinese, too, danced to fox-trots and waltzes to the music of Western-style bands. Ballroom dancing became so popular that a troubled reader wrote to the *China Weekly Review* on 17 November 1934 under the title 'Can Chinese Students be Banned from Cabarets?' Jazz music played by native or imported artists was to drive the sing-song girls from the scene.

Chinese patronage of Caucasian prostitutes did not seem to break through the stage of hesitancy until after the October Revolution. The earliest report of such a thing is to be found in the *Shen-pao* on 24 May 1872 – 'not a word being exchanged during dinner', perhaps due to the lack of a common language; 'lying on the couch with a handkerchief over her face', perhaps to neutralize the smell of someone's breath. English-speaking Chinese in the 1890s found it easier to 'get closer to the perfumed ones', 'but most of them have big teeth and tousled hair, as ugly as devils and as frightful as lionesses. They freeze the hearts of beholders. The Spanish, however, are different – brilliantly beautiful, with tender soft skin, and with a warm and delicate body.' The Russian invasion of the market lowered the charges to somewhere between $30 and $3.

At first the Chinese were debarred from the Huangpu Park. The first complaint against the exclusion of Chinese from the parks was recorded on 6 April 1881. In response, the Municipal Council put up the well-known signboard: 'No Chinese or Dogs', four years later. Apologists for this prohibition argued that the parks were for foreigners' recreation, and in some cases for that of their children.

If the Chinese were allowed in, there would be no way to prevent 'communicable diseases'. The prohibition required the rising tide of nationalism in 1928 to sweep it away. The first Chinese public garden came into being in 1890.

The Lyceum, the first foreign theatre, was built in 1867. Apparently it did not practise racial discrimination, but the tickets were prohibitively expensive at two or one *yuan* each. The theatre had a dome over the auditorium and gas lighting, and it struck the Chinese as spacious and tastefully decorated. In a Chinese opera house of that period, the spectator enjoyed the freedom to sip tea, eat, or call for a hot towel to wipe his face. He took his seat at any time he wished, not necessarily before the curtain went up. In fact, there was no curtain, nor scenery. The actors shared the stage with a small orchestra and a couple of helpers who arranged stage properties and offered a drink of tea to the actors. At the Lyceum the standard of behaviour expected was totally different. No one else appeared on the stage except the actors. What the *Shen-pao* reporter called 'screens' were probably flats. Judging by the records, what went on the stage, be it a play or an opera, was seldom understood by the Chinese patrons. When it was a play, the Chinese likened it to storytelling in a teahouse, but they did not know the plot. They enjoyed watching the reactions of the Western audience – clapping hands, stamping feet, and laughing uproariously – which they observed with puzzled amusement. When it was an opera the Chinese could at least appreciate the rhythm of the music. On 27 December 1879 the *Shen-pao* reviewed a Christmas performance of an Italian company:

There is no deafening noise of drum or gong [as used in the Chinese opera] only the harmony of the strings. [The actors] sing while they sit or dance, but [they] allow no such hideousness as acrobatics [as in Chinese opera]. The audience [80–90 per cent Caucasians] enjoys itself quietly. . . . The Westerners are happy with such a performance whereas the Chinese are not satisfied unless it is vulgar.

Occasionally, a Chinese opera was performed at the Lyceum, to attract Chinese customers. But what the Chinese liked most were Western conjuring shows and circuses. The *Shen-pao* reported the visiting French, American and Italian circuses in great detail and praised them as 'a truly great spectacle'. The dazzling performances of the Chiarinis Circus from the USA were not deemed as being beyond Chinese emulation, for, according to the same paper, the circus was, after all, a Chinese invention. The Chinese had had circuses once, had lost some elements of them and had become complacent, instead of perfecting the art as the Westerners had done.

Shanghai seems to have opened its first epidiascope theatre (*ying-hsi yuan*) on 7 March 1877. The slides or transparencies shown were likely to be on such marvellous but innocuous subjects as landscape, wildlife and architectural wonders. The first motion-picture show took place in a teahouse on 11 August 1896. The films were only one of the several 'numbers' on that day and admission charges were high, 50 *fen* for a front-row seat and 10 *fen* for one in the back row. Antonio Ramos, a Spaniard, was the man who put film shows in Shanghai on a permanent business basis. In 1906 he founded the first cinema, showing probably Pathé and Gaumont movies, which Duke Tsai-tse saw at a party given by the French consul on 14 July 1906.

Foreign films proved such a success that before long Ramos had a chain of cinemas in Shanghai, showing mostly French and other European movies. But after 1914, the US monopoly of the Chinese screen soon became established. Action films, with their simple plots which were explained to the Chinese audience by a commentator, were favourites, while pictures to do with social problems and middle-class family life usually played to empty houses. Gradually the Chinese became familiar with such names as Douglas Fairbanks, Charlie Chaplin, and the Keystone Cops.

The movies of the Gay Twenties brought to China jazz music and the image of frivolous, promiscuous and sophisticated Western women as portrayed by Garbo, Swanson, Crawford and Bow. The provocative gestures, the looseness in sexual relations, and the cynical attitude to life depicted on the screen worried such critics as Sir Hesketh Bell and M. Legendre. What was particularly disquieting was the mood of unquestioned admiration of the West which made the average Chinese audience gullible. This mighty mass medium exploited by the tycoons of Hollywood and Europe constantly undermined pre-war moral standards. In Chinese terms, the motion pictures being either 'licentious' (*hui-yin*) or 'larcenous' (*hui-tao*), they tended to cancel out much of the work done by the missionaries, and to create an entirely new image of Western life in the Chinese mind.

The arrival of sound and colour to Shanghai cinema screens in 1926 was a sensation, adding new dimensions to the image and making it compellingly real. By what other means could an ordinary Chinese find out, for instance, how a Western woman wept?*

Of the thirty-seven cinemas in Shanghai in 1935, eighteen specialized in showing only foreign films. In that year, 378 foreign pictures were imported, and of those 332 were American. The names of Hollywood stars were household words: films were frequent conversational subjects. But to the more critical minds like that of Lu Hsün, the American films were objects of sardonic comments:

In the grand circle sit white people and rich people; in the stall sit the middle and lower 'descendants of the Yellow Emperor'. On the screen appear white soldiers fighting, white gentlemen making money, white ladies getting married, and white heroes exploring [the unexplored]. All this evokes in the spectators envy, admiration, and fear that such things are beyond them.

and:

White men, well fed and well dressed, need highly-spiced amusements. Since they are growing tired of African savages and wild beasts, our yellow faces and yellow noses are now on the screen. So, there are films which insult China and make our patriots indignant.

In 1930 a concerned reader wrote to the *China Weekly Review*, an American paper published in Shanghai, deploring the effects of the cinema on youth. He blamed the cinema, as we still do, for violence and sexual indecency. Twenty years later, a Chinese criticism dug deeper down to the roots which nourished Hollywood films. The film under review was *Yes, Sir, That's My Baby*:

It shows the utter decay of American life. American comedies cease to be dramatic expressions of the delightful qualities which can be distilled from life itself. On the contrary, they are a dramatic form clapped on a jejune life for 'comedy effects'.

### The emergence of the compradore

The expansion of the Western community's economic activities caused the emergence of new social groups among the Chinese – the licensed head servants in their households who developed into

---

* When Jeanette MacDonald wept on the screen, it brought the house down. The audience burst out laughing, as if to say: 'So, this is how a beautiful American woman cries!' That was in the 1930s; the venue was the YMCA cinema in Ch'engtu. I was in the audience.

business associates in foreign firms, their Chinese competitors, and professional people such as journalists, publishers, writers and lawyers.

The first group, commonly referred to as 'compradores', a word with derogatory connotations, consisted of some 1000 people ranging from the very poor, who worked at the quayside, to the very rich in their luxurious executive suites. Their great wealth and important role in China's modernization far outweighed their small number.

An early English definition of the compradore was a simple one, for he was on more than a 'licensed head servant (later the No. 1 Boy) in a foreign household' whose job was to supervise domestic affairs, procure other servants, buy provisions, etc., according to the wishes of his employer. Even before the abolition of the *Co-hong* (the chartered merchants in Canton) monopoly of foreign trade in 1842, Chinese officials reported the existence of '*ma-chan*' (merchants)

who speak the barbarians' language and help in the barbarians' business.... At first they were employed in foreign firms to work on commission. Lately they have formed their own capital and traded with the barbarians.

The career pattern described in this brief report was transferred to Shanghai when Shanghai was opened as a treaty port. Compradores took the trouble to learn pidgin English and the Western ways of handling business affairs so as to gain the trust of their employers. In time, they acquired knowledge of market conditions and established business connections. Like the Banian brokers of India, they were immensely useful. As economic opportunities expanded after the Anglo–French Expedition, more compradores were needed as business assistants. Recruitment of trainees was perforce entrusted to the existing compradores, who made use of traditional ties – family relations and local affinity, which gave the compradore group a measure of cohesiveness and at the same time introduced factionalism based on geographic divisions. In addition to the Cantonese faction, Shanghai, Soochow, Ningpo and Chekiang cliques gradually formed.

All the compradores were paid a small salary plus business expenses; they also received a commission on the completion of a transaction. The transactions in tea, silk and so on were small; so were the commissions. Not until the twentieth century, when big deals such as the purchase of US $100000000 worth of arms were handled directly by a compradore, did the revenue from commissions become considerable. Far from being wealthy and powerful, the compradores in the 1850s and 1860s had to resort to goodwill (the trust of their employers) and their access to capital (in their employers' firms) to make money for themselves. On occasions, they even resorted to speculation. The fact that they worked for foreigners freed them from bureaucratic harassment and the necessity of giving large bribes. Their money was ploughed back into the foreign firms for which they worked, to raise their status to that of a partner or a creditor. Even the redoubtable Jardine, Matheson & Co. used compradore capital and handled arrangements for the voyages of ships owned by their compradores.

Having thus proved their superior abilities *vis-à-vis* the gentry officials with their background of classical training and land management, they were wooed by leading reformers, Tseng Kuo-fan and Li Hung-chang among them, to persuade them to participate in China's modernization. Tseng Kuo-fan seems to have recruited the more scholarly whereas Li Hung-chang, the wealthiest. Hsü Jun, a leading compradore of Dent & Co., was sent to the USA to supervise government students, probably at the turn of the century; T'ang Ching-hsing rose like a meteor from the time when he joined Jardine, Matheson & Co. as a compradore in 1861, and in 1871 was appointed the Director-General of the China Merchants' Steamship Navigation Co. Perfectly fluent in English, T'ang confidently wrote to W. A. P. Martin: 'The viceroy [Li Hung-chang] leads, but I am the man that pushes.' Compradore capital was to be found in Chinese mining, machine making and light industries as well as in banking, insurance and public utilities. The pattern was to be followed by such men as Yü Hsia-ch'ing, a leading member of the Chekiang group of compradores, who co-operated with Chiang Kai-shek in controlling the money market of Shanghai. A street in Shanghai was even named after Yü.

Compradore participation in China's economic modernization led to the emergence of a new business structure – the 'merchant management under government supervision' system (*kuan-tu shang-pan*) – with capital investment from the revenue of the maritime customs and of certain compradores. Such an institutional innovation as this naturally created a new ethos which was an eclectic mixture of Confucian values and bourgeois practice. As this new system grew, the new ethos settled into a pattern: Confucian values dominated the social and cultural aspects of the enterprises and bourgeois practice their financial management. The growth was a process of Confucianization of China's modern industries interacting with a simultaneous Westernization of Confucianism. Since both sources of capital investment depended on foreign trade, peace with the West was the basic condition of China's industrialization in that period. The tragedy was that neither the Confucianization of industry nor the Westernization of Confucianism was a success.

The compradores as a group were not politically motivated. They were specialists in a Confucian society ruled by amateur gentlemen whose exclusive concern was its political and administrative control. Their apolitical attitude made them a genus of political chameleons capable of co-operating with whoever was in power, so long as private ownership was tolerated. During the century of their existence, they worked by turns with imperial bureaucrats, republican officials, Western businessmen, and the Japanese occupation authorities. They could remain neutral even when China was at war with Britain, France, or Japan. However, to say that they possessed no political principles would be a gross over-simplification. A number of them wrote and published their views on political and economic reform in the closing years of the nineteenth century. Yung Wing, Wang T'ao, Shao Tso-chou, Cheng Kuan-ying and Ho Ch'i were the most notable of these. But even then their views were not particularly distinguishable from the more eloquently and more elegantly presented views of the 'enlightened' scholarly gentry (the Westernized Confucians). The divergence between the Westernized Confucianism and the Confucianized compradorism was hardly perceptible.* Hence it would not be quite accurate to say that the compradores were thoroughly Westernized in Wu Yen-jen's crude terms – 'even a foreigner's fart being perfume'; nor would it be quite right to say that they accepted Confucian values and norms without a murmur of defiance.

. Wealthy as they were, compradores commanded little social prestige and had no intellectual standing. Though they could purchase the former in some cases, the latter was hardly ever to be had for money. They developed a parallel upward mobility pattern

---

* For the institute for training compradores, St John's College, see Y. P. Hao, *The Compradore in Nineteenth Century China*, Cambridge, Mass., 1970, p. 198, and Lin Yutang *From Pagan to Christian*, London, 1960, pp. 29–30. Li-Po-yuan's novel, *An Informal History of Civilization*, was a satire on the life of the compradore. Wu Yen-jen, too, wrote. critically about the compradore in his *Fa-ts'ai mi chüeh* (The Secret of Money-Making) See also Marie-Claire Bergère in M. Wright, *China in Revolution*, New Haven, 1968, pp. 249–53.

reminiscent of the first generation Chinese or Jewish immigrants in a Western country. Having made good financially, they sent their children to work for academic degrees and become professional people with the prestige and sophistication belonging to that class. This higher position in the social scale would spare the young people the unpleasantness and insults their fathers had had to endure. In this sense, the Chinese compradores were also comparable to the middle-class Negroes in the USA like Booker T. Washington.

The compradores bought their way into the gentry class by contributing money to the government in exchange for official titles so that they could enjoy all the outward trimmings of gentility. They also shared in some of the traditional obligations of the gentry by donating money to charity, social welfare and education. When in the company of Caucasian colleagues, they donned mandarin costumes and affected a refined courtesy and studio-names to pretend to a measure of culture; when in a Chinese milieu, they wore Western clothes, assumed Christian names, displayed Western habits (e.g. pipe-smoking, horse-racing, low-voiced speech, etc.) to show that they had a better command of Western culture than the Westernized Confucians. The compradore's home was a Western-style house appointed with both Chinese and European furniture and *objets d'art*, but he ate Chinese food. Some of them embraced Christianity but at the same time practised Confucian ethics. Such a life-style was possible, even enviable, only when neither the foreign nor the Chinese community in Shanghai had any profound intellectual judgement. Therefore Lu Hsün defined his 'image of the compradore (*hsi-sai-hsiang*) as someone 'flitting between Chinese and foreigners, frisking between slaves and masters'.

## The growth of Chinese industry and finance

In the centre of China's foreign trade, finance and light industries, the Shanghai bourgeoisie was divided into two, not entirely unconnected, sections – the compradore and national. Because of an absence of information on capital structure, management personnel and business operations, it is impossible to decide which enterprises were completely Chinese-owned and Chinese-controlled and which were not. Some Western firms even had Chinese shareholders. What can be said with a measure of safety is that there was a growth of Chinese national industrial and commercial enterprises rivalling the

# Misconceptions

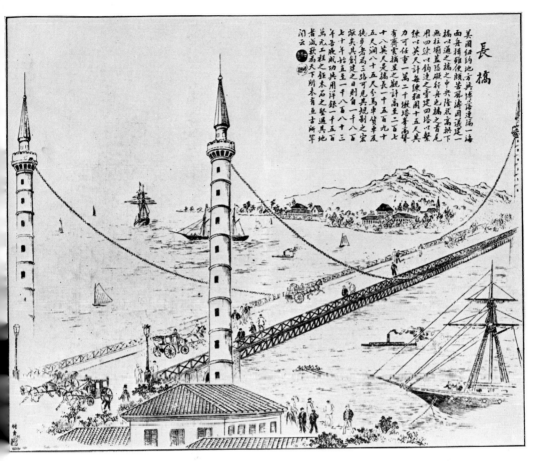

長橋

美國紐約地方其博話達隔一海面舟楫雖便顧苦風濤因議建一橋以通之橋之中央隆然高拱于典橋盖恐艘行舟此橋之者尾用四株以鉤連之空建四塔以繫練以鐵人許每練粗鋼十五人其力可任重一萬二千斤塔峯高聳有橋霓之勢塔之頂高至二百七十八英尺是橋長一千五百九十五尺闊八十五英尺全馬貨車及徒步者每三路可見其規制之宏歷失其創建之日閱自一千八百七十年始至一千八百三年告欲成功共用詳銀一千五百萬元工程之鉅木石之整通其地皆成歟為天下所未有亘古所罕閎云

*Brooklyn Bridge, New York,*
*1880s. A Chinese artist's impression*

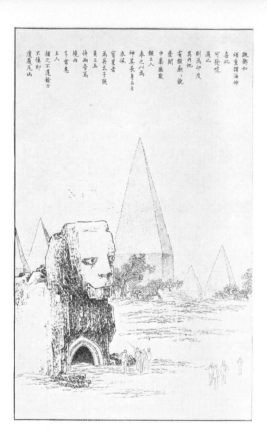

*The Sphinx and the Pyramids,*
*1880s. A Chinese artist's impression*

*St Paul's Cathedral, London,*
*1880s. A Chinese artist's impression*

*An American theatre, 1880s. A Chinese artist's impression*

# The Chinese in Western eyes

*Reception of the Chinese family by Her Majesty Queen Victoria, at Osborne, late 1840s*

*Collection formed by an American, Nathan Dunn. His exhibition lasted from 1843 to 1851*

*1851*

# "One of the Chief Lions' of the Day."—Times.

# THE CHINESE LADY,

## PWAN-YE-KOO,

### With Small Lotus Feet, only 2½ Inches in Length!

## HER NATIVE FEMME DE CHAMBRE,

## CHINESE PROFESSOR OF MUSIC,

### TWO Interesting CHINESE CHILDREN,

Male and Female—5 and 7 Years of Age,

## AND SUITE,

### Exhibiting Daily from 11 till 1, 2 till 5, and 6 till 10,

AT THE

# CHINESE COLLECTION,

## ALBERT GATE, HYDE PARK.

The LADY PWAN-YE-KOO will sing

## A SELECTION OF CHINESE AIRS,

And will be accompanied by the Professor, on Chinese Musical
Instruments, each Hour during their Exhibiting.

ADMISSION TO THE

# TWO EXHIBITIONS,

## ONE SHILLING.

R. S. FRANCIS, Printer, Catherine Street, Strand.

San Francisco Chinatown just
before the earthquake of 1906. Photo
by Arnold Genthe

'They don't trouble him any more.'
Note the Caucasian expression and
the big hands and feet. Frederick
Opper, Puck's Opper Book,
New York, 1888

" Too muchee bad boys alound here; all
callee me names; fixee up little supplise-part

*An American smile under an American hat, and above a Chinese jacket. Chinatown leader, New York, 1915*

THEY DON'T TROUBLE HIM ANY MORE.

"Hey, Chinaman, Chinaman!"

"Supplise-party workee first-latee!"

"Heap chilly day when Hop Sing gettee left!"

# Changing city life

*The Confucian village, Ch'ufu, Shantung, 1931. The village post office is on the left and is the only Western-style building. Photo by White Bros.*

Street scene in Peking,
showing traditional and modern
means of transport. Photo by White
Bros.

Rickshaws in Peking in 1931,
symbolizing the social positions of
foreigners and Chinese in
China

*American warehouse at Hankow. Bain Collection*

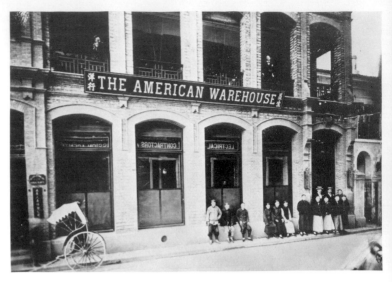

*The reception room of a well-to-do Peking home, 1931. The clock, photographs, chandeliers, spittoons and other Western paraphernalia are set against a Chinese background*

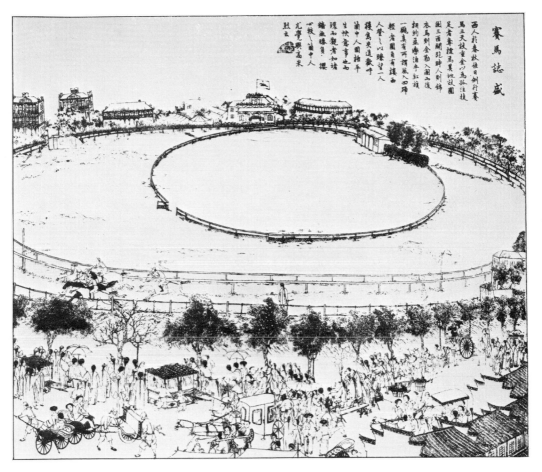

賽馬誌盛

西人酷好跑馬每當春秋佳日例行賽馬五天技皆兩圖少為跑注技足奪魁接馬其美觀故圍園三面開跑時人別錦衣馬剰金勒入圖而後相約並馳洎手紅後一頭真有�...風之四瑋輕者園皆有諸西人肇之以贈望之一人禄寫矣道駛行圃中人圍拾平生快睹言也西隄和觀者如堵播無煤目探...叙...喜歡興高采烈云

*Shanghai Race-course, 1880s*

*A game of cricket, Shanghai,*
*1880s*

*French opium addicts, Shanghai,*
*1880s*

*Explanation of Western diving*
*techniques, 1880s*

# Changing fashions and clothes

*Ladies' fashions, Shanghai, 1921*

*A Chinese couple, 1931. Photo by White Bros.*

*A wealthy Manchu family, 1931. Photo by White Bros.*

*Dr Wellington Koo – Western hair-style and Western clothes*

*A Chinese Christian pastor and family, Canton, 1900*

foreign establishments in all fields of economic activity in Shanghai except the most modern and highly capital-intensive industries. This was partly due to the awakening of a patriotism bent on the recovery of national economic interests; partly to the introduction of modern methods of business management and production, especially after the Sino–Japanese War of 1895; and partly to the spread of a new life-style which gave rise to demand for new manufactures.

Prior to the expansion of private enterprise, the 'merchant management under government supervision' initiative had met with a shortage of private investment and a lack of popular demand for machine-made goods. The reformist leaders referred to this shortage as 'a lack of proper atmosphere' (*feng-ch'i wei-k'ai*). The atmosphere changed after 1895 when Japan and other powers acquired the rights to set up manufacturing industries at the treaty ports. This new pattern of business organization, without the obstructive 'government supervision', and new industrial technology developed as rapidly as the national industries. At the time of the 1911 Revolution, Shanghai had some ninety privately owned light industries processing silk, cotton and food, publishing books, magazines and daily papers, and operating public utilities. The most notable was the Commercial Press, founded in 1897, which still exists today.

Soon the First World War followed, offering Shanghai industrialists a golden opportunity for expansion. Producers' and consumers' chemical products, machines and machine tools, water and power supplies and building materials were the new ventures. By 1934 the city boasted 5418 factories with a total capital investment of nearly US $175 000 000 and a total employment of 300 000. The average scale of production – $3000 capital and fifty employees – was very small and many of the factories survived precariously. An international business fluctuation or internal political upheaval was likely to take a heavy toll. Even so the Commercial Press and the Chunghua Book Co. (started in 1912) succeeded in breaking the monopoly of the Christian Literature Society in the publication of books on secular subjects; the Five Continents Dispensary replaced the Japanese in the cosmetic market; the Three Friends Industrial Society developed a successful line in textiles; the Heavenly Kitchen with its 'Essence of Taste' (*wei-ching*) drove the Japanese 'Ajinomoto' out of China. Even in Western-style food, a Chinese-owned bakery under the trade name of Sullivan, laid the foundation for several nationwide chains of shops selling biscuits, candies and cakes.

C.A.T.W.—H

In the money market, the Chinese challenge was no less effective. The first Chinese bank was founded in 1897; there were no fewer than eighty-six in Shanghai on the eve of the Japanese invasion of 1937. The modern Chinese financial agencies practically monopolized domestic operations and handled the remittances from overseas Chinese in south-east Asia, leaving European and American banking business and much of the insurance to the foreigners. The foreign Sharebrokers Association of 1891 (renamed the Shanghai Stock Exchange in 1904) was rivalled by the Chinese Stock and Merchandise Exchange which was started in 1920. Thereafter holding companies, brokerages, savings associations and discount houses multiplied. In these varied ways, Shanghai capitalists responded to the West, laying the foundation, however inadequately, of China's modernization.

## Publishing

It was British enterprise that gave Shanghai its first modern newspaper – the weekly *North China Herald*, founded by Henry Shearman in 1850, whose affiliated daily, the *North China Daily News* (Tzu-lin hsi-pao), began publication in 1864. Both were authoritative but conservative English-language papers in China; both survived into the twentieth century, only to be overtaken by China's political progress. American initiative was represented by T. F. Millard who in 1911 created the *China Weekly Review*, for many years under the editorship of J. B. Powell. The *China Weekly Review*, growing up under the influence of the ideals of self-determination and anti-colonialism put forward by President Wilson and inheriting the American tradition of republicanism and democracy, had a greater impact on Chinese politics in the 1920s and 1930s than its British competitors. Also influential locally was the American-owned *Shanghai Evening Post and Mercury* commencing in 1929. These papers and foreign news agencies and newspapers like Reuters and the *New York Times* had a number of notable reporters of different political persuasions, ranging from the sinophobe J. O. P. Bland and the astute and pragmatic Dr George Morrison (both of *The Times*) to the critical and cynical Hallet Abend (of the *New York Times*) and the radical Edgar Snow (of the *Chicago Tribune*).

Early Chinese newspapers in Shanghai were also founded by foreigners. The authoritative *Shen-pao* was the brain-child of E. Major, a Briton. It first appeared on 30 April 1872. The first issues reached a circulation of only 600, which was doubled in 1874 when Japan invaded Taiwan, and reached 5000 when the inauguration of a modern postal service enabled the paper to be delivered to other cities of the country. Up to 1876 it relied almost exclusively on foreign sources of news. Thereafter it appointed its own correspondents at Tientsin, Peking and other cities. Major hired Russian correspondents to cover the Sino–French War of 1884–5 on the spot, thus beginning the paper's tradition of reliable and conscientious reporting. In 1912 it came under exclusive Chinese ownership and management, that of one of the most celebrated Chinese journalists and industrialists, Shih Liang-ts'ai. Shih made it one of the most powerful papers in the country with a circulation of 15 000 throughout the 1920s and 1930s. The Japanese invasion of Manchuria in 1931 and Shanghai in 1932 turned the *Shen-pao* away from its apolitical tradition to being critical of Chiang Kai-shek's weak-kneed policy of reconciliation; hence the assassination of Shih in 1934. The *Shen-pao*'s life ended on 26 May 1949.

At first the *Shen-pao*'s reports read like traditional short stories or jottings. News items and poetry and prose were juxtaposed on the same page; advertisements, an important source of historical information, looked like present-day classified advertisement columns. The first illustrated advertisement in the *Shen-pao* was in the issue of 25 April 1873, and introduced lithographic printing in addition to moveable lead types. Machine-printing of the paper began on 13 December 1873, enabling an increase in circulation to 4000 copies a day, 'printed by only six people in two hours', as the paper boasted.

Right from the beginning, the *Shen-pao* carried news about foreign countries, new scientific inventions, Chinese immigrants overseas and notes on European history. This general interest in news from abroad led to its supporting the publication in 1875 of the *Ke-chih Hui-pen* (the Chinese Scientific Magazine), edited by John Fryer, and the *Tien-shih-chai Hua-p'u* (Illustrated News of the Tien-shih Studio). The latter, a lithographically printed periodical, contained line drawings of subjects taken from current affairs and marked the beginning of modern cartoons in China.

With modern printing facilities and a distribution network, Shanghai had established itself as the centre of China's publishing industry. This achievement must be attributed to the joint efforts of foreign journalists, missionaries and Chinese entrepreneurs. In the years of reform, Shanghai attracted nearly all the important papers –

*Shih-wu-pao* (Current Affairs), *Ch'iang-hsüeh-pao* (National Strength), and *Hsin-min ts'ung-pao* (New Citizens' Tribune) – to itself. However short-lived, these reformist papers, like the reform itself, profoundly influenced the political life of China in the closing years of the nineteenth century. Later, revolutionary papers like the *Su-pao* and radical papers like the *New Youth* also made their home in Shanghai. Despite political persecution and censorship, Shanghai's position as the centre of publishing remained unchallenged.

The end of the nineteenth century saw the emergence of the so-called 'yellow press'. These popular papers, lowbrow but with wide circulations, could support a large number of journalists whose main concern was not so much news gathering and editorial comment but juicy and appealing gossip and scandal to entertain the readers and make money. These journalists served as observers of the dark facets of the social life of Shanghai. They wrote as professional writers for money. Generations of writers of this kind churned out articles from simple and straightforward gossips, exposés, supernatural stories, sentimental romances and detective thrillers, to sharp social critiques. Before the emergence of this new rash of journalists, Chinese writers were gentlemen; after it, they were comrades. Neither were professional. To be sure, the yellow press was never scholarly, never stodgy, always earthy, always readable, but sometimes sensational, sometimes acidly satirical. It was none the less a unique phenomenon in the history of Chinese literature. From its ranks, there emerged the sentimental 'mandarin duck and butterfly' school of novelists who specialized in physically unrequited love soaked in wells of tears to please the teenagers. There also emerged the satirists who exposed the stupidity and corruption of the establishment, even the irrationality and illogicality of Chinese society and culture. From the beginning of this century, the satirical tradition established by such journalist novelists as Wu Yen-jen and Li Po-yuan was to blossom in the short essays of Lu Hsün, comparable in elegance and wisdom to those of Steele and Addison. This in essence is what the academicians refer to as the 'Shanghai school' – the producers of a decidedly modern and decidedly urban culture.

## The theatre and film industries

Inspired by the foreign theatres, some large teahouses where operas used to be performed were transformed into modern theatres by

Japanese-trained students at the turn of the century. They produced *Napoléon* and *La Dame aux Camélias*, on a modern stage using modern scenery, but it is not clear whether these were operas or plays. Just before the 1911 Revolution, the *'wen-min hsi'* ('civilized plays') were invented by a group of enthusiasts who formed a repertory school, the T'ung-chien Hsüeh-hsiao, to train actors for such productions as *Uncle Tom's Cabin*\* – a reformed, new-style opera and a total flop. The anti-Manchu, revolutionary operas staged by the Ch'un-liu (the Spring Willow) Group were slightly more successful and survived from 1907 through the revolution and the First World War. The 'civilized plays' laid the foundation of the later development of both Chinese modern drama and the Chinese film industry.

The dramatic tradition was carried on and improved upon by playwrights like Ou-yang Yü-ch'ien, Hung Shen and T'ien Han, whose Drama Study Society and Southern Country Society staged plays on social problems, youth and love, and translated works such as *Lady Windermere's Fan* and *Dear Brutus*. This line of development of the new theatre in the 1900s eventually merged with the new literature movement after the May 4th Movement, thus becoming part of the main literary trend. Another line of development, also led by capable dramatists like Cheng Cheng-ch'iu and Chang Shih-ch'uan, became divorced from social and political problems and from the mainstream of the literary movement to become sentimental, sensational and mercenary, eventually producing films of farces, thrillers and tear-jerkers.

Chang and Cheng, first employed by an American film producer in 1912, started what was to become the Chinese film industry. Their early productions were mostly based on traditional operas. The *Difficult Couple*, a critique of the Chinese marriage system, directed by Cheng Cheng-ch'iu, was probably the best film made in the first, uncertain and barren, period of the industry. With the founding of the Star Co. in 1922, a new era began. The company's capital was mostly foreign; its employees were compradores; and its concern was money. Screenplays were normally written by writers of 'the mandarin duck and butterfly' school – talented, urbanized and compradorized Confucian scholars – who laboured on contemporary themes of detectives and prostitutes and ancient themes of supernatural beings and swordsmen. In social problems, these writers and directors went no further than an anxiety to Westernize Chinese

---

\* The book was translated into Chinese in 1905 at the height of an anti-American boycott in protest against the exclusion of Chinese immigration of 1904.

society and life-style. Westernization on the Chinese screen went so far as to make up traditional swordsmen to look like cowboys in broad-brimmed hats and drain-pipe trousers with 'futuristic' scenes in the background. The use of actresses to play female roles, Western costumes, and scenes of picnics and a church wedding made the *Oath* (Hai-shih) of 1921 another such incongruous marriage of East and West. An actor and director, Wang Yuan-lung, even attempted to raise the bridge of his nose, dye his hair brown, and copy Western manners in acting Chinese roles. In his films, jokes were often at the expense of those who did not know Western etiquette. A series of farces under the general title of *Wang Lao-wu* provided the Chinese answer to Laurel and Hardy. Through the 1920s and 1930s screen playwrights often shamelessly plagiarized foreign works such as Maupassant's 'Necklace', *Tosca, Pillars of Society* and the *Inspector General*, all of which were of course sinocized.

In the 1920s and more especially in the 1930s, a small crop of good Chinese films was produced. Even the profit-conscious Star Co. brought out *The Orphan Rescues his Grandfather*, a critical and box-office success which marked the peak of the careers of Cheng Cheng-ch'iu and Chang Shih-ch'uan. After the outbreak of the anti-imperialist demonstrations and strikes of 1925, the film industry sank back into its dark age of tear-jerkers and supernatural stories, with its market now extending to the Chinese communities in Hong Kong and south-east Asia. It was in this stage, when the industry turned its back on art and taste, that Shao Tsui-weng founded his T'ien-i Co., the forerunner of the Shaw Brothers of the *kung-fu* film fame. But in the 1930s there were more serious and socially concerned films made, such as the *Great Road, Fishermen's Song, Angels in the Street* and *At the Crossroads*, with an artistry and subtlety that even Chiang Kai-shek's censorship failed to stifle. These films, described by Jay Leyda as 'the underground films' of the 1930s, raised the whole industry from the abject depths to which it had sunk and linked motion pictures to the prevailing social and literary movements, thereby giving them a degree of seriousness.

### The legal profession

Law reform in China will be dealt with elsewhere in this volume. It suffices here to mention the emergence of a small group of professional lawyers. Up to 1876 only magistrates and law clerks administered the law of the empire. The magistrate (a Confucian amateur) depended on his clerks (who were trained in judicial procedures and familiar with precedents) throughout a hearing and in passing a sentence. There was no modern lawyer with any knowledge of Western law. The first time modern lawyers, the American- and British-trained Wu T'ing-fang, appeared in a Chinese court was in Foochow in 1877, in a case involving an American plaintiff. In other words, since the establishment in 1868 of the Mixed Courts in Shanghai where lawsuits concerning citizens of the treaty powers were dealt with, legal representation of the Chinese parties had been deemed unnecessary. Step by step the Chinese, like the Japanese, came to an acceptance of European concepts of law and European practices, and this acceptance lay behind a series of law reforms. The training of professional prosecutors, advocates and lawyers formed a part of these reforms. No one knows how many lawyers there were in Shanghai before 1925. They numbered only 235 in 1926 for a population of nearly three million. This figure was doubled in 1930 and doubled again a year later. In 1935 some 1250 lawyers were in practice in that city.

The Mixed Courts in the International and French Settlements were eventually renditioned in 1927 as a result of the anti-imperialist demonstrations and strikes of 1925. In their place five local courts were set up, handling, with the help of 1174 Chinese lawyers, a total of 15 276 civil and criminal cases in 1934. This made an average of 3055 cases a year for each of the courts, or some ten cases a day if the court sat six days a week. If all the cases had legal representation, each lawyer should have received thirteen briefs per annum beside his legal work outside the court. There seem to have been too many lawyers but too few courts to improve the situation which had existed before the rendition of the Mixed Courts.

In a sense the new system was slightly better than the old Mixed Courts, for it provided a machinery for appeal and had properly trained law officers instead of Chinese magistrates and foreign consuls. Like the old system, it was overladen with work. The fact that some 80 per cent of the cases were not actually dealt with suggests a serious lack of thoroughness in investigation and court examination.

## Acculturation in Shanghai

How much contact and communication was there between the two communities in Shanghai? Before 1880 hardly any, as the foreigners struck a dignified posture and maintained a united front of aloofness towards the Chinese. Foreigners had to deal with the Chinese servants in foreign households, Chinese officials and merchants. According to the prevailing image of China and the Chinese, none of these groups could be regarded as 'friends', not even the compradores, despite their close association with foreign businessmen. Novels written in the closing years of the nineteenth century could not even imagine inter-racial friendship, only ill-tempered and haughty Westerners who frightened the wits out of those who had the misfortune to be in their company. With the passage of time, some more liberal Westerners pulled down this barrier. Still, a hard core of contemptuous and conservative whites always existed who absolutely refused to come to terms with the natives they worked with. When Chinese travellers gained some knowledge of Westerners in the West they realized the difference between the humane and helpful whites at home and the proud and unapproachable ones in Shanghai, Bombay, or Aden. The isolated and closed foreign community bred quarrels and intrigues within itself. It was a sin to be friendly with a Chinese; it was utterly ridiculous to marry one.

Mixed marriages did happen. The American soldier of fortune, F. T. Ward of Ever-Victorious Army fame during the anti-Taiping campaigns, married the daughter of a wealthy compradore who financed Ward's fighting. In the 1890s, another American, one Merit, married a Chinese woman. C. W. Mason, an Englishman who joined a Chinese secret society, reports this story and goes on:

If Merit hadn't married the woman – if she had been merely his mistress – everything would have been all right. As it was, of course, he and his pretty daughter were completely ostracized.

In the context of nineteenth-century Shanghai (or anywhere else for that matter) the children of mixed marriages were the insoluble problem. They were unacceptable to their relatives on both sides. Cohabition with a Chinese woman disguised as a housekeeper was the 'gentleman's' solution. If the woman became pregnant, her wages rose from $10 a month to $30.

Lower down the social scale, there were poor but educated whites who advertised for positions in Chinese firms, asking only about $15 a month. There were also White Russians employed as body-guards and chauffeurs of rich Chinese businessmen. The blacks working on white men's ships which docked at Shanghai were the loneliest of all. 'With a skin as black as if it were lacquered and an intelligence as low as that of a deer or a pig', these people, in the eyes of the Chinese, were degrading to associate with.

The discriminating endured discriminations. In the foreign commercial buildings, the Chinese had to use a separate lift; on French trams, they were not allowed to ride in the first-class com-partment. All dinner parties where the company was mixed were held in restaurants, clubs, hotels or office buildings, never in a Chinese or Western home. Some of the social clubs opened their doors to Chinese membership after 1918. Of course the Chinese who were eligible were English- or French-speaking leading citizens of Shanghai.

The pattern of acculturation in Shanghai was not then one where the majority was to change the minority, but vice versa. As neither community was profoundly intellectual and few intimate friendships existed between them, the acculturation of the Shanghai Chinese depended more on mass media than on the aloof Caucasians them-selves. It was confined to visible and superficial things. Ideas and philosophies, art and literature were of little importance.

New things and new notions, unavoidably modified the Shanghai dialect. Those who could not speak English transliterated or trans-lated English words into manageable expressions such as *yang-p'an* (Russian roulette – dazzling and deceptive), *wai-kuo huo t'ui* (foreign ham – being kicked or insulted by a foreigner), *kang-po-tu* (compra-dore) and *shih-lao-fu* (shroff). Even a barefoot milkman signed receipts 'A. F. Wu', a name given to him by his foreign boss. The Chinese who could speak English sometimes punctuated their Chinese conversation with English nouns, adjectives and even verbs, somewhat like the Russian aristocrats' habit of using a few French words late in the nineteenth century. Shallow as they may have been, these manifestations of Westernization were status symbols, intel-lectual distinctions, and practical conveniences and amusements. Their adoption was in most cases spontaneous, unpremeditated and indiscriminate; all was done in the name of modernity (*mo-tun*).

The modernization of Shanghai had its positive phases, notably in municipal planning and administration and to a lesser extent in the administration of the law. The introduction of such mass media as newspapers, magazines, theatres and cinemas helped, on the one hand, to spread new ideas and new information and, on the other, to import fads and fashions and a spirit of consumerism which China could well have done without. The agents of change were the Western businessmen, their ways of conducting business, their ideas of municipal modernization, and their pressure on the Chinese to change their ways. There were other agents like the missionaries and educators at Western schools and universities, some of whose influence has been discussed already. Later in this century of foreign influence in Shanghai, the adventurers came; their role was almost totally negative. Predominantly guided by the motive of money-making, the new things introduced into Shanghai destroyed the old order without enough thought of what the new order would be. The result was a jumble of old and new, a sprawling city with neither generally accepted values nor generally observed norms, a modern sorrow of China.

## San Francisco

### Emigration and the growth of Chinatown

It is not known under what conditions the first thirty-six Chinese made their journey to San Francisco in 1849. The Manchu government did not have a policy towards the emigration of its subjects until the recruitment of labourers in South China by foreign and native agents grew to serious dimensions, and the outbreak of anti-Chinese feelings in North America and Australia impelled the government to adopt a definite attitude and take some action. The Burlingame Treaty of 1868 marked the Chinese acceptance of the inalienable right of free emigration, but it was the visit of James B. Angell, the American envoy, to Peking in 1880 which impressed upon the Manchu government the need for a policy.

Before the first Exclusion Act of 1882, the only factors which affected the emigration of Chinese to the USA were the conditions of life and work within China and the opportunities for employment and making money in the USA. It was a *laissez-aller* situation. The coincidence in time of the age of rebellions in China (the Taiping, Nien and the Muslim Rebellions from the 1850s to the 1880s) and the opening of the American West contributed greatly to this demographic movement. The demand for cheap and unskilled labour in California in the early 1850s was immense, due to the increase in the Californian population in the wake of the discovery of gold, the growth of light industries, e.g. cigar and garment manufacture, the development of mining, railway-building and horticulture, and the need of service industries like laundries and restaurants. On the part of the Chinese emigrants, there was a willingness to go; on the part of the shipping companies, there was a willingness to carry them, since the 'human cargo' saved them from having to send empty ships back to the USA. The China trade was then adversely affected by the rebellions and there was a glut of goods of Western origins in Hong Kong to which the Chinese found it difficult to provide a return. Tea, China's most important export, was still subject to heavy duties. Chinese were declared to be the most valuable immigrants by Governor McDougal of California in 1852, on account of their industry and contribution to the prosperity and comfort of the State. Few Californians knew how the Chinese got there in the first place.

The business of contracting and delivering Chinese emigrants to Australia, America and later the Transvaal was called the 'coolie trade' in the West and the 'piglet trade' by the Chinese. The discovery of gold in Ballarat, Sacramento, and later in the Transvaal, stimulated its growth at Macao, Hong Kong and Whampoa in the Canton Delta, Amoy and Machiang in Fukien, and Shanghai, where recruitment stations were set up by private businessmen of Portuguese, British, French, American, Chinese and probably other nationalities. At a time when rebellions were raging and the Anglo–French Expedition was in progress, it can be imagined that neither the central nor the local governments of China did much to thwart this operation. The protests of the local gentry and of the common people fell on deaf ears. The Chinese foremen first signed a contract with a foreign agent laying down the number of coolies to be found and the period within which their recruitment was to be completed. Then the coolies, mostly illiterate, signed a contract with the foreign agent in the manner described by W. A. P. Martin:

The coolies were marched up [the ship], the contract was read in a rapid manner by a Portuguese to a coolie, who probably did not understand a word of it. Then his hand was seized, and the impress of his thumb forcibly made on paper. This was the voluntary signing of the compact.

Generally speaking, the agent paid for the coolie's passage, about Mexican $80 (or US $40), to San Francisco, this sum being deducted from his earnings after he began work at a predetermined destination. On board the ship, the coolies were treated no better than the black slaves of a slightly earlier age. They lived below decks and were not allowed to leave the area where they were confined; the sanitary conditions were appalling in spite of British and American legislation to improve them. In protest at this and other kinds of inhuman treatment, the Chinese 'human cargo' mutinied on several occasions, drawing the attention of the Chinese government and the press in Shanghai and Hong Kong. The *China Mail* of 2 May 1873 lamented:

China is the greatest country on earth and the Chinese are the greatest nation. . . . Once they are deceived into becoming slaves, these Chinese are treated like the blacks. This is indeed an everlasting woe.

But these hardships did not deter the Chinese from sailing. The ones who had returned from San Francisco to Hong Kong early in the 1850s with their savings of $200 or $300, were proof enough of a dream of gold that had come true. Their income of approximately $200 a year gave these diligent and frugal workers a chance to send some money home, to ameliorate their families' living conditions. That, too, was an incentive to depart for America. In California at large, the Chinese worked in the mines and on the railways and farms; in San Francisco, which is the focus of our interest here, they worked as laundrymen, cigar-makers, boot- and shoe-makers, woollen-mill operatives, hotel and restaurant keepers, and domestic servants. From 1870 onwards, merchants and industrial workers began to emerge from among their ranks. This pattern of occupational distribution continued till the time of the earthquake.

In San Francisco they lived in the Jackson and Dupont area, where the famous Chinatown grew out of the ashes of the 1850 fire. For the next two decades, the concentration of Chinese there was not perceptibly larger than in some other places in California. But the anti-Chinese sentiment which was rife around 1870 gradually drove Chinese into this haven of security, Chinatown, whose population grew from just over 3000 in 1860 to 12000 in 1870 and 22000 in 1880. From that high point it steadily declined to 13954 in 1900, 10582 in 1910 and 7744 in 1920. It was the economic insecurity of the Great Depression that sent many Chinese back to Chinatown to find jobs and community help.

## The Six Companies

The community, in the absence of a gentry class, organized itself under the leadership of the merchants and coolies. The merchant organizations were founded on traditional ties symbolized by the district and clan associations. Challenged by anti-Chinese whites from without and anti-establishment secret societies from within, these associations were compelled to form themselves into a confederation under the name of the Chinese Consolidated Benevolent Association, commonly referred to as the Six Companies. Although the Companies came into being some time between the 1860s and 1880s, they were not registered as a legally recognized body until 1901. They were not merely a local organization. Their affiliations extended to district associations in China and coolie recruitment agencies in Macao and Hong Kong. Though they claimed to be apolitical, they tended to strike an ambivalent posture at times of political change in China to fail to give their support to new regimes until long after their establishment.

The political leadership of the Companies had always been uncertain and they were conscious of this. Therefore, at the beginning of their history, they invited scholarly people from China to be their titular heads and function as political advisers, thus giving the Companies a hue of respectability. In China itself contemporary organizations without gentry leadership would be under suspicion as potentially subversive. The actual power derived from the support of the component associations, and the discharge of normal duties of the Companies rested with the merchant leaders who, at the same time, provided a livelihood for most of the Chinese in San Francisco. After the abolition of the traditional examination system in 1905, the practice of inviting scholars to preside over the Companies seems to have been discontinued.

In the early stages of their existence, the Six Companies took it upon themselves to settle disputes among their members – the discharge of this function by an extra-legal body was traditional and perfectly acceptable to the Chinese. It made the Companies into something like a civil court dealing with mining claims, trading posts, gambling houses and even brothels. They also represented the Chinese by handling matters involving the world outside Chinatown, a function usually performed by a consulate. With the cooperation of the district associations which gave temporary lodgings to, and arranged employment for, visitors from their respective home towns, and which cared for the aged and the sick and buried the dead, the Companies acted as a charity organization. These functions continued after the revision of their constitution in 1930. Before that, the charity work was broadened to include the provision of schools and hospitals.

To perform these duties the Companies needed independent finance, which came from contributions made by the constituent associations and from fees charged for the business they handled. For instance, when a Chinese decided to return home, he had to have a sailing permit from the Companies, the prerequisite of which was the repayment of all his debts. In such a situation, the Companies charged a fee on both the departing Chinese and his creditors. The impersonal, business-like way in which the Companies handled matters of this kind necessarily contradicted the spirit of local affinity or clan sentiment on which their infrastructure rested. The contradiction was often seen as exploitative or oppressive. The bureaucratic style and corruption of the Companies' officials helped confirm this image. Although the board of directors of the Companies was elected *pro rata* according to the size of the membership of each constituent association, the elections were often rigged. Corruption and apathy together created an oligarchical domination of the Companies by the strongest district associations and the strongest clans, giving rise to frequent factional feuds and disappointment among the younger members.

## The secret societies

The dispersal of rebels to places where the long arm of the law cannot reach them is a familiar pattern found wherever rebellions occur. From the failure of the uprising of the Small Swords Society in Shanghai in 1853 to the defeat of the Taiping Rebellion in 1864, many rebels fled either to remote parts of the Ch'ing Empire or overseas to south-east Asia, India, or the USA. They were the founders of the secret societies in San Francisco and elsewhere in the USA, which carried on the anti-Manchu, anti-establishment tradition. Obviously poor, with no or unclaimed clan affiliations, they were antagonistic to the domination of the big clans and the rich merchants in Chinatown. At the same time, they also needed economic security and mutual help, which being the goals of the secret societies determined their nature. As they were not organized on the basis of local affinity or clan loyalty, they had less respect for seniority than equality; the guiding principle was on a form of brotherhood. Since the merchant community had more or less cornered all legitimate business interests, the secret societies could hardly do other than draw revenue from gambling, prostitution and smuggling to finance their activities. They protected the under-privileged such as the cigar-makers, shoe-makers and laundrymen who formed the majority of their membership, and can thus almost be seen as prototype trade unions.

International organizations with branches among Chinese communities all over the world, these secret societies yet had a surprisingly parochial political concern. Their illegitimate operations inevitably antagonized the established authority – the government and the Church in particular – wherever they happened to be. Political alienation in their case seems to have justified their in-difference to, even ignorance of, all respectable institutions, except in so far as an understanding of these institutions might facilitate their own operations. Their image of the polity and society at large was just as stereotyped as the image which society had of them. At the same time they were radical with regard to Chinese political change, in the sense that whatever was radical for China was also radical for them. Therefore one finds that the secret societies sup-ported both reform and revolution in China as well as her wars against foreign enemies.

Out of their various ramifications emerged the main organization of the secret societies, the Chih-kung-t'ang (variously spelt Chee Kong Tong, Gee Kung Tong, or Chee Kung Tong). Much of its history is that of the two-front struggle against the Six Companies over the control of Chinatown and against the American authorities in the city at large. The rises and falls in its fortunes correlated not so much with police surveillance and control over its operations but with its internecine fights caused by personality clashes, factionalism and the general economic conditions. The prosperity of the 1880s enabled the Chih-kung-t'ang to infiltrate and dominate the Six Companies. Later in the 1890s, when the influence of the Six Companies declined in the wake of their hopeless campaign against Thomas Geary's anti-Chinese Act, the Chih-kung-t'ang practically took over Chinatown for a period of time. The change of its name from a *t'ang* (society) to a *tang* (party) in 1925 epitomized the irreconcilable differences between the society's branches in east and south China, and committed the San Francisco branch to the cause of the south without seriously affecting its strength or activity. However, the change opened the door for the branch's future co-operation with the Chinese Communist Party shortly before 1949. The Depression and the consequent unemployment of many members of the society impoverished and enfeebled it for a time. Without 'teeth', it could no longer command widespread fear and respect, and relapsed into a shadowy existence.

The society used violence, sometimes quite indiscriminately, in personal vendettas or to obtain control of business interests. In San Francisco itself, this seldom assumed the scale of a *tong* war as it so frequently did in other parts of California. It had among its members a number of 'salaried soldiers' or hatchetmen, and even white thugs who assassinated at the orders of the society's leaders, but it may be an exaggeration to say that some 20 per cent of its membership were such people.

## Business and community life in Chinatown

Under the diarchy of the Six Companies and the secret societies, Chinatown developed. The first-generation Chinese immigrants, many of whom belonged to both organizations, spoke a barely understandable pidgin English and did unskilled work. In the city, a few of them worked as carpenters while others dug ditches in the streets. Successful San Franciscans during the Gold Rush adopted the Yankee custom of wearing starched shirts which had to be laundered frequently. Since all the able-bodied men were preoccupied with digging for gold, the Spanish–American and Indian women charged $8 per dozen shirts while the tea clippers from San Francisco in an attempt to cut laundry costs, carried dirty shirts and other garments to Canton to be washed. The Chinese in the city took the opportunity of invading the laundry business, charging only $2 per dozen shirts. By 1876 the city boasted 300 Chinese laundry shops. Also during the Gold Rush, miners coming back to the city for a good time found Chinese restaurants cheaper than American and Spanish ones. The food was excellent and for $1 a person could have as much as he could eat.

Up to the Second World War, the Chinese remained happy in these two major occupations in which the whites either showed no interest or could not compete effectively. Even in the 1930s the chances for a young Chinese with good qualifications of getting a white-collar job were slight. The few who were lucky enough to have succeeded, e.g. Miss Faith Sai So Leong, the only woman dental surgeon in the USA in 1905, and the two Chinese graduates from Stanford who were employed by an oil company in Texas in 1916, were headline news. The discrimination against Chinese lasted all the way from the cradle to the grave. In spite of their demonstrated skill in Western technology – 'the Chinese mechanic is a wonder' as the *San Francisco Chronicle* reported on 18 October 1903 – employment opportunities and security for most of them existed only in Chinatown, unless one preferred a small business of one's own in a small town or a small village. That was why, even in 1951, out of 596 leaders of Chinese communities in North America, 209 were engaged in the traditional businesses – restaurants, laundry, grocery, medicine and curios – and 169 were employed in Chinese schools and organizations.

Southern Chinese cuisine was quickly accepted by San Franciscans and Chinese restaurants flourished. The work was hard, but the financial return was better than from laundry work or domestic service. Chinese cooks also worked in Caucasian restaurants or as servants in Western households where they learnt to cook European and American dishes. Another development in the catering business was designed to please the Americanized second and third generation; this was the first bakery fountain in Chinatown, opened in 1935. It had the latest stainless steel equipment and uniformed waiters to serve French pastries and lychee or ginger ice-creams. Culinary eclecticism may have been good for business, but it tended to blur the memory of genuine Chinese cooking, with the result that Chinatown food normally displeased the educated palate.

Just as the Chinese restaurants were subject to strict sanitary inspection, Chinese laundries were subjected to discrimination. Before the advent of the motorized van, a licence fee of $2 was levied on those laundry shops which could afford a horse for delivery, but a fee of $15 on those (mostly Chinese) which could not. Even so, the Chinese laundry business survived, producing about $8 to $20 a week for each laundryman. The widespread use of the washing machine finally dealt the fatal blow to hand laundries. Other declining industries which had once engaged many Chinese were cigar-making and shoe-making. At the peak of their prosperity in the 1860s and 1870s, the small cigar workshops run by the Chinese each employing no more than fifty people, virtually monopolized the entire supply of cigars and cigarettes along the West Coast. The cheap Chinese labour, usually about a half or one-third cheaper than similar white labour, drove the Caucasians out of the cigar trade. In retaliation the white manufacturers invented such charges as that the Chinese cigars were unclean, which incited the Cigar Makers' Union to expel the Chinese from the business and consequently to kill it altogether. A similar prejudice against Chinese hand-made shoes existed. To overcome it, an ingenious Chinese industrialist and gangster leader, Little Pete, marked the shoes made in his factory 'F. C. Peters and Co., S. F.'. The decline of the Chinese shoe manufacture, like that of the hand laundries, was due to a lack of capital for mechanization. It died out before the First World War. The sweatshops, however, flourished from the 1870s through to the 1930s. They employed a couple of thousand machinists, mostly non-English-speaking new immigrants who could not find other jobs. Their low wages, a target of the attack for the seamsters' union, ensured the sweatshops a measure of economic security.

The Chinese grocery store, selling both Chinese and American goods, including Chinese medicine together with medical treatment and a barber service, was also the nerve centre of community life where business men and consumers came for supplies and news of San Francisco and China. The management's relationship with its customers was partly that between friends and partly that between creditor and debtors, as business was frequently done on credit. This practice rendered banks and credit houses unnecessary in Chinatown. The Chinese did not take an interest in modern credit and stock-market operations until the 1920s.

On the surreptitious side, prostitution, gambling and opium dens throve. Open prostitution in San Francisco came to an end in September 1907, when Dr Edward R. Taylor became mayor. Before that, there were some 2700 Chinese whores out of a Chinatown population of 12022 – i.e. 22.5 prostitutes to every 100 inhabitants who must obviously have been overwhelmingly adult male bachelors. In an attempt to lessen the impact of this shocking picture, Mary R. Coolidge maintained that the density of white prostitutes among the Caucasian population of San Francisco in 1906 was far higher. Since by then the sexual ratio of the white population was almost at par, Miss Coolidge's assertion is likely to be strongly biased. Even as late as 1900, the sexual ratio of the Chinese in Chinatown was still unbalanced – one woman to every thirteen men, while the immigration law allowed no more than 150 Chinese women a year to enter the US. Sex was so hard to come by that a Chinese bachelor, unless he was happy to frequent brothels, had to sail across the Pacific, marry a woman in China, perhaps sire a child, and come back to San Francisco to resume his bachelor life. Chinese wives of American citizens were not permitted to join their husbands until the 1924 Immigration Act was revised in 1930. Considering all these factors, one may accept as true the statement that the great majority of the Chinese women in San Francisco in the nineteenth century were whores.

Prostitution was controlled by the secret societies (*tong*) in co-operation with their white partners. Brought over from China, the girls were sold at a market on Dupont Street at $1000 or so per head. If the girls were to entertain only Chinese customers, they would be told of the fearsomeness of both white men and women, thus, it was hoped, killing their curiosity in venturing into the other side of the business. Their usual charge was $1 to $1.50 for a young girl, who might be as young as only twelve, or 50c for an older one. The really beautiful girls, kept exclusively for white customers, could charge as much as one ounce of gold dust a time, as Ah Toy and Selina did. The belief that a Chinese woman was physiologically different from a white woman led to the 'lookie' show at 50c. Many white men would even pay for a peek at the bound feet of a Chinese woman. Caucasian whores competed with their Chinese sisters, but they were generally 'beastlier and filthier . . . than the Chinese'. In 1885 there was a ring of white brothels around Chinatown in which Caucasian whores worked well with their Chinese pimps, whom they preferred to white madames.

What caused the municipal authorities to introduce inspection and control of Chinatown pleasure houses were the use of violence against white prostitutes by Chinese hatchetmen and the employment of Chinese and Caucasian girls under the age of consent to entertain white boys of only eight or ten years of age. Some of the boys paid as little as 15c for their initiation into sex, with disease included in the bargain.

Gambling is not an uncommon vice among bachelors and Chinese gamblers unwittingly violated Californan law by indulging in *fan-t'an*, dominoes, lotteries, etc., instead of the permissible poker, bridge, horse-racing and pool. The secret societies, led by such men as Little Pete, Big Jim, Wang Yow and Chiu Tin Sen (Tom Chu), gained complete control of this lucrative business, with branches in all the big cities of California. Chinatown alone had more than 300 gambling clubs catering mostly for Chinese and for some Japanese and Caucasian patrons. Wong Yow's own house, a gambling den on Waverley Street, was lavishly appointed with telephones, electric lights and a victrola.

The opium trade, too, was a lucrative business in the hands of the secret societies and was illegal. Smuggling of opium reached the disconcerting quantity of 60000 lb in the 1880s. The drug was served in almost every Chinese home and restaurant as a gesture of common courtesy like a cup of tea. At $8 a tin it was more expensive than tea. None the less it was smoked by no less than 40 per cent of the adult population of Chinatown. What made it intolerable to San Francisco authorities was the presence of white people in Chinese opium dens. Blind Annie's Cellar, Ah King's Place and other establishments in Chinatown or on California and Pine Streets specialized in receiving white addicts, while at cheaper dens white men and women, boys and girls, blacks and Chinese lay on the same couch to smoke themselves away into their hallucinatory worlds. The white addicts numbered some 5000 in 1887. Only the heavy penalties laid down by the ordinances of 1890 and 1892 succeeded in curbing this habit among the whites, but the Chinese persisted with it in spite of the imposition of prison sentences. The Congressional prohibition of opium import merely raised the price of the drug from $12 a lb to $70.

Since the Chinese were forbidden from buying land outside Chinatown and bachelors' hostels there admitted no Chinese lodgers, the increase in the Chinese population necessarily led to overcrowding. To the Chinese with a sojourner's mentality and an anxiety to save money for his planned return home, the discomfort of living did not seem to matter. Therefore 'two or three men slept on each bunk in shifts' and there were 15180 such bunks in Chinatown in 1885. Health inspectors discovered rooms of 8 × 10 or 10 × 12 ft accommodating as many as twelve people, and the Globe Hotel on Jackson Street at Grant Street housed 800 to 1000 in its sixty rooms.

In the 1850s most Chinese homes were humble and filthy, whereas the houses of a few wealthy merchants were sumptuously appointed with magnificent chinaware and a white linen cloth on the table.

Interior decoration and furnishing showed considerable changes half a century later when even a comparatively moderate home was noticeably cleaner, simply appointed with a mixture of Chinese and American furniture, and also displayed such reading material as the English Bible and San Francisco newspapers. The exterior of shops and restaurants, temples and clan associations was a mixture of American structure and Chinese ornamentation. Elaborate lattice-work on the windows and balconies, curved eaves and glazed roof tiles, wood and bronze lanterns, Chinese shop signs and porcelain pots created the uneasy mixture of harsh and loud colours, Chinese rococo curves, and sharp Victorian straight lines which charac-terized Chinatown before the earthquake of 1906.

When his son was leaving China to study abroad, Tuan Fang, a distinguished minister of the realm warned the youth: 'You are my only son and this is your only pigtail. I'd rather have no son than that you should ever do without your pigtail!' Many Americans regarded the pigtail as a great social barrier between them and the Chinese: few appreciated that it was a token of loyalty to the Chinese throne, a badge of Chinese citizenship. The mutiny on board the *Robert Bowne*, a coolie carrier, in March 1852, was caused by the captain's decision to have all the coolies scrubbed clean and their pigtails cut off. Many Americans – see, for instance, Charles Nahl's drawings of the Wild West and Bret Harte's *Plain Language for Truthful James* (a best seller) – poked fun at the queue; some, e.g. the police officer James Curtis, forcibly cut queues off and hung them on the railings of the city hall. Practical jokes like this one played by Curtis led directly to litigation until the passing of the Queue Ordinance in 1876. Still many Chinese wearing the pigtail appear in Arnold Genthe's pictorial record of Chinatown. The spread of revolutionary sentiments and the downfall of the Manchu dynasty in 1912 hastened the disappearance of this hair fashion. Even the Chinese consul of San Francisco abandoned it in 1910. That by 1915 pigtail hunt was a sport suggests its rarity. When Quan Hoy died in 1936, the last pigtail receded into history.

Out of necessity, the Chinese adopted a black felt hat to protect his head and eyes against the bright light and intense heat of the Californian sun. An early Chinese immigrant or sojourner in San Francisco therefore wore a queue under such a hat, a pyjama-style jacket and trousers, and slipper-like cloth shoes with a thick white soles. For durability and the protection of one's feet when doing heavy work, leather shoes proved to be more suitable. For convenience at work, the relatively tight-fitting denim trousers were preferable. Only on formal occasions, a festival or a ceremony, would the Chinese go back to their national costume of the time. The gradual change in Chinese attire, induced a change in the Chinatown tailoring trade as new-style tailors, shoe-shops and hatters began to appear early in this century. Sartorially a Chinese gentleman became hard to distinguish from an American. Women, on the other hand, were guided by the fashions in China rather than those in the US. Such a daring display of Western finery as an orange shawl and bonnet sported by the well-known prostitute, Ah Toy, was rare indeed.

## Education and entertainment

'Chinese scholarship as the essence of learning while Western scholarship merely for practical use' seems to have been the dominant philosophy of education in Chinatown as well as in China in the closing decades of the last century. As the Chinese put Chinese learning first, education in Chinatown was divided between Chinese and American schools. At first, in the 1880s, the Chinese schools, numbering a dozen or so, were privately run by individual tutors in exactly the same manner as in the Chinese Empire. Each tutor took on twenty or thirty students, held classes from 5 p.m. to 8 p.m., and collected $4-5 from each student every month. The syllabus consisted exclusively of the Confucian classics, with the aim of nurturing the students' loyalty to the Chinese throne and cultivating their minds and personalities. Among the students of this vintage, perhaps the most famous was Liao Chung-k'ai, who was to become Dr Sun Yat-sen's important assistant and the leader of the left wing of the Kuomintang. Influenced by the structure of American schools, leaders of Chinatown founded the Great Ch'ing College (*Ta-ch'ing shu-yuan*) in 1884 to systematize Chinese education. Some sixty students enrolled and were divided into two classes taught by Confucian scholars from China. The hours of teaching were from 4.30 to 9 p.m., allowing the students to attend the American school (the Oriental Public School) during the day. But on Saturdays they stayed at the College from 9 a.m. to 9 p.m. Outstanding students could go back to China to sit in the traditional examinations if they chose to do so. With the collapse of the Manchu dynasty, the name of the College was changed to Overseas Chinese Public School; it was changed again to Chinese Middle School in 1927 when the campus was expanded. In the next year, its curricula were completely modernized in line with the changes in China. The College was not of course the only school in Chinatown. The 1900s may have been an exceptional period when monarchists and revolutionaries inaugurated a number of short-lived schools, mainly for political purposes. But even as late as 1940 Chinatown still could boast six Chinese schools. Neither the monarchists and revolutionaries in the 1900s nor the Kuomintang in the 1930s and 1940s endeavoured to break away from the Confucian tradition. This orientation suited the conservative leaders of Chinatown who continued to worship Confucius and the God of Scholars.

The need to sustain conservatism may have sprung from an identity crisis of the denizens of Chinatown in an entirely alien environment, which was more acutely felt by the second and third generations. For the first-generation immigrants, the outside world was 'bad', riddled with vice and hostility, and they advised their children never to venture into it. Turning inwardly, Chinatown denizens had to strengthen their faith in their cultural identity which was expected to unify them in spite of their internal dissensions *vis-à-vis* the hostile, 'bad world' outside. In educating their children, they deemed it necessary to instil the three major components of cultural identification – racism, political philosophy and Confucian ethics – through the vehicle of language instruction. This programme of education suited the Manchus, monarchists and revolutionaries alike.

The dilemma facing the Chinese educationists in Chinatown was that Chinese children had to go to American schools to learn the English language and useful subjects so that they could earn a living in American society, and this was precisely what the 'melting pot' required from them. In the 1850s and 1860s, these children showed little interest in adopting 'our habits or learning our language, or institutions', according to a report of the San Francisco superintendent of common schools in 1861. This lack of interest cannot be explained as a result of discrimination against the Chinese as such discrimination had hardly begun. In 1859 a separate public school was established for some seventy Chinese boys, but attendance remained poor. Another attempt was made in 1885 by creating a day school on the edge of Chinatown. This was the moment when the dual system of the American education during the day and Chinese education early in the evening came into existence. In addition, misionaries set up schools for Chinese boys and girls with the aim of converting them to Christianity. Thereafter the success of the public and religious schools threatened the authority and security of the Chinese parents, whose endeavours to Confucianize their children encountered increasingly insurmountable difficulties. From the 1920s onward, American-born Chinese youth, often with only a smattering of Chinese or none at all, found the courses offered at American schools more stimulating and certainly more useful. At school they came into contact with white children and learnt an entirely different way of thinking and style of life. The 'bad world' outside ceased to be believably bad. After school, the white children went home to be given food and affection, to play and do homework while the Chinese children were shepherded into Chinese-language and ethics classes which were irrelevant to their needs, especially when they were tired. The teachers, normally recent arrivals from China, spoke a kind of English which struck the children as funny, and their pedagogical methods were not appropriate for teaching Americanized pupils. Their unfamiliarity with American ways and their poor pay ensured that their pupils would have hardly any respect for them. Linguistically, politically and ethically their instruction was a farce, a total failure.

For the adults, reading material consisted chiefly of traditional Chinese romances, books on useful knowledge, and newspapers from Hong Kong and Peking. The *Golden Hill News* (*Chin-shan Hsin-wen*) – a periodical published twice a week – was inaugurated in April 1854 for the utilitarian purposes of making living more comfortable and the customs and general conditions of San Francisco more familiar. This was followed by a weekly founded by the Reverend W. Speer in 1855 to spread general information and Christianity. During the period of intensive politicization of the Chinese in Chinatown in the 1900s, when both the monarchists and republicans were struggling to influence them, a spate of Chinese newspapers came into circulation. The fact that six newspapers were published for a population of only 20000 evoked the envy of a distinguished visitor, Liang Ch'i-ch'ao. The information and comment printed in these papers involved Chinatown people in

Chinese home politics, since they were chiefly political periodicals edited or written by such party politicians as Lin Sen (titular head of the Republic of China from 1931 to 1943) in the 1900s and Chang Wen-t'ien (who was to become a leading figure in the Chinese Communist Party) in the early 1920s.

As for entertainment, a Chinese theatre gave its opening performance on 23 December 1852. New theatres replaced it in the 1870s. The audience observed all the traditional manners and etiquette of the Chinese theatre-goer – smoking and eating, talking and kneading the toes while watching the performance on the stage which, too, was entirely traditional. Cantonese operas were what Sarah Bernhardt saw on her two visits to San Francisco Chinatown in 1887 and 1891. While Bernhardt was impressed by the clever technique of the female impersonators, Edwin Booth found these Chinese theatres boring. To the American ear, the operatic music was an 'infernal din' and the singing 'howls and screams'. Despite criticisms and complaints from modernized Chinese, traditional Cantonese operas continued to thrive in San Francisco. The Chinese government even sent a troupe of thirty-eight actors to San Francisco in 1924, but they did not make the theatre page of the San Francisco papers. With the passing away of the older generation, operas based on traditional scenarios and idioms became less and less relevant and understandable to the American Chinese in the Depression era. They were replaced by the cinema.

## Crime

In its initial stages when the population of Chinatown was still small, criminality was not one of its prominent chracteristics. The industrious, docile and inoffensive Chinese, like little ants, did no harm to anyone and were welcomed by the Americans. The organization of the secret societies and the *tong* wars drew public attention to the crimes committed by the Chinese, which fell mainly into the categories of petty larceny and burglary – 412 and 115 cases respectively in the 1875–8 period in contrast to only nineteen cases of murder and one of manslaughter. Also, due largely to their ignorance of the laws governing immigration, gaming and the opium traffic, the Chinese often found themselves liable to somewhat unexpected punishment. This trend of criminality continued into this century (1900–1927) with:

| | | |
|---|---|---|
| Offences against the person | 671 | 1·03 % |
| Offences against public policy and morals | 53322 | 82·05 |
| Offences against public health and security | 10366 | 15·95 |
| Offences against property | 626 | 0·96 |
| Total | 64985 | |

In its entire history, even at the height of the *tong* wars and anti-Chinese riots, Chinatown was more tranquil than the rest of the city. The San Franciscans in the first decades of their residence in the city were mostly sojourners who, having failed elsewhere, 'came in the hope that they could quickly plunder California of her treasure and return to their homes'. They were a floating population, rowdy and lawless. In an endeavour to impose a measure of social order into San Francisco, Sam Roberts organized his Regulators of the Hounds to deal chiefly with the Spanish–Americans and other foreigners. This was succeeded by Sam Brannan's Committee of Vigilance of 1851. These self-righteous men deluded themselves into taking violent action according to their own concept of justice, while in effect they were vengeful law-breakers themselves. Criminality was, then, open-faced and 'as plentiful as blackberries'. It reached such a point that Governor Johnson had to declare San Francisco in a state of insurrection. As the city gradually settled into a pattern of law and order, crimes by Chinese stuck out like a sore thumb, not because they were frequent but because they were committed by Chinese, to receive adverse publicity and to be used as a reason for the exclusion of the Chinese from California.

The crime rate among the Chinese in the city had never been noticeably higher than that among any other ethnic group. If the number of prisoners at San Quentin can be regarded as an indicator, the average proportion of Chinese prisoners was about 1.76 per cent of the total. The impression that the Orientals or Celestials were prone to criminality was a newspaper exaggeration helped in many cases by stripping the Chinese of their right to testify in a court of law either in favour of or against a white person.

The strangeness of the Chinese, their supposed criminal tendencies, and the filthy overcrowded living conditions in Chinatown did not create a pleasant image in the minds of the white San Franciscans. The nausea accumulated since 1854 was accentuated by the economic depression and cultural hostility of the late 1860s and the 1870s. The community was declared a nuisance on 10 March 1880 and described as 'injurious to the prosperity of California, morally and commercially'. But when the anti-Chinese hysteria died down in the 1880s, the same strangeness, filth and overcrowding made Chinatown the 'mecca of tourists', which even attracted the interest of Sarah Bernhardt and Robert Louis Stevenson. It was this same strange, filthy and overcrowded Chinatown which was consumed by the great fire of 1906.

After the fire, there was no question of obliterating Chinatown from the face of San Francisco, only of the manner of its resurrection. At the insistence of the Chinese themselves, it was to be on the same site or in Oakland. The city bowed to the Chinese demand. However, apart from a new telephone exchange which looked like a temple, new neon lights, new shops and bazaars, and a large increase in the number of Chinese claiming to be American citizens taking advantage of the fact that the fire had destroyed their files, the old life-style and business patterns remained. Superficial as it was, the Americanization of Chinatown began from its destruction in the fire. Thereafter the tension between Chinese conservatism and Americanization assumed a new meaning. Excessive Americanization might end by destroying Chinatown's traditional character, and with its character its tourist attraction. The effort to preserve conservatism was no longer made for its own sake but for money-making; the nature was bourgeois and modern. In spite of these efforts, American modernity irresistibly invaded this conservative citadel, causing the writer of a series of reports in the *San Francisco Chronicle* early in March 1929 to lament the fading away of the traditional colour of Chinatown. Then came the Depression, during which Chinatown stores grew larger, night life grew longer, and new dance halls and bars sprang up for the fashionable Caucasian visitors, rivalling Harlem of New York City as a tourist district. Chinatown's importance in the tourist trade was eventually acknowledged and honoured, in February 1934, by the Downtown Association and the Junior Chamber of Commerce, thus enhancing the prestige of the conservative Six Companies which wielded considerable influence in re-zoning San Francisco so that the Oriental quality of the community would not be harmed.

*Anti-Chinese feeling and exclusion*

Robert Louis Stevenson was horrified by the American prejudice against the Chinese, whose forbearance under insult evoked only his admiration. Mark Twain directed his scathing satire against the 'individuals, communities, the majority of the state itself . . . hating, abusing, and persecuting those humble strangers'. Another literary figure, Bret Harte, who wrote:

> That for ways that are dark
> And tricks that are vain,
> The heathen Chinese is peculiar.

also described how a poor Chinese was ill treated on his way to Sacramento – thrown down from the top of a stage coach and beaten and robbed by Caucasians. But these voices were faint compared with the uproar against the Chinese in the 1870s. The *Illustrated Wasp*, a weekly which enjoyed a wide circulation, was probably the most virulent and acrimonious of all the anti-Chinese publications of that period.

The background to the Chinese question in California shows two strands of thought. In the first place, there was a racist wish, backed by the anthropological science of the time, to create an exclusively white California; in the second place, there was a fear of a new form of slavery. Based on the information gathered by diplomats, traders and missionaries, the *Anthropological Review* of 1866 wrote:

As the type of the Negro is foetal, that of the Mongol is infantile. And in strict accordance with this we find their government, literature and art are infantile also. They are beardless children, whose life is a task, and whose chief virtue consists in unquestioning obedience.

This poor image of China and the Chinese seems to have received confirmation from the sight of thousands of Celestials roaming the streets of San Francisco, reminiscent of the thousands of Indians roaming the beautiful hills and plains of California. Why should these people be allowed to live among the white settlers? Then there was the memory of the recently discontinued slave trade which was responsible for the anti-slavery stance of the Constitution of California of 1849, and made the state a free one. Would the influx of 'indentured' Chinese immigrants establish a new form of slavery there?

However, the state needed labour. The import of coolies believed to be under the same sort of contract as the bond-servants shipped from Britain to America in the seventeenth century, provoked a sharp debate among the leaders of California. Governor McDougal and Senator Tingley were in favour of legalizing the immigration of Chinese contract labourers because they were cheaper, more industrious, more docile, and in no way competitive with American workers. Furthermore, these labourers were allowed to stay and work at fixed wages only for a period of ten years or less. Senator Roach, on the opposing side, argued that free labour should be the foundation of the new state, which was also a Christian state committed against all pagan beliefs such as the Chinese superstitions. Although the need for and the influx of Chinese immigrants continued, the embryonic sinophobia of California had already begun to grow at the time of the debate of 1852.

After the Civil War, railway construction demanded even more cheap and unskilled labour which the Chinese could supply while the railway builders were willing to employ them. This situation led to the Burlingame Treaty of 1868, whose Article V ensured a free flow of the needed labour. In the three years after the signing of the Treaty 36000 Chinese passed through the customs of San Francisco and nearly all of them were contract labourers handled by the district and clan associations at the Californian end of their journey. They were prepared to accept low wages and do the most menial work. The unfortunate thing was that this Chinese invasion coincided with the economic recession of the late 1860s and early 1870s when employers preferred the cheap and docile workers to the more defiant Caucasians. Often the Chinese were used to break strikes. Industrious and thrifty, these Chinese spent very little to benefit Californian commerce. They also showed a business acumen which threatened small white businesses. An anti-Chinese campaign therefore broke out in 1871, to be sustained throughout the decade. It was chiefly urban, designed to drive the Chinese out of the cities of California; it was supported by the organized labour, the Irish (the Sand Lots) and the Catholic Church.

Cultural and social differences added fuel to the fires of wrath against the Chinese. The *Illustrated Wasp* furiously assaulted the Chinese precisely on social and cultural grounds – 'What is it?' (9 March 1878) on the Chinese life style; 'Judge Righteous Judgement' (9 August 1879) on the question of the queue and Queue Ordinance; 'Scrubbing the City of Scrubbs' (21 February 1880), one of the cruellest cartoons, on the filth of Chinatown. At the height of the campaign, Frank Pixley, the Democratic spokesman on the Chinese issue, described Chinatown as a lair of gamblers, opium smokers, bandits and prostitutes who lived on robbery and blackmail. The highbinders and crimes in Chinatown never failed to arouse intense sinophobia or contemptuous amusement in the 1870s and were thereafter reported in a sensational and exaggerated manner, as with the case of 'Celestial' Lui Fook who was accused of murdering his wealthy and eccentric mistress, Rosetta Baker. The murder trial remained on the front page of the *San Francisco Chronicle* from 13 December to 28 February 1930, competing successfully with the case of the blackmail of Clara Bow by her secretary. The despicable image of Chinatown was thus created and sustained; the demand from the hearts filled with racial hatred was 'Destroy it! Let the plow run through the filthy streets!'*

The Chinese reluctance to integrate themselves with the mainstream of American culture offended the American pride – the melting pot having thus failed to melt the Chinese! – and threatened their white civilization. Despite his denial of racism, Governor W. D. Stephens' charge of Chinese unassimilability epitomized a long racist tradition; hostility to the Chinese discouraged them and intimidated them from venturing out of Chinatown to become acculturated, and was in turn fed by the Chinese failure to be Americanized. Take the naturalization of the Chinese for instance. On the one hand, the Chinese were accused of having a sojourner's mentality – making a fortune and then returning home to spend the rest of their lives in comfort and ease – exactly like the Caucasians in Shanghai. They were quite unappreciative of the rights and duties conferred by American citizenship. On the other, they were disqualified from testifying in a court of law either for or against a white person and also from naturalization. The Celestials could do no right when the whites wanted to have their cake and eat it.

The Chinese response to Californian sinophobia is significant for the understanding of the American policy of exclusion. As has been pointed out before, the Chinese government had not had any immigration policy until it was awakened to the need for one by James B. Angell's visit to Peking in 1880. Its failure to formulate such a policy until then can be attributed to two reasons. First,

* The Reverend William Roder's statement of 1901 quoted in R. H. Dillon, *The Hatchet Man*, NY, 1962, p. 348.

Chinese citizenship was a cultural rather than legal concept and it was based on *jus sanguinis* rather than *jus soli*. Wherever he or she might be, a Chinese subject was a person who spoke the Chinese language, accepted Chinese norms and values, and was born of Chinese parents. Neither a nationality law nor an immigration law was necessary. Second, Chinese emigrants who were willing to jettison the world's only civilization to live in barbarian countries were usually people of the lower classes motivated by profit-seeking. Such people were of no importance; and the same applied to all problems connected with them. Although the anti-Chinese movement in California drew Chinese official attention, the government's way of thinking about and handling the problems of immigration remained traditional. The officials and gentry, in the first place, regarded the whole matter as trivial and unworthy of close attention. Since the immigrants were of low birth and uneducated, the American allegations of their immortality and anti-social life style were probably irrefutable. This was the view of the Chinese government and press throughout the 1880s. Even those who were influenced by the social Darwinism of a later period, Ts'ai Yuan-p'ei, the Chancellor of Peking University for example, began their arguments with the acceptance of the premise that the Chinese were inferior and it was the inferiority of the immigrants which had provoked the wrath of the whites. It followed that the Chinese Empire or republic should forbid its labourers to leave its shores while allowing only substantial merchants the privilege of representing their country and race for the sake of China's prestige abroad. This was precisely what the anti-Chinese Californians wanted.

The response from the Chinese immigrants themselves, by definition unskilled and uneducated labourers, was totally different. They insisted on pressing home the point that, humble and modest as they were, they had made considerable contributions to the prosperity of California by their sweat and toil. This was their *raison d'être* in the USA. Any attempt to exclude them was therefore unjust and must be resisted. The issue in their eyes was one concerning the nation and race; it was not merely a matter of honour and 'face'. In this perspective, it is understandable that their indignation, echoed by their like at home, was transmuted into action in 1905 in the form of an anti-American boycott, a show of strength by which they hoped to influence both the Chinese and the American governments.

When James B. Angell arrived in Peking in 1880 to discuss the exclusion of Chinese labourers from entering the USA, the Tsungli Yamen was already prepared to accept the propositions that too many Chinese had gone to that country and that it was impossible for the Empire to protect them if the anti-Chinese rioting in California became uncontrollable. The Yamen compromised by proposing a restriction of the number of immigrants while resisting total exclusion. The agreement reached was that 'the government of the US may regulate, limit, or suspend' the coming and residence of the Chinese, 'but may not absolutely prohibit it'. Subsequently, due to the dissatisfaction of the Californians, Congress announced the first Exclusion Act, to be in force for a period of ten years, in 1882. The Act calmed down anti-Chinese sentiment as the number of Chinese in California decreased. The Scott Act of 1888 which prevented the return of departed Chinese labourers was followed by the Geary Act of 1892 which extended the period of exclusion by another ten years. The Geary Act also stipulated the registration of all Chinese residents in the USA, probably for two purposes – to subject all Chinese to income tax and to ferret out illegal immigrants. The Six Companies reacted strongly to this Act, calling for a campaign to resist it, but failed. On this issue, the Chinese officials again sided with the USA. Then came the Exclusion Act of 1904, permanently forbidding Chinese immigration, which provoked the 1905 boycott. And the prohibition was extended to Chinese wives and children of American citizens by the Immigration Quota Act of 1924. Not until 1943 were these racist Acts repealed; not until 1952 did the Chinese become eligible for naturalization.

Long before exclusion became a policy, 'John is probably the best [*sic*] abused foreigners we have among us', declared the *Hutching's California Magazine*. When the Exclusion Act came into force, Chinese immigrants and visitors had to go through humiliating and discriminatory entry procedures before admission into the USA. To begin with, the Chinese had little understanding of the significance of a passport. Even a highly educated man like H. H. Kung, later Dr Kung and brother-in-law of Dr Sun Yat-sen and Chiang Kai-shek, and holder of many ministerial posts, carried with him a dubious piece of paper without even his photograph on it, thereby causing a good deal of trouble at the customs of San Francisco in 1902. Then the Chinese developed the illegal practice of selling their return permits and American birth certificates in Hong Kong and

Macao, thus arousing the suspicion of American customs officials as to the authenticity of such papers when presented at the customs. All Chinese immigrants and visitors on entering were carefully inspected and examined by health officers and vaccinated. The onus was on the Chinese to prove that he was not a labourer, and therefore exempted from the exclusion, and the proof might take several months to come. Meanwhile the visitor was kept in a wooden shack on Angel Island. Even eminent visitors like Liang Ch'i-ch'ao and Sun Yat-sen were subjected to this humiliating experience.

Once in California, the visitors or immigrants encountered all kinds of ill-treatment and discrimination. Early ridicule evolved into organized riots and massacres, such as occurred in San Francisco on 4 August 1863 and in Los Angeles on 23 October 1871. Often hooligans

follow the Chinaman through the streets, howling and screaming after him. They catch hold of his cue, and pull him from the wagon. They throw brickbats and missiles at him.

Even Chinese diplomats were sometimes beaten up by rowdy Caucasians. Chinese papers reported these atrocities; Chinese diplomats gave accounts of them to the throne. The Ch'ing government, however, had no effective means of doing anything about the problem, except by appealing to and arguing with the American authorities. With the promulgation of the Exclusion Acts, the anti-Chinese riots and massacres subsided, although discrimination has continued in mild or severe forms up to this day.

### Acculturation of the Chinese community

Surrounded by hostility and disdain, Chinatown was a culturally deprived community. At best, the merchants and workers had only a feeble grasp of cultural traditions and trends in China or the USA; even their command of English or Chinese left much to be desired. The cultural and social chasms between them and their children can be imagined, once the young people became educated. The young Chinese either left Chinatown or reluctantly remained for the lack of alternative possibilities. Rosie, a girl of thirteen, having learnt the piano and developed ambitions to become a real artist, felt the only way to fulfil her aspirations was to break away from the gambling and smells of Chinatown. In this manner, the brains of the commun-

C.A.T.W.—I

ity became unavailable to help its cultural growth. The Chinese
students at Berkeley and other universities close to Chinatowns also
refused to help in such growth. For as sojourners, they had neither
the time nor the interest to tackle the roots that clutched and
strangled these communities, turning the Chinatowns into cultural
wastelands. With their more progressive and more Westernized
outlooks, they generally disapproved and, indeed, felt ashamed of
the life-style and intellectual aridity of the Chinese immigrants.
Competent Chinese scholars usually rejected Chinatown overtures
designed to tempt them into leaving their academic colleagues in
China and coming to work in San Francisco. Thus cut off from the
cultural life of China, these immigrants could turn only to missionaries and teachers in the USA, e.g. Otis Gibson and Donaldina
Cameron, who, well meaning, compassionate and helpful, devoted
themselves to the social rather than cultural needs of the immigrants.
In Gibson's words:

They [the Chinese in the San Francisco Chinatown] may be called greatly
in wanting in good taste not to appreciate our superior fashions, yet it is a
fact that they looked upon this American fashion of mopping the streets
with the skirts of ladies' dresses as exceedingly nasty and barbarous.

The missionaries and school teachers tried scarcely anything beyond
the level of ladies' fashions.

   In such an atmosphere and in such an environment, the Chinese
immigrants evolved a defensive attitude *vis-à-vis* American criticism.
The traditions they defended gave them pride, cohesion and acceptability at home when the sojourners decided to return with their pots
of gold. As antagonism from outside quietened down into contempt
and smirk, into curiosity and amusement, the solemnly preserved
traditions were turned into a money-making business. In either case
there was good reason for the elders of Chinatown to resent the
trend of 'going white'. In either case, the preservation of conservatism had a utilitarian motive. These attitudes convinced the Americans that racially and culturally the Chinese could not be thoroughly
Americanized.

   The Chinese adopted a similar utilitarian attitude towards their
own limited Americanization or acculturation. Cutting off the queue,
freeing the bound feet, changes in their eating habits, donning of
Western clothes, partaking in civic celebrations, using English
Christian names, staging fashion shows and baby shows, were

designed to impress the outside world that, though proud and honourable, the immigrants were also adaptable and solid citizens when the pretence of being sojourners ceased to have any meaning. At no time did they make an effort to understand the Americans as human beings, or American culture as a fine and sophisticated heritage. To illustrate this, one only has to search for a Chinese account of, say, a dinner party at an American home. One might imagine that such rare occasions would deserve a space in a Chinese newspaper to satisfy the curiosity of its Chinese readership. No such account can be found! On the other hand, equally rare dinner parties where the guests were racially mixed were reported in American books, magazines and newspapers. The disparity in curiosity and observation, in sensitivity and orientation, cannot be denied.

At dinners given by Chinese hosts food tended to smother conversation, while such conversation as there was often focussed on food. There the language barrier was real. The Chinese who spent most of their time in kitchens and laundry rooms, or after work in Chinese teashops and *mahjong* clubs with their Chinese friends, needed very little English. Waiters and house-boys, on the other hand, spoke English better and knew some American etiquette. Government interpreters, mostly bilingual second-generation Chinese, were, as one would expect, more Americanized. But people of other kinds of occupation, the fringe elements – gangsters, prostitutes, *et al.* – had to be somewhat acculturated in order to make a success of their business. The Reverend O. Gibson regretted that before the 1870s, the Chinese had learnt English from 'bad people' – the vicious, immoral and profane – in other words, harlots, their customers, hoodlums and police from whom the Chinese picked up American slang and living habits. An outstanding example was the Chinese beauty, Ah Toy, who spoke almost no English on her first appearance in court. But on subsequent appearances, her command of English impressed her audience. She even led and won a legal battle against the Six Companies on the issue of levying a tax on Chinese prostitutes. Another highly Americanized, dubious character was Little Pete, who introduced American business practice – employing white salesmen, white book-keepers and white bodyguards – into his shoe factory. He had vast business contacts with the Caucasian world and a fluent command of English. Other gangster leaders like Chin Tin-sen and Big Jim likewise became Americanized with the help of their white wives.

Mixed marriages based on romantic impulse or sheer convenience did not normally survive for long under public censure and newspaper criticism. Take Wong Suey Wan's attempted marriage to Sarah Burke in 1883 for instance. This courageous woman demonstrated her love by kissing Wong in public, but those who witnessed the kiss were disgusted, police charged Wong with enticing the poor woman, county clerks refused to issue them a licence, and no minister would marry them. On 16 January 1892 the *Morning Call* even published an editorial, 'Lamentable Misalliance', to condemn the marriage of Miss May Foster to Li Ling. In San Francisco, as in Shanghai at the same period, such miscegenation of Chinese *yang* and Caucasian *yin* invariably led to the ostracization of the couple from both communities and ended in despair, disharmony and alcoholism.

How far these few white women who married Chinese husbands succeeded in acculturating their spouses is impossible to assess. Contemporary records on their marriages are so biased as to allow no serenity of mind to look into the positive side of their union. Any sexual contact between the two races was perceived in the vilest terms – white slavery, baby snatching or the desperate act of white 'trash' in need of a husband – any husband, not excepting a Celestial. Even the employment of white women workers in a Chinese canning factory for entirely respectable reasons was given a sinister interpretation by the *Morning Call* on 24 August 1893.

Wedding ceremonies and matrimonial relations between Chinese spouses underwent changes. As far back as 1855, iconoclastic immigrants wedded in the American fashion. Civil and church ceremonies became more and more common in the twentieth century. Divorces, however, remained rare. Women's position at home and in society showed some superficial improvement; for instance, Chinese women appeared for the first time at formal dinners in 1914, and voted in the municipal elections in 1931 and 1933. Although it was a far cry from the days of the slavery of women in Chinatown, the trend, guided by American feminism before the First World War, still fell a long way short of real female emancipation.

The inescapable conclusion is that, compared with other ethnic groups in the USA, the Chinatown Chinese were the least acculturated and perhaps made the least cultural contribution to American life. No great writer, actor, musician, or critic emerged among them or their descendants to place them in a position comparable to the blacks, Italians, Irish, or Mexicans, not to mention the Jews. Surely their own cultural deprivation, ambivalence and incoherence must have been responsible for this. There is enough evidence to prove their anxiety to excel in intellectual pursuits, and there was enough money for them to invest in learning and research. But both their ambition and their investment were misdirected, producing an intellectual barrenness almost unique in the cultural history of man.

## The emigrants and China

Did these Chinese make a significant contribution to the cultural modernization of China? There is a paucity of material and the very paucity suggests that they did not. Whatever contribution they did make was confined to bringing back tangible things and disjointed pieces of information about the USA which they passed on to their less knowledgeable friends and neighbours. Thus the Canton Delta, whence most of the San Franciscan Chinese came, exhibited some signs of change towards modernity similar to some areas in Shantung whence many Chinese porters and trench diggers set out for the Western and Eastern fronts during the First World War. Even the strident protests against the Exclusion Act of 1904 failed to inspire an immigrant to translate *Uncle Tom's Cabin*: the work was left to Lin Shu, a Chinese who had never set foot abroad, who saw it as a way of expressing the inhuman sufferings of the Chinese immigrants. Apart from Tom Gunn (T'an Ken), an aeroplane pilot, who went back to China in 1915 and aroused a measure of interest in aviation, the San Francisco Chinatown made scarcely any impact on the cultural modernization of their home country.

Dominated by the Six Companies, Chinatown's participation in Chinese politics tended to be conservative and hesitant, except when China was fighting Japan. The majority of the inhabitants always supported the regime in power in China, be it the Manchu dynasty or the republic. That none of them was inspired to introduce American republican democracy to their compatriots and thereby to assist Chinese political reform and revolution at the end of the last and the beginning of this century can be ascribed only to their ignorance or imperfect knowledge of American politics. They needed Chinese political leaders, e.g. Liang Ch'i-ch'ao, Sun Yat-sen and the anti-Japanese hero, General Ts'ai T'ing-k'ai, to articulate their goals and policy proposals for them. Although Yuan Shih-k'ai and the warlord government in Peking set up a bureau in charge of overseas Chinese workers because of the request for coolie labour at the Western front put forward by the Allied powers of the First World War, it was the Kuomintang government in Canton and later in Nanking which formulated the first coherent policy towards over-seas Chinese, encouraging them to co-operate with the American authorities, integrate themselves in American life, and at the same time strengthen their ties with China in order to improve their own status. In reality they, with their donations to the monarchical or republican cause, did more for China than China, in her impotence, did or could do for them.

The patriotism of these Chinese, eloquently demonstrated in the period of the Japanese invasion of Manchuria and Shanghai in 1931 and 1932 and the Sino–Japanese War of 1937–45, had its economic importance. The fact that San Francisco Chinese remitted no less than 8 000 000 taels of silver to China in 1890 alone attracted the attention of an eminent Chinese diplomat, Hsüeh Fu-ch'eng. However, the Manchu government had little success in attracting overseas Chinese capital for investment in China. Overseas Chinese remittances grew as overseas Chinese themselves became more affluent. By 1936 they offset 97.6 per cent of China's deficit balance of trade. They also began to invest in civil aviation, banking, rail-ways and light industries in China throughout the 1920s and 1930s. In return, Chiang Kai-shek's government showered honour and prestige upon them, satisfying their needs for recognition which would never have been satisfied otherwise.

# Part 2

# *Changes*

# Chapter 5
# *Process of change*

The stimulus of the first Sino–British war of 1839–42 revealed to the Ch'ing government the ineffectiveness of China's traditional navy and warships. Reforms in her maritime defences were urgently needed, 'not necessarily according to known methods or styles as long as the new ships and guns were well made and useful'. Soon afterwards, when the costliness of building ships for coastal waters was ascertained, a shift in defence policy occurred. An imperial edict early in 1843 stressed the fortification of some key points along the coast. The retreat of the Confucian empire from traditional methods of ship-building and cannon manufacture was thus symbolized by its retreat from sea to land. Initial difficulties there still were – gun barrels cracked and cannon grew rusty; nevertheless, China's improved defences gave her some excuse for the complacency of the 1850s. The Viceroy of Canton, Hsü Kuang-chin, for example, felt comfortably safe behind a wall of casemates. Relying on barrages of cannon and small arms to defeat invading barbarians on land, he asked: 'What would be the point of learning from any foreigner?' Confidence born of complacency took the place of the initial urge to learn from the foreigners in order to deal with them effectively. Meanwhile the efforts of the lower gentry, Wei Yuan's and Hsü Chi-yü's compilations of gazetteers, Ting Kung-ch'en's and Yeh Shih-huai's studies of gunnery, rudimentary and faulty as they were, were forgotten. China's ephemeral zeal for national strengthening was dissipated for the time being, as if waiting for another defeat to prick it back into life again.

That defeat came in 1860 when the Summer Palace in Peking was destroyed almost simultaneously with the south Yangtze headquarters of the government troops by the Anglo–French expedition and the Taiping rebellion respectively. The life of the empire hung in the balance. A more systematic and sustained effort was evidently needed if the empire was to regain its prestige by self-strengthening. In the metaphor of perhaps the most important memorial presented to the throne by Prince Kung and his colleagues seeking peace from the foreigners, the perils near the heart of the empire were the internal rebellions, near its armpits were the Russians, and at the extremities of its limbs were the British. Accordingly the empire must deal urgently with the rebels, then with the Russians, and finally with the British. In other words, it had to make peace with the invaders and concentrate on quelling the peasant uprisings in the short term, while in the long term pursuing the goal of strengthening its defences. 'War and defence are the real thing', in the words of the memorialists. The time bought through appeasing the barbarians was for reviving the empire so that when reinvigorated, it could drive them away. There was no question of Confucianism abdicating from its position as the guiding philosophy of the state or the Confucian elite withdrawing from its position as the ruling class. Both the short-term policy of suppressing the rebels and appeasing the foreigners and the long-term programme of strengthening, including learning their martial skills from the barbarians, fell perfectly within the confines of the resurgent modern-text school of Confucian teaching in the 1820s.

Before 1870, 'strength' meant military strength pure and simple to all Confucian modernizers. This narrow perception bred a narrow response; the minimum goals were the maintenance of peace and the preservation of territorial integrity and the maximum goal was 'doing what one wishes to do myriad leagues away' from China. The basic assumptions were that the Chinese people had the intelligence to acquire Western skills; that China had the natural resources for fulfilment of her policy goals; and that the bureaucracy was equal to the tasks.

Undoubtedly this approach was myopic and its inherent dangers were pointed out by Robert Hart, the British inspector-general of Chinese imperial maritime customs. In his essay of 6 November 1865, Hart was outspoken on Chinese indirectness and bureaucratic corruption and on a lack of knowledge of both the internal and the external situations; he advised reform and the adoption of modern transport and communication systems, the establishment of mechanized industries, and the standardization of currency in addition to defence arrangements. In the following year Sir Thomas Wade, the British *chargé*, with the consent of the British Minister, Sir Rutherford Alcock, presented a note to the Chinese government, advising the Chinese to give up the Confucian view that good government depended solely on the appointment of good men and instead to adopt modern institutions, modern industries and modern medicine. Following closely on Wade's heels, the French Minister, Henri de Bellonet, advised China on the urgent tasks of military, trade and transport reforms and, above all, to eliminate the corruption that permeated every level of the civil service. Their words fell on indignant ears. Prince Kung, heading the newly created Tsungli Yamen (Foreign Office and Board of Trade), thought the motives behind their proposals were dangerous and malevolent; Tso Tsung-t'ang, the Viceroy of Chekiang and Fukien and the founder of the Foochow Shipyard, fumed over the blunt words and the supposed self-interests of Hart and Wade. None of those who discussed Hart's and Wade's suggestions disagreed that there was a need to strengthen China's defences; none agreed with such shockingly new ideas as the construction of railways.

The Tientsin Massacre of the French missionaries in 1870 and the Japanese invasion of Taiwan in 1874 heightened a long-felt frustration on the part of the more enlightened Confucian modernizers. China's efforts at strengthening her maritime defence were judged to be inadequate to deal with the possible repercussions of these events. The meagreness of her defence achievements evidently could not be attributed to an unyielding archaic attitude alone; her subsistence agricultural economy was far from being sufficient to support her defence modernization. In fact, her defence projects had been up till then, and continued to be funded from the more reliable customs revenue and less certain *likin* (excise), respectively under foreign and Chinese managements. The defence industries themselves cried out for related industries which the empire had no capital to set up. Li Hung-chang, now promoted to the metropolitan viceroyalty, concluded: 'The weakness of China lies in her poverty.' As Li saw it, the wealth of much smaller countries in the West came from coal and iron, railways and telegraph systems. China must therefore plan for as drastic and as urgent a change as she could, if she too was to possess wealth. Since she had no capital for investment in such industries, Li developed the idea of merchant shipping and materialized it in 1872 in the hope that this would save China the expense of hiring foreign ships and facilitate the export of her native goods.

As expected, Li's view was shared by his protégés. Kuo Sung-t'ao, China's first Minister to the Court of St James, refused to accept that a country could be wealthy and strong when its people were in dire poverty; Ma Chien-chung and Hsüeh Fu-ch'eng concurred. The consensus in Li's secretariat now was that there was an inseparable link between wealth and strength. Representing the younger generation of the Confucian modernizers, Chang Chih-tung went a step further. His joint memorial with Liu K'un-yi (he and Liu were the Viceroys of Wuch'ang and Nanking respectively) in 1901 maintained that the wealth of Western countries was derived not from trade but from manufacturing industries. Ten years earlier, Chang had conceived a scheme for increasing the wealth and strength of China – training talents for the mining of coal and iron, using coal and iron for the manufacture of machines and weapons, producing machines and weapons for the utilization of talents. Three years after the war of 1895, he evolved his *t'i–yung* (essence–application) dichotomy in which industries were given the role of the essence and trade the role of application of essential knowledge for the enrichment and strengthening of China.

## Bureaucratic reform

The Confucian approach to changing China foundered on an unspoken but utterly unrealistic assumption that the entire bureaucracy was efficient and reliable. All those who partook in making the short-term and long-term policies based on this approach and all those who tacitly supported them were Confucian scholars in the government service, and the great majority of them were corrupt and inefficient. K'ang Yu-wei, in his seventh letter to the throne in February 1898, was not exaggerating when he spoke of there being but a few dozen officials who could be regarded as 'upright'. Indeed, Hart and Wade had already pointed out the reality behind the virtuous façade, only to be met with strong and hostile reactions from the entire officialdom. Corruption and the resultant deception were perhaps the greatest enemies of China's endeavours to modernize.

The reality, though unspoken, was not left out of consideration by the high leaders of the Confucian revival that began in the 1860s.

Tseng Kuo-fan made an attempt to discipline the civil service through Confucian persuasion or education. His successors, Li Hung-chang in particular, perhaps realizing the hopelessness of the task, shifted the emphasis from rectifying the civil service to the acquisition of new knowledge for new tasks.

But if one were to base one's study of the Chinese bureaucracy on the archives written by officials themselves, one can easily come to an impression as follows:

They [the Confucian modernizers] did not imagine that they were improving upon the traditional and lasting principles of good government; they sought only to adjust their methods in order to realize the original aim under new conditions. The two immediate problems were the suppression of rebellion and the stabilization of foreign relations. The long-term solution of these two problems, however, involved much more than the mastery of the techniques of diplomacy and modern armament. It required in addition, . . . restoration of the system of government by superior civil officials; re-establishment of the elaborate network on which local control depended; rehabilitation of the economy, with attention to the interests both of the state and of the people; fundamental military reorganization; a new outlook in foreign affairs; and in each of these spheres, education and scholarship aimed at reasserting the Confucian ideology.

However, if one turns one's attention to the writings of the lower gentry and merchants outside the civil service, one uncovers a totally different reality. Still within the Confucian framework, Feng Kuei-fen's essays in the 1850s and 1860s pointed out China's four shortcomings – unemployed talents, unused natural resources, imperfect communication between the monarch and his subjects, and the discrepancy between appearance and substance – and went on to suggest the selection of not only the talented but also the virtuous and the elimination of the superfluous staff of the government. Beyond any doubt, Feng focussed this attention on men rather than on mines, warships and railways as did Li Hung-chang and Chang Chih-tung. Other members of the lower gentry developed their arguments in the same vein. Wang T'ao, writing in the 1880s sarcastically listed dilatoriness, perfunctoriness, deception, concealment, corruption, conceit, etc., as China's 'excellences'. Shortly after him, Ho Ch'i and Hu Li-yuan minced no words, saying that: 'The decline of our country is due to many reasons, all of which have their roots in the turpitude of the officials.' The reassertion of the Confucian ideology, it seems, had achieved miserably little; so had the policies of self-strengthening. In the absence of popular participation and supervision of the political process, an unreliable civil service like that of China in the second half of the nineteenth century could distort, weaken and/or tear to shreds any edict, any decision, any programme.

## The crisis of 1895

So long as the fiction of Confucian moral superiority remained, the supremacy of bureaucratic control was unbroken. Its fictitiousness was known but not mercilessly exposed until the war against Japan in 1895. Once exposed, Confucianism was to become a political issue, an alternative among other contending ideologies which threatened to change the polity of the empire. The question then would be: if Confucianism together with its institutions and personnel were to be banished to the museums, what practically meaningful ideology would there be to replace it?

However, in the crisis of 1895 and immediately afterwards no answer to this question could be offered. Even with the advent of the modern printing press, the inauguration of periodicals and newspapers, and the organization of political societies, the inculcation of any new ideology, e.g. Huxley's interpretation of Darwinism, or the scientism in Robert Mackenzie's *History*, needed time and time was short in a crisis. Instead, fresh attempts were made to revitalize Confucianism, trimming it to suit the circumstances. Chang Chih-tung summed up the *t'i-yung* (essence–application) approach in his essay, *On Learning* of 1898, to express a Confucian adaptability, a willingness to yield, and also a limit beyond which Confucianism would not retreat. Its supremacy could never be conceded to any other ideology; the position of governance of the Confucian bureaucracy could not be abandoned; the polity of the Confucian empire could not be changed.

The fatal flaw of Chang's attempt at Confucian revitalization lay in the piecemeal modernization that was to be managed by the same old corrupt and inept bureaucracy. Persuasive rhetoric apart, this approach, having already been proved incapable of coping with the crisis of 1895, inspired no faith in its ability to cope with future crises of the same magnitude. Therefore, the policy proposals of the leading statesmen at the time appeared hesitant and unconvincing.

## The reform of 1898

A more extreme attempt at Confucian revitalization was a thoroughly radical reinterpretation of the doctrine – the 1898 Reform. For K'ang Yu-wei, Liang Ch'i-ch'ao and their fellows, Confucianism had always been reformist. The process from disaster to order and then from order to prosperity was an evolutionary change; the law of heaven as revealed in primal times to the sagacious kings was itself subject to change. The primitive form of Confucianism had come into being in the transition between the age of oligarchy (the eighth to the fifth centuries BC) and the age of monarchy (the fifth to the third centuries BC) and had promoted the transition; now a later and more sophisticated form promised to lead the empire to democracy.

The reformers saw no need to break away from tradition. There was, however, a need for them to adopt a more systematic approach than the segmentary *t'i–yung* school as represented by Chang Chih-tung. Their priorities were the preservation of both 'the sacred teachings of thousands of years *and* the 400 000 000 people of the yellow race'; their concerns were at once eclectically culturalistic and nationalistic. The way to reconcile the tensions between nationalism and culturalism was to accept that change was the norm of historical evolution, and to regard Confucian laws and institutions including the sovereign, as the commonwealth of people. The reigning emperor himself said, in 1898, to one of the reformers: 'We decide to change the laws and institutions in order to save the people. So long as this can be done, the power of the ruler is not our concern.'

The transformation of the laws and institutions into the commonwealth of the people implied a transformation of the universal sovereign, the patriarchal ruler, into the monarch of a nation-state who could lead his subjects to defend both the country and the faith. This was to be done by the proclamation of a constitution and the convocation of a parliament so as to attain the diarchy of the monarch and people. In such a way, the 400 000 000 Chinese would be involved in a political process which would arouse their interest in understanding and defending their country.

The bureaucracy would also have to share its powers of decision, if not its power of administration, with the people. The reformers were prepared neither to subvert the patriarchal sovereign nor to undermine the patrimonial bureaucracy; they merely wanted to reform both. They thought people's rights and people's intelligence could be linked together with almost mathematical precision – a degree of right to a degree of intelligence, the greatest right to the greatest intelligence. The most intelligent, 'holy and wise' (*sheng-ming*), was of course the sovereign; next to him, his officials. What was necessary, however, was the acquisition of knowledge by the bureaucrats to remedy their ignorance. Therefore, the educational and examination systems had to be changed while political societies were to be organized in order to facilitate the flow of knowledge from the concerned people who had it to the civil servants in power. The ultimate goal might be something akin to the constitutional monarchy of Meiji Japan or, even better, that of Britain.

The positive example of Japan and the negative example of the partitioned Poland were both presented to the emperor by K'ang Yu-wei in 1898. From its foundation in 1887, the Society for Diffusion of Christian and General Knowledge in Shanghai had been the fountain of information and inspiration for reformers like K'ang. Its leaders, Young J. Allen, Timothy Richard and Gilbert Reid, were in frequent contact with the reformers. Timothy Richard, in particular, published a pamphlet on a new policy for China (*Hsin-cheng-ts'e*) in 1895 to explicate the need for educating, protecting, pacifying and renewing the people. For the immediate future Richard proposed that China should extend the rule of the synarchy by appointing foreign advisers and administrators in the entire governmental structure, in effect, to reduce the empire to a semi-colony of the West. His daring views were listened to by the high dignitaries of the imperial court and powerful ministers of the realm with polite acquiescence. The position of the foreigner in the crises of 1895 and 1898 was vastly different from that of Hart and Wade a generation before. Confucian confidence had gone and China was open to the penetration of foreign ideologies.

For Yen Fu, the Confucian approach to the power and wealth of China had failed because of the decline of people's strength, the poverty of their knowledge, and the tenuity of their morals. Following Herbert Spencer, he regarded physical strength, intelligence and morality as the very foundation of the power of a state; consequently any policy aiming at building up the power of a country must begin from enhancing and liberating the energy of its people.

Like other contemporary reformers, Yen focussed on the people rather than on the economy, defence, finance and transport, for in Darwinian terms China's weakness lay in the unfitness of her people. The ignorance and moral weakness of the Chinese – both educated and uneducated – could only be remedied by an adherence to truth and intellectual honesty, which was the foundation of Western scientific achievement. Yen therefore launched an attack on the scholastic trends and educational institutions of his time, exposing their futility and proposing their complete re-examination, and advocated the inculcation of a new scientific spirit through education. This would be an arduous and long process requiring steadfast and sustained effort from the Chinese ruler and his subjects for decades or even centuries. In the meantime, the reformers had to maintain law and order so that the work of reform could be done uninterruptedly.

Freedom and democracy were not Yen's ultimate ends; he saw them only as a means to the end of national power and wealth. This was where he parted company with Spencer. In his perspective, freedom was the essence (end) with democracy as its application (means); national power and wealth were the essence (end) with freedom as their application (means). With freedom, the Chinese people would have their energy of faculty liberated to increase the honour and status of the country. What was application (science and technology) in the view of the Confucian modernizers was in Yen's view the essence. In spite of his attack on the essence–application approach, he fell back to it in more than one instance.

By what means could Yen's reform programme be materialized? Yen's own simple solution of education under the tutelage of the enlightened elite ruled by an enlightened monarch, impressed very few, but his translations of Huxley, Spencer, Smith and Mill became the common heritage of a generation of reformers and revolutionaries.

## Towards revolution

After the Boxer fiasco, there emerged a consensus that insisted on a drastic modification or total destruction of the *ancien régime*. How could this be done? To what extent should the cultural tradition of China be preserved? Few of the reformers and revolutionaries went as far as to abandon the past *in toto*: none was prepared to take the view that the history of China had been completely bleak and the efforts of the Chinese people entirely worthless. After all, China was a 'divine continent' (*shen-chou*) and the Han-Chinese were direct descendants of the Yellow Emperor. The ideal China that both reformers and revolutionaries wanted to bring about was therefore a dualist one, at once traditional and modern, not purely traditional or purely modern. It was to be both Chinese and Western.

The memories of the failure of 1898 which had lasted only a hundred days and the fiasco of 1900 were still fresh in the minds of the progressives in the 1900s. The failure considerably soiled the image of reformism. In this light, the government-led reforms of the 1900s, aiming at both the preservation of the dynasty and the strengthening of the country, aroused two doubts – whether reform alone would be enough to make China strong, and whether the Manchus were capable of accomplishing the feat. Peking's reform programme was apparently intended to create a better administration and to regain some of China's lost rights and its actions seemed to serve the same purposes. This gave K'ang Yu-wei heart to combat the theory that the Manchus were inferior to the Han-Chinese. If they were not, and if the regime was equal to its tasks, then a revolution to overthrow them would be unnecessary. More fundamentally, he did not believe that in a country ruled by old traditions and unclear principles, a revolution would contribute to the welfare of the people; revolution offered only the prospect of civil wars and disorders. In the 1900s there was a considerable body of opinion which felt that revolution would provoke internal unrest and external intervention. It might be wiser to allow the Peking leaders the power to control and plan China's reforms so that constitutionalism, new education, industrialization, defence, rights recovery, etc., could be realized step by step, whereas a revolution from below, with all the terrors of mob violence, would upset law and order, inducing foreign powers to demand more concessions and more territories. Ultimately there might be no China for anyone to change.

The leading spokesman of reform, Liang Ch'i-ch'ao, admitted the need for the destruction of the old according to well-established principles of evolution. But he asked who could take the lead in bringing this about, since the people's party (the revolutionaries) were just as corrupt as the government. If the resurgence of China required a change in her polity from monarchical despotism to 'democratic' despotism, like that of Jacobin France, a charismatic leader of extraordinary gifts, legitimized by popular sovereignty, was needed. Without such a leader, the ignorant masses could only propel their country towards chaos.

Liang was by no means oblivious to the turpitude of the elite, which was 'superior' in name only but 'inferior' in practice. Here was Liang's dilemma to which he provided no cogent solution. Perhaps in the final analysis he would choose the amoral elite rather than the amoral and ignorant masses, for 'childish people, like monkeys, who have been bathed and put on human clothes, easily become self-satisfied and apt to abuse whatever power is in their hands'. The fatal flaw in Liang's pragmatism was its inability to map out a strategy for political reform in China. His brilliant discussions of ideals and goals tended to omit problems of processes and procedures. The omission may have implied a traditional reliance on good government to be run by good men like the reigning emperor and reformers of his own kind.

## Anti-Manchuism

The revolutionaries justified the means they intended to use on purely Darwinian grounds. The inferiority of the Asian races having apparently been proved, the Chinese fear of sharing the fate of the American Indians and Australian aborigines seemed to be verified. But the inferiority of the Han-Chinese was far from being innate, because as descendants of the legendary Yellow Emperor – an obvious parody of the Japanese belief that they were the descendants of the Sun Goddess – the brilliance of the Chinese needed no proof.* The decline of the Chinese from their past brilliance to this present inferiority *vis-à-vis* the European races was due to their enslavement by the Manchus. The process also needed no proof. None of the revolutionary writers asked or answered the question as to how the superior Han-Chinese could have been subjugated by the inferior Manchus for 260 years. Irrational as it was, anti-Manchuism, accepted on Darwinian grounds, was the core and the rallying cry of the revolutionary nationalism of the 1900s. The Manchus became the

* There was even a magazine called the *Huang-ti hun*, the Spirit of the Yellow Emperor. Numerous articles appeared in many revolutionary periodicals presenting this legendary character as the progenitor of the Han-Chinese. See Chang Nan and Wang Jen-chih, *Hsin-hai Ke-ming ch'ien shih-nien-chien shih-lun hsüan-chi*, 1903, vol. II, pp. 485, 528–9, 580 and 721.

target of the revolutionaries' invective because of their misgovernment and their sycophancy and treachery in dealing with the outside world. Under Manchu rule, the Han-Chinese had lost their
capacity for self-government and allowed their concern for the fate
of their country to be dulled. They were slaves of a tradition which
the Manchus manipulated to rule them. To rescue them from permanent servitude and final extinction, it was necessary to throw
them into the process of a revolution.

Could the reforms, including the avowed constitution, sponsored
by the Manchus in the 1900s, do what they set out to attain? Chu
Chih-hsin, a radical revolutionary, argued that since the Manchus
were a different race, with practical aims and emotional attitudes
different from the Han-Chinese, it was impossible to believe that
they could sincerely grant sovereign rights to the ruled for the
benefit of the ruled. To assume that after 260 years the Manchus
could suddenly become altruistic and treat the Han-Chinese as
equals was to run an unacceptable risk. Hence leading revolutionary
theorists like Wang Ching-wei, Ch'en T'ien-hua, Wu Yueh and
Liu Ya-tzu all shared Chu-Chih-hsin's doubts and refused the
assumption. Time was to prove that the mild and gentle efforts of
the Manchus at rights recovery and their constitutional initiative did
indeed fall short of being sincere. A revolution, with the ousting
of the Manchus from positions of power and the overhaul of the
administration as its goals, was the only solution.

Revolution itself was regarded as a political education for all its
participants, for in its process the differences between ethnic groups
would become clear and the love of one's nation would be affirmed.
What the revolutionaries called 'the soul of a nation' (*kuo hun*) would
develop to serve as the incentive for people to do honour to their
own nation. That in essence was patriotism which would bind the
people together into a truly self-strengthened nation. The Chinese
would feel proud of their country as John of Gaunt had loved
England. Such a new ethos would transform both China and the
Chinese. In other words, revolution was *the* process of nation-making.

It was also a transition from barbarity to civilization, as it followed
the law of human evolution (as had, for instance, the revolutions of
England, America, and France), hacked out what was old and rotten
and encouraged fresh and healthy growth, and elevated people from
slavery to citizenship. The prospect of a republic of popular sovereignty similar to the USA lay at the end of it, with promises of the

restoration of the natural rights of man to the Chinese and a happiness a myriad times greater than they had ever experienced before.

How was such a civilizing revolution to be conducted? What would be its strategy? One way to conduct it was 'to strangle the reaction' (*e-hang*) by storming the central seat of power (Peking). In the absence of a powerful bourgeoisie, this strategy was hardly applicable to China. Another way was to occupy a portion of the empire which the revolutionary army could use as a base for defence or attack. This, however, could only be done in the initial stages, in order to give the revolution a base area (*ken-chü-ti*); it was scarcely feasible to attain a complete victory by this method. The third way was 'to swarm', staging simultaneous and co-ordinated uprisings all over the country, to hasten the disintegration of the reactionary government. In Chinese conditions, this would prove to be the most effective. In the actual event, the revolution of 1911 adopted the last of the three strategies which, incidentally, was not followed by a war against reaction.

## Anti-imperialism

The revolutionaries were aware of the presence of the foreigners and their interests in China, but none of their programmes, from whatever point of view, included an anti-Western policy. The government officials led a moderate attempt to regain some lost rights and prevent further losses without any substantial gain, while the revolutionaries, however radical they might be, adopted a two-pronged policy towards the Western powers. In the immediate future, the revolutionaries were prepared to accommodate the West, but in the distant future they would restore China's integrity.

Imperialism was known only in a social Darwinian sense as the natural outcome of the process of evolution from nationalism to expansion. It was justifiable and admirable. Once China had developed into a strong nation-state, she too would attain the status of another Russia or another USA. The Taiping rebellion, the Boxer Uprising and the 1911 Revolution, like the Japanese struggle to achieve the status of a great nation in the Meiji reign, cannot be proved anti-imperialist in intent or in act. Chinese nationalism, from a social Darwinian perspective, was introspective, looking inwards for an explanation of its weakness and unfitness and for a way towards strength. When it was developed fully it would spill over into a just and proud imperialism.

## Nationalism and the KMT

The importance of anti-Manchuism and the absence of anti-imperialism in the Chinese nationalism of the 1900s can be seen from the removal of nationalism from the political programme of the Kuomintang when it was instituted in 1912. With the Manchu abdication, China's nationalistic aspirations were thought to have been fulfilled. Hu Han-min, a leading member of the party, summed up the development of the party's nationalist thought and policies, albeit apologetically and with some distortion, as follows:

The goals of the revolution then [1911] were not merely the overthrow of the Manchu government, but also the subsequent transformation of the semi-colonial China into an independent China. This was self-evident. However, our mistake then was our exclusive emphasis on anti-Manchuism and our omission of anti-imperialism. As a result, when the Manchu government collapsed [we] thought our nationalism had succeeded. During the period of the revolutionary war and the provisional government [of Nanking, 1912–13], our declarations recognized all the treaties and agreements, indemnities and loans concluded with foreign powers by the Manchu government. Even the disposal of the maritime customs revenue and consular jurisdiction were unconditionally handed over to the powers. This set a bad precedent and was a grave mistake, contributing significantly to the failure of our national revolution.

But the Japanese Twenty-One Demands of 1915, the activities of the White and Red Russians in Mongolia and Manchuria after the October Revolution, and the Chicherin Manifesto of 1918, together with Wilson's principle of national self-determination and later Lenin's theory of imperialism, revived China's nationalistic concerns. Eclectic as he had always been, Sun Yat-sen made the first plank of his Three Principles of the People an admixture of Confucian ethical tradition, Confucianized Darwinism, Wilsonian anti-imperialism, and Leninist anti-imperialism. Sun talked in one breath of the restoration of China's traditional virtues and glory, elevation of China's international status, and rights recovery. Even when Sun's thinking reached its fullest and final form of 1924, his lectures on nationalism, like those on the other two principles, were concocted 'on the spur of the moment. It all depended on the political situation and the audience' as his widow recalled. For the first time, Sun assigned to China the status of a semi-colony or 'hypo-colony' under the yoke of foreign cultural, political and economic oppression. In spite of his consistent efforts to eliminate foreign interests in China through diplomatic means, he still maintained in his 1924 lectures that this 'hypo-colony' 'must aid the weaker and smaller peoples and oppose the great powers of the world'. A year later, when he was dying in a Peking hospital, his last will and testament exhorted his comrades to unite with the oppressed peoples of the world in a common struggle against imperialism. Only then did he give up the idea of China's becoming a great chauvinistic power.

Before 1937 Chiang had added little to the doctrinal arsenal of the KMT. Like Sun Yat-sen he was a syncretist. His nationalism had gone through two periods of change. Starting from a firm anti-imperialist stance in 1926, he assured the powers exactly a week after the Nanking Incident of 1927 that he would not change the status quo of the foreign settlements and concessions by force. Thereafter, he and his party ruminated over the dilemma of intolerable foreign oppression and China's need for international aid in her reconstruction. Nevertheless, the order of priorities – abrogation of the unequal treaties before national reconstruction – remained intact. A year later, when the Third Congress of the KMT was convened, the order was reversed, as the manifesto of the Congress argued that no diplomatic victory could be hoped for unless the country became united and strong first. In the years of the Great Depression Chiang's slogan was domestic pacification before any diplomatic settlement (*an-nei jang-wai*). Unfortunately for him this was also the period of intensified Japanese aggression, in the face of which the Fifth Congress of the KMT advised the nation

to exercise great patience and determination to safeguard the nation's existence and its road to recovery. We shall not foresake peace until there is no hope for peace.

The KMT of Chiang Kai-shek did not delimit its final position until 10 July 1936 when it announced: 'We shall not tolerate any aggression against our territorial sovereignty.' From the autumn of 1936, on, with the help of the Sian Incident, Chiang's nationalism went through its second change, from 'patience and determination to safeguard the nation's existence' to 'patience and determination to resist territorial encroachment'.

Between these two changes, Chiang drew closer to the Confucian tradition for the purposes of external tolerance and internal pacification (the anti-communist campaigns), culminating in his New Life Movement – an effort at psychological reconstruction of the Chinese nation so that the Chinese could achieve equal status with the citizens of the advanced nations. His basic assumption was the Darwinian unfitness of the Chinese; his remedy Confucian cultivation. Both doctrines were beyond his critical faculties. His nationalism, conditioned by Darwinism and Confucianism, was losing its grip on reality in an age of fervent anti-imperialism, and in 1935 and 1936 there were popular demonstrations and protests against his 'weak-kneed' attitude towards Japan. With neither progress towards democracy nor improvement in the people's standard of living to show for his years in power, had Chiang lost his leadership in nationalism the KMT would have forfeited its mandate to rule.

The national revolution, according to Sun Yat-sen in 1905, was to pass through three stages – martial law, the constitutional compact, and the formulation of the constitution. In 1923, however, Sun reformulated his theory of revolutionary stages which were now the military government stage, the tutelary government stage, and the constitutional government stage. Before the final transition, political power was invested in the KMT, in a form of party dictatorship. Sun's insistence, and later Chiang's, on party dictatorship originated from a belief that 'the 400 000 000 sovereigns are either politically infantile or unconcerned with political affairs', and the party therefore had to shoulder the responsibility of protecting and training them. This belief implied firstly that the KMT was the vanguard of the nation as a whole, an elitist party with a heightened political consciousness and a demonstrated ability to lead the nation after the military stage; secondly, that the masses as conceived by the revolutionaries during the era of the great debate in the 1900s were immature and ignorant, in need of preparatory education to fit them to assume their rights and responsibilities as citizens of the republic. 'To force the pace will inevitably repeat the errors of the early years of the republic' when parliamentary democracy was reduced to mockery by the powerful beasts of the political jungle. As laid down in Sun Yat-sen's *Fundamentals of National Reconstruction* (1924), local self-government would be the training-ground where the masses received their political education under the tutelage of the party in preparation for constitutional rule.

The first assumption was questioned by, among others, Ch'en Chiung-ming, an early follower of Sun and a southern warlord. Was the KMT competent enough to tutor the nation? 'What magic powers do they have' he asked, to transform the tradition of bureaucratic rule of so many thousands of years into a popular self-government? Like the Confucian modernizers in the seond half of the nineteenth century, who trusted the integrity and ability of the gentry, the KMT had faith in its members' fitness to rule. But the party under Chiang Kai-shek became predominantly military and its members, once admitted to its ranks, underwent no more than perfunctory political training. The party's fitness to tutor a nation was open to doubt. If the KMT performed no better than the gentry before it, the tutelary rule did no more than furnish excuses for Chiang and his comrades to delay the arrival of constitutional democracy.

The second assumption – the need for preparatory education of the masses – was challenged by a handful of liberals led by Hu Shih. Democracy in Hu's understanding was perhaps the most childish and the easiest form of government to practise and required very little preparatory political training. Dictatorship, whether a personal or a party's monopoly of power, on the other hand, was government by specialists, by professionals, and thus far more complex than democracy. If, as the KMT insisted, tutelage was necessary to prepare for democracy, still more was needed to prepare for dictatorship. Since China had no party, no class, no charismatic leader astute enough to dictate efficiently as in Stalin's Russia or Mussolini's Italy, party tutelage might help train the functionaries of a totalitarian regime; it would not lead to democracy.

For reasons of vested interests or ignorance, the discussions on the problems of party tutelage and constitution in the 1930s were pale, pedestrian and uninspiring compared with the controversy between the reformers and revolutionaries in the 1900s. Whatever progress in political thinking China had made in the thirty intervening years was either driven underground or banished to the countryside while the cities regressed into political apathy. The limited amount of democracy that could conceivably be practised, whether by default or on purpose, had to be guided by an elitist party. The prevailing political culture, in the tutelary stage remained status-conscious and attached undue stress to personal considerations – hence the spread of corruption, factionalism and repression without any vestige of an impersonal discipline. The modern mirage of the KMT political infrastructure concealed only the age-old political and moral tradition, preserving the Chinese 'essence' with a Western 'application'.

## Chinese communism

The founding of the KMT government coincided with the establishment of the first soviets in central China. In the ensuing ten years between the breaking up of the first and the formation of the second united front of the two major parties, the Chinese Communist Party carried on its revolution while experimenting with governing a state – two intertwined facets of a single effort to create a 'lovable' China. In the words of a pioneer Marxist, Ch'en Tu-hsiu,

what we love is a country whose people will patriotically resist foreign oppression, not a country whose government will make use of popular patriotism for aggression. What we love is a country which will strive for the welfare of its people, not a country which will treat its people as sacrifices.

China in 1919 was of course not in any position to act aggressively, but the warlords and self-serving bureaucrats acted against the interests of the people internally for their own benefit and externally to appease the imperialists. Far from being 'lovable', China's condition alienated the radicals who diagnosed that only democracy and science could attack the malignant disease at its root. As a liberal commentator put it at the time of Ch'en Tu-hsiu's trial and imprisonment for treason in 1932,

new politics can never be built upon the foundation of archaic ethics; the morality which supported the social structure of the feudal age can never be applied in an age of democratic rights; no citizen of a modern country can love his relatives more intensely than his nation. It cannot be denied that the monarchical restorations [in 1915, 1917 and 1932] and reverence for Confucius are cause and effect of paternalism and despotism.

The revolutionaries would engage the conservative forces on the political, economic, social and cultural fronts to bring about a total change and to create a 'lovable' China. They regarded tradition as a ball and chain from which the nation should seek to free itself. When liberation came, China was not to chain herself anew to some modern form of this. 'In place of the old bourgeois society, with its antagonism between class and class, we shall have an association in which the free development of each is the condition for the free development of all.'

The goals of the communist revolution were consequently anti-feudalism (or total iconoclasm) and anti-imperialism. The revolution itself was to go through two phases – the bourgeois democratic and the socialist. The revolutionary party and its mass following would use the party's ideology (Marxism–Leninism and later Mao Tse-tung's thought also) and organization as weapons of destruction and tools of construction. The cement of the party was to be different from the KMT's personal ties and personal considerations; it was to be the ideology, a firm grasp of which was one of the major qualifications for party membership, and 'iron discipline', which regulated and helped foster a mode of party life with its own values and norms. The old, particularistic familial and friendship ties would be replaced by a universalistic comradeship.

In its initial stages the party worked mainly in the cities. Its forced migration to the countryside when in the autumn of 1927 the party was ruthlessly persecuted, brought it face to face with the vast peasantry, opening up fresh possibilities and confronting fresh problems. The trained cadre of the party provided leading personnel for the soviets' governments, the Red Army and the mass organizations. It evinced a new attitude towards the masses and developed a new style of life and work which Mao was to describe as 'the mass line'. In spite of all its imperfections, the cadre was the first new leadership corps that China had evolved since her modernization. As bureaucrats, the communists proved themselves more efficient and less corruptible and more faithful to their political principles and party discipline than the members of any earlier elite. As army officers, they were far more democratic and far more astute fighters. In both capacities they demonstrated a tighter unity, as the party history recorded fewer factional disputes and even less separatist dissension than the KMT, and the Red Army knew no internecine wars among its units. In every sense, the cadre is modern, capable of playing a key role in China's modernization.

Of all the schools of thought that sought to change China, neither Westernized liberals, nor anarchists, nor social democrats had ever grown into an effective force exercising any decisive influence on the strategy of China's modernization while the others, from the Confucian modernizers to the 'democratic tutors' of the KMT, were culturally ambivalent between tradition and modernity. Their institutional innovations were often undermined by their own cultural conservatism; thus wittingly or unwittingly they never managed to break through the constraints of the formula of 'Chinese essence and Western application'. Only the iconoclasm of the CCP had enough strength of logic and resolve for clarity, supported by its organization and mass following, to dissipate the ambivalence. In the process of dissipation, a new cadre grew up with the new institutions, to prepare the way for the transformation of the ancient country into a socialist state and of the Chinese into socialist men.

# Chapter 6
## Politics and law

### Attempts at constitutional government

The rumblings of demand for a constitution were heard in the 1898 Reform and at the height of the Boxer War. The advocates then perceived a constitution as being the source of vitality of a nation and the only polity capable of putting an end to the cycle of order and disorder which had recurred throughout China's dynastical history. However, its adoption had to come in scheduled stages – a declaration of intention to be followed by careful investigation and institutional preparation lasting ten to fifteen years. The inspiration for having a constitution was undoubtedly of Western origin, but the event that convinced the politically concerned Chinese of the absolute necessity of having a constitution was Japan's defeat of Russia, the defeat of an autocracy by a constitutional monarchy, in 1905.

In the wake of Japan's victory, two official missions were dispatched by the Chinese Emperor to Europe, America and Japan to study the practice of constitutional governments. Upon their return in 1906 a conference in front of the throne decided that the key to the power and wealth of the empire was to improve communications between high and low, the government and the people, in a gradual process beginning with the reform of the civil and military services and ending in the proclamation of a constitutional monarchy. In 1909 and 1910, the Political Advisory Council (Tzu-cheng-yuan) was instituted, with half of its 200 members appointed by the throne and the rest selected jointly by the governors and the Political Advisory Bureaux of the provinces. Although dominated by the

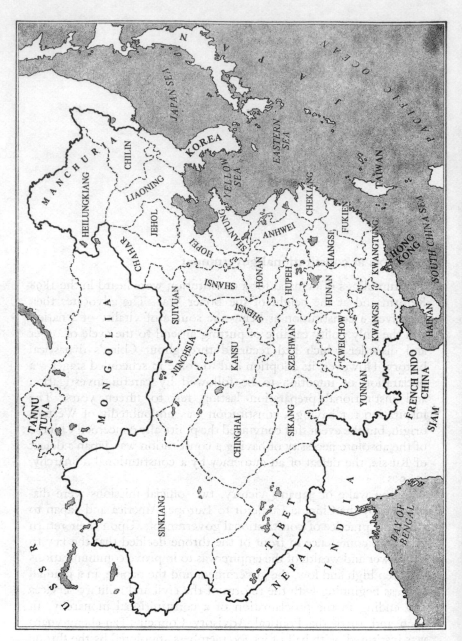

The provinces of China in the 1920s

aristocracy and the gentry, the minority on the Council and Bureaux, representing the nascent bourgeoisie and enlightened intellectuals, played an active role in hastening progress towards constitutionalism. Its petitions forced the reluctant imperial court to fix the period of preparation as nine years from 1908 and to declare its intention in 1910 of convening the planned national assembly in 1913.

Up to then the Constitutional Studies Bureau and the Advisory Council had completed the drafting of nothing except the principles of a future constitution, which, bearing an unmistakable resemblance to the Japanese model, were based on the recognition rather than the curtailment of the existing powers of the monarch and his government. Hardly any thought of safeguarding the freedoms and rights of the people had ever occurred to the constitutionalists, and whatever freedoms and rights they were to have were qualified by the phrase, 'as far as the law allows', without at the same time indicating what the law was. These principles, though never promulgated before the end of the dynasty, show three trends of the constitutional thinking of the time: (a) China needed a constitution to help build up her national strength and wealth, not to promote democracy; (b) with the goals so defined, there was a failure to realize that the laws of the empire had to be brought into harmony with the projected constitutional rule; and (c) without an awareness of the need for a total legal reform (not just a limited amount of change to comply with international usage), no one could have any serious objection to China's superficial aping of the Meiji constitution.

The political reality of the time, nevertheless, pointed to a different direction of development. In the context of the rising tide of revolution which demanded nothing less than monarchical abdication and republicanism, the activists in the Advisory Council and Bureaux, supported by chambers of commerce and overseas Chinese, planned their fourth petition. This was presented at the end of 1910, and was mercilessly nipped in the bud by the government. It was only after the outbreak of the revolution on 10 October 1911 that the panic-stricken imperial court presented its only constitution of 19 articles to the Ancestral Temple (another example of imitating Meiji Japan) on 3 November 1911. The court promised a British type of constitutional monarchy with executive powers in the hands of a representative cabinet. This belated attempt proved to be too late to stem the tide that washed away the empire.

The Provisional Government in Nanking was based on its own organic law of 3 December 1911 which incorporated the American presidential system, the Articles of Confederation, and the New Jersey Plan of one house and a single, equal vote for each of the provinces. To press the American parallel further, the entire constitutional structure was cut to fit one man, Dr Sun Yat-sen, whose overriding concern was how to hold the country together. It is curious that in Sun's inaugural statement as the Provisional President of the Republic of China, he relied on power rather than political consciousness to forge China's unity. Power, however, was precisely what he and his revolutionary colleagues did not have, and this deficiency necessitated his abdication in favour of the conservative Yuan Shih-k'ai. The transfer of the government from Nanking to Peking, and of the presidency from Sun to Yuan, precipitated a drastic change in the constitution of the infant republic in order to suit another man and another situation. The Provisional Constitution of 1912 was designed to use political consciousness to control power.

The new constitution was drafted by Sung Chiao-jen, a romantic democrat, and adopted by the Provisional Senate on 8 March 1912. Replacing the organic law of the 1912 Provisional Government, it changed the government from the American presidential system to the system of a responsible Cabinet whose ministers had to be appointed with the approval of the Senate. It also stipulated that the bicameral legislature, consisting of a Senate and a House of Representatives, could not be dissolved by an executive order. Another important revision was that from confederacy to a unitary state. Beyond that the constitution, like its successor of 1914, remained reticent on the structure of the provincial governments and their relationship with the central authority. With regard to the people's rights and freedoms, the Provisional Constitution was progressive, perhaps the most progressive of all the constitutions drafted before 1936. In its first chapter the principle of popular sovereignty was clearly stated and in a complete reversal of the Confucian legal principles, every citizen was made equal before the law. Its second chapter (Articles 5–15) granted unconditionally all the fundamental rights and freedoms of a democratic republic to the people, these were to be restricted only during a national emergency or for the maintenance of law and order.

After the general elections for the first National Assembly in

1912–13, a committee for drafting a proper constitution gathered at the Temple of Heaven to commence its work. In what was to be known as the Temple of Heaven Constitution, the people's rights and freedoms were subject to the law and the laws were to be made by the National Assembly. Only within the scope allowed by the laws could the people enjoy their rights. However, the Constitution accepted the Anglo–American writ of *habeas corpus*. Unfortunately, while the Constitution was being drafted, the political situation of the country took a sharp turn – the president's forces fought and defeated the forces supporting the Kuomintang in the war of March 1913, and soon after that the majority party of the Assembly, the KMT, was outlawed. Thus having reduced the Assembly to a shambles, Yuan Shih-k'ai interfered with the drafting by sending his henchmen to the committee to present his own views on the Constitution. When they were rejected, he rallied regional military powers to launch an attack on the work of drafting itself. At least three members of the committee were murdered and four were arrested. Finally the committee was disbanded by Yuan on 10 November 1913.

The man whom the Provisional Constitution aimed to restrain revealed a peculiar understanding of constitutionalism and republicanism in his presidential inaugural address:

As Western scholars often say, a constitutional country is ruled essentially by law, whereas a republic [*kung-ho*] is ruled by virtue. Virtue is the essence [*t'i*] and the law the instrument [*yung*]. Now if we are going to elevate our people to the status of citizens of a republic, we must use law to assist virtue. Having consulted scholars of various countries, I come to this definition: a republican government is one that has an all-embracing system of laws based on the wishes of all and to be strictly observed by all.

Yuan went on to say that 'any freedom beyond the scope of law will be treated by everyone with disdain. Law-abiding habits like these will take time to develop.' In his view, the dialectic between virtue and law was and had to be conducted in traditional Confucian terms. The country, be it monarchical or republican, must be first and foremost ruled by virtue with the assistance of law. The reign of virtue, being essential, could stand alone, while the rule of law, being subsidiary, could not. The perfect system of law was based on the wishes of the people, which were the virtue. When the virtue and the law clashed, it was the law, not virtue, that had to give way. If

C.A.T.W.—K

virtue dictated that China be strong and wealthy but the law stipulated that the Chinese should be free and self-governing, personal freedom and self-government could then be jettisoned or restricted for the sake of virtue. In Yuan's mind as in the minds of other 'enlightened' traditionalists, standards of right and wrong were more important than, or different from standards of what was lawful or unlawful. With such a man at the helm of power, a fatal clash between him and the legislature was only to be expected. As soon as the legislature was weakened, Yuan proposed a series of constitutional amendments to give him greater power over appointment and dismissal, in the declaration of war and conclusion of peace, and in issuing decrees with the same validity as law in times of emergency when the National Assembly was in recess.

As a matter of fact, when these amendments were presented to the National Assembly, the KMT had been defeated and outlawed and the legislature was sent into recess. On 10 January 1914 the latter was dissolved. The restraint of power by political consciousness had thus failed. Even so, the president needed legitimacy through constitutional revision, for which purpose he convened the Political Council of sixty-nine members two months before dissolving the National Assembly. Less authoritatively and less of a forum for popular views than Bismarck's *Rechtstaat*, the Political Council's major function was to produce a Constitutional Compact Conference for the purpose of drafting a new constitution. Of the sixty or so members of the Conference present on 18 March 1914, at least forty-five were holders of high traditional degrees – i.e. they were Confucian scholars. In social composition and ideological orientation, the Conference was a contrast to the defunct National Assembly. Its convocation connoted the reassertion of the reaction. Constitutionalism was no longer regarded as the panacea of all China's ills, with the chairman of the Conference setting the tone in his opening speech:

A good constitution such as that of Britain, Germany, or the United States of America can promote the strength and wealth of a nation whereas a bad one such as that of Mexico or any Latin American country leads only to incessant disorder.

Since both the president's and the speaker's addresses severely criticized the Provisional Constitution, everyone knew specifically which 'bad constitution' was meant. 'Parliamentary dictatorship' was decried and replaced by a presidential dictatorship under the

Constitutional Compact proclaimed on 1 May 1914. Under the president, there were to be a legislative council and an advisory council, but the president was supposed to be responsible to a non-existent national assembly. He was, of course, the chief executive to be assisted by a secretary of state and a number of ministers who were appointed by him and responsible to him. What was particularly ominous was that the Compact did not even pay lip service to the concept of popular sovereignty. Instead, the president affirmed in a formal statement that his powers came from the imperial abdication in 1912.

The death of Yuan Shih-k'ai in the summer of 1916 posed a constitutional question: who should succeed him and according to what law? If the 1912 Provisional Constitution and the 1913 Presidential Election Law based on it were to apply, Vice-President Li Yuan-hung was the obvious successor; if, on the other hand, the 1914 Constitutional Compact was, Li could only act as temporary president pending an election. There were a host of procedural and realistic problems involved. For instance, could the 1912 Constitution be revived by a presidential decree? Indeed, had it been abrogated by Yuan's presidential decree? If it had not, was its application in 1916 both natural and logical? If the 1914 Compact was to apply, would this automatically imply the discontinuation of the Provisional Constitution and the acceptance of all the other laws promulgated by Yuan as the president? Furthermore, the latter alternative would open the field of presidential election to several probable contenders, mostly strong military leaders including Tuan Ch'i-jui, the premier. Tuan understandably was in favour of the 1914 Compact, on the grounds that the 1912 Constitution put excessive powers in the hands of the Assembly, obstructing the efficient functioning of the government, and that the confirmation of the authority of the Compact could at least avoid the procedural anomaly of reviving a constitution by decree. But Tuan was almost alone, facing a barrage of insistent views in favour of the 1912 Constitution. The hatred of Yuan was such that all his legislation had to go. In the end, the presidential edict of 29 June 1916 re-established the Provisional Constitution and the Presidential Election Law of 1913. In the wake of this the old Assembly elected in 1913 met again on 1 August to resume the work of drafting a permanent constitution.

From 5 September 1916 to 10 January 1917, the Constitution

Committee had held no less than twenty-four meetings to deal with a host of new problems – the establishment of Confucianism as the state religion, the emergency powers of the president, and above all, the organization of provincial governments – in the light of the proposed Temple of Heaven Constitution of 1913. The powerless idealists represented by the splinter groups of the KMT wished to add a new chapter on provincial governments in the old hope that political consciousness would be able to control power. The critical issue was whether provincial governors were to be chosen by election or by appointment. Their pragmatic opponents were opposed to this addition, fearing that a legislation rendered unworkable by the defiant military powers could only harm the dignity of the constitution being drafted. A dilemma thus confronted both parties. If the new constitution could do nothing to arrest the trend towards separatism and disorder, what would be the point of it? If it aimed at preserving the status quo and improving on it by strengthening national unity, how could this be done? A resolution of this dilemma clearly lay outside the power of the Assembly and the Constitution Committee. In other words, China would have to settle her political problems before a constitution could be introduced. Her unreadiness for constitutional rule was symbolically exposed by heated debates between the two factions on the Committee which soon deteriorated into a fist fight, followed by the suspension of the Committee's work on 8 December 1916.

At this juncture, the seemingly unimportant issue of China's participation in the First World War developed into a threat to the survival of the National Assembly. What lay behind this was the fear that once China was in the war, the military clique led by Tuan Ch'i-jui might receive enough foreign aid, chiefly from Japan, to upset the balance of power between the factions, with complicated political and economic consequences. The issue evolved into an open conflict between the president and the premier in Peking and a realignment of the military forces in the country at large. In the Assembly itself, there was deadlock on this issue, much to the annoyance of the military leaders –

The members of the Assembly can make or unmake any law at will. They behave as if they are the law and threaten to deprive the government of its executive and judiciary powers. All the officials follow on their likes and dislikes in carrying out government functions. How can our country be ruled and ruled well in such a manner?

A demand for parliamentary dissolution and re-election thus gathered momentum, ending in the premier's disbanding of the Assembly and the president's dismissal of the premier in May 1917. Thereafter the constitutional history of China entered a period known as that of the wars for the protection of the constitution.

As Peking bled during the constitutional crisis and monarchical restoration of 1917, some members of the Assembly migrated south to Canton to rally around Dr Sun Yat-sen, who had since 1916 repeatedly defended the 1912 Provisional Constitution. In his view, it was the foundation on which the republic rested and its survival was synonymous with the survival of the republic. Through the vicissitudes of the next few years, he remained firm in this conviction. For the purpose of defending the 1912 Constitution, Sun set up military government in Canton with the legal approval of the Extraordinary National Assembly – the 1913 Assembly now reconvened in the south – and the military support of the warlords in the south and south-west. His incongruous and puzzling reliance on warlords to protect the constitution was probably due to a change in his thinking on revolutionary strategy. The problems of China in 1917 could not be solved by parliamentary ballots; they would have to be solved by a clash of arms –

There is no way to fulfil the goals of a true republic and the welfare of the people unless through the use of powerful armies and the navy.

But the warlords gathering around him cherished their own aims – either to safeguard themselves against encroachment by the northern military forces, or to expand into areas vital to their interests. The paradox in the southern government remained the same – the powerless Sun was still trying to control military power with political consciousness while the decorative Extraordinary National Assembly began again its work of drafting a permanent constitution. Unsurprisingly, this work foundered once more on the question of the organization of the provincial governments. When the members insisted on elective governors, they were simply beaten up and dispersed by the soldiers who had professed to protect them. 'What is the meaning of defending a constitution of this sort?' Ch'en Tu-hsiu asked:

The old-fashioned curse the Provincial Constitution because it obstructs the government; the ultra-modern do so because it restricts people's rights. In fact, those who have violated the law, accepted bribes, made themselves emperors, restored monarchies, and dissolved the National Assembly carry on as before. The Constitution has not obstructed them in any way. It has only deprived the people of their freedoms of publication and assembly to a lamentable degree.

In Peking, the triumphant premier, Tuan Ch'i-jui, having suppressed the monarchical restoration of 1917, proceeded to organize the second parliamentary election since 1912. It was held in the face of the opposition of five southern and south-western provinces while at least three provinces of central China were at war. Nevertheless he succeeded in convening a new National Assembly dominated by his henchmen (members of the An-fu Club) through extensive use of bribes. Bravely the new Assembly undertook the thankless task of drafting a constitution, a work which it completed in 1919. Before the draft had become law the war of 1920 not only overthrew Tuan's government, but also destroyed his military power base and outlawed his An-fu Club. The An-fu Constitution was thus stillborn.

The victors of the 1920 war – the Chihli Clique – reconvened the 'Long Parliament' and resumed the drafting of a constitution, to provide a legal foundation for the position of the new president and his new government. The new president, General Ts'ao K'un was, elected on 9 October 1923 and the constitution published the next day, in time to celebrate the National Day. The question of whether the republic was a unitary or federal state was deliberately left vague, as the draft constitution contradicted itself in Article 1 and Chapter V while conceding some crucial powers and interests to the provincial governments, e.g. the land tax now being formally recognized as a local tax. In the event of a dispute between the central and provincial governments over the division of power, the supreme court would have the final decision, thus involving the judiciary in the process of politics. Jurisprudentially perhaps the best constitution in the whole republican period, the 1923 constitution and the reconvened Assembly became the most hated and most objectionable to democrats because of the manner by which Ts'ao K'un was elected president. Each vote cast in support of him was rewarded with a cheque for 5000 *yuan* (about $1000). Therefore the adoption of the constitution on 18 October 1923, contrary to its avowed purpose of stabilizing the political situation in Peking, hastened the coming crisis. Ts'ao's government fell as a result of the civil war of 1924.

By then, a constitution of China was no more meaningful than a Delphic oracle; it was certainly no longer worth fighting for. Both the Provisional Administration in Peking now headed by Tuan Ch'i-jui and the reorganized KMT in Canton approached the affairs of the state along new lines. Both came to the conclusion that the basic issues of China had to be settled outside the context of the Assembly before another constitutional rule could be tried again. The political struggle in 1926–8 took the form of a violent revolution against the warlords and their Chinese and foreign supporters. Between the success of the revolution and the scheduled inauguration of another constitutional era, the people had to be trained in the use of their citizens' rights under the tutelage of the KMT. Under the six articles of the Tutelage Programme adopted by the Central Executive Committee of the KMT on 3 October 1928, the party entrusted all the power to the National Government in Nanking which consisted of five councils – the Executive, Legislative, Judiciary, Examination and Supervisory – with the Legislative Council as the only law-making body in the country. The Constitutional Compact of the Tutelary Period proclaimed in June 1932 specified that the people were to enjoy their freedoms and rights according to the law while the law, including the Compact, was to be interpreted by the KMT alone.

Anxious to bring about a constitutional rule, the Legislative Council worked out a schedule for the drafting and adoption of a new constitution in 1933. The time allowed for public discussion of the draft constitution was only thirty days, from 16 July to 15 August 1933; however, no date was fixed for the publication of the draft! What appeared to be even more inappropriate was that the document was published in the name of the member of the drafting committee, and in Shanghai instead of in Nanking where the government was located. The informality surrounding the publication of such an important document and the general dismay over the endlessness of the tutelary period contributed to the cold reception given to the draft. However, the draft was adopted on 16 October 1934 and proclaimed by the National Government on 5 May 1936, becoming known as the May 5th Constitution.

The situation of 1936 was not entirely unlike that in 1895 when for the first time China began to think in terms of a constitutional rule. Once again, China's existence was menaced by Japanese aggression. Her constitutional history had come full circle. Both the emperor in the 1890s and Chiang Kai-shek in the 1930s were more concerned with the survival of the nation than the promotion of democracy. After all, the situation as perceived by a weak nation was not particularly conducive to the confirmation of individual rights. In an atmosphere such as that of 1936 and 1937, KMT tutelage continued till the defeat of Japan when the mounting challenge of the Chinese Communist Party swept it away.

## The provincial issue

Before the KMT's accession to power, the strongest opposition to constitutional rule emanated from the conservative forces in the provinces, an informal alliance of military and gentry leaders. Foreseeing this possible source of opposition, the constitutionalists of the 1900s proposed the formation of provincial councils to involve the local elites in decision-making and power-sharing. After the demise of the empire, these councils came under the influence of the KMT, which regarded them as the foundation on which a form of provincial self-government could be constructed. When Yuan Shih-k'ai launched his attack on the KMT, he deemed it necessary to destroy this foundation in order to put a stop to the federal tendencies and so the councils were abolished in February 1914. For Yuan, China's first political needs were unity and strength, to which self-government and democracy had nothing to contribute. Furthermore, being unfamiliar with democratic procedure and resentful of legislative intervention in the administration, local conservative forces had been treating the councils with brutal disdain and now welcomed Yuan's decision, while the councils themselves, as long as they existed, had abused power by accepting bribes and revelling in factional feuds.

A champion of local self-government, the KMT was in fact divided over this issue. Sun Yat-sen's idea for self-government to be built up from the county level had nothing in common with a confederacy of autonomous provinces dominated by a military–gentry alliance, for he was interested in training the people to use their democratic rights and not in a division of power between the military–gentry coalitions in Peking and the provinces. His more pragmatic followers, however, entertained different views. Tai Chi-t'ao, for example, was in favour of a confederacy based on his observation that most Chinese would put their provincial concerns over national concerns and that Peking had always concentrated too much power in its hands at the expense of the provinces. A confederacy might advisably redress the imbalance and sort out the chaos of China. A local leader in his native Shensi, Yü Yu-jen spoke in support of regional self-government as a device to defend Shensi against external encroachment and invasion.

Through the years Peking also showed its equivocation. When it was militarily weak, for instance in 1920–1 after the first major civil war since Yuan Shih-k'ai's death, it evinced a willingness to accommodate the wishes of those who held local power by moderating its insistence on a unitary state and its policy of unification by conquest. But when it was strong, for instance in 1919 and 1922, both Tuan Ch'i-jui and Wu P'ei-fu, leaders of the Anhwei and Chihli Cliques of warlords respectively, opposed the idea of a confederacy on the grounds that China needed a strong central government to deal with the powers and that her richer provinces had traditionally to give grants in aid to the poorer ones.

Political commentators in the 1920s offered divided counsels on the question of confederacy. A veteran revolutionary and eminent classicist, Chang Ping-lin, thought the republic was in anarchy because the governments in Peking and Canton were no more than havens for political vagabonds. Chang scornfully described the election of 1917 as a bustling temple celebration. In his view, it was far better to do away with such central governments by taking steps towards provincial autonomy and a confederacy. Hu Shih, the liberal scholar, saw a confederacy as the only way to increase the powers of the civil governments of the provinces and to weaken the domination of the military leaders, for China, according to him, was singularly unsuitable for dictatorship or for a unitary system of state. The secretary-general of the CCP, Ch'en Tu-Hsiu, writing for the party organ, the *Guide*, on 13 September 1922, voiced no special objection to the principle of confederacy; 'however, [my party] dare not support the confederacy of warlords' separatism which in reality means the division of China by the consent of provincial military governors'.

What actually mattered was of course the views and actions of the confederalist warlords themselves, whose concerns diverged widely. Some used the slogan of local autonomy and provincial confederacy only to ward off outside influence and justify their own defiance of higher authorities. These included Ch'en Shu-fan's (Anhwei Clique) resistance to Yen Hsiang-wen's (Chihli Clique) military invasion of Shensi after the defeat of Tuan Ch'i-jui in 1920, Wang Chan-yuan's recalcitrance against Wu P'ei-fu's penetration into Hupei, Lu Jung-t'ing's attempt to consolidate his control of Kuangsi after his defeat in Kwangtung, Szechuan military leaders' refusal to submit to the meddling of Peking, T'ang Chi-yao's and Lu T'ao's endeavours to preserve their holdings in Yunnan and Kweichow, and Chang Tso-lin's efforts to salvage his diminishing powers in Manchuria after his disastrous military adventures in 1922. Based on similar considerations but also in more far-reaching and more coherent advocacies were other exponents of the policy of confederacy – Generals Lu Yung-hsiang of Chekiang, Chao Heng-t'i of Hunan, and Ch'en Chiung-ming of Kwangtung.

For expediency alone, General Lu Yung-hsiang linked up his own provincial self-government with that of Hupei, Hunan, Kuangsi, Yunnan, and even Shensi and Szechuan in an attempt to coerce Kiangsi and Fukien (where there were already scattered army units in favour of self-government) into adopting the same policy. If this could be realized, the south would be able to shake off the harassment of the north and then take a step further and make a bid for a new federal polity. The width of his vision made Lu different from the usual type of confederalist. He proposed that each of the self-governing provinces should make its own constitution. When autonomy and confederacy were achieved, each component province would possess absolute power over its own affairs, leaving the central government to deal with China's international relations. In that way, Lu hoped the movement would lead to the abolition of military governorships and disarmament, to peace and political order. To prove his sincerity, he and his provincial government did adopt a constitution of 158 articles on 7 September 1921 and had it promulgated two days later.

General Chao Heng-ti also wanted to free his province, Hunan, from outside interference. For one thing, autonomy might possibly extract Hunan from the uncomfortable position of being caught in the middle of the power struggle between the north and south; for another, it might also help eliminate the miscellaneous military forces in Hunan which relied on external and local requisitioning aid for their existence. For him and for T'an Yen-k'ai and other leaders of Hunan, autonomy would be useful as a means of attaining internal order, while confederacy would help promote peaceable relations with other provinces. It was for pragmatic considerations like this that Hunan adopted its constitution on 1 January 1922.

General Ch'en Chiung-ming of Kuangtung expounded perhaps the most radical federalism. Kuangtung's geographic location was in itself a bulwark against effective Peking intervention, and as a result Ch'en's main concern was the immense concentration of military factions which turned his province into a huge army camp. In a secret document published in the Hong Kong newspaper, the *China Mail* (Hua-tza Tih-pao), on 16 and 17 May 1922, Ch'en argued that local self-government was the general trend in all the advanced countries of the world which China had every reason to emulate. A large modern state was too complicated to be efficiently ruled from a single centre; it had to be administered by its provinces with a high degree of popular participation. As to China, the ambiguous division of power between the centre and the provinces had for a long time been the source of disputes and civil wars which could be stopped by instituting local self-government. Hence, General Ch'en proposed a constitutional federal government responsible for diplomatic relations, national defence, and justice and a constitutional government in each province to take charge of economy, transport, education, etc. All the ministerial posts were to be elected by the central or local legislature, and the legislatures should agree on the distribution of fiscal revenue to defray the expenses of central and local governments. Obviously following the American federal system, Ch'en in his radical mood in the early 1920s went so far as to suggest a local self-government system all the way down to the grass-roots level; an elector would have to do at least three days' manual labour before becoming qualified to vote. For him, this was the only way to break the stranglehold of the big warlords (e.g. those in north China). After that, the first step was to let small warlords share the power, and the second step was for the organized masses to take power from the lesser military leaders.

In a more constructive sense, the movement for provincial autonomy and a confederacy of 1921–2 represented an endeavour on the part of warlords to end warlordism with Lu, Chao and Ch'en as its staunchest champions. Lu and Chao could see no further than using the political consciousness of the gentry and a system of constitutions to curb the abuse of power, whereas Ch'en wanted, in the final analysis, the participation of the masses to put an end to warlordism. Nevertheless, none of them was coherent, as none of them was precise as to how their goals could be achieved. Even Ch'en Chiung-ming in 1923 still believed that to mobilize the masses in a revolution remained a distant dream. Chao Heng-t'i and Lu Yung-hsiang gave no thought to the basic rights of the people in their self-government programmes, whereas T'ang Chi-yao of Yunnan was blatantly hostile to any idea of democratic rights.

## The National Assembly

The 'Weimar Republic' of China possessed a liberal democratic regime without liberal democrats. The Provisional Senate of 1912 and the National Assembly elected in 1913, which continued to exist with incredible resilience till 1924, were the institutional arrangements, the democratic edifice without democratic content. The Assembly's composition by party and educational background was as follows:

*Distribution of seats in the 1913 National Assembly*

|  | House of Representatives | Senate |
|---|---|---|
| KMT | 269 | 123 |
| Republican Party | 120 | 55 |
| Unity Party | 18 | 6 |
| Democratic Party | 16 | 8 |
| Members of more than one party | 147 | 38 |
| Independents | 26 | 44 |
| Total | 596 | 274 |

Source: Tsou Lu, *Tang-shih-tkao*, vol. I, pp. 145–6.

And the members of the Assembly were elected in a manner reported by Mr Clennell, the British consul at Foochow:

The election of members, whether of National Parliament or of provincial assemblies, is absolutely unreal. . . . In Newchang, which is a town of some 100,000 inhabitants, the election of a parliamentary representative took place while I was there. Thirty-five voters recorded their votes, and of those 35 the majority were employees in the Taoyin's [the local intendants'] yamen. The public took no part, and exhibited no interest in the proceedings.

*Educational background of the 1913 National Assembly*

| | Traditional degree-holders (1) | Educated in modern schools (2) | (1)+(2) | No formal education |
|---|---|---|---|---|
| Chinese education only | 54 | 105 | 26 | 98 |
| Partly Japanese and partly Chinese education | 37 | 45 | 9 | |
| Japanese education only | | 71 | | |
| Partly Western and partly Chinese education | 1 | 5 | | |
| Western education only | | 1 | | |

Source: Jerome Ch'en, *Yuan Shih-k'ai*, Stanford, 1972, p. 211.

The *China Mail* of Hong Kong also published a report on 8 November 1913 which described the KMT bullying voters and the practice of bribes and rigging the election.

When elected, the Senators and later the Representatives also discharged their public duties in a rather cavalier manner. When it was the only legislature, the Provisional Senate was stricken with absenteeism, as it was reconvened in Peking; it had less than half of its thirty-eight members on 22 March and only twenty-three four days later. The elected Senate of 1913 had never had more than ninety-nine members present at a meeting out of a total of 274 and sometimes as few as only fifty-six. Their light-hearted treatment of their legislative duties evoked the empathy of the president who, instead of attending the opening ceremony in person, sent his secretary in his stead! The grandiloquence of his opening speech, written in the Han dynasty style and read on his behalf by his secretary, could not compensate for his conspicuous absence. In fact, the president's disrespect for the Assembly was such that he had never once set foot inside either of its Chambers! Putnam Weale justifiably wrote:

Probably no National Assembly in the world has been held up to greater contempt than the Parliament of Peking and probably nobody deserves it more.

During its brief working life from April 1913 to January 1914, the Assembly showed a grievous lack of democratic discipline, a susceptibility to factionalism and a propensity to corruption. Liang Ch'i-ch'ao commented bitterly on its performance:

In less than three months all that the nation expected from it has evaporated. The 800 ant heads ... have failed to elect a Speaker after 20 days and to institute a supreme court after 100 days. Absenteeism is reported every day while suspensions of meetings and truancy have established themselves as a normal practice. If by chance a meeting is held, there is an uproar like quarrelling village wives or uncouth screaming school-boys. Having wasted half a day in such bedlam, they disperse like birds and beasts. They have deliberated less than one per cent of the nation's business, but each of them draws an allowance of 6000 *yuan* a year. All this is only the more conspicuous part of it. If one takes a closer look, ... one discovers hundreds more of their dirty deeds. I shall not, nor do I wish to, list them here.

What Liang did not enumerate included the price of votes and price of party allegiance.

The bickerings inside the Assembly Chambers were coupled with physical pressure from the president and regional military leaders outside them. On the occasion of the presidential election, the Assembly was besieged by soldiers, police, and the so-called Citizen's Corps of riff-raff, threatening to kill off the Assemblymen unless they voted for Yuan Shih-k'ai. As soon as the election was over, the majority party was outlawed amid a clamour for parliamentary destruction. In the end Yuan justified his order of dissolution in these terms:

After four months of regular meetings the Assembly has not passed a single law. ... All its other duties have been obstructed by partisans, creating a situation akin to mob dictatorship. ... In consequence, the legislature has no law for it to discuss and the executive has no law to act upon.

The members of the Assembly were elected in a dubious manner rather than by public choice. To call them representatives is to deceive the nation. Indeed, among them there are patriots, but the majority of them are interested only in selfish partisan ends, with scant concern with the survival or the livelihood of the people.

The conservative Political Council that succeeded the National Assembly at the end of 1913 represented a step backward from a parody of American democracy to a parody of Bismarckian limited democracy. All its sixty-nine members were hand picked by the central and provincial administrations. Their high social status and personal wealth may have fortified them against easy corruption, but they were pliable tools for the president and his military henchmen. At its opening ceremony in the Presidential Palace on 15 December 1913, the president, instead of giving a speech, sent down instructions which reminded one of Bismarck's famous address on Iron and Blood:

The strength of a nation depends on the state of its domestic and foreign affairs; the state of its domestic and foreign affairs is determined by a powerful government, not at all by a monarchical or democratic polity. Although I admire the republican form of state as the highest development of constitutional politics, I cannot say that once 'the shop sign' is changed [from an empire to a republic], the strength of the country is enhanced.

Take the present state of domestic and foreign affairs, for instance. It is incredibly chaotic. Generally speaking, the people have the misconception that once the polity has been changed, they are all equal. Therefore, children now disobey their fathers, wives their husbands, subordinates their superiors, and soldiers their commanding officers. Defying orders is interpreted as equality, whereas obedience to them is regarded as extraordinary humiliation. Political unity is thus lost.

In other words, Yuan ascribed the disorder China was in to liberty and equality, to the adoption of a misconstrued republicanism.

The brief five months' existence of the Political Council and the interlude of Yuan's monarchy were followed by the reconvocation of the 1913 Assembly in 1916 and 1921. The Assembly continued to be subjected from time to time to the bare-fisted threats of the warlords, as in the siege of the Assembly by soldiers and paid strong-men during the debate on China's participation in the First World War.

What strikes one as curious is that the great intellectual ferment in Peking and elsewhere before and after the May 4th Movement of 1919 does not seem to have made any impact on either the style of the government or the behaviour of the Assembly. On the contrary, the executive and legislature furnished a negative image of the movement, acting clearly counter to the demands for democracy, science and iconoclasm. The rationale for the monopoly of power by the military–gentry coalition rested on the hypothesis that the ordinary people did not know how to use their rights, if the rights had been granted to them. The truth is that the elite lacked the discipline not to abuse its power.

## The growth of political parties

In the transition to constitutional republicanism and parliamentary democracy, politically concerned Chinese broke away from the age-old Confucian tradition against gentlemen organizing themselves into parties. The societies formed in 1896–8 for the promotion of reform evolved into the China Reform Association of Victoria, British Columbia, in 1899. Hitherto, they had all been study groups with no commitment to action. The political atmosphere changed with the throne's declaration of its intention to adopt a constitution in 1906, and so the Reform Association underwent a transformation, becoming the Constitutional Party, while Liang Ch'i-ch'ao organized his Political Information Society in Tokyo, both being groups of action. As yet, the throne was not prepared to tolerate a loyal opposition or to recognize minority rights; the intention to grant a Constitution did not imply freedom of assembly. The Political Information Society was therefore disbanded by decree a few months after its removal from Tokyo to Shanghai. Its highly respected and enlightened sympathizers, the scholarly industrialist Chang Chien and the political commentator Yang Tu, for fear of offending the government, withheld their support from it. However, as the country willy-nilly progressed towards a constitution at the end of the 1900s, the newly structured Political Advisory Council had at least three recognizable groups in it – the Friends of the Constitution Association (successor to the Political Information Society), representing the elected members; the Constitutional Promotion Society, representing the appointed members (mostly aristocrats); and the 1911 Club, representing the bureaucrats.

China's party politics thus began with her nationalist awakening, and so most of her early parties and groups strove for national honour and strength rather than individual rights and welfare. A newspaper commented: 'The Western view is that parties represent the vitality of a nation or the root of a nation's strength.' But it also understood that a party had to have three essential ingredients, enabling it to shoulder the responsibility of the state. It must possess a set of commonly accepted principles, a commonly agreed *modus operandi*, and unity. When in 1911 the prohibition on political association was finally lifted, a large number of parties sprang up with only vaguely defined principles, if they had any principles at all, and hurriedly improvised tactics and stratagems for the realization of their goals. Though they acted in the name of patriotism, these early parties relied on personal ties for their internal cohesion. This was possible because many of them were so small as to consist of only a handful of friends, colleagues, fellow provincials, and masters and disciples. For instance, the Transcendence Society had a membership of thirty, the Political Friends Society sixty-seven, the Mutual Benefit Society twenty, and so on. Vague and pliant principles, on the one hand, helped the parties and groups survive the rapid changes of the general political situation, since they, small as they were, had little influence on the course of the changes, and, on the other hand, provided room within the party structure for compromise and unity. Some of them were so vague and flexible in their principles that they could adopt only the addresses of their meeting places as their names – e.g. 200 Shunchihmen Street, 3 Shihfuma Boulevard, and Wu's Residence in Hsimahsien Lane, etc. Others, with no platform at all, were formed purely on ties of local affinity – e.g. Heng-she, Yu-jen-she, Ch'ien-yuan, Ching-lu, etc. Others still were organized at the suggestion or instruction of the president for dealing with a specific issue of the time, e.g. the election of a cabinet, or simply to split up a large party. They were not vastly different from the old-fashioned gentlemen's societies or traditional clan and local associations.

Two examples of this type of party may suffice to illustrate these points. The first is the Communications Clique (Chiao-t'ung hsi). This had no formal organization except that all its 'members' had been high officials of the Ministry of Communications, with a common background of education in Japan or the USA and common interests in the management of the railways, the Bank of Communications, government tax revenue, and other business enterprises. Nor did it have a political platform except for an inter-linked pro-Japanese and anti-Chihli Clique orientation. Because its founder and leader, Liang Shih-yi, was a Kwangtung man, its members were recruited mostly from among the natives of that province working in the Ministry. Its subdivision into the so-called 'old' and 'new' cliques implied perhaps a generation gap rather than anything else. Even so, their different outlooks are difficult to ascertain. The Clique as a whole played a considerable role in supporting

Yuan Shih-k'ai's presidential election and monarchical adventure when Liang Shih-yi organized the Citizen's Party in 1913. After Yuan's fall, it created the 1919 Club as a venue where the Anhwei Clique warlords' policy of unity by conquest might be moderated, since it did not believe in the capacity of the northern military leaders to bring such a policy to success.

The other, slightly more modern group, was the An-fu Club (An-fu Chü-lo-pu) of 1919–20, named after the street in Peking where the club headquarters were. An adjunct of the Anhwei Clique, it had nearly 400 members. In its headquarters, there were a secretariat in charge of the finance and paper work of the club, an executive body and a political research committee. In spite of its extravagant claims, it had perhaps only one or two provincial branches; there was certainly one in Hupei. In order to influence public opinion, it had a number of newspapers under its control in Peking, Tientsin, Shanghai, and perhaps also in Hupei. With the Japanese loans to Tuan Ch'i-jui's government, the club had money, and so each of its members in the National Assembly was subsidized to the tune of 300 *yuan* a month. Since there were 380 members of the club, including military leaders who were ineligible for parliamentary candidacy, and the club had 330 seats in the Assembly, practically all its civilian members were Assemblymen. At the height of its influence, the club had the backing of six military governors (Hunan, Shantung, Fukien, Shansi, Shensi and Anhwei) and the National Assembly under its domination. In the government, it had five ministers, four vice-ministers, a supreme court judge, the commissioner-general of the police, and the director of the Salt [gabelle] Administration. None the less, apart from its loyal support of Tuan Ch'i-jui and a firm pro-Japanese stance, it enunciated no other programme or policy of its own.

## The Kuomintang

The KMT started its revolutionary career as the China Revival Society in 1894. It differed from other contemporary political groups in the sense that it was an alliance between modernized intellectuals, small merchants and urban workers among overseas Chinese in Hawaii and Hong Kong, and that it was also a traditional secret society with a modern, nationalist penchant. Its rudimentary platform consisted of republicanism and the equalization of the right

to own and use land. Its social composition and its republicanism
determined its revolutionary nature, and the failure of the 1898
reform confirmed its commitment to revolution. By then, it had a
mass following of perhaps a few thousand.

The transformation of the China Revival Society into the Alliance
Society in 1905 marked a new orientation towards intelligentsia;
the society now formed a coalition with other revolutionary groups
among the Chinese students in Japan. The old mass base, however,
was not abandoned. An indication of this was that revolution
remained for the members of the Alliance Society the only feasible
strategy to achieve China's nationalistic goals and social modernization. Furthermore, the Alliance Society, like the China Revival
Society, continued to agitate for popular uprisings in south China.
Guided by a council of thirty and the official organ, the *Min-pao* (the
People), Sun Yat-sen formulated his three-stage revolutionary
strategy – the initial stage of military destruction, followed by six
years of party tutelage in which local self-government was to be
developed before the coming of the constitutional stage. Though it
is generally regarded as the first modern political party of China, the
Alliance Society's platform was initially crude and its strategy
imprecise. Its members were required to take an oath of loyalty to
its revolutionary principles, but it is doubtful whether the oath was
strictly observed or the members showed any discipline in committee
life or in the conduct of party affairs. Their personalization of
essentially impersonal issues and their penchant for letting personal
feelings affect matters of principle riddled the history of the society
until the revolution of 1911.

The success of the revolution brought new prospects to the
Society and necessitated its transformation from a popular, secret
organization into an open, elitist, parliamentary party. Under the
energetic leadership of Sung Chiao-jen, a Japanese-trained champion
of democracy, the Alliance Society broadened out to amalgamate
with the Unity Republican Party, the National Progressive Society,
the Republic Promotion Society, and the National Public Party. It
was at the insistence of the Unity Republican Party that the name,
New Alliance Society, was changed to the Kuomintang.

In the process of the formation of the KMT, the old ties with the
secret societies of people of little or no education were severed, as
the party now added education as a qualification for membership.
In consequence, it came under gentry domination. Sun remained

the director and Huang Hsing his associate director, assisted by seven executives including Sung Chiao-jen and a number of erstwhile bureaucrats. In the elated spirit of 1912, Sun's three-stage strategy was obviously forgotten or rejected; the republicans of whatever persuasion were to lead the country straight to constitutional rule. With that prospect apparently so near, the need was for an apparatus to enable the sovereign people to participate in government, and its provision was a task the KMT had to work for in both the legislature and executive of the Provisional Government in Nanking and later in the republican government in Peking. It was faced with the task of making a state at a constitutional convention and, through debates, discussions and compromises, of arriving at the Provisional Constitution. It was a task without historical precedent in China and the state-makers had neither a fearful bourgeoisie nor a resentful proletariat to contend with. The miserable peasantry, who were similar to the Negro slaves in America, could safely be ignored. It was then a unique opportunity comparable to the creation of the USA at the Philadelphia Convention. But there was a difference – whereas the USA possessed no aristocracy, China inherited a tenacious bureaucracy and many unruly military men, far more powerful than the handful of liberals.

Thus the KMT's programme of national unity, local self-government, racial assimilation, economic progress and international peace had to combat the political culture brought into the party by the gentry and bureaucrats. Their personal ties and particularistic values and norms were familiar to the modernized intellectuals and could easily evoke a compromise from the liberals. In the first place, it struck the gentry and bureaucrats as strange that one's views had to be debated and voted on before adoption. In the Confucian tradition, a gentleman engaged himself in no other form of contest than the sport of archery and when gentlemen disagreed, they quietly parted. To remain and fight for one's advocacy was perhaps the most ungentlemanly behaviour imaginable. In the second place, when committee life was affected by traditional considerations like this, the only alternative short of coercion was to take the matter under discussion out of the context of a party or assembly and turn it into an issue for behind-the-scene negotiations and compromises, which was to open the door to indiscipline, factionalism and corruption.

That was the *modus operandi* of the KMT before the brute power of

Yuan Shih-k'ai was let loose upon it. With a feeble organization, tenuous in its ideological cohesion, the KMT was easily crushed by Yuan. The parliamentary KMT was scattered and the party's military members – Li Lieh-chun, Po Wen-wei, Ch'en Chiung-ming, Hsiung K'e-wu, and even Huang Hsing, who was without a command – refused to accept Sun's proposal to reorganize the KMT. But between the spring and summer of 1914 Sun did reconstruct his party, as the Chinese Revolutionary Party. Its membership was a sorry 500, mostly people without prestige or status in established society, e.g. Chang Ching-chiang, Liao Chung-k'ai, Chü Cheng, Chiang Kai-shek, *et al.*, but with firm overseas ties. The restoration of its overseas ties betrayed the fact of its illegality in China and its recourse to secret society support. Indeed, in explaining his move to the overseas Chinese in south-east Asia, Sun defined the Chinese Revolutionary Party as a secret society, not a modern political party. Chang Hsi-man, another veteran of the KMT, described the new organization as 'a small group of oddly-assorted people coming from old-fashioned secret societies without the slightest political training'.

The Chinese Revolutionary Party demanded that its members should be loyal to its leader, Sun, and to fight for people's democratic rights and a better livelihood through only two stages – the military and tutelary. Their loyalty to the leader was to be so absolute that they were required to swear to risk their lives if necessary in carrying out his instructions. Having now lost his elitist following in China and commanding only scanty support from overseas Chinese, Sun felt the need to train his men for his goals, but the party was not an underground organization waging underground struggles. It carried out little propaganda work to win the support of the masses and was planning no assassination or other conspiracy to enhance its political influence. Sun's question in 1913–14 was Lenin's in 1902 – 'What is to be done?' The Chinese Revolutionary Party still lacked a clear political as well as organizational line; it was anything but a Bolshevik party.

In the years of fighting to protect the constitution, Sun depended on his personal prestige and the warlord's support rather than his party. Then the tide of the First World War turned in favour of the Western democracies and the Revolutionary Party was ready for liberalization and another reorganization. On 10 October 1919 Sun renamed it the Chinese Kuomintang and carried out a superficial reorganization; in November 1920 he reorganized it again and again superficially. In spite of his efforts to revitalize it, the party's discipline remained lax, relying almost exclusively on personal ties with Sun himself.

After his defeat by the Kwangtung warlord, Ch'en Chiung-ming, in the summer of 1922, Sun went back to Shanghai to reflect on his revolutionary principles and strategies: Ch'en, having rejoined the party in the autumn of 1920, had now turned against him; and many other military leaders, who had also joined the party, sometimes even *en bloc* with their command, had rebelled against him. The reorganizations aiming at tighter discipline had failed ignominiously. An overhaul of the party centre, when it had scarcely anything but a centre, was comparatively easy, but how could the party as a whole be reorganized? This was the question that preoccupied him in the winter of 1922. New inspiration now came from his conversations with G. Maring, the Comintern representative, and A. Joffe, the representative of the USSR, for the Executive Committee of the Comintern in its resolution on 12 January 1923 appraised the KMT as 'the only serious national-revolutionary group in China'. By all accounts, the reorganization of the KMT in 1922 affected only the central leadership, and all the departments and committees at its headquarters seemed to be research and planning bodies. In view of this, and in view of Sun's agreement with Joffe to admit individual members of the Chinese Communist Party into the KMT, this reorganization may have been preparatory for a more thoroughgoing one which was to follow. The admission of the communists and the arrival of M. Borodin as Sun's political adviser late in 1923 set the scene for the best-known reorganization of the KMT along Leninist lines in the following year.

The startling increase in the 'white-collar class' after the 1923 reorganization meant an influx of both gentry and petite bourgeoisie (doctors, lawyers, journalists and civil servants) into the party, while a relative decrease in the proportion of workers suggested a shift of the party's work away from the overseas Chinese. The KMT was back to China again with the centre and local branches now being drawn under the dominance of the white-collar class and the students. In 1923, the total membership of the party was estimated at 16000 by the Central Executive Committee; by 1924–5, it had expanded to 50000.

The basic unit of the party now moved down to the district level

*Class composition of the KMT*

|  | Kwangtung province 1925 | Nation as a whole October, 1926 |
|---|---|---|
| Workers | 34% | 29% |
| Peasants | 3 | 7·5 |
| Students | 11 | 10·5 |
| Merchants | 4 | 4·3 |
| Soldiers | 37 | 23 |
| White-collar class | 11 | 25·7 |

Source: Central Executive Committee's figures, *Hua-tzu,jih-pao* 9 April 1925.

which was below the county; above the county was the province and finally the national centre. Power theoretically belonged to the general meetings at the district level and the congress of the representatives at the higher levels, while the exercise of the power was in the hands of the executive committees at all levels. For speed of action and efficiency, the Central Executive Committee (similar to the central committee of a communist party) resolved to organize a Central Political Council (similar to the political bureau) on 11 July 1924, which had three leftists among its members (including a communist, T'an P'ing-shan, as the head of the Organization Department) and three rightists, with Sun as chairman and Borodin as adviser. In the government, if it was under the tutelage of the party, and in other organizations – the army, police, labour unions, etc. – the party blocs were to be responsible for the realization of KMT policies and programmes. The unity of the KMT was provided by the ideology based on the Three Principles of the People as expounded by Sun himself during and immediately after the First National Congress in January 1924. In addition, the KMT also adopted the Leninist principle of democratic centralism as its organizational line. Of the two unifying forces, much greater emphasis was placed by Sun on ideology through propaganda and persuasion than on organization and party life. He probably realized that the organization of his party was far from being robust and that party life, if it could be fostered at all in the context of the KMT, would take a long time to evolve. When Sun's lieutenant Liao Chung-k'ai spoke of 'the party controlling the gun' at the central cadres' conference on 9 December 1923, his thoughts were probably running on the lines of propaganda and persuasion among the soldiers rather than on actual control of the finance and supplies of the army or the physical presence of a large number of party members in the army. It was doubtful if he was thinking in terms of the politicization of the KMT army.

For the first time, the party's discipline received close attention, and the new party constitution was vastly different from those of 1919, 1920, and 1923. Even in the 1923 constitution, where the KMT showed an inkling to learn from the Bolshevik party, its chapter V on discipline remained crude. Those who had joined other parties, betrayed KMT secrets or harmed the KMT's honour or reputation, were to be punished by nothing short of expulsion. When a party could mete out dismissal so readily, dismissal either meant very little to the recipient's political and social life or was the only feasible way of penalizing a wrong-doer. Records of that and later times demonstrate that the KMT membership could easily be lost and regained.

The 1924 constitution was adopted at a time when the KMT had acquired a base area in Canton and its environs. It could now elaborate its disciplinarian principles and methods in a separate resolution which regarded discipline 'as the first and foremost necessary condition of the victory of the revolution'. Wherever the KMT was not in administrative control, the penalties for those who had acted against the party's discipline would be moral sanction or retraining until they became fit to shoulder party tasks again. Wherever the party was in control, the penalties could take the form of dismissal or demotion from official positions, expulsion from the party, or even deportation from the controlled area. By rigorous discipline, Sun and his more radical colleagues hoped to turn the ailing party into an integrated, vigorous organization equal to its revolutionary tasks.

But the practical difficulties of applying the new resolution on discipline were insurmountable. In the areas beyond the KMT's administrative control, for instance in Peking and Shanghai where the KMT Comrades' Club and the 1911 Comrades' Club flourished unrestricted, the party's discipline proved to be without teeth, whereas in the revolutionary base in Kwangtung, the focus of attention of most KMT members was on the governmental structure rather than on the party itself. This explains why nearly all the bureaux of the party centre fell into the hands of the leftists and communists, while the more substantive government posts, be it at the generalissimo's headquarters or later in the National Government, were the domains of the rightists. As to the lower organizations of the KMT, even in May 1925, nearly a year and a half later after the reorganization, Kwangtung had less than five county branches. In 1926, when a veteran rightist, Tsou Lu, wrote to Chiang Kai-shek, the situation was growing ominous for the KMT:

How many non-communists are dispatched to other provinces from our headquarters in Canton? How many non-communists are sent to other places to organize peasants' associations? How many non-communists are responsible for organizing workers? Need I ask you more before you are aware of the situation?

The fact was that by then the lower and middle echelons of the KMT had become communist enclaves.

To blame the sorry state of the KMT, and especially of the local KMT branches, during the years of the KMT–CCP alliance, on the machinations of the CCP alone was the rightist stance. The rightists' fear that the CCP would usurp the authority of the KMT drove them to take separatist action – early in 1925 after the death of Sun Yat-sen, the right-wing West Hill Clique emerged. The formation of the Clique was an evident violation of the party's discipline, in spite of its claim, in common with all factions, to be representing the majority and upholding the orthodoxy of Sun's teachings. One of its members, Tai Chi-t'ao, wrote to Chiang Kai-shek on 13 December 1925, admitting the incompetence and decay of the KMT: 'Most of the combative youths of today are communists while the corruption and cowardice of our KMT comrades cannot be denied.'

Why then did Tai decide to go to Peking and join the West Hill Clique? He wrote again on 22 January 1926: 'Firstly, I wanted to seek a way of stopping the left–right dissensions in our party. Secondly, I just could not give up the friendship of so many of them.' Friendship and other personal ties, Tsou Lu maintained, were the orthodox, traditional relations which bound the party together, and not its impersonal discipline nor its vague and flexible ideology. And this same friendship and personal ties were the criteria by which the separatism of the West Hill Clique was to be judged at a time when all the KMT factions were reunited under the openly unfurled anti-communist banner at the end of May 1927. Hu Han-min looked back on this episode:

[The West Hill Clique] did nothing seriously wrong. It was unlucky and unwise with regard to the methods it had adopted. That was why it fell into the trap laid for it by the CCP. After all its members did not meet on the West Hill [outside Peking] for selfish reasons. Therefore we must stop such irresponsible talk of doing away with them.

The West Hill Clique episode marked an end to discipline in the party. The separatists were not penalized; they continued to be respected for their contribution to the revolution and for their seniority. The same leniency and toleration were to be shown later to violators of the party's threadbare discipline; Wang Ching-wei, Ch'en Kung-po, Hu Han-min and many other celebrities were dismissed and re-admitted with considerations other than the discipline. The party, like the country at large, had a legality and a tradition which frequently contradicted each other. Often it was the tradition that prevailed. The consequences of this were observed by Hu Han-min, who remarked in May 1927 that the party was an empty shell, the masses were confused, and the communication between the leadership and the grass roots onwards was blocked. From 1928 onward, the KMT was to be riddled with factionalism, dissensions, even open splits caused by personal rivalries and personal ties.

The party was ready to return to Confucian particularism and tolerance. Its public exhortation to revere Confucius in May 1928 was to gain momentum, and culminated in the New Life Movement of 1935. The substitution of Confucian values and norms for strict discipline opened the way to the admission and re-admission of old-fashioned members of the gentry and warlords, even corrupt and dubious characters, into the party. Moreover, as another eminent KMT leader, Huang Shao-hsiung, candidly acknowledged:

Our party's admissions policy pays attention only to the orientation and understanding of a person before his admission. Once in the party, he is neither reformed nor trained.

The training department of the party branches were soon abolished after 1927, while the party itself drifted from one internal crisis to another.

To compound the gravity of the situation, the military wing of the party grew to become the dominant faction led by Chiang himself. The *élan* had to change from the limited democracy of 1924–7 to centralism and unquestioned obedience after 1929. Liao Chung-k'ai's dream of the party controlling the gun remained a dream. At the Third Congress, for instance, 80 per cent of the delegates were appointed by Chiang's faction. With a party so deficient in political awareness and in discipline, it was not surprising that the government under its tutelage was corrupt, inept and bureaucratic.

The masses were left to propaganda and persuasion in the hope that their spontaneity could one day be awakened. Under no circumstances was the party to 'kidnap' them into political action in the communist style. In Chiang's view, since the KMT repre-sented the whole nation, it naturally represented the less privileged also. China being a nation of the poor and poorer, there was no sharp social stratification, let alone class struggle. Under the existing conditions of primitive political communication among the illiter-ate masses, particularly the peasantry, it was a mystery how Chiang could expect to mobilize the masses by propaganda and persuasion. Indeed, after the purge of the communists from the KMT, it would not be impertinent to ask if the KMT had an ideology for its cadres to propagate. How was the party to purge itself of the communist influence on its ideology and organization after the break-up of the alliance?

The KMT held power twice, briefly in 1912 and for a longer period after 1928, and was both times overcome by the tenacious political tradition of China. Instead of cultivating an impersonal discipline through political education, it bowed to the ancient sages and founded its institutional structure on their teachings while aiming at the modernization of the country it tutored. In so doing, it lost all its revolutionary impetus and became a traditional Confucian gentleman dressed in a Leninist tunic, too old-fashioned and too confused to carry out its task of reconstructing China. What was worse, when others who were more coherently modernistic en-deavoured to change China by means of a different policy and a different strategy, the KMT of Chiang Kai-shek would discard all its pretentions to tolerance and unleash a ruthless persecution. Its impressions of the CCP and the League for the Defence of People's Rights of 1933 were examples of the utter incoherence of the party.

Law reform, like political change, was China's response to foreign stimulation. In other words, the Confucianized justice system proved to be unacceptable to Europeans who came to live in or visit the country. A handmaid of the rule of virtue, Chinese law rested on Confucian ethics as its theoretical foundation instead of having a fully developed jurisprudence of its own. When guidance on reaching a verdict was not to be found in the written law, the Chinese judge was apt to resort to the predominant philosophy of the state and society which often contradicted European usage. For instance, the hierarchical society, justified in terms of Confucian philosophy, denied the principle of equality before the law. Furthermore, the inquisitorial procedure ran counter to the British common law by assuming the guilt of the accused until his innocence was established. The disgrace of being accused, with its implication of guilt, deterred people from appealing to the law for the settlement of disputes. The prevalence of this attitude was the reason for the existence of a whole network of extralegal bodies and institutions like the clan associations, guilds, etc., which were available to the Chinese but not to the foreigners in China.

As to foreign diplomats and army and naval officers, the rule of thumb was not to punish them with death, but any leniency shown to them depended on the pleasure of the Chinese sovereign. There was no recognized concept of extraterritoriality as such. Indeed, in the culturalist empire, even the concept of inalienable sovereign rights was vague. On the one hand, this vagueness made it easy for China to accept foreign demands, e.g. consular jurisdiction, the most-favoured-nation treatment and negotiated tariffs; on the other, it encouraged European and American powers to ask for such things. Before the Opium War of 1839, prison reform in the West had just begun. When Europeans arrived in China in the 1830s, therefore, they were particularly struck by the cruelty of torture, the severity of punishment and the insanitary state of prisons in China. The Chinese empire these visitors saw was in an advanced stage of decay, and corruption was the rule rather than the exception in the judicial system. For all these reasons, the idea of transplanting a more familiar and fairer legal administration on to the Chinese soil occurred to the British and Americans.*

* China of course was not the only country in which consular jurisdiction was applied. Japan, Siam, Turkey and Egypt had it also. See Cleveland Perkins, 'Extraterri-

## The establishment of consular jurisdiction

A series of cases involving Chinese and foreigners (mixed cases) had been dealt with by Chinese law officers between 1780 and the conclusion of the Nanking Treaty in 1842. Although the Chinese principle of 'blood for blood' as used in the case of the *Lady Hughes* in 1784* appeared unreasonable to the Westerners, no serious resistance to Chinese law was heard until the end of the 1820s. In 1833, the British decided to establish a naval court in China, and five years later Lord Palmerston attempted to set up a judicial system there. The former decision was carried out by Lord Napier, but the latter was not realized till the 1840s. Strictly speaking, consular jurisdiction, in China or elsewhere, had no legal foundation if all states were equal before the international law. That such a structure was erected and preserved up to 1943 implied a hierarchy among the states – some being more equal than others.

Article 13 of the Treaty of the Bogue on 8 October 1843 stated that British subjects involved in criminal cases in China were to be tried by British officials according to British law. There was no indication of how the court was to be structured and how the accused was to be arrested. Article 17 of the Sino–British Tientsin Treaty of 26 June 1858 was equally vague. Since in China criminal and civil cases were never clearly distinguished, the Treaty of the Bogue was imperceptibly extended to civil cases as well. In 1844 when Caleb Cushing, the American envoy, was negotiating a commercial treaty with China, an American beat and killed a Chinese. Instead of handing the man over to Chinese authorities, Cushing had him tried before an American jury according to American law, and he was acquitted on the ground that he had acted in self-defence. That this verdict was accepted by the Imperial Commissioner Kiying (Ch'i-ying) was used by Cushing as a valuable precedent for his argument that only a Christian state could try an American citizen. Conceding consular jurisdiction to the USA, the Wanghia Treaty of 1844 left the geographic scope of the application of American law in China

toriality – Its Origin, History, and Present States', *China Weekly Review*, Extraterritoriality Supplement, 19 June 1926, p. 68, and Liang Ching-ch'un, *Tsai Hua ling-shih ts'ai-p'an-ch'uan lun* (On the consular jurisdiction in China), Shanghai, 1930, p. 2.

* When the Chinese authorities had the British gunner on the ship strangled because three Chinese had been injured and one of them had subsequently died by the salute fired by him (Mary G. Mason, *Western Concepts of China and the Chinese*, NY, 1939, pp. 127–8).

and the consul's power of arrest undefined. In the French Treaty of Whampoa, 1843, the scope of consular power was confined to the five treaty ports and the consul was unambiguously given the power of arrest. All the treaty powers then as later enjoyed whatever legal privileges China conceded to anyone of them separately.

The establishment of consular jurisdiction raised a number of legal questions. In a case involving the citizens of two or more treaty powers, the treaties did not indicate whether a consular court should use the law of the plaintiff's or the defendant's country. In a mixed case, it was customary to use the law of the defendant's country and this was specified in some of the treaties. Here again vagueness could arise from practical difficulties which the treaties did not foresee. For instance, if the defendant happened to be a Brazilian and there was no expert on Brazilian law in China, what other law should then be applied? Should the other law be applied to criminal cases only, or to both criminal and civil cases?

To administer the consular jurisdiction, the treaty powers set up eleven consular courts and the court of consuls in the foreign settlements of Shanghai. The former dealt with all cases concerning foreign nationals alone and mixed cases in which a foreigner was either accused or a defendant. The court of consuls (1882) handled only cases in which the Municipal Council of Shanghai was the defendant. The consular courts were courts of first instance. In the British system, there were also a supreme court for China and an appeal court based on the Consular Ordinance of 1844 and the Foreign Jurisdiction Act of 1890 to link up with the British system of justice as a whole; in the American system, the consular courts were regarded as the equivalent of American minor municipal courts, while the US Court in China established in 1906 corresponded to a federal district court, whence all cases of appeal would be sent to San Francisco to link up with the American system of justice.

## The mixed courts of Shanghai

Foreign legal practice had the greatest impact on China in the mixed courts of Shanghai, which dealt with all cases involving a foreign plaintiff. The practice of having a foreign observer at a Chinese trial can be traced back to 1807 when a sailor employed by the British East India Company killed three Chinese. Although consular jurisdiction had been conceded in 1844, mixed cases continued to be heard in a Chinese court within the Chinese jurisdiction. It was during the Taiping Rebellion, when the British consul in Shanghai tried some 500 minor cases in the British Concession, that the new trend was set. In 1863 the International Settlement further acquired the right to arrest any accused resident who had no consular representation. This of course affected all the Chinese inhabitants. By the time when the mixed courts of the International Settlement in Shanghai were formally founded according to the agreement of 1868, the judicial system of the Settlement was practically independent from China and capable of dealing with all mixed cases having a Chinese accused or defendant, including those involving foreign inhabitants without consular representation. They were courts which stood alone, as they belonged to neither the Chinese nor any other legal system of the world. Their verdicts were dangerously final.

Nominally they were still Chinese courts presided over by a Chinese magistrate. The consul or his deputy appeared as the assessor, whose concern was to see that the trial was conducted fairly. If he was not satisfied, he might protest or refer the matter to his legation in Peking. However, in reality, the Chinese magistrate could easily be brow-beaten by such blustering characters as Sir Harry Parkes. The Chinese magistrate may well have been steadily losing control over the proceedings before the end of the dynasty. In the disorder of the revolution of 1911, the Chinese law officers, like many other officials, fled, taking with them the funds deposited by the litigants. The assessor therefore became the judge and the court a foreign institution. The consul was normally untrained in the law; the courts had no legal foundation. Nevertheless they continued to function, handling fifty to sixty cases a day in the light of the consul's common sense.

Through the years the biased assessors and consuls gave the impression of favouring their fellow nationals by bending the rules to suit them. The *cause célèbre* in the 1870s concerned an Englishman in Chefoo who shot and killed a Chinese. The Chinese magistrate obtained the Englishman's confession through torture and convicted him of murder, but the British consul retried the case before a British jury which overturned the Chinese verdict and released the man. When the British verdict was made known, Chefoo went up in an uproar while a *Shen-pao* commentator, writing under the *nom de plume* Ho Wei-kung (What is Justice?), on 3 October 1874, asked: 'If a Chinese shot and killed a Westerner and obtained such a verdict, would the people in the West regard it as fair?' One may attribute the Chinese indignation to Chinese ignorance of trial by jury, but one would be hard put to answer the question posed by another *Shen-pao* commentator on 13 August 1877: 'Why is it that since the opening of the treaty ports there has not been a single case of homicide ending in a death sentence on an accused Westerner?'

The assessor was introduced to guarantee a fair trial. When he discharged his duties unfairly, the system itself was open to doubt. The treaties stipulated that he was 'to watch the proceedings'; he actually 'supervised over a Chinese tribunal'. He extended his jurisdiction far into the areas where the stipulations were unclear by giving legal protection to Chinese legal persons registered with a foreign consulate, Chinese employees of a foreign firm or foreign church, and even Chinese residents in foreign settlements. Records show that the British mixed court dealt with mixed cases between Japanese and Chinese parties; the French court did likewise. The most perplexing of them all was the mixed court's handling of the case of the revolutionary newspaper, *Su-pao*, in 1903. From the point of view of the imperial government, the only legally recognized government, it was a simple case of subversion and treason, but the consular authorities decided to try it in the mixed court of the International Settlement.

## The decline of consular and extraterritorial jurisdiction

The abuse of power by the consuls and the awakening nationalism of the Chinese accounted for Chinese reaction against the assessor system and the concept of consular jurisdiction as a whole. With some fifty treaty ports for eighteen treaty powers which had nearly a quarter of a million of their citizens living and working in China, consular jurisdiction considerably undermined the Chinese judicial system, which was itself in the process of reforming to comply with the Western usage. The tide of Chinese resentment began to set in 1909. In the case of the slaying of a British sailor in Tientsin, for instance, the British consul insisted on being present at the trial. The republican Ministry of Justice, which had earlier instructed all modern Chinese courts to refuse the presence of an assessor, relented only on condition that the consul would not under any circumstances interfere with the proceedings.

The situation changed rapidly and immediately after the First World War. With China in the war, the Peking government cancelled its treaties and agreements with the Central Powers by the presidential declaration of 14 August 1917. The Treaties of Versailles, St Germain and Trianon acquiesced in China's action. However, the formal abrogation of German consular jurisdiction had to wait till the Sino–German agreement of 1921, since China refused to sign the German peace treaty in 1919. In 1925, by the Sino–Austrian Treaty of Commerce, the Austrian privileges were abolished. Before that, in 1920, the Chinese authorities took over the Russian courts along the Chinese Eastern Railway in Manchuria, although Russia kept some of her privileges, including consular jurisdiction, until her new treaty with China signed in Peking on 31 May 1924. After the founding of the National Government in Nanking in 1928, Belgium, Denmark, Italy, Mexico, Portugal and Spain in theory gave up their consular jurisdiction.

As for the greater powers, the suspension of their privileges came in two stages – the transfer of the Shanghai mixed courts and the renunciation of their extraterritorial jurisdiction. With many unprofessional sovereign judges, unprincipled lawyers ready to exploit the chaotic judicial system of China, and too many cases to try,* even the foreigners themselves felt that the mixed courts were a nuisance. But it required the nationwide anti-imperialist movement, the May 30th Movement of 1925, touched off by the killing and wounding of Chinese workers and students, to change the Anglo–American view of Chinese popular nationalism, and to hasten the progress towards the rendition of the mixed courts. The agreement of the transfer was reached on 31 August 1926 and the courts were handed over on 1 January 1927. Even so, the warlord who actually controlled Kiangsu turned the court in the International Settlement into a provisional court of the province and required it (a) to handle all the mixed cases occurring not only in the settlements in Shanghai but also in Shanghai and Paoshan counties; (b) to have a foreign assessor present at all the criminal hearings which had a direct bearing on the law and order of the settlements; (c) to obtain the approval of the doyen of the consular corps in Shanghai before appointing or dismissing the chief clerk of the court; and (d) to retain foreign counsel in nearly all mixed cases. The rendition was a

* In 1921 alone, this French court listed no less than 3352 cases (Jean Escarra, *Chinese Law and Comparative Jurisprudence*, Tientsin, 1926, p. 17).

farce. It was Britain (in the form of a memorandum) and the USA (in the form of a note) who proposed to the Chinese government in 1927 that they were willing to forgo their right to appoint an assessor in all cases involving a British subject or an American citizen as the plaintiff. It took another agreement, that of 17 February 1930, to eradicate the last vestiges of the mixed courts. By this, the provisional court was replaced by a Special District Court, which formed an integral part of the judicial system of China and in which only Chinese law was applied.

On the larger issue of extraterritorial jurisdiction, the treaty powers first officially mentioned the possibility of its abolition in Article XII of the Mackay Treaty, the Sino–British Commercial Treaty of 5 September 1902, 'when the state of the Chinese laws and the arrangement for their administration warrant us in so doing'. Newly defeated in the Boxer War, China then expressed her strong desire to reform her judicial system in accordance with Western usage, and Britain's lead induced the USA, Japan and Sweden to follow in 1903. The initiative for the recovery of her sovereign rights being largely fruitless, China delayed her official demand for the cancellation of extraterritorial jurisdiction until the conference at Versailles, only to be bitterly disappointed. Up to then, the powers' objection to the cancellation had been largely technical and practical – founded on the anarchy in China, the imperfection of her legal codes and judicial system, the fact that in the 1920s the country had at best only 150 modern courts, fifty modern prisons and less than 1000 trained judges, and the trial procedures and attitude towards law that were unbridgeably different from those of the West.

The fervent nationalist movements that arose between May 1919 to May 1925, drawing their support from the urban masses of students, merchants and workers, made their impact on the question of extraterritorial jurisdiction; they also received Soviet aid to an alarming extent. Against this background the treaty powers met at Washington and resolved on 10 December 1921:

The Governments of the Powers shall establish a Commission to inquire into the present practice of extraterritorial jurisdiction in China, and into the laws and the judicial system and the methods of judicial administration of China, with a view to reporting to the Governments their findings of fact in regard to these matters, and their recommendations as to such means as they may find suitable to improve the existing conditions of the administration of justice in China, and to assist and further the efforts of the Chinese Government to effect such legislation and judicial reforms as would warrant the several powers in relinquishing either progressively or otherwise, their respective rights of extraterritoriality.

The considerations here were still technical in nature, being based on the powers' concern for the interests of their citizens rather than the interests of the Chinese. This being so, the Washington Conference showed no feeling of urgency and little inclination to treat the matter as a political issue. Caution therefore outweighed far-sightedness. First of all, all Chinese codes had to be rendered into English and data on the judicial system of China collected. Technically, it was impossible and premature to convene the Commission on Extraterritoriality within three months of the Conference as had been decided. In May 1923 the Chinese government proposed that the Commission be convened in Peking, but Japan's objection followed by that of France delayed any action till after the May 30th Movement of 1925.

Perhaps the greatest contribution of the 1925 Movement was to politicize the entire issue of extraterritorial jurisdiction, as it sharpened the contrast between the co-operative policy of China's ruling elite, which was seriously weakened by continuous civil wars, and the anti-imperialism of the masses who evinced an uncompromising militancy. London and Washington were at the same time moving towards a recognition of the potency of China's nationalism, although neither Austen Chamberlain nor Frank Kellogg was ready for abolition.

At last, the Commission on Extraterritoriality of twelve countries, including Germany, Sweden, Peru and Brazil, which were not the powers of the Washington Conference, in spite of China's objection, met in Peking at the beginning of 1926 when China had no effective central government and the country was torn asunder by several simultaneous civil wars. While the Commission sat, the war situation deteriorated progressively. Critical of the extraterritorial jurisdiction in China and satisfied that Chinese law had been reformed, the Commission by implication played down the technical hindrances to abolition, though the actual surrender of the privileges would have to wait for further legal reform and the return of peace to that country. Under the existing conditions, the Peking authorities paid little attention to legal niceties; for instance, they ordered the summary execution of a radical journalist, Shao P'iao-p'ing, on 26 April 1926, to the embarrassment of the Commission. As might have been expected, the Commission had achieved almost nothing of practical importance while the mood of the nation, especially the anti-imperialist forces, changed from reform to revolution.

After the revolution of 1926–8, both Sir Miles Lampson and Nelson Johnson, the British and American ministers, favoured a gradual approach towards a final renunciation; this view was shared by France, Italy and the Netherlands. China's unilateral declarations of her intention to abolish all extraterritorial jurisdiction on 28 December 1929 and 4 May 1931 amounted to nothing more than mere gestures. Then there occurred Japan's invasion of Manchuria, her steady ingress into Inner Mongolia and north China, and finally the outbreak of the Sino–Japanese War of 1937. As Japan's occupation of China expanded, the residue of the extraterritorial jurisdiction diminished till it was finally given up on 11 January 1943, ironically just two days after agreement on the abolition of Japanese privileges in China was concluded between Tokyo and the Wang Chin-wei government in Nanking. Even then it was agreed to maintain 'appropriate safeguards' for the US citizens and British subjects for five more years. When this period had elapsed China was once again in the throes of a revolution.

## Law reform

The manner in which the Henry A. Burgevine affair was handled by the Chinese government revealed both the spirit of Chinese law and a misconstruction of European law by the Chinese leaders. Burgevine was an American soldier of fortune who, having fought for the imperial government, surrendered to and served the Taiping rebels. Prince Kung, head of the Tsungli Yamen, reported the incident to the throne on 27 June 1865:

[The Westerners] generally regard the death penalty as too heavy. Therefore they prefer to have a man who has committed a capital crime killed on the spot. Once he is arrested, he must be tried and his case must be argued in various ways in order to have him released. This has been established as a Western tradition.

In the light of this, the prince proposed that Burgevine should be executed as soon as he was caught so as 'to avoid unnecessary complications'. Later, when consular jurisdiction firmly established itself and its judicial procedure became better known, Chinese reaction can be seen in newspaper comments on a number of occasions. For instance, the French mixed court in Shanghai once sent a case to the Shanghai magistrate court for trial and the magistrate had the accused, one Hsü Jen-k'uei, tortured for confession until the man was crippled. Thereupon the French consul lodged a strong protest against torture before conviction. Reporting the news, the *Shen-pao* commented on 12 March 1873:

Although the Westerner's argument against torture before hearing the case sounds reasonable, he is oblivious of the Chinese intention to use law as a deterrent against crime. Since Hsü Jen-k'uei is plainly guilty, a hearing would be superfluous. His notoriety coupled with the magistrate's known enmity to evil-doing inevitably led to the grave manner in which the case has been handled.

Ten years later, the same paper showed an appreciation of the painstaking way a foreign court tried a case. Neither torture nor corporal punishment was ever used to exact a confession; capital punishment was employed with the utmost care. Even when strong language was uttered, the bench remained perfectly calm but absolutely firm in its search for justice. The paper then underlined the meticulous care taken before a Western court passed a death sentence, because the Westerner valued life; the frequent use of imprisonment as a form of punishment was because the Westerner attached great importance to money-making. Obviously no money could be made when one was confined in a prison. However, as the paper pointed out on 9 February 1881, imprisonment could not be applied to Chinese criminals, for they would enjoy free board and lodgings and have no thought of repentance. As to the system of engaging legal counsel to present one's case, the paper thought it was no better than the use of Chinese law clerks, 'for silver-tongued people can always twist words to confuse right and wrong'. But it was conscious of a general ignorance of Western law, and went on to propose a systematic translation of Chinese and Western laws so that mixed cases could be handled more satisfactorily. Then the public hearing of a divorce case between an American couple opened the eyes of the paper, whose editorial on 2 October 1877 showed amazement at the possibility of a wife accusing her husband in a court of law and at the court's order for the husband to pay his wife's legal costs and alimony.

At this stage law reform in China had scarcely advanced beyond scattered and unsystematic ideas which emanated from the treaty ports and Chinese legations abroad. Kuo Sung-t'ao, in a dispatch from London, advised the Tsungli Yamen to compile a modern commercial code in order to facilitate China's international trade, and he also exhorted the government to send a delegation to the international conference on penal reform in Stockholm. Coming only seven years after the revision and publication of the new Ch'ing Code, Kuo's initiative fell on reluctant ears.

The humiliating defeat of 1895 awakened China's consciousness of her sovereign rights; Japan's success in cancelling all consular jurisdiction within her territory soon afterwards set an example for China; the waning authority of the imperial court after the Boxer War softened the resistance to law reform. In 1901–2 the government took the first step by creating the Bureau of Legal Reform, which naively copied Japanese laws on corporations, navigation, stocks and bonds, bankruptcy, etc. The commercial code drafted in 1902 unwisely neglected the realities of Chinese commercial practice, and therefore was of little value. When the Trade-mark Law was promulgated in 1904, more foreign than Chinese firms applied for registration of their trade-marks. The governmental reform of the same year saw the Board of Punishment superseded by the Ministry of Justice, while the Supreme Temple of Justice was replaced by the Supreme Court. In the provinces, a three-tier system of courts was to be set up, corresponding to the three-tier local administration at the provincial, prefectural and county levels. All litigation was to be dealt with by the courts which now lay beyond the jurisdiction of the Ministry of Justice and the local governments. Justice, it seemed, might be separated from administration for the first time in Chinese history. Under the influence of students and scholars trained in the Anglo-Saxon tradition, China for a brief moment hoped to adopt the system of jury trial, of legal counsel and of clearly demarcated civil and criminal codes, to bring the Chinese judicial system in line with its Western counterparts. Under a government leadership apparently liberal and enlightened, an ebullient mood bubbled through the words of a comment of the influential newspaper, *Ta-kung-pao*, on the rule of law and the reign of virtue:

A reign of virtue depends not upon public morality but upon the stupefaction of the masses to achieve an orderly rule. It is organized on despotic principles which in effect turn the people into slaves. It resorts to oppressive punishment to cramp the natural and precious personality of the individual.

So the comment advocated a change from the reign of virtue to the rule of law, whose tangible components consisted of legislation, judiciary, law administration and a law-abiding habit, with its intangible components including morality, ethics, religions and philosophies.

By the time the Russo–Japanese War ended in 1905, the work of translating foreign criminal laws was under way, while the Bureau of Law Codification engaged itself in revising the 1870 Ch'ing Code. During the course of this work, two significant memorials were presented to the throne, advocating the abolition of torture before a trial, because it had made China a laughing stock among the nations, and the abolition of extremely cruel penalties, e.g. slow death, decapitation, corpse mutilation, etc. But before the draft criminal code was completed in 1907, conservatives like the Minister of Justice and the Grand Councillor, Chang Chih-tung, attacked the liberal trend in defence of the Confucian tradition which they called the 'special conditions of China'. They argued against the principle of equality before the law, for its adoption would injure the dignity of the throne and the respect owed to elders by the young and to man by woman. Once respect and dignity were lost, social order and national cohesion would be lost also. The civil code, the criminal code and the code of criminal procedure compiled and promulgated before the fall of the dynasty therefore showed the influence of these Confucian views.

In the period of transition from 1912 to 1915 the codes drafted just before the end of the dynasty remained in force, only the parts 'which obviously contradict the republican polity' being deleted. Meanwhile the Law Codification Commission set to work in July 1912. Two drafts of the criminal code were completed, in 1915 and 1918, to be inherited by the Legislative Council of the National Government in Nanking and finally published in 1928. Two drafts of the civil code were also completed, in 1912 and 1925, to be revised and published in 1929. In addition, the code of civil procedure was promulgated in 1925 and the commercial code in 1936. In the meantime the constitution had changed several times, thus providing as the background for this legislation an uncertain concept of the rights and duties of the citizen. Take the uncertain

declaration of principle of the Legislative Council for instance. It
followed neither familialism nor individualism, but nationalism.
That is to say that the laws of the Kuomintang government protected
only those individual interests which did not run counter to the
interests of the nation as a whole. The question, however, remained:
what were the interests of the nation as a whole and who could
define them? Without a constitution, the process of legislation was
unavoidably anomalous. This was the case with all the legislation
of the Peking as well as of the Nanking governments.

## Modern law courts and judicial independence

*Modern law courts in China*

|                                    | 1926 | 1930 | 1935 |
|------------------------------------|------|------|------|
| Supreme court                      | 1    | 1    | 1    |
| High courts                        | 23   | 28   | 28   |
| Branch high courts                 | 26   | 32   | 42   |
| District courts                    | 66   | 106  |      |
| Branch divisions of district courts| 23   | 207  | 232  |
| Old-fashioned courts               | 1800 | 1743 | 1558 |

Sources: *China Yearbook*, 1938, p. 230; Liang Ching-ch'un, *Tsai-hua ling-shih
ts'ai-p'an-ch'uan lun* (Consular Jurisdiction in China), Shanghai, 1930, pp. 155–6;
D. Borg, *American Policy and the Chinese Revolution*, NY, 1947, p. 172.

The establishment of modern law courts progressed painfully
slowly, due chiefly to a shortage of qualified personnel. According
to Wang Ch'ung-hui's statistics, China had less than 1000 trained
judges by 1926, and according to the *Shanghai Year Book* of 1936,
there were only 1174 practising lawyers (including sixty-six foreigners) in that treaty port where most Chinese lawyers were
concentrated. Many of them, educated at institutions other than the
National Law School of Peking or the missionary Aurora University
and Soochow University, were so poorly qualified that the Educational Convention of 1922 described them as 'disorderly'. The
salary scale of the judges, ranging from 100 to 400 *yuan* a month with
the salary of the president of the Supreme Court fixed at 1000 *yuan*,
compared well with that for civil servants and teachers, although it

was much lower than that of the judges of the mixed courts. Like other government employees, the judges were not paid regularly, and so in November 1921 they and their colleagues went on strike. Modern prisons developed even more slowly, and consequently in the early 1930s China had only sixty or seventy of them out of a total of some 1500 prisons. Efforts were made to provide better accommodation and better food for foreign prisoners, but none the less corporal punishment and torture remained the rule and in general the prisons were appallingly dirty and intolerably over-crowded.

The only constitution which guaranteed the independence of the judiciary was the Provisional Constitution of 1912, whose Article LI protected them from the interference of higher officials and Article LII secured them against arbitrary transfer or dismissal. But two years later when he instructed the Political Council to design a legal system, Yuan Shih-k'ai attacked the principle of judicial independence on moral and pragmatic grounds. Because of a serious shortage of trained personnel and of the financial resources which might help keep the personnel there above corruption, the modern courts accepted bribes and bent the law, turning judicial independence into a farce. Yuan hoped to remedy the situation by strengthening the control of the leader (Yuan himself) whose moral example and moral persuasion, supplemented with harsh punishment, might eventually bring some order into the present chaotic system of justice. This was clearly a return to the reign of virtue of the Confucian tradition. For the revolutionaries at the height of the revolution in 1927, Confucian ethics were replaced by 'the principle of the Party [KMT] and of the revolutionary nation' to serve as the foundation of justice. Hsü Ch'ien, Minister of Justice of the KMT Wuhan Government, who was incidentally a Christian, reported on the reform of the judiciary and was obliged to

frankly declare that the revolutionary jurisdiction will be controlled by the Party, that the judiciary will further the interests and principles of the Party, inasmuch as the interests of the Party and those of the Revolution are identical.

Chiang's government in Nanking, in spite of all its differences from Wuhan, observed the same principle of party control over the judiciary.

In theory, all Chinese citizens* were equal before the law since the Provisional Constitution of 1912, but in practice Confucian ethics continued to play their role in both legislation and the administration of justice. To begin with, there was no juvenile law while the age of legal responsibility was fixed at twelve *sui* which could be either eleven or even ten years of age in Western terms. Polygamy, though forbidden, remained widespread and the law could do little about it. The favoured treatment, which seniors and males enjoyed under Confucianism and which had in the past dominated Chinese legal thought, still remained strong. The *China Mail* of Hong Kong on 17 March 1919 recorded a case of a young man who had killed his father's murderer. The court of Hsinhui which heard the case changed it from a criminal to a civil trial on the basis of filial piety. Compare this with the case of two sons who killed their father in Shanghai on 4 October 1939, where the judge, having passed the death sentence on both brothers, commented: 'Unless merciless penalty is meted out to them, there is no way of warning the others.' The criminal code of 1935 fixed considerably heavier penalties for those who inflicted bodily injury on their parents or adopted parents than for those who committed ¦similar felonies against other people. In the same Confucian spirit, the Central Political Council of the KMT decided on 23 July 1930 to omit the question of concubinage in its directive on the kinship law, and in the criminal law of 1935 the section concerning public morality (sexual offences) was immoderate and harsh in tone. During both the Peking and Nanking government periods, people who possessed power or social status, like the gentry under the old system of justice, were treated leniently by the law; this leniency usually took the form of suspended sentences when other people of power and social status were willing to *pao* them (a form of bail without paying money and guarantee of good conduct in order to secure the release of the convicted).

In the forty years of political judicial change, the modernizers strove to introduce a constitution, parliament and party political system into Chinese political life, and to reform the law so as to bring it in line with the Western practice. Their aim was the power and wealth

* From 1909 to 1929 all the nationality laws of China adopted the principle of *juis sanguinis*. This means that practically no Chinese could lose his or her Chinese nationality unless by marrying a foreign husband, establishing one's foreign parentage, or voluntary renunciation. These laws were a direct result of foreign discrimination and ill-treatment of the Chinese living abroad.

of the nation; their strategy had varied from gradual reform to violent revolution. Reform depended on a readiness to concede and compromise for the common good on the part of the conservatives. When this did not happen and the strife became more violent, revolution was the only course to take. The first attempt at reform in 1898 was ruthlessly suppressed by its opponents; then parliament, constitution and party politics were subverted by their enemies in 1913–14; and finally the united front of the KMT and CCP was destroyed by its foes in 1927–8. Socially, the modernizers were enlightened intellectuals and businessmen; intellectually, they were social Darwinians, liberals, or Marxists. Their most powerful enemies were found among an alliance between the gentry and the military with varying degrees of tolerance of commercial and industrial interests and of social Darwinism and liberalism. But in the final analysis, their major political and intellectual concern was the preservation of the Confucian tradition, their own political culture, with which they endeavoured to Confucianize all the laws and political institutions they cared to borrow from the West.

To say that the conservatives were unaware of the incompatibility between the old and the new is to overlook their suppression of what they deemed unsuitably new; to say that they were perfectly conscious of what they were doing is to open the gate to a conspiracy interpretation of history. The first alternative would require the acceptance of the premise that they were completely sincere in their intention to make China strong and wealthy; the second would require the rejection of such a premise. Sincerity or insincerity of intention may be difficult to establish, but ignorance can be proved quite easily. Without exception, the gentry–military alliance laid bare in its important policy statements a dismaying ignorance of the politics and law of China and the West. When this intellectual deficiency was linked up with practical interests and power, the opposition of the alliance to what it regarded as unacceptably new hardened to become a stumbling block in the way of China's progress towards modernity.

# Chapter 7

# Economy

| | Import of opium in chests (1 chest = 133 lbs) | China's deficit trade in Mexican $ | Net outflow of silver taels |
|---|---|---|---|
| 1821 | 4244 | 1911082 | −908237 |
| 1825 | 12434 | 1039269 | 1572120 |
| 1830 | 16257 | 9212295 | 3887972 |
| 1835 | 21885 | (1833) 13418592 | 4340589 |
| 1839 | 40200 | | |

Sources: H. B. Morse, *The International Relations of the Chinese Empire*, Shanghai, 1910, vol. I, p. 210, and *Chronicles of the East India Company Trading to China*, vols. III and IV, *passim*; R. M. Martin, *China: Political, Commercial, and Social*, London, 1847, vol. II, p. 94; Yen Chung-p'ing, *Chung-kuo chin-tai ching-chi-shih t'ung-chi tzu-liao hsuan-chi*, Peking, 1955, p. 33.

## The growth of international trade and tariffs

The importance of opium as an international commodity carried from Bengal, Bihar and Orissa to Canton was not in dispute; nor was the increasing weight of that trade since 1820. The Napoleonic wars had considerably eroded the monopoly of the British East India Company, and the consequent competition between Malwa and Bengal forced down the price to increase the sale. As a result the Chinese government reaffirmed its prohibition of the traffic, and drove the trade out of the Canton system of trade. What was, and still is, in dispute was the economic impact of the drug on China.

In the perspective of British India,

From the opium trade the Honourable Company have derived for years an immense revenue and through them the British Government and nation have also reaped an incalculable amount of political and financial advantage. The turn of the balance of trade between Great Britain and China in favour of the former has enabled India to increase tenfold her consumption of British manufacture; contributed directly to support the vast fabric of the British domain in the East, to defray the expenses of His Majesty's establishment in India, and by the operation of exchange and remittances in teas, to pour an abundant revenue into the British Exchequer to benefit the nation to an extent of £6 million a year without impoverishing India. Therefore the Company has done everything in its power to foster the opium trade.

From the Chinese point of view, as expressed in two nation-wide debates on the opium issue in 1836 and 1838, one aspect of deep concern was the loss of silver through the import of opium which impaired the monetary equilibrium between the *de jure* legal tender, the copper *cash*, and the *de facto* legal tender, the silver *sycee*. The disequilibrium cannot be, nor was it, explained in terms of such long-term factors as the debasement of the copper coin and the habit of hoarding the better of the two currencies, for these factors had been in operation for more than fifty years before the balance of trade turned against China in 1808. Before that date, the rate of exchange between silver and copper had remained quite stable around the legal par of one *tael* of silver to 1000 *cash*, often with a bias favourable to copper. When silver began to flow out of Canton from 1808 onwards, the rate fluctuated more violently and frequently against copper than ever before. In the 1808–56 period it rose first to 1200–1300 *cash* to one *tael*, and then to 2000 *cash*. The record year was 1845 when a *tael* could fetch 2300 cash! Neither the range nor the frequency of the fluctuations can be accounted for by traditional factors; opium import and the resultant outflow of silver were responsible for it.

Since it was impracticable to stop the trade altogether, and therefore impossible to forbid the use of silver as the medium of exchange at Canton, the only feasible alternative left open to the Chinese government was to prohibit the import of opium. The war caused by the prohibition is well known, but Britain was fighting for larger issues than the simple right to trade in opium – to uphold the principle of free trade and safeguard the trade by devising a system of legal arrangements. By the Nanking Treaty and the accompanying treaties, the international trade of China ceased to be restricted to the port of Canton alone. There were now to be a number of treaty ports with Hong Kong as the British commercial base in East

Asia. At the ports, the foreign traders were no longer subject to legal or monopolistic constraints. They and their property were protected by a negotiated tariff of five per cent *ad valorem* and by consular jurisdiction backed by the stationing of men-of-war at the ports. To ensure that the economic advantages gained by the powers from China were shared fairly, the most-favoured-nation clause was introduced to guard against the possibility of China falling under the domination of one power, and also against that of the powers being played off against one another by China.

The new system underwent modifications and revisions under the Tientsin Treaties of 1858 and the Chefoo Convention of 1876. By these diplomatic agreements more ports were opened to foreign trade and foreigners were allowed to travel in the hinterland of China. In order to free foreign goods from cumbersome inland taxes, the Tientsin Treaties made sure that the transit dues were not to exceed half of the value of the tariff itself, and inland excise (*likin*) on imported opium was to be collected simultaneously with this duty. 'Inland' now meant the length and breadth of the whole country and these arrangements were hammered out, through tempestuous sessions of negotiations, to fulfil the age-old hope of opening the unlimited market of the ancient empire to the penetration of Western commodities. The system forged in the turbulent years between 1842 and 1876 was to last without any major breach till 1917.

Immediately after the Nanking Treaty, Western merchants at large, particularly the British, shared Sir Henry Pottinger's optimism in regarding China as a market of 300 000 000 customers for London pianos and Sheffield cutlery. These great expectations led to a glut of Western goods in Hong Kong and a parliamentary report:

We find that the difficulties of the trade do not arise from any want of demand in China for articles of British manufacture, or from the increasing competition of other nations, . . . The sole difficulty is in providing a return.

The 'return' was, of course, the same thing as the demand. The logical flaw in the parliamentary report was to be exposed by an assistant magistrate at Hong Kong, one Mitchell, whose exhaustive report to Sir George Bonham in 1852 pointed out that the self-sufficient nature of the Chinese economy was chiefly responsible for the British inability to expand sales in China.

Although the Western merchants' dream of China being the El Dorado of the East was modified by experience, they never quite awakened from it. Western merchants continued to create demand for Chinese goods at home, for instance by obtaining the reduction of British tariff on tea under Peel and Gladstone, and for Western goods in China, for example, by the building of railways and the acquisition of the right to navigate in China's inland waters. Their efforts evoked a positive and conscious response from their Chinese partners from the 1870s onward. With the awakening of Chinese nationalism, trade came to be regarded as a form of human struggle for survival and development. Even so, international trade never played an important part in the economic life of that populous country whose share in world trade was never of any great significance. In its peak years in the 1920s the total value of China's foreign trade scarcely exceeded 1 per cent of world trade; the total value

*Imports, exports and trade balances 1871–1936 (in million yuan)*

|  | Export | Import | Surplus ( + ) or deficit ( − ) |
|---|---|---|---|
| 1871–3 | 110 | 106 | +4 |
| 1881–3 | 108 | 126 | −18 |
| 1891–3 | 167 | 219 | −52 |
| 1901–3 | 311 | 473 | −162 |
| 1909–11 | 570 | 702 | −132 |
| 1919–21 | 921 | 1203 | −282 |
| 1929–31 | 1464 | 2082 | −618 |
| 1933 | 612 | 1346 | −734 |
| 1934 | 535 | 971·7 | −436·7 |
| 1935 | 576 | 919 | −343 |
| 1936 | 706 | 942 | −236 |

Sources: Yen Chung-p'ing, op. cit., p. 64, based on the Maritime Customs Reports.

per capita was no more than US $2; and the trade itself took only 6 to 8 per cent of China's gross national product. Take Britain, for instance. China's share of her overseas trade in the 1920s hardly went beyond 1 per cent of her imports and only about 2 per cent of her exports.

As to the terms of trade, the general trend had been unfavourable to China due chiefly to the rising price of gold in terms of silver.

This rise accelerated after 1895 as most of the major powers went over to the gold standard while China remained on silver. Take the rate between the *tael* and sterling for example. The *tael* stood at 6s 11¼d when the Taiping rebellion ended; in 1895 it fell to 3s 3¼d; and in 1905 it was only 3s 1d. Although the European war arrested the trend temporarily, the advent of the Depression, which hit the prices of primary products the hardest, further worsened China's terms of trade.

The restoration of peace and the construction of the great railways in the USA, the opening of Japan and the opening of the Suez Canal contributed to the changes in the China trade in the 1870s. The trade expanded but was not yet aided by a flow of capital to help China's international balance of payments. The Treaty of Shimono-seki of 1895, by which the right of the treaty powers to invest in manufacture in China was recognized, turned a new page in her international economic relations. Capital inflow from the treaty powers and from overseas Chinese remittances enabled the trade to grow more rapidly than before, culminating in the wartime and post-war boom of her exports and imports.

## Exports

Of her major exports, China tea monopolized the world market until the competition from Assam became a considerable force and until the opening of Japan. Its share of the world tea supply fell from 90 per cent in 1867 to only 29 per cent in 1905. By 1875 China had lost much of her British market to India and her American market to Japan, leaving Russia as the most important buyer of China tea. Then came the First World War, the October Revolution, and the 2d surcharge on every pound of tea from outside the British Empire which sent the Chinese tea trade to its lowest point yet, from 55.5 million *taels* (or 13 per cent of her total export) in 1915 to a mere 8·9 million (or 1·6 per cent) in 1920. The tragedy of this once valu-able commodity must be ascribed to a host of reasons: small-scale production and processing which offered no guarantee of the quality of the product, archaic methods of packaging and marketing which meant that goods were easily damaged, and also increased cost, and the lack of capital and technical knowledge which retarded the modernization of the industry. In spite of the fact that two Rus-sian tea-processing plants were established in Hankow, in the 1870s,

Chinese tea merchants still needed British and Russian agents to teach them modern methods of firing and packaging in the 1890s and they did not set up their own tea-brick factories, which were even then on a very small scale, till 1906. The Peking government's initiative aiming at the modernization of the trade came in the good year of 1915. Unfortunately it was to be affected by Yuan Shih-k'ai's fall which entailed the demise of the government initiative. The costliness of the marketing procedure can be seen in the fact that a picul of Anhwei tea could be bought on the spot at Mexican $1·50, but when it reached Shanghai its price was $14!

Could China's tea trade have been saved if she had opened her door to foreign investment, turning the small tea gardens into large-scale plantations, and also modernizing processing and marketing so that the trade would have been put on a competitive footing with Assam and Japan? The question of course cannot be answered by considering the tea trade alone; it involved China's status as a politically and economically sovereign state as well as her own attitude towards and competence in modernizing this and other business enterprises. Even if China had given up her tea trade to a synarchy of the Chinese and foreigners, to be managed like her maritime customs service or her railways, it is still doubtful whether she would have been able to compete with India. In the first place, the Assam tea plantations were started in the 1820s when China's sovereign status was still intact and, in the second place, unless China had become a part of the British Empire, she would not have been able to enjoy the privileges within the British imperial trading system. Furthermore, there were also wider issues concerning international and domestic politics of China, and stubborn and complex cultural problems which were beyond the ability of anyone at that period to tackle successfully.

Despite strong Japanese competition, China's export of silk held its primacy till the Depression, though her share of the world silk market declined from almost six times that of Japan in 1880 to less than half of that of Japan in 1925. In absolute terms, the increase in the export of silks was unspectacular, from 74000 piculs in 1871 to twice as much forty years later, and by 1929 it was no more than 223844 piculs. Thereafter the trade declined as silk was superseded by synthetic fibres. In all three areas of China's silk exports – cocoon production, raw silk and silk piece goods – the basic problem lay not in marketing, which was almost entirely in the hands of foreign businessmen in China, but in quality standardization and in understanding of the consumers' tastes. Chinese brocade, damask, taffeta, satin, etc., were manufactured in more or less the same measurements, designs and colours for a long time without noticeable changes to meet or stimulate demand in the West. Chinese raw silk, reeled in an unstandardized manner, was a nightmare for the Western weaver. Her exported cocoon products were often diseased. It was only at the urging and with the help of foreign technicians that the cocoons were pasteurized from the 1880s onwards, but foreign intervention in silk reeling, much to the chagrin of the Chinese producers, failed to compensate for the political and administrative interference which resulted in frequent bankruptcies of the small-scale filatures under Chinese management.

The decline of tea and silk exports freed her trade capacity in foodstuffs at the beginning of this century; the Mackay Treaty of 1902 helped diversify her exports by including such commodities as beans and bean products, eggs and egg products, wheat and vegetable oil. Meanwhile, her exports of raw cotton and cotton goods, wood oil (*t'ung*), hog bristles and minerals (chiefly coal, iron ores, antimony, wolfram, etc.) expanded. Before 1914, no machine-made goods appeared on her export lists, and even in the 1930s China remained principally an exporter of primary goods. The only Chinese machine-made commodities which could hold their own in international markets were cotton yarn, shirtings and sheetings, wheat flour and matches. It was an irony that China, a country of food shortages, should have become a supplier of food, also raw materials, to the belligerent powers of the First World War, to the improvement of her trade position during and after the war. However, with the onset of the Depression even her exports of foodstuffs decreased.

## Imports

The import of opium continued to increase in the years after the peace of 1842, rising to an average of over 50000 chests in the first half and over 70000 chests in the second half of the 1850s. With some fluctuations it declined slightly thereafter, due to local competition and the levy of the inland excise on opium. Although the drug's relative share of China's total imports was clipped from 46 per cent in 1867 to a mere 7·5 per cent in 1905, its value showed a slight increase from 32 million *taels* to just over 34 million. The European War dealt a heavy blow to Indian opium from which it never recovered. But on the other hand British exports of morphia and heroin to Japan and then to China rose from 600000 oz in 1917 to 800000 oz in the early 1920s. Between the Depression and the outbreak of the Sino–Japanese War the smuggling of heroin, cocaine and other opiates from Japan and Japanese settlements in China to Korea and China proper was the world centre of this illicit traffic.

Imports of cotton yarn and piece goods increased at vastly different rates – the former twenty-four times while the latter merely doubled in the period from 1871 to 1911, thanks chiefly to the cheap yarn from Bombay and Japan and China's lack of purchasing power for the more expensive cloth from England. As far back as 1885, cotton yarn represented 25·7 per cent of China's total imports, which made it the leading foreign commodity in the Chinese market; its value then was greater than that of China's silk exports. In the 1890s, it surpassed the combined value of her exports of silk and tea. The import of yarn began to decline from the outbreak of the First World War, which gave a chance for the nascent Chinese mechanized textile industry to develop. In less than twenty years, it shrank from 800000 piculs in 1919 to only 6000 piculs in 1936, a rate as impressive as the spectacular increase in the 1860s and 1870s. Imported piece goods, however, went through a period of sturdy growth when Japan replaced Britain as China's chief supplier of cloth and fine yarn. Even this failed to withstand the down-swing of the Depression as the import of cotton piece goods fell from the dizzy height of 221 million *yuan* in 1919–21 to just over 12 million in 1936.

Next in importance to cotton goods, China imported from the beginning of this century a great amount of foodstuffs, including rice, wheat, flour and sugar. If we include alcohol, or soft drinks and tobacco, their share of total imports leapt from 4 per cent in the 1860s to over 30 per cent in the 1930s. After this came a host of other goods – kerosene, perfumes, dyestuff, machines, and machine tools locomotives and other vehicles, etc. – to make up the rest of China's import list.

The salient features of China's foreign trade in the century after the first Anglo–Chinese War were that she was an exporter of primary goods and importer of secondary commodities and technical knowledge. After the decline of her silk and tea sales in the international market and the replacement of imported opium by native drugs, her foreign trade became diversified – a development which distinguished her trade from that of colonies like India or Indonesia. Although capital goods took an increasingly important share of her imports, rising from about 8 per cent of the total value in 1873 to over 16 per cent during the European War and over 35 per cent during the 1930s, the lion's share of this consisted of building materials, vehicles and fuel. Both finance and shipment of the trade were in the hands of foreign firms, especially British firms, e.g. the Hong Kong and Shanghai Banking Corporation, Butterfield and Swire, and Jardine and Matheson. Since China's share in international trade was so small and her political influence negligible, she was in no position to manipulate prices or promote the sales of her exports. There was even a lack of determination and skill to do either. On the contrary, the marketability of her goods depended on fashions and demand in the West and on the availability or otherwise of substitutes. The rise and fall of the trade in tea, silk, bristles, *t'ung* oil, straw plaits, etc., told an eloquent story. The small producers of these goods possessed neither the information about changing market conditions abroad which would have enabled them to prepare themselves against changes, nor the research facilities or capital to improve their products, so as to create demand.

## Balance of payments and the maritime customs

The secular trend in the balance of trade had been consistently adverse. This meant that any expansion of China's trade was conditional on the inflow of capital so that her international payments could be balanced. In other words, China's purchasing power depended on foreign loans, foreign investment and particularly overseas Chinese remittances, the last of which reached an amount of 84 million *taels* a year in the 1870s and was to leap to 364 million *taels* in the 1890s. By 1936 over 97 per cent of her trade deficit was offset by these remittances. Even then they were almost completely handled by foreign banks.

Of cardinal importance to the whole treaty system of trade was the maritime customs service organized by the Chinese government according to the Nanking Treaty. The Taiping Rebellion of the 1850s threw it into total chaos, partly because of the timidity and corruption of the officials in charge of it, and partly because of the arrogant foreign merchants who fished in the resulting muddy water, defying the Chinese authorities. Shanghai itself was threatened from within by the Small Sword Uprising and from without by the Taiping armies. The British consul, Rutherford Alcock, with the consent of his American colleague, organized the Provisional System for tariff collection which lasted from September 1853 to February 1854 in an attempt to impose a measure of order and to ensure a degree of fair competition on the legal foundation of the Nanking Treaty: 'British consuls were obliged to see that the just duties and dues of the Chinese Government should be duly discharged by Her Britannic Majesty's subjects.' Though the system worked better than the anarchy left behind by the Chinese official in charge, Wu Chien-chang, neither the willingness nor the mechanisms to enforce its regulations were present, the inefficiency of the system had become evident by the beginning of 1854. Therefore, a tariff conference was called in June 1854, to initiate a board of foreign inspectors appointed by the Chinese district officer of Shanghai.

The Shanghai model was to be adopted on a national scale in 1859 by the appointment of a foreigner as the Inspector-General of the Chinese Imperial Maritime Customs with, under him, a number of foreign inspectors. The reason for so doing was, according to a high official, Wen-hsiang, that the Chinese 'could not manage the indemnity question [this refers to the indemnity of the Anglo–French Expedition] without foreign assistance'; according to a Shanghai official, Hsüeh Huan's recommendation of H. N. Lay for the post of Inspector-General, it was 'to prevent corruption';* and according to Prince Kung, it was that 'the whole matter [of maritime customs] was too complicated [for us] to see all its pitfalls.' Lay's attitude when accepting the appointment was typical of the ebullience and arrogance of the triumphant Westerners in China at that time:

My position was that of a foreigner engaged by the Chinese Government to perform certain work *for* them not *under* them. I need scarcely observe in passing that the notion of a gentleman acting *under* an Asiatic barbarian is preposterous.

Drawing princely salaries (the Inspector-General received about

* See Hsüeh's memorial, *Chou-pan i-wu shih-mo*, HF, ch. 71, December 1860, 33a. Hsüeh himself had not sent any account of the ports under his control for three years. See FO 17/350, Bruce to Russell, despatch no. 14, 12 March 1861.

£3500 a year, his deputy £2600, and even the lowest inspector about £1200), the foreigners working in the Chinese maritime customs service enjoyed great comforts which they were reluctant to give up by training their Chinese colleagues to replace them. Take C. W. Mason in Chenkiang in 1890, for example. He received a salary of 250 *taels* of silver a month and a rent-free house fully furnished and heated in winter, he paid less than 7 *taels* to each of his three house-boys, less than 3 *taels* to each of two grooms, one boatman, and two chairbearers, sing-song girls cost him less than 1 *tael* a night, and *geisha* less than 30 *taels* a month. All his imported wine, cigars, canned food, etc., were duty free. In this synarchical arrangement, about 55 per cent of the foreign employees in the services were British and about 62 per cent of the high officials were also British. The rest of the lucrative and powerful posts were shared by citizens of the other treaty powers. Their authority increased as China steadily sank into the quagmire of foreign loans after 1895, when the revenue of the customs was pawned as security against loans. It was further enhanced during the 1911–12 revolution, when their power was extended from supervision to the actual collection of the revenue. With all this power and comfort, it was widely believed that the foreigners were incorruptible. But the cost of collection was never lower than 11 per cent of the total revenue!

*Maritime customs revenue*

| | | | | |
|---|---|---|---|---|
| 1845 | 5 526 439 HK *taels* | | 1895 | 21 390 000 |
| 1865 | 8 297 000 | | 1905 | 35 110 000 |
| 1875 | 11 970 000 | | 1915 | 34 177 000 |
| 1885 | 14 470 000 | | 1925 | 78 100 000 |

Sources: BBP (4187), Alcock to Clarendon, Peking, 1 April 1869; *Ch'ing-ch'ao hsü wen-hsien t'ung-k'ao*, ch. 66, k. 8229; *The Times*, 7 January 1918, 3 January 1927, and 3–4 January 1928; J. K. Fairbank, *Trade and Diplomacy*, Cambridge, Mass., 1953, p. 257.

The customs revenue, the traditional land-poll taxes (*ti-ting*) and the salt gabelle were the three legs of the new financial tripod of China. In the 1890s the customs revenue equalled the land-poll taxes in importance and later overtook them, especially after 1912 when the latter were intercepted by provincial authorities. The salt gabelle had never been as remunerative as the other two, being only about one-third of the amount of the customs revenue, but it increased considerably after its reorganization by foreigners in 1913. The inland tariff, which had once been a major source of income for the government, fell far behind the *likin* excise. In the 1890s the former brought in no more than 5 per cent of the amount that the maritime customs did, while the latter brought in close to two-thirds as much.

The amounts received by the government from land and salt taxes did not, of course, represent the actual amounts borne by those who paid them. The traditional system of tax assignment and corruption were responsible for their being stable rather than increasing sources of revenue. Neither of them could be relied upon as a source of additional income for the government to deal with emergencies such as the suppression of rebellions and the finance of modernization projects. Against this background, the development of maritime customs and *likin* on commodities, a more flexible source, was of great significance to government spending in the second half of the nineteenth century. The synarchical administration of the customs service made sure of its relative incorruptibility and the growth of foreign trade increased its volume. Therefore, in the 1890s, tariff and *likin* made up over 45 per cent of the government revenue, compared with only about 10 per cent from commodity taxes in the 1840s. Once the salt gabelle had been reformed and the *likin* transformed into the consolidated taxes, they joined the maritime tariffs as sources of financial support for Chiang Kai-shek's government in Nanking.

Important as it was, the maritime customs, kept under foreign control by means of treaty stipulations and of the foreign inspectorate, was consistently biased in favour of the importers. The basis of valuation was always lower than the prevailing market prices. As a result, Japanese goods, for instance, actually paid only 3·5 per cent import duties instead of the agreed 5 per cent *ad valorem*. The tariff negotiations in 1858, 1902, 1918 and 1922 were all concerned with the revaluation of the prices of imports in order to keep the rates of duties in line with price increases. On each occasion these negotiations suffered from delays and political bargaining. Another thorny problem concerning the maritime customs cropped up after the Washington Conference of 1921–2 at which a surtax of 2·5 per cent was promised. This would increase the revenue of the Peking government by about 250 million *taels*. As the projected tariff conference was delayed; the Chinese regional authorities began to collect this surtax without waiting for an international agreement. The KMT government in Canton (later Wuhan) set the example; Peking followed; then Shanghai and Shantung authorities joined them. The rates collected by these various authorities ranged from 2·5 to 57 per cent *ad valorem* in 1926 and 1927, creating a situation close to anarchy which the British Inspector-General, Sir Francis Aglen, could not control. The same anarchy existed to an even less controllable degree in the salt gabelle, from which local military authorities began to take a share as far back as 1919. In the worst years of the gabelle, 1926–7, the government and the foreign consortium of banks suffered from a decrease in revenue while the military magnates managed to increase theirs from 47·6 million *yuan* to 52·5 million *yuan*.

From 1895 onward, especially after 1911, there arose a peculiar problem known as 'the balance of the customs revenue' (*kuan-yü*). Because of indemnities (that owed to Japan and the Boxer indemnities) and the consequent foreign loans, the revenue was to be deposited in foreign banks in China, chiefly the Hong Kong and Shanghai Banking Corporation, which would see to it that the loans and indemnities were properly served before the Chinese government could lay its hands on what was left. As China's debts piled up and the rate of tariff remained constant, the balance available to the government diminished, aggravating the poverty of Peking. The situation eased to some extent when China recovered a degree of her tariff autonomy after 1930.

The size of the customs revenue alone prompted some Chinese to contemplate the possibility of tariff autonomy. Marquis Tseng was in favour of it, but his voice went unheard, and the creation of the Tax Bureau in the fatuous wave of 'rights recovery' in the 1900s proved to be useless. The gathering force of nationalism tended to furnish ammunition for the government leaders in Peking to demand a larger share in the revenue to alleviate their financial straits. This trend, after the interruption of the First World War, culminated in the promise of a tariff conference and a surtax of 2·5 per cent at the Washington gathering in 1921.

The tariff conference eventually took place in October 1925 after much wrangling between China and France and Japan. The thirteen powers gathered at Peking were to discuss the interim arrangement of a 5 per cent surtax on ordinary goods and 20–30 per cent surtax

*The balances of the maritime customs (in million yuan)*

|      | Net revenue | Loan service | Balance |
|------|-------------|--------------|---------|
| 1923 | 88          | 94·25        | −6·25   |
| 1924 | 121         | 91·5         | 29·5    |
| 1925 | 124         | 88·7         | 35·3    |
| 1926 | 127         | 90·5         | 36·5    |
| 1927 | 130         | 84·15        | 45·85   |
| 1928 | 132         | 85·5         | 46·5    |
| 1929 | 134         | 81·1         | 52·9    |
| 1930 | 136         | 77           | 59      |
| 1931 | 138         | 66           | 72      |
| 1932 | 140         | 65           | 75      |
| 1933 | 142         | 55·5         | 86·5    |
| 1934 | 144         | 55·5         | 88·5    |
| 1935 | 146         | 55           | 91      |
| 1936 | 148         | 55           | 93      |
| 1937 | 150         | 54·5         | 95·5    |

Source: G. Padoux, *The Financial Reconstruction of China and the Consolidation of China's Present Indebtedness*, Peking, 1923, Table III.

on luxuries to ease the financial difficulties of the tottering regime in Peking. The larger issues on the agenda consisted of China's abolition of the *likin* and the powers' eventual recognition of her tariff autonomy. Economically the interim arrangement was to China's detriment, if the *likin* was to be abolished as a quid pro quo. The surtax might yield some 30 million *yuan* while the abolition of the *likin* would mean a loss of 70 million. There was, however, a difference between the recipients of the gains and losses – the surtax would go to Peking while the local military authorities would be deprived of the benefit of the *likin*. Even Peking would not be the final beneficiary, for the powers insisted on the income from the surtax being used for the liquidation of foreign loans.

There was, none the less, a community of interests between the government in Peking and the powers in strengthening the status quo, regardless of the shakiness of the foundation on which the work would have to be done. To rely on the dilapidated regime of Tuan Ch'i-jui to realize the dreams of the Washington Conference was itself a historical irony and stupidity if it was not disingenuous. Outside Peking there were Feng Yü-hsiang's armies in Inner Mongolia and the north-west, Wu P'ei-fu and his associates along the Yangtze valley, the armies of Sun Ch'uan-fang which were hostile to Tuan Ch'i-jui's in Chekiang, Chang Tso-lin's armies in Shantung, and the KMT in Canton, all of whom were opposed to the tariff conference; some even went as far as to initiate civil wars to sabotage the deliberations of the powers. Coming after the anti-imperialist demonstrations and strikes in the summer of 1925 and in the midst of several civil wars, it was inconceivable that any of the tasks of the tariff conference could be accomplished. No wonder that the delegates were reduced to playing golf and riding Mongolian ponies in the brisk, but not uncomfortable, early winter in Peking, as reported by *The Times* on 14 December 1925.

The surtax was introduced regardless; Sir Francis Aglen protested against it and was dismissed. The appointment by Peking of A. H. F. Edwardes as Aglen's successor revealed an interesting attitude. The anti-imperialist government in Wuhan objected. By then, the rising tide of China's nationalism had been recognized by London, Washington and Tokyo, although the Japanese Minister to China still preached to the Chinese in the light of Japanese experience, that it would be futile to negotiate for tariff autonomy from a position of weakness. The futility of it indeed became obvious after the powers had shown their strength in the Nanking Incident when Chiang Kai-shek's soldiers molested foreign residents and damaged their property in March 1927; and so in July the Nanking government, reverting back to the introspective nationalism of the Darwinian brand, announced its intention of recovering tariff autonomy and abolishing the *likin* simultaneously. Now that the sharp edge of the Chinese nationalism of 1925–7 had been blunted, the powers could come to terms with China's demand for tariff autonomy. With the USA leading the way, a series of treaties were signed with Britain, France, Holland, Norway and Sweden in the second half of 1928, when the Nanking government accepted Edwardes's appointment and the pledging of both the maritime customs and the salt gabelle against foreign loans.

Finally, with the agreement of Japan to China's tariff autonomy in 1930, Chinese nationalist aspiration in this respect at least seems to have been sated. The average tariff rate rose from 4 per cent before 1929 to 10 in 1930 and to 25 in 1934–7. This led to an increase in revenue and also in smuggling from Manchuria, Taiwan, Macao and Hong Kong. The revenue was now deposited in Chinese central banks instead of foreign ones so as to be at the disposal of the Nanking government, which undertook to repay all the outstanding foreign loans. True, a few Chinese were promoted to be commissioners and deputy commissioners in 1928–9, and more American-trained Chinese took over important posts in the maritime customs service from foreigners, but Britain retained the privilege of having one of her subjects as the Inspector-General, and the service itself remained international in character till 1938, when much of it was taken over by Japan.

The crucial importance of the maritime customs from the 1860s to the 1930s was due not only to the size of its revenue, but also its synarchical administration which warded off corruption and the interception of the revenue. The impersonal discipline of its administration was exemplary, but could hardly be imitated by the Chinese bureaucracy, riddled as it was with traditional particularism. The need to continue the synarchy after the recovery of tariff autonomy is a proof of this. The availability of this additional income to the government before 1895 was welcome for two major purposes: first, to deal with an international crisis such as the Japanese expedition against Taiwan in 1874, when China's additional defence needs had to be financed from this source of revenue; second, nearly all her defence industries established in the 1860s and 1870s drew much of their capital from the customs. The Kiangnan Arsenal, the Foochow Shipyard, the Tientsin Arsenal, the purchase of warships, and even the finance of Li Hung-chang's Huai Army resorted to the *yang-shui* (maritime customs). In the Taiwan crisis, Li Hung-chang saw the customs revenue and foreign loans secured by it as the only money available for China's self-strengthening or modernization.

China's dependence on this income, which came increasingly under the control of the foreign Inspector-General, the foreign banks and the diplomatic corps in Peking, explains the powerful position held by such a man as Sir Robert Hart and the importance of such institutions as the foreign banks in modern Chinese economy. The revenue itself, in turn, depended on her foreign trade. When the trade was threatened by the prospect of, for instance, a war against France in 1884, Li Hung-chang's chief anxiety was that there might be a drastic reduction of the revenue, and hence of China's ability to pay for the war. Those who saw this danger had been consistently against a tough foreign policy in 1884 and later.

To a considerable extent this explains China's unwillingness to fight an international war between 1900 and 1937, despite intolerable encroachments on her sovereignty.

The 5 per cent *ad valorem* tariff, the 2.5 per cent transit dues, and the surtax, low as they were, brought in a tax revenue upon which the Chinese government relied for the repayment of loans and the defraying of government expenses. But the rates debilitated the customs as a protective shield for China's infant, indigenous industries. The limited revenue from the maritime customs provided a minimum amount of capital for industrialization, but at the same time the low rates actually prevented industrialization from becoming endemic. Therefore, it was, at the same time, both a blessing and a curse.

### Industrial development: the growth of government-financed industries

The presence of Western military forces and merchandise was a challenge to which China was compelled to respond. In so doing, the decaying empire had to change its attitude towards modernization (the question of *feng-ch'i*), to accumulate capital in the absence of a modern money market, and to learn from the West not only science and technology but also business management and accounting. All this required strong leadership from the traditional elite which ruled alone and took the initiative in bringing in innovation, and which alone, in theory, had the far-sightedness and moral integrity to lead. That the first wave of China's modernization came after the suppression of the Taiping Rebellion was significant, for the suppression had been justified on the grounds of upholding the great Confucian tradition so that the polity and society could be consolidated against the threat from these insurgents inspired by Christianity. During the campaigns of suppression, regional leaders, e.g. Tseng Kuo-fan, Li Hung-chang and Tso Tsung-t'ang, played a deciding role and grew to crucial importance. It was they who knew China's military weaknesses; it was they who co-operated with foreign assistants in the campaigns; it was they who controlled local financial resources. Therefore it was they who were destined to lead the self-strengthening movement.

The leaders in the centre as well as in the regions were all men of high classical training, and hence firmly committed to the Confucian canons. Holding fast to this tradition, they stood in sharp contrast to the lower *samurai* engaged in promoting the modernization of Japan at about the same time. Again they were different from the *Junkers* of Germany and the liberals of Russia who were also leading the modernization of the countries. In the years of rehabilitation after the Anglo–French Expedition and the rebellions, to be faithful to the Confucian canons meant to restore the prosperity of the small farmers through the resettlement of the depopulated areas, and to encourage agricultural production through tax exemptions and by the government's refraining from competing with the people in profit-making.

This last consideration resulted in leaving industrial growth to regional initiative without an overall policy to curb the development of local interests; the commitment to restoring the prosperity of the small farmers resulted in the separation of agricultural surplus capital from these industrial projects, forcing them to rely on the only available funds – the newly instituted maritime customs service.

## The Foochow shipyard

To illustrate the success and failure of the first generation of the self-strengthening movement, the characteristics of which were that it aimed at maritime defence only, that it was under the control of the gentry and was dependent on government capital, especially the customs revenue, we shall choose the shipyard founded by the Viceroy of Chekiang and Fukien at Mawei near Foochow in 1866.

Tso Tsung-t'ang fostered an interest in ships and guns when he was in Huich'eng, Hunan, in 1854. Spurred on by the unpleasant experience of buying ships from England in 1862–3, known as the Osborn Flotilla Affair, Tso proposed to establish a shipyard for maritime defence and for the transfer of technological knowledge so that 'China will not be complacent about her lack of the skill [of ship-building]'. However, his proposal did not show a clearly conceived strategic plan. Assisted by two French colleagues, Giquel and d'Aiguebelle, in the days of the anti-Taiping campaigns, he optimistically estimated an initial outlay of 400000 *taels*, to be followed by an annual budget of 600000 *taels* for five years during which sixteen ships were to be built. The money was to come from the customs revenue of Fukien, Chekiang and Kwangtung, and to a lesser extent from the *likin*. In addition, the shipyard was to have a school for training students in foreign languages, navigation and manufacture. Unfortunately, neither Giquel nor d'Aiguebelle was well versed in shipping affairs; they were soldiers. The machines bought and foreign experts recruited by Giquel in France were becoming superseded by the introduction of iron and steel, for ship-building was making rapid progress.

Before production began Tso was sent to Kansu and Sinkiang to quell the Muslim rebellion, leaving the affairs of the shipyard to Shen Pao-chen, a man of great integrity and competence but also of firm traditional values. Shen believed that officials must rule and lead while the merchants and people should never be allowed to perform such functions.

Merchants are the people, who should not be trusted with any responsibility. Once they are so trusted, they will employ their relatives and friends, on whom neither punishment nor reward will have the slightest effect. They grumble and complain whenever their demands are not met.

The founders of the shipyard, and for that matter of all the other defence enterprises of the time, saw no need for a different ethos or different practice from those established by tradition in the bureaucracy.

Regarding the affairs of today, it is necessary to train the Chinese mind to understand foreign skills, but it is absolutely unnecessary to change the Chinese character by adopting foreign habits and customs.

The management of the shipyard was in the hands of members of the gentry – candidates for the bureaucracy and military officers – and of one Hu Kuang-yung, a compradore who had purchased his way into officialdom. In spite of Tso Tsung-t'ang's strong recommendation on the grounds of his fine mind and foreigners' trust, Hu commanded scant respect from his official colleagues and found it difficult to discharge his duties as the chief buyer and personnel manager. He was forced to have an official assistant. The combination of a compradore and an official presented a new problem to Shen Pao-chen: 'A merchant would cause more social problems than an official and an official would embezzle more money than a merchant!' Even with the backing of Tso Tsung-t'ang's prestige, Shen endured no end of trouble from the new Viceroy of Chekiang and Fukien, Wu T'ang.

After Shen's retirement from the shipyard in 1875, his successors, who were of lesser stature and lesser abilities, opened the door to over-staffing, absenteeism, nepotism and other irregularities. The management had no technical training and so were easily deceived by the specialists; when the ships that were built were found to be of poor quality and performance, the management resorted to its usual practice of shifting the blame to the foreigners, especially those who had gone back to France. Time and again the shipyard was instructed to cut down its redundant staff, but the problem seemed to be insoluble.

Another perennial hazard of the shipyard was lack of funds. Tso's original budget of 600000 *taels* a year for five years proved to be much too low, for it included neither the cost of maintaining the ships and machinery nor the expenses of the foreign staff's home leaves. The allocation from the Fukien customs office was seldom paid in full – for four months out of eighteen from 1874–5 the shipyard received nothing from the customs; before 1881 the normal practice was for the customs to pay only half of the annual amount due each year; and during eight months of 1883 only one month's payment was made. According to a report of the Tsungli Yamen in 1883, the Fukien customs and Rehabilitation Bureau owed the shipyard over 4 million *taels* since 1879. In spite of its insufficient income, the shipyard continued to struggle to fulfil its plan as long as it was still producing only wood and composite ships. The introduction of iron and steel ships after 1876, drastically increasing the shipyard's expenditure in capital outlay and hiring new foreign experts, led the enterprise into a financial impasse; the only solution was to reduce the number of ships constructed at the yard.

Production at the shipyard began in 1869, but by the end of 1871 only six ships of a total of 5315 tons had been launched. The end of Tso Tsung-t'ang's first quinquennium came in 1872, when the initial optimism and high expectations had turned into anxiety. A high official of the Grand Secretariat who was concurrently the vice-president of the Board of Rites, Sung Chin, fired the first shot at the policy of ship-building. Sung seriously doubted the efficiency of the Mawei ships in dealing with the foreign men-of-war in battle; if they were to be used only for patrolling the coast, it would be an appalling waste. To cut the losses, he proposed that the whole project be abandoned. Echoing this view the Viceroy of Kwangtung and Kuangsi, Jui-lin, suggested a reversion to the old policy of buying ships from abroad. What was most disturbing was an imperial edict issued on 7 April 1872, inquiring whether the types of ships built at Mawei, regardless of their costliness and the slow rate of production, were really any use for the maritime defence of the empire.

Springing to the defence of the shipyard, Tso Tsung-t'ang and Wen-yü (the Tartar General in Foochow) admitted that there was delay, but said that production was not too far behind the original schedule, and that there had been overspending, but not greatly in excess of the original budget. For the sake of China's maritime defence and national honour, Tso insisted, the shipyard must under no circumstances be closed down. Li Hung-chang shared these views, but also offered his own criticisms and solutions for the shipyard's problems. In his view the gunboats manufactured at Mawei were too small (these were generally between 500 and 600 tons) to be of combat value, and therefore larger and faster vessels should be built. To alleviate the financial stringency of the shipyard, Li suggested the building of merchant ships for profit and the opening of iron and coal mines in south China to reduce costs. With the supporting voices of such highly respected ministers as Tso and Li, the shipyard survived. From 1873 onward, its line of production switched to the building of more transports than warships, but Li's other suggestion, the opening of mines, was shelved.

From 1869 to 1902 Mawei built thirty-nine or forty ships. Shen Pao-chen, the first director, accomplished his task by producing sixteen ships before his retirement in 1875, at a total cost of nearly twice as much as the original estimate of 3 million *taels*. Thereafter, the rate of production slackened to eight in 1875–80, five in 1883–7, six in 1889–94, and five in 1897–1902. From the more complete statistics of the 1869–74 period, one can arrive at the cost of 350 *taels*,* or just under £120 per ton. The cost was high, and was made higher by the losses in the French, Japanese and Boxer Wars. By 1902, only fourteen (or it may have been twenty-one) Mawei ships were still in service.

The yard employed two foreign supervisors and seventy-five foreign technicians, teachers and medical staff, all of whom were well paid. Giquel himself drew an enormous salary of 96000 francs per month while a foreign workman received a wage ten times and a foreign foreman five times that of his Chinese equivalent. That is to say that in 1874, when a Chinese foreman was paid about 6s a day,

* A total of 15,932 tons was produced at a cost of 5356948 *taels*.

his French colleague received 30s. The total wage bill for the foreign staff was considerable, and as a consequence of the 1872 crisis some of the foreign employees were repatriated, leaving behind only fifty-one. The yard hired 1600 Chinese workers to begin with, and when the scale of production was enlarged the number increased to about 2000. Judging from the reports available, the management paid little attention to labour problems, except that the French- or English-speaking workers tended to bully those who had no foreign languages, and the different dialects spoken by the workers recruited from a province known for its linguistic diversity and mutual incomprehensibility of its dialects created a veritable tower of Babel.

In 1883 the yard had not built a single ship for at least two years; during that period many workers may have been dismissed by the then director Li Chao-t'ang. It was Li, a man of meagre abilities and strong bureaucratic habits, who decided to scale down the production of the yard. The riot which occurred in March 1883 may have been caused by the dismissals.

The yard took on some 300 students, all of whom were given generous stipends, under the supervision of the two Frenchmen, Giquel and d'Aiguibelle. In 1873 Shen Pao-chen tried out their skills in building and navigation. Shen's initial expectations proved to be too sanguine, as ten years later these students' performance came under heavy censure. Both production and navigation remained under the guidance of foreign technicians. As to the navy itself, its performance in the French and Japanese wars with the ships built at Mawei and elsewhere in China or bought from abroad was dismal. The mortgaging of the maritime customs drained away the funds needed for ship-building and ship purchasing. After 1895 China ceased even to aspire to become a naval power. By 1937 her few naval vessels, already thirty or forty years old, were obsolete and useless.

## The Hanyehp'ing foundry

The pioneer project at Mawei was daringly conceived and daringly put into practice with maritime defence as the sole aim, but there was no awareness of the need for supporting industries to make it work. Meanwhile other defence industries were being developed along the coast at Shanghai, Nanking and Tientsin, only to face similar economic problems – the need for coal and iron, transport

C.A.T.W.—M

and training of technical staff. Therefore by the beginning of the 1870s, the leaders of the self-strengthening movement came to understand what the economist calls 'the external economy' of an enterprise. In his letter to one of his assistants, Ting Jih-ch'ang, in 1872, Li Hung-chang argued for the necessity of developing railways and mining; in the following year, he gave his opinion that the strength of Japan lay in six key items: rifles, railways, coal mines, foreign books, foreign loans and coinage of currency. These external economies were what Li called '*fu*' (wealth) on the basis of which the nation could be strengthened. Such an understanding, shared by other self-strengtheners, was to become the guiding philosophy of China's industrialization strategy in the 1870s and 1880s, with the founding of the Merchants' Steamship Navigation Company in 1872, the K'aip'ing Coal Mines in 1877, the Tientsin Telegraph Office and Lanchow Woollen Textile Factory in 1880, the T'angshan-Hsikechuang Railway in 1881, and the Shanghai Cotton Textile Factory in 1882 as its main landmarks.

Carried away by this new trend of thought, Chang Chih-tung, the governor of Shansi, communicated with the Tsungli Yamen concerning the exploitation of iron deposits in his province in 1883. Persisting with this idea and aiming primarily at national defence capabilities, Chang evolved his three-point plan of iron and coal, armament and technical personnel – 'only a good technical staff can perfect weapons; only iron and coal mines can assure a plentiful supply of weapons; and only the mines and arsenals can make good use of the technical staff.'

The opening of the K'aip'ing mines for the Tientsin Arsenal and coal mines in Taiwan for Mawei had already clearly brought out the urgent need to improve both overland and waterway transport for the efficient delivery of the bulky fuel. C. W. Kinder, the British engineer at K'aip'ing, convinced his Chinese colleagues that the 'Rocket of China' which he had secretly built, and which ran at a speed of 20 mph, was far superior to the traditional coal cars pulled by mules. The seven-mile track constructed by Kinder in 1881 was the first railway China possessed then. At the same time, a famous general and protégé of Li Hung-chang, Liu Ming-ch'uan, was received in an audience by the Emperor at which Liu presented his plan for the building of a strategic railway either from the capital via Shantung to Ch'ingchiangp'u or from the capital via Honan to Hankow. In spite of Li Hung-chang's support, the opposition to railway construction remained strong enough to delay the implementation of Liu's plan.

Li Hung-chang's proposal to extend the rail transport system from the K'aip'ing mines to T'ungchou, south-east of Peking, touched off a discussion on the building of railways in 1888. The conservatives opposed Li on the grounds that the railway might be used by foreign missionaries and invaders for their own purposes, might displace the people engaged in traditional means of transport, and would certainly disturb the geomantic features along its route to the annoyance of the inhabitants. Chang Chih-tung, then Viceroy of Kwangtung and Kwangsi and about to be transferred to the viceroyalty of Hupei and Hunan, participated in the discussion, repudiating the conservative views but also differing from Li Hung-chang. His ambitious alternative was to lay a line from the Marco Polo Bridge on the outskirts of Peking to Hankow, a trunk line which promised both economic and strategic advantages. 'In no sense is this designed to compete with Western merchants for trivial profits in an unworthy manner.' But

coal and iron are said to be possibly the most lucrative minerals found in China and the best quality deposits are concentrated to the north of the T'aihang Mountains. But there transport is generally inconvenient, more so for such bulky and heavy goods as coal and iron. Assuming a railway is constructed there, the mining machinery can be sent to the mines and production can proceed according to Western methods. . . . The output would be a great help to us for reducing our need for imported coal and iron.

Chang had a personal interest in this project; the iron foundry planned during his term of office in Canton could be transplanted to Hankow to make rails for this trunk line. He was hoping that the money already sunk into the purchase of furnaces for the foundry could still be rescued, even though his successor at Canton refused to take over his over-ambitious project. The imperial authorization of both of Chang's plans did not exactly please Li Hung-chang, who bowed to the decision of the throne but refrained from giving any financial help out of the vast maritime customs funds under his control. In a private message to the Chinese Minister in Berlin, Li cuttingly remarked: 'His [Chang Chih-tung's] memorial is a model of exquisite writing which, however, can be regarded only as "utopian".'

Chang Chih-tung's iron foundry of 1890 illustrates the problems of the second generation of China's industrialization efforts. Like his predecessors, Chang also believed firmly in official initiative and leadership, even though the foundry was only partially intended to supply materials for defence. The unavailability of private capital for investment in such an ambitious project with little prospect of quick and attractive returns may have been a deciding factor in his belief that this should be an official enterprise, and this was also why, even at Canton, an important treaty port, he had to resort to the gambling tax to finance the purchase of the two Bessemer converters. At Hankow, a central China river port, he had the further hindrance of the *feng-ch'i* – the general attitude towards modernization – which was reluctant if not antagonistic. Now without financial aid from Li Hung-chang, Chang fell back on a subsidy from the central government (950000 *taels*) and local resources from the inland tariff and *likin* (50000 *taels*) for the first year. Relying on this same pattern of investment, he hoped to gather together some 2·5 million *taels* in two years so that the foundry could begin production in 1892 or 1893.

The transplant of the foundry to Hankow was technically a costly mistake. The iron ore found at Tayeh, some sixty-six miles down the river from Hankow, contained a high percentage of phosphorus and was therefore unsuitable for use in the Bessemer converters originally ordered for Canton. To add to Chang Chih-tung's difficulties, the coal mine at Maanshan could not be used for coking. Instead of placing the foundry where the ore was, Chang wanted it where he and other high officials at Wuch'ang could keep a close watch on it. Therefore it was situated in Hanyang, one of the three Wuhan cities, near the Yangtze river and on marshy ground. The land had to be drained before the foundations of the foundry could be laid. This, too, proved to be costly. Furthermore, the location required the iron ore and coal to be transported up and down the river, which increased the cost of production even more.

Now Chang Chih-tung needed a new furnace, a Siemens Martin for the available Tayeh ores, which was blown on 28 June 1894. In November shortage of capital and coal forced the foundry to suspend production, which was not resumed until the autumn of 1895. At that stage, the iron ore had to be carried by porters to the riverside, a distance of fifteen miles, and then pulled up the river to the foundry. Transport costs alone amounted to nearly 2 *taels* a ton, and it took four to five days to deliver the ores from the mines to the foundry. As for coke, this came from Germany and from K'aip'ing to the north-east of Peking. It cost over 13 *taels* a ton. In August 1895 the subsidy from the central government stopped. Under these circumstances Chang Chih-tung's iron proved to be too expensive and yet not good enough for making rails. The total expenditure mounted up to 5·8 million *taels* with nothing to show. Even the imperial court began to express its deep concern, asking Chang to make a reliable and factual report – 'In short, you should not waste money; nor should you be deceived. Only then will it [the foundry] be of practical benefit. You should try to understand our concern.'

Reluctantly Chang agreed to let this government enterprise be taken over by Sheng Hsuan-huai and be transformed into a commercial enterprise under official supervision in 1896. Sheng, a bureaucratic capitalist with extensive foreign contacts and considerable business experience, floated one million *taels* of shares to keep production at the foundry going under the condition that the rails for the projected railway from the Marco Polo Bridge to Hankow must be bought from the foundry, while for each ton of iron produced the foundry must pay 1 *tael* to the government in repayment of the official investment. Sheng also found suitable coal for coking at P'inghsiang in Hunan, some 300 miles south of the Yangtze, and floated another million *taels* of shares for exploiting the coal. The coke at P'inghsiang was cheaper than that from K'aip'ing, but the distance of ninety miles from the coal mines to the nearest river port had to be covered by a railway which was not completed until 1905, at a cost of 1·5 million *taels* borrowed from Germany. In the meantime, the Tayeh mines produced a total output of about 84000 tons of ore which could not be made into pig iron for lack of coal and coke. In an attempt to keep the enterprise afloat Sheng, entered into an agreement with the Yawata Iron and Steel Works of Japan to exchange Tayeh ores (at ¥3 and ¥2 for a ton of the first and second grade respectively) for Yawata coal and coke for a trial period of fifteen years. Further financial needs compelled the Hanyang Foundry to borrow more from Yawata in 1903. The amount borrowed was ¥3 million, at 6 per cent, to be repaid over thirty years in terms of 60000 tons of iron ore per year at ¥3 per ton. This meant that Hanyang could afford to pay only ¥180000 per annum, which cleared the annual interest but did not touch the principal. Over thirty years the total repayment would be ¥5·4 million, leaving

Hanyang with the same amount of debt as at the beginning. As time went on and debts piled up still more, and as further loans were obtained in 1908, 1910, 1911, 1912 and 1913, this gigantic industrial complex was practically reduced to being a mere supplier of raw materials, an adjunct of Yawata. Out of its estimated total output of 11 767 241 tons of iron ore processed from 1893 to 1934, 64 per cent was sent to the Japanese firm. In the meantime, the Penhsihu Iron Works under Japanese management could produce pig iron at Mexican $24.54 per ton against the Hanyang cost of Mexican $48.50, and the amounts of both iron and coal produced in southern Manchuria, also under Japanese management, out-stripped Hanyang and P'inghsiang.

In 1908 the three units – Hanyang Foundry, Tayeh Iron Mines, and P'inghsiang Coal Mines – were combined into the Hanyehp'ing Company, a private enterprise now employing some 10 000 workers, with a paid-up capital of $13 million and net assets of nearly $50 million. This structural change to free the company from government supervision was designed to attract private investment. None the less, official intervention never ceased. After the 1911 revolution, both Sun Yat-sen and Yuan Shih-k'ai attempted to nationalize it without success, and civil wars such as the Northern Expedition of 1926 forced all three departments of the company to suspend production.

Leaving aside the constant problems of an acute lack of capital and a lack of coal, the foundry during its initial period as a government enterprise had to endure endless bureaucratic harassment. The personal animosity between Chang Chih-tung and Weng T'ung-ho, the President of the Board of Revenue from 1886–98, was well known. This made sure that after the allocation of 2 million *taels* there would be no more subsidy from the central government. From the beginning of the project, Li Hung-chang had neither trusted Chang nor co-operated with him. When Chang was temporarily transferred to the viceroyalty of Nanking in 1894, his successor at Wuch'ang, T'an Chi-hsün, dismissed a large number of the managerial staff and manual workers, with the intention of closing down both the foundry and the iron mines. This bureaucratic infighting, coming after the humiliating and impoverishing defeat of 1895, only exacerbated the sufferings of the enterprise.

In the foundry itself, the overhead costs were enormous. The monthly outlay on management salaries was 70 000 *taels*, while the cost of buying coal was just over 10 000. The staff not only embezzled funds but also stole machines to equip privately owned factories belonging to the thieves themselves or to their friends. With such a poor record and such low morale in the works, it was no wonder that when private capital was needed for transforming the foundry into a private enterprise in 1896 and 1908, Sheng Hsuan-huai encountered a cool response from investors. He was forced to rely on short-term and foreign loans which led Hanyehp'ing along a disastrous path.

## Foreign concessions: the railways

*Railway construction 1895–1937 (in kilometres)*

| Years | Total length | Increase in each period | Annual increase |
|-------|--------------|-------------------------|-----------------|
| 1895–1911 | 9618·10 | 9253·83 | 544·34 |
| 1912–27 | 13 040·48 | 3422·38 | 213·89 |
| 1928–31 | 14 238·86 | 1198·38 | 299·60 |
| 1932–7 | 21 036·14 | 6797·28 | 1132·88 |

(Including Japanese constructions in Manchuria, see Yen Chung-p'ing, *T'ung-chi tzu-liao hsuan-chi*, Peking, 1955, p. 180)

In railway construction foreign dominance was evident. The percentage control of Chinese railways by Britain, Japan, Russia, France, the USA and other powers taken together increased steadily from 78 per cent in 1894 to 93 in 1911, 98 in 1927, and 91 in 1937, partly because the Chinese customs revenue was mortgaged after 1895 to pay foreign indemnities so that there was no fund available for building railways, and partly because Western financial capital was seeking profitable outlets. The 1895–1911 period was one of great activity in railway construction, coinciding with what Lord Salisbury called 'the battle of the concessions'. The capital-exporting countries struggled among themselves for concessions to build, to finance and sometimes even to control and manage railways in China. In a few cases concessions were granted but no railways were constructed. The most prominent example was the concession to the USA to build the Hankow–Canton Railway in 1898 which, in the years of the so-called 'rights recovery', became a target of Chinese nationalist aspirations. 'Rights recovery' was of course an empty slogan, an illusion. Of the thirty-two projected railways conceded to foreign companies and consortia, only the American rights to build the Hankow–Canton line were returned to China, at a cost of US$6 750 000. That was the year of the Chinese boycott against the US exclusion of Chinese immigration, at which time only the thirty-mile Canton–Sanshui section had been built. On the whole, the 'rights recovery' movement saw more railway rights conceded than regained by China. Another period of busy activity was 1932–7, in which the Japanese began their extension of the Manchurian (or Manchukuo) railways.

Most of the instances of concessions being granted and loans contracted while no railway was actually built occurred in the chaotic years between 1913 and 1922, when the government in Peking relied on foreign loans for survival. By 1928 the Ministry of Communications owed its foreign creditors a total of $590 million, much of which had been spent on purposes other than transport and communications. In that period there was hardly any noticeable difference between political and industrial loans.

China had the shortest mileage of railways in a given area and yet the locomotives, passenger coaches and freight cars were all under-utilized or unevenly utilized. As a result, the overhead costs were extremely high. Compared with the Japanese South Manchurian Railway, the Chinese railways reaped a low rate of profit – an average 7·4 per cent in 1916–36. Even this 7·4 per cent existed on paper only, as all the railways were treated by local military leaders in any way they wished. The Provisional Government of 1912 made a law that the presidential office, ministries, and provincial governors could issue certificates to soldiers and police allowing them to use the train service free of charge. This established practice persisted after 1922 in spite of the revocation of the law. Whenever there was a civil war, trains were requisitioned at will for the transport of troops and supplies; whenever the warlords needed money for military or personal use, they compelled the railway authorities to meet their needs. Some of the warlords simply took over control of sections of trunk lines and collected money from them. This anarchical situation did not come to an end until after 1928. Occasionally bandits harassed railway transport; the most famous case was the train robbery and kidnapping of the foreign passengers on board in May 1923, when a north-bound train on the Tientsin–P'uk'ow line was stopped by a thousand bandits at Linch'eng.

## Private enterprise

Indigenous private industries began to appear in 1872, but it was the peace treaty with Japan in 1895 which broke the official control or gentry leadership of China's modern industry through the depletion of government capital and the concession to foreign nationals of the right to set up manufacturing concerns at the treaty ports. In the year of the Hundred Days Reform, 1898, the emperor even issued an edict to encourage his subjects to establish their own factories. Freed from official supervision and on the bases of existing handicraft industries, privately run factories sprang up to compete with foreign firms in the rising tide of the post-1895 nationalism.

*Foreign control of mechanized industries in China (percentage of total output) 1936*

| | |
|---|---|
| Coal | 65·7 |
| Iron | 96·8 |
| Cotton yarn | 29 |
| Cotton cloth | 64 |
| Matches | 11 |
| Cigarettes | 58 |
| Electricity | 55 |

Source: Yen Chung-p'ing, *T'ung-chi tzu-liao hsuan-chi*, Peking, 1955, pp. 124–31.

These indigenous private enterprises proved to be more successful when on a small scale and engaged in light industries, with an already existing market, requiring a limited amount of investment, with a quick rate of turnover, and demanding relatively simple technical skills such as silk-reeling, food-processing, cotton-spinning, printing, etc. In the initial period of their development, they had to compete with foreign firms in China and foreign imports, with the further disadvantages of a shortage of capital and the absence of a modern money market. Their technical staff lacked sophistication, and managerial staff were unfamiliar with modern methods of rationalization and modern accounting. Even in the 1930s their technicians were still poorly trained; their foremen usually took no part in the productive work; their managerial personnel carried with them traditional attitudes and modes of operation; and their depreciation allowance was often insufficient to compensate for their careless treatment of capital goods. Hence, their production costs were generally higher than those of the foreign firms in China, and their profit rates were generally lower.

These inefficient infant industries obviously needed tariff protection, which they did not enjoy until after 1930. Their golden opportunity for expansion came during the European War when foreign competition, except that of Japan, withdrew temporarily from the China market. It was in that period that the indigenous textile, food-processing, silk-weaving, enamel-ware, glassware, toilet articles and other industries developed at a rate unknown before or afterwards. Take Jung Tsung-ching's cotton yarn and flour empire, for instance. The number of spindles increased more than fivefold from 1916 to 1920, and the productive capacity of its flour mills nearly seven times. Thereafter the rate of growth slowed down even in the early 1930s when it had the advantages of tariff protection and strong anti-Japanese feeling in China.

## The failure of industrialization

For seventy years, China's industrialization proceeded along a tortuous course at the end of which her mechanized industries accounted for less than 4 per cent of her total industrial output and her total industrial output for a mere 5·6 per cent of her gross national product. Compared with the other powers which started to industrialize in the same period, Japan and Russia, China's performance was deplorable. One can think of a host of reasons to explain this failure, but here we shall concentrate on four major ones: capital shortage, irrational management, foreign competition and the resilience of the traditional handicrafts.

*Investment and banking*

*Total foreign investment in China and capital outflow*
(*US$ million*)

|  | Total investment |  | Net capital outflow (annual average) |
|---|---|---|---|
| 1902 | 787·9 | 1902–13 | 22·3 |
| 1914 | 1610·3 | 1913–30 | 56·1 |
| 1931 | 3242·5 |  |  |
| 1936 | 3483·2 |  |  |

Source: C. F. Remer, *Foreign Investment in China*, NY, 1923, pp. 58 and 160.

As we have remarked before, the early industrialization of China depended primarily on the customs revenue for capital formation. But from 1895 onwards foreign investment made directly into foreign-owned businesses in China or indirectly through government loans* played an increasingly important role. The total foreign investment of US$3·5 billion up to the 1930s may give an impression that China had been a capital importing country. But C. F. Remer's careful study, the conclusions of which are widely accepted, has shown that, apart from a brief period from 1894 to 1901 during which China had a net inflow of capital of US$1·5 million, she was in fact a capital exporting country, if overseas Chinese remittances are not considered. The returns from direct foreign investment and the payments of the interest on and principal of the foreign loans were chiefly responsible for the outflow. Even then, Remer does not include the irregular repayments of the Boxer indemnity which amounted to US$14 million annually from 1902 to 1918. Thereafter they decreased to US$3·4 million in 1923 and 1924 and about 7·5 million yearly from 1925 to 1936. If these were included, China's export of capital would have been even greater.

Of the foreign loans, 60 per cent was spent on administrative and military requirements and on loan services, 34 per cent on railways, and only 6 per cent on manufacturing industries. The lion's share of direct investment went into exports and imports, banking and finance, transport and communications, real estate and public utilities at the treaty ports, and only 19·6 per cent into manufacturing industries. These industries failed to attract foreign investors for the same reason as they failed to attract the funds of Chinese landlords, pawn-brokers and rural money-lenders. The profit rates they offered compared unfavourably with the prevailing rates of interest, rent and commercial profit. Take the Tasheng Cotton Mill at Nant'ung, for instance. When it floated its first shares before production actually began, they bore a rate of dividend of 8 per cent while the market rates of interest ranged between 12 and 30.

Foreign investment in China stood at US$3·75 per capita of the Chinese population of 1931, of which less than 20 per cent was sunk in manufacturing industries. Its contribution to China's industrial growth was as meagre as was her industrial growth itself. To make this picture even more distressing, less than 2 per cent of China's

* Individual borrowing from abroad had always been negligible.

total investment in the 1930s was in the production of capital goods. In other words, this was hardly enough for the maintenance of existing equipment, let alone for capital accumulation.

During the first period of industrialization, between 1860 and the 1890s,

The *status quo ante* in land titles was restored, and land tax relief was directed primarily toward the relief of landlords. The right of the gentry to appeal to Peking against provincial and local officials was confirmed.

This was hardly surprising, since the agricultural policy of that period was based on Confucian principles, and one of its aims was to establish the tradition that agricultural development was not to be involved in capital formation for industrial growth. This, however, is not to say that foreign investment did not affect Chinese agriculture at all. On the contrary, there were direct investments by the Mitsui group in the growing of American long-staple cotton around Shihchiachuang in Hopei in 1916, and by the British–American Tobacco Company in the growing of Virginia tobacco in Shantung, Honan, Anhwei, Hupei and other places. Indirectly, the development of foreign trade and modern transport opened up rural China and linked it with international markets, thus influencing the marketability and prices of agricultural products. But on the whole, the subsistence agriculture, which was the mainstay of rural China's productivity, remained unaffected by foreign investment and played a negligible role in her industrialization. This experience, vastly different from that in Japan or Russia, resulted in a painfully slow rate of capital formation from domestic sources. The United Nations estimated that in 1931 China's net capital formation was a mere 2·7 per cent of her gross national income, i.e. about US$0·85 per capita. If we accept the hypothesis that from 1911 to 1937 China had a zero growth in her gross national product, hence that the average income per person before that date was slightly higher, but thereafter slightly lower, her capacity for capital formation might have been greater in the last decades of the Ch'ing dynasty and probably much smaller during the war against Japan from 1937 to 1945. This dire shortage of capital forced up rural rates of interest and land rents, making industrial investment singularly unattractive to landlords and village money-lenders.

We have more than once mentioned the absence of a modern money market in China. This of course was no longer true by the

Republican period. In response to the establishment of foreign banks in the treaty ports, e.g. the Shanghai branch of the Chartered Bank of India, Australia and China in 1857, the Hong Kong and Shanghai Banking Corporation in 1865, the Banque de L'Indo-Chine in 1875, etc., Chinese banks (*yin-hang*, a distinct from the traditional remittance houses and money-shops) began to appear from 1897 onwards. By 1937 there were 164 Chinese banks, including four central government banks, with 1627 branches in existence. Immediately after the First World War, Peking and Shanghai acquired their stock markets.

The foreign banks were founded to facilitate trade, hence the concentration in their hands of all international operations. From the beginning of the use of customs revenue, and later of the revenue from the salt gabelle, as security against foreign loans, until 1929, these banks acted as the depositories of the revenue from these sources. Their high reputation made them attractive to Chinese individual depositors too, but their operations were confined chiefly to foreign trade, foreign exchange, land speculation at the treaty ports and acting as the bankers of Chinese banks and money-shops. They did not actively mobilize Chinese floating capital for industrial investment.

The Chinese central banks, e.g. the Bank of the Board of Revenue, the precursor of the Bank of China, established in 1904, acted as the treasury of the central government. This tradition continued into the 1930s when Chiang Kai-shek controlled China, but by then there were four central banks: the Central Bank, the Bank of China, the Bank of Communications and the Bank of Agriculture. Their chief operation was to accept government bonds and treasury notes as reserves against the issue of paper currency. Even the Bank of Communications and Bank of Agriculture were no exception to this rule. They, too, had little to do with channelling floating capital to industrial or agricultural use. Take the Bank of China for instance. Apart from accepting government bonds and issuing bank notes, it played an important role in foreign exchange and land speculation. It accepted deposits from business enterprises and wealthy individuals (officials, military leaders and landowners) to be invested in government bonds, commerce and other banks. Industrial financing had never been its major function.

The same pattern of business operation was to be found in private Chinese banks which, instead of being agencies of the central

*Deposits and loans of the Bank of China (in percentages)*

| Deposits: | Industry and commerce | Government | Individuals |
|---|---|---|---|
| 1930 | 54·23 | 9·89 | 35·88 |
| 1931 | 33·29 | 0·25 | 58·64 |
| 1932 | 33·86 | 4·46 | 61·68 |
| 1936 | 30·73 | 7·14 | 62·13 |

| Loans: | Commerce | Industry | Government | Individuals | Banks |
|---|---|---|---|---|---|
| 1930 | 22·14 | 6·57 | 49·97 | 6.44 | 16·92 |
| 1931 | 21·79 | 10·14 | 48·27 | 4·78 | 15·02 |
| 1932 | 22·38 | 11·46 | 43·8 | 3·44 | 18·92 |

Source: Chang Yü-lan, *Chung-kuo yin-hang fa-chan shih*, Shanghai, 1957, pp. 71–3.

government, were associated either with political cliques, e.g. the Chin-ch'eng Bank of Shanghai, associated with the Political Study Group, or with local military forces, like the banks of Szechuan, Yunnan, Shansi and so on. They too invested in local government bonds, commerce and land. When they accepted the bonds of local governments, the nominal rate of interest was usually between 6 and 8 per cent, but they also imposed a discount sometimes of 40 per cent. They invariably preferred high interest rates and quick profits and because of this, secondary industries could never compete with trade, land speculation and public bonds for the banks' investment funds.

The traditional money-shops (*ch'ien-chuang*) issued money orders and promissory notes backed by the foreign banks in Shanghai; thus their credit before the First World War was even better than that of some modern Chinese banks. Their main functions included financing the sale of foreign goods in the interior of China and the purchase of Chinese goods on behalf of foreign exporters; they also acted as intermediaries through which foreign banks could lend money to Chinese borrowers. These operations inevitably involved the money-shops in rural financing and land speculation, and exposed them to great risks when the Depression came and when the American Silver Purchase Act of 1934 drastically reduced prices of imports, exports and land. Many of the money-shops went out of business or transformed themselves into modern banks in 1935.

It was then that the Bank of Agriculture came into existence, to fill the vacuum left by the money-shop bankruptcies and to finance the rural rehabilitation programme in the areas recovered from communist occupation. Through deposits and loans, the collection of savings and the financing of transport, the Bank hoped to 'return capital to the villages' so that the peasants would not be exploited by landlords, rich peasants and merchants whose lending accounted for 67·6 per cent of rural credit and was usually at a monthly rate of interest of 2–4 per cent. To fulfil this hope, the Bank would have had to lend money to peasants not merely for consumption but, more important, for production, and the rate of interest on its loans would have had to be low enough for the peasants to pay it from net income. Neither of these conditions proved realistic and as a result the Bank's operations, like those of any other bank, became concentrated in the cities and in speculation in public bonds. Agricultural loans took up no more than 3 per cent of its total assets, a mere $4 million.

Therefore, with or without the infrastructure of a modern money market, Chinese industrial growth continued to depend on a limited amount of foreign investment and bureaucratic and compradore capital, while Chinese agriculture, plainly the most important productive enterprise of the country, was not brought in to play a part in capital formation. Available capital for industrial investment being already small, its misuse for administration, warfare, commerce and excess consumption could only limit the scope and slow down the rate of China's industrialization.

## Management

The pioneer pattern of business management evolved during the incipient stage of China's modern industrial development was either government enterprise or private enterprise under government supervision. This was necessary because the enterprises needed government capital, a market guaranteed by the government and government protection, the last of which was of course against the government's own exactions. Even an enlightened official like Li Hung-chang used his authority to discourage the organization of private cotton mills and shipping lines in order to protect enterprises of the same kinds under his own auspices. In these enterprises, gentry and merchants worked together and their capital was merged, setting in motion two simultaneous processes – the bureaucratization of the merchants and the transformation of bureaucrats into capitalists. An inevitable question therefore arose: how was one to resolve the tension between bureaucratism and capitalism? Which of the two was to become the predominant ethos and *modus operandi* of these enterprises?

The power to appoint and dismiss the directors and managers of these enterprises was in the hands of regional government leaders; through the directors and managers the bureaucrats could also control the appointment and dismissal of the lower-ranking managerial staff and the technicians. In other words, selection, at least for management posts, was based not only on ability but on status. Their classical training and particularistic ties would be regarded as a guarantee of their integrity and their being able to mix and communicate with their gentry colleagues. Backed as they were by regional government leaders, there was no doubt that the bureaucrats in these enterprises had the upper hand over the merchants who, also suffering the additional disadvantage of being less articulate, tended to be browbeaten and overawed by their better educated colleagues. Chang Chih-tung could arbitrarily decide to scrap the plan for a privately owned textile factory under government supervision and turn it into a government concern while contemptuously refusing to refund the money paid for the shares already bought by investors. This was by no means the only example of its kind.

The bureaucratic preponderance determined the locations of enterprises of this type – Tso Tsung-t'ang's shipyard was near Foochow, Li Hung-chang's arsenal and textile factory were in Tientsin, Chang Chih-tung's foundry near Wuch'ang, etc. The stated reason, that placing these industries near the centres of administration enabled the regional leaders to keep a close watch on them, seems to be in contradiction with the insistence on official leadership, on the grounds that the officials with classical training were morally more upright. Shen Pao-chen's dilemma – 'A merchant would cause more social problems than an official and an official would embezzle more money than a merchant' – was a real one. But to determine industrial location on this consideration would sometimes lead to economic disaster. Tso Tsung-t'ang's woollen textile mill in Lanchow, where Tso set up his headquarters during his Muslim campaign, was a case in point. The place had no soft water for washing wool nor adequate facilities to transport the products to the markets. It became a white elephant like the Hanyang Foundry.

The bureaucrats who supervised these enterprises granted privileges to government offices. The Telegraphic Service of Tientsin, for instance, allowed Li Hung-chang's administration to send telegrams free of charge. Their total lack of technological training, even of common sense, could be alarming: the officials in the Board of Revenue were perplexed by the need for repairs and maintenance of ships manufactured at Mawei; and Sung Yun-tzu, who was in charge of industrial development in Szechuan, founded a *mei-yu* (coal-oil, kerosene) factory in Chungking, where he tried to squeeze oil out of coal. These people generally neglected to allow for the wear and tear on plant, and so made insufficient provision for depreciation, which led to decapitalization. The worst case of this again involves Chang Chih-tung, who bought machines for the cotton textile factory in Hupei but left them in Shanghai to rust. Because of their technological ignorance, these bureaucrats relied excessively on the judgement and advice of foreign technicians, to the extent that they were often fooled by these technicians.

With regard to technical matters, the merchants were not necessarily better informed, but their motives were more clearly defined. They sought profit; therefore they would not join officials in an enterprise unless a reasonable rate of profit was guaranteed. That was why the shares in the private enterprises under government supervision were more like bonds than shares and holding such shares was the same as lending money at a fixed rate of interest. The bureaucrats, on the other hand, were more concerned with the political and military significance of these enterprises than with their economic gains. For them and for the merchants, the only rational solution to the conflicting motivations and objects was either for the bureaucrats to become majority shareholders or for the shares to assume the nature of bonds. Otherwise, the merchants would much prefer to play an active role in their own private businesses without government supervision or to join forces with foreign partners.

The ethos and *modus operandi* of the enterprises under government supervision were not, unfortunately, confined to such business establishments. In varying degrees, they permeated all the other forms of business organization, for the merchants, lacking a culture of their own, accepted the values and norms of the gentry. Even in the private firms established late in the nineteenth or early in the present century there was a lack of organizational rationalization, functional specialization, and impersonal discipline. It is probably in this sense that the nascent bourgeoisie of China was weak. Their growth, like the growth of the enterprises under government supervision, was not meant to subvert the *ancien régime*. On the contrary, they themselves had accepted the ethos of the high value set on particularistic ties of that regime. They did not even have enough pluck to fight for legal protection of their interests.

When Chiang Kai-shek came to power the Chinese bourgeoisie was stronger, better informed and better trained. Under his regime, bureaucratic business organization took five different forms – full government management, joint management by government and private individuals, private management by officials, joint management by foreign and Chinese government agencies, and joint management by central and local governments. To harness these enterprises, Chiang's regime set up the four central banks, a central trust company, a central savings bank and the National Resources Commission. In the year before the Japanese war, the four central banks issued 78 per cent of all the notes in circulation, possessed 42 per cent of the total assets of all the Chinese banks and received 59 per cent of all the deposits. At the same time, the National Resources Commission controlled 10 per cent of the total industrial investment of the country. By these means, the government tried to exercise a more centralized control over finance, commerce and industry. It also reformed the *likin*, transforming it into the consolidated taxes on cigarettes, cotton yarn, matches, flour and cement, thus putting itself in a position to influence these important light industries also.

Under Chiang, bureaucratic capitalism developed to an extent never known before. As foreign-trained students were absorbed into this gigantic infrastructure, the new bureaucracy became more knowledgeable and more efficient than the old. None the less, they still maintained the traditional particularistic values and ties, for Chiang and the KMT under him were committed to their own kind of Confucian restoration. Government and party interference in all forms of enterprise did not always conform to the canons of capitalist rationality. Corruption, nepotism, favouritism and other irregularities were rife in most of them. Furthermore, the dividing lines between the government and the party and between the government and the military were often unclear. Cutting across the three power bases of the government, party and the military forces were the family ties of the Chiangs, Soongs, K'ungs, and Ch'ens – the four leading bureaucratic capitalist families of modern China.

Judging by Western or capitalist criteria, Chinese business management was particularistic and irrational, and the conclusion built into these Western criteria was that if China was to become a modern industrialized nation, she must give up this particularistic irrationality. There are, however, two arguments against this conviction which do not simultaneously require defence of the traditional values and norms of China which had been carried over into her industrial life. The first is that in small-scale and handicraft industries and in agricultural production, as they stood in the China of the 1930s, particularistic ties were of paramount importance. To suggest the replacement of this traditional particularism by bourgeois universalism was to ask for the disintegration of small-scale production. This was tantamount to industrializing the country at the cruel expense of destroying the small producers and small peasants, thus creating a virtually revolutionary situation. The second is that bourgeois universalism might be too weak *vis-à-vis* the Chinese tradition or totally unsuitable for Chinese economic development. In other words, bourgeois universalism may not be synonymous with the modernization of the industries of a country and to combat this deep-rooted tradition China might have needed a stronger ideology than rational scepticism. To put it another way, the Western ideas of technological progress and institutional reforms had been presented to the Chinese since the 1860s, but the old Chinese institutions were too rigid and the new institutions were too feeble to pursue them. One could justifiably blame the institutions and urge their transformation; one could equally justifiably blame the ideas for being too weak or too outlandish for China to adopt.

The conflict between institutional hindrances and technological progress was nothing new; nor was it peculiarly Chinese. When the hindrances proved to be too deeply entrenched to be shaken by new ideas, the logical solution was to seek even stronger ideas instead of merely lamenting the hindrances. It was at this point that the Chinese turned to the Marxist theory of productive relations shackling the growth of productive forces. It was here that they radicalized themselves. In the process of radicalization, they found their own methods of business management which turned out to be neither traditional and particularistic nor bourgeois and universalistic. But the conservatives of the second half of the nineteenth century and the 1920s and 1930s paradoxically yearned for national power and wealth while still clinging to tradition. They brought the tradition into the enterprises in an attempt to tame technological innovations so that the innovations would not be subversive. In doing so, they defeated their own purpose.

*Foreign competition*

The heavy industries – ship-building and shipping, coal and iron, and defence industries – introduced in the 1860s and 1870s did not, on the whole, stand up successfully against foreign competition. The Merchants' Steamship Navigation Company, for example, failed even to compete against the British and Japanese firms in inland waterway and coastal services.

Even in light industries like cotton textiles, China's performance *vis-à-vis* foreign competition was highly unsatisfactory. Nine years after the first machine cotton mill in Shanghai began production, the south and central China markets were monopolized by Indian yarn and the north and north-east China markets by Japanese. This situation continued till the outbreak of the First World War, causing China to lose 50 per cent of her cotton yarn production. Spurred on by the 1895 war, which freed Chinese private industry from the bureaucratic stranglehold, and then by the First World War, during which European, chiefly British competition withdrew, China's cotton textile industry made a great leap forward in spite of growing Japanese imports. Its spindles and looms increased in number; so did its share of the domestic market. But from 1921 onward, Japanese competition took the form of direct investment in setting up new Japanese factories and in buying shares of Chinese-owned mills, resulting in Japanese domination of cotton yarn production.

In 1887 a bale of native cotton yarn sold at Newchuang, Shantung, for 87 *taels* of silver while a bale of foreign yarn only cost 57 *taels*. This price differential gave Indian and Japanese cotton goods a chance to penetrate the Chinese market. In the 1920s, a bale of yarn cost the Chinese producer 43·70 *yuan* while it cost the Japanese producer in China only 20·40 *yuan*. As long as the market conditions were good and prices were favourable, the Chinese producer could hold his own. But when there was a down-swing in the market, he would be in serious jeopardy. In addition to the higher cost of production, the Chinese producer was normally more heavily taxed. Before the recovery of tariff autonomy, the infant Chinese industry had enjoyed no protection. Even after that, the consolidated taxes instituted by Chiang Kai-shek's government had a bias in favour of fine quality yarn, produced chiefly by the Japanese, at 2·41 per cent *ad valorem* against 4·27 per cent on the coarser yarn made mostly by the Chinese. Shortage of capital often deprived the Chinese producer of the opportunity of stockpiling raw materials when they were cheap; it also made it more difficult for him to equip his factory with newer and more modern machines. All these factors together with poor management and the lower productivity of his workers contributed to his lack of competitiveness *vis-à-vis* the foreigner.

There were also circumstances beyond the control of the Chinese producer which crippled productivity and hence the competitiveness of his product. From the founding of the Republic onwards, civil wars frequently disrupted production and transport. Even after Chiang Kai-shek's accession to power, disorders continued, and Chiang's economic policies solved none of the basic problems of industry and agriculture. His Ten Year Reconstruction Plan announced at Geneva in August 1931, with its hopes pinned on the League of Nations for capital, technology, and even institutiona control, came to nothing. It was, for one thing, doubtful whether the League had such resources, and, for another, within a month of the submission of the plan, the Japanese occupied Manchuria.

The opening of China gradually incorporated that ancient country into the world economic system, and thus made it subject to the influence of world economic fluctuations. Being of negligible significance as a trading nation, she had never been in a position to turn an international situation to her own advantage. The European war, it was true, benefited her industries. However, this very fact established what could happen to modern Chinese industries once foreign competition was removed. It was foreign competition which depressed China's tea and silk production. Both their commercialization and decommercialization as international commodities were the work of foreigners and in this process of change the livelihood of millions of Chinese was affected. Changes in fashion and the invention and marketing of substitutes in the West punctuated the

vicissitudes of Chinese producers of straw braids, bristles, *t'ung* oil,
etc. When the Depression came, China was at first benefited by the
fact that the world silver price dropped faster than the average level
of prices and so her general level of prices measured in silver showed
an increase. Then the major powers left the gold standard in 1931
and the American Silver Purchase Act was adopted in 1934.

At the end of 1932 the price of silver stood at US$0·25 per oz. In
order to save the silver industry in the USA Roosevelt raised the
price to US$0·64½ per oz at the end of 1933. Then the Silver Pur-
chase Act of 19 June 1934 caused an outflow of silver from China
to the tune of some US$100 million. Inside China, the price level
fell sharply; outside China, the rapid rise in the value of her currency
drastically reduced her exports of primary goods. The Act brought
the Depression with all its violent consequences home to China.
But the USA hesitated to help China out of her predicament, for
fear of offending Japan. The British initiative, the first major one
since the 1920s, to rescue China by sending a financial mission under
Sir Frederick Leith-Ross, resulted in the transfer of the Chinese
monetary system on to a foreign exchange standard with British
backing. The currency reform of 1935 did contribute to China's
industrial recovery and monetary unity. Other powers followed
Britain's lead.

*China in the Depression (million yuan)*

|                  | *1931* | *1932* | *1933* | *1934* | *1935* | *1936* |
|------------------|--------|--------|--------|--------|--------|--------|
| National income  | 24871  | 23822  | 20417  | 19443  | 21102  | 26758  |
| Investment       | 698    | 808    | −24    | −617   | −573   | 1472   |

Source: United Nations, *National Income Statistics*, 1948.

Although by 1936 China had made an impressive industrial recovery,
her national income showed no noticeable increase compared with
1931. If investment in 1936 is deducted from the national income,
her standard of living indicated almost no improvement. In the
agricultural sector, the picture was even more chilling. There, the
total product in 1934 was a mere 54 per cent of that of 1931.

*Handicrafts*

Under the double pressure of imports and the mechanized native industries of consumer goods. Chinese handicrafts are said by some economic historians to have declined, and by others to have shown a splendid resilience. A. Feuerwerker writes:

Anyone who would claim that the Hunan or Szechuan peasant in the 1930s dressed in Naigaiwata cottons, smoked BAT [British-American Tobacco Company] cigarettes, and used Meiji sugar has a big case to prove. In 1933, the output of handicrafts accounted for an estimated 68 per cent of the total value of industrial output . . . and *a fortiori* that handicrafts industry as a whole was not seriously undermined between 1870 and 1911.

What Feuerwerker means is that from the 1870s, when mechanized civilian industries emerged in China, until the outbreak of the Sino–Japanese War in 1937, handicrafts as a whole stood up against their mechanized competitors and held their ground. On the other hand,

*Modern and traditional industries 1933*

|               | Modern  | Traditional |
|---------------|---------|-------------|
| Manufacturing | 28·24%  | 72·76%      |
| Shipping      | 14      | 86          |
| Exports       | 23      | 77          |
| Coal          | 78      | 22          |
| Pig iron      | 82      | 18          |
| Banking       | 66      | 34          |

Source: Hou Chi-ming, *Foreign Investment and Economic Development in China*, Cambridge, Mass., 1965, p. 166.

Hou Chi-ming's statistics show that in heavy industries and finance the traditional sector had been in retreat, giving ground to modern competitors. Our chief concern here must be with cotton-spinning and weaving which, together with farming, formed the very foundation of China's rural economy. The disintegration of this foundation meant a loss of livelihood, or, at least, impoverishment of the peasants.

At first, Lancashire cottons made inroads into the Chinese markets around the treaty ports, but the fine shirtings and sheetings did not meet the peasants' demand for thick, coarse, and durable clothing material. The turning point in the competition between imports and handicrafts came during the American Civil War when the demand for Chinese raw cotton abroad suddenly increased, thus raising its price and also the price of homespun. This was followed by the expansion of Indian and Japanese production of coarse yarn at a steadily decreasing cost. Both its quality and price suited the taste of the peasants and their hand-operated looms, and therefore the coarse foreign yarn began to replace native spun yarn, first as the warp only and then as the woof also. Economically this change meant the commercialization of handicraft weaving, for the imported yarn had to be paid for by woven cloth, and the separation of spinning from weaving. At this stage of development, say, since the 1890s, the penetration of foreign yarn into the Chinese market was no longer restricted to the environs of the treaty ports, but went deep into the interior of the country. With the machine-spun yarn from Chinese mills, which became a considerable competitive force, home-spun yarn lost more ground, while hand-loomed cloth continued to show resilience. Even in the 1930s, the latter still represented up to 61 per cent of all the cotton cloth produced in the country.

In other handicraft industries, more markets were lost to machine-made substitutes; kerosene replaced vegetable oil for lighting, the modern printing press replaced wood blocks, matches replaced flints, and toilet soaps, dye-stuff, and a host of other machine-made commodities invaded the market. Judging by Hou Chi-ming's figure of 28·24 per cent as the share of modern manufacturing industries in the Chinese market, the rural marketing system yielded more than 10 per cent to the modern trading system. The cumbersome traditional transport probably served as a shield to protect the rural handicraft industries.

Earlier on we argued that the cost of production, say, of Chinese yarn was higher than that of yarn produced in a Japanese factory in China. This applied to some handicraft industries also. Part of the cost was of course the rate of interest borne by the producer. The small handicraft producers in the villages bore an usurious rate of interest which lessened their competitiveness.

No one is sure whether in absolute terms the traditional sector of Chinese industry declined or maintained its position against the competition of machine-made goods. Assuming that the secular trend of the gross national product of China from 1911 to 1949 was of zero growth, then *a fortiori* the relative decline of Chinese handicraft industries, which is generally accepted as a fact, must mean that there was an absolute decline also. Furthermore, the resilience of handicrafts was not necessarily a good thing for China: the tougher the handicrafts, the slower the industrialization. At the very bottom of this toughness lies the basic desire for survival. The peasants had to make as much use as they could of the labour power in their families for productive purposes, and to buy as little as possible in order to make ends meet. To industrialize at the expense of this type of subsistence economy in the twentieth century could be justified only if a complicated system was constructed to safeguard the interests of the peasants, out of humanitarian considerations. Alternatively, China's rural economy had to be modernized at the same time, either under the leadership of the elite or by the efforts of the peasants themselves. None of these solutions could be hoped for while China remained largely under the control of the military and the gentry, that is, until the downfall of Chiang Kai-shek.

## The benefits of imperial economic penetration

If the foregoing analysis can be accepted, China's economic modernization was hampered by a lack of capital, a lack of rational institutional breakthrough and by foreign competition. The removal of these obstacles required a change of attitude, or a change in economic culture, and the recovery of national integrity. For these reasons economic change had of necessity to be closely connected with the political and cultural changes which are discussed elsewhere in this volume. Few now believe that China's traditional attitudes and institutions were defensible. The problem at issue is whether imperialist economic penetration had yielded, on balance, benevolent or malevolent results in that country.

When the economic penetration was left to individual citizens of the Western countries, and when their governments undertook to protect their economic interests, imperialism could not possibly be intentionally beneficent. After all, the individuals who were willing to take the risks involved in trading with or investing in that distant country sought profit, a higher rate of profit compared with other opportunities, not the fulfilment of a humanitarian mission or the amelioration of the standard of living of the Chinese. By the 1930s, their predominant position in China's heavy industries, banking, foreign trade, transport and some light industries betokened that the trade and investments had been highly profitable, and this profitability was guaranteed by such institutional arrangements as the treaty port system, the synarchical control of major sources of government revenue, consortia of banks, etc. In quantitative terms, the results of these informal imperialist arrangements were shown in China's continuous trade deficit and continuous export of capital. But imperialism in China did not stop at informal arrangements; it also forced China to make territorial concessions, particularly to Russia and Japan.

It has been argued that since the 1860s modern Chinese industries had been growing steadily and not sporadically, and that this proves the beneficial impact on China of foreign economic contact. China's pig iron output increased at the rate of 9·8 per cent *per annum* from 1900 to 1937; her coal at 8·2 per cent *per annum* from 1912 to 1936; her cotton yarn spindles at 11·6 per cent *per annum* from 1890 to 1936. By looking at the long-term growth rate we naturally eliminate or assume away short-term fluctuations such as those caused by the First World War and the Depression. But the effect of the war is a good example of how the absence of foreign competition could encourage indigenous industries and trade to grow at a much faster rate, just as the effect of the Depression proves how disastrous foreign competition and other forms of foreign economic entanglement were to the Chinese economy.

It has also been argued that the imperialist economic presence hastened a change of attitude towards the defence and economic life of the country, imparted modern knowledge to the Chinese workers, specialists and capitalists, and started a series of linkage or multiplier effects which spread from banking and railways to other industries. Leaving aside the linkage effects which were negligible anyway, this is essentially a culturalist apologia for imperialism. As it is couched, it ignores, first, the economic and political losses which China suffered in acquiring a new economic culture, and second, the efforts of the people, students, scholars, missionaries, *et al.*, whose task it was to import that culture into China. In the light of the Japanese experience, so different from that of China, one might conclude that such a culture could have been acquired without the accompaniment of such heavy losses if China had had a leadership like that of Meiji Japan.

The fact that China did not possess a leadership of a comparable calibre to that of Japan raises another set of questions. Was the new culture palatable to the Chinese elite? Was it strong enough to change its attitudes? Would the new culture, if accepted in toto, have ensured the successful industrialization of China as it had in Japan? What would China have been, had she succeeded as Japan did? Would the world have been capable of accommodating another East Asian imperialist power, nearly twenty-five times the size of Japan? The answers to the first two questions are obviously negative. The tenacity of the Chinese tradition was the proof of the weakness of the Western economic culture. The answers to the last two questions are too abhorrent to contemplate. The Chinese tradition was too deeply rooted to allow the acceptance of the Western model in toto which would have enabled China to industrialize herself as successfully as Japan. In the actual event, the tortuous and arduous road of Chinese economic modernization was too costly and its results too shamefully meagre. China had to look for another model, another method, in order to transform herself into a modern economic entity.

What we have been arguing against may be described as economic modernization from above, depending on the initiative of the elite. After the suppression of the great rebellions of the 1850–75 period, the pressure on the elite came from the imperialists, not from the people below. Under such circumstances, the elite was inclined to co-operate with the stronger pressure group through a process of identifying its own interests with those of the imperialists. This was all the more so as the government in Peking or Nanking depended on the maritime customs, foreign loans and foreign backing for the monetary stability which enabled it to mobilize national resources for administration, military campaigns and economic control. But when mass nationalism began to gain momentum, the elite found itself sandwiched between two active pressure groups, for the mass nationalism of the 1919 vintage was decidedly anti-imperialist.

# Chapter 8

# *Society*

## Emancipation of women

The missionaries were the first to draw Chinese attention to the irrational, traditional ways in which men treated women. Polygyny, infanticide, foot-binding and the exclusion of women from education all came under attack from the churches. Under such severe strictures, a handful of enlightened Chinese began to rethink their attitude to women. The *Shen-pao* of Shanghai published an editorial on 9 August 1878, which said:

The social intercourse between Western men and women seems to be less strict [than ours], but their methods of preventing immorality compare favourably with our way of confining women in their chambers so that they are not even seen by their close relatives. A slight relaxation of this sequestration usually ends in vile scandals and for this our over-emphasis on propriety (*li*) is to be blamed. The West allows men and women to take part in social functions with ease and freedom. Paradoxically elopment and adultery among them are few and far between.

Even the Chinese elite came to be aware of this serious social problem. The Chinese delegate at the Philadelphia Exhibition of 1876, Li Kuei, was awed by the women workers of that city. 'Women are as intelligent and sometimes even more so than men. . . . Therefore the Westerner is just as pleased to have a daughter as to have a son.' This observation caused Li to consider the possibility of reforming such attitudes as the idea that 'ignorance is a feminine virtue' and putting an end to such practices as female infanticide. The Chinese Minister to the USA, Ts'ui Kuo-yin, had no answer to Americans who asked him why Chinese women did not possess even the most basic human rights and why they were subject to inhuman male domination.

These scattered efforts and revelations did not gather into a strong enough force to change the tradition; it required the shattering defeat of China by Japan in 1895 to bring women and youth on to the agenda of social and political reform. Chinese youth broke their silence by urging political changes in their petitions of 1895 and a leading reformer, K'ang Yu-wei, audaciously sent a memorandum to the throne in June 1898:

In our country, houses are shacks and clothes are rags. In addition, our air is polluted by the smoke of opium and our streets are lined with beggars. For some time now, foreigners have taken photographs to circulate among themselves and to laugh at our barbaric ways. But the most appalling and the most humiliating is the binding of women's feet. For that, your servant feels deeply ashamed.

Shame served as the spur for reforms in the attitudes towards and treatment of upper-class urban women, proposed by upper-class urban and enlightened men. The women of the lower orders of society, who were to remain ignorant and to suffer foot-binding and ill-treatment for many more years than their sisters in the cities, showed a remarkable activism in the Boxer Uprising. While women of gentle birth fled from or submitted to the invading foreign marines, the organized lower-class women, the Red Lanterns of Boxer girls and the Blue Lanterns of Boxer widows, resisted the invasion and spread the influence of the movement.

When the dust of 1900 had settled a Women's Conference was held in Shanghai with the home life of Chinese women as its theme. Nearly all the speakers were foreigners with church connections and among their subjects of discussion were family life, prostitution and, of course, foot-binding. 'We are here not to criticize; we are here as students to collect facts about the social and home life of the people we want to help, only as sociologists.' Help naturally implied criticism and action; thus the professed scholarly objectivity contained an element of emotional involvement, an urge to ameliorate the fate of Chinese women. It was for the same purpose that Young J. Allen published his *Women in All Lands or China's Place Among the Nations* (Ch'uan-ti wu-ta-chou nu-su t'ung-k'ao) in 1903. Allen's effort was part and parcel of the churches' work right from the beginning of proselytization in China. However, he was daring enough to attack the Emperor as the man who led in the practice of concubinage and to say that the ladies of the Imperial Household were probably the worst treated anywhere.

On the opposing side, an edict prohibiting foot-binding was issued on 10 February 1902 and in response to this regular meetings for the liberation of women's feet were instituted in Soochow on 2 July 1905. However, the more radical thinkers went further than the mere physical emancipation of women's feet. Since they denied sexual differences in intelligence and moral sentiments they advocated equal economic, political and educational rights for women.

The 1900s saw two trains of thought on this question: the silence of the majority of the gentry rulers did not in any sense suggest that the position of the conservatives was weak; while the more vocal radicals urged for a reform of the family system and equal rights for women. The girl revolutionary Ch'iu Chin, who planned an armed uprising and was arrested and executed, was an exception in a society where change went no further than from the attitude that 'female ignorance is female virtue' to an admiration for good mothers and good wives who would encourage their sons and husbands to promote social progress. Unmarried girls came out of their secluded chambers and began going to school. On the eve of the 1911 Revolution the new elite in power had to contend with and weigh the claims of the stronger but silent and the weaker but more vocal elements.

In the course of the revolution several contingents of armed female troops were organized in Shanghai, Nanking, Chekiang, Wuhan and other places, fighting for women's rights such as the right to marry whom they chose, participation in public activities, and equal opportunity in education as well as the chance to play an equal role in politics. Both the Women's Political Participation Alliance in Nanking and the daily paper, *Women's Rights* (Nü-ch'uan), of Ch'-angsha were short-lived. They failed to win suffrage for women, as the Provisional Constitution of 1912 granted the right to vote and to be elected to men only. During the period of Yuan Shih-k'ai's reaction, women were denied the right to own property; they were bound by law to declare their husband's residence as their own residence; they were also deprived of the right to join any political association according to the Police Regulations, Articles 8 and 12. An Act promulgated in October 1917 stated that only good wives, kind mothers, chaste widows and fiancées who refused to enter into another matrimonial arrangement, and women who committed suicide after being raped would be given a citation as a reward for their virtuous conduct. The revised Act governing the practice of law in October 1916 excluded women from joining that profession.

In spite of the scholarly opinion in favour of equal rights for women, the chaos of the warlords' rule from 1916 to 1928, like that in Japan in the sixteenth century, witnessed a general deterioration of the position of women except in the sanctuaries of the cities, where the educational institutions and the churches spread a cloak of protection over them. Yet the scholarly opinions expressed in the May 4th Movement in 1919 had an impact on the movement for provincial constitutions early in the 1920s. There then emerged for a short period of time, another wave of demands that women's rights should be incorporated in these constitutions. In addition to suffrage, women now asked for property rights and economic independence. In the province of Hunan, where the constitutional movement was the strongest, not only did the constitution itself give women the right to vote and to be elected to public office, but a few women actually were chosen for the provincial council. However, the 1923 constitution, like all its predecessors, granted no rights to women.

The scholarly opinion expressed in the May 4th Movement also made its impact on the KMT when the party was reorganized in 1923–4. The inauguration of a women's department at its centre, besides other departments dealing with mass movements, showed the party's positive support for women's political and social demands. The activists in this department were KMT leftists and women communists trained in France, e.g. Madame Sun Yat-sen, Ho Hsiang-ning, Hsiang Ching-yü and Ts'ai Ch'ang. The second congress of the KMT resolved to establish not only women's political rights but also their economic rights, including the right to inherit property. But the women's associations set up in this period of KMT–CCP coalition were to be disbanded when the coalition split.

In Peking, the situation at the Women's Teachers Training College had been explosive for nearly a year before the arrival of foreign gunboats at Taku, the port of Tientsin, to bombard the garrison troops on 12 March 1926. Six days later Peking students demonstrated against the incident in front of the Provisional Government building only to be mowed down by the guard's guns.

Forty-seven were killed and 150 more wounded. Students from the Women's Teachers Training College took part in the demonstration; two girl students lost their lives and one was severely wounded. Lu Hsün, the celebrated writer, who was one of their teachers, wrote:

. . . a bullet hit [Miss Liu Ho-chen's] back and wounded her in the heart and lungs. The wounds were fatal, but she did not die instantly. Another girl, Miss Chang Ching-shu, rushed to help her up, but was shot four times. One of the bullets came from a pistol and Miss Chang fell. Yet another girl, Miss Yang Teh-ch'un, went to help her; she too was hit in the left shoulder and the bullet pierced the right side of her chest. Miss Yang also fell, pulled herself up, and was struck twice by a soldier with a wooden stick. Then she died.

Their teacher preserved the memory of the smiling faces of the three girls, their determination to fight for their country, and their courage in aiding each other 'in the forests of guns and showers of bullets'. Lu Hsün continued:

Since last year I have been watching how Chinese women handle public affairs. Although there are only a few of them, their competence, resolution, and undaunted spirit have impressed me more than once. And this time, the fact of their helping each other regardless of their own safety in a shower of bullets has proved, beyond any doubt, their bravery which, after thousands of years of oppression and suppression by schemes and conspiracies, continues to live. If we are seeking a meaning for the future in these deaths and injuries, this is probably where the meaning lies.

This was on the eve of Chiang Kai-shek's unification of China. Up to that moment, modern Chinese women's struggle for their emancipation had shown two separate strands of development: one under the influence of Western feminism which was limited to family reform, women's education and women's welfare; the other, a militancy and a political involvement which tended to combine feminine problems with the general political problems of the country. In the former tradition were a number of women doctors, educationists, and social welfare workers; in the latter, Ch'iu Chin, Liu Ho-chen, and others.

Of the intellectuals who took part in the May 4th Movement and its aftermath, the gradualists put their emphasis on education, through which Chinese women might achieve equality some day in the future. This was essentially John Dewey's view contained in one of the lectures he gave in China. Beyond that, opinions diverged.

Hu Shih, the liberal scholar, thought Chinese women should go further than merely being 'good wives and kind mothers' and acquire a measure of the 'self-reliance' of American women. But Hsü Chih-mo, the Anglophile poet, was much less sanguine about the future of women's liberation in China. Taking England as a model, Hsü argued:

China is backward in every respect, including women's liberation. They [England] liberate their minds first; we begin from our bodies – our feet, our chests. It will take us three or four generations to achieve just that and it will take much, much longer to achieve anything else.

Hsü wanted every Chinese woman to become truly liberated like, say, Katherine Mansfield. But then, 'have women [in China] really been suppressed?' Lin Yutang asked:

I often wonder. The powerful figure of the Empress Dowager immediately comes to mind. Chinese women are not the type to be easily suppressed ... Women have ruled ... at the [*sic*] home. ... And what is still more important, women have been deprived of every right, but they have never been deprived of the right to marry. ...

The more one knows Chinese life, the more one realizes that the so-called suppression of women is an Occidental criticism that somehow is not borne out by a closer knowledge of Chinese life. ... The only ... possibility is that daughters-in-law may be oppressed by the mothers-in-law and this is often what actually happens.

For Lin, if one took a relativist view and sprinkled life with a bit of spicy humour, the so-called suppression of women simply disappeared.

But others, e.g. Ch'en Tu-hsiu, Li Ta-chao, Chou Tso-jen, and Lu Hsün, took the problems of women's liberation seriously. Ch'en's essays in 1916 exhorted women to shake themselves free from male domination so that they might regain their 'independent and self-reliant personality'. His call for respect for women's rights in the *New Youth*, 1 December 1919, was echoed in a series of articles written by Mao Tse-tung regarding the suicide of a girl in her bridal sedan-chair. As if to answer Hsü Chih-mo's argument about ten years before it was written, Li Ta-Chao reminded his readers that what the English suffragettes wanted represented the demands of middle-class women. They had nothing to do with the wishes of the poor, proletarian women. 'One group aspired to rule others; the other merely asked to liberate themselves from poverty.' Therefore the advancement of the rights of middle-class women could not be identified with women's liberation. In Li's view 'we must unite with all women to destroy the social system under male domination and at the same time unite with the proletarian women of the whole world to destroy the system of male and female bourgeois domination.' After the killing of girl students in Peking in March 1926 even the moderate classicist and essayist, Chou Tso-jen, came to the same conclusion as Li Tao-chao.

What steps towards women's liberation did the May 4th Movement achieve? An article in the periodical *Yü-ssu* (IV:19, p. 34) answered succinctly and sarcastically: 'The flower pots have been transferred from ladies' chambers to offices.' Lu Hsün made the same observation when he wrote in 1933:

Now some ladies can stand side by side with well-off gentlemen to have their photographs taken on the quay or at a conference, or to step forward to smash a wine bottle before a ship or a plane is launched. . . . Then there are all sorts of jobs [for them]. . . . On the one hand, they are nicknamed 'flower vases'; on the other, there are the glorious advertisements – 'You will be looked after by women only'.

For ten years Lu Hsün had been consistent in his advocacy of women's liberation and the kernel of his argument lay in economic equality between the sexes. Without that, women could not achieve their goals either at home or in society, for freedom could be sold for money even if it could not be bought with money. In a speech delivered at the Peking Women's Teachers Training College under the title, 'What Happened to Nora after Her Departure from Home?' in 1923, he concluded: 'I know that you need to struggle more and perhaps more ferociously than just for your right to participate in politics.' In an article under the title, 'On the Emancipation of Women', in 1933, he concluded: 'Without the same economic rights as men, I think all the enticing names and titles are just so many empty words. . . . Before true emancipation there must be struggle.'

Neither gradualist nor militant feminism would allow the government of Chiang Kai-shek to deny equal rights to women any longer when the new penal and civil codes came to be compiled. Both the penal code which came into force on 1 July 1928 and the civil code which was promulgated on 24 January 1931 recognized sexual equality. Even so, Article 256 of the Penal Code said: 'A married woman who commits adultery shall be sentenced to imprisonment for up to two years and the co-respondent shall be similarly punished.' After a fierce debate among the law-makers about sex equality in relation to this clause, the article remained unchanged except the 'two years' was reduced to 'one year'. When this revised article became public knowledge, women in Peking and Shanghai protested strenuously, forcing the Political Council and the Legislative Council to reconsider it. Not until 29 November 1934 was it changed to read: 'A married person who commits adultery shall be sentenced to imprisonment for up to one year.'

## Morality and love

The laws were one thing: the reality was another. Since the adult male had pitifully few rights under Chiang's government, the law led women to think they had even less. In the meantime, Chinese views on sex, love, marriage, family life and divorce gradually changed. As Chou Tso-jen pointed out, the frustrations of Chinese sex life did not date from the May 4th Movement, but it was the attack on Confucian ethics during that movement which made the Chinese conscious of their sexual problems. The translations of romantic literature – *La Dame aux Camélias, The Sorrows of Young Werther, Madame Bovary, Sonnets from the Portuguese, Cyrano de Bergerac,* and even the letters of Abelard and Héloise – gave impulse and energy to the unmarried to challenge the status quo with little concern for the objectives and possible achievements of this challenge, and scant respect for the existing values and norms. The translation of *A Doll's House* and the publication of the Ibsen Supplement by the *New Youth* (IV:6) provoked widespread discussion on marriage and family life which influenced a generation of intellectual youth. Literary writers* began to expose their own or fictionalized problems of sex and marriage; scholars like Chou Tso-jen, having studied Freud and Havelock Ellis, asked their readers and friends to contribute anecdotes of personal experiences in love and sex. Once more the vocal minority assaulted the silent majority.

To start with, women's fashion changed from the pre-First World War bodice and full skirt, two side buns and tinted glasses, short socks and narrow shoes to the long and tight-fitting gown, necker-

* For example, Tseng Meng-p'u, Chang Tzu-p'ing, Yü Ta-fu, Chang Yi-p'ing, Feng Yuan-chun (f), *et al*.

chief, high-heeled shoes and short hair with a fringe and side sweeps. The gown (*ch'i-p'ao*), with short sleeves and side slits exposing elbows and knees, offended the sense of decency of the government, which promptly took it upon itself as a matter of morality and law, to forbid it. A year later the Ministry of Home Affairs enforced the prohibition by imposing a fine of 5 *yuan* or five days in prison. But women went on to expose more and more of their bodies. Towards the end of the 1920s they even appeared in swimsuits in newspaper pictures and at the seaside. Traditional writers may still have been comparing feminine beauty to natural beauty (the crescent moon for the eyebrow, autumnal water for the eyes, willow for the waist, etc.), the physical beauty of woman had now acquired its own value and had its own attraction.

Those who were involuntarily cut off from this exposure to modern sex appeal, the peasants, for example, continued to regard sex as dirty but necessary for the procreation of children. Those who voluntarily shut themselves off from it, for instance the traditionalist scholars, might be led by their moral weakness into embarrassing situations or spurred into stubborn reaction by their strong moral inhibitions. The new trend towards indecency according to their judgement either confirmed their belief that women were the source of all men's troubles or necessitated this sort of advice to young men:

If the sexual desire is not curbed, the sexual organs will weaken through wear and tear. This in turn will affect the physical strength of our sons and grandsons, eventually leading to the disappearance of our race.

But the modern-minded, under the influence of the romantic writers of the 1920s and a spate of books on sex, were fostering admiration for women, their beauty and their characters. Some, like Chang Ching-sheng, went as far as to encourage stimulation of the sexual urge and of more frequent intercourse so that men and women would develop their sexual differences more fully. What Chang wanted to see were He-men and She-women. Most of Chang's books were proscribed, but had a wide clandestine circulation.* He was by no means the only writer of his kind, although he was the best known. This fact indicated a commercial exploitation of sex by publishers and film-makers. And some women, too, took advantage of the trend for their own benefit, described by Lu Hsün:

* I am now universalizing my own experiences as a secondary-school pupil.

[They] are displaying something while preserving something else; [they] are luring men on but also resisting. They appear to be endearing and at the same time hostile to the opposite sex. They seem to like and also dislike the opposite sex.

Three attitudes towards love gradually emerged after the May 4th Movement. The poet Hsü Chih-mo personified the first, romantic, attitude. For him 'love is the centre and essence of life: its success is life's success; its failure life's failure'. He believed that a good life must be motivated by love and guided by intellect, since only love could help one to understand and only understanding could perfect love. Such extreme individualist love was possible only for a man as deeply immersed in the individualist tradition of the West as Hsü, although many others after the May 4th Movement might have shared his feelings and sentiments to a lesser degree. The second attitude, the platonic, evinced a greater element of self-control and rationality which might take the form of 'a correct view of life and society' or 'a friendship built on mutual respect and common interests'. For the proponents of this attitude, women were not merely people of the opposite sex, they were complete personalities and should be treated as such. For the platonists love was never the entirety of life. A good example of this type of love was a letter to the editor of the *Hsi feng* (Western Wind), No. 49, pp. 90–5, in September 1940:

Mr Chi is well-educated, upright, and good-looking. He is eight years older than I. It is true that I have congratulated myself for having him as my friend to compensate for the loss of my elder brother. I do treat him as such while I play the rôle of his younger sister. . . . But his eyes are clearly burning with love and his lips spell out his most tender emotions. He certainly lowers me from the position of a younger sister to that of a lover! In despair and a feeling of loss, my tears stream down my cheeks. He has even written to ask me to marry him, but my reply is that I am too young still, and therefore not yet ready to be a good wife for him.

Disappointed, Chi sank into a life of debauchery and married someone whom he did not love. It was the news that Mr Chi was destroying himself that prompted the girl to write the letter. In spite of her own regret and pity for the man, she made clear in her letter the helplessness of an ideal and ethically correct love that had vanished like a burst bubble.

The third attitude was to sublimate individual love into collective love, a love for one's country or for a revolutionary cause. Many of the soldiers and political workers during the Northern Expedition of 1926–8 and the civil war between the KMT and CCP that ensued adopted this attitude because of their total lack of experience in individual love. But a few of them may have turned to collective love after a bitter experience of the romantic variety. Hsieh Ping-ying was such an example. She fell in love with M at first sight, but resolved not to let him know. After a whole year of letter-writing, diary-keeping, tears, and even thoughts of suicide, her reason eventually overcame her emotions and she left her home to join the Northern Expeditionary army. All the time M was unaware of the fact that she loved him.

The traditional segregation of the sexes made young men and women extremely self-conscious in each other's presence, hence the difficulty of communicating with one another. Even the most active students seldom approached a girl student directly. Their usual method was to write notes or letters. On one occasion a college girl student bravely gave a public speech on freedom in love, only to be rewarded during the speech by cat-calls and boos and after it by jeers and general contempt. In the 1920s one began to see young couples holding hands and walking in parks, and perhaps also kissing in such places after dark. But the government and public opinion were definitely against such open displays of affection for fear of corrupting public morals.

It required tremendous courage for women of the 1920s and 1930s to live with their lovers without going through the ceremony of marriage. The cases of Hsieh Ping-ying and Ch'i and Ting Ling's affairs with various young men were in bold defiance of tradition, almost cocking a snook at gossips and scandal mongers. Such happenings were few and Ting Ling was a bohemian writer. It required the same courage for the playwright Ou-yang Yü-ch'ien to rewrite a popular story into a drama in praise of an unconventional woman, turning her into a great heroine. Through the mouth of the heroine of the play, P'an Chin-lien,* Ou-yang said: 'What you call chaste women have all been ill-treated by men till their deaths. Those whom men have failed to wear out are called sluts.'

The traditional forms of marriage came under severe criticism

---

* The career of this woman is described in the *Golden Lotus*.

from the early 1870s onwards. Comparing the Chinese system of arranged marriages with American freedom of choice, a pastor in Soochow attacked the former on the grounds that there was inevitably a lack of understanding between the groom and the bride; he also attacked the custom of the relatives and friends at the wedding party 'teasing the bride' with jokes and practical jokes in a manner verging on cruelty till the small hours of the wedding night. The lack of understanding was responsible for many unhappy marriages and the teasing, if excessive, the estrangement of friends. After the May 4th Movement, arguments against the arranged marriage ran in terms of personal freedom and the injustice of preventing those who were sincerely in love from marrying. Lu Hsün, however, put his views in the bitterest manner:

Since the invention of the valuable thing, money, the progress of men has been spectacular. Everything under the sun can be bought or sold, sexual satisfaction being no exception. . . . Having been abused, the woman has to say: 'Thank you, sir.' Can even beasts behave in this way? So to patronize prostitutes represents a rather high degree of men's evolution. At the same time, the old-style marriage based on parental command and match-makers' messages is better than visiting brothels. Under that system, a man can possess his live property in perpetuity. When a bride is put in the bed of the groom, she has only obligations, not even the freedom to bargain [like a prostitute] let alone love.

Other aspects of marriage, e.g. early marriages including the arrangement of marriages when the couple were still in the womb, child brides, ghost brides (married to dead husbands), polygyny, etc., were based on convenience or the traditional concept of chastity, both of which were strongly censured by the churches and enlightened opinion in the 1900s and especially after the May 4th Movement.

Chastity, particularly feminine chastity, was of the highest importance in Chinese sexual relationships. A politically active girl in Shanghai drank poison because her fiancé believed that she had not been faithful and therefore broke off their engagement. This was before the 1911 Revolution. On the eve of the May 4th Movement the magistrate of Shanghai recommended that a citation should be given to a wife who killed herself when she heard of the news of her husband's death. All well-known writers agreed that chastity was sacrosanct, though it must be applied equally to both sexes. In Hu Shih's words,

Chastity is an attitude of one individual to another. . . . If a man cannot reciprocate the chastity of his woman, he does not deserve her chastity. This is by no means an imported heresy; it is what Confucius once said: 'Do not do to others what you do not want others to do to you.'

Lu Hsün posed four questions about feminine chastity: how could unchaste women damage our country? Why should the responsibility of preserving public morality be on the shoulders of women alone? What would be the results of giving citations to chaste women? What right had polygamous men to give such citations to chaste women? The elaborate system of chastity, in Lu Hsün's eyes, was perfected by men to trap women.

Neither premarital nor extramarital sex was permissible, even for the modernized Chinese. What they sought to abolish was the one-sidedness of the principle of chastity and what they sought to establish was voluntary chastity on the part of both men and women. They were against governmental interference in this entirely private matter and also against the arbitrary preservation of chastity by widows; none of them went as far as to advocate the preservation of chastity by widowers.

In the process of modernization, new matrimonial problems arose from the clash between old ideas and modern practice. How should enlightened youth break away from arranged marriages? For young men, it was easier to leave home for another place and another woman; for young women, the question might be insoluble. Such occurrences as Hsieh Ping-ying's three escapes from home and her final enlistment in the army were extremely rare. There were also the problems which arose between a highly educated, Western-trained husband and his uneducated wife or fiancée as posed and immortalized by Ou-yang Yü-ch'ien's play *On Returning Home* and Wu Fang-chi's epic *Wan-yung*.

To these problems the philosopher Liang Shu-ming gave an answer which may have been realistic, but also was conservative. He doubted that Chinese could adopt Western individualism and ignore the demands and predilections of their families. He also doubted whether young people, unaided by their parents or teachers, could decide rationally and wisely on a matter of this importance. 'Marriage is a family affair and therefore should be decided by the head of the family.' The sociologists Yi Chia-yüeh and Lo Tun-wei proposed three ways of dealing with these problems – cancellation of the marriage contract by mutual consent, proper consideration for the interests of the fiancée or wife, and schooling for the woman so as to bring her up to the educational standard of her partner.

In all cases, modern writers on the question of marriage stressed pure and sincere love as the only solid foundation for a happy marriage. Hu Shih tried to define this elusive concept of 'love' by the simple formula of sexual love plus 'self-consciousness'. This 'self-consciousness' was nothing more than moral and emotional sincerity and monogamous chastity. Any marriage according to him, if it was not based on this kind of love, was no better than two people living together for convenience. Monogamous, solemn and sacred love was also the basis of the ideal successful marriage held up by Mai Hui-t'ing in her monographic study of marriage. She replaced the traditional marital morality with her undefined concept of love. To make the marriage work, she urged considerations of such factors as physical health, adequate education, economic independence, small age difference, common interests, an understanding of the meaning of marriage, and, if necessary, parental consent.

These writers were obviously concerned only with the marriages of educated and well-off young people who had opportunities of meeting the opposite sex on equal terms and falling in love. If the parties were too young, say, still in the secondary education stage, parental interference could easily nip love in the bud. For instance, after a certain boy had taken a girl out two or three times, her father invited the boy to dinner and remarked: 'The discipline of us people in Ningpo it pretty strict. If a girl goes out with a man, other people will talk. But if you are serious I think you ought to get engaged to my daughter. If you are not, you'd better stop seeing her.' Outside school campuses men and women did not often meet on equal terms. Even in the process of social modernization it was not always convenient for a man and woman to approach each other directly. They sometimes had to advertise for a partner in the papers or resort to an informal matchmaker. Even an Americanized liberal like Hu Shih thought it was demeaning for a woman to learn music and dancing and expose herself in the 'marriage market' for the sole purpose of finding a husband. In criticizing this middle-class American custom Hu was in fact defending the traditional Chinese matrimonial arrangement.

Beginning at the turn of the century the so-called 'civilized wedding ceremony' (*wen-ming chieh-hun*) gradually came into fashion, first in the metropolitan cities and then in the hinterland of China.

This ceremony required a privately provided certificate, the presence of parents or their deputies, witnesses and introducers, in addition to the bride and groom and the inevitable banquet. When the Minister of Finance, Chou Tzu-ch'i, gave away his niece in February 1913, the bride and groom merely bowed to each other instead of performing the traditional *kowtow*. The schoolmates of the bride then sang a song after which the parents and senior guests each made a speech and the groom replied. The whole party of several hundred people finally had tea and cakes. At another wedding, that of the son of a bank manager in Hsiangshan, Kwangtung, in May 1913, photographs were taken and the proceedings were enlivened by letting off strings of firecrackers. The speeches made by the senior guests before the banquet attacked old-fashioned weddings and supported freedom of marriage. The whole proceedings ended with shouting slogans – 'Long Live the Republic of China!' The conservatives naturally shook their heads in disapproval of this 'neither new nor old, neither Chinese nor Western, neither a horse nor a donkey' type of wedding. In their judgement, it was not a wedding at all.

Could one free oneself from the tribulations of an unhappy marriage? Leaving the seven traditional reasons for the dismissal of a wife out of consideration, the novelist, Lao She, correctly pointed out two strong reasons against divorce – the married couple had to respect parental views and feelings for the sake of filial piety and they had to obey social sanctions. Sociologists who had studied the causes of matrimonial failures in the West, especially in the USA, took a middle-of-the-road position between a denial of the right to divorce and a *laissez-faire* attitude towards it. Under the impact of individualism, women's liberation, growing urbanization, the rising standard of living, and changing attitudes towards marriage, it was impossible to prohibit divorce. When it became unavoidable, the feeling was that divorce should be based on mutual consent and on considerations of its wider consequences for society, morality and the children. Speaking for the more conservative body of opinion, the philosopher Liang Shu-ming thought the Western pattern of divorce was too dangerous for China to emulate. Not only would it cause social disintegration, it would also lead the divorced to despondency and loss of interest in life.

Marquis Tseng's daughter was one of the first Chinese women to divorce her husband, but the reasons for her action and the procedure adopted remained unclear. About the time of the May 4th Movement a highly educated young man annulled his marriage on the following conditions: the dowry to be returned to the wife, an agreed sum was to be paid as alimony, and the daughter of the marriage was to live with her mother. There were two celebrated divorce cases in the 1920s and 1930s brought on the grounds of total lack of love. Hsü Chih-mo's divorce was a logical consequence of his highly developed individualism; none the less when it occurred, it shocked his friends and mentors. The artist, Hsü Pei-hung had also developed his individualism with the help of the left-bank community of Paris. His divorce took the form of an advertisement in a newspaper in Kueilin, 1938, and was to be made legal by signing a document in the presence of a couple of friends and a lawyer in 1945.

No statistics on divorce in China at this period are available, except for the city of Shanghai where the modern legal system probably offered the best facility for people seeking divorce. Even there, in 1928–9 the monthly average of divorce cases was only 68·8 among a population of 2·7 million. The annual average of 30·58 compared favourably with the American average of 165 among every 100000 people. Most of the Shanghai divorces were initiated by mutual consent (57·92 per cent). As for the rest of the cases, 23·67 per cent were initiated by women and 17·41 per cent by men.

As for remarriage after divorce, one can safely speculate that it occurred more frequently among men than among women. Hu Shih, influenced by the example of Woodrow Wilson's second marriage, thought it was a purely personal matter; no one else had any right to interfere. Liang Shu-ming, however, argued against the experience of having sexual intercourse with another person. The memory of the first marriage would cause embarrassment and unhappiness if a divorcee remarried.

Sex only for enjoyment, not for reproduction, was not unknown to the Chinese. But sex for enjoyment without the fear of pregnancy was an idea introduced to China by the visit of Margaret Sanger in 1922. She was welcomed by the educated middle-class women of Shanghai and her lectures and discussions were translated on her behalf by none other than Hu Shih. Her question was: should women be the mistresses or the slaves of childbirth? This highly important question received an enthusiastic response from Chang Ching-sheng who was China's best-known apostle of sex for pure enjoyment. Mrs Sanger's influence can be seen in the establishment of the Birth Control Consultation Clinic in Shanghai in 1934, sponsored by Christian leaders like Dr F. C. Yen and Mrs Herman Liu, it became the Shanghai Birth Control Study Society in 1936. In co-operation with the Chinese Medical Association it ran a clinic which gave free treatment to upper- and middle-class ladies; it also attempted to manufacture cheap birth control medicine for the less well off. Its *Birth Control Quarterly* was distributed to all the public organizations. As Lin Yutang pointed out, it was the poor who needed birth control. But neither he nor any of the others involved in the family-planning work made any effort to bring the message to the poor, let alone any medicine or devices.

## The family revolution

The stability of the old family system depended upon the authority of its senior generation and of the men of the family. This authority pattern was disintegrating under the assault of both institutional and ideological forces. The growth of modern industry and commerce in China attracted young people of both sexes into factories and offices and this gave them not only a chance to leave home but also economic independence. In many cases the old generation, deficient in physical strength, mental flexibility, and untrained in modern skills, had to rely on the financial help from the young, thus becoming dependent on their children for their living. The result was that the authority of the seniors was enfeebled. By the same token, some women achieved economic independence and freed themselves from male domination. Modern education, especially girls' education, both contributed to the economic self-reliance of the young and helped them in forming new ideas of human relationships with their seniors and with the opposite sex. It was hardly possible for a student trained at Cornell University to return home happily into his old-fashioned arranged marriage merely to produce a grandson for the satisfaction of his parents. Equally, it was hardly possible for an illiterate mother with bound feet to give guidance to a daughter who was fond of the music of Schubert.

In a changing society the inadequacies of the older generation were mercilessly exposed for everyone to see. Their fumbling management of affairs of state apart, they either mismanaged the property of the family through their lack of modern business skill or through their persistence with old spending habits, or indulged in modern extravagances which led to insolvency, thus forcing their children to seek economic independence. The incompetence of the seniors and the problems it brought to the family inevitably upset the harmony of the home, especially when the seniors tried to defend themselves in order to preserve their authority. In such circumstances, it was small wonder that a writer like Chou Tso-jen described the traditional Chinese family system as a system totally devoid of emotional ties and a poet like Hsü Chih-mo bitterly dismissed propriety and family ties as utter rubbish.

On the other hand, a fortunate minority of Chinese youth found a chance to leave home either to receive education at school or to work in a business. With their peers, they learnt to arm themselves economically and intellectually to combat whatever senior or male irrationality they felt to be unjust. Away from home, these young people had to assert themselves in making decisions and solving problems, especially those concerning their marriages and careers. Some of them even became politically concerned and active. With their greater mental agility, they quickly acquired modern views and skills through formal education, training, or extracurricular reading of books and periodicals on politics, society and, most important, literature. These concerned and active young people were the champions of modern China's family revolution.

The revolution actually began at the turn of the century, with the emphasis on emancipating the young so that they could participate in the political revolution. Through the industrial growth during the First World War, which sharpened the clash between the generations, the attack on the theoretical foundation of the traditional family system, intensified. Confucian critics like Wu Yü, Lu Hsün and Ch'en Tu-hsiu described the entire traditional ethical system based on familial considerations as 'cannibalistic' while Ibsen's *A Doll's House* served as a mirror of the selfish, enslaving, hypocritical and cowardly family life and family system of China. It was in this intellectual atmosphere, Lu Hsün wrote his *Madman's Diary* and Hu Shih his 'Biography of Miss Li Ch'ao', posing the question: how long should the tyranny of family and clan heads continue to warp the sturdy growth of the young? In criticizing the old system, the scholars also suggested a modern substitute. The up-and-coming young scholars, Fu Ssu-nien and Yü P'ing-po, both gave the answer that the claims of the individual should be asserted, for no right or wrong, good or bad could be properly assessed independently of the individual. 'One must be oneself', maintained Fu; 'independent individuality must be respected', said Yü.

Following this trend of thought, the YWCA organized a series of discussions on the 'model family' in the big cities between 1920 and 1925, while the sociologists Yi Chia-yüeh and Lo Tun-wei established their Family Study Society, publishing a periodical whose aim was to promote family reform. Now under the influence of the Protestant Church and their authoritative magazine, the *Chinese Recorder*, and such writers as Ellen Key, George Bernard Shaw and Edward Westermarck, the superiority of the Western form of the nuclear family based on monogamy was unreservedly accepted among the enlightened minority. Only in such a family system, as seen by its Chinese advocates, could sex equality be realized and love be the foundation of a matrimonial union.

Idealizing the nuclear family system, Mai Hui-t'ing thought it would produce a more harmonious atmosphere at home, foster economic independence and the good habit of saving, realize equality between the sexes, eliminate the clan-centred way of thinking, facilitate the proper socialization of children, and make the home more hygienic to live in. She even went as far as to encourage the study of home economics by the wife and the learnings of modern methods of bringing up children, so that the urban middle-class Chinese family would one day become a copy of the urban middle-class American family. But the reality bore no resemblance to her ideal. Even in the cities, long after the KMT government had incorporated the principle of sex equality into the codification of law and forbidden traditional forms of marriage, concubinage, child brides and the relentless effort to produce a male heir continued. To give just one example, a mother of four girls was expecting another child and her husband warned her that if the fifth was a girl, he would take a concubine. When the baby turned out actually to be another girl, the mother paid 15 *yuan* to the nurse to have her baby exchanged secretly for a male child. Unfortunately for the mother, the male baby soon died and thereafter she was subjected to inhuman treatment by her husband and mother-in-law. This happened in February 1940. Only Pearl Buck could have praised the Chinese method of bringing up children like this: 'it was simple and clarified by the usage of centuries and so the growing personality was poised and calm'. Only Lin Yutang could have written:

Every family in China is really a communistic unit, with the principle of 'do what you can and take what you need' guiding its functions. Mutual helpfulness is developed to a very high degree, encouraged by a sense of moral obligation and family honor.

The problems of the Chinese family system existed precisely because this idealized picture was utterly untrue and the other idealized picture of the American style nuclear family was unattainable. Between the two ideals, the inconclusive battle between tradition and modernization went on.

## Chinese youth

The problem of the youth of China began with the awakening of nationalism in the wake of the 1895 War. Nationalism posed a set of questions which her culturalism and traditional political culture could not answer. The problems were many and varied, but they all to some degree demanded inconoclastic solutions for they were concerned with fundamental elements in the culturalistic tradition. Although this questioning was stimulated by the war with Japan, it arose from either Western or Soviet Russian inspiration. Because of the problems, the young sought for a new literature, new music, new art, a new life-style, new modes of sexual love, new forms of political struggle, new knowledge and new education, and even a new image of themselves. All these had their traditional equivalents which the young people either submitted to (a way of avoiding all difficulties), or endeavoured to change (a way of raising further problems). In spite of the political elements permeating all these problems, the problems themselves were essentially cultural. It would be no exaggeration to say that modern Chinese culture was a youth culture. To overlook this point is to be unappreciative of the problems of Chinese youth in this century and is to misunderstand them.

Since some of the cultural problems will be dealt with in the following chapter, we shall concentrate here on two aspects only of the activities of the young – their education and their role in politics.

*Educational reform*

Educational reform was perhaps the most successful of all the modern reforms in China. Initially it had two directions: the modernization of the examination system to bring new subjects into the curriculum of students outside the school system and the establishment of modern schools to train interpreters, diplomats and defence technicians.

Li Hung-chang was one of the first to notice the obsolescence of the traditional examination system. The general attitude towards scholarly pursuits being as it was in 1874, he could not suggest more radical changes than discarding calligraphy as a criterion for grading the examinees and hoping for a gradual expansion of the modern school system so that perhaps eventually education would serve practical needs. He did not advocate the total abolition of the system until after his European tour in 1896. Meanwhile the opposition to the system was gathering momentum before and after the 1894–5 War. Representing this trend of thought in the 1898 Reform were K'ang Yu-wei, Liang Ch'i-ch'ao and Yen Fu, who attacked the futile formalism of the system and proposed to change it by introducing papers on specialized subjects without at the same time doing violence to the basic Confucian discipline. The Reformers saw this as an interim arrangement, their eventual aim being the abolition of the system and its replacement with modern schools. Viceroy Chang Chih-tung, however, feared that any attempt to departmentalize the system might result, first, in the neglect or misinterpretation of the classics, which would weaken the ideological foundation of society, and, second, in undue emphasis on specialized subjects which would produce a crop of morons devoid of both refinement and integrity. In his view the traditional essay style could be changed, but the examination system must be preserved in an improved form, with three parts – one on Chinese statecraft, one on Western statecraft, and one on the classics. The waxing and waning of these two views accounts for the institutional reform of the system in 1898 and the reversion to the old form immediately after the failure of the Hundred Days Reform. But the vacillations of government policy concerning such a basic institution of the empire inevitably damaged the public image of the system. The number of candidates at all grades of the examinations held after 1898 dropped alarmingly.

Even Chang Chih-tung himself knew that the system was riddled with irregularities such as impersonation and kidnapping, bias and corruption. After a sensational discovery of irregularities in the metropolitan examination of 1858, a Grand Secretary and three other officials were executed. In Kwangtung, gambling on the county and provincial examinations (*wei-hsing*) was organized like that on a Western horse-race. The betting was on such a scale that the government considered it worthwhile to tax it and Chang Chih-tung used the revenue from this tax to finance the purchase of his two Bessemer converters.*

The reform of the examination system along the lines suggested by Chang Chih-tung was adopted by the Board of Rites in 1901 and the first of the reformed metropolitan examinations was held in 1903. Ill-planned and ill-prepared, this examination showed a lack of standard of judgement on the part of the examiners and a tendency to use fashionable words and arguments without much solid understanding on the part of the candidates. The twenty-seven successful examinees, apart from those who had already received the highest traditional degree, were neither admitted into the Hanlin Academy as promised nor given promotion from their existing posts. The reformed examinations in the provinces were in most cases fiascos. In 1904 only some 260 candidates took part in the Hangchow prefectural examination and in 1905 only forty-two candidates out of a total registration of 1200 actually sat for the military examination at Canton. At long last, the system was dying a natural death; it was formally abolished on 2 September 1905.

Now Chinese education was at a crossroads in urgent need of correct direction. Chang Chih-tung's well known essay *On Learning* laid down self-strengthening as the supreme goal of education.

Chang saw the proper aims of education as collective, political and, at the same time, pragmatic. Chang Po-hsi's important memorial on education of 1902, written in the same spirit and with the same aims, was to be formulated into the six goals of modern Chinese education of 1906. That the aims were 'loyalty to the emperor, reverence to Confucius, devotion to public welfare, admiration for martial spirit, devotion to truth or respect for industrial pursuits' showed the strength of the example of the Imperial Rescript on Education of Japan of 1890. This was hardly surprising, for in the opening years of this century Japanese influence on China through the thousands of Chinese students in Japan was

* See above, p. 355.

enormous. Education could not conceivably be for the development of individual personality or intellect only; it had to be for the benefit of the state and society. This trend of thought remained dominant even after the 1911 Revolution.

The different opinions voiced by the revolutionaries of the 1900s were inspired by the same source and followed the same model – Japan. Their disagreements with the official policy lay in politics rather than in education itself. What the revolutionaries meant by 'the state' was not the dynasty; what they meant to strengthen was not the realm of the emperor but the country of the people. Otherwise, the education they favoured was equally political and equally pragmatic. If there was any Western doctrine on education which became accepted by the Chinese, it was social Darwinism, leading to an interest in the strengthening of the physique as well as the morality and intellect of the students.

The principles of education announced by the Ministry of Education in September 1912 and the Outline of Compulsory Education in February 1915 were based on morality, utility and martial spirit. The continuity between these goals and those of 1906 was evident. Not in evidence was the Western liberal influence of the then Minister of Education, Ts'ai Yuan-p'ei. Ts'ai's original proposal contained two other principles – cosmopolitanism and aesthetics; his aim was to break away from the Confucian tradition and cultivate a new personality for the scholars. The elimination of Ts'ai's two principles in a Ministry firmly dominated by traditionalists during the presidency of Yuan Shih-ka'i was only to be expected.

The Japanese influence continued to be evident in both the principles and institutions of Chinese education till the May 4th Movement and the coming of John Dewey to China.

Dewey opened the Chinese mind to the need for a philosophy of education and a training in pedagogical methods. He argued:

... in an authoritarian country with a class society, mere pouring in of instruction could conceivably constitute an adequate education, because the child is merely being trained to occupy a predetermined position and role, and this sort of education can condition him to this end.

But China was changing and the Chinese consciously wanted change. If the child was to be denied his predetermined position or role in a changing society, what would be his new position and new role? To this question, Dewey gave no answer. For him, education meant growth in relation to all life situations; and 'growth' meant the development of the child's intellectual, moral and physical potential. The methods of teaching, therefore, far from consisting merely of pouring knowledge into the young mind, should be flexible and experimental, preparing the child all the time for social life in the milieu of the school.

The legacy of Dewey's visit was historically significant. He gave education a new goal – the growth of life, a new centre – the child, and a new pedagogy – the flexible and experimental method. In all three respects, his ideas ran counter to the Japanese tradition which had now been adopted as Chinese. His lucidity and prestige, combined with the work of his students, were to reorient Chinese educational principles and educational system throughout the difficult years of the 1920s.

After Dewey's visit an invitation was sent to Paul Monroe, whose theory of education was the subject of a special supplement of the journal *New Education* in February 1922. W. A. McCall was invited in 1922–3 to supervise the conducting of school tests, and in 1927 Helen Parkhurst brought with her the Dalton Plan for the free pursuit of knowledge. The famed educationist Ts'ai Yuan-p'ei now wrote, obviously in the spirit of Dewey, that the development of the potential of the student and his personality was the ultimate goal of education. If followed that he and the other liberals were opposed to training students as means to an end irrelevant to the students themselves. Political or religious interference in education was to them utterly intolerable. Another famed educationist and a student of John Dewey's, T'ao Hsing-chih (or Chih-hsing), aimed at applying the theory of his mentor to mass education in the hope that at least the ordinary townsmen, if not the peasants, could learn enough to cope with the situations they met within their ordinary life and ultimately to break down the barriers between classes and occupations.

From the point of view of education, the chaos of the 1920s was both a blessing and a curse. True, modern education in China regressed at that time, but the weakness of the government also meant less effective interference, at least in the higher seats of learning. When the country became nominally united again in 1928 the KMT's control over education tightened. At first, riding on the crest of nationalism, the party tackled the question of Chinese control over missionary schools. The Universities Council headed by Ts'ai Yuan-p'ei was replaced by a Ministry of Education headed by Tai Chi-t'ao – the veteran educationist thus being displaced by a veteran party functionary. With the publication of Tai's 'Aims of Education' in the same year the KMT took over the making of educational policies. The Three Principles of the People was decreed as a required subject even in primary schools in order to achieve the party's aim of ideological unity of the nation. In the name of fulfilling the minimum scholastic requirements a standard curriculum for secondary schools was introduced and this was followed by a compulsory military training. The party made skilful use of the mounting threat of Japan in the early 1930s to push through educational reforms, converting in the process even some of the erstwhile liberal educationists. Herman Liu, a Christian and liberal, for example, now sophisticatedly argued that Chinese education should produce a real synthesis, true to Chinese genius, 'not an external amalgamation of old and new values'. There was an implied criticism here of the earlier indiscriminate borrowing from abroad. Jen Hung-chun, another liberal educationist and scientist, having attacked the KMT intervention in education in 1932, took up the theme of relevance to China, also criticizing indiscriminate borrowing, chiefly that from the USA.

The establishment of modern schools came with the founding of the Language Institute in Peking in 1861. Other such schools were founded in Shanghai and Canton in 1863 and defence technology and telecommunications were added to language study in the 1880s. In the 1890s there were also polytechnic institutions in Shanghai and Wuch'ang and medical colleges in Tientsin and elsewhere. Before 1895 most of these schools were sponsored by the government and the successful students were given the equivalent of traditional degrees or ranks as an encouragement. Since the future career patterns of the students were uncertain, enrolment was a serious problem and this was exacerbated by a high drop-out rate. Those who remained and graduated served as secretaries and clerks in the Chinese legations abroad or at the Tsungli Yamen. These graduates rose to positions of distinction as Chinese ministers to Europe and America, Ministers of Foreign Affairs, or high-ranking officers of the Chinese navy, in the 1890s.

Modern schools began to appear in Peking and elsewhere after 1895, some under government sponsorship and some others

*Progress of Chinese modern education*

| A. | Primary education | Schools | Students |
|---|---|---|---|
| | 1912 | 86318 | 2795475 |
| | 1916 | 128525 | 3843454 |
| | 1922 | 120097 | 6601802 |
| | 1929 | 212385* | 8882077 |
| | 1932 | 262496† | 12179994 |
| | 1936 | 318797† | 18285125 |

| B. | Secondary education | Schools | Students |
|---|---|---|---|
| | 1912 | 500 | 59971 |
| | 1916 | 653 | 75595 |
| | 1922 | 547 | 118658 |
| | 1928 | 954* | 188700 |
| | 1932 | 1914† | 409586 |
| | 1936 | 1956† | 482522 |

| C. | Higher education | Universities | Colleges |
|---|---|---|---|
| | 1912 | 4 | 111 |
| | 1916 | 10 | 74‡ |
| | 1922 | 19 | — |
| | 1925 | 47* | 57 |
| | 1932 | 41† | 35 |
| | 1936 | 42† | 36 |

\* Statistics of education became even less systematic at the height of the civil wars from 1924 to 1928.

† The KMT's policy was to curb the growth of universities and expand primary and secondary education.

‡ The decline of colleges was due to the closing down of a large number of Japanese-style law schools and also due to the failure of attempts to popularize vocational education.

Sources: Sun Pang-cheng, *Liu-shih-nien lai Chung-kuo chiao-yü*, Taipei, 1971, *passim*; Ch'en Ch'i-t'ien, *Chin-tai Chung-kuo chiao yü-shih*, Taipei, 1969 edn., ch. 19; Ministry of Education, *Chung-kuo chiao-yü nien-chien*, 1934, Shanghai, 1943, no. 3. pp. 1224–6; *Tung-fang tsa chih*, 25 October 1924, p. 134.

privately run. This modest beginning became a fashion after the imperial edict of 3 September 1902 which urged local governments and private citizens to set up primary schools in the counties, secondary schools in the prefectures, and universities or colleges in provincial capitals. By the time the traditional examination system was formally abolished in 1905, four schools were in operation; even at remote places like Chiating (now Loshan), Szechuan, at Kunming, Yunnan, there were more than a dozen, and at Lanchow, Kansu, nine. Co-existing with earlier government schools and missionary institutions, these new schools differed from traditional tutors' classes by offering courses such as English, arithmetic, natural sciences, and sometimes even physical education in addition to classics and calligraphy. Furthermore, the courses were actually given as lectures in classrooms, a totally new form of teaching.

Many of the primary and secondary schools used the buildings of old Taoist and Buddhist temples while the traditional higher seats of learning in the provinces, the *shu-yuan*, were transformed into modern colleges. In the imperial capital there were the University (later the University of Peking) and its affiliated Institute of Advanced Studies (an amalgamation of the Shih-hsüeh-yuan, Chin-shih-kuan) for the newly selected holders of the *chin-shih* degree.

According to the School Act of 1902, the government intended to provide free primary and secondary education for the first five years and thereafter a small tuition fee would be required. In the time of financial stringency after the Boxer Uprising, when most provinces had to shoulder a part of the indemnity, this was hardly possible. In fact, students were required to pay tuition fees from 1903. In addition, they had to pay for new textbooks which, unlike the classics, they could not easily borrow from their relatives or friends, for their board and lodging, and for tunics. The new-style education was therefore considerably more expensive than the old. This fact had two significant consequences: first, education tended to become the preserve of the wealthy, thus offering fewer opportunities for upward mobility to the poor and underprivileged; second, in an endeavour to advance their careers, the poor and underprivileged turned to other avenues of advancement such as the military schools, so that talented youths were channelled into the army and navy, among whom there were to emerge a few brilliant scholars like Lu Hsün and a large number of warlords. With the introduction of modern education, the old Chinese saying, 'Good iron is not used to make good nails; good men do not become soldiers', no longer held true.

In the early years of the Republic and immediately after the founding of the KMT government, attempts were made to adopt a uniform system of primary and secondary education in order to

make sure of a minimum standard of training. But, apart from the
mere duration of each stage of education,* little else was stan-
dardized. The imperial government had the intention of publishing
all school textbooks after the Japanese model and a bureau was
established for this purpose in 1906. But in reality the publication
of school books was left in the hands of private publishers, except
that later the KMT Ministry of Education had to approve these
publications. The KMT's efforts to impose a standard curriculum
on the schools also failed to a large extent.

At one end of the educational hierarchy was the compulsory
primary education which the Yuan Shih-k'ai administration planned
to initiate in 1915. But Yuan's monarchical attempt put an end to it
along with much else and it was not considered again until 1935.
The KMT aspired to provide a system of free, compulsory education lasting four years for all children in China at an estimated
budget of 280 million *yuan* and the scheme also required nearly
1·5 million teachers and one million classrooms. However, the
money the government actually allocated for this purpose was no
more than 3·2 million *yuan*. Mass education was then left to small-
scale individual efforts like those of James Yen in Tinghsien,
Hopei, Liang Shu-ming in Tsoup'ing, Shantung, and T'ao Hsing-
chih in Hsiehhsien, Anhwei and Hsiaochuang near Nanking.

At the other end of the hierarchy was university education, which
may be illustrated here with a brief description of the University
of Peking. The university came into being in 1898, incorporating
the old government publishing house and translation bureau into
what was then called the Institute of Advanced Studies for the
Officials (Shih-hsüeh-yuan). In 1900 it was suspended because of
its Chancellor's open hostility to the Boxers and the government's
supportive policy towards them. When it resumed its work in 1902
it looked for the first time like a modern university, consisting of
eight departments (classics, politics and law, literature, medicine,
natural history, agriculture, engineering and commerce). It offered
extramural courses in government administration and teacher
training. Like Indian universities, it became the centre of learning
with all the other colleges and schools of the empire loosely attached

---

* Six years for the primary stage (four for the junior section and two for the senior
section), another six for the secondary stage (equally divided between the junior and
senior sections), and four for the university stage. See the *Social and Political Journal*, vol.
IX, no. 1, p. 49, 3 March 1925; *Tu-li p'ing-lun*, no. 11, 31 July 1932.

to it for intellectual guidance. In 1903, its affiliated institutes included the old Language Institute (T'ung-wen-kuan) founded in 1861, which became its bureau of translation, the Institute of Advanced Studies and the Institute of Medical Research (for both Western and Chinese medicine). Three years later the Institute of Advanced Studies was transformed into the faculty of law.

At this stage, few took the entrance examination of the university; enrolment depended therefore more on students being recommended by the various government offices. Once admitted, the students were required to attend eight lectures a day, leaving no time for their own home work, research and reading for pleasure. Since they were officials, they treated their teachers, mostly foreign-trained and with a poorer command of the Chinese language and literature than the students, with open contempt. They carried their customary modes of recreation, e.g., gambling, drinking and patronizing prostitutes, into the university dormitories.

Although this institution acquired the name of the University of Peking in 1912, it did not undergo any drastic modernization until Ts'ai Yuan-p'ei assumed its Chancellorship in 1916. A classical scholar who had received a modern training in Germany and had close associations with Japan and France, Ts'ai's liberal outlook left an indelible impression on that institution which he reshaped into a true seat of higher learning. His institutional innovations at the university included a research institute attached to each department which was now administered by its faculty council, a senate which took over the making of all the academic policy decisions, and a division between required and optional courses for students. He abolished the department of engineering but added those of history and geology. Another important step Ts'ai took was to allocate funds for the students to publish a daily campus paper so that democracy was extended to grass-roots level. Among the faculty members of his day there were old-fashioned conservatives like Liu Shih-p'ei and Huang K'an and also liberals and radicals like Hu Shih, Ch'en Tu-hsiu and Li Ta-chao. The intellectual stimulation and campus freedom prepared the university for its future academic distinction and for the political role it played in the May 4th Movement of 1919.

Ts'ai's infectious intellectual attitude and liberal leadership evoked in his students a new mood, a new spirit which they themselves described in the inaugural issue of their paper, the *New Tide*:

[We] are fortunate to be engulfed in the tides of the world so that we may be prepared to give guidance to the Chinese society of the future. We shall follow this spirit and this road in the hope that ten years hence our university of today will be the fountain of scholarship and the trends of thought at our university will influence the whole country.

When the government used violence against the students on 4 May 1919, Ts'ai resigned in protest. But he was soon persuaded to return to his Chancellorship and remained till 1923. In that period the university began to admit girl students (in the autumn of 1920) and set up its institutes of Chinese Studies and Music in 1921 and 1922 respectively. Increasing government interference culminated in its temporary dissolution in the summer of 1927 when the warlord Marshal Chang Tso-lin wanted to combine all the nine universities and colleges in Peking into one institution. After Chang's departure and assassination, it was restored to its former state and Ts'ai Yuan-p'ei was once again appointed Chancellor in 1929.

University education, like all other forms of modern education in China, was constantly hampered by financial difficulties. The general situation was particularly bad in the 1920s when the government budgeted less than 1 per cent of its total annual expenditure for education; consequently the half-starved teachers, whose salaries might be in arrears for many months, often went on strike. In the 1930s the pay scale of the teachers was, on the average, 20–30 *yuan* a month at the primary school, 80–200 *yuan* at the secondary school, and 300–400 *yuan* at the university level, while the student's expenses amounted to 4–17 *yuan* per annum at the primary stage, 60–120 *yuan* (including board and lodging) at the secondary stage or in a vocational training college, and 600–800 *yuan* at a university. Education being so expensive, it was no surprise that the university student population in 1936, numbering 37330, was less than 0·01 per cent of the total population.

The demands for women's rights led to more girls being admitted into schools and universities. The rate of growth was, however, painfully slow. In 1923 only 3·14 per cent of the total secondary school population were girls and at the universities the percentage was 2·43. In 1931 3887 girls were at universities or colleges, forming less than 9 per cent of the student population. The slow rate of growth was due more to personal or family financial reasons than educational discrimination. The lack of employment opportunities for all graduates, especially for women, may also have been responsible for this slowness.

The explanation of the paradox of an extremely small educated elite with a high rate of unemployment must lie in the underdevelopment of modern industries and commerce. This must also have been the reason why the general trend of education in China was to put ordinary primary and secondary schools before teacher training, polytechnic schools, or any other form of vocational education. In 1936 the ratio of secondary schools to vocational institutes was 100 to 25 and that of their students number was 100 to a mere 12!

## Student political movement

In the fateful year of 1895 the best of the young scholars gathered in Peking for the metropolitan examination, only to be shocked by the news of the Treaty of Shimonoseki. Their immediate petitions to the throne suggesting the rejection of the treaty and the continuation of the war marked the beginning of an active role in politics for youth. After that they participated in the 1905 anti-American boycott, the 1911 Revolution, the demonstration in 1915 against the Twenty-One Demands, the anti-missionary movement early in the 1920s, the Northern Expedition and a series of anti-Japanese demonstrations reaching their highest point in 1931–2. The May 4th Movement of 1919 and the December 9th Movement of 1935 were the great landmarks.

When thousands of Peking students demonstrated, beat up one pro-Japanese official, and burned the house of another on May 4th 1919, they were demanding the rendition of former German possessions in Shantung to China instead of Japan, the abolition of secret agreements between China and Japan, the cancellation of the Twenty-One Demands, and the unification of the country. It was a patriotic demonstration against imperialist encroachment and militarist misgovernment. To further their political action the students used, in addition to demonstrations, organizations (the Peking Students' Union), propaganda, strikes, and the boycotting of Japanese goods, and alliance with businessmen, workers and students of other cities. In response, the central and local governments suppressed the students' expression of their political views by law and by force. The government's attitude was formed on the assumption that the students were too young and too ill-informed to interfere with matters of state. They should concentrate on their studies and help the government maintain law and order by refusing to listen to trouble-makers and agitators.

The May 4th Movement thus set the pattern for students' political action and government reaction. For the students, the fortunes and misfortunes of their country were the responsibility of every citizen; for the government, their being young disqualified them from intervention. But what distinguished the May 4th Movement from its successors was the cultural revolution following in its wake, which was to make an impact on Chinese state and society unmatched by any other students' movement before 1935.

The students' action divided opinion on students' political role among their teachers and mentors. Radical scholars like Ch'en Tu-hsiu, Li Ta-chao and Lu Hsün praised the selflessness of the students as 'an important element for the reconstruction of China' and continued to encourage their political participation, to show their concern 'with the very life and death of the nation and people'. Eleven years after these events, Lu Hsün was still exhorting the students:

Now is not the time to put one's nose between the pages or stay in one's studio discussing religion, law, literature, and art. Even if you must discuss [these subjects], you must first of all know the circumstances and have the courage and tenacity to face the forces of darkness.

Moderate and conservative scholars, on the other hand, maintained that the primary task of the students was to learn and study, for the only way in which they could help their country was by perfecting their knowledge while waiting for their leaders to put the country in order.

At the time of the May 4th Movement the KMT was not strong enough to give aid and leadership to the students and the CCP was not yet in existence. However, in 1924 when the KMT was re-organized and the alliance between it and the CCP had been formed, the situation changed radically, as was shown by the anti-imperialist demonstrations and boycotts in 1925–6. By then the KMT had set up its youth department and the CCP its Youth League, to lead and train young people in political action. The situation underwent another radical change when the alliance split up and the KMT's persecution of the CCP began. The fourth plenum of the KMT in February 1928 resolved to abolish its youth department and forbade students to take part in political agitation. In place of the departments dealing with mass movements the KMT now instituted the Committee for Training the Masses under Ch'en Kuo-fu, one of the two leaders of the right-wing C-C clique.

Even after its reorganization the KMT was still bedevilled by intra-party factional disputes over internal and external problems of both the party and the government. Consequently its major policies evinced an uncertainty and hesitation that weakened the party's leadership. Furthermore, the bureaucratism and corruption of its functionaries disillusioned the young, who either showed a negative attitude towards the party's lead or sought other channels for political expression. The students could not be assumed to be blind to the predicament of their country, especially after the Japanese invasions of Manchuria in September 1931 and of Shanghai in January 1932. Nor could they be assumed to be preoccupied with their classwork and sports only. The CCP, too, sank into a period of interregnum. Its leadership in urban work was frustrated by Chiang Kai-shek's persecution and its own misjudgement. Therefore in the early 1930s the students relied almost completely on their own patriotic *élan* and political experience in carrying on their anti-imperialist struggles, with a feeling that their seniors had deserted them.

In the wave of anti-Japanese action after 18 September 1931, the students added village propaganda, fund-faising for the volunteers fighting the Japanese in Manchuria, and the organization of detachments of volunteers among themselves to their arsenal of political weapons. Their petitioning of the government assumed unprecedented dimensions; they even seized a train on the Tsin-p'u Line and operated it themselves from Tientsin to Nanking in an endeavour to change Chiang Kai-shek's conciliatory policy towards Japan. As Chiang continued to make concessions to Japan to such an extent that the sovereignty of Hopei was in danger, the students in Peking came out on to the streets again, on 9 and 16 December 1935.

The December 9th and 16th demonstrations, like the May 4th, had a nationwide impact, but unlike the May 4th Movement they were simply an anti-Japanese political movement. Women played a more prominent role in the December 1935 demonstrations and the planning and orderliness of the operations showed a much stronger organization behind them. To follow up the activities in the city, the students revived the suppressed and languishing Peking Students' Union and sent out propaganda teams to agitate among the peasants in the vicinity of Peking. Moreover, they also made friendly overtures to the garrison troops, the 29th Army, and created a strong left-wing body of high political consciousness and cohesion called the Anti-Japanese National Salvation Vanguard (*Min-hsien*). These political experiences were of great value and great importance, for when the war broke out in July 1937 the Peking activists worked as cadre under the leadership of the CCP and in co-operation with peasants and soldiers to create guerrilla war bases.

## The labour movement

The industrial work force* in China is estimated to have been approximately 100000 strong on the eve of the 1894–5 War, growing to about 1·5 million at the end of the First World War. Geographically, it was distributed around the Yangtze estuary, at Wuhan, Tientsin and Canton, and in southern Manchuria, central Shantung and north-eastern Hopei. If handicraft labour is also included, the total labour force in manufacturing after the First World War stood at somewhere between 10 and 11 million.

Against a background of deepening agrarian crisis, there was an abundant supply of unemployed or displaced peasant labour for industrial use. This, together with the urban poor and small craftsmen, formed the major source of labour supply in the cities. Between the supply and the demand, there emerged a number of 'middlemen', the labour contractors, who were sometimes compradores and sometimes members of secret societies, travelling out into the countryside for the purpose of recruiting labourers, including women and children. These contractors provided funds to pay for the travelling expenses, board and lodging of the labourers when

* The bourgeoisie was, of course, another important social group to appear in the course of China's modern social changes. A brief discussion of the 'compradores' is to be found in ch. 4, pp. 220–4, and one on the growth of modern industry in ch. 9, pp. 348–59. Marie-Claire Bergère's study, 'The Role of the Bourgeoisie,' in M. C. Wright (ed.), *China in Revolution* (New Haven, 1968), covers too short a time span to be of any help to us here. At present, researches on the Chinese bourgeoisie and proletariat are only just beginning and there are more primary sources and secondary works on labour than on capital. We are in difficulty in drawing even an impressionist picture of the capitalist class after the rise of Chiang Kai-shek. I have therefore decided to leave any further analysis of the bourgeoisie here.

they went to work in the cities. From the employers, the contractor received wages to be distributed among the labourers he had recruited under contract according to the work done by the labourers, and from this amount the contractor deducted his own expenses, interest on the expenses, and whatever fees he cared to charge. The system was essentially the same as the one used for recruiting Chinese labourers to work abroad in San Francisco, Sydney and the Transvaal.

Under the watchful eyes of the foreman, sometimes Sikhs and white Russians who did not as a rule take part in productive work, the workers usually worked more than ten hours a day and rested only on traditional holidays like the lunar New Year Festival. Sundays were not observed, even in the factories owned by Westerners. Protection against accidents hardly existed and compensation for death or disability was meagre. In the coal mines of T'angshan, to the north-east of Peking, the compensation for the death of a worker was 30–40 *yuan*, whereas the price of a mule was at least three times as much. The worst treated were the apprentices in small-scale workshops who had neither wages nor fixed hours of work.

Wage levels varied from place to place, depending chiefly on the cost of living. An unskilled worker earned only 8 *yuan* a month in Canton where the warm climate required less expenditure on clothing and accommodation, against 7–15 *yuan* in Ningpo, Chekiang and 12–15 *yuan* in Newchuang, Shangung, in the same period. As the cost of living increased with the passage of time, wages also increased, but at a slower rate. According to Ch'en Ta, the price of rice increased by 90 per cent between 1918 and 1920 while wages rose by only 50 per cent. The average rate of wage increase may have been even slower, if the wages of five different trades in Shanghai are taken as typical. Between 1911 and 1921 wages in these trades rose less than 20 per cent. At all levels of skill the difference between the wages of men and women was startling. The skilled and semi-skilled factory workers in Shanghai are used here to illustrate this point. The average wages for men were four times those for women in 1912 and the gap widened to more than five times in 1923.

Being uneducated and mostly illiterate, the nascent proletariat was conscious neither of its economic interests as a class nor of its potential strength as a force which could fight for those interests. The traditional guilds organized on the basis of specialization were in decline under the challenge of modern industry and commerce, while the secret societies in their modern transformation tended to side with the bourgeoisie. After the anti-American boycott of 1905 and anti-Japanese boycott of 1908, scattered efforts to organize industrial workers were made, but were soon suppressed during the Yuan Shih-k'ai reaction.

To be sure, the boycotts were not organized chiefly by workers, nor primarily in their interests. They were an expression of popular nationalism, which provoked a variety of reactions from government leaders. Some of the leaders, for example the Viceroy of Kwangtung and Kwangsi, considering regional interests, supported the boycotts while the others, considering their diplomatic implications, opposed them. The government's final decision to suppress the 1905 boycott was based on the fear that mob nationalism might involve the country in diplomatic difficulties. There was as yet hardly any class consciousness to divide the government and the people.

The rapid industrial growth during the First World War with its accompanying labour problems drew the attention of the intellectuals, including students, who were at the same time imbibing Western socialist thought, including Marxism. Their field investigations and theoretical studies brought about a change of attitude towards manual work and the proletariat. Thus Li Ta-chao could write in 1920:

Some self-styled gentlemen say: 'The social movements of the intelligentsia must not copy from those of the lowly workers.' This is strange. Let me ask: 'What is the difference between the high and the low?' All those who work are high and noble, far better than the gentlemen, celebrities, and politicians who do nothing else but sucking other people's blood.

And Ch'en Tu-hsiu could say: 'I think it is the workers who are the most useful and the most noble people.'

Because of this changing attitude an informal alliance between the proletariat and radical intellectuals was in the making, as observed by the British consul in Chengtu, Sir Meyrick Hewlett: 'Labour looked entirely to the students and not to the ruling authorities to represent them in political matters.' This radical attitude was *mutatis mutandis* to be inherited by the CCP.

The moderate intellectuals and the Protestants, especially the

YMCA and YWCA, advocated a gradual improvement in the living and working conditions of female and child labour. There were children aged six or seven who frequently worked twelve hours a day while suffering from skin or other diseases and these naturally evoked the humanitarian sympathies of these intellectuals. Through the YMCA's efforts, an Industrial Department was set up and the Municipal Council of the International Settlement of Shanghai appointed a Child Labour Commission in 1923–4. The Commission's report of 1924, which suggested a voluntary abstention from employing any child under the age of ten in any dangerous or exhausting work for more than twelve hours a day, did not win much admiration nor produce any noticeable result. The moderates were in fact so weak that they failed to evolve a social democratic tradition based on an understanding of the conflicting interests of capital and labour. Indeed, their 'populist' approach to labour problems in the hope of bringing about class co-operation fitted in eminently well with the political philosophy of the KMT. When the party first came to power, it professed to represent the interests of the nation as a whole instead of those of a particular class. On the one hand, it exhorted the big capitalists to curb the growth of their private capital; on the other, it controlled the trade unions, preventing them from taking extreme action. The difference between exhortation and control in the party's earlier policies developed into an antagonism to labour and the labour movement. When the labour movement threatened to disrupt China's international relations with the major powers, such as the anti-Japanese boycott in 1931, the KMT government came down on the side of suppressing the workers.

The hideous living and working conditions of the proletariat were the creation of the employers and contractors who were certainly hostile to the labour movement. But the political consciousness of the proletariat itself was growing, partly because of workers' living away from their extended families, partly because they were learning from experience and becoming more adept at empirical ways of thinking, and partly because there was easier access to information and propaganda in an urban milieu.

Other factors also contributed to hasten the growth of proletarian consciousness on the eve of the May 4th Movement. The Chinese labourers returning from both the eastern and western fronts after the First World War brought with them not only rudimentary political ideas but also the experience of racial discrimination on a mass scale. Those who had worked in France were known to have gone on strike against low wages and poor working conditions and those who had worked in Russia had taken part in the October Revolution. The strength of industrial labour was now greater and the attitude of the intellectuals towards it was changing. When radical intellectuals went to agitate among the workers in 1920, they were bound to ignite what was already a combustible situation. With the founding of the CCP in 1921, the union of labour and intellect became systematically organized. The modern trade union movement in China thus began and it was to free itself from the influence of the traditional district associations and secret societies in a long and arduous process.

On Labour Day 1922 the first Trade Union Congress of China took place in Canton. Its 162 delegates came from twelve cities, representing more than 100 unions with a total strength of 230000 workers. They discussed the political problems of imperialism and warlordism as well as economic and social problems such as the eight-hour working day, the support of strikes, workers' education, the elimination of secret society influence among the unions, and the formation of a national federation of trade unions. Unionization was greatly helped by the nation-wide strikes of 1925–6 and the Northern Expedition. Take Shanghai for example. Union members there before May 1925 numbered about 20000 and this number was to increase to 120000 by the beginning of 1926. Hupei showed the same trend with a union membership of less than 40000 in 1924 but over 300000 at the beginning of 1927. When the fourth Trade Union Congress was held in Wuhan on 19 June 1927, the total number of unionized workers stood at some 3 million.

That was the peak of the trade union movement, although its members were already under persecution by Chiang Kai-shek's troops and under attack from the secret societies in Shanghai. When the final split between the KMT and CCP occurred, less than a fortnight after the fourth Congress, the membership of the unions dwindled and was less than 2 million in 1928, of which the CCP could influence only about 60000 in Shanghai in 1929. The subsiding of the union movement in the late 1920s and early 1930s was adequately described by the second issue of the *Labour Year Book* (Lao-tung Nien-chien), compiled by the Social Survey Institute of Peiping:

C.A.T.W.—O

In the four years [since 1928], the Chinese labour movement has come completely under the supervision and guidance of the KMT. The dissolution of the General Trade Union of Shanghai on 12 April 1927 marked the beginning of this period. . . . In sum, in the four years of KMT control the party seems to have made no positive contribution to labour. . . . [On the contrary,] the spontaneity of the labour movement has been grievously damaged. Any union that was not recognized by the KMT has either been disbanded or reorganized. The loss of vitality of the union movement under official supervision is only to be expected.

The most potent weapon unionized labour had was, of course, the strike; next came the use of boycotts. It is estimated that between 1895 and 1918, Chinese workers struck either alone or jointly with others for political or economic reasons 152 times. Perhaps the most noteworthy of these occasions were the strike of women workers at Hungk'ou, Shanghai, on 27–8 June 1909 and the Kirin-Ch'angch'un railway workers' strike in June 1910, both for higher wages. The participation of the workers in the May 4th Movement marked a new era for China's labour movement, for it was at this time that Chinese nationalism moved out of its introspective stage into its anti-imperialist stage. Not only was its political consciousness heightened, but its scale was now nation-wide. With the ground so prepared, the alliance between labour and students was more easily formed when the CCP came into being. The first notable creation of this alliance was the union of the Peking–Hankow Railway workers in 1921. At the beginning of 1923 the union had sixteen branches and a membership of 13000. The famous strike, an economic one, staged by the union on 4 February 1923 had the support of the railway unions of the Peking–Suiyuan, Chengting-T'aiyuan and Hankow–Canton lines as well as that of the workers of the Hanyang Foundry, the Third International, and the workers of Korea and Japan. Three days later, however, the military leaders in control of the railway ordered their troops to open fire. In Chengchow alone thirty-seven workers were killed and twenty-seven wounded and there were casualties at other places along the line. This serious setback in the labour movement, coming after the great wave of strikes in 1920–1, had its political repercussions: it considerably but temporarily weakened the confidence of the CCP in proletarian hegemony in the projected revolution and consequently changed its policy concerning the formation of a coalition with the KMT.

The most celebrated single wave of strikes in the modern history of China occurred on 30 May 1925. The prelude to this great movement was that the workers at the Japanese-owned Naigai Wata Kaisha demanded an increase in wages and went on strike; all the workers at Japanese-owned cotton mills in Shanghai joined them. This was in February; and some 30 000 workers took part. Through the good offices of the Chambers of Commerce of Shanghai an agreement was reached and the strikers went back to work. But the management refused to comply with the agreement and the workers struck again at the beginning of May, affecting the third, fourth and seventh mills of the Naigai Wata. On 15 May a clash took place between the management and the strikers at the seventh mill, resulting in the killing of one and wounding of seven other workers. The fact that the factory was situated in the International Settlement involved the British police in the incident. A number of workers were arrested by the police of the Settlement in an attempt to restore order.

The storm gathered during the apparent calm of the next fortnight as the workers and students were forming their alliance and forging their political weapons. The thirteen demands they formulated included the punishment of the culprits who had opened fire on the workers, compensation to the families of the dead and the wounded, better working conditions and higher wages, and also the abolition of unequal treaties, extraterritorial rights, foreign police, etc. On the 30th May the students and workers staged a demonstration and marched to Nanking Road where some workers and students were detained in the police station.

The 30th was a Saturday when most of the Chinese working people were resting in the afternoon while most of the Europeans were out enjoying themselves. With no higher authority available for consultation, the five British police officers and constables had to make a decision of their own in the face of the challenge of some two thousand demonstrators who were threatening to break into the station. They opened fire, precisely forty-four rounds, killing forty to fifty people. In the fracas that followed, four more people were trampled to death there and then, seven died later, eight were seriously injured, and a dozen or so received light wounds. The matter thus became completely out of hand, while the target of the Chinese attack shifted from the Japanese cotton mills to the British imperialists.

At least ten cities, including Peking and Canton, went on strike to show their sympathy with Shanghai, where martial law was declared as workers, merchants and students continued with their agitation and protests. The mobilization of the volunteers of the International Settlement, the bringing up of twenty-six gunboats, and the landing of marines only added fuel to the fire. Now nearly 150000 workers in Shanghai alone were on strike and the strike was against imperialism.

The government in Peking three times protested to the legations against the way the British and Japanese were handling the Shanghai situation; it also sent a delegation, nominally to give support to those who had suffered, but in fact to start negotiations on the spot. Although the discussions with the diplomatic corps failed to reach an agreement, the Naigai Wata, instructed by Tokyo, came to an arrangement with the workers to punish the people responsible for the casualties, to give 10000 *yuan* to the dead worker's family and the wounded as compensation, and to increase wages by 20 per cent. Thus Japan adroitly pulled herself out of an extremely difficult situation.

Of the triumvirate in Peking, Marshal Chang Tso-lin expressed his support for the head of the Provisional Government, Tuan Ch'i-jui, while the Christian general Feng Yü-hsiang was prepared to fight the British. The local military authorities of Hankow and Tientsin suppressed the demonstrations there with the mailed fist. At the time scholarly opinions represented by the venerable Liang Ch'i-ch'ao, the geologist V. K. Ting, the philosopher Hu Shih and the diplomat Wellington Koo, condemned the pipe-dream of the strikers and boycotters as masochistic and 'Boxeristic' and proposed long-term and short-term solutions through peaceful negotiations.

The attitude of the most authoritative British paper in China, the *North China Herald*, as expressed on 6 June was considerably tougher than that of its American equivalent, the *China Weekly Review*, in its issue of 4 July 1925. While the British paper demanded nothing less than 'the unconditional surrender of the students and other agitators', the American weekly expressed its sympathy with 'the pent-up wrath and racial antagonism fostered by half a century of contact between East and West'. Of the foreign residents in Shanghai, the businessmen feared Bolshevism but the missionaries wanted an investigation and eventually some treaty revisions to assuage Chinese nationalist aspirations.*

* For the reactions of the British press, see ch. 1, pp. 51-2.

In Britain, the Trade Union Congress of Britain wrote to the Prime Minister advising the withdrawal of British troops from Shanghai. In the debate on the May 30th demonstrations in the House of Commons, Sir Austen Chamberlain was cautious, refusing to accept the simple theory of Bolshevik conspiracy and proposing the appointment of an international commission of judges from Britain, the USA, France and Japan whose duties would be to investigate the truth and to discuss ways to trammel up the consequences. What was significant in Sir Austen's speech was his recognition of 'a real nationalist spirit' now abroad in China.

By June, there existed a considerable area of common ground between Chinese and foreign public opinion and also among official attitudes towards the whole incident. The strikes and boycotts had quietened down; the ranks of the students were broken by their own dissension; and the merchants had deserted the workers. At the beginning of July the workers of Shanghai became almost completely isolated, and peace was restored throughout the country except in Canton where there was still strong anti-British feeling. This was the time for the government in Peking to advise the nation to wait patiently for an official settlement of the whole affair and it did so. The International Commission of Judges began its investigation in October. There was no Chinese on it; nor was any Chinese witness called to testify throughout the whole investigation.

When the May 30th incident broke out in Shanghai, the KMT headquarters in Canton was preoccupied by the unification of the province of Kwangtung. It did not respond to the then nation-wide wave of strikes and boycotts until 23 June. On that day a mass meeting of some 50000 workers was held after which they marched to Shameen where the foreign community lived. The confrontation led to some fifteen minutes of heavy fire exchanged between the foreign marines, chiefly British and French, and Chinese soldiers; eighty-three people were killed and 500 wounded. Thus began the year-long boycott against Hong Kong.

There were the usual charges that the *other* side had fired the first shot which were followed by protests and demands, counter protests and counter demands. The immediate results of this event were the formation of the National Government of the KMT so that, among other things, the diplomatic affairs could be handled on the spot instead of through Peking, and a strike committee organized to mobilize mass support for the government's diplomacy. A strike

in Canton had the unique feature that it entailed the Hong Kong
workers' going on strike in sympathy and the tightening of the
boycott against Canton–Hong Kong trade. Foreign cargo ships
which used to unload in Hong Kong could now, under special
licence, sail directly to Canton. At first both British and Japanese
ships were refused licences because of the boycott. As the summer
wore on, only British ships were prevented from coming to Canton.
To reinforce the boycott, the workers of Canton and Hong Kong
organized a contingent of 300 pickets to maintain law and order,
stop smuggling and search for traitors.

The strike committee, with the help of the KMT labour department which was largely in the hands of the communists, gathered
together a strike fund of nearly 5 million *yuan* to pay the living
expenses of the 200000 workers from Hong Kong. They took over
gambling houses, opium dens, vacant buildings, etc., to house the
Hong Kong workers while they were on strike. Supplies of food and
fuel were carried by American, Japanese, German and Russian
ships with the co-operation of the peasants and peasant associations
in Kwangtung. This was the first and only time when even a small
number of peasants were involved in this nationalistic movement.

Hong Kong languished under the impact of the boycott. Many
shops and trading firms went out of business and the entrepôt trade
was slashed by half.

Certainly, in October 1926, even after the boycott had ended, Hong
Kong had all the appearance of a deserted village. Business was dead.
Buildings were empty, offices were closed, and there was little activity of
any kind.

Canton, too, suffered grievously. The administration of the boycott
alone cost the KMT government 15000 *yuan* a day. As the KMT
military forces under Chiang Kai-shek urged an early expedition
against the north, the need for money, supplies, and the consolidation of the Canton area made it imperative that the boycott should
end. Chiang's coup of 20 March 1926 weakened the left-wing leadership in the party and the KMT–CCP alliance. After that, feelers
were put out to the Hong Kong authorities while right-wing propaganda against the continuation of the boycott and the strike circulated among the inhabitants of Canton. Then came the proclamation
of martial law in the city in conjunction with the launching of the
Northern Expedition, which put all public organizations, including

the strike committee, under one military authority. By July 1926, the boycott was broken by Chiang's military force and the negotiations with Hong Kong formally began.

The strikes and boycotts of 1925–6 were chiefly political in nature and it is in terms of political gains that they should be judged. Apart from international recognition of the strength of Chinese nationalism and the benefit reaped by both the KMT and CCP during this great movement, the workers of Shanghai had their general trade union organized and recognized. The trade union movement as a whole was also benefited as its membership swelled and its influence was expanded. Unlike previous nationalist movements, e.g. the 1905 boycotts and the May 4th demonstrations, both the leaders and the rank and file of the May 30th Movement came from the proletariat, whose militant anti-imperialism evoked widespread international sympathy and support. The workers of Britain, America and France and the left-wing intellectuals of these countries, including Bernard Shaw, Upton Sinclair and Henri Barbusse, not to mention the Third International, openly declared their admiration and openly condemned the actions of their governments.

During the strikes and boycotts, patriotic businessmen joined forces with the workers and students at first, but gradually cooled off and left the ranks; warlords in Chang Tso-lin and Wu P'ei-fu adopted a hostile attitude, suppressing the workers' movement and trade unions. The military operations in Kwangtung preoccupied Chiang Kai-shek, who maintain an appearance of neutrality to begin with and then revealed his hostility in the spring and summer of 1926. His bloody persecution of the communists and workers in Shanghai in April 1927 intensified his antagonism to any form of class conflict.

In the early stages of the Northern Expedition in Hunan and Hupei Chiang's armies received support from the workers in the form of strikes and sabotage behind the enemy lines and the organization of transport teams to supply Chiang's troops. When his troops were knocking at the gate of Shanghai, the workers there, following the waves of strikes in 1926, rose up to disrupt the economy and defence of the city. Though on a smaller scale, the strikes of 1926 were even more frequent than those of 1925. After the suppression of communists in 1927 the picture changed rapidly. Whereas there had been 318 strikes in 1925 and 535 in 1926, there were only 140, mostly economic and spontaneous, strikes in 1928, involving only a quarter of the number of workers of 1926. Liu Shao-ch'i, an important labour leader, admitted in 1927 that the union organization and political consciousness remained weak after the all too swift expansion of 1925 and 1926. These weaknesses were mercilessly exposed under Chiang's persecution.

The CCP was not willing to abandon the idea of the proletarian hegemony under any circumstances, in spite of the fact that, under persecution, the exodus of its members, some workers but largely students and scholars, from the cities to the countryside was shifting the centre of the party's activities to rural China and was beginning to involve the vast peasantry. The party's leaders in 1927 and 1928 were mostly urban-intellectuals whose urban-centred views on revolutionary theory and strategy were sanctioned by the resolutions on the trade union of the party's sixth congress held in Moscow. The policies were to encourage party members to join what were called 'the yellow unions', to struggle for the legal existence of 'the red unions', and to intensify economic strikes since political strikes were now almost impossible. Proletarian hegemony was deemed by the Executive Committee of the Communist International in its letter to the CCP on 9 February 1929 to be the very foundation of a communist leadership in the Chinese revolution.

Therefore when the party was under his leadership, Li Li-san tried to prop up the hegemony by stirring up strikes in Shanghai, Wuhan, Tientsin and Nanking. On the one hand, he was anxious to prove that any talk of the labour movement lagging behind the peasant movement was unacceptable; on the other, he aimed at the promotion of a general strike in preparation for armed insurrections in major cities, eventually hoping to win preliminary victories in one or several provinces. On the feeble base of only 32000 members in the secret 'red unions', Li's efforts to restore the proletarian hegemony were defeated in the summer of 1930.

The Russian-trained leaders who succeeded Li commanded scant respect from either the communist trade union leaders or the rural soviet leaders. Their assumption of power under extremely difficult conditions alienated the trade union movement. Fortunately for them, the Japanese invasions of Manchuria and Shanghai in 1931 and 1932 offered them an opportunity to consolidate and expand the party's work in the unions. They organized political strikes against Japan, supported the Chinese army fighting in Shanghai and the volunteers in Manchuria, and hoped eventually to turn these scattered pockets of resistance into a national war under the proletarian hegemony. When these efforts came to nothing, the party withdrew into the countryside while the waves of labour movement ebbed.

From 1895 to the early 1930s, the major trends of China's social changes under Western and Russian influence meant the changes in the social and political roles of women, youth and labour. The struggle for their rights meant the gradual decline of the patriarchal and gentry domination of society and state. To landmark these changes the nuclear family system was to a limited extent adopted by the urban educated while the traditional examination system was replaced by modern schools teaching modern curricula and the guilds and secret societies gave way to trade unions among the industrial workers. These metamorphoses brought out the voices of women, youth and labour, which were chiefly political voices, for the struggle for their rights could not be separated from politics. They were sometimes militant and strident voices, for the struggle could and did assume violent dimensions.

Any attempt to curb or suppress the struggle had to be justified, in terms of internal and external peace and order. When it was so justified it implied either a total preservation of the status quo or a slowing down of the process of change in order to avoid provoking a violent reaction. In either case, the ruling elite had to explain why the status quo was worth preserving and why the traditional values were preferable to any other values women, youth and labour wanted to introduce. When the explanation became unconvincing, social and political polarization was bound to occur.

The masses in the struggle were urban masses whose agitation and action affected chiefly urban life. Their numbers compared with the enormous peasantry were small. As long as they failed to stir rural China into political participation, they remained weak *vis-à-vis* the government and foreign intervention. In this sense, the exodus of some of them to the countryside in the summer of 1927 when the KMT–CCP alliance split and the communists were being persecuted was an event of epochal significance. From there on, the peasantry was to become an active participant in Chinese politics. To put it in Napoleonic terms, the awakening of the peasantry of China meant the awakening of the titanic China. However important that may be, it does not fall in the scope of this study.

# Chapter 9

# *Culture*

Unwilling to concede its superiority and yet unable to ignore the two defeats it had suffered in twenty years (1840, 1860), the culturalist empire began its response to the challenge of the West. As we have seen, its initial efforts at consolidating maritime defence grew into a halting industrialization. In this process, the policies, piecemeal though they were, had to be argued out so that their underlying principles, goals and finally efficacy could convince the imperial court, silence the opposition and justify the cost. That the challenge from overseas differed from earlier challenges which had come overland was dimly perceived by the better informed, although the challengers were still labelled 'barbarians' (*yi*). Tradition had taught the Chinese, including the sinocized Manchus, to believe that to learn from the barbarians meant degeneration, with perhaps the borrowing of their martial skills and the study of their languages as the only exception. Therefore, when on 11 December 1866 the Tsungli Yamen proposed to add astronomy, mathematics and other Western natural sciences to the curriculum of the Language Institute in Peking, it was taking an unprecedented step which had to be justified.

By then, the regional leaders in some of the coastal provinces had already had a few years of experience in the foreign ships and guns and had realized that the knowledge needed for such industries was by no means as uncomplicated as people like, for example, Tseng Kuo-fan, had initially expected. Reluctantly they came to the conclusion that Chinese students had to learn science and technology from the 'barbarians'. Aware of the epoch-making nature of their proposal and anxious to have it approved by the throne without provoking unnecessary controversy, Prince Kung and his pragmatic colleagues at the Tsungli Yamen couched their memorial in the routine officialese, offering only one reason for the proposed innovation. Astronomy and mathematics were basic training for defence and defence industries; they were therefore crucial to China's self-strengthening. The employment of foreign teachers for these new subjects was treated by the memorialists as a matter of course.

However, imperial approval did not stifle opposition. Between 11 December 1866 and 28 January 1867, the capital seems to have been buzzing with rumours and excitement. Few had the temerity to challenge Prince Kung, who, as the uncle of the reigning emperor and the leading Grand Councillor, was at the peak of his power; fewer dared to defy the approval of the throne. The matter was not so much a power struggle as a cultural shock. It was in cultural terms that the controversy over the added subjects developed.

What Prince Kung, and his supporters in the provinces such as Li Hung-chang and Tso Tsung-t'ang, meant by astronomy and mathematics for industrial use could not be comprehended by their critics. These *shu* (crafts) had been traditionally applied to calendar-making, irrigation, seismology and meteorology chiefly for the benefit of agriculture; they were also used by heretical Taoists in what Joseph Needham terms aurifaction, aurifiction and macrobiotics as well as in geomancy and fortune-telling. The government appointed *shu* specialists for the first kind of uses while private individuals appealed to them for the second sort. Neither category was of any great significance to the rise and fall of a dynasty. Accordingly they were regarded as *yung* (application) or *mo* (branch) of knowledge, in contrast to the Confucian classics which cultivated the finer qualities of men, making them virtuous rulers or solid citizens. The classical training therefore was the *t'i* (essence) or the *pen* (stem) of knowledge. In other words, what knowledge did depended on what it was, as only good knowledge could guide men to apply useful knowledge to do good things with good results. Despite their excellence in 'weird and obscene' arts the barbarians knew nothing of the Confucian classical cultivation. There was no guarantee that, once in contact with Chinese students, they would refrain from utilizing their *shu* for evil purposes. Furthermore, the master–disciple relation, one of the cardinal human relations in Confucian society, required benevolence and loyalty, hence the necessity that it should be guided by Confucian ethics. Taught by foreigners, the students of astronomy and mathematics would be bound by this traditional tie to their teachers, thus to become untrustworthy and unusable from the point of view of the throne, however skilled in their *shu* they might become.

Forestalling possible objections to his proposal, Prince Kung, in his second memorial on this subject dated 28 January 1867, reinforced his urgent plea that China's defences should be strengthened, and cited none other than the most revered Emperor of the dynasty, the saintly and humane K'ang-hsi (r. 1661–1722), as having set an authoritative precedent. K'ang-hsi had relied on the visiting Jesuit fathers for Western scholarship. As to the shameful feeling of learning from barbarians, Prince Kung reasoned ingeniously:

The Western *shu* of evolution came originally from the Chinese *t'ien-yuan* [the theory of evolution] which the West accepted as an Oriental art. Due to the punctiliousness and thoughtfulness of the Western mind, this mathematical method was further developed to become widely known overseas. It was, in fact, a Chinese innovation.

Prince Kung was not alone in tracing Western genius back to a Chinese origin; this dialectical device was to become hackneyed in the years to come. He went on to quote from the *Analects* – 'ignorance', not an eagerness to learn, even from foreign teachers, 'is the shame of a scholar'.

On 5 March 1867 a minor official dared to send in a memorial, criticizing the undue importance and urgency ascribed to the training, and eventual appointment, of Confucian scholars in the *shu* of manufacturing ships and guns. The main concern of a Confucian scholar was to understand the essence (*ming-t'i*) of his culture so that he knew how to apply his learning (*ta-yung*). The classics alone could foster his loyalty and integrity from which discipline, good government and justice might be derived to strengthen the empire.

Thus far, the debate was unequal, a minor official having pitched himself against the puissance of Prince Kung. The critic's memorial was shelved and the matter was dismissed in a few sentences by an imperial edict of the same day. Then a highly respected classicist, the chancellor of the Hanlin Academy, Grand Secretary Wo-jen, threw his immense authority behind the minor official. In an elegantly composed representation to the throne on 20 March 1867, Wo-jen argued:

The foundation of an empire rests on propriety and righteousness, not schemes and stratagems. Its roots lie in the hearts of men, not skills and crafts. Now for the sake of a trivial knack, we are to honour barbarians as our masters. Even if these guileful aliens impart their secrets sincerely and our students learn likewise, all we shall gain will be a number of professional artisans whose adroitness has never been known as a means of strengthening a country. The empire is vast and abundant in human talents. If astronomy and mathematics must be studied, there are bound to be some Chinese who are well-versed in them. Why do we have to approach barbarians? What reason is there to respect them as our teachers?

Wo-jen feared that barbarianization might lead to a dissipation of the righteous spirit (*cheng-ch'i*) of the people. The loss of such a vital asset would sadly outweigh the gain of 'a trivial' knack.

Wo-jen went on:

Victory needs loyal and trustworthy people to win it; self-strengthening needs upright and righteous people to attain it. We need no outstanding intelligence to appreciate this truth. Having studied the ancient *Odes* and *History*, scholars are now required to pay homage to barbarian teachers. Their willingness to do so is an indication of the state of their integrity. Even if they learn well, can they be expected to retain morality in their hearts so as to render their best service of which they are to the empire? [I am] afraid that most of them will be used as mere tools by their barbarian masters.

The farthing candle of the minor official could easily be snuffed out; the Grand Secretary's fume required more serious attention. Prince Kung stuck to his pragmatic primary considerations, the defence of the empire. Avoiding the main thrust of Wo-jen's argument, but charging him with spreading rumours irresponsibly so that no one would be willing to take these new courses, the prince challenged him on a matter of fact. Since the Grand Secretary had asserted the possibility of discovering Chinese scholars well versed in these subjects, the prince claimed to be overjoyed that the arduous search for such people that he had been conducting for twenty years could now come to an end. He requested the throne to direct Wo-jen to send in a few names. After the names had been given, he suggested, Wo-jen should be appointed the head of another institute at another place for the students to study astronomy and mathematics under Chinese instructors. The imperial directive was issued as requested and the Grand Secretary retired from the debate.

But before long, probably at Wo-jen's instigation, another minor official, one Yang T'ing-hsi, elaborated in a memorial of 23 June 1867 what Wo-jen had omitted. The immediate reason for Yang's memorial was the inauspicious astrological phenomenon of the drought in the spring of that year; what he wanted was to have the Language Institute abolished altogether. Yang's logic rested on the correlation theory of Han Confucianism which maintained that there was a mystic link between astrology and human affairs – the famine was the result of the creation of the Institute. Beseeching the throne to concentrate on improving moral discipline instead of adopting arts and crafts to increase the prosperity of the empire, Yang was puzzled by the speed with which yesterday's enemy became today's master of astrological skills (*hsing-hsü*). He was puzzled by the great importance attached to ships and machines in warfare. In his view, man, not guns, was the factor which determined victory or defeat. Yang was also puzzled by the disregard of the distinction between the Chinese and the barbarian, the respected and the disrespected, principles and mere skill of doing things.

If we send [Confucian scholars] to pay respect to barbarians as their tutors and let them live and work with barbarians day in and day out, they may be misled and even duped by the scheming barbarians so that they will become so confused as to pledge their loyalty to their teachers and their teachers' religion. That will be the end of their loyalty and sense of righteousness, of their incorruptibility and sense of shame.

Yang was puzzled by the idea that these scholars so trained would in twenty years be promoted to positions of importance and would be influential enough to sway ministers in the court and governors in the provinces. 'What then will become of the morale of the civil service?'

Nevertheless, although Yang's memorial was ignored and Wo-jen received an imperial warning which rounded off the whole matter, the cultural issues which had been brought out in the memorials were highly significant. None of the debaters of 1867 was a scientist who knew anything about the scope and methodology of science. Wen-hsiang, Prince Kung's associate at the Yamen, refused to believe that the earth circled round the sun. The obvious confusion of astronomy with astrology in his opponents' argument was not pointed out by the prince. To those on both sides of the controversy, science possessed no other value than its practical utility as if it was a cutting which could be grafted onto the stem of Confucianism, Christianity, or any other philosophical system. No one in the debate had any inkling that science and Confucianism might be incompatible; no one suspected that Confucianism was becoming historical and needed changing.

Although Prince Kung had his new courses successfully mounted, the authority of Confucian orthodoxy as the stem or the essence of learning was reaffirmed. It had conceded little, a mere branch, an application, in which the Chinese could condescend to learn from the barbarians who, after all, had a measure of punctiliousness and thoughtfulness of mind. This debate may thus be regarded as the beginning of the formula – Chinese learning as the essence with Western learning only for application. The training of scientists in Peking and the manufacture of ships and guns near Shanghai and Foochow were the beginning of China's industrialization in every sense, however limited their scope might have been. Now the formula spread a cloak over the industrialization to give it an extraneous value since it had no value of its own. The useful knowledge borrowed from the West was not for the benefit of the West, not even for any purpose inspired by cosmopolitan thinking, but for the defence of the Confucian culture the scholars and officials cherished. The formula was to guide China's first and only industrialization policy for a whole generation.

Wo-jen's influence was to be seen in the number and quality of the candidates for the new courses. Of the ninety-eight enrolled, few were degree-holders, though it was degree-holders that Prince Kung had had in mind in his original plan. When the qualifying examination was held on 21 June 1867, only forty-two participated; eventually thirty of them were selected. To make things worse, the Language Institute engaged as astronomy instructor one Johannes von Gumpach, 'an impostor' in the words of W. A. P. Martin, perhaps also a little mad, who aspired to do no less than to overthrow the Newtonian theory of gravitation. The fact that Gumpach had to be dismissed and died in destitution tended to confirm Chinese suspicions of the turpitude of barbarians. Even the building of an observatory for the astronomy students caused an argument and a compromise. The traditional geomancists laid down that the building must not have more than three storeys.

A year after the 'astronomy–mathematics' debate in China, Emperor Meiji of Japan in his Charter Oath announced Japan's resolve: 'Knowledge shall be sought for all over the world and, thereby the foundations of the imperial rule shall be strengthened.' No such unequivocal statement was heard at any time during the entire history of Chinese modernization before the May 4th Movement. The difference between the first generation of the essence-application school of modernizers of the 1860s–1890s and the second generation of the 1890s–1910s lay not in one being more eclectic than the other, one being more sociological than the other, but in one being more confident than the other. The theoretical formulation of the first generation was hammered out at the beginning of China's modernization when the Western *yung*, application, had not yet made enough inroads into the Confucian *t'i*, essence. At the same time, the *yung* itself, as yet untried or just being tried for the first time, promised success and radiated a glow of optimism about the solving of China's defence problems. The confidence was a confidence in Confucianism as still being able to encompass and answer all questions posed by life as a whole. No other schools of thought, indigenous or imported, could possibly challenge its authority. It remained monolithic.

After some thirty years of practical experience of industrialization, the *t'i-yung* modernizers grew aware of the strains and stresses, anxieties and disappointments brought by their approach. The first warning that something had gone gravely wrong, when France threatened China in 1884–5, was allowed to pass and be forgotten. The test case of the Japanese War of 1894–5 sealed the fate of the first generation of the *t'i-yung* policies. From the ashes of the war, the second generation of the *t'i-yung* theory and policies emerged. In one sense, the circumstances of 1860 and 1895 were not radically different, for the dynasty was in jeopardy at both times. But the fact that the second shattering defeat came after thirty years of the self-strengthening movement made it all the more unnerving. Domestically, the sphere of the Western *yung* had been expanded greatly to invade the domain of the traditional *t'i* as if to show that it had a *t'i* of its own, independent from Confucian values; externally, the same *yung* had been so successfully exploited in Japan, a country clearly not part of the Great West and much smaller than China, that she was now able to humble the empire. If the *t'i-yung* dichotomy was to remain valid, the Chinese had to explain what *t'i* the Japanese had preserved in order to make the Western *yung* victorious.

The concern over preserving the *t'i* still cut deep, but now with less assurance, more trepidation. The periodical *Hsiang-hsüeh-pao* (Hunan Scholars), of 21 February 1898, taking exception to the interference in China's internal affairs by some notable missionaries, and the barbarianization of a large number of urban Chinese, worried about the coming disaster, 'the emergence of an unimaginable and unclassifiable species of cultural hybrids (*tsa-jen*)'. The Shanghai *Shen-pao* of 13 June 1898 attributed the fact that all the American-trained students of the 1870s became disgustingly 'foreignized' and took up jobs with foreign firms instead of serving their country to their ignorance of the great traditional virtues. Both T'an Ssu-t'ung, a staunch reformer, and Chang Chih-tung, an enlightened conservative, expressed anxiety over the preservation of the country, the Confucian teachings and the Chinese race. In a letter to his teacher, Ou-yang Chung-ku, in 1896, T'an showed an intense fear that it would be impossible to save the sagacious teachings of thousands of years and the yellow race of 400 million people from coming to an abrupt end.

The kernel of Confucian teachings had to be protected to preserve the cultural identity of the Chinese. What came to an abrupt end was the self-strengthening policies, not the *t'i-yung* formulation. Liang Ch'i-ch'ao, despite his vehement criticism of Li Hung-chang and Chang Chih-tung, still posed the questions he asked in this fashion: what would be the use of Chinese scholarship without Western learning? What would be the foundation of Western learning without Chinese scholarship? Cheng Kuan-yin, a compradore, asked his questions in a similar manner: 'Without the [Chinese] essence, how could [the Western application] stand by itself? Without the [Western] application, how could [the essence] have any function?' Both these voluble reformers of the 1890s were still thinking in terms of the *t'i-yung* formulation. But the diffident *t'i* depended on the much enlarged *yung* so that it might have any practical meaning. Evidently unable to go back to the days before the Opium War, *t'i* and *yung* became now symbiotic in a dialectical relationship which, it was hoped, would promote the growth of both in harmony.

When formulated in this way, both the permanency and the absolute authority of Confucianism were open to doubt. In his *Hsin-hsüeh wei-ching k'ao* and *K'ung-tzu kai-chih k'ao* (On the Forged Classics of the Hsin Learning, and On Confucius as a Reformer,

1891 and 1897 respectively), K'ang Yu-wei refuted the traditional interpretation of the role of Confucius by dressing up the sage as a progressive reformer. The sage and other thinkers of his kind were anxious to use the teachings of the past to reform the politics of their time; his writings and compilations were therefore no more sacrosanct or permanently valid than those of his contemporary philosophers. This démerche of K'ang Yu-wei liberated the intellectual life of China and opened up the possibility of comparative study of all the ancient philosophies, including perhaps even a comparative study of Chinese and Western philosophies. For K'ang the primary concern was *jen*, the Confucian humaneness, which must control a scholar's intellectual pursuits, e.g. practical statesmanship, textual criticism and poetic literature. If *jen* was the essence with intellectual pursuits (statecraft, for instance) as its application, then traditional morality, largely Confucian, would be the foundation for such intellectual products as a constitution and a parliament. What could be permanent was the system of morality; what should be changed were the institutions, methods of production, etc.

K'ang's *jen*, which was also T'an Ssu-t'ung's, differed significantly from Chang Chih-tung's *jen-cheng* (humane government, paternalism) although both schools of thought stressed the importance of 'rectifying the heart' (*cheng hsin*). When the emphasis was on *jen* alone, all institutions, political, legal, economic, as well as societal, were alterable; when the emphasis was on *jen-cheng*, those institutions which made up the structure of paternalism could not and should not be changed. *Jen-cheng* as expounded by Chang Chih-tung in his famous essay 'On Learning' (1898), was therefore syncretic, aiming at the preservation of both the traditional morality and some of the traditional institutions, the sum total of which he called *ming-chiao*, the name and the teachings or the teachings and their forms. In choosing what was to be preserved and what was to be changed, one must apply one's judgement fairly and cautiously so as to achieve the optimum result or strike the golden mean (*chung-cheng*), and in a way that was neither obscurantist nor radical. On this ground, Chang was opposed not only to the reformist interpretation of Confucianism but also to such dangerous ideas as people's rights, equality before the law and sexual equality.

The British-trained Yen Fu lashed out at the Chinese essence–Western application approach.

An ox *yung* (uses) its *t'i* (body) to carry weight; a horse uses its body to run fast. I have never heard of making the body of an ox to run fast. . . . Chinese learning has its essence and application just as Western learning has its. They both thrive when [the Chinese and Western] are separated, but both would wither if they were mixed up.

To Yen, what his contemporaries called 'application' chiefly consisted of Western science. This total travesty of the truth, Yen thought, 'overlooks the fact that the good government of the West comes precisely from the application of science. Science is the *essence* of Western government.' Yen was more concerned with what was contemporaneously regarded as 'right', which the Chinese knew all about, than with what they regarded as 'wrong', of which they knew little. It was the 'right' which was obsolete and should be eliminated, and its elimination, to Yen, was much more difficult than the introduction of the 'wrong', which was new and progressive.

To show the essence of Western government and society in order to promote China's modernization and her progress towards national power and wealth, Yen translated some of the works which expounded social Darwinism. His enterprise, in the first place, explained the international milieu in which China then found herself – the competition among the nations in which the fittest would survive, and in the second place, instilled an evolutionary view of history which gave the pariah empire a gleam of hope. If China could educate her people by strengthening their intellect, morals and physique, the country would survive and flourish. But in the absence of an individualistic tradition, social Darwinism in China came to focus on the nation and its culture rather than on individuals and their welfare. The strengthening of the individual was for the revitalization of the nation and its culture. This was possible because the nation and its culture had had a glorious past, while all the individual and collective weaknesses were remediable.

The reform of 1898 failed to achieve its political goals and at the same time the essence–application formula failed to defend the absolute authority of Confucianism. The catch phrase of *t'i-yung* continued to circulate, but the doctrine had now become a political and intellectual battleground. If the Chinese trained in the Confucian tradition were no longer morally, intellectually and physically fit, the concept of the Confucian gentlemanship must go. It was two years after the Boxer fiasco that Liang Ch'i-ch'ao in exile sat down to work out a new concept of a model personality, the new citizen, in his essay under that title. The intellectual device Liang used to define his new citizen was the bifurcation of morality into the public and the private without indicating which of the two was the *t'i* and which was the *yung*, for morality as a whole was the *t'i*. Unifying the country and society, public morality qualified a man to participate in politics and other public affairs, and his loyalty was to the nation in contradistinction to the particularistic Confucian loyalty to the monarch and one's family. The Confucian ethics based on the traditional family system were particularly weak in their exposition of public morality or in giving guidance for conduct in any association which was not derived or extended from the family system. Here Liang stepped outside the Confucian bounds to introduce what was new to the Chinese. And private morality? There Liang could not think beyond Confucian ethics, for he was familiar with neither individualism nor privacy. As a Confucian personal moral discipline acquired through one's socialization at home and the modern impersonal moral discipline acquired, if all went well, through a similar process at school were not always compatible, let alone integrated, how was one to resolve the differences? How was one to reconcile the moral relativism of one's public life with the moral absolutism of one's private life? Liang could furnish no cogent answer. The threat of an invasion by Confucian ethics of the realm which should be dominated by modern morality still loomed large.

The general political scene in the early years of the Republic with all its accompanying problems favoured a Confucian revival. K'ang Yu-wei, joined by two foreign-trained scholars – Ku Hung-ming (Edinburgh) and Ch'en Huan-chang (Columbia and Chicago) – equated Confucianism in a most un-Confucian way to the great religions of the world, and pleaded for its inclusion as the state religion in the constitution being drafted. If it was transformed into an organized religion like Christianity, Islam, or Shinto, Confucianism could help unify the nation and at the same time become separated from the administration. If this was done, its unifying power could contribute to good administration in one sense and its separation from the administration, in another sense, could dissociate it from the weakness of China. The material evidence that religion could perform the former function was the rise of the Protestant nations of the West, and that it could perform the latter function was evidenced by the survival of the Jewish, Muslim and Catholic peoples in spite of the destruction or languidness of their countries.

A parallel development was the concept of national quintessence (*kuo-ts'ui*) which began to occur in the writings of 1905. This was not an intellectual tool, but simply a banner used to rally all defenders of Confucianism, scholars, politicians and warlords. They founded the *National Quintessence Monthly* in that year and the Society for the Preservation of National Studies and the Society for National Honour of the Divine Country soon afterwards. Even the Rotary Club was used as a vehicle for the promotion of Confucian studies. Warlords publicly exalted Confucian doctrine and ordered schools everywhere to increase the hours devoted to Confucian classics. They also sponsored the reprinting of the classics and established colleges for classical studies while they themselves worshipped the sage in Confucian temples. For them, the quintessence was purely spiritual with no utility value, whereas the Western learning was chiefly material in nature. Derived from the spiritual quintessence were morality, merits and literary brilliance which, instead of hindering, would help vitalize material Western studies. The two branches of knowledge now became interdependent; one would shrivel away without the other. Although the quintessentialists did not seem to have advanced beyond the position held by Liang Ch'i-ch'ao and Cheng Kuan-yin nearly ten years earlier, their methodology of contrasting the East and West, spiritual and material, static and dynamic continued to influence even such radical thinkers and Ch'en Tu-hsiu and Li Ta-chao. Hu Shih also commented in 1919: 'Too many people nowadays talk about the preservation of the national quintessence without understanding what the quintessence is.' In his view, a critical and scientific method was needed to define and re-examine what was the quintessence and what was rubbish before one could say what should and should not be preserved.

The aim of the defenders of Confucianism was to arrest the disintegration of the Republic and the decay of morality which affected the conduct of public and private affairs. The quintessence was an intensely moral issue. It was on moral grounds that the iconoclasts fired their salvos against it. For Li Ta-chao and Ch'en Tu-hsiu, moral standards changed with social changes. What had been suitable standards in the past could not be applied to the present. Neither 'the teacher for a myriad generations' nor 'the universally valid doctrine' was logically or practically possible.

What had been proved beneficial to imperial China was now detrimental to the Republic. Filial piety and chastity were notable examples: they denied the individual the right to independent development of his personality and were in fact the moral standards of slaves.

In this intellectual context, an eccentric scholar, Wu Yü, who had publicly accused his father of misconduct in April 1911 and had since lived under a cloud of unfiliality, stepped forward to attack Confucian ethics as 'cannibalistic':

In the hierarchical Confucian system the respected and disrespected were based on the observation of the lofty heaven and the humble earth, there were the noble sovereign and his humble subjects, respected fathers and their humble children, respected husbands and their humble wives, and respected officials and the humble people they governed.

In a rigidly stratified society of this kind, everyone was assigned a position in the hierarchical order and its ethics were those of despotism; therefore they should be abolished.

The debate between the Confucian conservatives and the modern iconoclasts continued. The European War with its exposure of the weakness of Western civilization bolstered the traditionalists' confidence; the Confucian revival now acquired another *raison d'être* beside the preservation of the Chinese identity, namely, the avoidance of a repetition of Western mistakes. Intellectually, however, it became increasingly barren, while the iconoclasts tried to define a new model personality, the *new youth*. The new youth of China were active in their service to society and iconoclastic in their attitude towards tradition. Armed with their new values, science and democracy, they hoped to bring about a new China which was materially comfortable and socially free and equal. Now that iconoclasm and individual emancipation had been added, the concept of the new youth of 1919 differed from Liang Ch'i-ch'ao's idea of the new citizen of 1902. The liberal Hu Shih could go as far as to say:

Children did not voluntarily choose to be born in the homes of their parents. Instead, the parents gave them their lives without much consideration of their consent. . . . How can the parents then claim to have performed some wonderful service and insist on having done a great favour for their children? . . . Having brought a human being into this world, the parents must be responsible for his happiness or unhappiness, his merits or demerits. Let me put it in an extreme fashion. When we give life to a child, we are in fact sowing the seeds of trouble, trouble for society. . . . As we educate and look after the child, we are in fact redeeming our sin. . . . In short, what I have been saying is that we have done our children no favour. As to their feelings about us, that is their business, completely beyond our control.

Confucian filial piety on the part of the children thus became original sin on the part of the parents; even the heart of the essence was threatened by Westernization. Following this train of thought, Hsü Chih-mo, the Cambridge-educated poet, could write: 'First, I must examine myself in order to find out what I am, and then decide how I should proceed from here on this road of life I did not choose to take.' Therefore propriety, the family, society, etc., were all nonsense and should be treated as such; therefore the essayist Chou Tso-jen could, in 1926, sever his relations with his teacher, the classicist Chang T'ai-yen on account of Chang's political activities; and Chou Shu-jen (Lu Hsün) could advise the young people:

Let us shout aloud, [pleasantly] like an oriole or [unpleasantly] like an owl. There is no reason whatever for us to imitate the tones of those who have just left a brothel but brag about 'the Chinese morality being the best in the world'.

Seen in this way, the introduction of Western philosophies and literature in the years after the First World War was not as completely without rhyme or reason as the buddhologist, T'ang Yung-t'ung, suggested. Goethe's *Werther*, Ibsen's *Nora*, and Wilde's *Lady Windermere* all fell into their place in the line of battle deployed against the 'quintessence'.

But the West was not for the exclusive use of the iconoclasts; Confucianism could be dressed up to look modern. The debate between the metaphysicians and scientists in 1923–4 was in a sense an extension of the long drawn out battle between the Confucians and their critics,* but now the protagonists of spiritual values enlisted Eucken, Bergson and other Western sages to reinforce Confucius. In his introduction to Mrs Katherine Fullerton Gerould's *Modes and Morals* (1920), Irving Babbit's Chinese disciple, Wu Mi, pointed out to his readers that the Westerners also had their rules of conduct, and in his introduction to Babbit's comparison of European and Asian civilizations, Wu stressed the fact that in the

* See above, p. 188.

West moral discipline also played an important part in society. Morality West was thus borrowed to reinforce morality East. More ingenious but less cautious, Professor Miu Feng-lin, in his discussion on the meaning of life, identified Nietzsche's individualism and Tolstoy's humanitarianism with the ethos of the Confucian *Four Books* which, in his view, started from the premise of individualism (the cultivation of oneself) to end in humanitarianism (love of others). In this sense, modern Confucianism represented a synthesis of these two separately developed schools of modern Western thought. Its renewal would therefore strengthen China without at the same time committing the mistakes of the West. Wu, Miu, and other admirers of the traditional quintessence who put forward programmes of action to save China failed to structure any coherent theoretical system; their scattered incidental observations and reflections amounted to little more than a repetition of old theories East and West.

It was left to Liang Shu-ming in his *Tung-hsi wen-hua chi ch'i che-hsüeh* (Oriental and Occidental Civilizations and their Philosophies, 1921) to systematize the position of the essence–application school after the May 4th Movement. At this stage of China's intellectual development, the conservatives aimed at the preservation of her cultural identity in order to save China and avoid falling into Western mistakes, while their critics wished to bring up a generation of new youth, combative in spirit and iconoclastic in attitude to take up the task of reconstructing China. The barrenness of conservatism left the essence of the Confucian tradition seriously eroded. Liang Shu-ming, to be sure, did not fall into the trap of contrasting the spiritual civilization of the East with the material civilization of the West. For him, all cultural achievements stemmed from man's spiritual activities; therefore all differences between the great civilizations were reducible to different spiritual orientations. The West was oriented towards advancement and progress; India towards backwardness and retrogression; China towards a compromise, a golden mean between the two. When faced by a problem, man searched for a total solution for his total satisfaction, escaped from the need to tackle it by having a firm disbelief in its solubility, or handled it pragmatically while doubting its solubility. These varied patterns of reaction to a problem were, in Liang's view, characteristic of the three civilizations. They also marked the three stages of cultural development – the youthful West anxious to have all its problems solved to its satisfaction, the mature China unsure that all problems were soluble, the aged India denying that any problem was soluble.

In more specific terms, these characteristics and stages were symbolized by the declining interest in religion and metaphysics in the West, the thriving interest in them in India, and the nonchalance to them prevalent in China. The West, in the midst of a religious decline and having reached a metaphysical impasse, excelled in epistemology, the total absence of which in India was due to the dominance of religion and metaphysics, while China had surpassed both of them in developing a philosophy of life, the totality of her philosophical research which now found its parallel in the views of Russell and Kropotkin.

The Westerners' eagerness to solve problems, armed as they were with a highly developed epistemology, had been the cause of their material affluence and superior standard of living, but had also led them into egotism and rationalism. On the one hand, the Westerner satisfied his desires and emancipated his personality; but, on the other, he also attenuated, if he did not break off, his relationship with others because of a clash of interests. His rational attitude towards others became calculated. At the other extreme, India, shrugging off her problems and indulging in religious meditation, wallowed in dire poverty and suffered from a general cultural destitution. Hers was a civilization to be rejected. Between the two extremes, and therefore striking the golden mean, the Chinese had a material standard of living far below that of the West, but drew greater enjoyment from whatever was at his disposal than the Westerner. He cherished what he had instead of craving for what he had not. His contentment therefore made him socially more acceptable, a happier person in the company of others. For him, the search for happiness depended on one's intuition and feelings, on one's compassion for others, rather than on rational analysis and egotism. Compassion, in Liang's view, had its defects also; it thwarted the growth of individuality, thus making China a country without beauty in her religion or music and scarcely any beauty in her literature.

Since all these three civilizations had evolved differently, it was futile for China to talk about Westernization or to catch up with the West. For Liang, even the superiority of the West was not sufficiently certain to warrant Chinese emulation. Who could tell that in the final analysis the West would not come round to see the merits of Chinese civilization and decide to embark on a course of sino-cization? The attractiveness of the Chinese model was overshadowed by the present cultural crisis in which China's traditional values were in decay. Who could tell what the future would be, once China had successfully restructured her culture, revitalized it and made it articulate? In so doing, she should critically refurbish her tradition (Confucianism) and blend it with elements borrowed from abroad and put them through a process of sinocization so that the inherent values and attitudes of these elements were made to harmonize with Chinese tradition and thus made suitable for Chinese use. Only in this way could the civilizations of the world be propelled into a stage of human understanding from the stage where man only understood nature. Having reached that understanding, man would have both material satisfaction and the spiritual serenity to enjoy the comfort which he could draw from himself and his environment. It would be a civilization of compromise, of the golden mean, of the Chinese orientation.

Liang was repelled by Western acquisitiveness, which he tried to moderate with Confucian compassion, probably unaware that to harness the uninhibited Western man to Confucian virtue was to return to the essence–application dichotomy, this time in the disguise of the dichotomy of compassion and desire. However, he did not elaborate on how desires could be controlled by compassion, so as to spare China the agonies of a capitalist society; nor did he depict what sort of society China would have once compassion and desires were held in a delicate balance. Hu Shih criticized him precisely on these points. According to Hu, the contentment derived from a compassion for others had led China into her present complacency and ignorance. Nature was left unexploited and irrational institutions were allowed to continue unreformed. On the other hand, the divine discontent of the West had produced science and industry, the rights and freedoms of man, the equality of the sexes, and a respect for labour. It would be sheer folly for the Chinese to sit there like a lazy wise man, devoid of thought and action, happily accepting whatever fate should come. Hu wanted to see that the Chinese embraced a critical attitude in the search for truth.

This was not the first time that Hu expressed his support for total Westernization; nor was he the first to express this view. At the other extreme, the radical iconoclasts of the May 4th Movement generation began to examine the mistakes in their intellectual conviction and political action. The alliance between the KMT and CCP broke up in 1927; the revolution had changed its nature. In the aftermath of these events, Marxists and non-Marxists opened the debate on the nature of Chinese society from which ensued another, more detailed discussion on the problems of rural China, seeking to ascertain the position of the gentry and its ideological role. The outcome of the debates was a general agreement that Chinese society was semi-feudal under the influence of the feudal ideology of Confucianism among others. Thus the left became more deeply committed to the eradication of the tradition as a step towards laying the foundation of a socialist China.

Of those in favour of total Westernization, Ch'en Hsü-ching, an American-trained sociologist, thought it was illogical to characterize Oriental culture as essentially spiritual and Occidental culture as essentially material. Equally illogical was to describe one of them as static and the other as dynamic. All civilizations had to solve both material and spiritual problems; all were dynamic in the process of constant change. He seriously doubted the validity of Liang's psychological analysis of desire. In his view, desire was never completely satiable and was therefore always seeking satisfaction, making it a powerful driving force for social progress. It never stood still in a perpetual state of contentment or went back to deny its own existence. Furthermore, Liang's sequential development from the West, through China, to India in three stages was logically impossible. What would be the future of the Indian stage, if one assumed that all civilizations, even that of India, were in a state of constant flux? What would be the future of the Western and Chinese civilizations if one of them did not fuse with the other?

In Ch'en's appraisal, modern European civilization had in every aspect outstripped China. Not only its material standard of living, but its politics, education and morality were also more advanced. An organic entity which defied compartmentalization for the convenience of comparison, civilization, in Ch'en's view, could not and should not be handled in the way it had been handled by Liang. The only valid comparison was through time in a linear progress from the less to the more advanced stages. Civilizations could be old and new, of a higher or lower stage of development. Any other method of comparison was bound to be meaningless. In the present stage of growth, Western civilization threatened to become universal while Chinese civilization was in rapid decline. It was consequently inconceivable that the two could mix in any proportion, as essence or as application, to produce a harmonious new entity.

Those who argued in favour of creating such a new entity on the ground of China's special conditions omitted to define their terms. If the special conditions meant China's historical tradition, then the act of creation could mean only an admixture of the old with the new in an attempt to preserve the old as the essence. If the special conditions meant that there were some strong points in the Chinese civilization, what were the strong points?

The decline of the Chinese civilization was due to a host of reasons which had inhibited and stifled the individualities and abilities of the Chinese. For the emancipation of the individual it was imperative that the tradition as a whole should be jettisoned. Total Westernization was the only answer.

Hu Shih's own position vacillated between that of the preservationists and that of the total Westernizers in the 1926–30 period, perhaps due to the American-trained sociologist P'an Kuang-tan's criticism of his initial stance. His essay of 1929, 'The Cultural Conflict in China', published in the *Christian Year Book*, favoured wholesale and wholehearted Westernization and it was to the word, 'wholesale', that P'an strongly objected. An essay he wrote in the next year, 'Introducing My Own Views' (*Chieh-shao wo-ti ssu-hsiang*), avoided advocating such sweeping change. Like all those of his contemporaries who had a deep concern with Chinese cultural problems, Hu did not flinch from accepting any foreign culture wholeheartedly as long as it could resurrect and rejuvenate China.

Judging by the debates in the 1920s and 1930s, the May 4th Movement had not completely discredited the essence–application formula. To add to the tribulations of the Westernizers, the decline of Western prestige stimulated a resurgence of the cultural confidence of the traditionalists. The seesaw battle between the two schools of thought left the new intelligentsia as confused as before in the early 1930s, with no clear conclusions or strategies in view. In this confusion, the KMT took a hand by founding the Association for Cultural Reconstruction with Ch'en Li-fu, leader of the C–C Clique of the party, as its president. Its official organ, the *Cultural Reconstruction Monthly* (Wen-hua chien-she yüeh-k'an), began publication. Two conferences, in Shanghai on 19 January 1935 and in Nanking on 31 January 1935, were held, and to which a number of scholars were invited. They listened to the organizers' report, expressed their views, but developed no criticisms or discussion. The conference held in Peking on 31 March 1935 was made noteworthy by the absence of all the academic luminaries.

These conferences were designed to sound out the reactions of the leading intellectuals of the time to the Declaration on the Reconstruction of Chinese Indigenous Culture published on 10 January 1935 over the names of ten professors with close K M T ties. The basic theme of the Declaration was the fear of the loss of Chinese identity through the loss of cultural identity. In such an eventuality, the term 'Chinese' would cease to have any meaning. To save China from this lamentable fate, the ten professors bravely undertook to initiate a reconstruction of the indigenous culture to meet the needs of present-day China. In order to do so, they intended to redefine the national characteristics of the Chinese through a study of the tradition and present conditions of the country. Only then could the professors decide what theories and institutions were to be kept and which were to be discarded, what was to be absorbed from abroad and what was to be rejected. The preserved and absorbed elements would thereafter be blended in a process of creating, of reconstructing a new culture. Guided by neither obscurantism nor a blind admiration of the West, these scholars would critically examine both China's past and Western present, keeping a firm grasp on current needs in their efforts to lay the foundations of a bright future for their country.

More a political statement than an intellectual challenge, the Declaration was general and imprecise. It did not specify the criteria used in the selection beyond the vague expression, 'the present needs of China'; nor did it give details of the methodology of selection. The strong K M T ties of the signatories and the fact that Ch'en Li-fu had presided over the enterprise tended to discourage genuine criticism of the Declaration. Hu Shih, in his two articles on the subject, advised his fellow countrymen not to fear a total exposure to the new culture of the West, for culture, always conservative and resistant to change, had an inertia of its own which ensured its continued survival under any circumstances. Total Westernization would never result in total eradication of the Chinese tradition; it would arrive only at a reconciliation of the two, preserving what was strong and obliterating what was weak in a natural process of selection. The term, 'total Westernization', appeared inadequate to him. A better alternative would be 'total internationalization', for he was in favour of accepting whatever, from any quarter, was beneficial to the country. There was a tinge of inconsistency in Hu's views. It was uncertain whether he supported total Westernization or internationalization at the expense of tradition, or only wanted to see what part of the curate's egg was still good enough for the Chinese palate. This slight ambivalence may have originated from his own uncertainty about the wisdom and practicability of a total change. Torn between his anxiety to integrate Chinese culture into the mainstream of world culture and his concern to meet China's nationalistic needs, Hu the cosmopolitan liberal and Hu the patriot came into conflict. Divided by this conflict, he remained unable to conclude in choosing whether cultural interchange should be conducted freely as a natural, uninterrupted process, or dictatorially under the surveillance and selection of a higher authority.

None the less, Hu judged the attempt of the ten professors to be another version of the essence–application formula. This the professors denied in their reply of 10 May 1935. In their perspective, each civilization had its own essence and application, hence it would be foolish to propose either a total restoration which would deny a place to anything foreign of value to the Chinese, or a total Westernization which would deny a place to anything Chinese of value to the Chinese. Thus, they rejected Hu Shih's charge while confirming its truth by their very words. Lying underneath their compromise between the two extremes was the formula of essence–application, for they feared, as indicated in their reply, that the loss of Chinese cultural identity would be a disaster. Again, they omitted to define what they meant by the cultural identity of China. Neither Hu Shih nor Ch'en Hsü-ching could see any good theory or institution in the Chinese tradition worth keeping in order to preserve Chinese cultural identity, while the ten professors vaguely felt that there must be something worth the trouble of safeguarding. In their reply they did, however, define the basic requirements for a reconstructed indigenous culture. It should (a) enrich the material and spiritual life of the people, (b) develop the economy of the country, and (c) defend the existence of the nation. When these demands were fulfilled, they hoped the confidence of the Chinese would be restored.

As Ch'en Hsü-ching pointed out in his critique of the reply, the three demands could be combined into one – the first in effect encompassed the other two. Although no one would dispute the need to raise the material standard of living of the people, the method of attaining this might be open to discussion. The real bone of contention lay in the enrichment of spiritual life. Since the ten professors denied that they were obscurantists or compromisers, what alternative was open to them but total Westernization?

The interesting point in the three demands had to do with the question of life, its material and spiritual continuation and enrichment. The point becomes clearer when one considers the list of recommended reading for an organization affiliated to the Association for the Reconstruction of Indigenous Culture, which consisted exclusively of books on the Three Principles of the People, and the vitalism of Ch'en Li-fu. This, together with Ch'en Li-fu's presidency of the Association and the professors' tie with the KMT, laid bare the party's attempt at intervention in cultural matters.

The inaugural issue of *Cultural Reconstruction* carried an article by Ch'en Li-fu who, quite oblivious of the intellectual progress made since the May 4th Movement, set the Chinese and Western civilizations in the old spirit–matter dichotomy: 'The Westerner discovered the centre of matter (centre of gravity) and the energy locked up in matter while the Chinese discovered the centre of spirit (the golden mean) and the energy latent in the human spirit (sincerity).' The energy of matter was used for manufacturing things; the energy of spirit was used for the practice of proper conduct. An optimum combination of the two would be an ideal cultural pattern meeting all the needs of life. The necessity for learning from the West was evidently stated here, but by implicating the knowledge gained was to supplement the deficiency of the spiritual civilization, and the centrality or essential nature of the spirit would be in no sense threatened by the West. So Ch'en's framework remained the essence–application formula.

He then pushed his logic a step further to produce an essence of the essence – life itself. Both the essence and the application were for the continuation and enrichment of the life of the nation. The emphasis on life and the concepts of 'centre of spirit' and 'energy of spirit' were the basis of Ch'en's vitalism.

In fact, life being the centre of life and progress coming from the struggle to live were Sun Yat-sen's conception. He was to expand this crude idea, influenced by social Darwinism, into the 'existential' interpretation of history (*min-sheng shih-kuan*), in opposition to both the idealist and materialist interpretations. But to say that life was the centre of life and that the struggle to live was the history of human life was to commit an elementary tautology, which left Sun's theoretical innovation in a hopeless impasse. Aware of this weakness, Ch'en Li-fu came to the rescue of the basic philosophy of his party by borrowing from Henri Bergson's *élan vital*. Like Bergson, Ch'en's philosophy was concerned with action, with man's conquest of matter, and was dualistic, with a greater stress on spirit than on matter. In Ch'en's everchanging world, as in Bergson's, life, the great force, surged forward to crush the resistance of matter; its purpose was to promote the progress of life itself (the creative evolution). But here Ch'en parted company with Bergson by defining the force of life as coming from the traditional concepts of *yin* (positive) and *yang* (negative). In Ch'en's theoretical framework sincerity occupied a position similar to that of the *élan vital* in Bergson's.

Applying his theory of life to politics, Ch'en relied on sincerity and love to strengthen the character of the Chinese nation and eventually to restore the past glory of the Chinese race. He borrowed Bergson's terminology merely to effect a moral reconstruction of China, which for him was the very foundation of China's future revival. In these political goals, he and Sun Yat-sen were in perfect agreement. In the revived China, people being guided by sincerity, love and other virtues of the great tradition, would be ruled by moral standards rather than by coercion. Loyal to the country, the leaders would treat the people with propriety (*li*) and the people would reciprocate with respect. Both would be anxious to do their best for the benefit of society.

The first step was to reinvigorate the character of the people which had always been 'extremely great, courageous, moderate, and upright'. The revival of these qualities would strengthen the people's resistance to temptations. Neither egoistic individualism nor extremist egalitarianism should be encouraged; neither feudalism nor class struggle should be allowed. The progress of change and growth must be controlled by wisdom of the party, which, representing the people as a whole, carries out the functions of nurturing people's morality during the period of party tutelage. In that period the party was to enlighten the unenlightened, leading them to partial and then to full consciousness of their moral character and their political rights and duties.

Ch'en did not conceal his fidelity to the Confucian tradition nor his intention of reviving it. In his preface to a collection of essays on cultural relations between China and the USA (*Chan-hou Chung-mei wen-hua kuan-hsi lun-ts'ung*, 1941) he wrote:

The Chinese culture is firmly planted on the foundation of orthodox Confucianism which has always been the predominant school of thought in China. The essence of this orthodoxy lies in the Confucian teachings of sincerity and humanity . . . which are in complete agreement with the spirit of Jesus Christ.

Indeed, Ch'en's party was in full agreement with him. The head of its Department of Propaganda, Yeh Ch'u-ts'ang, believed that China had been 'a country built of the golden bricks of her beautiful virtues'. On 14 February 1933, the Central Executive Committee of the KMT resolved to instruct all party branch offices and each office of the country's voluntary organizations to hang a sign across the centre of their conference halls with the inscription, 'Loyalty, filial piety, humaneness, love, reliability, righteousness, harmony, and fairness', on it. Even as late as 1966, Chiang Kai-shek was still writing the praises of the 2500 year-old-orthodox tradition of China and of Sun Yat-sen as its great inheritor. The government and party of Chiang Kai-shek consistently defended the teachings of the sage, notwithstanding Chiang's other commitment to Methodism.

From the controversy in 1866 over the new courses on astronomy and mathematics to be given by foreigners, to Chiang's commemorative essay in 1966, the century of China's response and reaction to the cultural challenge of the West had come full circle. The new intelligentsia, shackled by the *t'i-yung* dichotomy, tried to break free from it while the traditional gentry and those who shared their ideology remoulded and strengthened but never abandoned it. Aware of the incompatibility of the particularistic doctrine of Confucius with China's modern needs, the former group re-interpreted it by turning it into a reformist and dynamic theory by drawing a clear distinction between public and private morals, even by reinforcing it with foreign ethical theory and practice. In sum, the aims of the new intelligentsia were to universalize Confucianism and at the same time relativize it so that it could be applied to fulfil China's nationalistic aspirations, economic growth and social reconstruction. To be sure, none of the new intellectuals demanded an immediate abandonment of all the existing moral standards and the existing institutions structured on them, not even the radicals whose ultimate aim was, to borrow a term from the late Professor Joseph Levenson, the museumification of Confucianism. Instead, the new intellectuals in most cases proposed only a liberal and gradual approach to their reformist ends.

But in the absence of a system of new values and a workable rule of law, the conservatives, the gentry and warlords who had consistently been in power, feared that the loss of the traditional virtues would mean the loss of Chinese identity and, worse still, the loss of restraint and orderly conduct. They therefore endeavoured to retain the reins of control, by hook or by crook. Ignoring the theoretical revisions which were taking place, they held fast to the absolute pre-eminence of Confucian orthodoxy and imposed it on the nation by legalist methods. From the suppression of the reform in 1898, through Yuan Shih-k'ai's destruction of parliament in 1914, down to Chiang Kai-shek's tutelage in the 1930s, the uncompromising authority muzzled the moderates crying for reform in the political wilderness and drove the radicals to rebellion.

The wrangle was between tradition and modernization; the bugbear was ideology which opened some Chinese minds and closed others. Ideology, to be sure, interested only a small sector of society; the masses were unconcerned, in spite of the lip service paid to involving them in the political process through party tutelage. The wrangle thus engaged only the conservative and modernizing elites, a relatively small number, all of whom evinced a concern for the welfare of the country and all of whose views and actions were ostensibly intended to promote its welfare.

What then prevented the moral absolutists from giving a sympathetic hearing to the advocacies of the moral relativists? What bogeys prohibited them? The missionaries and their religion did not divide the ranks of the gentry; the introduction of science and industry, path-clearing action as it was, caused only minor misgivings. But when the reign of virtue itself and its institutional bulwarks came under attack, the defenders of the faith reacted with ferocity and fought with tenacity. The bogey of nationalism was a threat, for in the final analysis it aspired to defend the nation instead of the dynasty; the bogey of democracy was also a threat, for it defended people's rights rather than government power, which the conservatives deemed to be essential to national unity and strength. The loss of central control over state and society, in the assessment of the conservatives, might lead to separatism and disorder in the midst of which another bogey, imperialism, might easily encroach further upon China's sovereign rights. There was also the reality and rhetoric of the unruly mob, which, too, was a bogey. It could spring into action as in the rebellions in the 1850–70s period and the Boxer uprising. This bogey was to become more menacing when it joined hands with the communists, as in the case of the anti-imperialist strikes in 1925–6. Of them all, the most fearful was the bogey of communism, whose challenge to the Confucian tradition was the most thorough-going. Unless a new system of values and new institutions could be built to face this challenge, the authorities had hardly any choice but to reinforce Confucianism as their Maginot line.

However, not all these spectres were real. The masses, whose strength was dormant most of the time, presented no threat to the cultural tradition. The articulate critics of Confucianism were mostly non-violent, except the nationalist revolutionaries in 1911–12 and 1927–8 and the communists after 1927. On the contrary, violence was much more frequently resorted to by the defenders of the tradition, as witnessed by the incessant civil wars launched by the warlords who were the true destroyers of law and order.

If the preservation, reform or abandonment of the Confucian tradition was purely a cultural issue, it would not have precipitated government intervention. It had been a political issue ever since the 1860s. The government had given three reasons for the preservation of Confucianism in addition to the need to maintain law and order. These were the centralization of power to strengthen the nation, the consolidation of civil service morale in order to improve the efficiency of the service, and the discipline of the people so that the nation, through its moral and psychological reconstruction, could become equal to other great nations of the world. The fact was that, except for the attempts to centralize power, all the other tasks and goals remained only rhetoric throughout the whole period up to 1937. It was not only the civil service morale which continued to degenerate; the cadre of the KMT also became bureaucratized and dysfunctional. With the party corrupt and inept, all its programmes of political education for the masses rang hollow. The country stood weak, poor and unmodernized.

What then was the purpose of the centralization of power? The absence of a coherent plan for industrialization, the disregard of the short-term problems of rural China, and the relentless pursuit of the war against the CCP suggested that the retention of power by the defenders of Confucianism was to protect the vested interests of whoever was in control of Chinese industries and agriculture, the status quo as it existed, *mutatis mutandis*, from the second half of the nineteenth century to the 1930s. The ownership and use of resources, the tax revenue drawn from them, and the disposal of the revenue were all geared to this end. Consequently, a China dominated by Confucian defenders could neither democratize herself in order to arrange a more rational disposal of her resources nor accept the communist alternative for the same purpose before 1949.

The Confucian essence took a firm grip on the Western application for the protection of traditional vested interests, while leaving China's nascent industries and other modern programmes to languish on a diet of crumbs of domestic and foreign resources.

Seen in this light, the cultural issues were inseparably bound together with the political, economic and social issues. Cultural changes had to be preceded by changes in other spheres, if all the changes were to become endemic and meaningful to the nation as a whole. While the conservatives and modernizers wrestled over their cultural problems, another China was growing up, first in the scattered soviets and then in the Border Region around Yenan and the guerrilla war bases. There, an entirely new cultural orientation was developing in the context of entirely different institutions, all of which were committed to a firm iconoclasm. It was there that the cultural issues were simplified and settled, to lay the foundation for an unhampered modernization, in spite of the occasional reactions. The revolution of 1949 was thus not merely a test of the relative military strength of the belligerents; it was a test of the relative moral and cultural strength also.

# Select bibliography

In this bibliography I do not propose to include books on the modern history of Europe and North America or those on Western thought and philosophy, although many of them have obviously been consulted in preparing this book. The following lists, therefore, refer only to books and articles concerning China either in English or in Chinese.

## English sources

For general information on China, the *China Yearbooks* compiled by the British journalist H. G. W. Woodhead from 1913 to 1939 and the Chinese official *Chinese Year Book* (Shanghai, 1937) contain a wealth of data. Earlier, J. Dyer Ball, *Things Chinese or Notes Connected with China* (London, 1904), and S. Couling, *The Encyclopaedia Sinica* (London, 1917), are useful. As to the eminent Chinese who had played a significant role in this period, one should consult A. Hummel, *Eminent Chinese of the Ch'ing Period* (Washington, 1943), H. L. Boorman and R. C. Howard, *Biographical Dictionary of Republican China* (NY, 1967), and the *China Weekly Review*'s *Who's Who in China* (Shanghai, 1925). A. H. Smith, *Chinese Characteristics* (NY, 1894), and S. W. Williams, *The Middle Kingdom* (NY, 1848), are indispensable for this study. H. R. Isaacs's *Images of Asia* (NY, 1972) and M. G. Mason's *Western Concepts of China and the Chinese, 1840–1876* (NY, 1939) tell the readers the early and more recent Western conception of that ancient country, while J. Spence's *To Change China, Western Advisers in China* (Boston, 1969) and C. K. Yang's *Religion in Chinese Society* (Berkeley, 1961) prepare a solid ground for the readers to understand many of the events and issues in this book.

Of the many general histories on modern China, *East Asia, the Modern Transformation* by J. K. Fairbank, E. O. Reischauer and A. M. Griag (Boston, 1965) is probably the most comprehensive in coverage and most reliable in information and analysis. From the Harvard University Press there come a series of useful monographs for this study, including W. Ayers, *Chang Chih-tung and Educational Reform in China* (1971), Banno Masataka, *China and the West, 1858–1861, the Origin of the Tsungli Yamen* (1964), Chang Hao, *Liang Ch'i-ch'ao and Intellectual Transition in China 1890–1907* (1971), Chang Hsing-pao, *Commissioner Lin and the Opium War* (1964), Chow Tse-tsung, *The May 4th Movement* (1960), M. B. Rankin, *Early Chinese Revolutionaries: Radical Intellectuals in Shanghai and Chekiang, 1902–1911* (1971), J. E. Schrecker, *Imperialism and Chinese Nationalism, Germany in Shantung* (1971), and B. Schwartz, *In Search of Wealth and Power* (1964). Other monographs which should be mentioned here are R. S. Britton, *The Chinese Periodical Press 1800–1912* (Shanghai, 1933), R. Dawson, *The Chinese Chameleon, An Analysis of European conceptions of Chinese civilization* (London, 1967), M. Elvin and G. W. Skinner, *The Chinese City between Two Worlds* (Stanford, 1974), M. Gasster, *Chinese Intellectuals and the Revolution of 1911, the Birth of Chinese Radicalism* (Seattle, 1969), and M. Wright, *China in Revolution, the First Phase, 1900–1913* (New Haven, 1968) and *The Last Stand of Chinese Conservatism* (Stanford, 1957). For a general study of the intellectual trends in modern China, J. R. Levenson's *Confucian China and Its Modern Fate* (London, 1958, 1964 and 1965) is most stimulating.

Now let us turn to archival and periodical materials. This study has consulted extensively the archives of the Council for World Mission, the China Inland Mission, the American Methodist Mission, the other American Protestant missions in China, and the United Church of Canada which have thrown a great deal of light on the life and work of the Western missionaries in China. It has also used the *Chinese Recorder* – an official organ of the Protestant missions in China, the *Chinese Repository* (Macao, 1832–51), *A Selection of Leading Articles from the Peking and Tientsin Times*, 1 January – 23 April, 1927 (Tientsin, 1927), the *New China Review* (Shanghai), *North China Herald* (Shanghai), and the *China Weekly Review* (Shanghai). The rich collection of pamphlets on China in the Hankow Club Collection housed in the Library of the University of Hong Kong is of immense usefulness.

On general cultural matters there are J. Dewey, *Lectures in China, 1919–1920* (Honolulu, 1973), Hu Shih, *The Chinese Renaissance* (Chicago, 1934), D. W. Y. Kwok, *Scientism and Chinese Thought* (New Haven, 1965), and G. R. Twiss, *Science and Education in China* (Shanghai, 1925). On education, one should refer to K. Biggerstaff, *The Earliest Modern Government Schools in China* (Ithaca, 1961), M. E. Ferguson, *Chinese Medical Board and Peking Union Medical College, a Chronicle of Fruitful Collaboration, 1914–1951* (NY, 1970), A. Foster, *Chinese Schoolgirls* (London, 1909), H. E. King, *The Educational System of China as Recently Reconstructed* (Washington, 1911), and C. H. Peake, *Nationalism and Education in Modern China* (NY, 1932).

Hitherto general works on modern Chinese literature of this period are still very few. Mention should be made of C. T. Hsia, *A History of Modern Chinese Fiction* (New Haven, 1961) and L. O. F. Lee, *The Romantic Generation of Modern Chinese Writers* (Cambridge, Mass., 1973). About the more popular cultural aspects of the country, one may find the following informative and entertaining: P. S. Buck, *The Good Earth* (NY, 1931), *The New Adventures of Charlie Chan* (Illinois, 1958–9), G. Cockburn, *John Chinaman: his ways and notions* (Edinburgh, 1896), M. Collis, *Foreign Mud* (London, 1946), T. de Quincey, *China: a revised reprint of articles from 'Titan' with preface and additions* (Edinburgh, 1857), W. P. Fenn, *Ah Sin and His Brethren in American Literature* (Peking, 1933), R. Gilbert, *What's Wrong with China* (London, 1923), D. Jones, *The Portrayal of China and India on the American Screen, 1869–1955* (MIT, 1955), J. Leyda, *Dianying* (MIT, 1972), and Lin Yutang, *My Country and My People* (NY, 1939).

Changes in the modern Chinese family system and the position of women are to be found in Lady Hosie's *Portrait of a Chinese Lady* (London, 1929), O. Lang, *Chinese Family and Society* (New Haven, 1946), M. J. Mevy, *The Family Revolution in Modern China* (Cambridge, Mass., 1949), and M. B. Young, *Women in China* (Michigan, 1973).

Students and student movements are treated in J. P. Chu, *Chinese Students in America: Qualities Associated with Their Success* (NY, 1922), J. Israel, *Student Nationalism in China* (Hoover Institution, 1966), W. H. Kiang, *The Chinese Student Movement* (NY, 1948), and Y. C. Wang, *Chinese Intellectuals and the West, 1872–1949* (N. Carolina, 1966).

There are too many studies on China's domestic politics, but I think the following should help the readers of this book. Ch'ien Tuan-sheng, *The Government and Politics of China* (Cambridge, Mass., 1950), Hu Shih and Lin Yutang, *China's Own Critics* (Shanghai, 1931), T. T. Meadows, *The Chinese and their Rebellions* (Stanford reprint, 1953), G. T. Wu, *Party Politics in the Republic of China, the Kuomintang 1912–1924* (Berkeley, 1966), and L. E. Eastman, *The Abortive Revolution* (Cambridge, Mass., 1974). For the growth of the Chinese communism, J. Harrison's *Long March to Power* (NY, 1972) is to date the most comprehensive account. Then there are C. and W. Band, *Two Years with the Chinese Communism* (New Haven, 1948), E. F. Carlson, *Twin Stars of China* (NY, 1940), O. E. Clubb, *Communism in China, as reported from Hankow in 1932* (NY, 1968), K. E. Shewmaker, *Americans and Chinese Communists 1927–1945* (Ithaca, 1971), S. R. Schram, *Mao Tse-tung* (Middx, 1967), A. Smedley, *The Great Road* (NY, 1956), E. Snow, *Red Star over China* (NY, 1938), and N. Wales, *Inside Red China* (NY, 1939). There is also my own contribution to the study of the Chinese communist movement, *Mao and the Chinese Revolution* (Oxford, 1965).

The international economic problems of China have always been the centre of attention of all the nations trading with China and about them there exists an immense corpus of literature. G. C. Allen and A. G. Donnithorne, *Western Enterprise in Far Eastern Economic Development, China and Japan* (London, 1954) is a convenient volume to use. In addition there are these general treatises: A. Feuerwerker, *The Chinese Economy ca 1870–1911* and *The Chinese Economy 1912–1949* (Michigan, 1969 and 1977 respectively) and A. N. Young, *China's Nation-Building Effort, 1927–1937* (Hoover Institution, 1971). Monographic studies of Chinese economy include Y. K. Cheng, *Foreign Trade and Industrial Development of China – a historical and integrated analysis* (Seattle, 1956), Y. W. Cheng, *Postal Communication in China and its Modernization, 1860–1896* (Cambridge, Mass., 1970) J. Chesneaux, *The Chinese Labor Movement, 1919–1927* (Stanford, 1968), A. Feuerwerker, *China's Early Industrialization* (Cambridge, Mass., 1958), and 'China's Nineteenth Century Industrialization, the case of Hanyuehping Coal and Iron Company', in C. D. Cowan, *The Economic Development of China and Japan* (London, 1964), E. M. Gull, *British Economic Interests in the Far East* (London, 1943), Y. P. Hao, *The Comprador in Nineteenth Century China* (Cambridge, Mass., 1970), C. M. Hou, *Foreign Investment and Economic Development in China, 1840–1937* (Cambridge, Mass., 1965), L. S. L. Hsu, *Silver Prices in China* (Shanghai, 1935), Liu Kwang-ching, *Anglo-American Steamship Rivalry in China, 1862–1874* (Cambridge, Mass., 1962), S. C. Lockwood, *Augustine Heard and Company, 1858–1862* (Cambridge, Mass., 1971), W. H. Mallory, *China: Land of Famine* (NY, 1926), G. Padoux, *The Financial Reconstruction of China and the Consolidation of China's Present Indebtedness* (Peking, 1923) and *The Gold Franc Case in the 1901 Indemnity Question* (Peking, 1923), C. F. Remer, *A Study of Chinese Boycotts* (Baltimore, 1933), *Foreign Investment in China* (NY, 1923), and *Foreign Trade in China* (Shanghai, 1926), and S. F. Wright, *Hart and the Chinese Customs* (Belfast, 1950).

On some of the general problems of China's international relations with the West, one should refer to J. Escarra's *Chinese Law and Comparative Jurisprudence* (Tientsin, 1926), and *the Extra-Territoriality Problem, being a memorandum presented to the Commission for Extra-Territoriality* (Peking, 1923), J. K. Fairbank (ed.), *The Chinese World Order* (Cambridge, Mass., 1968), W. R. Fishel, *The End of Extraterritoriality in China* (Berkeley, 1952), I. C. Y. Hsü, *China's Entrance to the Family of Nations, the Diplomatic Phase, 1858–1880* (Cambridge, Mass., 1960), A. Iriye, *After Imperialism* (Cambridge, Mass., 1965), and *Across the Pacific* (NY, 1967), J. N. Thomas, *The Institute of Pacific Relations – Asian Scholars in American Politics* (Seattle, 1974), and W. W. Willoughby, *China at the Conference, a report* (Baltimore, 1926), and *Foreign Rights and Interests in China* (Baltimore, 1927).

Readings on Sino–British relations should perhaps begin from

W. C. Costin, *Great Britain and China, 1833–1860* (Oxford, 1937). Then there are S. L. Endicott, *Diplomacy and Enterprise, British China Policy 1933–1937* (Vancouver, 1975), J. K. Fairbank, *Trade and Diplomacy on the China Coast* (Cambridge, Mass., 1953), H. N. Lay, *Our Interests in China: a letter to the Right Honorable Earl Russell* (London, 1864), H. B. Loch, *Personal Narrative of Occurrences during Lord Elgin's Second Embassy to China* (London, 1869), and L. R. Louis, *British Strategy in the Far East, 1919–1939* (Oxford, 1971). Those on the Sino–American relations should include D. Borg, *American Policy and the Chinese Revolution, 1925–1928* (NY, 1947), R. D. Buhite, *Nelson T. Johnson and American Policy towards China, 1925–1941* (East Lansing, 1968), J. K. Fairbank, *The United States and China* (Cambridge, Mass., 1958), A. N. Griswold, *The Far Eastern Policy of the United States* (New Haven, 1938 and 1962 reissue), T. J. McCormick, *China Market – America's Quest for Informal Empire 1893–1901* (Chicago, 1967), J. C. Thomson, *While China Faced West, American Reformers in Nationalist China, 1928–1937* (Cambridge, Mass., 1969), P. Varg, *Open Door Diplomat: the Life of W. W. Rockhill* (Urbana, 1952), and M. B. Young, *The Rhetoric of Empire: American China Policy 1895–1901*.

The missionaries left behind a massive body of literature on various facets of their life and work in China. But to begin with, I think one should read W. Eberhard, *Guilt and Sin in Traditional China* (Berkeley, 1967). Then in alphabetical order there are E. P. Boardman, *Christian Influence upon the Ideology of the Taiping Rebellion 1851–1864* (Madison, 1952), F. S. Brockman, *I Discovered the Orient* (NY, 1935), M. Bromhall, *The Jubilee Story of the China Inland Mission* (Toronto, 1915), P. S. Buck, *Is There a Case for Foreign Missions?* (NY, 1936), China Education Commission, *Christian Education in China, Committee of Reference and Council of the Foreign Missions Conference of North America* (NY, 1922), P. A. Cohen, *China and Christianity* (Cambridge, Mass., 1963), G. S. Eddy, *I Have Seen God Work in China: Personal Impressions from Three Decades with the Chinese* (NY, 1944), J. K. Fairbank (ed.), *The Missionary Enterprise in China and America* (Cambridge, Mass., 1974), S. D. Gamble, *Ting Hsien: A North China Rural Community* (NY, 1954), S. Garrett, *Social Reformers in Urban China, the Chinese YMCA, 1895–1926* (Cambridge, Mass., 1970), C. Gutzlaff, *China Opened* (London, 1838), and *Journal of Three Voyages along the Coast of China in 1831, 1832, and 1833* (London, 1834), R. Holden, *Yale in China* (New Haven, 1964), E. H. Hume, *Doctors East, Doctors West: An American Physician's Life in China* (NY, 1946), J. R. Hykes, *The American Bible Society in China* (Shanghai, 1916), A. M. Johansen, *Big Mark, One of China's Boys* (London, 1923), W. N. Lacey, *A Hundred Years of Chinese Methodism* (NY, 1948), K. S. Latourette, *A History of Christian Missions in China* (NY, 1929, 1967 ed.), J. G. Lutz, *China and the Christian Colleges 1850–1950* (Ithaca, 1971), D. W. Lyon, *The First Quarter Century of the*

*YMCA in China, 1895–1920* (Shanghai, 190), D. MacGillivray, *A Century of Protestant Missions in China* (Shanghai, 1907), C. N. Moody, *The Mind of the Early Converts* (London, 1920), M. T. Staiffer, *Christian Occupation of China* (Shanghai, 1922), H. and G. Taylor, *Hudson Taylor and the China Inland Mission* (London, 1925), and *Hudson Taylor in Early Years* (London, 1911), P. Varg, *Missionaries, Chinese and Diplomats, the American Protestant Missionary Movement in China, 1890–1952* (New Jersey, 1958), and H. R. Williamson, *British Baptists in China, 1845–1952* (London, 1957).

I have consulted many newspapers and periodicals about the overseas Chinese in California, especially in San Francisco. Here I shall mention only these: G. Barth, *Bitter Strength, a history of the Chinese in the United States, 1850–1870* (Cambridge, Mass., 1960), W. G. Beach, *Oriental Crime in California, a study of offenses committed by Orientals in that state, 1900–1927* (Stanford, 1932), D. T. C. Cheng, *Acculturation of the Chinese in the United States: a Philadelphia study* (Foochow, 1948), M. R. Coolidge, *Chinese Immigration* (NY, 1909), S. W. Kung, *Chinese in American Life: Some Aspects of Their History, Status, Problems, and Contributions* (Seattle, 1962), M.T.F., *My Chinese Marriage* (London, 1922), S. C. Miller, *The Unwelcome Immigrant* (Berkeley, 1969), V. and B. Nee, *Long Time Californ* (NY, 1972), A. Saxton, *The Indispensable Enemy, Labor and the Anti-Chinese Movement in California* (Berkeley, 1971), and R. Shepherd, *The Ways of Ah Sin* (NY, 1923).

Of the many journalists accounts of China, the following are perhaps the more noteworthy – H. Abend, *My Life in China 1926–1941* (NY, 1943), and *Tortured China* (NY, 1932), H. Abend and A. J. Billingham, *Can China Survive?* (NY, 1936), J. M. Bertram, *Crisis in China, the story of the Sian mutiny* (London, 1937), J. O. P. Bland, *China, the Pity of It* (NY, 1932), and *Recent Events and Present Policies in China* (London, 1912), H. G. W. Woodhead, *Adventures in Far Eastern Journalism* (Tokyo, 1935), and his unpublished *A British Editor in China, 1902–1942* (in my collection).

Finally, there are a large number of biographies and personal memoirs which are informative as well as colourful reading. They have certainly given me a great deal of insights towards the understanding of many facets of China's relations with the West. They are listed as follows: T. Allen and S. Gordon, *The Scalpel, the Sword: the Story of Dr Norman Bethune* (Toronto, 1952), N. F. Allman, *Shanghai Lawyer* (NY, 1943), A. A. Bennett, *John Fryer, the Introduction of Western Science and Technology in the Nineteenth China* (Cambridge, Mass., 1967), P. S. Buck, *My Several Worlds* (London, 1955), A. M. Cable, *The Fulfilment of a Dream of Paster Hsi* (London, 1918), H. Cahill, *A Yankee Adventurer, the story of Ward of the Taiping Rebellion* (NY, 1930), Chiang Monlin, *Tides from the West* (New

Haven, 1947), P. A. Cohen, *Between Tradition and Modernity* (Cambridge, Mass., 1974), J. and A. C. Dewey, *Letters from China and Japan* (NY, 1920), F. V. Dickens and S. Lane-Poole, *The Life of Sir Harry Parkes* (London, 1894), D. Fisher, *Calvin Wilson Mateer* (Philadelphia, 1911), C. Furth, *Ting Wen-chiang, Science and China's New Culture* (Cambridge, Mass., 1970), J. J. Gerson, *Horatio Nelson Lay and Sino–British Relations, 1854–1860* (Cambridge, Mass., 1974), J. Grieder, *Hu Shih and the Chinese Renaissance* (Cambridge, Mass., 1972), Han Suyin, *The Crippled Tree* (NY, 1965), T. F. Harris, *Pearl S. Buck, a Biography* (NY, 1969), M. Hewlett, *Fifty Years in China* (London, 1943), C. Holcombe, *The Real Chinaman* (NY, 1895), A. Hosie, *Three Years in Western China* (London, 1890), M. Huc, *Travels in Tartary, Thibet and China during the Years 1844–5–6* (Chicago, 1898), W. C. Hunter, *The 'Fan Kwai' at Canton before Treaty Days, 1825–1844* (London, 1882), J. Jackson, *The Sassoons* (NY, 1968), B. Jurgenson, *All the Bandits of China* (Minneapolis, 1965), G. N. Kates, *The Years that Were Fat* (MIT, 1952), M. F. E. Kelly, *Some Chinese Friends of Mine* (Cincinnati, 1924), P. King, *In the Chinese Customs Service: a personal record of forty-seven years* (London, 1924), J. R. Marsh, *The Charm of the Middle Kingdom* (London, 1922), W. A. P. Martin, *Calendar of the Tungwen College* (Peking, 1879), and *The Cycle of Cathay* (NY, 1896), A. Michie, *The Englishman in China during the Victorian Era as Illustrated in the Career of Sir Ruthford Alcock* (London, 1900), A. E. Moule, *Half a Century in China* (London, 1911), L. Oliphant, *Narrative of Earl Elgin's Mission to China and Japan in the Years 1857, '58, '59* (London, 1859), T. Pawley, *My Bandit Hosts* (London, n.d.), C. Pearl, *Morrison of Peking* (Sydney, 1967), G. Peck, *Two Kinds of Time* (Boston, 1950, 1967 edn), J. B. Powell, *My Twenty-Five Years in China* (NY, 1945), G. Reid, *Glances at China* (London, 1892), P. S. Reinsch, *An American Diplomat in China* (NY, 1922), T. Richard, 'Autobiography', in *Conversion by the Million in China* (Shanghai, 1907), J. F. Roche and L. L. Cowan, *The French at Foochow* (Shanghai, 1884), D. T. Roy, *Kuo Mo-jo* (Cambridge, Mass., 1971), B. Russell, *The Problems of China* (London, 1922), T. G. Selby, *As the Chinese See Us* and *Chinamen at Home* (London, 1901 and 1900 respectively), E. A. Selle, *Donald in China* (NY, 1948), S. Shaw, *The Journals of Major Samuel Shaw* (Boston, 1847), J. L. Stuart, *Fifty Years in China* (NY, 1954), E. Teichman, *Affairs in China* (London, 1938), B. W. Tuchman, *Stilwell and the American Experience in China, 1911–1945* (NY, 1971), F. W. Williams, *Anson Burlingame and the First Chinese Mission to Foreign Powers* (NY, 1912), and T. F. Wu, *America through the Spectacles of an Oriental Diplomat* (Taipei 1968 reprint).

## Chinese sources

This section of the bibliography may be more relevant to those who are interested in further research than to the general reader. I find that Wei Yuan's pioneer work, *Hai-kuo t'u-chih* (An Illustrated Gazetteer of the Maritime Nations) of 1847 is indispensable for an understanding of the Chinese knowledge of the West about the time when Britain opened the door of China. For bibliographical guidance, I often resort to Chang Ching-lu, *Chung-kuo chin-tai ch'u-pan shih-liao* (Source Materials on Modern China's Publication, Peking, 1954) and *Chung-kuo hsien tai ch'u-pan shih-liao* (Source Materials on Contemporary China's Publication, Peking, 1954). *Chin pai-nien-lai Chung-i hsi-shu mu-lu* (A Catalogue of the Chinese Translations of Western Books, Taipei, 1958) and *Chung-hua min-kuo k'e-hsüeh-chih* (Science in the Republic of China, Taipei, 1955–8) are also useful.

Newspapers are obviously an important source of information on social and cultural development. I have read the *Shen-pao* of Shanghai (from 1872) as much as I can in the holdings of the libraries I have used and the *Hua-tzu jih-pao* (the China Mail) of Hong Kong (from 1865) contains a wealth of data on the modernization and Westernization of south China. In addition, there are a number of periodicals which appeared briefly in the early years of this century. These include the *Chekiang ch'ao* (Tides of Chekiang, Tokyo, 1902), the *Chin-chung jih-pao* (Alarming Bell Daily News, Shanghai, 1904), the *Hsin-min ts'ung-pao* (New Citizens' Magazine, Yokohama, 1902), the *Wai-chiao pao* (International Relations, n.p., 1901–2), etc. The pictorials which I have consulted include the *Hsin-ming hua-pao* (New Records, Peking, 1909), the *Hsing-ch'i hua-pao* (Sunday Pictorial, Shanghai, 1906), the *Liang-jih hua-pao* (Every Two Days Peking, 1907), and of course the *Tien-shih-chai hua-pao* (the Tien-shih Studio Pictorials, Shanghai, 1884).

No one who studies modern China's social and intellectual development can afford to ignore such popular but highly respected periodicals as the *Tung-fang tsa-chih* (the Eastern Miscellany, from 1904) which began to introduce Western literature from 1920, the *Kuo-wen chou-pao* (National Affairs Weekly, August 1924 to December 1937), the *Lun-yü* (the Analects, 1932), the *Hsi-feng* (the Western Wind, 1936), the *Yü-chou-feng* (the Universe, 1935) and so on. All of these were published in Shanghai. Then there were the more scholarly *Min-to* (People's Bell, Shanghai, 1919), which took on the responsibility for introducing Western philosophies in a series of special supplements on Bergson, Darwin, Kant and others, the *Hsüeh-heng* (the Critical Review, 1922) which shared the responsibility of introducing Western thought as well as engaged itself in polemics of the time, and the *Hsien-tai p'ing-lun* (the Contemporary Forum, Peking, 1924) and the *Tu-li p'ing-lun* (the Independence, Peking, 1932) which were more concerned with the problems of the country. On the problem of cultural reconstruction, or more precisely on the development of the indigenous culture, there was the *Wen-hua chien-she* (the Cultural Construction, from October 1934) of which I have read only twelve issues.

I have also consulted a number of university journals, e.g. the *Tsinghua chou-pao* ('Tsinghua Weekly), the *Lingnan hsüeh-pao* (Lingnan Journal), and so on. There are too many literary preiodicals, e.g. the *Yü-ssu* (Gossamers of Words, 1924) and the *Hsin-yüeh* (the Crescent Moon, 1928), for me to mention. But I must mention the two powerful periodicals of the May 4th Movement period, the *Hsin ch'ing-nien* (the New Youth, 1915) and the *Hsin-ch'ao* (New Tides, 1919) which, together with many other magazines of the same period, influenced a generation of Chinese youths.

A generally neglected source of information is the travelogue which was read with pleasure and amazement, a fact borne out by the many editions of some of the travel books available throughout the whole period this study covers. From the *Ch'ing-mi lei-ch'ao* (Classified Jottings on the Little Known Facts of the Ch'ing Period, Shanghai, 1928) compiled by Hsü K'o, the *Chin-tai hsiao-shuo pi-chi hsüan* (Selected Modern Short Stories and Memoirs, Hong Kong, 1958 edn), the well-known *Hsiao-fang-hu-chai yü-ti ts'ung-ch'ao* (Collected Writings on Geography by the Hsiao-fang-hu Studio, Shanghai, 1877–1897), and the *Wai-kuo yu-chi hui-k'an* (Collected Writings on Travels Abroad, Shanghai, 1924) one reaps a rich harvest of facts, impressions, and comments on the West. Chang Chao-jung's *Tai-hsi ke-kuo ming-jen yen-hsing lu* (Words and Deeds of the Eminent People of the West, Shanghai, 1903) and Chang Yuan-sheng's *Wai-kuo shang-yu-lu* (Who's Who Abroad, Shanghai, 1902) are pioneer works to introduce famous Westerners to the Chinese reader. Many Chinese diplomats left behind accounts of their travels and life in the West; starting from Chih-kang's *Ch'u-shih tai-hsi chi* (An account of the First Mission to the West, 1890) this tradition continued to Ch'eng T'ien-fang's *Shih-Te hui i-lu* (My Mission to Germany, Taipei, 1963).

However, not all travelogues are informative or worth reading. In my research I have wasted a great deal of time on books and articles which were obviously copied by their authors from guide-books and brochures. The more rewarding ones are Fei Hsiao-t'ung's *Ch'u-fang Mei-kuo* (My First Visit to the USA, Chungking, 1945), Hsü Cheng-k'eng's *Liu-Mei ts'ai-feng-lu* (My Years in the USA, Shanghai, 1936), Hu Shih's *Liu-hsüeh jih-chi* (My Studies in the USA, Shanghai, 1948), K'ang Yu-wei's *Ou-chou shih-i-kuo yu-chi* (Travels in Eleven European Countries, Shanghai, 1905–33), Liang Chi'i-ch'ao's *Hsin-ta-lu yu-chi* (Travels on the New Continent, Shanghai, 1936), Sheng-huo chou-k'an-she's *Shen-k'e-ti yin-hsiang* (Deep Impressions, Shanghai, 1932), Tsou Lu's *Chiu-yu hsin-kan* (Fresh Feelings from Old Travels, Chungking, 1942), and Tsou T'ao-feng's four collections of his travel experiences published in Shanghai, 1937–8.

About the general history of the Christian missions in China, I would like to refer to Wang Chih-hsin, *Chung-kuo chi-tu-chiao shih-kang* (An Outline of the History of the Christian Missions in China, Hong Kong, preface date 1940), *Ch'in-hui tsai Hua pai-nien-shih* (A Hundred Years of Baptism in China, by A. R. Gallimore, Chinese translation, Shanghai, 1936), and the YMCA in Shanghai, *San-shih-wu chou-nien chi-nien-ts'e* (the thirty-fifth anniversary volume, Shanghai, 1935). On specific subjects of the work of the Church in China, there are Chu Chin-i, *I-ke shih-nien-ti hsiang-ts'un chiao-hui* (An Experimental Rural Church, Shanghai, 1940), Lin Chih-p'ing, *Chi-tu-chiao yü Chung-kuo chin-tai-hua lun-chi* (Discussions on Christianity and China's Modernization, Taipei, 1970), Liu T'ing-fang, *Chung-kuo chiao-hui wen-t'i ti t'ao-lun* (A Discussion on the Problems of the Church in China, Shanghai, 1922), Wu Lei-ch'uan, *Chi-tu-chiao yü Chung-kuo wen-hua* (Christianity and the Chinese Culture, Shanghai, 1936), Chao Shih-kuang, *Meng-chao san-shih-nien* (Thirty Years as a Christian, Hong Kong, 1960), Chao Tzu-ch'en, *Hsüeh-jen* (Learning to be Charitable, Shanghai, 1936), and all the writings by Hsieh Fu-ya, a considerable theologian. Then there are also the anti-Christian writings, e.g. the *Chiao-wu chi-lüeh* (An Account of the Anti-Christian Incidents, Shanghai, 1905) and Lü Shih-ch'iang, *Chung-kuo kuan-shen fan-chiao-ti yuan-yin* (Why Did Chinese Officials and Scholars Oppose Christianity?, Taipei, 1966) which represent the old antagonism and the *Fan-tui chi-tu-chiao yun-tung* (The Anti-Christian Movement, Shanghai, 1925) which represents the new antagonism of the 1920s.

Shu Hsin-ch'eng's compilations – *Chung-kuo chin-tai chiao-yü-shih tzu-liao* (Source Materials on the History of Modern Chinese Education, Peking, 1962) and *Chin tai Chung-kuo liu-hsüeh-shih* (A History of Studying Abroad in Modern Times, Shanghai, 1927) – are basic references to the subject of Chinese students abroad. Apart from Hu Shih's *Liu-hsüeh jih-chi* already mentioned above, Ch'en Ch'un-sui, *Liu-hsi wai-shih* (An Informal History of Studying in the West, Shanghai, 1928) and Sheng Ch'eng, *Hai-wai kung-tu shih-nien chi-shih* (My Odyssey in Europe, Shanghai, 1932) provide detailed information about the life of the Chinese student in the West.

About Shanghai, there are the journal published by the Shanghai T'ung-chih-kuan (the Office of the Shanghai Gazetteer) from 1933 to 1935 and the *Shanghai Nien-chien* (Shanghai Yearbooks). Ch'iu Chin-chang and Hsu Kung-su have compiled the *Shanghai kung-kung tsu-chieh chih-tu-shih* (A History of the International Settlement in Shanghai, Nanking, 1933), Ku Ch'i-chung has discussed the general implications of the foreign settlements in China in his *Tsu-chieh yü Chung-kuo* (Foreign Settlements and China, Shanghai, 1928), and Liang Chin-ch'un has commented on the consular jurisdiction in *Tsai-hua ling-shih ts'ai-p'an-ch'uan lun* (Consular Jurisdiction in China, Shanghai, 1930). As to the Chinese overseas and the problems of Chinese emigration, there are available general histories such as Sun Chen-t'ao, *Mei-kuo hua-ch'iao shih-lüeh* (A Brief History of Chinese Immigrants in the USA, Taipei, 1962) and Wu Shang-ying, *Mei-kuo hua-ch'iao pai-nien chi-shih (Chia-na-ta fu)* (One Hundred Years of Chinese in the United States and Canada, Hong Kong, 1954). Huang Chin-ch'u's *Hua-ch'iao ming-jen ku-shih-lu* (Tales about Eminent Overseas Chinese, Ch'angsha, 1940) and Liu Ling's *Hua-ch'iao jen-wu-chih* (Who's Who Among the Overseas Chinese, Los Angeles, 1951) are useful references. Ch'en Li-t'e's *Ou-chou hua-ch'iao sheng-huo* (Life of the Overseas Chinese in Europe, Shanghai, 1933) is one of the very few monographs on the Chinese in Europe. Looking out from China, there are Ch'iu Han-p'ing's *Hua-ch'iao wen-t'i* (The Overseas Chinese Problem, Shanghai, 1936), Hsüeh Tien-tseng's *Pao-hu ch'iao-min-lun* (On the Protection of Overseas Chinese, Shanghai, 1937), Huang Chin-wan's *Hua-ch'iao tui tsu-kuo-ti kung-hsien* (Overseas Chinese's Contribution to Their Motherland, Shanghai, 1940), Chang Ts'un-wu's scholarly study – *Kuang-hsü san-shih-i-nien Chung-Mei kung-yüeh feng-ch'ao* (The Crisis of the Exclusion Act of 1905, Taipei, 1966), and Liang-hsüeh-jen's (pseudonym), *Chü-yüeh ch'i-t'an* (The Strange Story of the Exclusion Act, Shanghai, 1906).

Books on China's political, legal and economic changes have been repeatedly and extensively used in many recent studies published in the West, especially in the USA. I propose to omit them from this bibliography. As to the social changes, Lin Lo-chih (Young J. Allen), *Ch'uan-ch'iu wu ta-chou nü-su t'ung-k'ao* (Women in All Lands or China's Place Among the Nations, tr. Jen Pao-lo, Shanghai, 1903) is a pioneer work and the obvious one to begin with. Then there are Liu-wang Li-ming, *Chung-kuo fu-nü yun-tung* (Chinese Women's Movement, Shanghai, 1934), Mei Hui-t'ing, *Chung-kuo chia-t'ing kai-tsao wen-t'i* (Problems of the Reform of China's Family System, Shanghai, 1935), Wang Ming-tao, *Chi-tu-chiao yü hun-yin* (Christianity and Marriage, Hong Kong, 1967), and Yi Chia-yüeh and Lo Tun-wei, *Chung-kuo chia-t'ing wen-t'i* (Problems of the Chinese Family System, Shanghai, 1926) represent the influence of Christianity and the Western sociology on a section of the Chinese intelligentsia. Curiously enough, recent writings on the Chinese family system and on women tend to overlook this trend in modern China's sociological thought. Also overlooked are the changes in modern China's attitude towards sex as represented by Chang Ching-sheng, *Hsin Wen-hua* (New Culture, Shanghai, published in 1936–7) and *Shih-nien ch'ing-ch'ang* (Ten Years of Romantic Experiences, Singapore, 192?), Chang Hsi-chen, *Hsin hsing-tao-te t'ao-lun-chi* (Discussions on a New Sexual Morality, Shanghai, 1925), and Lin Chao-yin, *Hsing-sheng-huo chih chuan-hua* (Changes in the Sexual Life, Shanghai, 1925).

This study does not place any emphasis on literature and art, but I have relied on Chao Chia-pi, *Chung-kuo hsin-wen-hsüeh ta-hsi* (A Systematic Compilation of China's New Literature, 10 volumes, Hong Kong, 1962 edition) and Ch'eng Chi-hua *et al.*, *Chung-kuo tien-ying fa-chang-shih* (A History of the Motion Picture Industry in China, 2 volumes, Peking, 1963). I find the early satirical novels, Li Po-yuan's *Wen-ming hsiao-shih* (An Informal History of Civilization, Shanghai, 1906) and *Kuan-ch'ang hsien-hsing-chi* (An Exposure of the Officialdom, n.p., preface date 1903) and Wu Yen-jen's *Erh-shih-nien mu-tu chih kuei-hsien-chuang* (The Strange Things Observed in the Past Twenty Years, Shanghai, 1907–9) extremely revealing. Lao She's novels – *Erh Ma* (Two and Horse, Shanghai, 1931) and *Li Hun* (Divorce, Shanghai, 1947) – are helpful social documentation; so is Mao Tun's *Tzu-yeh* (Midnight, Shanghai, 1940).

On cultural changes and designs for cultural change, there are many important works. By Hu Shih, there are *Wen-ts'un* (Collected Essays, Shanghai, 1921 and 1924), *Wen-hsüan* (Selected Essays, Shanghai, 1947), *Jen-ch'uan lun-chi* (On Human Rights, Shanghai, 1930), and *Ssu-shih tzu-shu* (Memoirs at the Age of Forty, Hong Kong, 1957 edition). By Lu Hsün, there is his voluminous *Ch'uan-chi* (Complete Works, Shanghai, 1946). Then there follow a large number of collected works by Ch'en Tu-hsiu, Li Ta-chao, Lin Yü-t'ang, Ts'ai Yuan-p'ei, Ku Yüeh-hsiu, and so on. At the extreme of conservatism, one finds Ch'en Huan-chang's *K'ung-chiao lun chieh-lu* (Brief Discussions on the Confucian Religion, Taiyuan, 1918) which should be read together with the writings of K'ang Yu-wei; slightly more moderate, one finds Liang Shu-ming's *Tung-hsi wen-hua chi ch'i che-hsüeh* Civilization and Philosophy of the Orient and the Occident, Shanghai, 1923) and T'ang Chun-i's *Chung-kuo wen-hua chih ching-sheng chia-chih* (The Spiritual Values of the Chinese Civilization, Taipei, 1953). From this kind of modern *t'i-yung* tradition, the Kuomintang sponsored 'cultural construction movement' grew and is represented by Chang Tao-fan, *Wen-hua chien-she hsin-lun* (New Discussions on the Cultural Construction, Chungking, 1944), Ch'en Li-fu, *Chung-kuo Kuomintang yü hsin-sheng-huo yun-tung* (The Chinese Kuomintang and the New Life Movement, Nanking, 1934) and *Sheng chih yuan-li* (The Principle of Life, Shanghai, 1946 edition) and other writings. On the other extreme, the extreme of total Westernization, there is Ch'en Hsü-ching's *Chung-kuo wen-hua chih ch'u-lu* (The Future of the Chinese Civilization, Shanghai, 1934).

In a study of this kind, one cannot avoid using many biographical materials. Personally I find Chiang Pi-wei's *Hui-i-lu* (Memoirs, volume I, Taipei, 1970?), Hsieh Ping-yin's *Nü-ping tzu-chuan* (Autobiography of a Woman Soldier, Hong Kong, 1962 edition), and Huang Lu-yin's *Tzu-chuan* (Autobiography, Shanghai, 1934) of high significance towards an understanding of the attitudes and life-styles of modern Chinese women who were not communists. Hsü Chih-mo's *Ch'uan-chi* (Complete Works,

Taipei, 1969 edition) contains much biographical material about a highly Westernized intellectual while Liang Hsiao-ch'u's *Wei-wan-ch'eng ti tzu-chuan* (An Unfinished Autobiography, Hong Kong, 1969) throws a great deal of light on the life of a Chinese Christian. Liang Shih-ch'iu writes about his studies at Tsinghua University in the *Ch'ing-hua pa-nien* (Eight Years at Tsinghua, Taipei, 1962) and about his friend, Wen I-to, in the *T'an Wen I-to* (On Wen I-to, Taipei, 1967). Mu Ou-ch'u, *Wu-shih tzu-shu* (At the Age of Fifty, Shanghai, 1926) and Yu-liang (pseudonym), *K'ung Hsiang-hsi* (Dr H. H. Kung, Hong Kong, 1935) are useful accounts of modern businessmen as are Wu T'ing-kuang, *Wu T'ing-fang* (A Biography of Wu T'ing-fang, Shanghai, 1922) and Yen Hui-ch'ing, *Tzu-chuan* (Autobiography, Taipei, 1973 edition) on the lives of modern China's diplomats.

# Index

Abend, Hallett, 54, 226
administration, 41–3
  Catholic interference, 93
  *see also* civil service; government;
  *etc.*
Aglen, Sir Francis, 344, 346
agriculture, 121, 153, 364, 374, 375
  Bank of Agriculture, 367
  European, 68, 75
Ah Toy, 243, 259
Alcock, Rutherford, 213, 267, 341
alcohol, 217
Allen, Young J., 77, 100, 108, 111,
  116, 117, 138, 213, 272, 381–2
Alliance Society, 307
  *later*, Kuomintang *q.v.*
American Oriental Society, 121
Amherst, Lord, 24
Amoy, 122, 123, 235
ancestor worship, 118
Anderson, J. G., 174
Andrade, Fernao Peres, 59
An-fu Club, 294, 306
  Constitution, 294
Angel Island, 257
Angell, James B., 234, 254, 256
Anglo–American Christian Union,
  114
Anglo–French Expedition (2nd
  Opium War), *see* wars, 1856–60
Anglo–Japanese Alliance, 32
Anhwei, 154, 297, 306, 337, 407
  Clique, 297, 306

anti-Christian Movement, *see*
  Christianity
anti-imperialism, *see* imperialism
Anti-Religious League, 143
Anyang, 174
archaeology, 94, 120, 174
architecture, 201, 209
arms, 221, 265, 268, 347
Army, 141, 175, 346
  conversion of soldiers, 106, 107,
  110
  education of officers, 153, 176
  Ever-Victorious Army, 232
  German officers, 193
  Huai Army, 347
  and politics, 413
  Red Army, 136, 283, 292
  treatment of wounded, 132
art, 40, 120–1, 158, 167, 175,
  199–202
  and revolution, 198
  Western, 69, 71, 116, 200–2
Assembly, *see* National Assembly
Associated Boards for Christian
  Colleges, 158
Association for Asian Studies, 121
astronomy, 94, 174, 175, 426–30,
  431
Australia, 121
  emigration to, 235, 414
Austria, 191

Ballou, Mr, 102

bandit theory, 52, 53–4, 56, 57
banking, 222, 226, 340, 344, 364–7, 370, 375
barbarians, 25–6, 28, 59–61, 203, 426
Bashford, Bishop James, 114, 125, 138, 147
Bauer, Col. Max, 193
Behrend, B. A., 161
Bentham, Jeremy, 97, 177, 181, 184
Bergson, Henri, 90, 177, 179, 186–8, 200, 439, 448
Bertram, James, 55
Bethune, Norman, 49, 149
Bible, 103, 125
Big Jim, 244, 259
Billingham, Anthony, 54
biology, 174, 175
Birkhoff, G., 179
Black, Davidson, 161, 174
blacks, attitude towards, 79–80, 81, 161
Bland, J. O. P., 51, 226
Blue-shirts, 86, 87
Bluntschli, Johan Kaspar, 181
Bolshevism, 50, 51–2, 56, 100, 188
Bonham, Sir George, 334
books, on China, 39, 40, 45, 69, 78, 85, 94, 98, 117, 120, 153, 270, 434
Boone, Bishop, W., 207
Borodin, Mikhail, 48, 162, 310, 311
bourgeoisie, 370–1, 413
*see also* compradores
Boutroux, 162, 177
Boxer War and Uprising, 28, 29, 30, 40, 50, 64, 72, 98, 110, 139, 141, 142, 153, 208, 273, 277, 285, 322, 326, 352, 381, 406, 407, 435, 451
Boxers, 100, 204
Indemnity, 154, 155, 156, 344, 363
boycotts, 50, 128, 410, 415, 421, 422, 423
by Chinese in USA, 255, 256
Brannan, Sam, 250
Briand, 33
Bridgman, Elijah, 77, 106, 116, 122, 123, 129
Britain
Chinese views of, 71–5

diplomats, 170
education of Chinese, *see* study abroad
missionaries, 94
and railways, 359–60
settlements, 30, 146, 206–7, 208, 212
*see also* language, English; war
British East India Company, 25, 318, 332–3
Brockman, F. S., 101, 134, 135, 148
Brown, Rev. S. R., 151
Buck, J. L., 121
Buck, Pearl, 45, 47, 48, 55, 58, 102, 133, 135, 149, 160, 398
Buddhism, 110, 112, 406
and Christianity, 115
Bureau of Law Codification, 327
Bureau of Legal Reform, 326
bureaucracy, *see* civil service
Burgevine, Henry A., 324
Burke, Sarah, 260
Burlingame, Anson, 62, 63
Treaty, 122, 234, 253
Burton, E. D., 125
Commission, 125, 127
business, *see* commerce
Butterfield, Kenyon, 135

Cairo, 33
California, 236
riots, 256, 257
*see also* San Francisco
Cameron, Donaldina, 258
Canada
collection of Chinese art, 121
student volunteers, 99
United Church of, 147
Canton, 25, 27, 28, 50, 59, 94, 106, 116, 128, 129, 130, 132, 151, 199, 221, 265, 293, 295, 297, 312, 332, 333, 355, 356, 401, 404, 413, 419, 420, 422
delta, 235, 261
railway, 359–60
capitalism, 189, 191–2
USA, 81
Carl, Miss, 199

Carlson, Evans Fordyce, 57
Catholic Church, 92–4, 98, 116, 141, 147, 149
  Chinese clergy, 93
  clothing, 118
  converts, 92
  priests, 93, 149
Celestials, 250, 254, 260
Chalfont, F. H., 120
Chamberlain, Austen, 323, 421
Chan, Charlie, 43
Chan T'ien-yu, 152, 155
Chang, Carsun (Chang Chun-mai), 177–8, 187–8
Chang Chien, 304
Chang Chih-tung, 108, 117, 153, 154, 268, 269, 270, 271, 327, 354, 355–8, 368, 369, 400–1, 433, 434
Chang Ching-chiang, 309
Chang Ching-sheng, 164, 388, 395–6
Chang Ching-shu, 384
Chang Chun-mai, *see* Chang, Carsun
Chang Fu-liang, 136
Chang Hsi-man, 309
Chang Hsing-lang, 162
Chang Hsün, 65
Chang Ping-lin, 297
Chang Po-hsi, 154–5, 401
Chang Po-ling, 75, 78, 111
Chang Shih-chao, 188
Chang Shih-ch'uan, 229, 230
Chang T'ai-yen, 213, 439
Chang Tso-lin, 108, 298, 346, 409, 420
Chang Tung-sun, 187
Chang Wen-k'ai, 108
Chang Wen-t'ien, 249
Chang Yin-huan, 76–7, 79, 88, 132, 162–3
Chang Yin-lin, 187
Ch'angsha, 51, 128, 133, 143, 382
Changteh, 141
Chao Heng-t'i, 298–300
Chao Shih-kuang, 119
Chao Yuan-jen, 195
Chaot'ung, 141
Chaplin, Maxwell, 101
Chavannes, Edouard, 120

Chefoo, 132, 319
  Convention, 138, 334
Chekiang, 221, 222, 267, 298, 342, 346, 349, 382, 414
chemistry, 175, 176, 178
  chemical industry, 225
Ch'en Chiung-ming, 281, 299, 300, 309, 310
Ch'en family, 371
Ch'en Heng-che, 165
Ch'en Hsing-shen, 178
Ch'en Hsü-ching, 443, 446–7
Ch'en Huan-chang, 436
Ch'en Kung-po, 314
Ch'en Kuo-fu, 412
Ch'en Li-fu, 188, 444, 445, 447, 448–9
Ch'en Shu-fan, 297–8
Ch'en Ta, 414
Ch'en Tai, 106–7
Ch'en T'ien-hua, 276
Ch'en Tu-hsiu, 85, 90, 144, 148, 177, 184–5, 189, 190, 191, 282, 293–4, 297, 385, 397, 408, 411, 415, 437
Ch'en Yi, 168
Ch'en Yuan, 74
Ch'en Yu-jen, 79
Cheng Cheng-ch'iu, 229, 230
Cheng Kuan-yin, 223, 433, 437
Cheng Man-t'o, 199
Cheng Yü-hsiu, 165
Chengtu, 125, 133, 415
Chiang Kai-shek, 33, 40, 42, 53–4, 55, 56, 86–7, 109–10, 111, 134, 136, 137, 146, 148, 150, 193, 194, 202, 208, 211, 222, 227, 256, 262, 279–80, 296, 309, 313, 315, 329, 343, 346, 365, 370, 373, 377, 384, 386, 412, 417, 422–3, 424, 449, 450; *see also* Kuomintang; Northern Expedition
  Madame, *see* Soong Mei-ling
Chiang Pi-wei, 200
Chiang T'ing-fu, 174, 193
*chiang-hsüeh*, 158
Chiangning county, 136
*Chiao-hui hsin-pao, see Chinese Christian Review*

*Chicago Tribune*, 226
Ch'i-ch'ao, 437
Chicherin declaration, 32, 278
Ch'ien Chung-shu, 195
Ch'ien Teh-p'ei, 130
Ch'ien Tuan-sheng, 193
Chih-Kung-t'ang, 239
Chihli Clique, 294, 297, 298, 305, 306
children, 76–7, 398–9
  *see also* youth
*chi-mi*, 60, 62–3
Chin Tin Sen, 244, 259
China Association, 139
China Foundation, 121
China Inland Mission, 44, 96, 114, 138
*China Mail*, 299, 301
China Merchants' Steamship Navigation Co., 222
China Reform Association, 304
  *later*, Constitutional Party, *q.v.*
China Revival Society, 306–7
  later, Kuomintang, *q.v.*
China Society for the Promotion of New Education, 184
*China Weekly Review*, 51, 53, 54, 55, 217, 220, 420
Chinatown, *see* San Francisco
*Chinese Christian Review*, 111
Chinese Church
  autonomy, 114–16, 127
  Christian theology, 112–16
  clergy, 93
  education, 128–9
Chinese Communist Party (CCP), 52–7, 90, 115, 129, 146, 166, 167, 189, 190, 191, 192–3, 240, 249, 282–4, 296, 297, 310, 390, 411–13, 417–18, 423–5, 452
  and Kuomintang alliance, 282–4, 310–15, 331, 418, 422, 425, 443
  women, 165–6
Chinese Consolidated Benevolent Association, *see* San Francisco, Six Companies
Chinese Exhibitions, London, 40
Chinese Ratepayers' Association, 211, 212

*Chinese Recorder*, 53–4, 398
*Chinese Repository*, 41, 116, 120, 163, 207
Chinese Revolutionary Party, 309
  *later*, Kuomintang, *q.v.*
*Chinese Scientific Magazine*, 116, 227
Ch'ing empire, 25, 26, 31, 106, 110
  biographies, 121
  government, 65, 257, 265
  penal code, 326, 327
Ch'ingchiangp'u, 354
*ch'ing'-i*, 29, 63
Chinnery, George, 199
*chin-shih*, 153, 154, 157
Ch'i-shan, 60
Ch'iu Chin, 382, 384
Chou En-lai, 33, 167
Chou Fu, 108
Chou Shu-jen, 439
Chou Tso-jen, 385, 386, 387, 397, 439
Chou Tzu-ch'i, 394
*Christian Century*, 145–6
Christian Literature Society, 117
  *see also* Society for the Diffusion of Christian and General Knowledge
Christianity, 45, 65–6, 68, 224
  anti-Christian movement, 50, 53, 128–9, 138–47
  Chinatown, 248
  Chinese Christian theology, 112–16, 149
  conversion to, 103–11
  *see also* Catholic Church; missionaries; Protestant church
chronicles, Chinese, 121
Chü Cheng, 309
Chu Chih-hsin, 143–4, 276
Chu Ching-yi, 136
Ch'ü Ch'iu-pai, 200
Chu Kuang-ch'ien, 202
*chü-jen*, 153, 154
Ch'un, Prince, 154
Chung K'ai-lai, 178
Ch'ung-hou, 63, 64
Chung-hua Book Co., 225
Chungking, 369

Church Self-Government Society, 114
cities, 135
Citizens' Corps, 302
Citizens' Party, 306
civil rights, 184, 212, 272, 289, 381
civil service, 27, 29, 42, 43, 123,
    138, 168, 267, 285
    bureaucratic reform, 268–70
    education for, 153
civil wars, 48, 297, 346, 360
    1913, 289
    1917, 293ff
    1920, 294
    1924, 204
    1926–8, 295, 324, 390; *see also*
    Northern Expedition
    *see also* revolution
clans, 42, 153, 253
Clarke, J. F., 99
Clennel, Mr, 300
Clubb, O. Edmund, 56
coal, 361, 375
    coal oil, 369
    mining, 354, 356, 357
    P'inghsiang, 358
Co-hong, 25, 27, 221
Colledge, 129
Comintern, 310
commerce
    commercial code, 326
    education, 153
    employment in, 220–4
    and the West, 66
Commercial Press, 117, 225
Committee of Vigilance, 250
communications, 266
    Clique, 305–6
    postal service, 209, 210, 227
    radio, 210
    telegraphs, 209, 210, 354, 369
    telephone, 210
    *see also* publishing; railways; *etc.*
communism, 34, 42, 52, 90, 102,
    115, 135, 139, 146–7, 161, 167–8,
    189–93, 211, 230, 282–4
    *Communist*, 191
    USSR, 33, 34, 50, 51–2, 70, 188
    *see also* Chinese Communist Party

compradores, 220–4
confederacy, 297–300
Confucianism, 26, 27, 29, 41, 68,
    69, 84, 87, 90, 96, 112, 158, 174,
    176, 180, 213, 266, 280, 292, 304,
    308, 311, 381, 430–5, 426–52
    *Analects*, 163
    and Christianity, 105, 115
    and civil service, 268–70
    classics, 44, 65, 82, 120, 148,
    151–2, 246, 427–8, 437
    Confucians, 98, 268
    education, 122, 400
    and industry, 268, 348–9
    and Kuomintang, 314, 315, 316
    and law, 327, 329, 330
    and literature, 196
    and medicine, 130
    neo Confucians, 110
    and philosophy, 183, 188
    Reform, 271–3
    revival, 268–73, 314, 436–52; *see
    also* New Life Movement
    and science, 174, 176, 177, 180, 181
    *Sinarum Philosophus*, 119
    virtues, 42, 222–3, 442
conspiracy theory, 52
constitution, 271, 285, 287, 288, 295,
    304, 327
    1923, 294–5, 383
    An-fu, 294
    Ch'ing, 285–96
    committee, 292
    Constitutional Compact Con-
    ference, 290–1, 295
    constitutional government, 285–96
    Constitutional Party, 304
    Constitutional Promotion Society,
    304
    Constitutional Studies Bureau, 287
    and judiciary, 329
    May 5th, 295
    Provisional Constitution, 288–94,
    308, 330, 382
    provisional constitutions, 296–30
    Temple of Heaven, 289, 292
    Ts'ao Kun, 294
    wars for protection of, 293 ff.

consular jurisdiction, 316, 317–18
  decline, 320–4
conversation, with Westerners, 162–3
conversion to Christianity, 92, 93,
  103–11, 123, 147
Coolidge, Mary R., 242
coolie trade, 235–7
co-operatives, 137
copper, 333
Cordier, Henri, 120
corruption, 42–3, 138, 161, 267, 268,
  316, 341, 347, 350, 359
  USA, 80–1
cotton, 338, 339, 354, 361–2, 363,
  364, 375–6
  textile industry, 361–2, 372–3
  workers, 419
courts, *see* law
Creation Society, 197
Crescent Moon Society, 196–7
Cressey, G. B., 121
crime
  Chinatown, 239, 240, 249–50, 254
  treatment of criminals, 324 ff.
culture, 426–52
  reconstruction associations, 444–5,
  447
Cunningham, E., 207
currency, 333, 374
Cushing, Caleb, 121, 317
customs, maritime, 340–8, 349
  revenue, 359, 363

Darwin, Charles, 97, 106, 139, 186
  Social Darwinism, 29, 69, 79, 162,
  180, 181–2, 255, 270, 273, 275,
  276, 277, 280, 331, 402, 435, 448
Davis, George L., 138
Davis, John Francis, 120
d'Aiguibelle, 349–50, 353
de Bellonet, Henri, 267
de Chardin, Teilhard, 94, 161, 174
de Groot, J. M., 120
de Laprade, Victor, 40
de Quincey, Thomas, 40, 45, 46, 74
de Valera, Eamonn, 88
December 9th Movement, 30, 410,
  412–13

defence, 265 ff., 349, 427, 428
  maritime, 349, 351, 352
Delamarre, Fr, 92
democracy, 42, 185, 188, 189, 193,
  273, 304
  democrats, 294
Denby, Charles, 72, 139
despotism, 41–3
Dewey, John, 70, 175, 177, 179,
  182–6, 384, 402–3
diet, 136
diplomats, 45
Dobson, W. H., 133
Dowager Empress, 63–4, 132, 154,
  199, 385
Drake, Samuel, 46
dress, 217
  of Chinese in America, 152, 156,
  245–6
  missionaries, 118
  Western, 171
  women, 387–8
Driesch, Hans, 177, 179
drugs, 339
  *see also* opium
Du Halde, Jean-Baptiste, 39
Dubs, H. H., 121

East Asiatic Committee, 121
*Eastern Miscellany*, 193
economy, 193, 332–79
Eddy, Sherwood, 53, 108, 136, 146,
  148
Edkins, J., 43
education, 111, 135, 183–4, 272
  of Chinese overseas, *see* study
  abroad
  Educational Act, 1922, 184
  examination system, 117, 154–5,
  272, 400, 401, 405–6
  mass education, 135, 403, 406,
  407
  missionaries, 122–9, 403
  *New Education*, 403
  reform, 400–10
  Western studies, 65 ff.
  *see also* missionaries; universities
  and colleges; women; youth

Edwardes, A. H. F., 346
elections, 288, 291, 297, 300–1
    presidential, 291, 294, 302
electricity, 361
Elgin, Lord, 30
Eliot, T. S., 90
emigration, 64, 234–6, 253
    conditions of travel, 236
    contribution to China, 261–2
    Immigration Act (US), 1930, 243
Endicott, Dr, James, 102, 147
engineering, 178, 203
Eucken, Rudolf, 90, 177, 179, 186,
    188, 439
Europe, Chinese views of, 75, 81, 88
    *see also under individual countries*
Exclusion Acts (USA), 152, 154, 155,
    156, 234, 256, 261
exports, 27, 335, 336–8, 376
extraterritoriality, 320–4

*Fa kuo Chih-lüeh*, 84
Faber, Ernst, 120
factories, 189, 225, 373, 414
family, 396–9
    conversion of, 106
    Family Study Society, 398
famine, 92, 150
Fan Shou-k'ang, 178
Fanchuang, 136
fascism, 86–7, 192–3
    *see also Mein Kampf*
Fen Nai-ch'ao, 197
Feng Kuei-fen, 61, 269
Feng T'i, 193
Feng Yü-hsiang, 110, 111, 345, 420
Feng Yu-lan, 176
*feng-ch'i*, 35, 225
Ferguson, J. C., 120–1
Feuerwerker, A., 375
films, 43, 47, 101, 219–20, 229–30
finance
    Depression, 374
    insurance, 222
    investment, 262, 362–4
    *see also* banking; currency
Fisher, Thomas, 106
Fontainier, H. V., 63

Foochow, 107, 231, 300
    shipyard, 153, 267, 347, 349–53,
    368
food
    exports, 338
    imports, 339
    processing, 225, 361–2
    Shanghai, 217
foot-binding, 119, 123, 160, 243, 258,
    380, 381, 382, 385
foreign concessions, 359–60
'foreign dogs', 59
foreign policy, 28, 29, 30–1, 59–91
    diplomatic office, 168
    Ministry of Foreign Affairs, 108,
    155
France
    Chinese views of, 82–6, 186–8
    and emigration, 235
    literature, 195, 197
    missionaries, 31, 92–4, 119–20,
    122, 267
    railways, 359–60
    relations with, 32, 63, 149, 165,
    346, 349–50
    settlement, 207, 208, 211, 212, 231
    *see also* study abroad; war
Friends of the Constitution
    Association, 304
Fryer, John, 41, 102, 116, 117, 174,
    227
Fu Ssu-nien, 398
Fukien, 54, 123, 135, 153, 166, 189,
    235, 267, 298, 306, 349, 351
*Fundamentals*, 99

Gabb, H., 141
gambling, 45, 103, 216, 401
    Chinatown, 239, 242, 243–4, 249,
    254
Gamewell, Frank, 148–9
gazetteers, 265
Geary, Thomas, 239
    Geary Act, 256
Geneva, 33
geography, 120, 121
geology, 94, 120, 174
    Chinese Geological Institute, 174

George, Lloyd, 91
Germany, 31, 32, 43, 72, 191–2
  Chinese views of, 86–8, 321
  literature, 195
  Nazis, 86–7, 160, 193
  Peace Treaty, 321
  refugees, 79
  and Shantung, 70, 188, 410
Gest Collection, 121
Gibson, Rev. Otis, 258, 259
Gilbert, Rodney, 44, 47, 49, 50, 58
Giles, Herbert, 120
Ginling College, 109, 111
Giquel, Prosper, 153, 349–50, 352, 353
*Globe Magazine*, 116–17
Go T'o, 106
Goebbels, Joseph, 87
Goforth, J., 106
*Golden Hill News*, 248
Goldsmith, Oliver, 39
*Good Earth*, 47, 135
Goodnow, Frank, 46
Gordon, Charles, 61
Goucher, Dr J. F., 131
government
  constitutional, 285–96
  reform, 271–3
  USA, 77–8, 81
  *see also* National government;
  Provisional government
Grabau, A. W., 174
Grand Council, 81
Great Harmony, 177
Gregg, Alice H., 127
Griswold, J. A., 207
*Guide*, 297
guilds, 42, 414–15
Gunn, S. M., 126, 133, 136
Gunn, Tom, 261
Gunther, John, 208–9
Gutzlaff, Charles, 39, 95, 96, 108,
  116, 138
  Mrs, 151

Hall, Ronald O., 137
Han Suyin, 164, 180
Han-Chinese, 274, 275, 276
Han-Confucianism, 430

handicrafts, traditional, 362, 371, 375–7
Hankow, 30, 56, 146, 164, 189, 336,
  354, 355, 356, 357, 420
  Hankow–Canton railway, 359–60
Hanoi, 120
Hanson, Haldore, 54
Hanyang, 357–8, 369
Hanyehp'ing foundry, 353–9
Hart, Sir Robert, 27, 62, 63, 70, 82,
  138, 213, 266, 267, 268, 272, 347
Harte, Bret, 252
Hatem, George, 55
Hawaii, Chinese in, 306
Hay, John, 82, 162
Hedin, Sven, 174
Hegel, G. W. F. 40, 97, 98
Hemingway, Ernest, 179
Hengshan, 135
Hewlitt, Sir Meyrick, 170, 415
Hill, Dr David, 107, 118
Hisao Yao-nan, 132
history, 120, 174
Hitler, Adolf, 86, 87, 193
Ho Ch'i-fang, 197, 202, 223, 269
Ho Chung-han, 193
Ho Hsiang-ning, 383
Hobson, J. A., 58
Hocking, W. D., 101
Hodgkin, Henry, 53–4
Holland, 59, 88, 346
Hollywood, 43, 101
Honan, 141, 354
Hong Kong, 27, 60, 72, 151, 156,
  168, 230, 235, 236, 237, 248, 256,
  299, 301, 306, 333, 334, 346, 421–3
  Hong Kong Conference, 114
Hopei, 135, 136, 407, 412, 413
hospitals, 129, 131, 132–3, 150, 209
Hou Chi-ming, 375, 376
Howard, Dr Leonora, 131
Hsi Liao-chu, 107
Hsiang Ching-yü, 168, 383
Hsiangshan, 394
*hsiang-yüeh*, 115
Hsieh Fu-ya, 112
Hsieh Ping-ying, 390, 392
Hsieh Wan-ying, 165
Hsien-feng, Emperor, 81

*Hsi-feng*, 389
*Hsin-min ts'ung-pao*, 170
*Hsin-yüeh*, 196
Hsiung K'e-wu, 309
Hsü, I. C. Y., 62
Hsü Cheng-k'eng, 80
Hsü Ch'ien, 329
Hsü Chih-mo, 71, 73, 74, 77, 83,
    148, 161, 162, 195, 197, 385, 389,
    395, 397, 439
Hsü Chi-yü, 66, 77, 84, 116, 265
Hsü Jen-k'uei, 325
Hsü Jun, 168–9, 222
Hsü Kuang-chin, 265
Hsü Pei-hung, 167, 200, 201, 395
Hsü Shih-ch'ang, 44
Hsu Yu, 83
Hsüeh Fu-ch'eng, 68, 69, 131–2, 262,
    268
Hsüeh Huan, 341
*Hsüeh-heng*, 171, 187
Hu Bo Mi, 107
Hu Han-min, 278, 314
Hu Hsien-hsu, 171
Hu Kuang-yung, 350
Hu Li-yuan, 269
Hu Ngieng Su, 107
Hu Shih, 50, 70, 78, 89, 90, 144,
    148, 159, 161, 173, 175, 180, 182,
    184, 198, 281, 297, 385, 391–2,
    393, 395, 397, 408, 420, 437,
    438–9, 442, 444, 445–6
Hu Sing Mi, 107
Hu Yong Mi, 107
Hua Lo-keng, 178
Huang Hsing, 308, 309
Huang K'an, 408
Huang Shao-hsiung, 314
Hubbard, Hugh, 135, 136
Hume, David, 39
Hummel, A. W., 121
humour, 74
Hunan, 135, 153, 154, 157, 165, 166,
    298–9, 306, 349, 355, 383, 423
Hundred Days Reform, 108, 361, 400
Hung Hsiu-ch'uan, 106
Hung Hsün, 67, 68
Hung Shen, 229

Hungary, 191
Hupei, 111, 153, 154, 298, 306, 355,
    417, 423
Huxley, Thomas, 69, 72, 90, 180,
    181, 270, 273
Hwang, Y. L., 125
hydraulics, 174

Ibsen, H., 387, 397
idolatry, 118, 141
I-liang, 82
illiteracy, 106, 135, 154, 161, 235, 414
*Illustrated Gazetteer of Maritime
    Countries*, 61, 65, 84
*Illustrated Wasp*, 252, 253–4
immigration, 152, 154, 155, 206–34,
    254–7
    *see also* missionaries
imperialism, 29–30, 190
    anti-imperialism, 30, 32, 138–47,
    212, 277–8, 283, 321, 346, 376, 451
imports, 335, 338–40
    opium, 332, 338–9
India
    Chinese views of, 160
    opium trade, 332–3
industrialization, 431
    and agriculture, 364, 371
    failure of, 362–77
    and money market, 364–7
    and private enterprise, 361–2
    shortage of capital, 362–3, 377, 378
    and traditional handicrafts, 362,
    371, 375–7
    *see also* investment
industry, 175, 222–3, 224–6, 265,
    268, 348–59
    employment in, 168
    foreign competition, 372–5, 376
    heavy, 349–60, 372
    iron, 353–9
    light, 361–2, 372
    management, 367–72
    private enterprise, 361–2
    Western, 68, 75
infanticide, 45, 380
Institute of Pacific Relations, 135
international relations, 27–34

investment, 262, 374
  foreign, 362-4
Ireland, 88, 189
iron, 361, 375, 378
  industrial centres, 356-8
Isherwood, Christopher, 179
Italy, 193
  Chinese views of, 86-7

Jaffe, Philip, 55
James, William, 99
Japan
  immigration, 207
  influence on language, 198
  and railways, 359-60
  relations with, 32, 34, 54, 70, 80,
    188, 193, 346, 410
  Twenty One Demands, 30, 278
  *see also* study abroad; war,
    1894-5; 1931; 1932; 1937-45
Jardine, William, 129, 214, 222
*jen*, 69, 434
Jen Hung-chun, 176, 404
Jen Pao-lo, 108
Jesuits, 93-4, 119
Joffe, A., 310
Johnson, Governor, 250
Johnson, Nelson, 56, 137, 324
Jones, J., 44
Jordan, Sir John, 163
journalism, 221, 228
judges, 328-9
*Jui-lin*, 351
Jung Tsung-ching, 362

K'aip'ing coal mines, 354, 357
K'ang Yu-wei, 83, 84, 85, 175, 180,
  200, 268, 271, 272, 274, 381, 400,
  434, 436
K'ang-hsi, 428
Kansu, 350
Kant, Immanuel, 183, 187
*Kapital, Das*, 203
Kautsky, Karl, 190
*Ke-chih hui-pien, see Chinese Scientific
  Magazine*
Kellogg, Frank, 323

Key, Ellen, 398
Kiangnan Arsenal, 116, 347
Kiangsi, 54, 135, 136, 298
Kiangsu, 108, 154, 157, 165, 189, 321
Kinder, C. W., 354
Kipling, Rudyard, 98
Kiu Kiang, 30, 146
Knatchbull-Hugessen, Sir H., 56
Koo, Wellington, 420
Korea, 160, 189
*kowtow*, 24
Kriebel, Col. Herman, 193
Ku Hung-ming, 173, 436
Ku Yü-hsiu, 157, 161, 162
*Kuan-tu shang-pan*, 222, 350, 357, 367-70
Kuangchow, 111
Kuang-hsü, 108
Kuangsi, 298
Kung, Dr H. H., 137, 202, 256
Kung, Prince, 61, 62, 82, 266, 267,
  324, 341, 427-31
Kung family, 371
Kunming, 56
Kuo Mo-jo, 197
Kuo Sung-t'ao, 62, 63, 67, 268, 326
Kuomintang (K M T), 52, 54, 87,
  109, 129, 134, 143-4, 146, 156,
  184, 185, 188, 192, 199, 211, 246,
  247, 262, 282-4, 289, 290, 295-6,
  300, 301, 306-15, 329, 330, 344,
  346, 370, 371, 383, 390, 398, 403,
  404, 406, 411-12, 416, 417, 421,
  422, 423, 444, 445, 449, 451
  and CCP Alliance, 282-4, 310-15,
    331, 418, 425, 443
  constitution, 312
  and fascism, 194
  formation, 306-8
  1st National Conference, 311
  membership, 310-11
  and nationalism, 278-82
  party factions, 314-15
  revival, *see* New Life Movement
  3rd National Conference, 315
  Tutelage Programme, 295-6, 450
Kwan Ato, 129
Kwantung, 152, 153, 154, 157, 166,
  298, 299, 305, 310, 312, 349, 394

Kweichow, 141, 298
    French Bishop of, 93
Kwok, D. W. Y., 182

labour
    cheap, 64, 234, 235, 253, 352–3
    child, 416
    conditions, 414–15
    contractors, 413–14
    female, 76
    political mobilization, 189–90,
        413–25
    protection, 414
Lampson, Sir Miles, 324
Lanchow, 354, 368
land, 306–7
    Catholic ownership, 92–3
    and immigrants, 206; *see also*
        settlements
    *Land and Labour in China*, 135
    Land Regulations, 206–7
    speculation, 366
    tenure system, 137
Langua, 199
language – Chinese, 46–7, 63, 119–20,
        247–8
    dictionary, 120
    dialects, 119, 122
    diplomatic service, 154, 169
    foreign language acquisition,
        124–5, 172
    interpreters, 168
    Language Institute, 63, 64, 96,
        116, 151
    and missionaries, 105, 147
    official language in church, 115
    study of, 119–20, 151–2
    vernacular, 196, 199
    Westernization, 198–9, 233
    *see also* translation
language – English
    at court, 154
    pidgin, 59
    Shanghai, 233
    teaching, 124–5; in USA, 247–8,
        258–9
Lao She, 161, 194, 195, 394
Lassar, Joannes, 103

Latourette, K. S., 95
Lattimore, Owen, 55
law
    Ch'ing codes, 326, 327
    civil code, 386
    commercial code, 326
    consular jurisdiction, 316, 317–18
    courts, 168, 231, 318, 326
    *Elements of International Law*, 62
    European, 66, 67–8, 73, 116
    lawyers, 168, 221, 230–1, 328–9,
        383
    Legislative Council, 295
    mixed courts, 231, 318–20, 321, 325
    modern courts, 328–31
    penal code, 120, 326, 327, 386–7
    reform, 271, 288, 289, 290, 316,
        324–38, 386–7
    rights of Chinese in USA, 250
    *see also* constitution
Lay, Horatio Nelson, 62, 341
Laymen's mission and inquiries, 101,
        127, 139
Lazarists, 93–4
Leaf, Earl, 54
League for the Defence of People's
    Rights, 315
League of Nations, 33, 88, 373
Lecomte, Fr Louis, 39
Left-wing Writers' League, 197–8
Legge, James, 44, 82, 120
Leith-Ross, Sir Frederick, 374
Lenin, V. I., 30, 91, 139, 191
    Leninism, 188, 278
Lew, Timothy, 145
Li Chao-t'ang, 353
Li Cheng-tao, 160
Li Chien-wu, 202
Li Chi-jen, 194
Li Chin-fa, 167
Li Ch'ing-yai, 194
Li Fu-ch'un, 168
Li Hung-chang, 62, 63, 64, 67, 86,
        108, 131, 151, 152, 221, 267, 269,
        347, 348, 352, 354–6, 358, 367,
        368, 369, 400, 427, 433
Li Kuei, 200, 380
Li Kung-p'u, 81

Li Lieh-chun, 309
Li Ling, 260
Li Li-san, 168, 424
Li Po-yuan, 172, 200, 223, 228
Li Sheng-lan, 96
Li Shih-ts'en, 166, 187, 200
Li Ssu-kuang, 174
Li Ta-chao, 90, 189, 190, 191, 385,
    386, 408, 411, 415, 437
Li Yuan-hung, 65, 108, 291
Liang Ch'i-ch'ao, 69, 72–3, 78, 79–80,
    81, 84, 85, 90, 144, 162, 168, 170,
    177, 180, 181, 186, 198, 248, 257,
    261, 271, 274–5, 302, 304, 400,
    420, 433, 435–6, 438
Liang Fa, 106
Liang Hsiao-ch'u, 108, 119
Liang Ju-hao, 152
Liang Shih-ch'iu, 196
Liang Shih-yi, 305–6
Liang Shu-ming, 136, 144, 157, 162,
    176, 188, 202, 392, 394, 395, 407,
    440–2, 443
Liang Ssu-ch'eng, 201
Liang Teng-yen, 152
Liang Tun-yen, 169, 202
Liao Chung-k'ai, 246, 309, 311, 315
Liao-tung Peninsula, 86
liberation, 115
libraries
    on China in West, 121
    Chinese, 126, 210, 212
*Life*, 55
*likin*, 267, 334, 343, 345, 346
Lim Jin-gi, 123
Lin, Commissioner, 130, 200
Lin Feng-mien, 167, 200, 201
Lin Sen, 249
Lin Shu, 75, 194, 261
Lin Tse-hsü, 61, 116
Lin Yutang, 42–3, 49, 50, 55, 73–4,
    76, 77, 78–9, 170–1, 194, 204, 223,
    385, 399
Lio Ho-chen, 384
literature, 120, 196
    visits by literary figures, 179
    Western, 69, 74, 75, 172–3, 195–6,
    198

Little Pete, 244, 259
Liu Hai-Su, 200, 201
Liu, Herman, 404
    Mrs, 396
Liu K'un-yi, 268
*Liu Mei ts'ai-feng-lu*, 80
Liu Ming-ch'uan, 354
Liu Shao-ch'i, 55, 424
Liu Shih-p'ei, 408
Liu Ya-tzu, 276
Livingstone, Dr, 129
Lo Chia-lun, 193, 194
Lo Tun-wei, 392, 398
Lo Wen-kan, 50
London, 68
London Missionary Society, 94
London School of Economics, 74,
    137, 163
Long March, 54, 55, 56, 136
Lu Cheng-hsiang, 108
Lu Hsün, 74, 90–1, 172–3, 197, 220,
    224, 228, 384, 385–6, 388, 391,
    392, 397, 406, 411, 439
Lu Jung-t'ing, 298
Lu T'ao, 298
Lu Yüeh-chang, 82
Lu Yung-hsiang, 298–300
Lui Fook, 254
Lyon, D. Willard, 101, 134, 149

Ma Chien-chung, 198, 268
Ma Liang, 111
McCall, W. A., 403
Macao, 41, 109, 116, 129, 235, 237,
    257, 346
McCartney, Lord, 26
McDougal, Governor, 235, 253
MacGillivray, Donald, 147
Machiang, 235
Mackay, T., 322
    Treaty, 338
Mackenzie, Robert, 69, 117, 270
Maclay, 47
MacMurray, J. V. A., 149
MacNair, H. F., 120
Mahan, A. T., 58
*mahjong*, 215, 259
Mai Hui-t'ing, 393, 398

Maio, 141
Major, E., 226, 227
Malacca, 103
management, 367–72
Manchuria, 132, 193, 298, 346, 413
    anti-Manchuism, 275–7, 278
    Manchus, 26, 234, 238, 247, 261,
    274, 426
    railways, 360
    *see also* war, 1931
mandarins, 41–2
Mao Tse-tung, 55, 168, 180, 283, 385
    Maoism, 116
Marconi, 179
Maring, G., 310
marriage, 118–19, 325, 390–5
    adultery, 386–7
    arranged, 391, 392
    divorce, 387–95
    love, 389–90, 393
    mixed, 163–4, 166, 168, 232, 243,
    259–60
    polygamy, 330, 380, 392
    weddings, 393–4
    women's rights, 382
Marsham, Dr John, 103
Martin, C. Currie, 46
Martin, W. A. P., 44, 62, 96, 108,
    116, 222, 235, 431
Marxism, 75, 88, 98, 143, 186, 188,
    189, 190, 191, 192, 203, 415
    Marx, 98
    Marxist–Leninist, 191–2, 283
*Ma-shih wen-t'ung*, 198
Mason, C. W., 342
Mateer, Calvin, 98
mathematics, 174, 178, 179, 426–30,
    431
Matheson, J., 116
Mawei, *see* Foochow
May 4th Movement, 30, 112, 127,
    175, 177, 189, 190, 199, 200, 229,
    383, 384, 386, 389, 391, 395, 402,
    408, 409, 410–11, 412, 416, 423,
    432, 442, 444, 447
May 30th Movement, 51–2, 143, 212,
    321, 323, 419–23
Mayer, Frederick, 120

Medhurst, W. H., 41, 47, 170, 213, 216
Medical Missionary Society, 129
medicine, 129–33, 143, 150
    Chinese Medical Association, 396
    surgery, 130
    teaching of, 126, 133, 203, 404
Mei Ssu-p'ing, 136
Mei Yi-ch'i, 111
*Mein Kampf*, 87, 194, 203
Mencius, 90
mercantilism, 66, 67
merchants, 221, 350, 368, 369
    Chinese in USA, 237
meteorology, 94
Metternich, 23, 42
Michie, Alexander, 214
*Middle Kingdom*, 41, 120
military, 28, 64
Mill, John Stuart, 41, 72, 90, 106,
    180, 184, 273
Millard, T. F., 226
Miller, Eddy, 209
Milnes, Dr W., 103, 106
Ming Wan-li, 59
mining, 153, 189, 222, 268, 354–6
*Min-pao*, 307
*Min-to*, 187
missionaries, 31, 44, 45, 49, 53,
    92–150, 380
    and Boxer uprising, 110
    Catholic Church, 92–4
    and communists, 53–4
    conversions, 103–11, 147
    and corruption, 138
    decline, 101–2
    dress, 118
    education of Chinese, 122–9
    Friends, 125
    hostility towards, 138–47, 267, 410
    influence, 116–18
    language, 105, 119–20, 147
    life style, 118
    medical, 129–33, 148, 209
    motives, 102–3
    Protestant Church, 94–5
    'Rice' missionaries, 102
    rural communities, 135
    in USA, 258

Mitchell Report, 27, 334
Miu Feng-lin, 440
modernization, 33, 35, 116, 268–84
    contribution of emigrants, 261
    defence, 267
    industry, 348 59
    modernists, 197
monarchy, 287, 289, 294
Mongolia, 345, 346
    Mongols, 43
Monroe, Paul, 179, 403
Montesquieu, C. de S., 39
moral rearmament, 110
moral standards, 43–4, 437–8
*Morning Post*, 189, 190
Morrell, Miss, 110
Morrison, Dr George, 121
Morrison, Robert, 94, 103, 106, 129,
    130, 138, 226
Mott, John R., 146
Mo-tzu, 68
music, 119, 201–2, 217, 409
    Chinatown, 249
    choreography, 165
    opera, 63, 202, 218, 228, 229
    singing, 158, 201
Muslims, 93
    rebellion, 234, 350
Mussolini, Benito, 86, 87, 162

Nagasaki, 216
Nanking, 53, 60, 62, 82, 109, 129,
    143, 156, 262, 268, 329, 343, 353,
    358, 379, 382, 407, 412, 424, 445
    government, *see* Provisional
    government
    incident, 30, 146, 279, 346
    Treaty, 60, 317, 333, 334, 340
    University, 136
Napier, Lord, 25, 317
National Assembly, 288–9, 290,
    291–4, 300–4, 306
    Extraordinary National Assembly,
    293
    Provisional Administration, 295
National Association for the
    Advancement of Education, 128
National Bureau of Translation, 198

National Christian Council, 53
National Government, 295–6, 313,
    324, 327, 328, 329, 330, 421
National Progressive Society, 307
National Public Party, 307
National Resources Committee, 370
Nationalism, 29, 30, 32, 33, 50, 52,
    127, 138, 158–9, 212, 271, 277–8,
    278–82, 304, 335, 346, 359, 361,
    379, 399, 418, 450–1
    and fascism, 193–4
National Day, 294
Nationalist societies, 437
Nationalists, 42, 162, 170, 322
    *see also* Manchuria, anti-Manchuism
navy, 153, 265
Needham, J., 174, 427
Netherland Missionary Society, 95
New Alliance Society, *see*
    Kuomintang
New Life Movement, 87, 109, 314
*New Tide*, 408–9
New York, 79, 81, 107, 226
*New Youth*, 189, 190, 228, 385
newspapers, 225, 226–8, 248, 270,
    306
    Chinatown, 248–9
    'yellow press', 228
    *see also under names of papers,* e.g.
    *Shen pao*
Nieh Jung-Chen, 168
Nien rebellion, 234
Nietzsche, F. W., 98, 200, 440
1911 Club, 304, 306
Ningpo, 122, 221, 393, 414
*North China Herald,* 209, 226, 420
Northern Expedition, 143, 146, 208,
    358, 390, 410, 417, 423
Norway, trade with, 346
*Notitia Linguae Sinicae,* 119

obscenity, 44, 45
Olymphant, D. W. C., 116
O'Neill, Eugene, 179
'Open Door and Equal Economic
    Opportunities', 32, 82
opera, *see* music

opium, 25, 27, 40, 103, 107, 116,
    130, 138, 214, 216
    Chinatown, 242, 244, 249, 254
    import, 332
    prohibition, 332
    refuge, 107
    trade, 332-3, 338-9
    wars, *see* war, 1839-42; 1856-60
oracle bones, 120, 121, 174
Osgood, W. F., 179
Ou-yang Chung-ku, 433
Ou-yang Yü-ch'ien, 229, 390, 392

'P', 56
Pa Chin, 50
paleontology, 174
Palmerston, Lord, 25, 30, 317
P'an Chai-hsün, 195
P'an Kuang-tan, 444
P'an Yu-ch'iang, 193
Paoan, 55
Paoshan, 321
Paoting, 110, 136
Paris, 82-3
Parker, Dr Peter, 41, 94-5, 129, 130,
    138, 168
Parkes, Sir Harry, 64, 319
Parkhurst, Helen, 185, 403
parliament, 294
Patterson, L. E., 161
peasants, 135, 136-7, 189, 190, 413
    *see also* labour
Peck, Graham, 137
Peffer, Nathaniel, 101
Peirce, C. S., 182
Peiping, *see* Peking
Peking, 31, 32, 44, 55, 59, 64, 65,
    108, 123, 128, 129, 161, 163, 166,
    197, 204, 211, 212, 227, 234, 248,
    254, 256, 274, 292, 295, 296, 297,
    298, 299, 301, 303, 306, 308, 312,
    313, 321, 328, 344, 345, 346, 347,
    354, 355, 387, 404, 412, 413, 419,
    420, 445
    opera, 63, 202
    Peking Man, 174
    Treaties, 61, 94, 140
    *see also* universities and colleges

Pelliot, Paul, 120
Pettus, Dr W. W., 102
Philippines, 189
Philosophes, 39
philosophy, 70, 120, 144
    Western, 69, 175-8, 179-202
physical appearance, 43-4
    Westerners, 59, 71
physics, 175, 178
Physiocrats, 39
'piglet trade', 235
Pin-ch'un, 70, 82
P'inghsiang, 357
Pingyang, 107
Pius XI, 93
Pixley, Frank, 254
Po Wen-wei, 309
police, 209
Political Advisory Bureau, 285, 287
Political Advisory Council, 285, 287,
    304
Political Council, 290, 302-3, 329
Political Information Society, 304
political parties, 300, 304-16
    *see also under names of major parties*
politics, 50 ff., 138, 183, 285 ff.
    Central College of Political
    Science, 136
    labour movement, 413-25
    political influences on China,
    179-94, 261
    societies, 270, 304
    women's role, 165-6, 168, 381,
    382-4, 412, 418
    youth, 410-13, 415
Portuguese, 59, 88, 235
    *see also* Macao
Pottinger, Sir Henry, 334
pragmatism, 182
President, 288, 290-1, 302, 303,
    306
Price, Dr Frank W., 121, 136, 147
printing and publishing, 103, 106,
    117, 361
prisons, 329
    San Quentin, 216, 250
private enterprise, 361-2, 369-70
property, private, 190

prostitution, 45, 102, 103, 119, 163, 209, 215–16, 217, 391
   Chinatown, 239, 242–3, 254, 259
   concubinage, 382, 398
   France, 83
   USA, 76
Protestant Church, 93, 94–5, 100, 114, 415
   Baptists, 100, 109
   Church of England, 147
   Conference of the Protestant missions, 96, 98, 102, 114, 116, 145
   converts, 93
   denominations, 113
   Methodists, 107, 108, 109, 110, 147
   Presbyterians, 94–5, 110, 149
   and science, 98
   statistics, 95
   *see also* missionaries; Chinese Church
Proust, M., 90
provinces, 296–300
Provisional government, 278, 288, 295, 308, 330, 347, 360, 379
Pruitt, Ida C., 121
publishing, 195, 221, 225, 226–8, 270
P'u-lun, 154
P'u-yi, 65

Quesnay, 39
queues, 118, 119, 152, 156, 245, 258
   Queue Ordinance, 1876, 245, 253–4
quintessence, *see* Confucianism, revival

racial discrimination, 79–80, 160, 164, 233, 274, 275–7
   against Chinese in USA, 79, 159–60, 232–3, 234, 236, 241, 250, 252–7
   *see also* Exclusion Acts; Manchuria, anti-Manchuism
Radcliffe-Brown, A., 179
radicalism, 48–51, 52–3, 88

railways, 354–5, 359–60, 363, 412, 418
   construction, 64, 335, 336
   Eastern railway, 321
   T'angshan–Hsikechuang railway, 354
rebellions, 31, 48, 61, 62, 64, 141, 207, 234, 266, 379
reconstruction, 373
'recovery of rights', 30
Red Army, 136, 283
Red Cross, 132
*Red Star Over China*, 55
'Reds', 54–7
   *see also* communism
reform movement, 228
   1898, 153, 190, 271–5, 285, 307, 331, 381, 435
   1900, 34, 190
refugees, 79, 92
Regulators of the Hound, 250
Reid, Gilbert, 100, 116, 139, 272
Reinsch, Paul S., 42
religion
   comparative, 99
   folk, 110, 120, 141
   religious incidents, 140
   *see also* Catholic Church; Confucianism; *etc.*
Remer, C. F., 363
Renan, Ernest, 99
Republic of China, 249, 288, 308, 394, 436
Republicans, 42, 300, 306–7
*Review of the Times, see Globe Magazine*
revolution, 190, 191, 192, 273–84
   French, 84
   1911, 40, 119, 155, 208, 225, 229, 277, 307, 358, 382, 402, 410
   1926–8, 295, 324, 390; *see also* Northern Expedition
   and law reform, 329
   Russian, 188, 190–1, 217
   songs, 201
   women's influence, 165–6, 168, 381, 382
   *see also* civil war

Ricci, Matteo, 59
Richard, Timothy, 69, 100, 107, 108, 116, 117, 125, 138, 162, 181, 213, 272
riots, 48, 60, 140, 141, 143, 256, 353, 383–4, 410
  anti-Chinese in USA, 257
Roach, Senator, 253
Roberts, Sam, 250
Robertson, C. H., 178
Rockefeller Foundation, 136, 197
Rockhill, William, 121
Roosevelt, Theodore, 139, 162
Rousseau, J. J., 39, 184
Royal Asiatic Society, 120, 214
rural reconstruction, 136–7, 144
Russell, Bertrand, 51, 99, 148, 162, 175, 177, 179, 186, 441
Russia, 31, 32, 34, 56, 59, 86, 119, 191, 266, 278
  Bolshevism, 50, 51–2, 56, 100, 188
  borders with, 25, 59, 321, 452
  Chinese views of, 81
  communism, 88
  industrial assistance, 337, 359–60
  literature, 195
  revolution, 188, 190–1, 417
  St Petersburg, 69
  White Russians in China, 208, 215, 233, 276

Sa Pen-t'ieh, 178
San Francisco, 206, 234–62
San Francisco Chinatown, 34, 64, 161, 234–62
  acculturation, 257–61
  Chinese Consolidated Benevolent Association, *see sub-entry below on* Six Companies
  Chinese immigration, 64, 234–6, 253–7, 414
  cigar shops, 241–2
  crime, 239, 240, 242, 249–50, 254
  culture, 248–9, 257–61
  dress, 245–6
  earthquake, 245
  education, 246–9
  fire, 251

gambling, 239, 242, 243–4, 249
influence on China, 261–2
language problems, 258–9
laundries, 240–1, 259
naturalization, 254
occupations, 236, 239, 253
opium, 242, 244, 249
overcrowding, 244, 250–1
patriotism, 262
prostitution, 239, 242–3
railways, 253
restaurants, 240–1, 259
secret societies, 238–40, 249–50
shoemaking, 241, 242, 259
Six Companies, 237–8, 239, 240, 251, 256, 259, 261
tourism, 251
Westernization, 245–6, 251, 254, 257–61
Sanger, Margaret, 395–6
sanitation, 136
Sanyuanli, 50
Sassoon, Sir Victor, 209
Scandinavia, 88
Schlegel, G., 120
Schmidt, W., 179
schools, 404–7
  American, 76–7, 151
  buildings, 118, 176, 406
  mission schools, 122–5, 129, 403, 406
  preparatory for study abroad, 154, 155, 166
  primary, 405
  secondary, 405
  *see also* education
science, 68, 94, 98, 116, 117, 126, 167, 174–9, 203, 426, 435
Scott Act, 256
secret societies (*tong*), 120, 141, 238, 249, 306, 415
  *tong* war, 240, 249, 250
  in USA, 238–40, 243
Selby, T. G., 46
Self-Strengthening Movement, 28
settlements, 31, 212
  Chinese in foreign, 208
  Hankow and Kiukiang, 30, 146

International (Shanghai), 206–10, 212, 213–20, 231, 319, 320, 419, 420
life style in, 214–15
sex
  birth control, 395–6
  chastity, 391–2
  France, 83
  immorality, 118, 164–5
  morality, 387 ff.
  segregation, 390
  sex education, 388
  sexual equality, 71, 119, 123, 380–7
  *see also* marriage; prostitution; women
Shanghai, 51, 61, 96, 98, 111, 114, 143, 145, 156, 164, 166, 168, 189, 191, 206–34, 235, 236, 262, 295, 304, 306, 310, 312, 318, 321, 328, 337, 341, 344, 353, 354, 365, 366, 381, 382, 387, 395, 404, 412, 414, 417–21, 423, 424, 445
  acculturation, 232–4
  administration, 208–9, 210–11, 212
  business, 220–6
  cinemas, 220
  College of Arts, 200
  courts, 318–20, 321, 325
  crime, 216–17
  entertainment, 218–20
  hospitals, 209
  moral degeneration, 214 ff.
  parks, 217–18
  police, 209, 210
  population, 207
  public services, 209 10
  publishing, 226–8
  *Shanghai Evening Post*, 226
  'Shanghai school', 228
  *Shen-pao*, 80, 131, 152, 172, 194, 207, 209–10, 215, 216, 217, 218, 226–7
  sport, 214–15
  stock exchange, 226
  Western community, 34, 45, 64, 134, 206–34, 254; *see also* settlements
Shansi, 54, 108, 306, 354

Shantung, 93, 123, 136, 188, 189, 261, 306, 344, 346, 354, 407, 410, 413
  question, 163
  resolution, 30, 32, 70
Shao P'iao-p'ing, 323
Shao Tso-chung, 223
Shao Tsui-weng, 230
Shaw, Bernard, 179, 398, 423
Shaw, Captain S., 45
Shaw brothers, 230
Shearman, Henry, 226
*Shen-pao*, 80, 131, 152, 194, 207, 209–10, 215, 216, 217, 218, 226–7, 319–20, 325, 380, 433
Shen Pao-chen, 350–1, 352, 353, 368
Shen Yu-ch'ien, 158
Sheng Ch'eng, 75, 86
Sheng Hsuan-huai, 357, 358
Shensi, 297, 298, 306
Shepherd, George, 135, 137
Shimonoseki Treaty, 336, 410
ship building, 175, 176, 265, 349–53
shipping, 222, 267–8, 375
Shuck, J. Lewis, 109
Shunhuachen project, 136–7
Sian incident, 279
Siberia, 64
silk, 27, 221, 225, 337–8, 339, 373
  reeling, 361
  weaving, 362
silver, 333, 335–6, 374
  American Silver Purchase Act, 366, 374
Simpson, Lennox, 52
Sinkiang, 330
Sinn Fein, 88
Sino–French Education Society, 166, 167
sinology, 119–21
Six Companies, *see* San Francisco, Six Companies
slavery, USA, 252
Sloane, Roy, 82
Small Sword rebellion, 207, 238, 341
Smedley, Agnes, 49, 55
Smith A. H., 43–4, 45, 46, 47, 57, 120

Smith, Adam, 72, 90, 180, 184, 273
Smith, E., 179
Smith, George, 98
Smith, Goldwin, 159
smuggling, 239, 244, 346
Snow, Edgar, 49, 55, 57, 149, 209, 226
social gospel movement, 54, 112, 134–7
social sciences, 159, 181
  social survey, 189
  sociology, 398
social work, 99, 113, 114, 134–7
socialism, 75, 188–90, 415
Society for the Diffusion of Christian and General Knowledge, 117, 225, 272
Society for the Diffusion of Useful Knowledge, 116
Society for Lectures on the New Learning, 179
Soochow, 221, 328
Soong Ch'ing-ling, 109, 165, 371
Soong, Charles C. J., 109
Soong Mei-ling, 79, 109, 165
Soong, T. V., 202
South Africa, 64, 235, 414
Soviets (Central China), 54
Spain, 88, 162
Speer, Rev. W., 248
Spencer, Herbert, 72, 179, 180, 181, 272, 273
Spengler, O., 87, 90
'spirit of the people', 28, 29, 30, 35
sport, 134, 136, 158, 214–15
  Western, 72, 76, 151, 161
Stalin, J. 48, 162
Star Co., 229, 230
Staunton, Sir George, 120
Stephens, W. D., 254
Stevenson, Robert Louis, 251, 252
Stilwell, Col. Joseph, 55, 57
Stone, Dr Mary, 165
street lighting, 209
strikes, 50–1, 143, 208, 212, 348, 409, 417, 418–23
  France, 167
  USA, 253

Stronach, Alexander, 104
Strong, Anna Louise, 55
Stuart, Dr, 125
Student Volunteer Movement, 99, 113, 121, 124, 147
students, 410–13, 423
  *see also* education; schools; study abroad; universities and colleges; youth
study abroad, 151–8, 170, 178
  administration, 154–6
  alienation on return, 189, 202–5
  art, 199–201
  Britain, 153, 154, 157, 174, 178
  employment, 168–73; *see also* translation
  examinations, 154–5
  France, 157, 158, 161, 165, 166, 174, 189
  Germany, 153, 154, 157
  Japan, 153, 155, 156, 169, 401
  language problems, 161–2
  music, 201–2
  scholarships, 156, 171
  social life, 159–66
  statistics, 157
  USA, 64, 77, 112, 151–3, 154, 155, 156, 158, 165, 168, 171, 174, 178, 258
  Westernization, 151–2, 158–9, 170–1, 258
  women, 165–6
Stuntz, H. C., 138
Sun Ch'uan-fang, 201, 211, 346
Sun Yat-sen, 69, 87, 90, 109, 157, 194, 246, 256, 257, 261, 278–9, 280–1, 288, 293, 296, 307–8, 309, 310–13, 358, 447, 448, 449
  Madame, 55, 149, 383
Sung Chiao-jen, 288, 307, 308
Sung Chin, 351
Sung Yun-tzu, 369
*Su-pao*, 320
superstition, 14|
Sweden, 346
Switzerland, 88
Szechuan, 53, 154, 166, 298, 366, 369, 406

*Ta kung-pao*, 326–7
Tagore, Rabindranath, 179, 196
Tai Ai-lien, 165
Tai Chi-t'ao, 296, 313–14, 404
Tai Wang-shu, 197
T'aihang Mountains, 355
Taiping rebellion, 31, 61, 62, 64,
  106, 140, 141, 207, 232, 238, 266,
  277, 319, 324, 336, 340–1, 348,
  349
Taiwan, 227, 267, 347
Taku, *see* Tientsin
Tan, Chester, 142
T'an Chi-hsün, 358
Tan Leang-li, 144
T'an Ping-shan, 311
T'an Ssu-t'ung, 133, 434
T'an Yen-k'ai, 298
T'ang Ching-hsing, 222
T'ang Chi-yao, 298, 300
T'angshan, 189
T'ang Shao-yi, 152, 154, 169, 202
T'ao Hsing-chih, 185, 403, 407
Taoism, 110, 406
tariffs, 334, 335, 341, 343, 344, 346,
  362
  Peking Conference, 344–5
Tawney, R. H., 135
taxes, 169, 267, 342–3, 344
  land, 66, 294, 342
  salt, 341–3
  settlements, 208, 211
  USA, 78
  *see also* customs; *likin*
Tayeh, 356, 357
Taylor, Edward R., 242
Taylor, Hudson, 44, 96, 114, 118,
  129, 130, 147
tea, 27, 63, 221, 335, 336–7, 339, 373
  tea houses, 229
teachers, 125, 168–70, 409
technology, 174, 176
  training, 361, 426
Teichman, Sir Eric, 171, 214
Teng Hsiao-p'ing, 168
textile industry, 175, 224
  *see also* cotton; silk
theatre, 228–30

Chinatown, 249
plays, 118, 120, 160
  in settlements, 215, 218, 228–30
  Western dramatists, 179
Three Principles of the People, 87,
  109, 121, 129, 194, 278, 311, 404,
  447
Tidman, Arthur, 104
T'ien Han, 195, 229
T'ien-i Co., 230
Tientsin, 62, 131, 134, 227, 306, 320,
  353, 368, 369, 383, 404, 412–13,
  420, 424
  Arsenal, 347, 354
  massacre, 63, 267
  negotiations, 92, 138
  railway, 360
  treaties, 317, 334
Ting Jih-ch'ang, 354
Ting Kung-ch'en, 265
Ting Ling, 390
Ting, V. K., 161, 174, 177, 178, 193,
  202, 211, 420
Tinghsien, 135, 407
Tingley, Senator, 253
*t'i-yung*, 268, 270, 271, 282
tobacco, 364
Tokyo, 121, 304
*tong, see* secret societies
Torba Wei, 26
T'oung Pao, 120
Toynbee, Arnold, 90
Toyo Bunko, 121
trade, 30, 59, 332–48
  balance of payments, 335, 340–8, 378
  employment in, 221
  envoys, 31
  with Britain, 24 ff., 30–1
trade union movement, 417–18
translations
  careers in, 194–5
  Chinese to English, 120, 121
  English to Chinese, 62, 65–6, 69,
  72, 75, 87, 90, 103, 108, 116, 117,
  179, 180, 190, 191, 194, 195, 198,
  203
  National Bureau of, 198
transport, 209–10, 266

treaty system, 30–1, 33, 122, 138, 333, 336, 340, 346
 ports, 31, 92, 214, 221, 225, 326, 333–4, 363, 376
tribute missions, 26
Trindle, J. R., 148
Tripartite Intervention, 86
Trotsky, L., 191
Ts'ai Ch'ang, 168, 383
Ts'ai Ho-sen, 144, 168
Ts'ai Shao-chi, 152, 169
Ts'ai Ti'ng-kan, 152, 162, 169, 261
Ts'ai Yuan-p'ei, 85, 145, 148, 176, 177, 200, 255, 402, 403, 404, 408–9
Tsai-chen, Prince, 73, 119, 154
Tsai-tse, 154, 219
Ts'ao K'un, 294
Ts'en Ch'un-hsuan, 108
Tseng Chao-lun, 178
Tseng Chi-tse, 67, 82, 108, 131, 157, 344, 394
Tseng Kuo-fan, 62, 64, 110, 151, 168, 222, 269, 348, 426
Tsou Lou, 313
Tsou T'ao-fen, 75, 76, 77, 78, 81, 83, 87, 88, 160, 161
Tso Tsung-t'ang, 267, 348, 349–50, 351, 352, 368, 427
Tsoup'ing, 136, 407
Ts'ui kuo-yin, 380
Tsungli Yamen, 61, 63, 153, 256, 267, 324, 326, 351, 354, 404, 426, 427, 430
Tuan Ch'i-jui, 65, 291, 292, 294, 295, 298, 306, 345, 346, 420
Tuang fang, 154, 245
Tung Hsün, 63
Tungan, 123
T'ung-chih restoration, 34
T'ungchou, 355
T'ung-wen kuan, *see* universities and colleges; Language Institute
Turgot, A. R .J., 39
Turner, J. J., 107
tutelage programme, 295–6, 450
Twain, Mark, 252
Twenty-One Demands, 30, 278, 410
Tz'uchow, 106

Tzu-wei, 79

USA, 31, 32, 57, 58, 63, 64, 72, 149, 162, 165, 184–5, 206–7
 Chinatown, *see* San Francisco
 Chinese view of, 75–82
 Exclusion Act, 152, 154, 155, 156, 234, 256
 medicine, 132
 missionaries, 94, 120, 122, 258
 naturalization, 254, 256
 racial discrimination, 79, 159–60, 234
 religion, 99
 settlements, 207, 208
 war, 146
Unity Party, 300
Unity Republican Party, 307
Universities and Colleges in China
 Language Institute, 63, 96, 116, 151, 404, 408, 426, 431
 National Peking University, 70, 85, 91, 176, 255, 406, 407
 others, 94, 109, 111, 123, 126–7, 128, 133, 155, 165, 167, 170, 223, 383–4, 404, 405, 407–8
 Universities Council, 403–4
universities and colleges, overseas
 Britain, 120
 France, 120, 160–7
 Germany, 120
 USA, 112, 120, 121, 151, 158, 246

vaccination, 209
van Hoorn, Pieter, 26
violence, 190, 240, 451
Vladivostok, 64
Voltaire, 39
von der Gabelentz, 120
von Kettler, Baron, 72
von Richthofen, Ferdinand, 120, 174

Wade, Sir Thomas, 42, 61, 120, 138, 267, 268, 272
Wang Chan-yuan, 298
Wang Cheng-t'ing, 108, 134, 202
Wang Chih, 74–5, 198
Wang Ching-wei, 166, 276, 314, 324
Wang Chi-ping, 108

Wang Ch'ung-hui, Dr, 160, 328
Wang Hao, 178
Wang Hsi-chih, 200
Wang Hsing-kung, 145
Wang K'ai-yün, 68
Wang Lung, 47
Wang Ming-tao, 119
Wang T'ao, 44, 82, 84, 85, 214, 215,
  223, 269
Wang T'ung-chao, 200, 201
Wang Yow, 244
Wang Yuan-lung, 230
Wang Yun-sheng, 50
Wanghai Treaty, 319
Ward, Frederick, 61, 232
warlords, 32, 42, 65, 129, 150, 211,
  262, 293, 295, 297, 299, 306, 309,
  321, 383, 406, 423
Warnshuis, A. L., 148
wars
  class war, 190
  constitutional, 293 ff.
  1839–42, 28, 30, 60, 61, 265
  1856–60, 28, 31, 40, 60, 110, 130,
  138, 143, 235, 265–6, 316, 333,
  341, 349, 433
  1884–5, 28, 31, 64, 98, 102, 153, 227
  1894–5, 28, 40, 64, 98, 132, 139,
  153, 225, 361, 432
  First World War, 32, 139, 144,
  177, 211, 225, 261, 262, 292, 303,
  309, 321
  1900, 28, 29, 64, 90, 139, 141, 142,
  153
  1917, 31, 32, 292, 303, 309, 321
  1931–2, 29, 33, 40, 88, 193, 227,
  262, 324, 412, 424–5
  1932, 262, 412, 424
  1927–45, 34, 57, 89, 262, 324, 375,
  413
  Second World War, 135
  *see also* civil war
Washington Conference, 32, 33, 40,
  322–3, 343, 344–5
water, 136–7
Weale, Putnam, 301
Weber, Max, 40
*Weekly Review*, 189, 190, 191

Wei Li-huang, 163
Wei Su-yuan, 161
Wei Yuan, 61, 65, 68, 77, 84, 116, 265
Wellesley, Sir Victor, 42
Wen I-to, 89
Wen Yi-to, 160, 195
Weng T'ung-ho, 108, 358
Weng Wen-hao, 174
Wen-hsiang, 341, 430
Wen-yü, 352
West Hill Clique, 313
Westermarck, Edward, 398
Western world
  Chinese view of, 59–91
  literature, 195–6
  view of China, 39–59
  Western studies, 65 ff.
Westernization, 33, 151–2, 158–9,
  176, 178, 210, 224, 230, 233–4,
  245, 261–2, 377–9, 399, 426–7,
  442–6
  Chinatown, 324–8
  of Chinese students, 169–73
  of law, 324–8
  Protestant influence, 116–18
Whampoa Treaty, 92, 122, 235, 318
Wheaton, Henry, 62
Whelpey, J. D., 52
Whitehead, Alfred, 112
Wieger, Fr Leon, 94
Wiener, N., 179
Williams, S. Wells, 41, 120, 138
Williamson, Alexander, 117
Wilson, Miss, 102
Wilson, President, 90, 91, 163, 226, 395
Wo-jen, 428–31
Wolff, Christian, 39
women, 71, 76, 119, 189, 190, 260,
  380–96
  dress, 387–8
  education, 165–6, 380, 382, 384,
  393, 396, 409–10
  emancipation, 380–7
  political role, 165–6, 168, 381,
  382–4, 412, 418
  professions, 383
  property rights, 382, 383
  suffrage, 382, 383

Womens' Conference, 381
*see also* foot binding; marriage;
family
Wong Fun, 129
Wong Suey Wan, 260
Woodforde, James, 43
wool industry, 354
workers, *see* labour
workstudy scheme, 157, 165, 166–8,
189, 200
World Student Christian Federation,
128, 143
Wu Chien-chang, 341
Wu Chih-hui, 164, 166, 177
Wu Fang-chi, 392
Wu Kuang-chien, 194
Wu Lei-ch'uan, 112–13, 148
Wu Lien-te, 160
Wu Mi, 195–6, 439–40
Wu Mo-ching, 199
Wu P'ei-fu, 297, 298, 345
Wu T'ang, 350
Wu Ta-yu, 178
Wu T'ing-fang, 72, 77–8, 79, 82,
157, 164, 231
Wu Yao-tsung, 113
Wu Yen-jen, 223, 228
Wu Yi-fang, 111, 165
Wu Yu, 428
Wu Yueh, 276
Wu Yu-hsun, 178, 397
Wuch'ang, 268, 356, 368, 404
*wu-chih-hsüeh*, 175
Wuhan government, 329, 346, 382,
413, 417, 424
Wylie, Alexander, 213

xenophobia, 50–1

Yang Chen-ning, 160
Yang Chu, 172
Yang Ju, 69
Yang Man-hua, 160
*yang-nu*, 170
Yang Teh-ch'un, 384
Yang T'ing-hsi, 430
Yang Tu, 304

Yangtze, 141, 152, 153, 215, 346,
356, 413
Yeh Ch'u-ts'ang, 449
Yeh Shih-huai, 265
Yellow Emperor, 274, 275
'yellow peril', 57–9
Yen, Dr F. C., 396
Yen Chi-tz'u, 178
Yen Ching-ming, 28
Yen Fu, 69, 90, 155, 175, 177, 180–1,
198, 272–3, 400, 434–5
Yen Hsiang-wen, 298
Yen Hui-ch'ing, 109, 151
Yen, James, 50, 111, 135–6, 407
Yen Yung-ching, 179
Yenching, 55, 128
Yi Chia-yüeh, 392, 398
*Ying-huan chih-lüeh*, 66
Yi-to, 201
Young, Mrs W., 122
Young China Study Society, 143
Young Men's Christian Association
(YMCA), 53, 108, 109, 111, 112,
113, 117, 134–5, 220, 416
Young Women's Christian
Association (YWCA), 398, 416
youth, 189, 190, 381, 399–412
and fascism, 193
and labour movement, 415
'new youth', 438–9
politics, 410–13, 415
*see also* education; students
Yü Hsia-ch'ing, 222
Yü P'ing-po, 398
Yü Yu-jen, 297
Yuan Dynasty dramas, 120
Yuan Han-ch'ing, 178
Yuan Shih-k'ai, 46, 108, 132, 155,
169, 202, 211, 261–2, 288, 289–91,
296, 297, 302–3, 306, 309, 329,
337, 358, 382, 402, 407, 415, 450
*yuan-ch'i*, 80
*Yu-li wen-chien tsung-lüeh*, 67
Yung Wing, 151, 168, 223
Yunnan, 141, 298, 300, 406

Zikawei Observatory, 94
Zola, Émile, 58